GREGG SHORTHAND

COLLEGE BOOK 1

CHARLES E. ZOUBEK
GREGG A. CONDON

D0144700

CENTENNIAL EDITION

Gregg Division/McGraw-Hill Book Company

New York Atlanta Dallas St. Louis San Francisco Auckland Bogotá Guatemala Hamburg Lisbon London Madrid Mexico Milan Montreal New Delhi Panama Paris San Juan São Paulo Singapore Sydney Tokyo Toronto

Sponsoring Editor: Elizabeth R. Shelapinsky
Editing Supervisor: Elizabeth Huffman
Design and Art Supervisor/Cover Design: Karen Tureck
Production Supervisor: Frank Bellantoni
Production Assistant: Mary C. Buchanan
Photo Editor: Rosemarie Rossi

Consulting Design Coordinator/Interior Design: Susan Brorein
Cover Photography: Karen Leeds/Everett Studio

Photo Credits
Jules Allen: pages 1, 9, 25, 211, 261, 267, 279. Will Faller: pages 7, 23, 32, 53, 73, 81, 107, 125, 131, 133, 144, 148, 157, 159, 184, 185, 202, 297, 303. Michal Heron: pages 11, 37, 46, 51, 60, 65, 78, 87, 94, 99, 105, 113, 119, 139, 164, 176, 194, 213, 229, 235, 237, 243, 248, 259, 292.

Library of Congress Cataloging-in-Publication Data

Zoubek, Charles E., date
Gregg shorthand.

1. Shorthand—Gregg. I. Condon, Gregg A., date. II. Title.
Z56.2.G7Z7 1988 653′.427042 87-31050
ISBN 0-07-073661-8 (college bok. 1)

The manuscript for this book was processed electronically.

Gregg Shorthand, College Book 1, Centennial Edition

Copyright © 1988, 1980, 1973, 1965, 1958 by McGraw-Hill, Inc. All rights reserved. Copyright 1953 by McGraw-Hill, Inc. All rights reserved. Copyright renewed 1981. Printed in the United States of America. Except as permitted under the United States Copyright Act of 1976, no part of this publication may be reproduced or distributed in any form or by any means, or stored in a data base or retrieval system, without the prior written permission of the publisher.

Formerly published under the title *Gregg Shorthand for Colleges*.

1 2 3 4 5 6 7 8 9 0 KGPKGP 8 9 5 4 3 2 1 0 9 8

ISBN 0-07-073661-8

CONTENTS

UNIT VII

UNIT VIII

UNIT IX

UNIT X

TO THE STUDENT

The Value of Shorthand

Gregg Shorthand is one of the most valuable subjects you will ever learn. There are several reasons why such a powerful statement is true.

First of all, shorthand is a lifelong personal skill which relieves one from the drudgery of writing longhand. Shorthand makes it possible for most people to write three or four times faster than their longhand writing speed. Over a lifetime this saves a tremendous amount of time.

All personal notes, such as shopping lists, telephone messages, reminders, and "to do" lists, can be written in shorthand. To the student, shorthand is particularly valuable. The shorthand writer takes notes completely and easily while the longhand writer struggles and often misses important information. In the library, the shorthand writer saves valuable time in making research notes.

Professionals in all occupations find their jobs made easier and more efficient if they know shorthand. News reporters use shorthand when listing facts for a news story. Lawyers use shorthand when listing facts for the presentation of a case. Managers in a wide variety of jobs use shorthand to record instructions given to them by their supervisors. Professionals in all occupations and citizens pursuing active roles in civic organizations use shorthand in order to make notes in meetings.

Most secretaries use shorthand. They use it for taking dictation of letters and for the personal and administrative uses already discussed. The best-paying secretarial jobs require shorthand. For those secretarial jobs which do not require shorthand, the person having shorthand skill is preferred for employment. Once a person has a secretarial job, shorthand skill is most likely to be required for promotion to even better jobs. Shorthand skill pays too. Typically, people who know shorthand earn between $1,000 and $3,000 a year more than those who do not have this skill.

Another benefit derived from the study of Gregg Shorthand is that other skills grow as one learns shorthand. Many people who have never considered themselves particularly strong students of English are amazed at how much the study of shorthand improves their knowledge of punctuation, grammar, and word usage.

A familiar old saying tells us, "You can't get something for nothing." Shorthand is something of tremendous value, but it can only be acquired through reasonable, honest effort. That is another reason why employers prefer to hire people who know shorthand—they are most likely to be dependable and take pride in their work.

The Study of Shorthand

The speed with which you learn to read and write Gregg Shorthand will depend largely on two factors—the *time* you devote to practice and the *way* in which you practice. If you practice efficiently, you will be able to complete each lesson in the shortest possible time and derive the greatest possible benefit.

Before you begin, select a quiet place in which to practice. Do not try to practice while listening to music, watching television, or carrying on a conversation.

Here are some features of the materials along with learning suggestions that will help you get the maximum benefit from the time you invest in shorthand practice.

LINE PLACEMENT

Gregg Shorthand can, of course, be written on either ruled or unruled paper. The printed lines of a shorthand notebook lessen the hesitation in writing and provide a guide for the eyes to follow as the shorthand outlines are read.

With the Centennial Edition of *Gregg Shorthand*, a commonsense approach to line placement has been adopted. The line placement of each outline has been selected as that which is the most reasonable for speed of writing and maintenance of proportion.

Shorthand writers are encouraged to "throw" outlines upon the page as rapidly as possible. Therefore, the placement may vary slightly because it is difficult when writing to begin at, or touch, the same place every time.

READING WORD LISTS

With the presentation of each shorthand principle is a list of words that illustrates the principle. As part of your out-of-class practice, read these word lists in this way:

1. Using the typed word and shorthand outline, spell—aloud if possible—the shorthand symbol in each outline in the list, thus: *s-e, see; f-e, fee.* Reading aloud will help impress the shorthand outlines firmly on your mind. Read all the shorthand words in the list in this way—with the typed word exposed—until you feel you can read the shorthand outlines without referring to the typed word.
2. Cover the typed word with a piece of paper and read aloud from the shorthand, thus: *s-e, see; f-e, fee.*
3. If the spelling of a shorthand outline does not immediately give you the meaning, refer to the typed word and determine the meaning of any outline you cannot read. Do *not* spend more than a few seconds trying to decipher an outline.
4. After you have read all the words in the list, read them again if time permits.

Note: In reading brief forms for common words and phrases, which first occur in Lessons 4 and 5, respectively, do not spell the shorthand outlines.

READING SENTENCES, LETTERS, AND ARTICLES

The presentation of each shorthand principle is followed by connected practice material. Each lesson concludes with additional practice material in which sentences, letters, or articles are written in shorthand. Proper practice of all this material will help you develop your shorthand ability.

First, *read* the material. Using the transcript to the shorthand in the back of the textbook, you should follow this procedure:

1. Read the shorthand outlines aloud until you come to a word you cannot read. Spell the shorthand symbols in that outline. If this spelling does not *immediately* give you the meaning, refer to the transcript.
2. To find the shorthand outline in the transcript, look for items that precede or follow the outline, such as the salutation, closing, or a new paragraph.
3. Determine the meaning of the outline you cannot read.
4. Return to the shorthand from which you are reading and continue reading in this manner until you have completed the material.
5. If time permits, read the material a second time.

By following this procedure, you will lose no time in finding your place in the shorthand and in the transcript when you cannot read an outline.

Remember, during the early stages your shorthand reading may not be very rapid. That is only natural as you are, in a sense, learning a new language. If you practice regularly, however, you will find your reading rate increasing almost daily.

WRITING THE READING AND WRITING PRACTICE

Before you do any writing of shorthand, you should acquire an appropriate notebook and pen.

Your Notebook. The best notebook for shorthand writing is one that measures 6 by 9 inches and has a vertical rule down the center of each page. It should have a spiral binding so that the pages lie flat at all times. The paper should, of course, take ink well.

Your Pen. A pen is a satisfactory instrument for writing Gregg Shorthand. A pencil is not recommended. Because writing with a pen requires little pressure, you can write for long periods of time without becoming fatigued. A fine ballpoint pen facilitates the fastest writing for most people. Pen-written notes remain legible almost indefinitely; pencil notes become blurred and hard to read.

Having selected your writing tools, follow these steps in writing the Reading and Writing Practice.

1. Read the material you are going to copy. Always read the Reading and Writing Practice before copying it. Make sure you can read the copy easily before attempting to write.
2. When you are ready to start writing, read a convenient group of words from the printed shorthand; then write the group, reading aloud as you write.

In the early stages your writing may not be very rapid, nor will your notes be as well written as those in the book. With regular practice, however, your notes will rapidly improve.

UNIT I

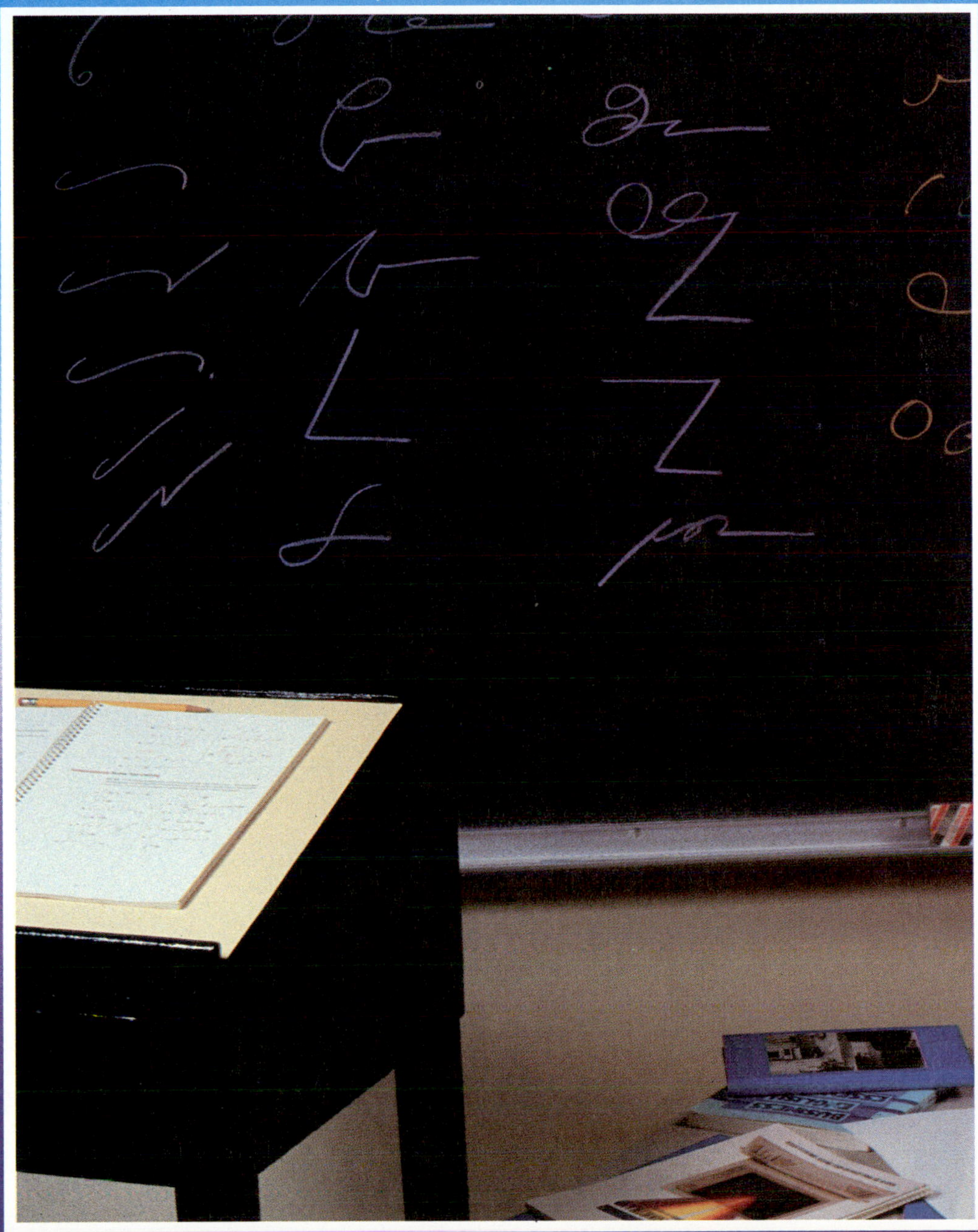

LESSON 1

NEW IN LESSON 1

- **Concept of *you write what you hear***
- **Concept of symbols representing sounds**
- **Symbols for the sounds of *a*, *e*, *n*, *m*, *t*, and *d***
- **Shorthand symbols for punctuation, paragraph, and capitalization**

You Write What You Hear

In shorthand silent letters are omitted and other letters may have different sounds. Following are some English words with their shorthand spellings and an explanation of the sounds.

Word	**Sounds**	**Explanation**
name	nam	*e* is silent
right	rit	*gh* is silent
navy	nave	*y* sounds like *e*
stay	sta	*y* is silent
face	fas	*c* sounds like *s*
phone	fon	*ph* sounds like *f*
snow	sno	*w* is silent
safe	saf	*e* is silent
age	aj	*g* sounds like *j*
home	hom	*e* is silent
lead	led	*a* is not heard
large	larj	*g* sounds like *j*
copy	kope	*c* sounds like *k*; *y* like *e*

Can you determine the shorthand spellings for each of the following words?

may	aid	eat
aim	main	tea
day	date	team

SOUNDS OF A, E, N, M

The shorthand symbols for *a* and *e* are circles that are differentiated by size much the same as they are in longhand.

The *a* is a large circle.

The *e* is a small circle.

The shorthand symbols for *n* and *m* are straight lines written forward along the line of writing.

The *n* is a short straight line.

Example: knee

The *m* is a long straight line.

Example: aim

A, E, N, M Words

The following words contain the long sounds of *a*, *e*, *n*, and *m*. The symbols for each sound in a word are joined together to form a word called an *outline*.

me	main	aim
may	knee	
mean	name	

A, E, N, M Practice

1.1

1 I to please.

2 She go to the game.

3 My hurts.

4 He did not meet .

5 What is her ?

6 Meet at 3 o'clock.

7 The gate is open.

8 His is Jim.

9 He is not .

10 I the dog.

Key:

1 I aim to please.
2 She may go to the game.
3 My knee hurts.
4 He did not meet me.
5 What is her name?
6 Meet me at 3 o'clock.
7 The main gate is open.
8 His name is Jim.
9 He is not mean.
10 I may name the dog.

SOUNDS OF T, D

The shorthand symbols for *t* and *d* are *upward* slanting straight lines differentiated by length.

The *t* is a short slanting straight line. 

Example: tea 

The *d* is a long slanting straight line. 

Example: day 

T, D Words

day 

date 

deed 

made 

mate 

meet, meat 

tea 

eat 

team 

tame 

ate 

aid, aide 

T, D Practice

1.2

1 The tiger is  .

2 The  has been signed.

3 The chef   .

4 Leon will  the train.

5 The  is warm.

6 Check the  on the calendar.

7 Our  won!

8 When will you  lunch?

9 Steve is a nurse's  .

10 We  lunch late.

Key:
1 The tiger is tame.
2 The deed has been signed.
3 The chef made tea.
4 Leon will meet the train.
5 The day is warm.
6 Check the date on the calendar.
7 Our team won!
8 When will you eat lunch?
9 Steve is a nurse's aide.
10 We ate lunch late.

PUNCTUATION, PARAGRAPH, AND CAPITALIZATION SYMBOLS

Since ordinary longhand marks of punctuation are similar to some of the shorthand symbols that will be presented in later lessons, special symbols are used to represent those punctuation marks. There are also special paragraph and capitalization symbols.

Punctuation and Paragraph Symbols

Special symbols are used to represent the period and question mark at the end of a sentence. Note that an ordinary comma is used within a circle.

A sentence ending with a period or question mark may also be the last sentence in a paragraph. In this case, if the last sentence in the paragraph ends with a period, the period is dropped and a paragraph symbol is used alone. If the last sentence ends with a question mark or an exclamation point, both the punctuation mark and the paragraph symbol are retained.

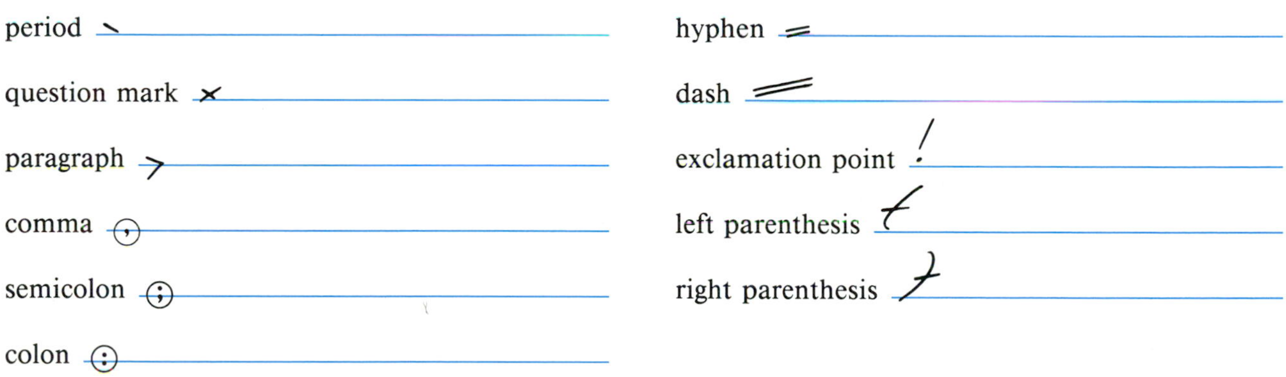

Capitalization

Shorthand capitalization is indicated with a pair of tiny upward slanting straight symbols. These capitalization marks are placed underneath the word to be capitalized at the end of the outline. While vertical placement is not critical, the capitalization marks should be close enough to the body of the outline to be unmistakably associated with it. In order to promote writing speed, the first word of each shorthand sentence does not contain capitalization marks. When shorthand notes are typed in English—which is called *transcribing*—the first word of each sentence is, of course, capitalized.

Salutations such as *William* or *Dear William* or sentences beginning with a proper noun will contain capitalization marks. However, when a letter begins with a salutation such as *Dear Mr. Franklin* or *Dear Ms. Harrington,* the proper noun will not contain capitalization marks. When the notes are transcribed, the names will be capitalized.

Capitalized Words

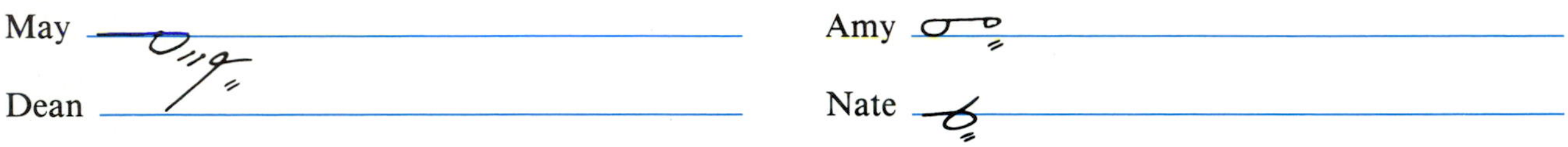

Punctuation and Capitalization Practice

1.3

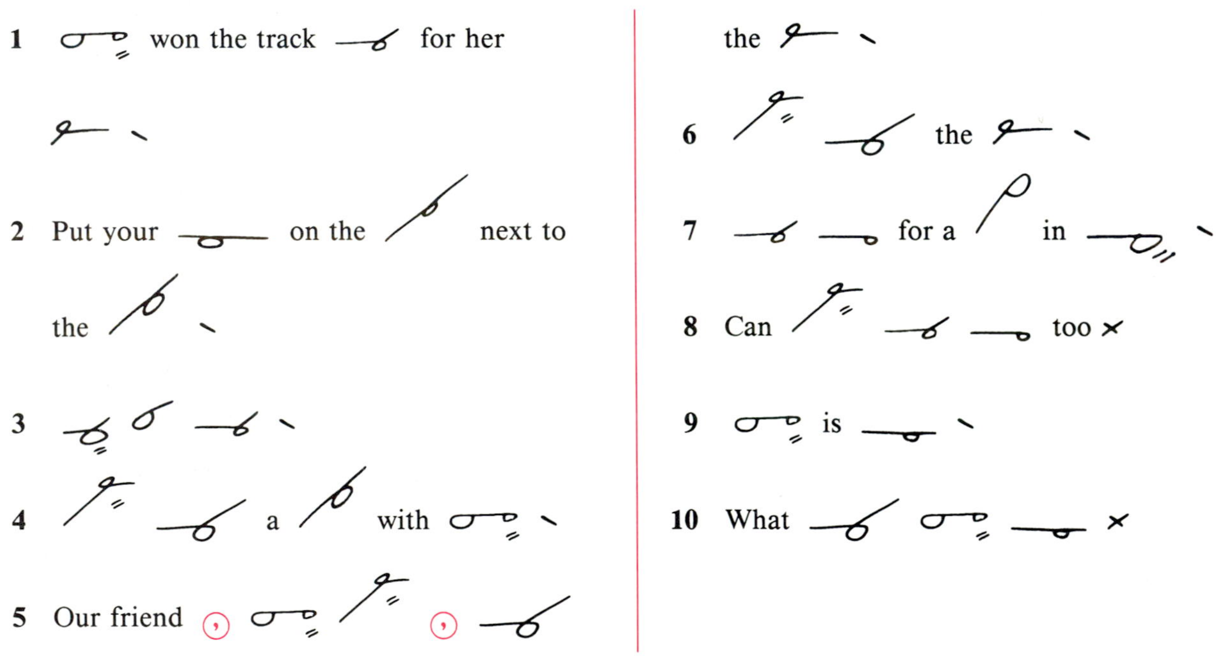

1 won the track for her
2 Put your on the next to
the
3
4 a with
5 Our friend
the
6 the
7 for a in
8 Can too
9 is
10 What

Key:

1 Amy won the track meet for her team.
2 Put your name on the deed next to the date.
3 Nate ate meat.
4 Dean made a date with Amy.
5 Our friend, Amy Dean, made the team.
6 Dean made the team.
7 Meet me for a day in May.
8 Can Dean meet me too?
9 Amy is mean.
10 What made Amy mean?

Shorthand can be used in any situation to record information quickly and accurately.

Reading Practice

1.4

1 My stop from going

2 will any

3 at 4 o'clock for

4

5 be on the

6 sign the in

7 He will the of the track

8 for the

9 on East to sign the

10 Mark the on the

LESSON 2

NEW IN LESSON 2

- **Symbol for the sound of *h* at the beginning of words**
- **Word ending *-ing***
- **Symbol for the sound of *long i***
- **Efficient use of a steno pad**

SOUNDS OF H, -ING

The shorthand symbol for the sounds of *h* and *-ing* is a dot.

h, -ing ·

The letter *h*, which almost always occurs at the beginning of a word, is represented by a dot placed above the vowel.

Example: he

The sound of *-ing*, which almost always occurs at the end of a word, is represented by a dot placed close to the end of the body of the outline.

Example: meeting

H, -ing Words

he	naming	taming
heat	meeting	heeding
heating	hate	dating

H, -ing Practice

2.1

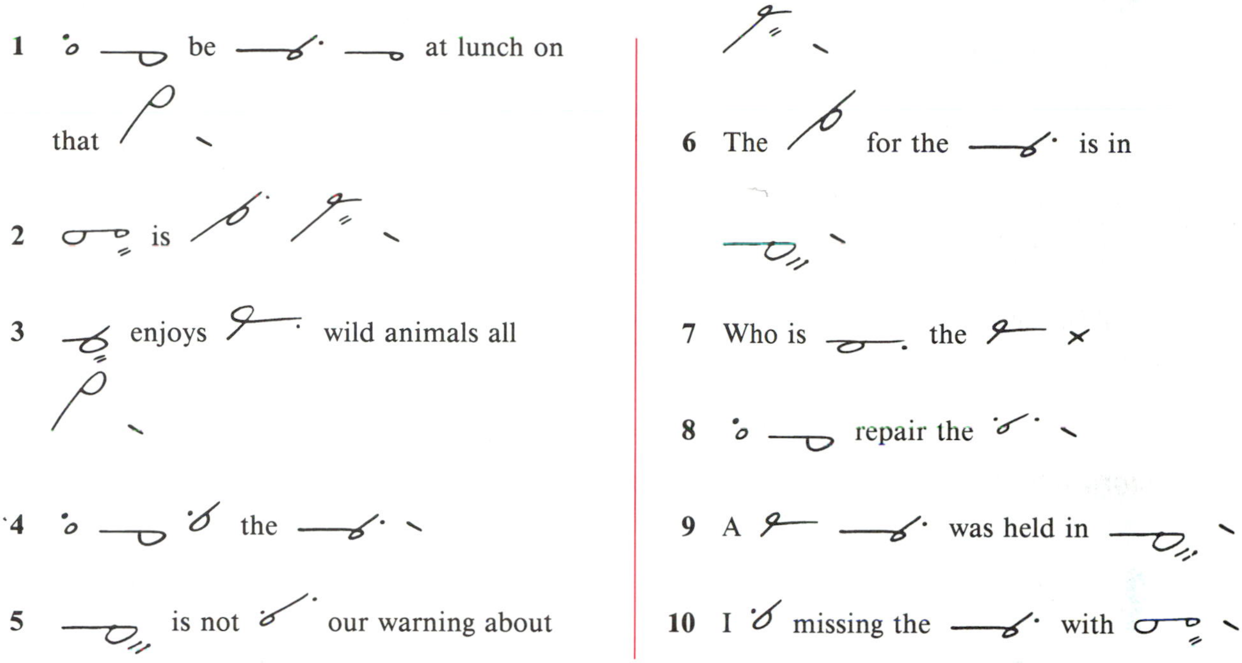

1 be at lunch on that
2 is
3 enjoys wild animals all
4 the
5 is not our warning about
6 The for the is in
7 Who is the
8 repair the
9 A was held in
10 I missing the with

Key:

1 He may be meeting me at lunch on that day.
2 Amy is dating Dean.
3 Nate enjoys taming wild animals all day.
4 He may hate the meeting.
5 May is not heeding our warning about Dean.
6 The date for the meeting is in May.
7 Who is naming the team?
8 He may repair the heating.
9 A team meeting was held in May.
10 I hate missing the meeting with Amy.

Shorthand notebooks are divided into two columns to gain writing speed.

SOUND OF LONG I

The shorthand symbol for *long i* is a broken *a* circle.

Example: high

Long I Words

high	mine	night
my	tie	die, dye
might	tied	dying

Long I Practice

2.2

1 write at in

2 is in the safe at

3 a fancy knot in

4 The price of is too

5 ended the game in a

6 The is in

7 go out at to her

8 did not before the

9 The rate on be

10 learn to his

Key:

1 He might write Amy at night in May.
2 My deed is in the safe at night.
3 Dean tied a fancy knot in my tie.
4 The price of my deed is too high.
5 My team ended the game in a tie.
6 The date is in May.
7 Amy might go out at night to dye her tie.
8 He did not dye my tie before the meeting.
9 The rate on my deed might be high.
10 He might learn to tie his tie.

Notebook Management

Use a two-column steno pad. This type of pad is best for writing shorthand.

Use one column at a time. In order to minimize wasted *return* writing motions, you should write your shorthand notes in one column at a time.

Use one side of paper. In order to avoid wasting time turning pages, you should write on one side of the page only. When you reach the end of the notebook, turn it around and proceed to write on the back of all the pages.

Use a rubber band. Group completed pages together with a rubber band so that the pad falls open at the first page available for writing.

Date the notes. Each day you use your steno pad, write the current date first. This will avoid much confusion later.

Separate your notes. Draw a line across the column to clearly indicate the separation between the letters or other notes.

Maintain good posture. You will have the greatest writing speed when your arms are fully supported by the writing surface. Use your free hand to steady the notebook. Have your steno pad opened flat. When turning pages, do not waste time tucking the used pages underneath the pad.

Select the right pen. You should select your writing instrument with care. Pencils should definitely be avoided. The ideal pen allows the ink to flow freely. It writes a relatively fine line with a minimum of friction on the paper. The ink should be dark enough to be clearly legible.

When writing shorthand near the bottom of the page, slide the page up with the fingers of your nonwriting hand instead of moving your writing arm down.

Reading Practice

2.3

1 be at the

2 at 10 at

3 The will be held with

4 We in the room at

5 The is not

6 will the

7 her

8 will the warning of

9 The rate gave is

10 The price of the is too

LESSON 3

NEW IN LESSON 3

- Symbols for the sounds of *o*, *r*, and *l*
- Minor vowels omitted as an abbreviating principle
- Symbol for the sound of *short i*
- Listening as a communication skill

SOUNDS OF O, R, L

The symbols for *o*, *r*, and *l* are short forward "under" curves differentiated by length.

o r l

Sound of O

The *o* is a tiny hook.

Example: no

O Words

no, know	own ■	total ■
tow	owning ■	note ■
dough	known ■	noting ■
home ■	tone ■	mode ■

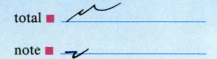

■ When the *o* is joined to the beginning of *t*, *d*, *n*, and *m*, it is written without an angle to make writing faster.

Sound of R

The *r* is a short forward curve.

Example: ray

R Words

ray	or	dear
rate	more	write
raid	row	ride
rain	wrote	try
train	road	tried
trade	near	hire

Sound of L

The *l* is a long forward curve.

Example: lay

L Words

lay	lane	line
late	lean	Dale
Lee	lie	mailing
leading	light	low

O, R, L Practice

3.1

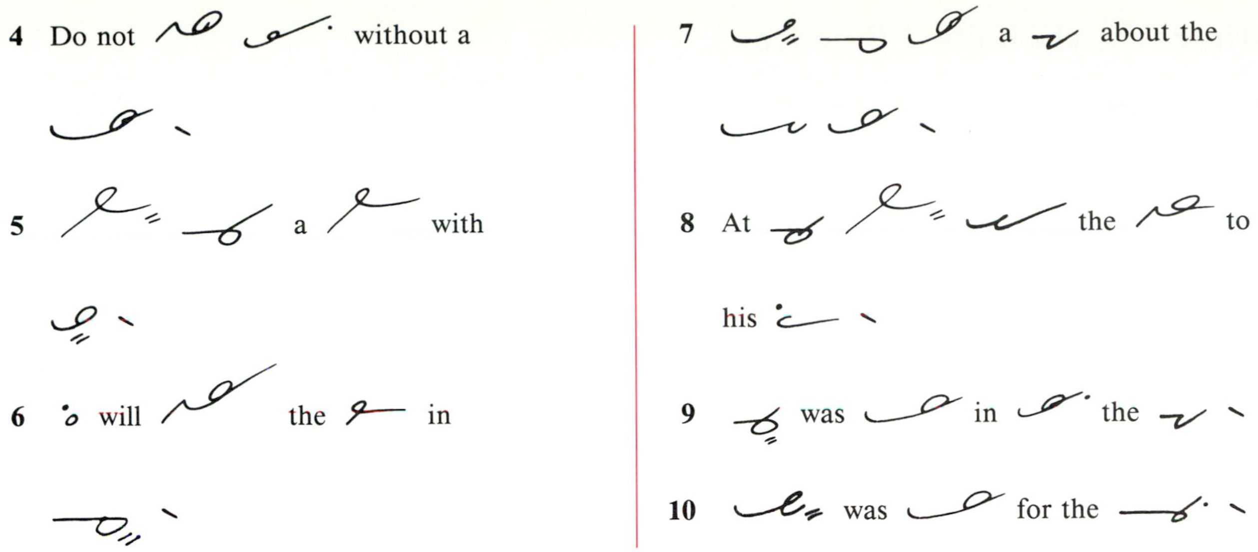

4 Do not without a
5 a with
6 will the in
7 a about the
8 At the to
his
9 was in the
10 was for the

Key:
1 Nate wrote a note home.
2 He may mail the note.
3 Dale may read without a light.
4 Do not try reading without a light.
5 Dale made a deal with Ray.
6 He will trade the team in May.
7 Lee may write a note about the low rate.
8 At night Dale rode the train to his home.
9 Nate was late in writing the note.
10 Leo was late for the meeting.

MINOR VOWELS OMITTED

Many words contain vowels that are barely pronounced in ordinary speech. Such vowels may be omitted from shorthand outlines if they do not contribute to speed or readability.

Example: later 

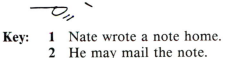

Minor-Vowel-Omitted Words

later		dealer		total	
leader		trailer		title	
lighter		meter		delay	
reader		motor		delight

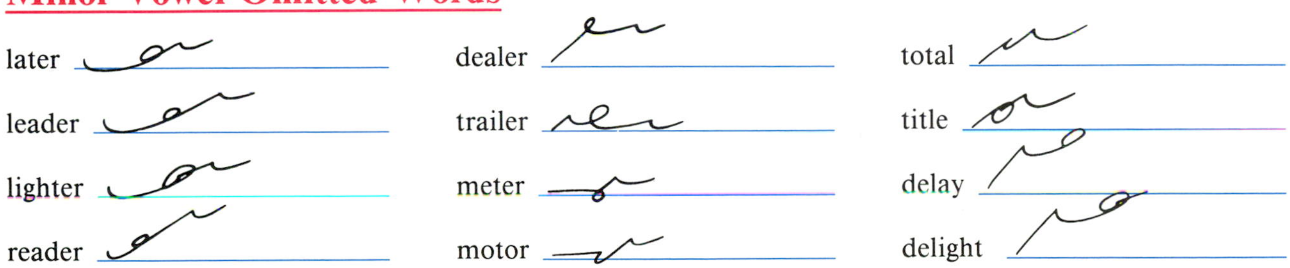

Minor-Vowel-Omitted Practice
3.2

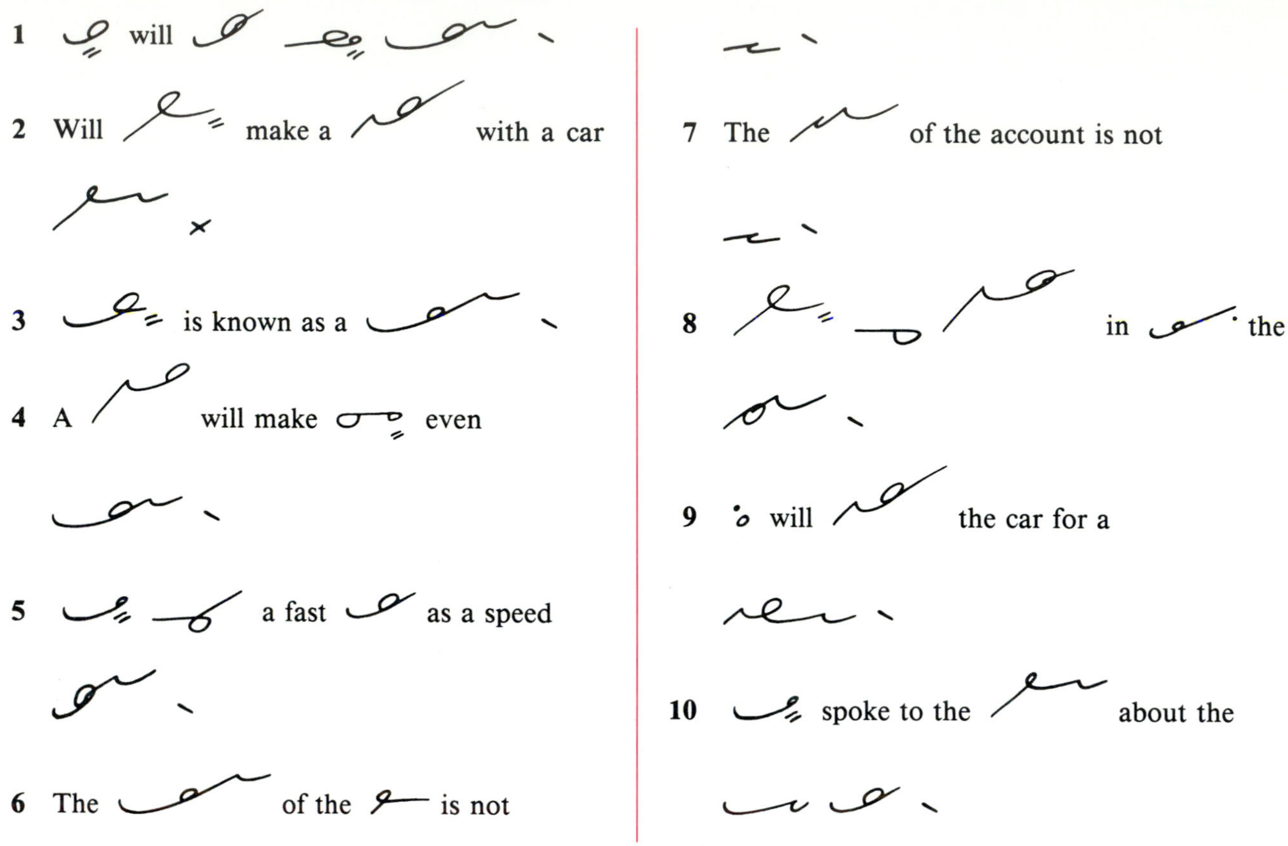

1 will
2 Will make a with a car
3 is known as a
4 A will make even
5 a fast as a speed
6 The of the is not
7 The of the account is not
8 in the
9 will the car for a
10 spoke to the about the

Key:
1 Ray will write Mary later.
2 Will Dale make a trade with a car dealer?
3 Lane is known as a leader.
4 A delay will make Amy even later.
5 Lee made a fast rate as a speed writer.
6 The leader of the team is not known.
7 The total of the account is not known.
8 Dale may delight in reading the title.
9 He will trade the car for a trailer.
10 Lee spoke to the dealer about the low rate.

SOUND OF SHORT I

The short sound of the vowel *i* is represented by the shorthand *e* symbol. Phonetically, they are the same family of sounds.

short i = 

Example: him 

Short I Words

him	Tim	little
hit	did	knit
hitting	litter	

Short I Practice

3.3

1 a sweater for

2 The is a better than they

3 The baseball on the ankle last

4 better than on the

5 pick up on the

6 the choose last

7 not the

8 Is at with his sister

9 not the to

10 will a to

Key:

1 Mary did knit a sweater for Lee.
2 The team is hitting a little better than they did.
3 The baseball hit him on the ankle last night.
4 Lee did better than Tim on writing the deed.
5 Did Tim pick up litter on the train?
6 Did the team choose him last night?
7 He did not trade the trailer.
8 Is Ray eating at home with his little sister?
9 Tim did not write the note to Dean.
10 Lee will need a little light to write.

Listening as a Communication Skill

Communication is a process whereby people are able to understand each other. One person may be very good at describing facts, ideas, or emotions. Other people will not *understand* these messages, though, unless they are effective listeners.

Effective communication is a two-way street, with listening skills being an essential part of the process. Good listening skills are among the many communications skills that you will refine through your study of Gregg Shorthand.

Reading Practice

3.4

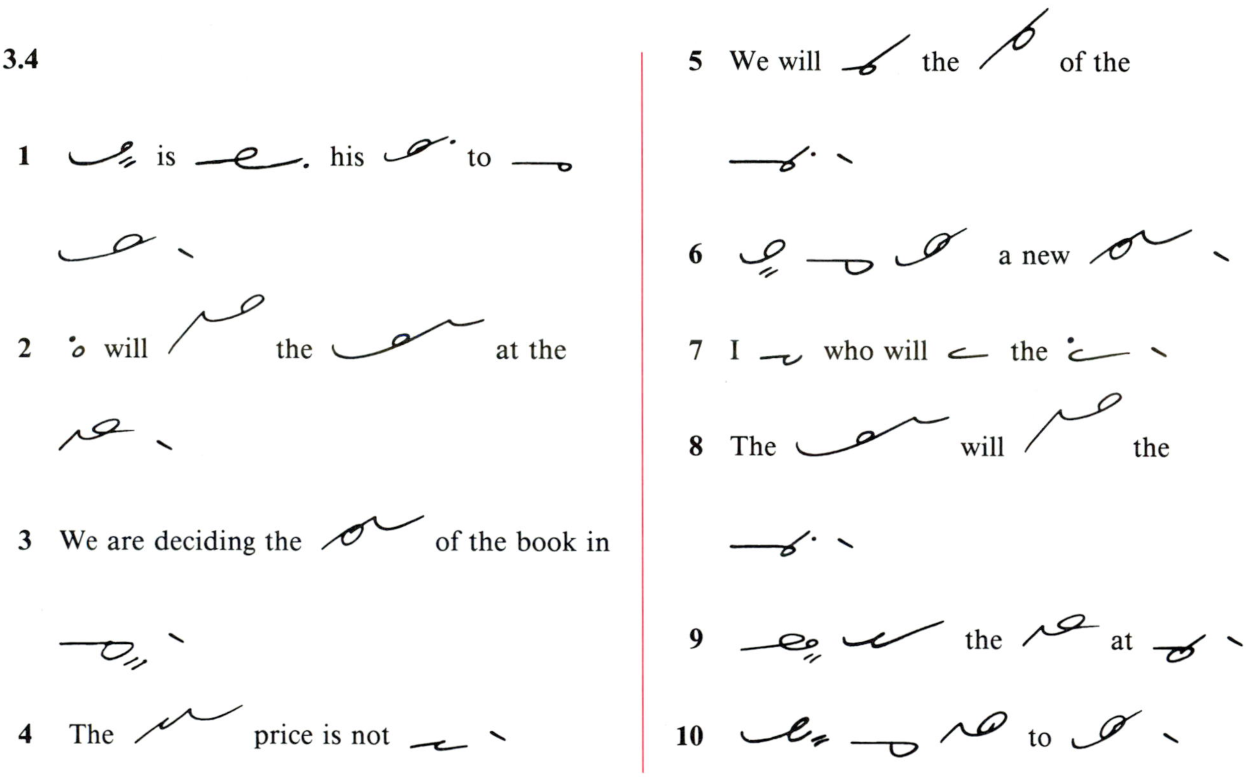

LESSON 4

NEW IN LESSON 4

- **Nine abbreviated words called brief forms**
- **Short and soft vowel sounds of *a* and *e***
- **Taking class notes**

Note: Outlines for brief forms will be highlighted in the practice materials.

BRIEF FORMS

Some of the most common words have abbreviated shorthand spellings called *brief forms.* The nine brief forms in this lesson are all written with single shorthand symbols. Since these words occur often in our language, their brief forms are a major source of writing speed. They must be learned for instant recall and are highlighted in the *practice* material.

it, at 

would 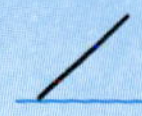

I 

in, not 

am 

of 

are, our, hour 

will, well 

a, an 

Brief-Form Derivatives

Some brief forms can be used for longer words by making the brief forms plural or past tense, or by adding a common prefix or a common suffix such as *-ing.* One brief-form derivative is possible using the alphabetic characters presented so far.

Example: will + ing 

Brief-Form Practice
4.1

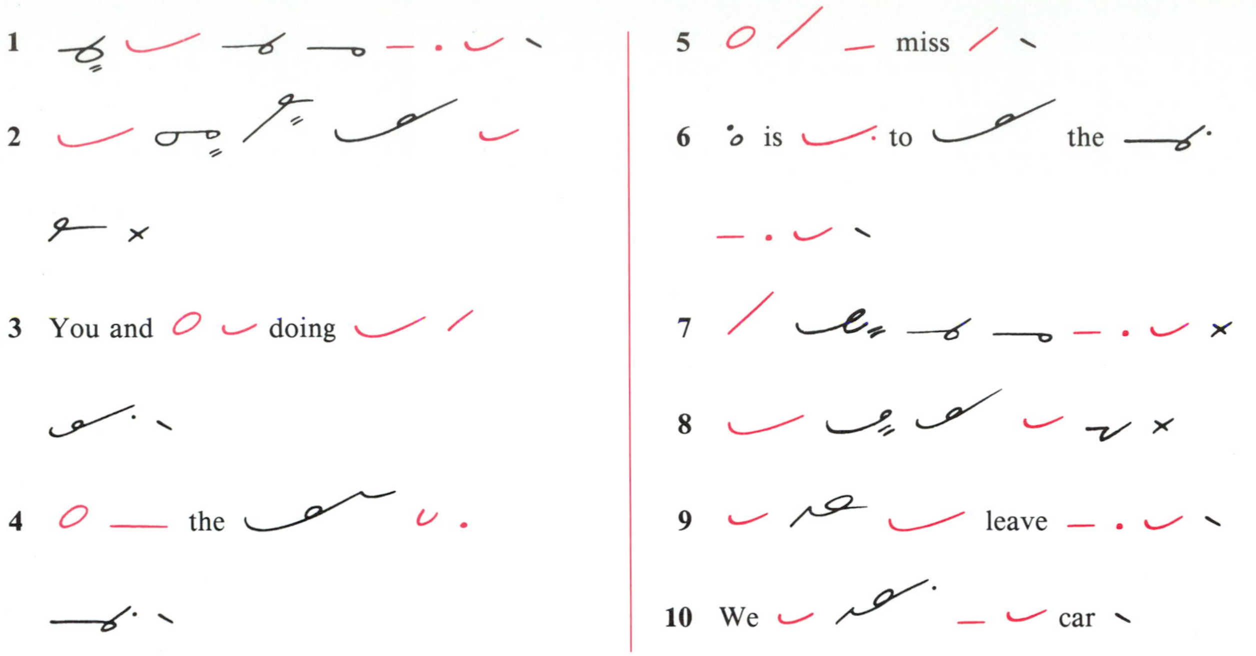

Key:

1 Nate will meet me in an hour.
2 Will Amy Dean lead our team?
3 You and I are doing well at reading.
4 I am the leader of a meeting.
5 I would not miss it.
6 He is willing to lead the meeting in an hour.
7 Would Leo meet me in an hour?
8 Will Lee read our note?
9 Our train will leave in an hour.
10 We are trading in our car.

SHORT AND SOFT SOUNDS OF A

The large *a* circle, which represents the long sound of *a* as in *made*, also represents the short sound of *a* as in *man* and the soft sound of *a* as in *arm*.

Example: man 

Short A Words

man 
dad 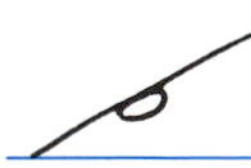
matter 
had 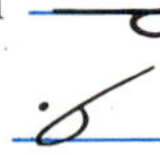
hammer 
ran 
hat 
Matt 
ladder 

Soft A Words

arm | harm | art
Army | heart | alarm

Short and Soft A Practice
4.2

1 to get .

2 bought . new

3 Is something the with his ×

4 to strengthen his

5 She . old from the

6 . the story —

7 .

8 go to the ×

9 The be settled —

10 . — . play

Key:

1 Nate ran home to get a hammer.
2 My dad bought a new ladder.
3 Is something the matter with his arm?
4 Matt ran to strengthen his heart.
5 She had an old hat from the Army.
6 A man will write the story in May.
7 Matt had a low reading rate.
8 Will my dad go to the meeting at night?
9 The matter will be settled in May.
10 My dad had a leading role in a play.

SHORT AND SOFT SOUNDS OF E

The tiny *e* circle, which represents the long sound of *e* as in *Lee*, also represents the short sound of *e* as in *let* and the soft sound of *e* as in *her*.

Examples: let her

Short and Soft E Words

let

letting

letter

heading

net

met

red

led

her

hurt

hurting

Short and Soft E Practice

4.3

1 was — the

2 have the

3 his on the

4

5

6 the

7 to

8 was sent to

9 is missing

10 What be the on the

Key:

1 Her dad was in the Army.
2 Let Amy have the red ladder.
3 Matt hurt his head on the ladder.
4 He read her letter.
5 He met her dad, Matt Dean.
6 Let Tim meet the leader.
7 He will mail a letter to Leo.
8 A letter was sent to my home.
9 My red tie is missing.
10 What will be the net rate on the loan?

Taking Class Notes

Most class lectures follow an organized approach which relates directly to the way the information will later be tested. A history teacher might, for example, start a class period by saying, "Today we are going to discuss the causes of the American Revolution." The discussion might then center on lack of governmental representation, physical isolation, and economic ties. Shorthand is the best way for students to capture the content of the concepts presented and to make sure that lists of details are complete.

Learning shorthand is an opportunity to acquire a personal and professional life skill.

Reading Practice

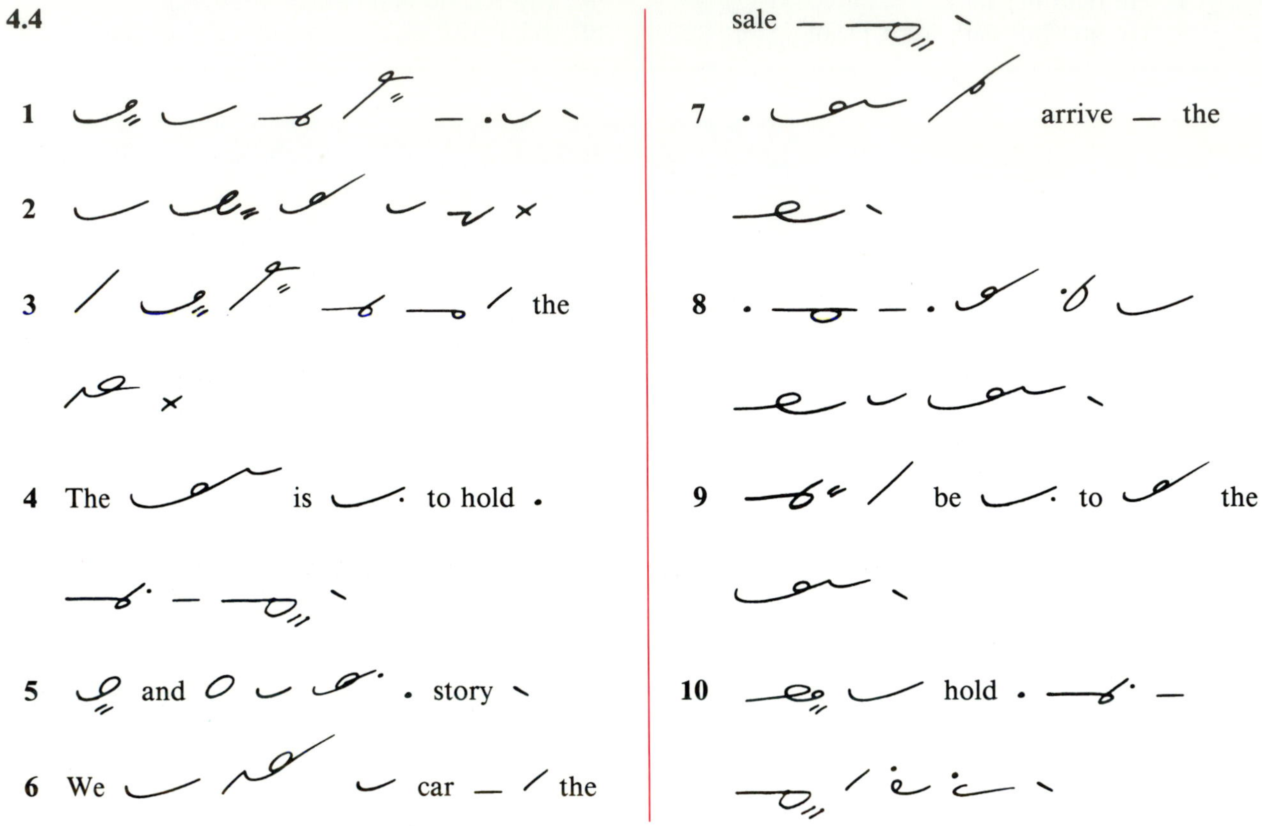

4.4

1

2

3 the

4 The is to hold

5 and story

6 We car the

sale

7 arrive — the

8

9 be to the

10 hold

UNIT II

1) Decrease in the number of
than fifteen fell 7%
2) Increase in the number of elderly
The number of people 65 or older
There was a sharp reduction in the
B) Gulf that Separates the old and
1) largest portion of public money spent on the

LESSON 5

NEW IN LESSON 5

- **Shorthand phrases**
- **Symbols for the sounds of *s*, *f*, and *v***
- **Shorthand blends for *fr* and *fl***
- **Short and soft sounds of *o***
- **Differentiating between sound-alike words *sight*, *site*, and *cite***

Note: Beginning with Lesson 5, outlines for new words and phrases will be highlighted in the practice materials.

PHRASES

In Lesson 4 you learned special abbreviations, called brief forms, for some very common words. Very often these occur together. Much of the writing speed of shorthand comes from combining these brief forms into a single outline called a *phrase*.

Example: in  + our  = in our 

I will 

will not 

I will not 

in our

are in, are not 

I am 

in it 

it will 

it will not 

I would 

I would not 

of our 

Phrase Practice
5.1

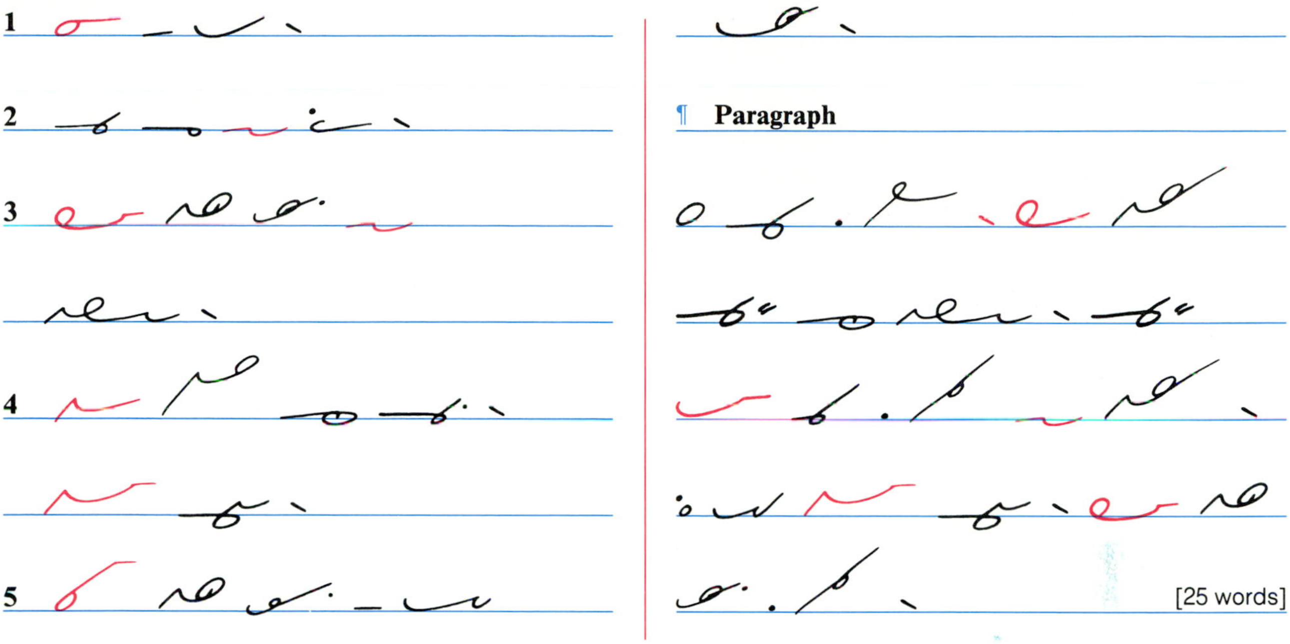

Key: 1 I am not well.
2 Meet me in our home.
3 I will not try writing in our trailer.
4 It will delay my meeting. It will not matter.
5 I would not try reading in low light.

You Write What You Hear

The *s* symbol represents the soft sound of *c* as in *face.*

sight = S I T	cite = S I T	nice = N I S
site = S I T	lace = L A S	face = F A S

The past-tense *d* has the sound of either *d* or *t*. In shorthand, remember, you write what you hear.

saved = S A V D	faced = F A S T	laughed = L A F T

SOUNDS OF S, F, V

The symbols for *s*, *f*, and *v* are *downward* right curves differentiated by length.

s f v

Sound of S

The *s* symbol is a short downward curve. Because of its size, slope, and direction, it is often called the *comma s*.

Example: say

S Words

say	seen, scene	as
see	seat, set, sit	has ■
same	sign	stay
seem	sight, site, cite	so

■ The letter *s* often has the *z* sound in longhand. In shorthand the *s* is always used for the sound of *z*.

Sound of F

The *f* symbol is a medium-size downward curve.

Example: fame

F Words

fame	feet	fast, faced
Fay	face	laugh
fee	safe	if
feed	safes	phone

Sound of V

The *v* symbol is a long downward curve. 

Example: vain 

V Words

S, F, V Practice

5.2

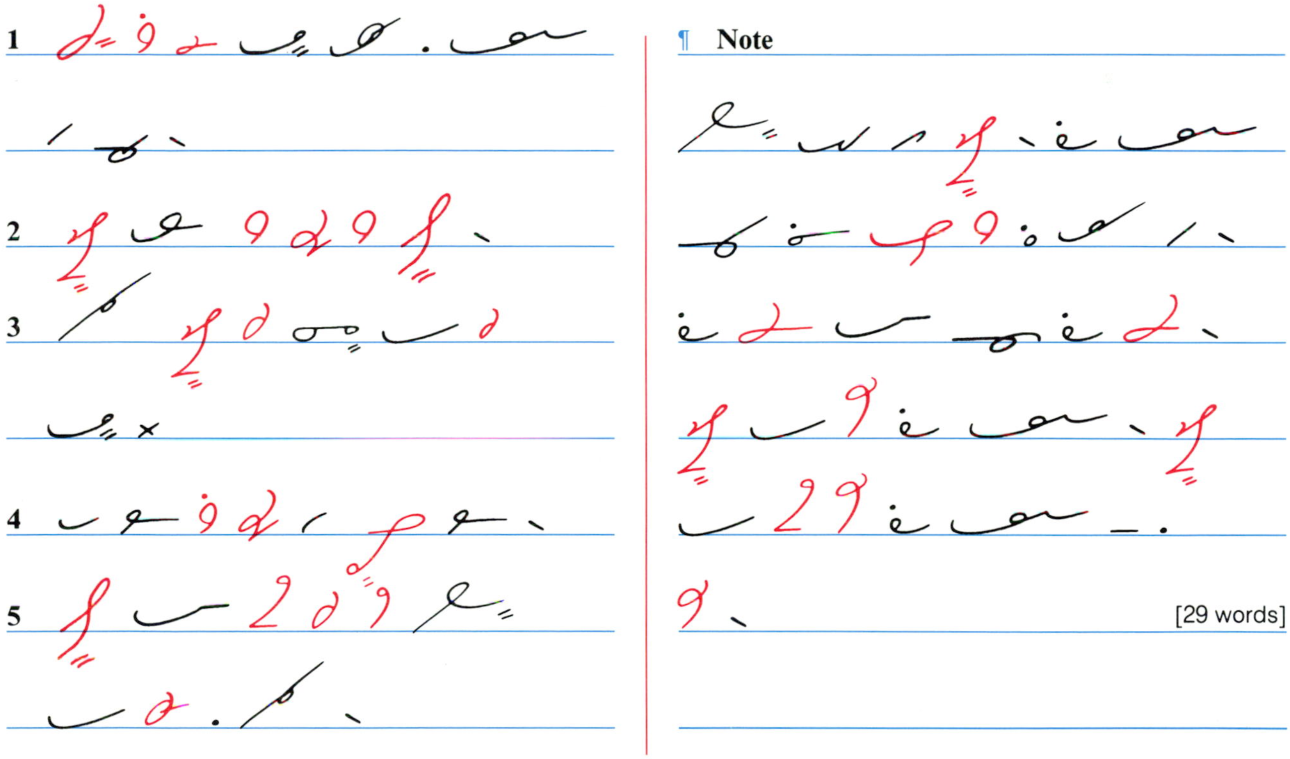

Key:
1 Fay has seen Lee write a letter at night.
2 Steven ran as fast as Dave.
3 Did Steven say Amy will see Lee?
4 Our team has faced the Navy team.
5 Dave will not even say if Dale will sign a deed.

FR, FL BLEND

Another way in which Gregg Shorthand provides writing speed is through several *blends* of symbols that frequently occur together. Writing speed is gained by eliminating the pen stop.

fr fl 

Examples: frame fly 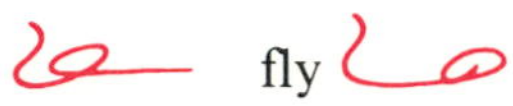

Fr, Fl Words

frame
Fred
free
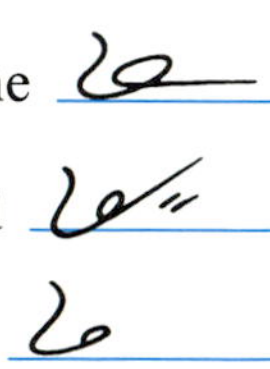

fry
flame
fly
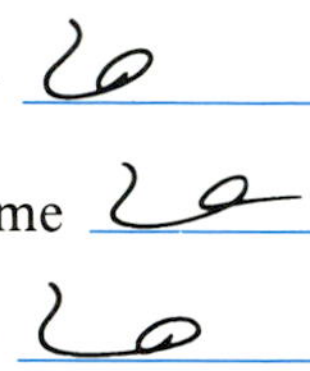

flying
flown
afraid
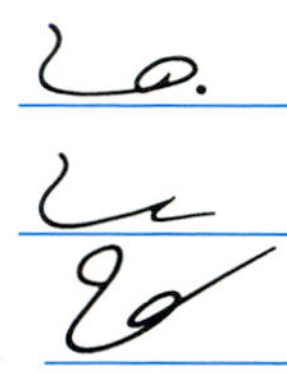

Fr, Fl Practice

5.3

1
2
3
4
5
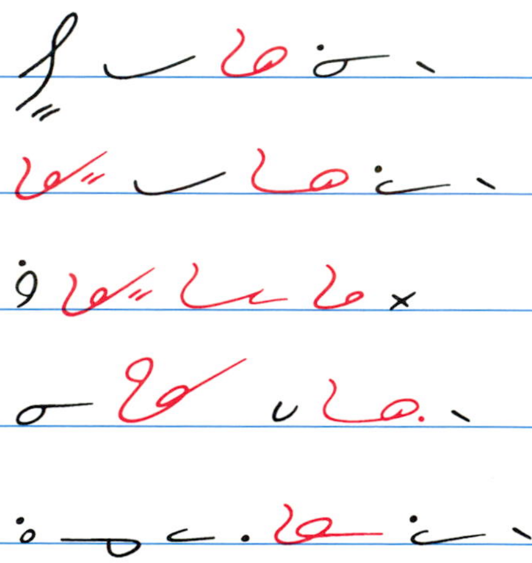

¶ **Phone Message**

To:
From:
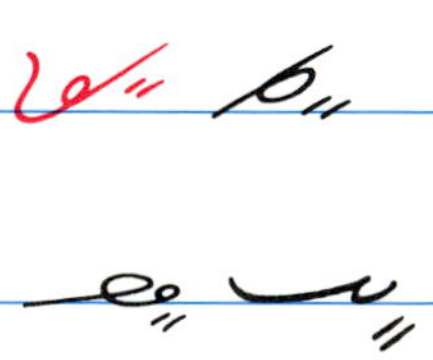

Date: 

Time: 12:15

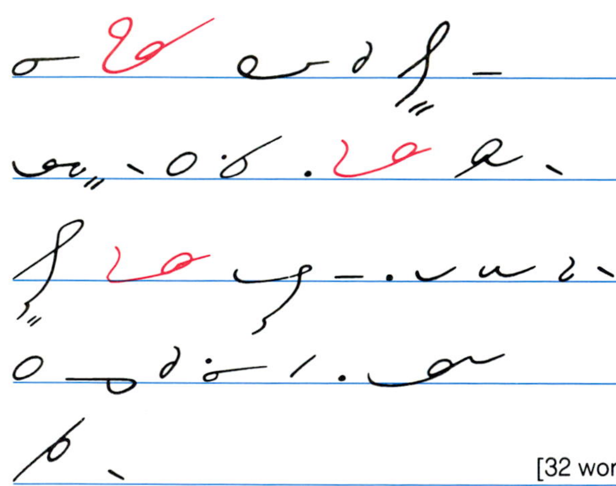

[32 words]

Key: **1** Dave will fry ham.
2 Fred will fly home.
3 Has Fred flown free?
4 I am afraid of flying.
5 He may own a frame home.

You Write What You Hear

The *o* symbol that represents the long sound of *o* as in *home* also represents the short sound of *o* as in *Tom* and the soft sound of *o* as in *thought*.

own = O N	Ron = R O N	saw = S O
hot = H O T	brought = B R O T	stop = S T O P
taught = T O T	stone = S T O N	tall = T O L
home = H O M	job = J O B	Paul = P O L

SHORT AND SOFT SOUNDS OF O

The *o* symbol represents the short and soft sounds of *o*, no matter how the word is spelled in longhand.

Short and Soft O Words

Short and Soft O Practice

5.4

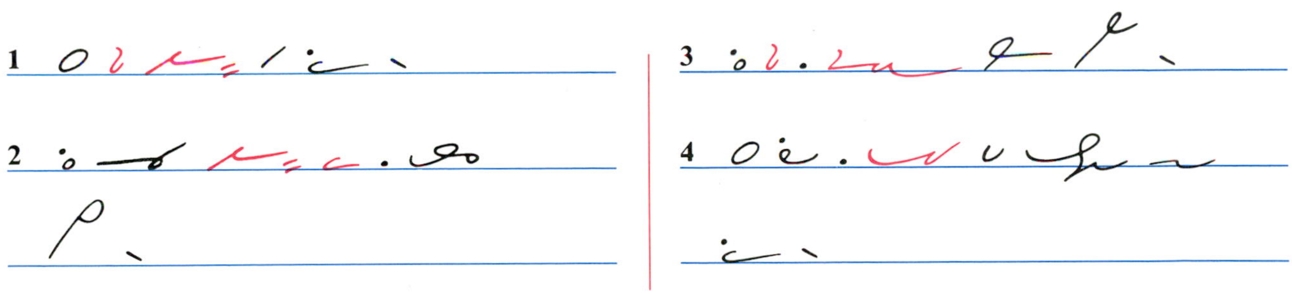

5

¶ Letter

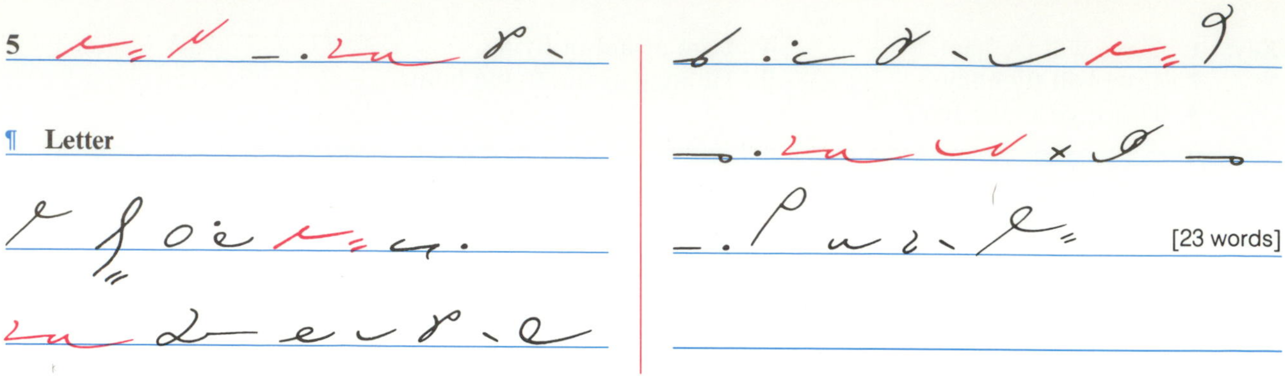

[23 words]

Key:
1 I saw Tom at home.
2 He met Tom on a rainy day.
3 He saw a small tame deer.
4 I hear a lot of laughter in our home.
5 Tom taught in a small city.

Shorthand skill enables the student to obtain a better position in the job market.

Communication Skill Builder

Similar Words: sight, site, cite

sight: having to do with seeing; vision
site: a location
cite: (v.) to make reference to; to quote

More light may harm her *sight*.

Dale has a small home *site*.

I will *cite* a name in my farm deed.

Reading and Writing Practice

5.5 Agenda for Yearbook Staff Meeting

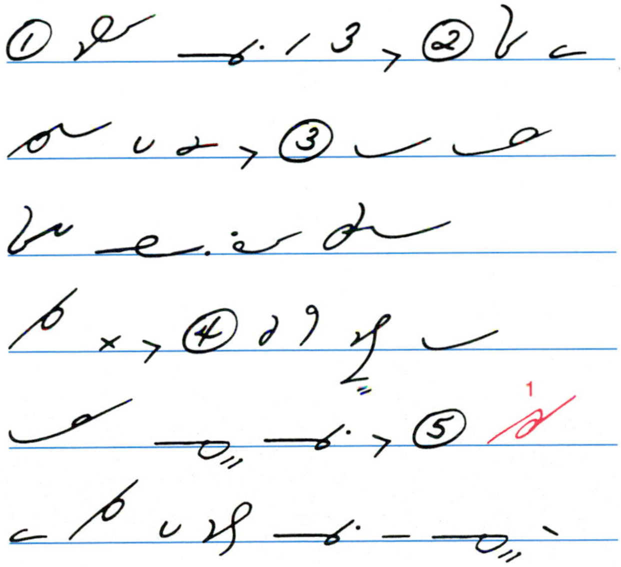

1 Decide

[31 words]

5.6 "To Do" List

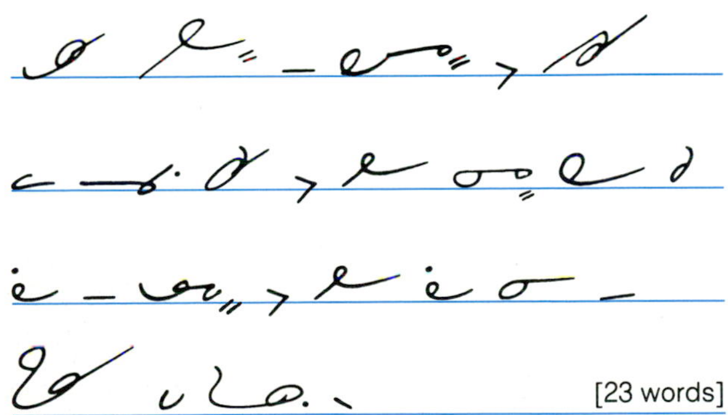

[23 words]

LESSON 6

NEW IN LESSON 6

- Word beginning *in-*
- Symbols for the sounds of *oo*, *k*, and *g*
- Symbols for the sounds of *w*, *sw*, and *wh* at the beginning of words
- Differentiating between sound-alike words *to*, *too*, *two* and *knew*, *new*

WORD BEGINNING IN-

The brief form *in* is also used as a word beginning, as in *invest*.

Example: invest 

In- Words

invest 

investing 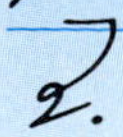

invite 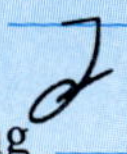

inviting 

indeed 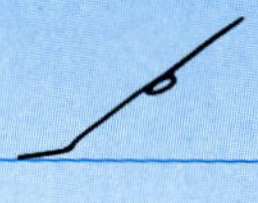

inside 

In- Practice

6.1

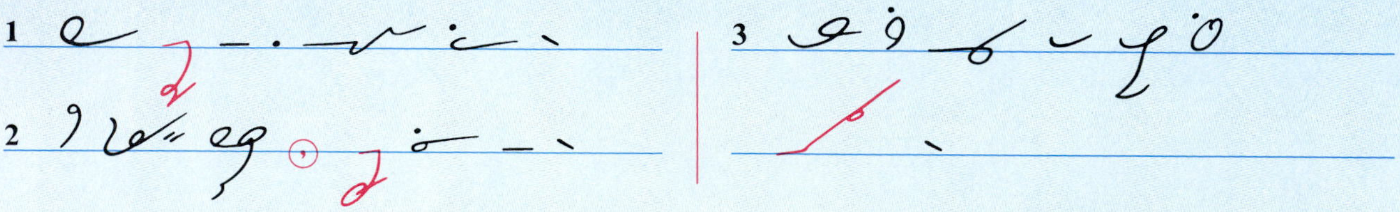

4
5

¶ **Phone Message**

To:

From:

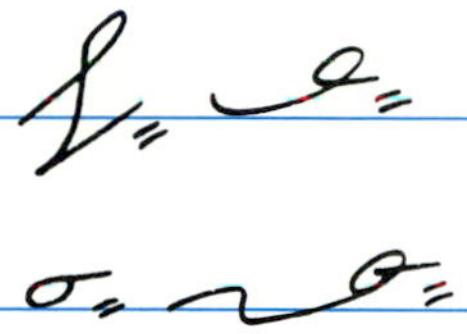

Date: 13

Time: 11:30

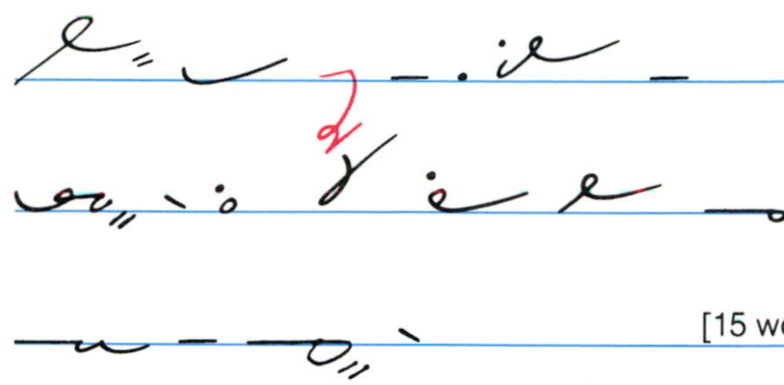

[15 words]

Key:
1 I will invest in a motor home.
2 If Fred arrives, invite him in.
3 Rain has made our river high indeed.
4 Light a fire inside our stove.
5 Invite him to our home.

SOUNDS OF OO, K, G

The symbols for *oo*, *k*, and *g* are forward "over" curves differentiated by length.

oo k g

Sound of OO

The shorthand *oo* is a tiny upward hook.

Example: do

OO Words

do	move	suit
duty	moved	food
to, too, two	who	room
knew, new	whom	fruit
noon	Sue	flew

Sound of K

The *k* symbol is a short over curve written from left to right across the writing line.

Example: came

K Words

came	cake	car, care
make	take	crate ■
making	like	clearing ■
Mike	liked	clean ■

■ Writing Tip: Curves of the same length, like *kr*, are written as somewhat flat reverse curves. Curves of unequal length, like *kl*, have an exaggerated joining to ensure readability.

kr kl

Sound of G

The *g* symbol is a long over curve written from left to right across the writing line.

Example: gain

G Words

gain	great ■	again
game	grade ■	eager ■
gave	green ■	regret ■
give	grain ■	glow ■
given	go	gleam ■
guide	goal	legal ■

■ Writing Tip: Curves of the same length, like *gl*, are written as somewhat flat reverse curves. Curves of unequal length, like *gr*, have an exaggerated joining to ensure readability.

gl gr

OO, K, G Practice

6.2

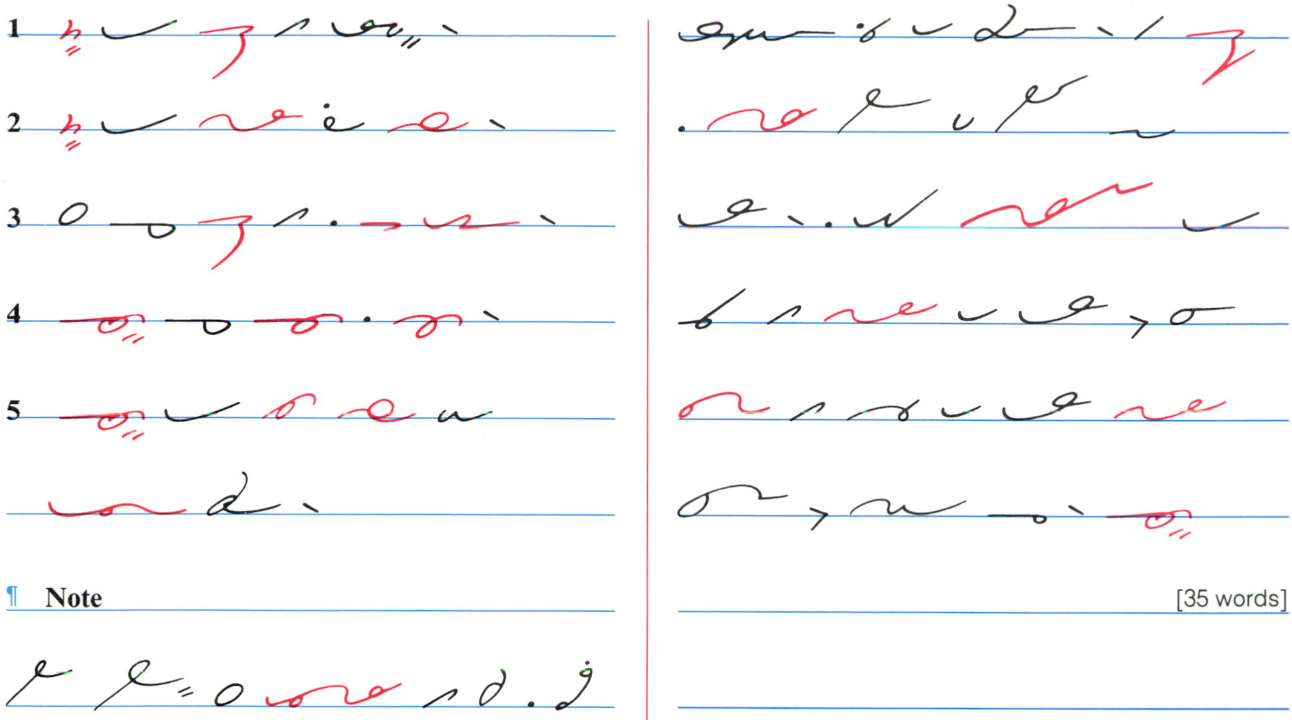

Key: 1 Sue will move to Reno.
2 Sue will clean her car.
3 I may move to a new room.
4 Mike may make a cake.
5 Mike will take care of our legal file.

Students can use their shorthand skill to draft a report for class assignment.

SOUNDS OF W, SW, WH

At the beginning of words, *w* is represented by the *oo hook*, as in the word *we*. The sound of *sw* at the beginning of a word is written *s oo*, as in *sweet*. The *wh* sound at the beginning of words, such as *why*, is represented by the *oo hook*.

Examples: we sweet why

W, Sw, Wh Words

we	wait	why
way	waste	white
week	sweet	while
weeks	swell	

W, Sw, Wh Practice

6.3

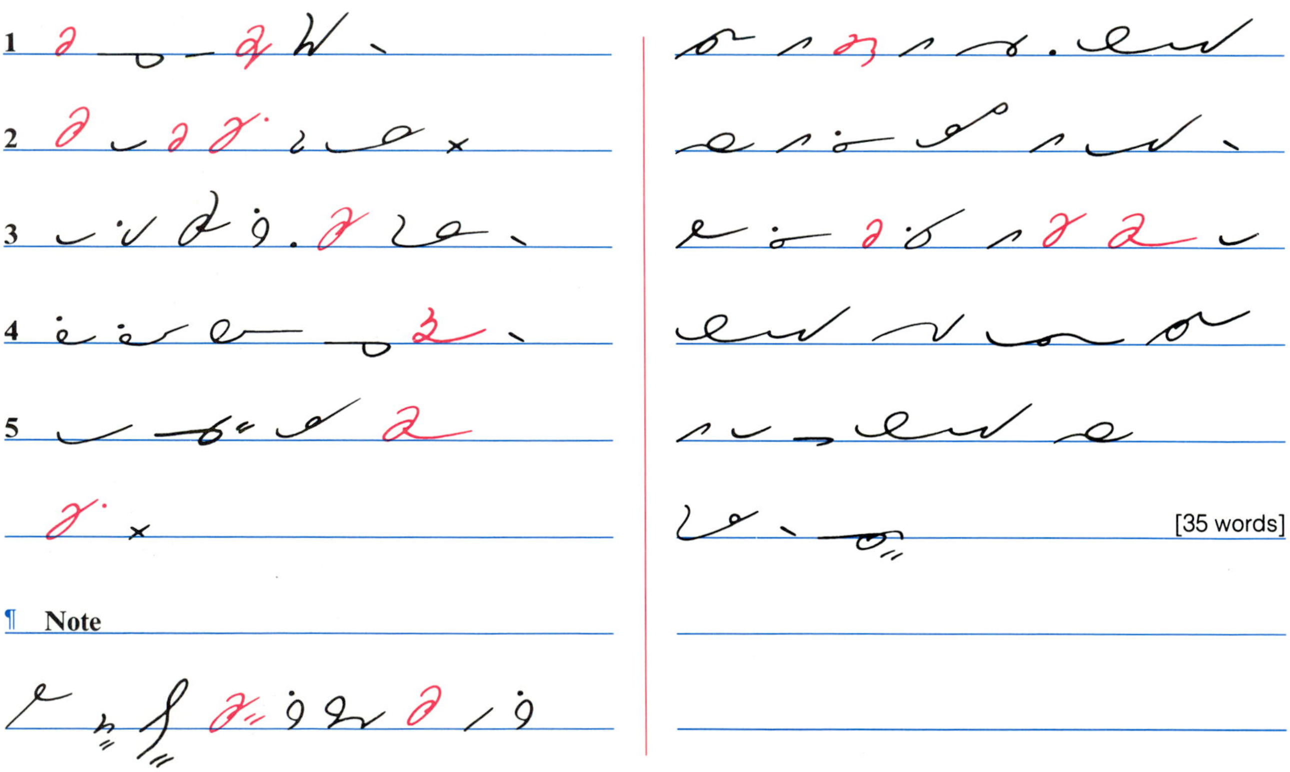

Key: 1 We may not waste food.
2 Why are we waiting so late?
3 Our hot fire has a white flame.
4 Her hurt arm may swell.
5 Will Matt read while waiting?

Communication Skill Builder

Similar Words: to, too, two

to: (prep.) toward

too: (adv.) excessive; also

two: a number

Give my letter *to* Fay.

Lee gave me a gift *too*.

Fred has *two* free airline flights.

Similar Words: knew, new

knew: had prior knowledge

new: not having existed before

We *knew* our trailer tire might go flat.

We will need a *new* trailer tire.

Reading and Writing Practice

6.4 List of Points for Phone Call

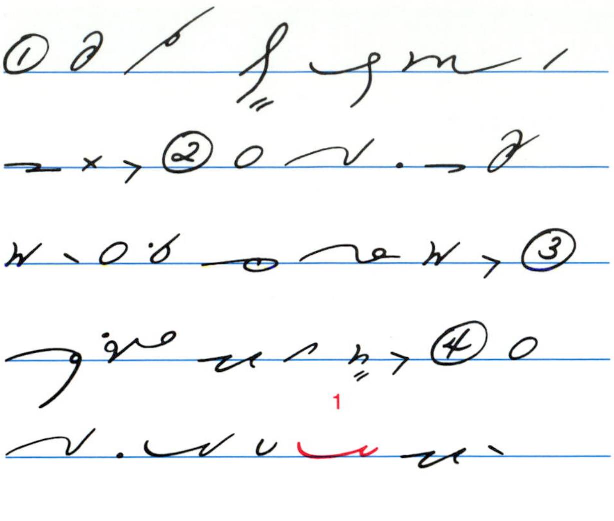

[26 words]

6.5 Personal Letter

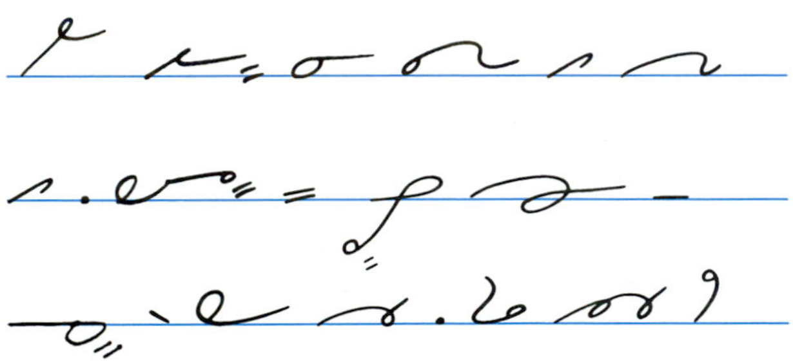

1 law

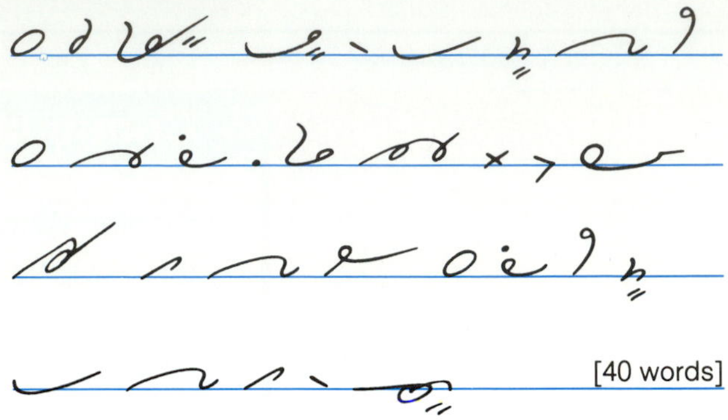

[40 words]

6.6 Memo

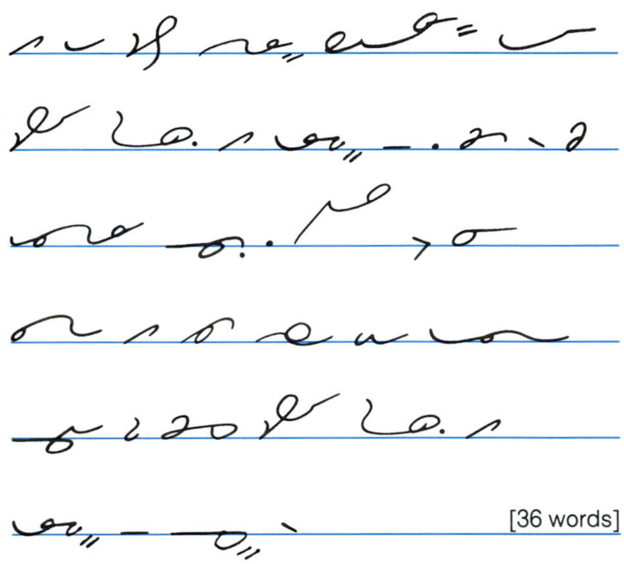

[36 words]

LESSON 7

NEW IN LESSON 7

- **Another way of writing *s***
- **Symbols for the sounds of *p* and *b***
- **Symbol *oo* for the short and soft sounds of *oo***
- **Intelligent notetaking**

SOUNDS OF S, P, B

The symbols for *left s* and for *p* and *b* are *downward* left curves differentiated by length.

left s  p  b 

Left S

The *left s* is a mirror image of the *comma s*. There are two symbols for *s* so that this frequent letter may always join curves in the same direction as the curve and so that it may join straight strokes with a sharp angle. Joining patterns will become clear through reading practice. 

Example: seems 

Left S Words

seems 	leads 	days 
names 	writes 	desk, disk 
needs 	nice 	leasing 

list, least

sales

increase

raised

readers

most

Sound of P

The symbol for the sound of *p* is a medium-size downward left curve.

Example: pay

P Words

pay

piece

post

pays, pass

paper ■

hope

please ■

people ■

opens

place ■

pipe

despite

space

price, prize ■

Paul

■ Writing Tip: The *p* symbol joins to the *l* and *r* symbols in a single curve.

Example: purple

Sound of B

The symbol for the sound of *b* is a long downward left curve.

Example: base

B Words

base

beats

blame ■

based

beds

bright ■

best

better

brief ■

buy

big

bought, boat

bay

label ■

neighbor ■

■ Writing Tip: The *b* symbol joins to the *l* and *r* symbols in a single curve.

Example: bright label

Left S, P, B Practice

7.1

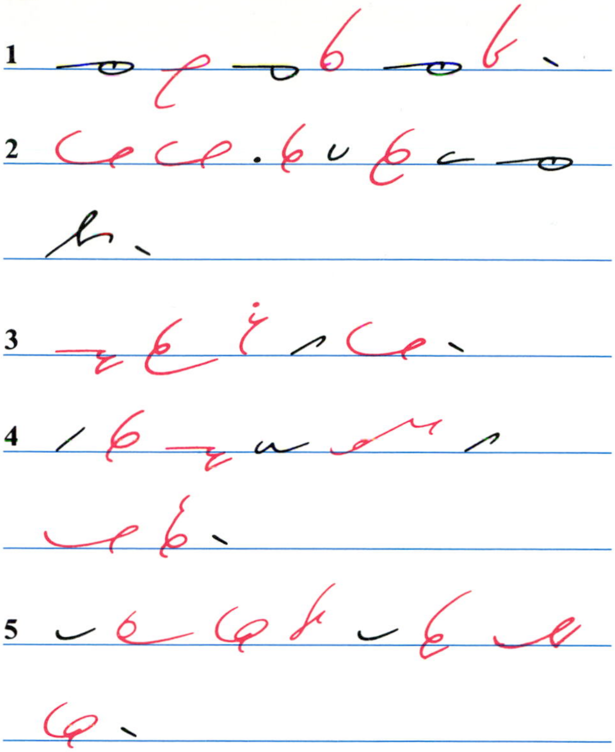

¶ **Memo to a Sales Manager**

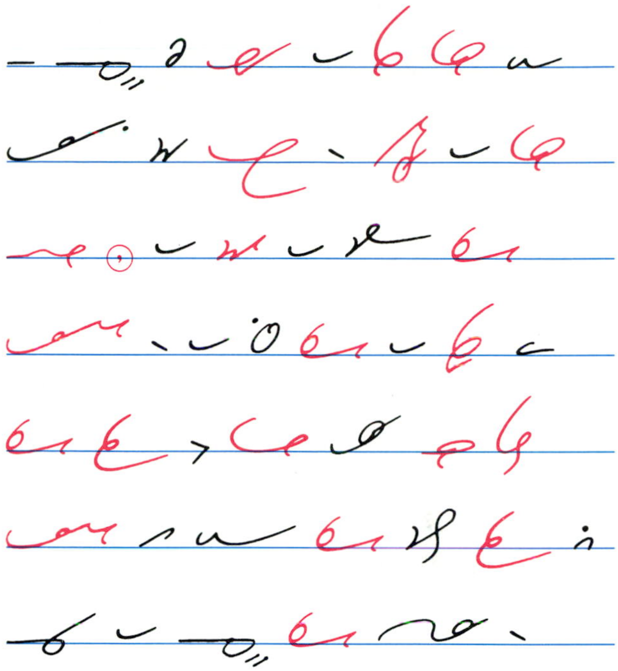

[39 words]

Key:
1. My neighbor may buy my boat.
2. Please place a piece of paper on my desk.
3. Most people hope to please.
4. It pays most of our readers to lease space.
5. Our sale price beats our best list price.

SHORT AND SOFT SOUNDS OF OO

The *oo* hook that represents the sound of *oo* in *too* also represents the short sound of *u* as in *up* and the soft sound of *oo* as in *book.* 

Examples: up  book 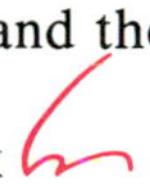

Short and Soft OO Words

up  does  must 

number  enough  us ■ 

■ *Us* is written *oo s* in a single pen motion.

book
cookbook
pull
books
foot
took
cook
put

Short and Soft OO Practice

7.2

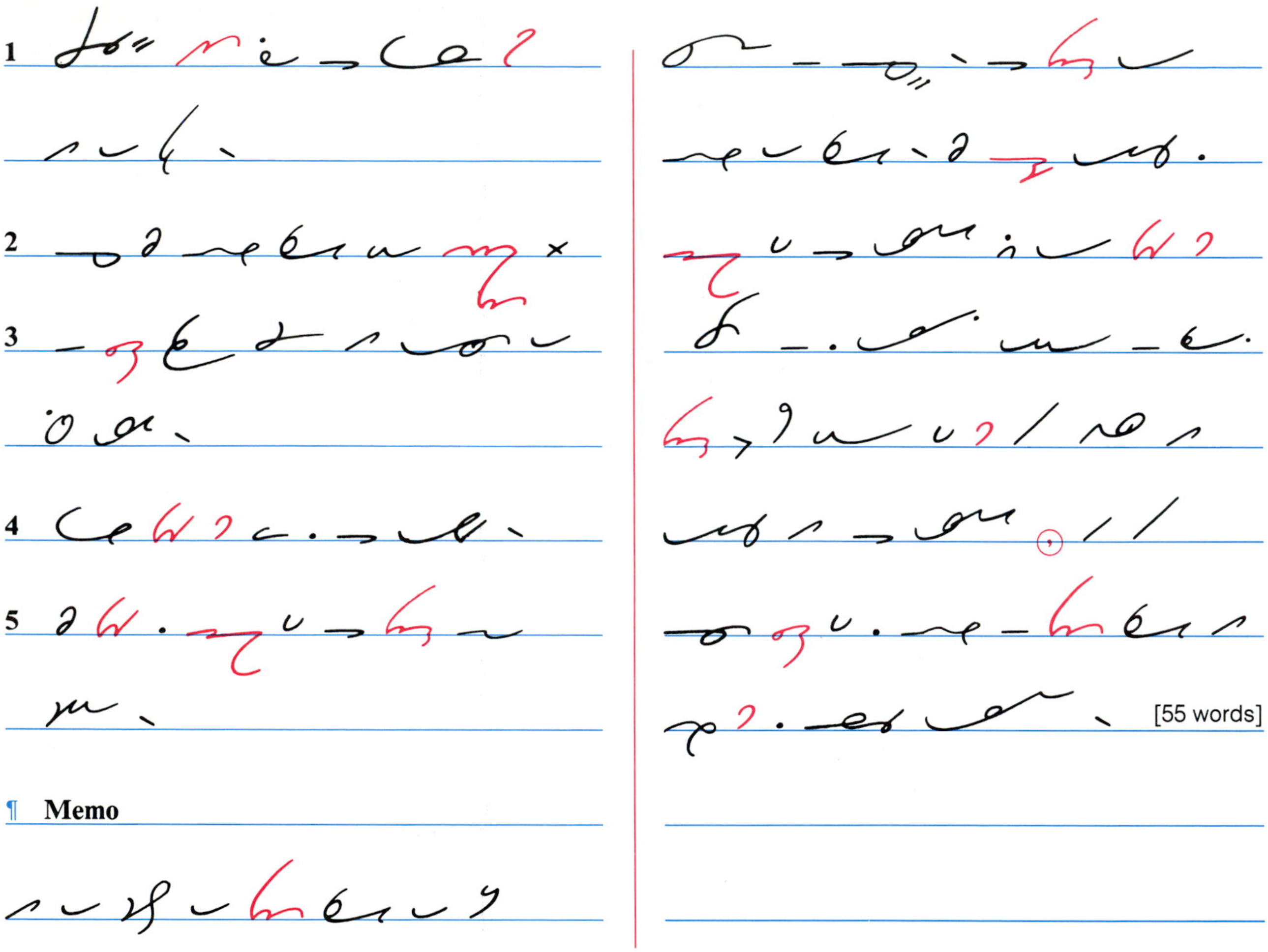

[55 words]

Key:
1 Janet took her new plan up to our boss.
2 May we increase sales of our cookbook?
3 Not enough people seem to like our high rates.
4 Please put us on a new list.
5 We put a number of new books in our store.

Intelligent Notetaking

One of the most valuable uses for shorthand is the taking of intelligent notes. The person who knows shorthand and has good listening habits has a tremendous advantage in terms of personal efficiency. To the student, taking notes in shorthand means that all the key points of a lecture will be recorded in class notes for later study. To the secretary, taking notes in shorthand means that all the elements of a list of instructions will be retained the first time the executive gives those instructions, which in turn will avoid mistakes and embarrassment later on. To the executive, taking notes in shorthand means that once a business meeting has been concluded, details of agreements will be remembered and commitments met.

Whether you are taking notes as a student, a secretary, or an executive, shorthand enables you to record all the pertinent information—and *only* the pertinent information.

Reading and Writing Practice

7.3 Letter

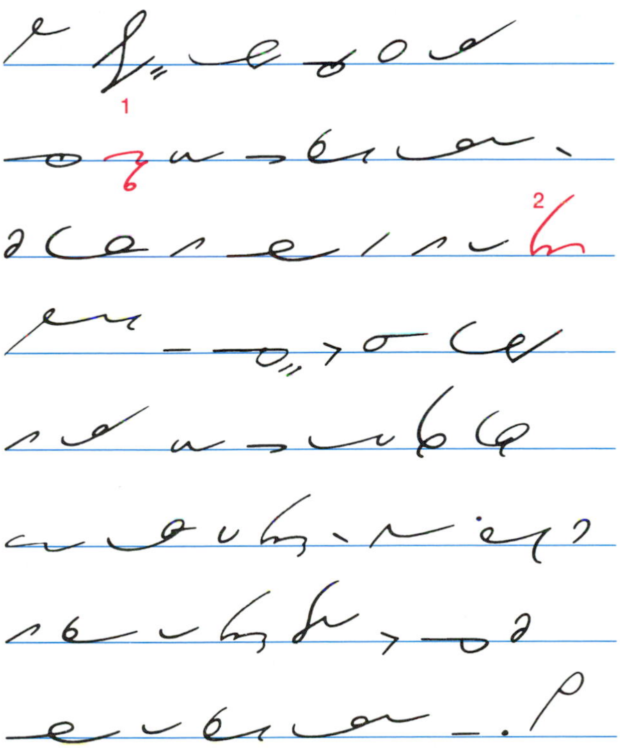

1 copy 2 book

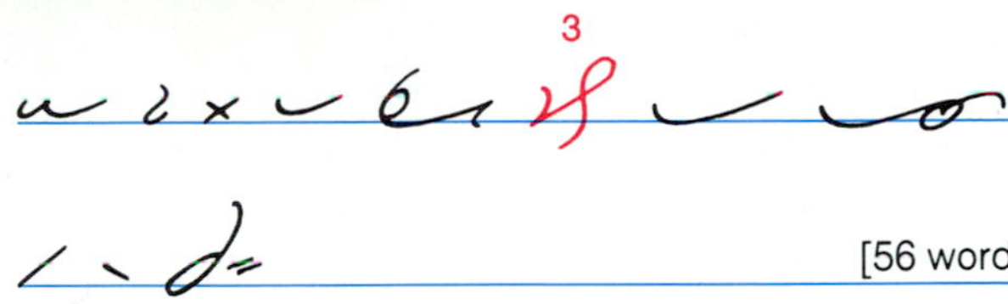

[56 words]

7.4 Notes From a Meeting

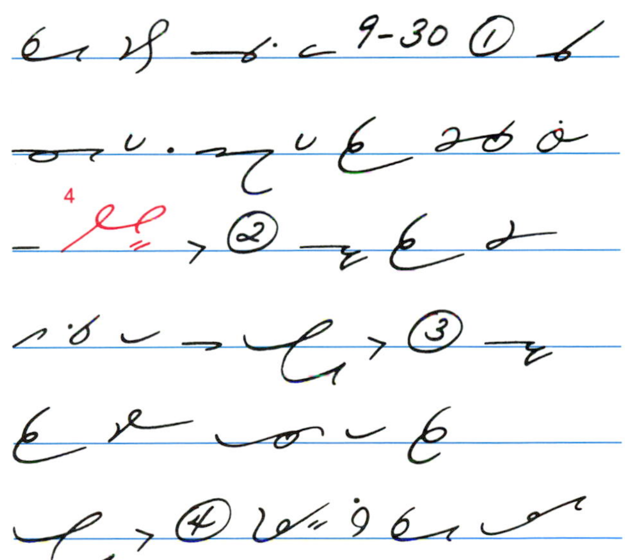

3 staff 4 Dallas

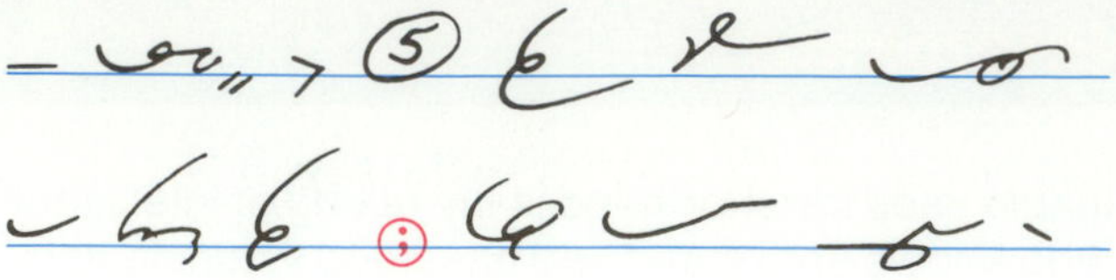

[51 words]

7.5 Note to a Roommate

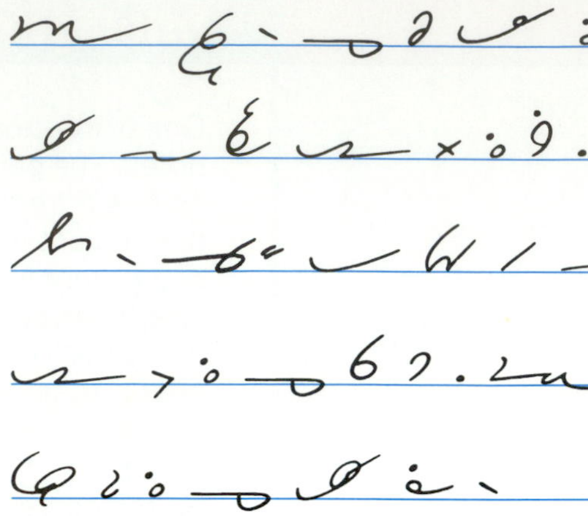

[30 words]

Taking lecture notes in shorthand is faster than in longhand, and it enables the student to edit so that only the key points are recorded.

LESSON 8

NEW IN LESSON 8

- **Eight brief forms**
- **Brief-form phrases**
- **Differentiating between similar words *it is* and *its***

BRIEF FORMS

is, his	for	have
you, your	can	good
be, by	Mr.	

Brief-Form Derivatives

form	forgive	because
forms	afford	beside
inform	being	before
force	believe	having
forced	became	goods
forget	began	cannot

Brief-Form Practice
8.1

1 2 3 4 5 6 7 8

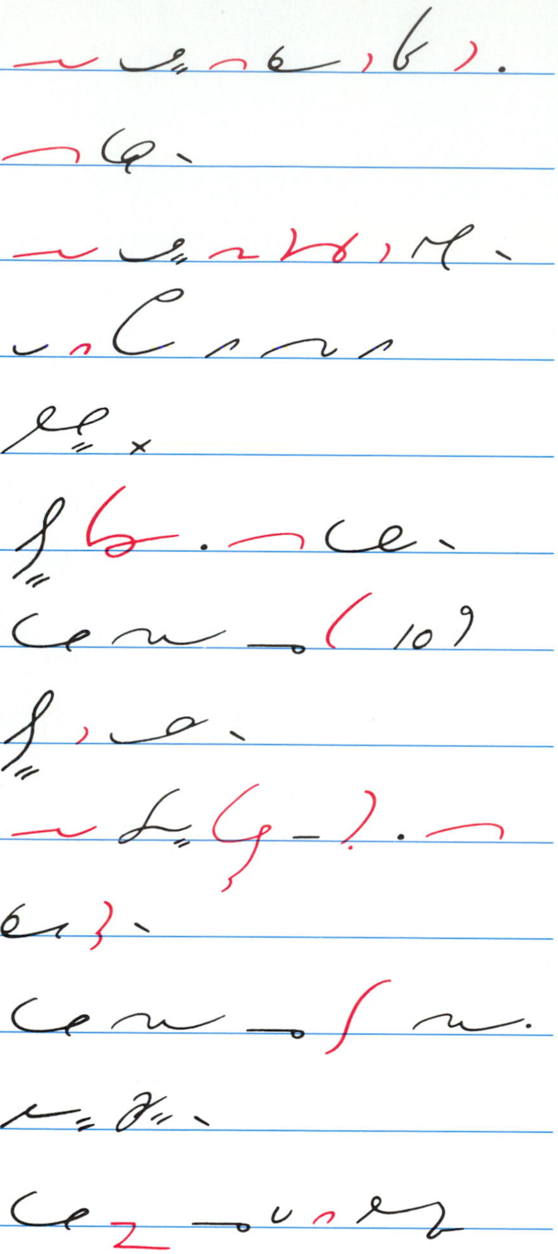

9 10

¶ **Personal Note**

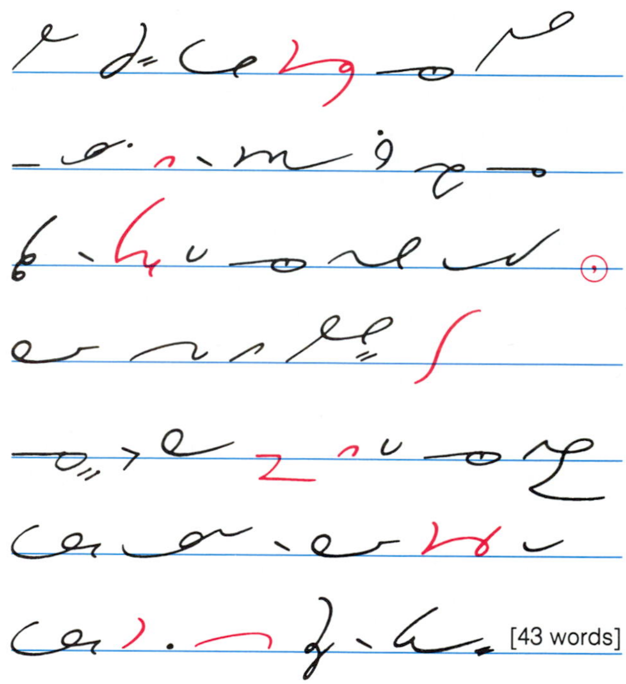

[43 words]

Key:

1 Mr. Lee can sell his boat for a good price.
2 Mr. Lee cannot forget his trip.
3 Are you able to go to Dallas?
4 Dave became a good player.
5 Please call me by ten if Dave is late.
6 Mr. Baker believes in having a good sales force.
7 Please call me before calling Tom White.
8 Please inform me of your telephone number.
9 Nate is being given a pay increase.
10 Our game is being delayed because of rain.

BRIEF-FORM PHRASES

The new brief forms in this lesson, together with those in Lesson 4, make possible a large number of high-speed phrases—so many that they cannot all be used in this lesson. The phrases presented here, along with additional similar phrases, will be used in the following lessons.

You, Your Phrases

of you, of your 

for you, for your 

you are 

you are not 

you have 

you have not 

Will Phrases

I will be 

I will not be 

I will have 

you will 

you will not 

you will be 

you will not be 

you will have 

you will not have 

he will 

we will 

we will be 

Would Phrases

I would 

I would be 

I would not 

you would 

you would be 

you would not be 

you would have 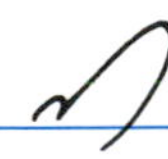

you would not have 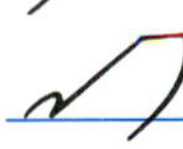

Can Phrases

I can
I can be
I cannot
I cannot be
can have
you can have
you can
you cannot
you can be
cannot be
we can
we cannot

Additional Phrases

it is
by the
by you, by your
I have
have not
I have not

Phrase Practice

8.2

1
2
3
4
5

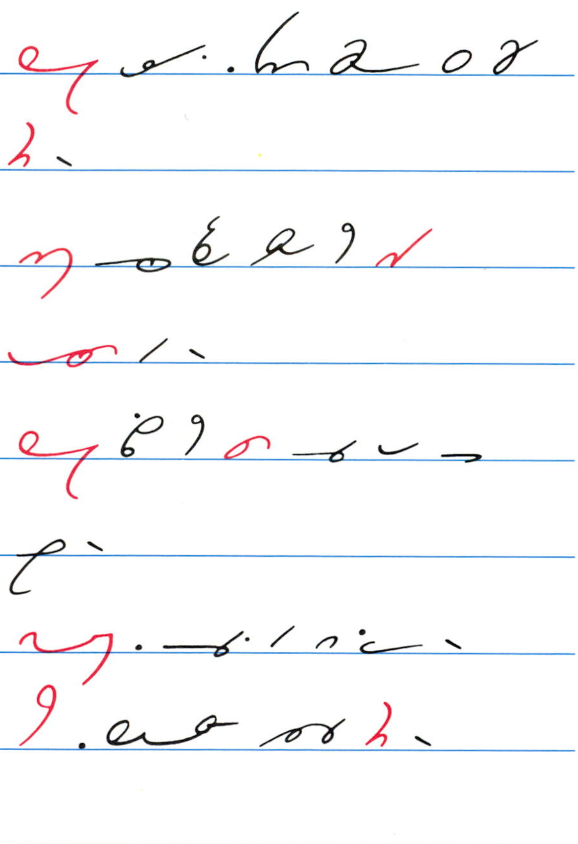

¶ **Note**

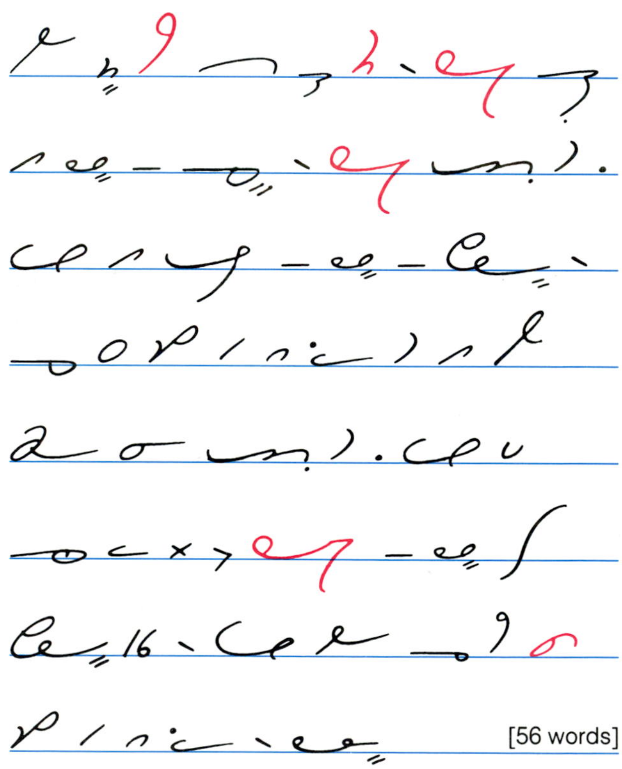

[56 words]

Key: 1 I will be reading a book while I wait for you.
2 You can have my spare tire if you would like it.
3 I will be happy if I can meet our new neighbor.
4 You will not have a meeting at your home.
5 I have an airline ticket for you.

Communication Skill Builder

Similar Words: it is, its

it is: shorthand outline for this phrase is identical with outline for the word *its*

its: possessive meaning "belonging to it"

It is a nice, bright day.

Our plane is flying off *its* course.

Students can use their shorthand to record information from textbooks for study purposes.

Reading and Writing Practice

8.3 Personal Note

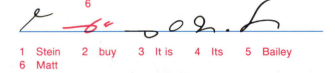

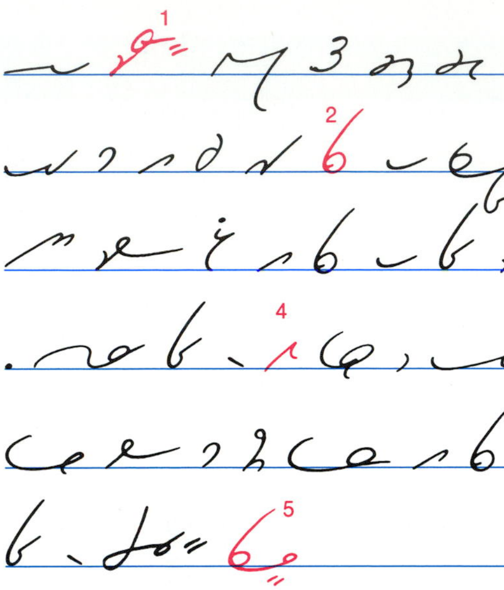

[35 words]

8.4 Business Letter

1 Stein 2 buy 3 It is 4 Its 5 Bailey
6 Matt

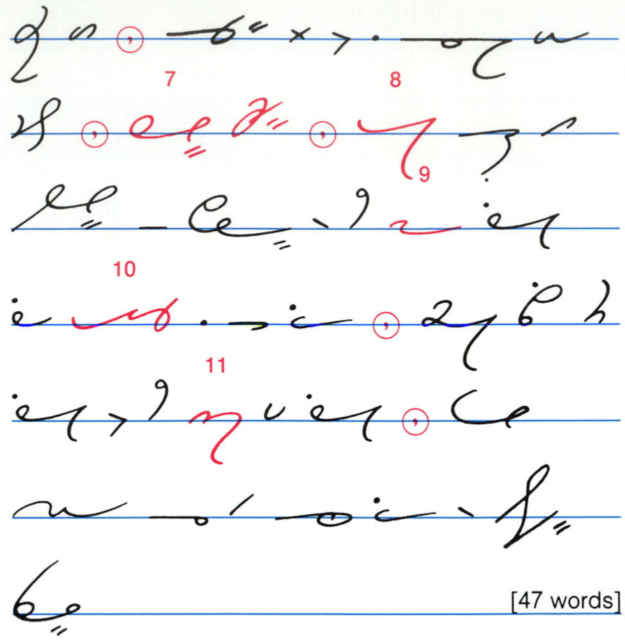

[47 words]

7 Alice White 8 will be 9 you will 10 locate
11 you can be

UNIT III

LESSON 9

NEW IN LESSON 9

- **Phrases containing theory words and brief forms**
- **Symbol for the sound of *th***
- **Symbols for the sounds of *sh*, *ch*, and *j***
- **Transcribing dates within sentences**

THEORY AND BRIEF-FORM PHRASES

A large number of high-speed phrases are possible by combining a few simple theory words with the brief forms already learned.

I know

we know

as you, as your

as you know

if the

if you, if your

if you have

if you are

if you will

if you can

if you cannot

we are

we are not

we have

we need

I need

I do

do not

I do not

we do

do you

do you know

to you, to your

to take ■

on our

for our

on it

■ This phrase does not contain a brief form.

Can Phrases

I can

we can

we cannot

can you

we can be

we cannot be

Will Phrases

we will

we will be

we will not have

we will have

we will not

we will not be

Would Phrases

we would

we would be

we would not have

we would have

we would not

we would not be

May, Might Phrases

I might

we might have

you might have

I might be

we might be

we may be

we might

you might be

we may have

Phrase Practice

9.1

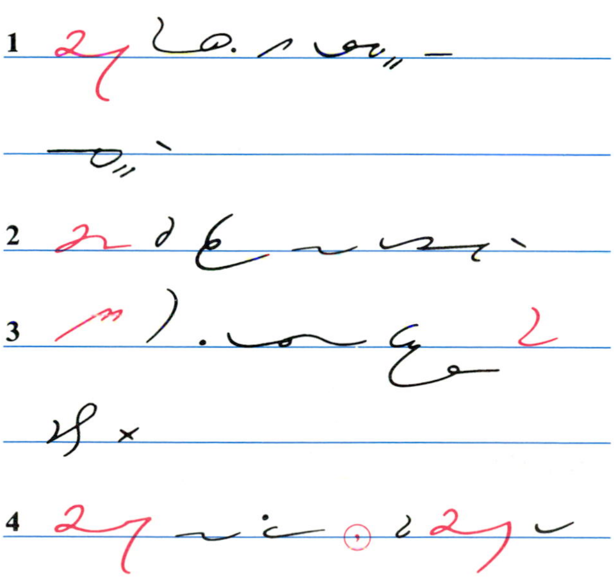

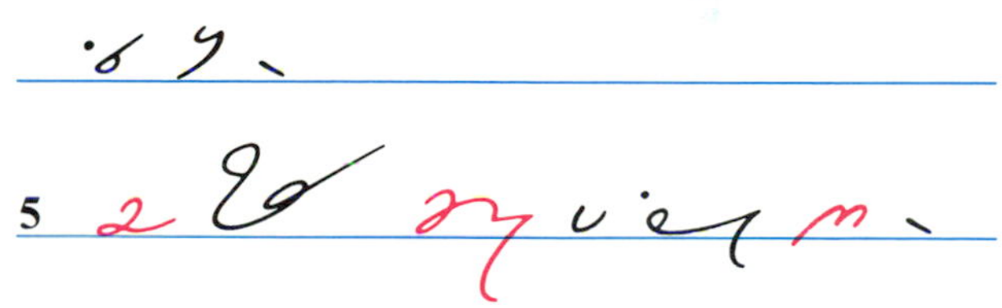

¶ **List of Points to Discuss With the Boss**

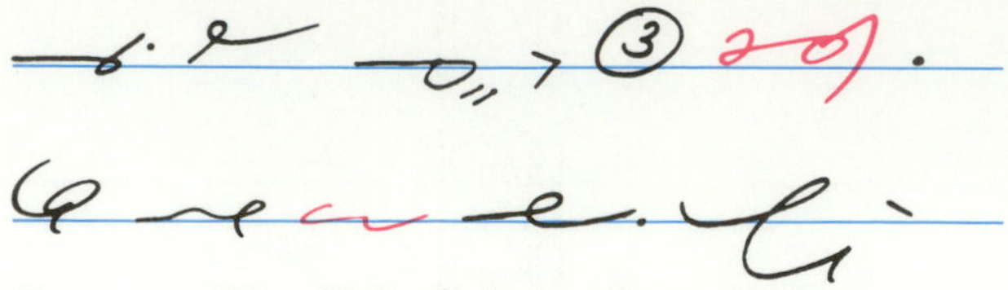

[16 words]

Key:
1 We will be flying to Reno in May.
2 We cannot see people in our rooms.
3 Do you have a legal problem for our staff?
4 We will not be in our home, so we will have our heat off.
5 We are afraid we cannot be of help to you.

SOUND OF TH

The sound of *th* as in *these* is written with an *upward* sloping short curve, much like a curved *t* symbol. This symbol is called *ith.*

Example: these

Th Words

these

then, thin

thick

math

Smith

Beth

Keith

Ruth

smooth

truth

faith

booth

Th Practice
9.2

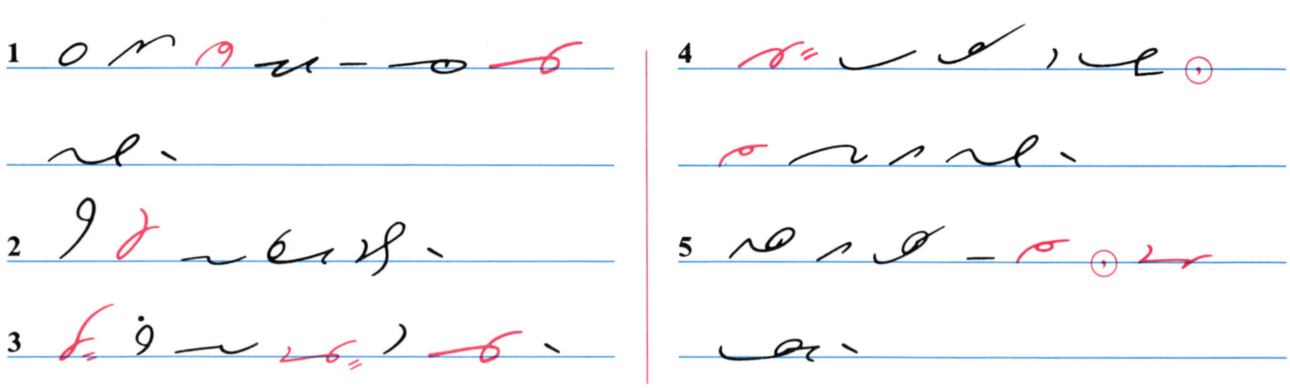

¶ **Personal Note**

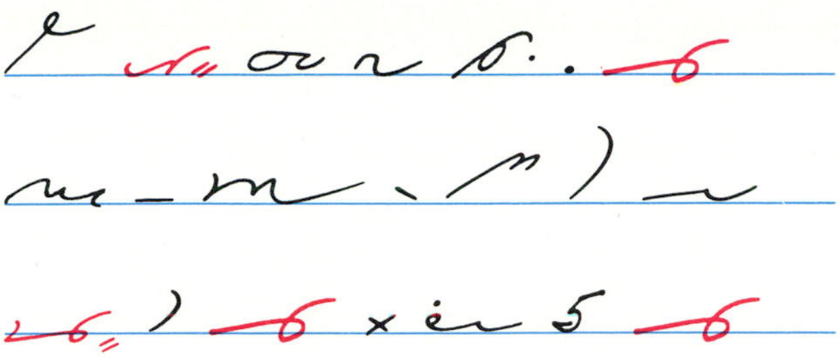

[29 words]

Key: **1** I took these notes in my math class.
2 I have faith in our sales staff.
3 Beth has Mr. Smith for math.
4 Keith will read his lesson, then go to class.
5 Try to write in thin, smooth lines.

SOUNDS OF SH, CH, J

The symbols for *sh*, *ch*, and *j* are *downward* straight symbols differentiated by length.

sh  ch  j 

Sound of Sh

The sound of *sh* as in *she* is represented by a short downward straight symbol called *ish.* 

Example: she 

Sh Words

she 
show 
showed 

share 
shade 
shape 

sure 
issue 
issued 

Sound of Ch

The sound of *ch* as in *check* is represented by a medium-size downward straight symbol called *chay*.

chay 

Example: check 

Ch Words

check ____ each ____ attach ____

checked ____ match ____ reach ____

chair ____ March ____ search ____

church ____ teach ____ French ____

You Write What You Hear

The letter *g* has two sounds in English. For the hard sound of *g* as in *go*, you write the *g* symbol in shorthand. For the soft sound of *g* as in *age*, you write the *j* symbol. Here are a few more examples of the *j* symbol for the soft sound of *g*.

page = P A J
change = ch A N J
large = L A R J
charge = ch A R J
changed = ch A N J D
college = K O L E J

Sound of J

The sound of *j* as in *job* is represented by a long downward straight symbol called *j*.

j 

Example: job 

J Words

job ____ age ____ change ____

jobs ____ page ____ large ____

Jane ____ charge ____ college ____

Jean ____ charged ____ George ____

Sh, Ch, J Practice
9.3

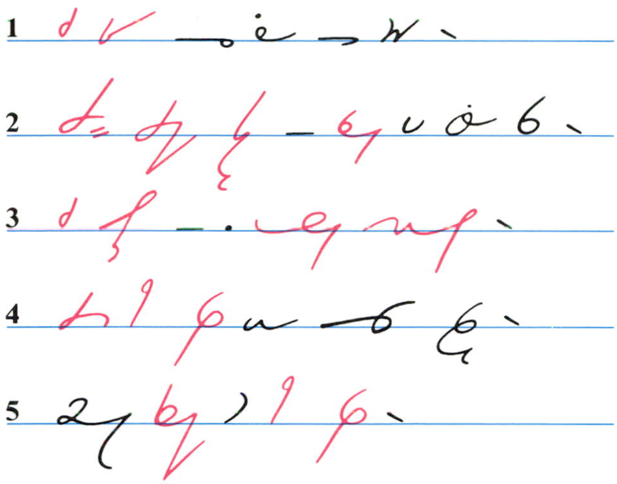

¶ **Personal Letter**

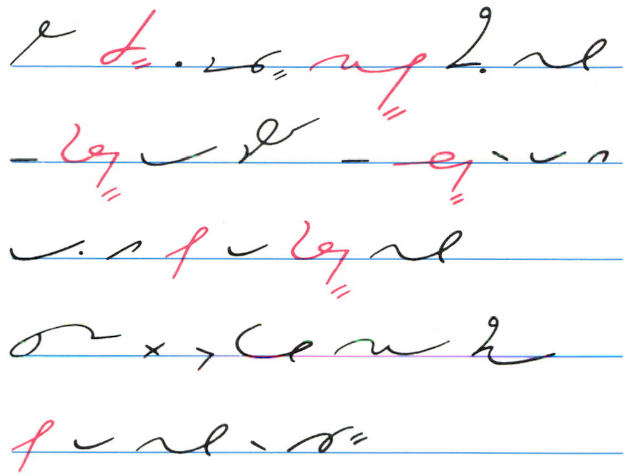

[27 words]

Key:
1 She showed me her new suit.
2 Jane changed jobs in search of higher pay.
3 She teaches in a large college.
4 Check each page of our math papers.
5 We will be charged for each page.

Dates Within Sentences

In business communications it is common practice for the month to precede the day. In expressing dates this way, it is not appropriate to use *th*, *st*, or *d*, and no punctuation is required.

Call me on *July 8* if you can.

If for some reason the day precedes the month, then it is appropriate to use *th*, *st*, or *d* in the transcript. For the sake of writing speed, the *th*, *st*, or *d* is not written in shorthand.

On the *17th of March* we select new members.

Reading and Writing Practice

9.4 Business Letter

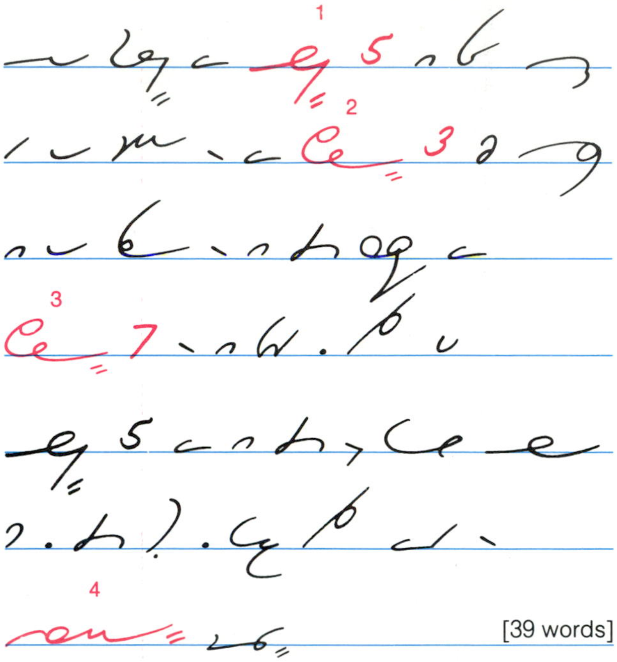

[39 words]

1 March 5 2 April 3 3 April 7 4 Carol

9.5 Personal Note

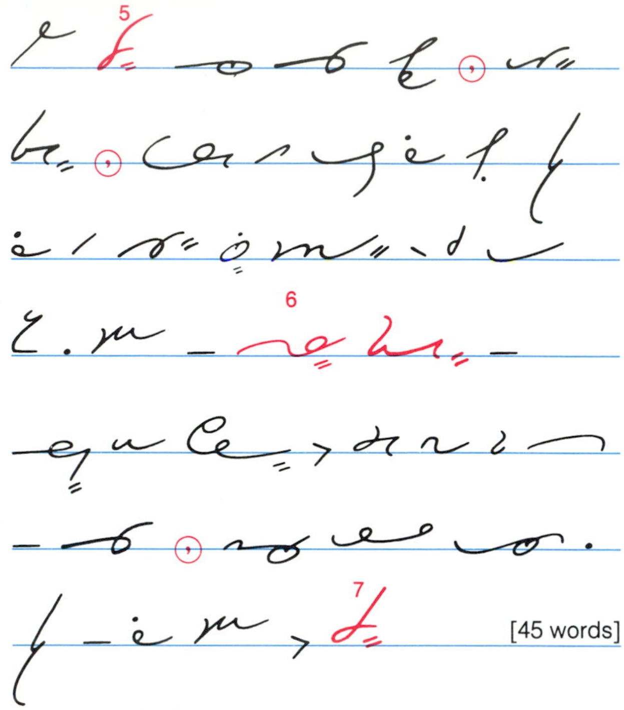

[45 words]

5 Beth 6 Great Falls 7 Jane

Shorthand can be a valuable skill in transcribing telephone messages quickly and accurately.

LESSON 10

NEW IN LESSON 10

- Eight brief forms
- Phrases containing theory words and brief forms
- Word ending *-ly*
- Tips on taking dictation

BRIEF FORMS

the	that	this
them	should	could
but	which	

Brief-Form Practice
10.1

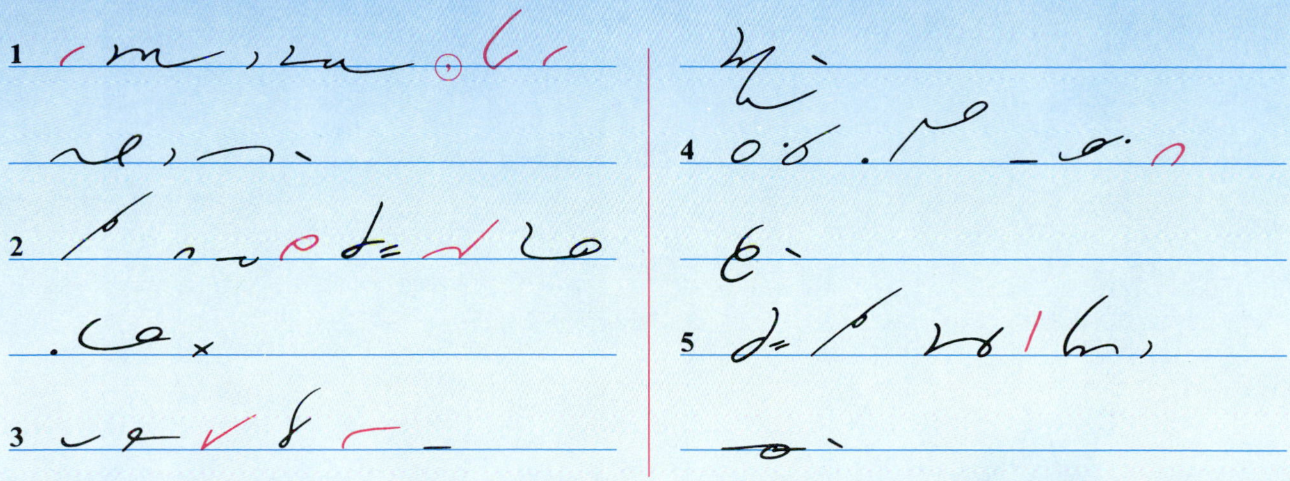

¶ **Agenda for a Meeting**

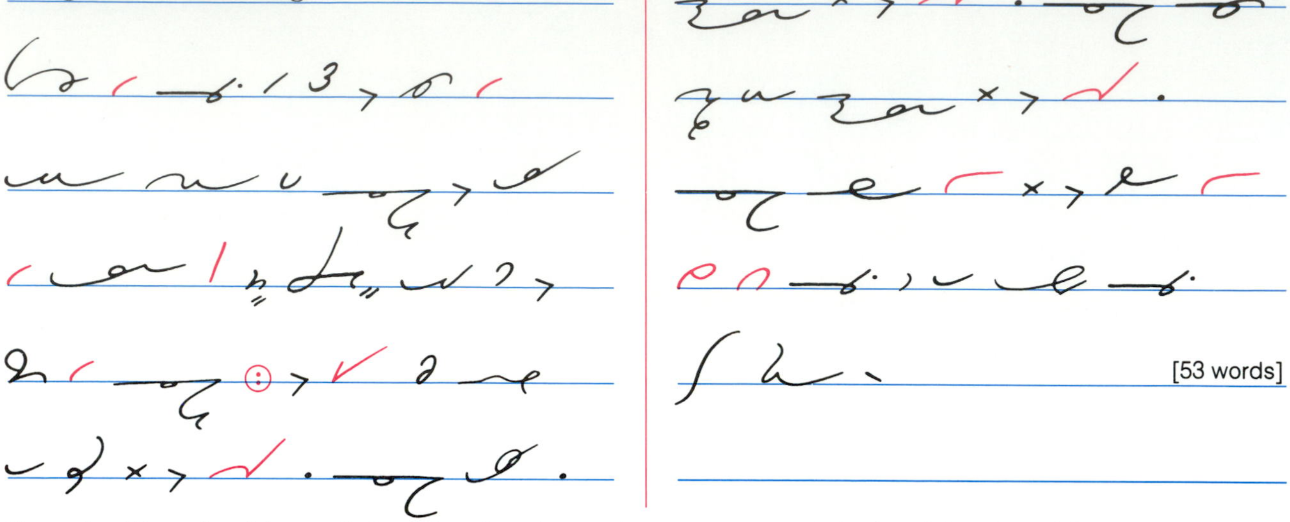

[53 words]

Key:
1 The school is small, but the class is good.
2 Did you know that Jean could fly a plane?
3 Our team should beat them in football.
4 I had a delay in writing this paper.
5 Fay did forget which book is mine.

THEORY AND BRIEF-FORM PHRASES

- of the
- of these
- of them
- on the
- as the
- by the
- to the
- for the
- for this
- for you, for your
- in the
- on the
- is this
- this is
- this is the
- in this
- on this
- this will
- this will be
- that will
- in which
- which is
- is in, is not
- should be
- should have
- I could
- I could not
- did not

Phrase Practice
10.2

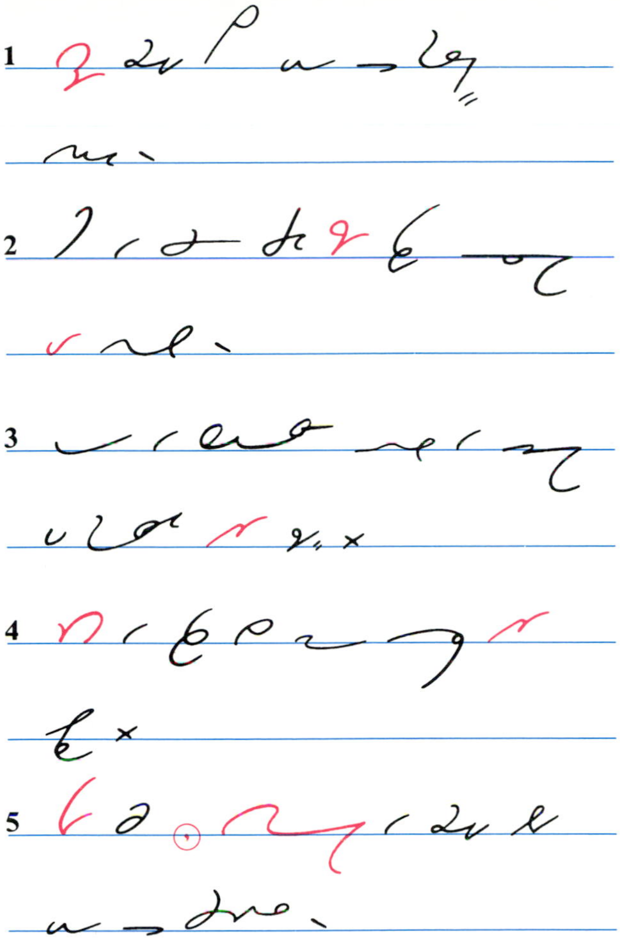

¶ **Business Letter**

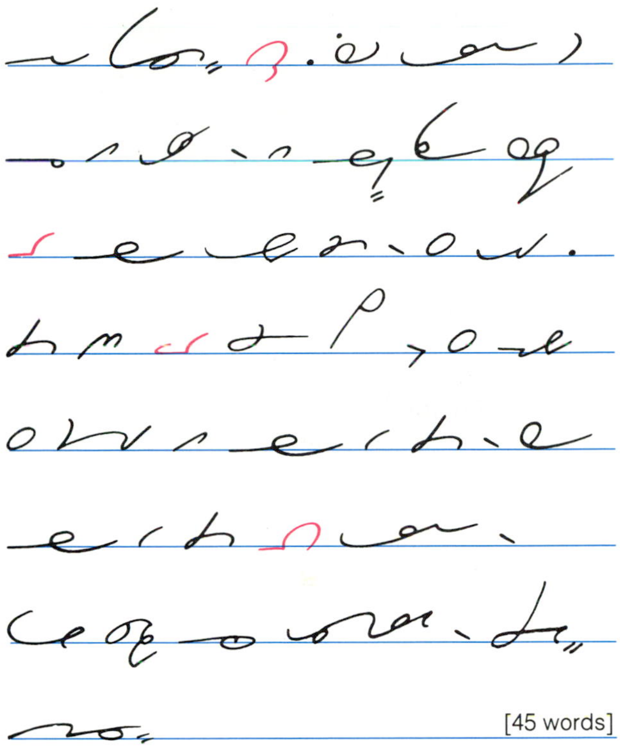

[45 words]

Key:
1 This is the first day of our new French course.
2 You have the same chance as the best member of the class.
3 Will the airline increase the number of flights to the East?
4 Is this the paper that you will give to the teacher?
5 By the way, this will be the first test of our new factory.

WORD ENDING -LY

The word ending *-ly* (which sounds like "lee") as in *only* is written with the *e* circle. 

Example: only 

-ly Words

only

likely

greatly

clearly

properly

highly

weekly

daily

mostly

early

sincerely

But: When the *l* is double, both the *l* and the *ly* are written.

really

finally

totally

-ly Practice

10.3

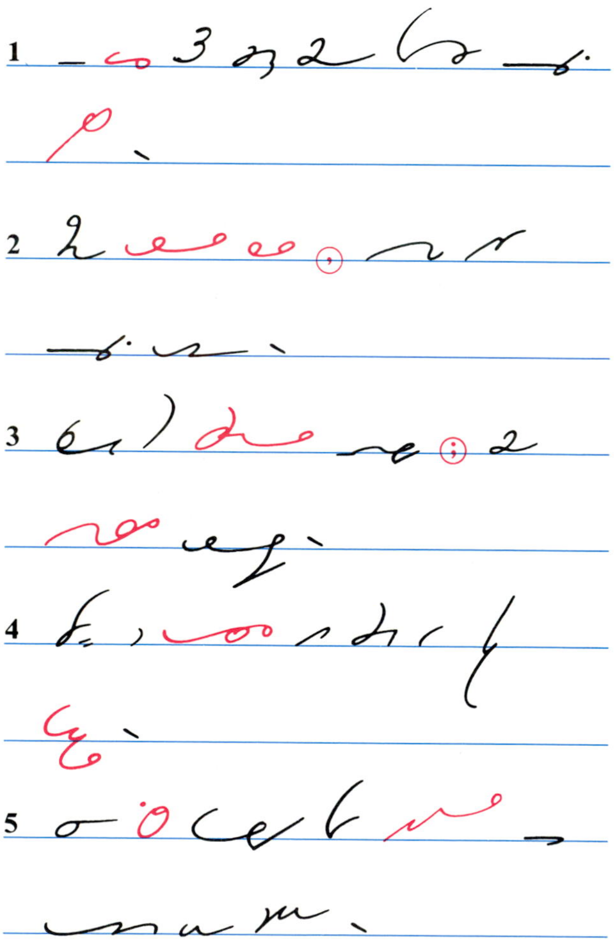

¶ **Interoffice Note**

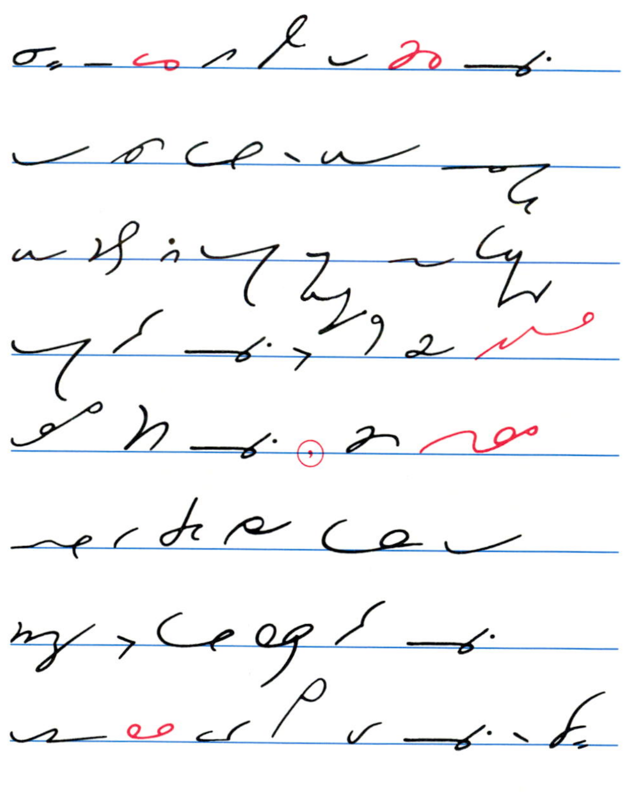

[55 words]

Key:
1 In only three weeks we will begin meeting daily.
2 If you are really early, go to the meeting room.
3 Sales have finally increased; we are greatly relieved.
4 Beth is likely to finish the job properly.
5 I am highly pleased by the totally new look of our store.

Taking Dictation

While shorthand has many personal and professional uses, taking dictation is what comes to mind when most people think of shorthand. Shorthand dictation is one of four basic ways executives may *input* to the information cycle.

Here are a few tips in taking dictation:

Write fluently. Shorthand must be practiced to the point where outlines can be "thrown" on the paper. Theoretical accuracy and proper writing proportions are important, but it is more important to get the work *done*.

Write something. When you do not know the outline for a word that is being dictated, write something. You may write the first sound of the word, the most distinctive sound of the word, or an outline that you consider to be a good guess.

Do not give up. If the dictation is so fast that you get too far behind, you should leave a gap in the notes and pick up what the dictator is currently saying. As soon as the dictation is completed, you should fill in the gap on the basis of memory and context clues.

Watch proportion. From the very start, you should concentrate on keeping the tiny characters tiny—specifically *e*, *n*, *t*, *s*, and *ish*. At very high speeds straight strokes tend to curve a bit. Therefore, it is very important that the symbols which are supposed to be curved are curved deeply.

When away on a business trip, the manager may mail in recorded dictation or may call and dictate to the secretary over the telephone.

10.4 Interoffice Note

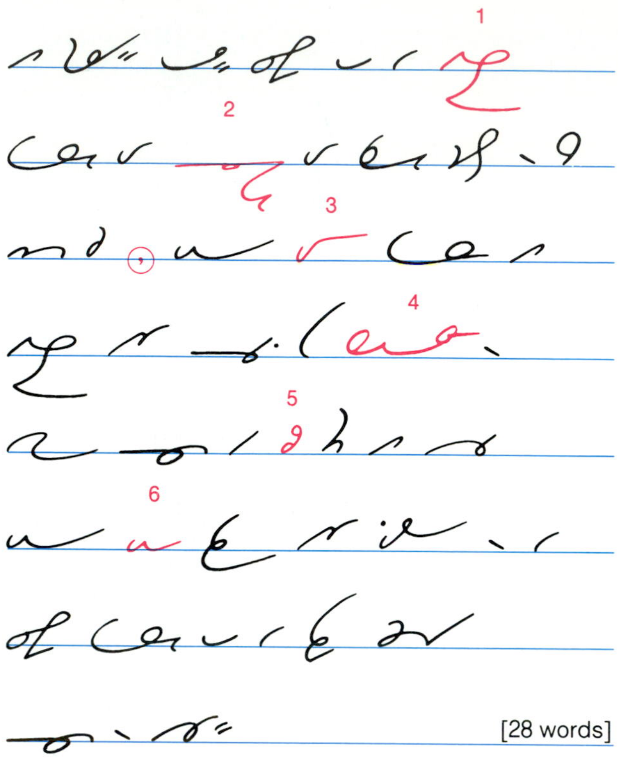

[28 words]

10.5 Insurance Adjuster's Notes About Accident

1 travel 2 members 3 of them 4 airline
5 easy 6 of our

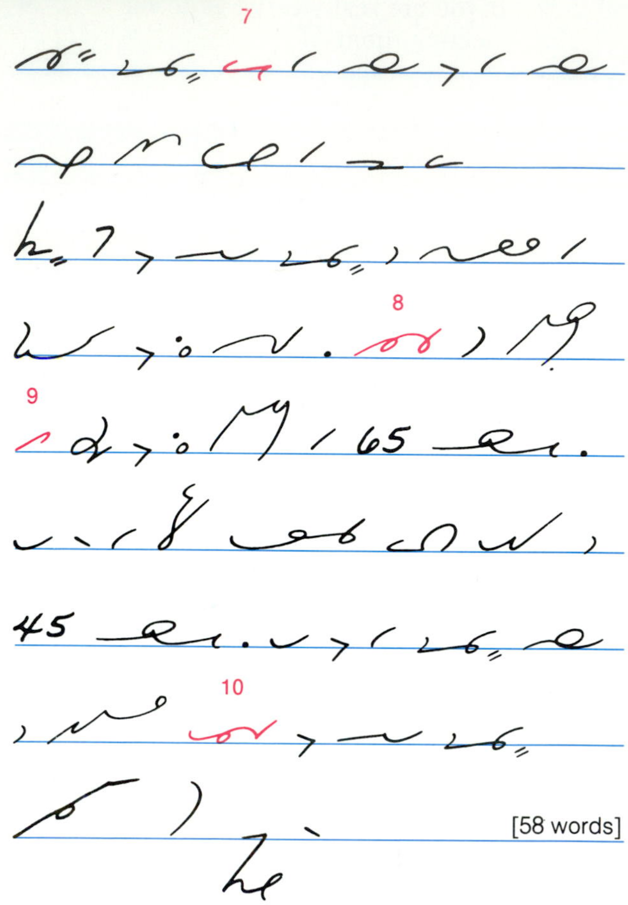

[58 words]

7 owns 8 ticket 9 too 10 wrecked

LESSON 11

NEW IN LESSON 11

- **Word endings *-tion*, *ciency*, and *cient***
- **Shorthand symbols for numbers**
- **Phrases containing *been*, *able*, and *to***
- **Transcription of numbers**

WORD ENDINGS -TION, -CIENCY, -CIENT

The word ending *-tion*, pronounced *shun* as in *nation*, *fashion*, and *decision*, is represented by the *ish* symbol.

The word ending *-ciency*, pronounced *shun see* as in *proficiency*, is written *ish, s, e*.

The word ending *-cient*, pronounced *-shunt* as in *patient*, is written *ish, t*.

Examples: nation  proficiency 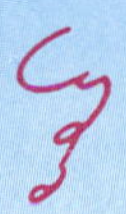 patient 

-tion Words

nation 	collection 	occasion 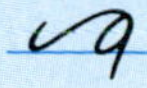
national 	selection 	occasionally ■ 
section 	application 	education 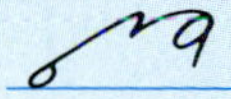
fashion 	decision 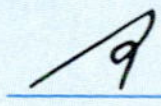	provision 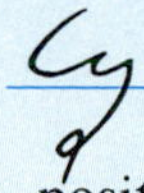
vacation 	location 	possession, position 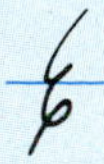

■ The sounds of *l* and *ly* are heard in the word *occasionally*.

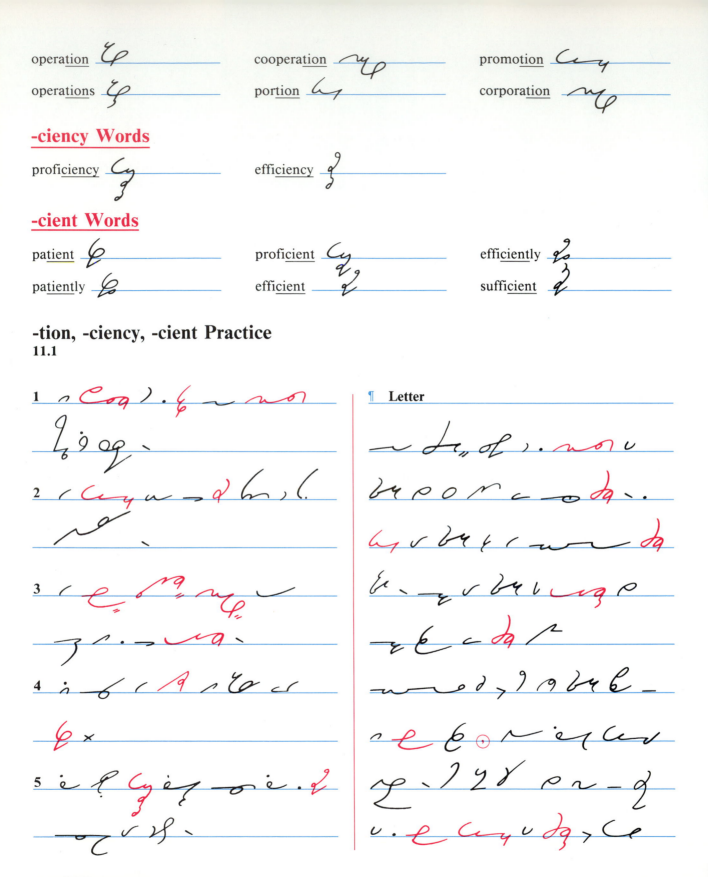

operation

operations

cooperation

portion

promotion

corporation

-ciency Words

proficiency

efficiency

-cient Words

patient

patiently

proficient

efficient

efficiently

sufficient

-tion, -ciency, -cient Practice

11.1

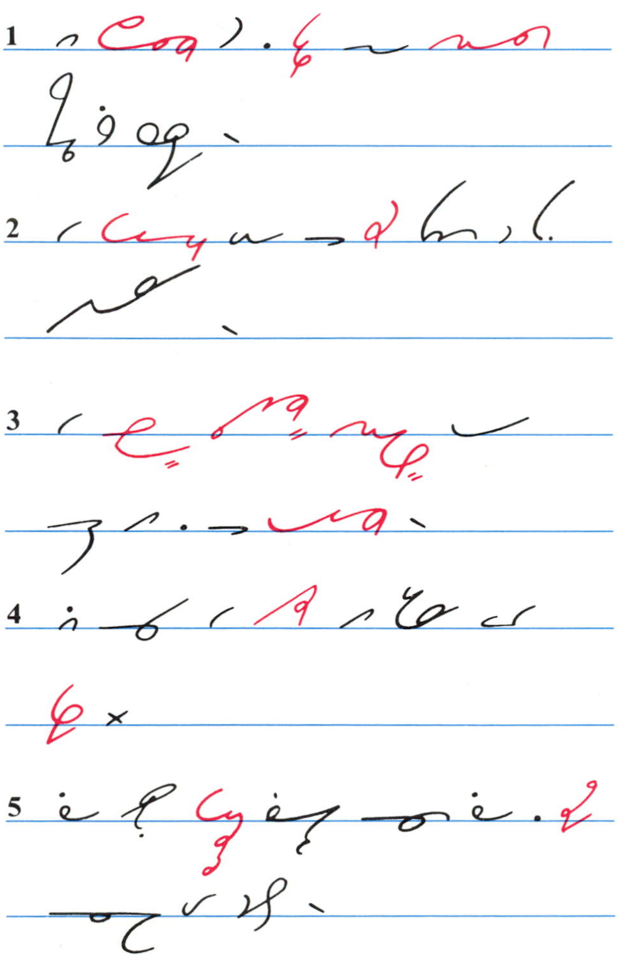

¶ Letter

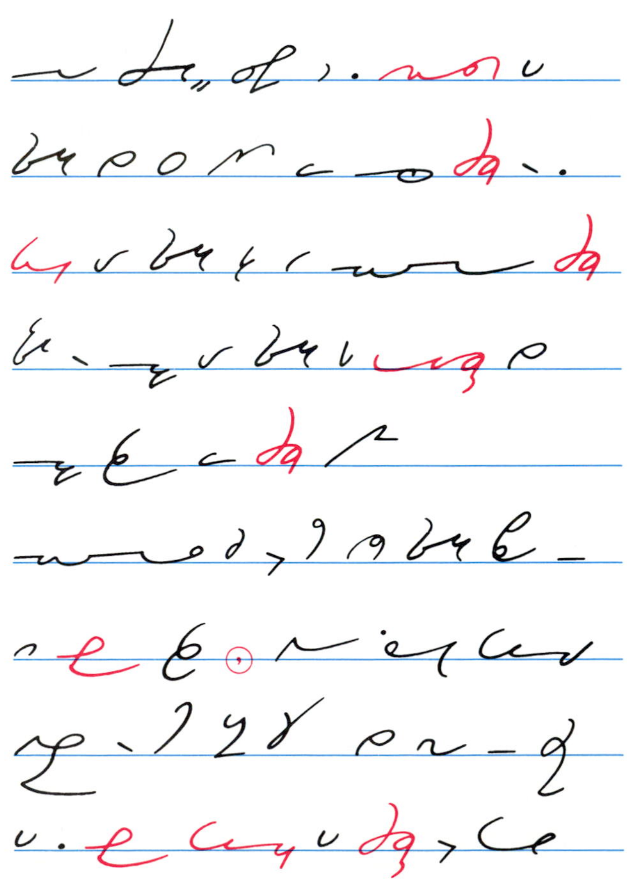

[95 words]

Key: **1** Your application for a position in our collection agency has arrived.
2 The promotion of our new fashion book is being delayed.
3 The National Education Corporation will move to a new location.
4 Who made the decision to operate on the patient?
5 Her typing proficiency helps make her an efficient member of the staff.

NUMBER EXPRESSIONS

The numerical expressions *hundred, thousand, million,* and *dollars* are given special shorthand abbreviations which greatly increase writing speed.

Hundred is written with the *n* symbol.

Thousand is written with the *over th* symbol. 

Hundred thousand is written with the *n* and *th* symbols. 

Million is written with the *m* symbol.

Dollars is written with the *d* symbol. 

Hundred dollars is written with the *n* and *d* symbols. 

Thousand dollars is written with the *th* and *d* symbols. 

Hundred thousand dollars is written with the *n, th,* and *d* symbols. 

Million dollars is written with the *m* and *d* symbols. 

An amount of money containing both dollars and cents is represented by writing the dollar figure in normal-size handwriting and the cents as smaller raised figures.

$2.50 

Number Examples

These expressions often occur in combinations.

200 ■	$8	$10 million ■
5,000 ■	$600 ■	$7.50
300,000 ■	$7,000 ■	a dollar
6 million ■	$800,000 ■	a million ■

■ The *n* for *hundred* and the *over th* for *thousand* are placed underneath the figure. The *m* for *million* is written beside the figure.

Number Practice

11.2

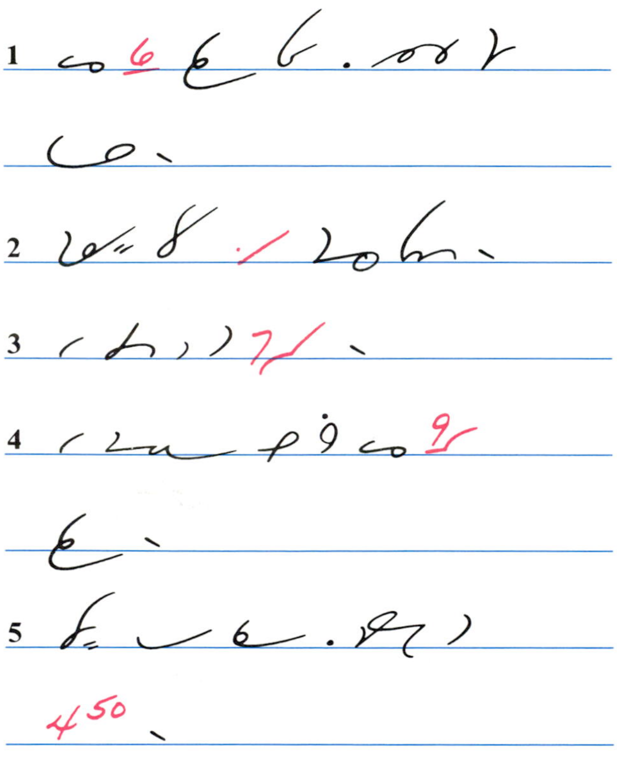

¶ **Letter**

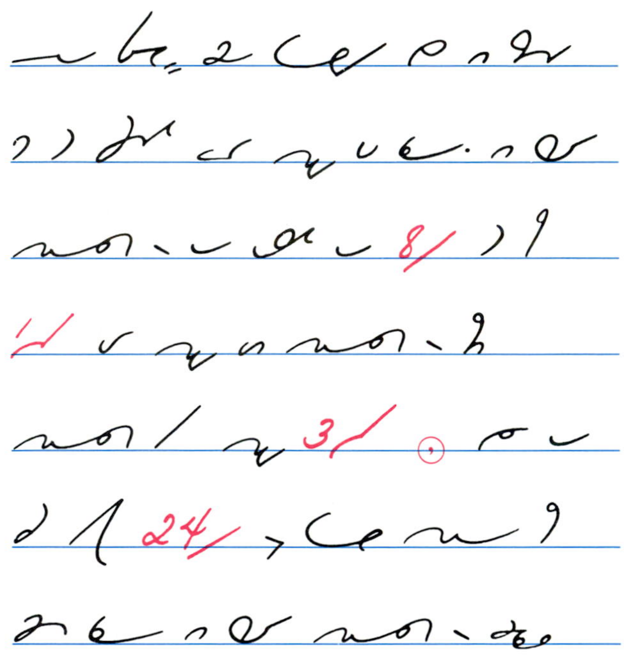

[59 words]

Key: 1 Only 600 people bought a ticket for the play.
2 Fred paid a dollar for my book.
3 The check is for $7,000.
4 The small nation has only 900,000 people.
5 Beth will sell a stamp for $4.50.

BEEN, ABLE, TO PHRASES

In phrases the *b* symbol may represent *been,* while the *a* symbol may represent *able.* Twenty-four such phrases are possible. A representative sample follows.

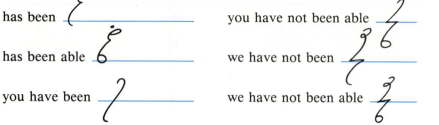

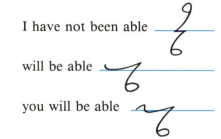

has been 

has been able 

you have been 

you have not been able 

we have not been 

we have not been able 

I have not been able 

will be able 

you will be able 

In two very common phrases the *t* symbol represents the word *to.*

to have 

to be 

Phrase Practice

11.3

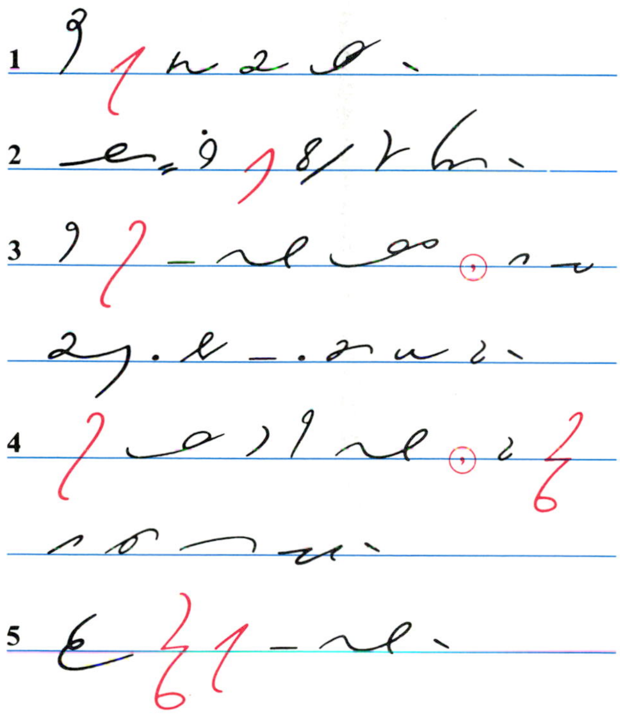

1 2 3 4 5

¶ **Personal Note**

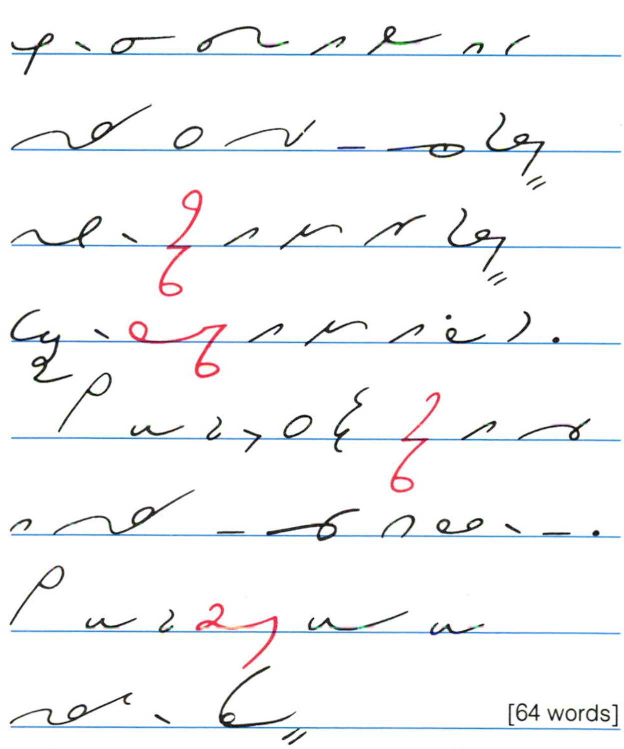

[64 words]

Key: 1 We have to be sure we are right.
2 Mark has to have $8 for the book.
3 If you have been in class lately, you know we will have a test in a week or so.
4 You have been late for each class, so you have not been able to take good notes.
5 People have not been able to be in class.

Transcription of Numbers

The basic rule of number expression is to spell out the numbers *one* through *ten* and to use numerals for numbers above *ten*.

Only *five* days of the vacation remain.

We need *17* books for class.

Numerals are used to express exact amounts of money. A decimal point and zeroes are not used with whole-dollar amounts.

Jean gave me *$10* for the tickets.

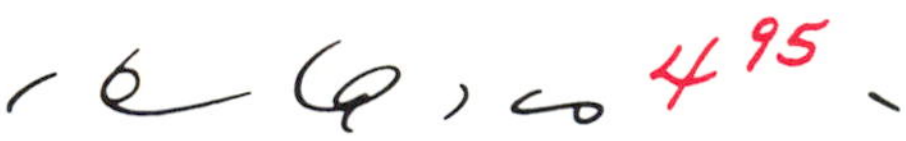

The sale price is only *$4.95*.

When transcribing, use a comma to express *thousand* and *thousand dollars*.

We need *3,000* books.

The price of the collection is *$12,000*.

When transcribing *million* and *million dollars*, replace the commas and ciphers with the word *million*.

Our company has *5 million* people across the nation.

We need *$10 million* for the project.

Telephone messages recorded in shorthand are transcribed onto a telephone message form at the conclusion of the call.

Reading and Writing Practice

11.4 News Reporter's Notes

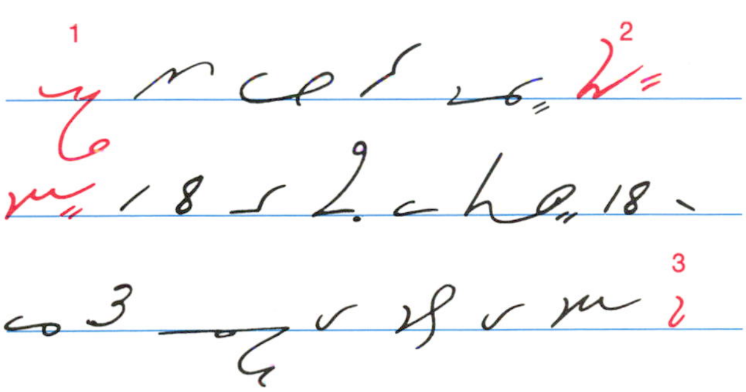

1 robbery 2 Food Store 3 saw

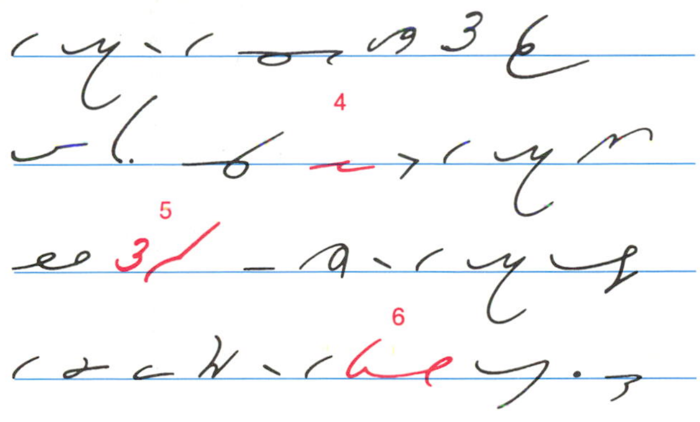

4 known 5 $3,000 6 police

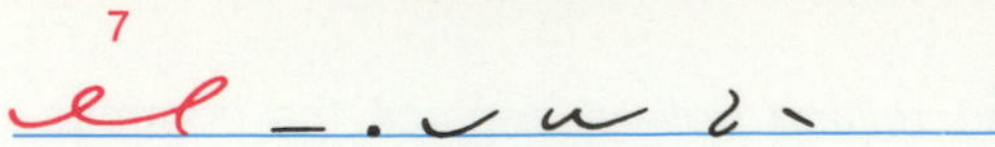

[66 words]

11.5 Business Memo

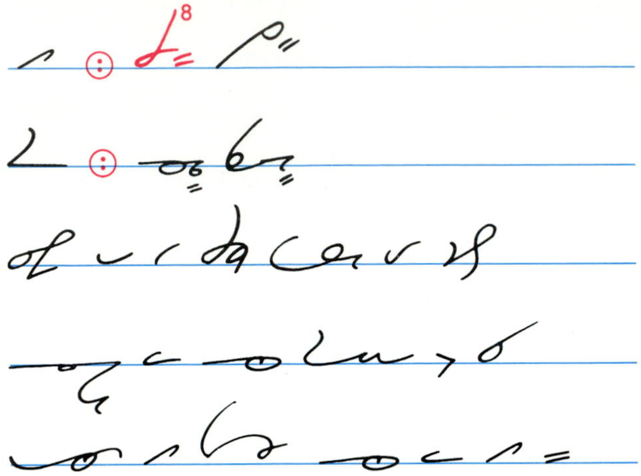

7 release 8 Jean

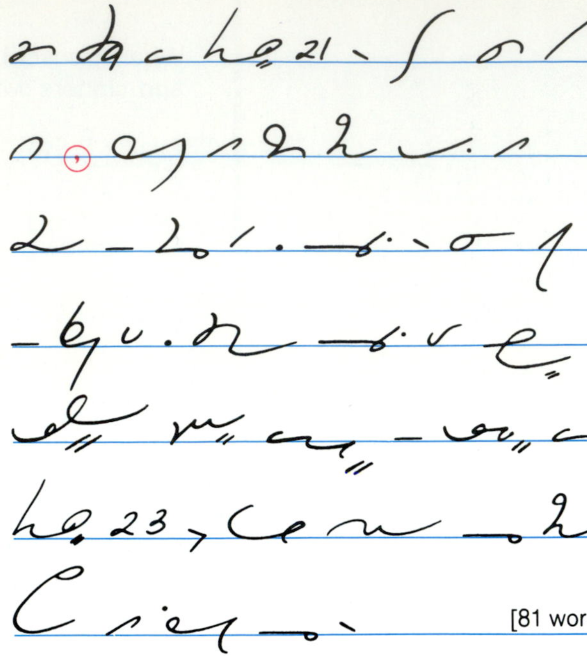

[81 words]

LESSON 12

NEW IN LESSON 12

- Eight brief forms
- Brief-form phrases
- Symbols for the sounds of *tem* and *dem*
- Salutations and complimentary closings
- Transcription tips

BRIEF FORMS

about 
after 
Mrs. 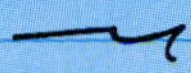
from 
street 
when 
glad 
with 

Brief-Form Derivatives

gladly 
streets 
afternoon 
within ■ 

■ Combining the brief form *with* and *in* would produce an outline that would be difficult to read; therefore an extra *e* is added for readability.

Brief-Form Phrases

about the 
with our 
I am glad 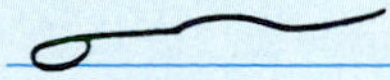
with you, with your 
from the 
I will be glad 
with the 
from you, from your 
after the 

Brief-Form Practice
12.1

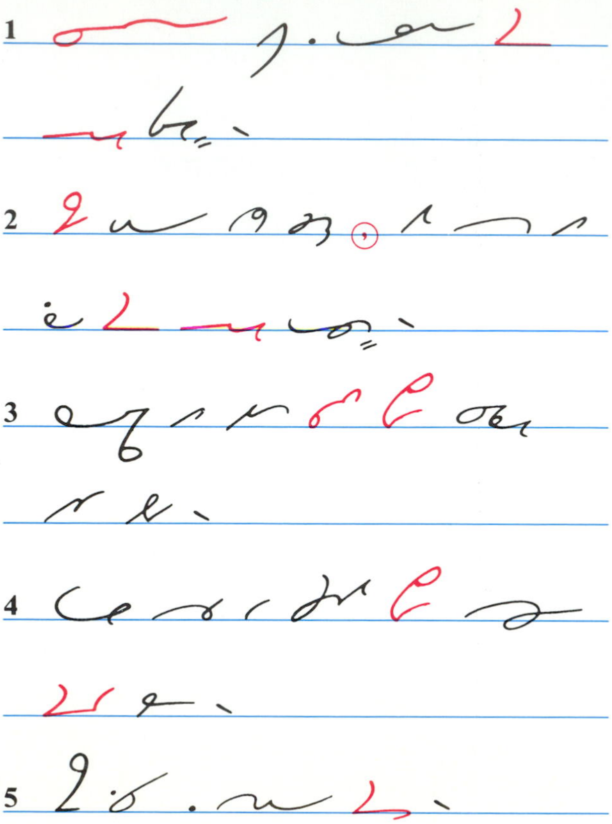

¶ **Letter**

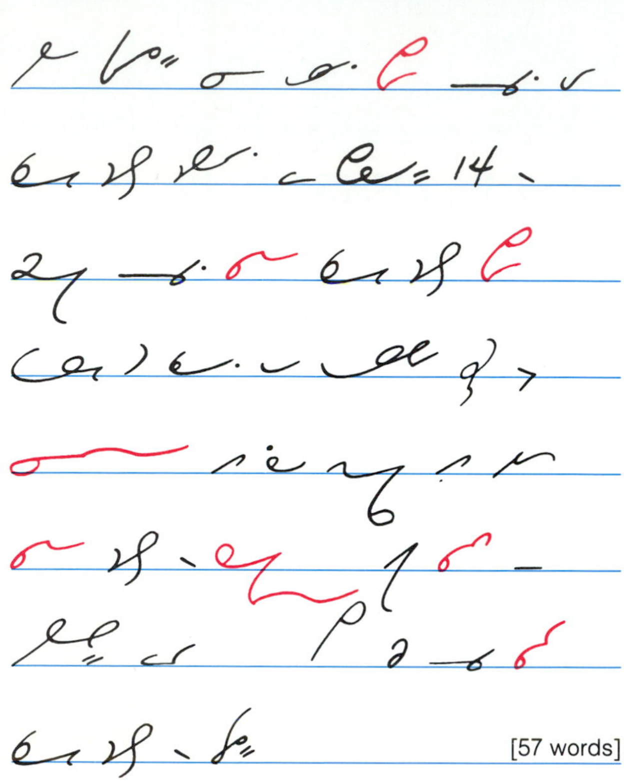

[57 words]

Key:
1 I am glad to have a letter from Mrs. Jones.
2 After all these weeks, it is good to hear from Mrs. Lake.
3 I will not be able to talk with you about the answers to the test.
4 Please get the facts about the game from the team.
5 I have not had a call from you.

SOUNDS OF TEM, DEM

The sounds of *tem* as in *item* and *dem* as in *freedom* are represented by a blend of *d* and *m.*

d  + m = dem 

Examples: item 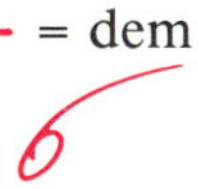 freedom 

Tem Words

item
items
temper
temporary
tomorrow
attempt
attempting
estimate
automobile
customer
customers
accustom

Dem Words

freedom
damage
damages
demonstrate
demonstration
seldom
medium
Adams
Dempsey

Tem, Dem Practice

12.2

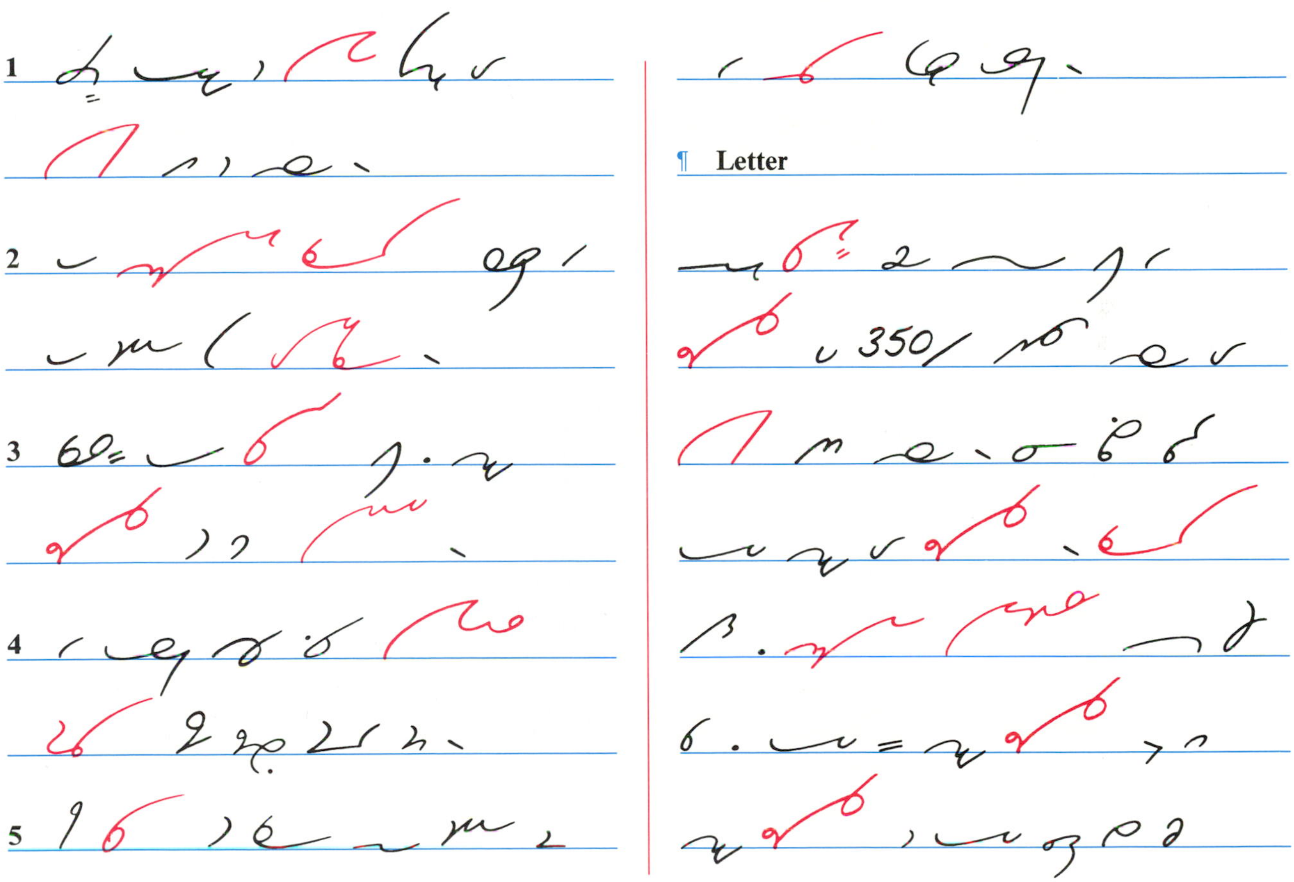

[92 words]

Key: 1 Jack lost his temper because of the damage to his car.
2 Our customers seldom arrive at our store by automobile.
3 Sarah will attempt to have a cost estimate for us tomorrow.
4 The large cat had temporary freedom after escaping from the zoo.
5 Each item for sale in our store is in the medium price range.

SALUTATIONS AND COMPLIMENTARY CLOSINGS

Dear Mr.

Dear Mrs.

Dear Miss

Dear Sir

Dear Madam

Very truly yours

Yours very truly

Cordially yours

A secretarial position may prove to be a stepping-stone for further advancement.

Salutation and Complimentary Closing Practice

12.3

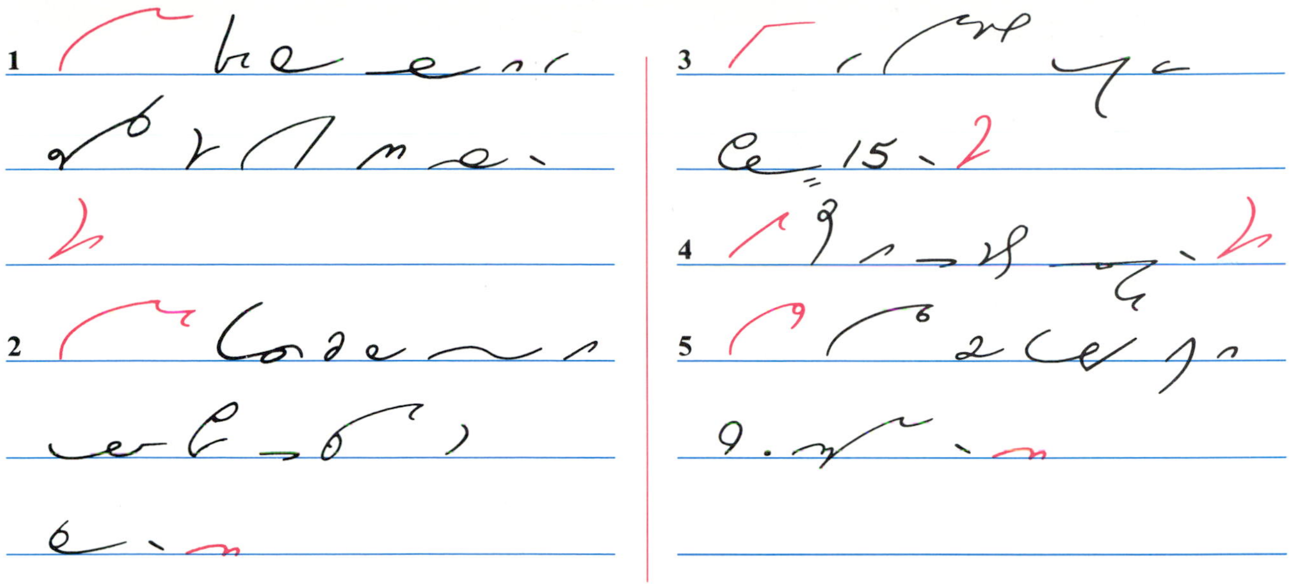

Key: 1 Dear Mr. Jones I will mail you the estimate for the damage to your car. Very truly yours

2 Dear Mrs. Black We were glad to learn about the new items for sale. Cordially yours

3 Dear Madam The demonstration will be on April 15. Yours very truly

4 Dear Sir We have two new staff members. Very truly yours

5 Dear Miss Dempsey We are pleased to have you as a customer. Cordially yours

Transcription Tips

When writing shorthand outlines for the names of places, such as streets and avenues, you should include capitalization marks below the outlines.

Therefore, when transcribing the names of places, you will remember to capitalize them.

When transcribing salutations such as *Dear Sir* and *Dear Madam*, capitalize the first letter of each word. When transcribing salutations such as *Dear Mr.* and *Dear Mrs.*, the words *Dear, Mr.,* and *Mrs.* are capitalized. A period follows *Mr.*, *Mrs.*, and *Ms.* When transcribing *Dear Miss, Miss* is capitalized but not followed by a period.

When transcribing a letter, it is customary to place a colon at the end of the salutation and to place a comma at the end of the complimentary closing. In order to promote writing speed, omit these marks of punctuation in your shorthand notes.

Reading and Writing Practice

12.4 Business Letter

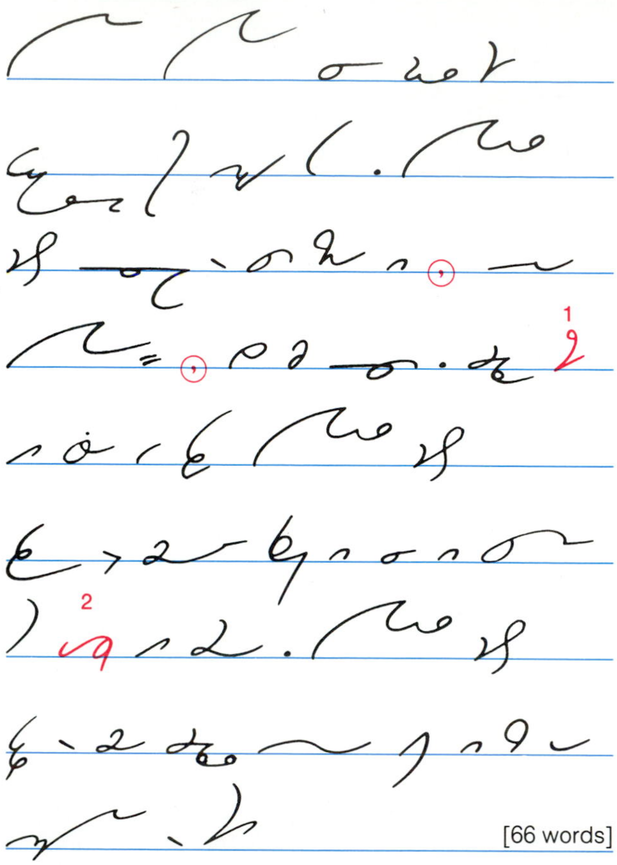

[66 words]

12.5 A Student's "To Do" List

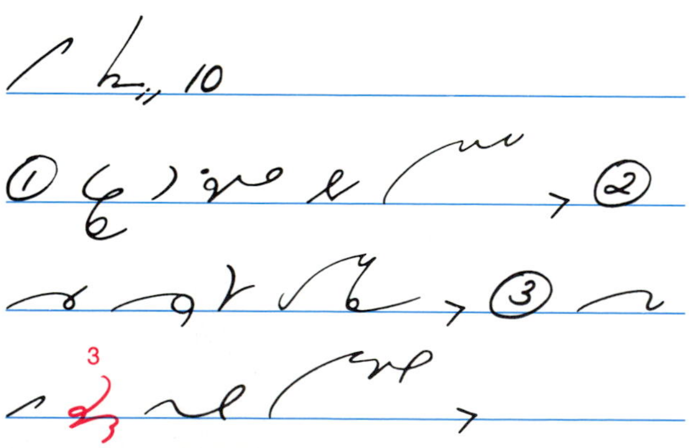

1 effort 2 occasion 3 physics

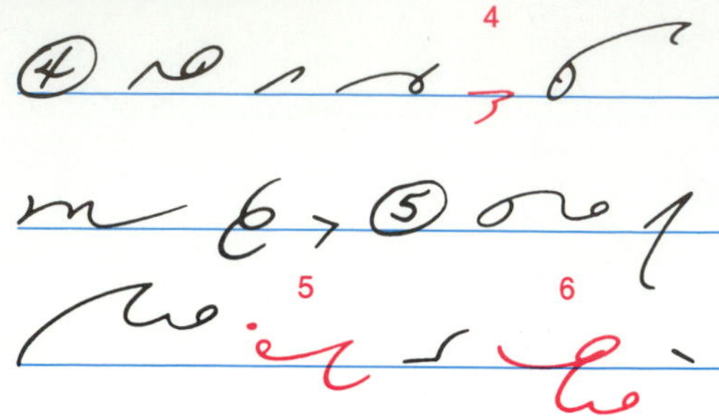

[45 words]

12.6 Business Letter

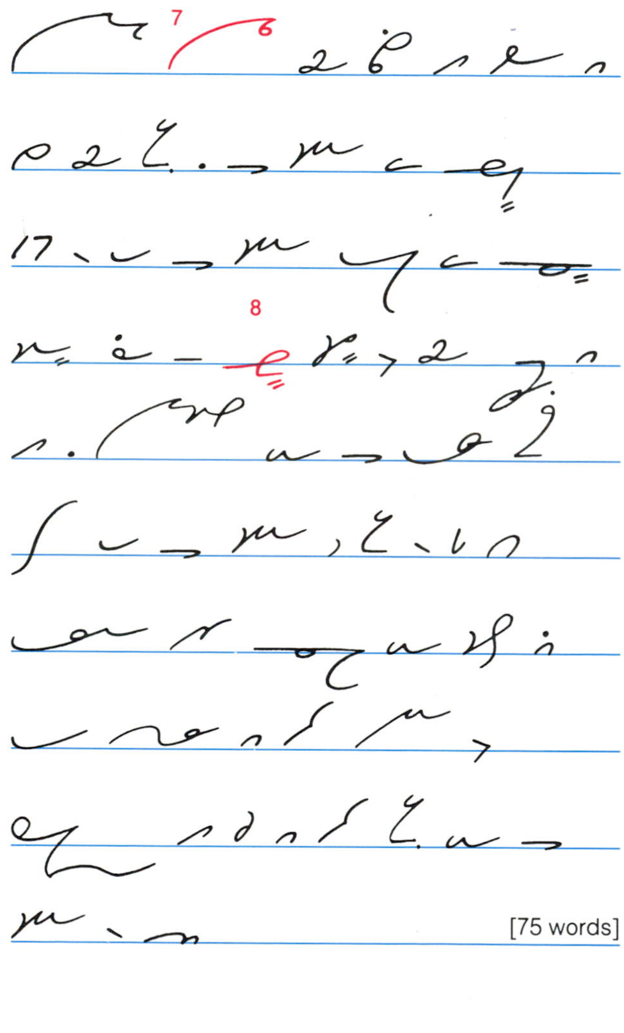

[75 words]

4 news 5 helper 6 library 7 Dempsey
8 Mason City

UNIT IV

LESSON 13

NEW IN LESSON 13

- Word beginnings *con-* and *com-*
- Second symbol for the sound of *th*
- Word beginning *re-*
- Using shorthand to compose rough drafts

WORD BEGINNINGS CON-, COM-

The word beginnings *con-* as in *control* and *com-* as in *complain* are represented by the *k* symbol.

Examples: control complain

Con- Words

control
contract
contracts
conduct
consider
consideration
concern
conference ■
conversation ■

■ When *k* is followed by an *f* or *v*, the outline is blended.

Com- Words

complain
complete
completely
completion
compare
comparing
compile
combine
combines

But: When *n* or *m* is double in *con-* or *com-* words, these word beginnings are represented by *kn* or *km*.

connect 	committee 	accommodate ■ 
connection 	commerce 	accommodation 

■ Transcription Alert.

Con-, Com- Practice

13.1

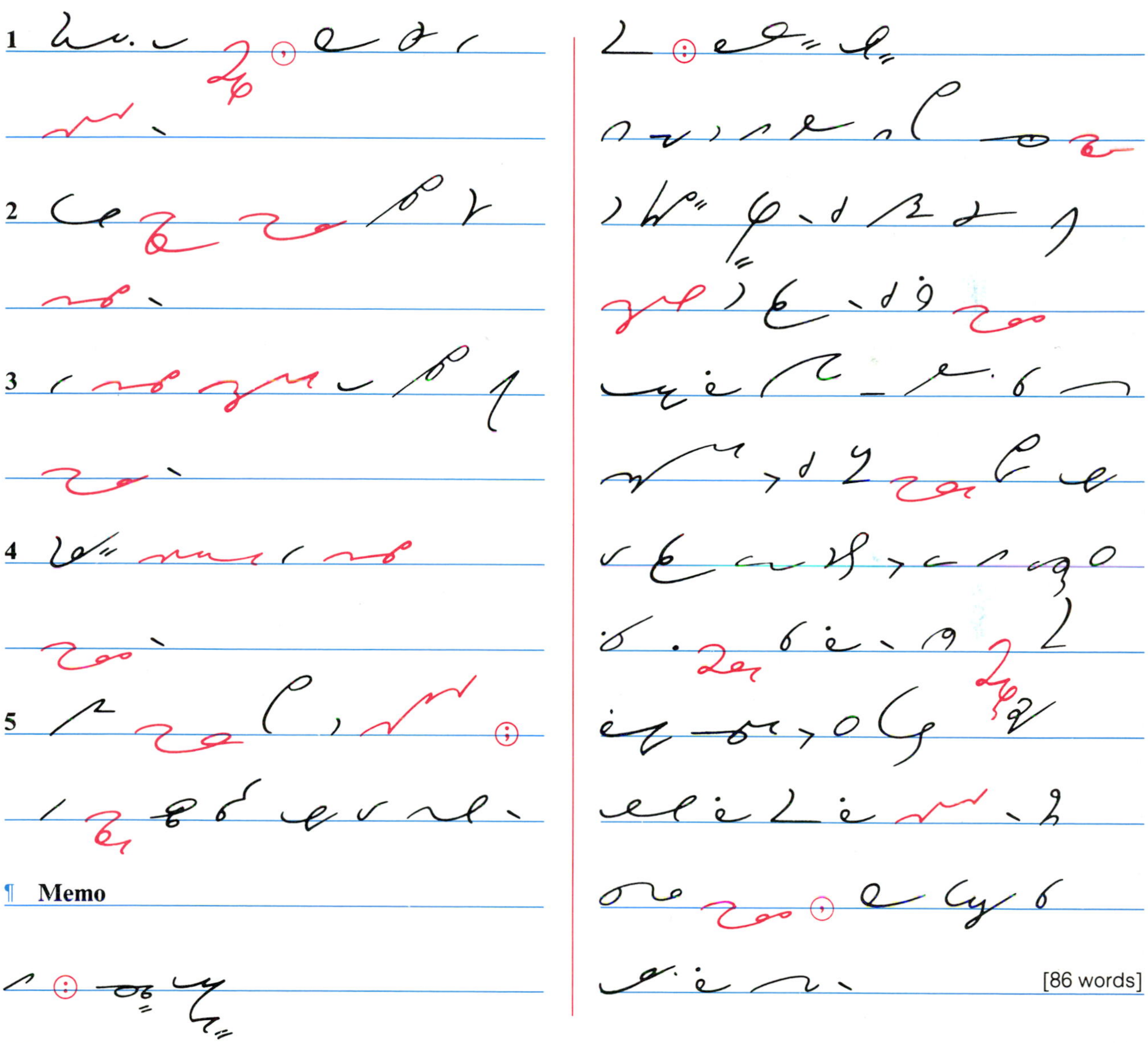

SOUND OF TH

Just as we have two *s* symbols to facilitate fluent joinings to other symbols, we have two *th* symbols for the same reason. The *th* you learned in Lesson 9 is called the *over ith*. The *under ith* is the mirror image of the *over ith*.

under ith

Example: though

Under Ith Words

though	health	thorough
thought	healthy	both
those	clothes	growth
threw, through	clothing	wealth ■

■ Brief-form derivative.

Under Ith Practice

13.2

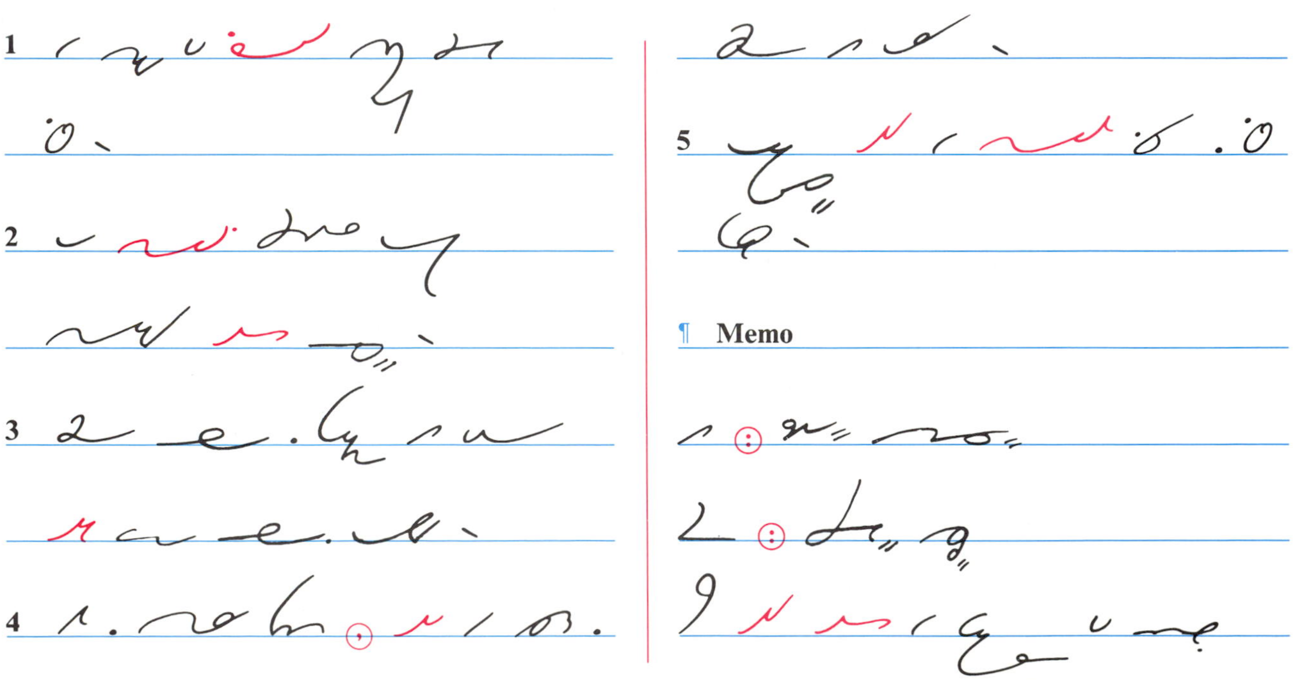

[49 words]

WORD BEGINNING RE-

The word beginning *re-* as in *reject* is represented by the *r* symbol.

Example: reject 

Re- Words

reject

replace

reply

replies

repair

research

receive

received

refer

referring

reference

reason

But: Before a forward or upward stroke, *re-* is written *re.*

relate

remain

retire

Re- Practice

13.3

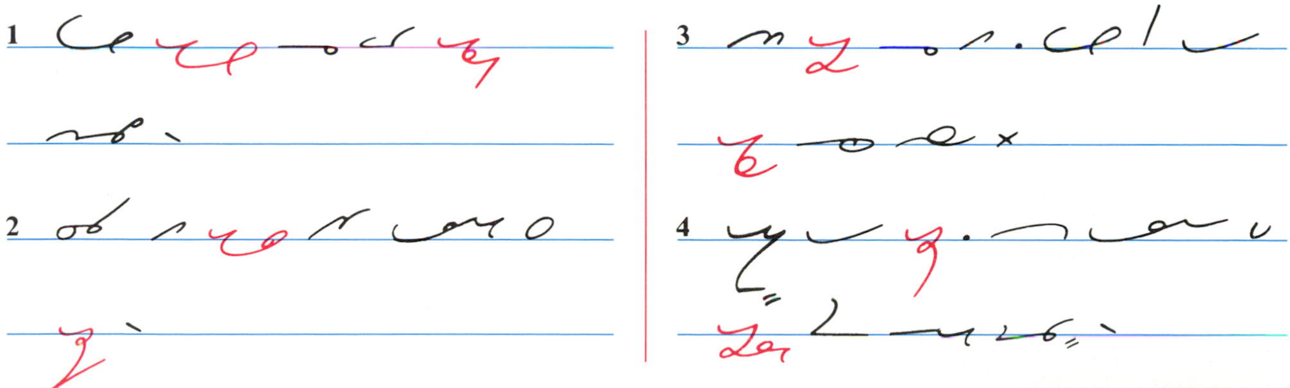

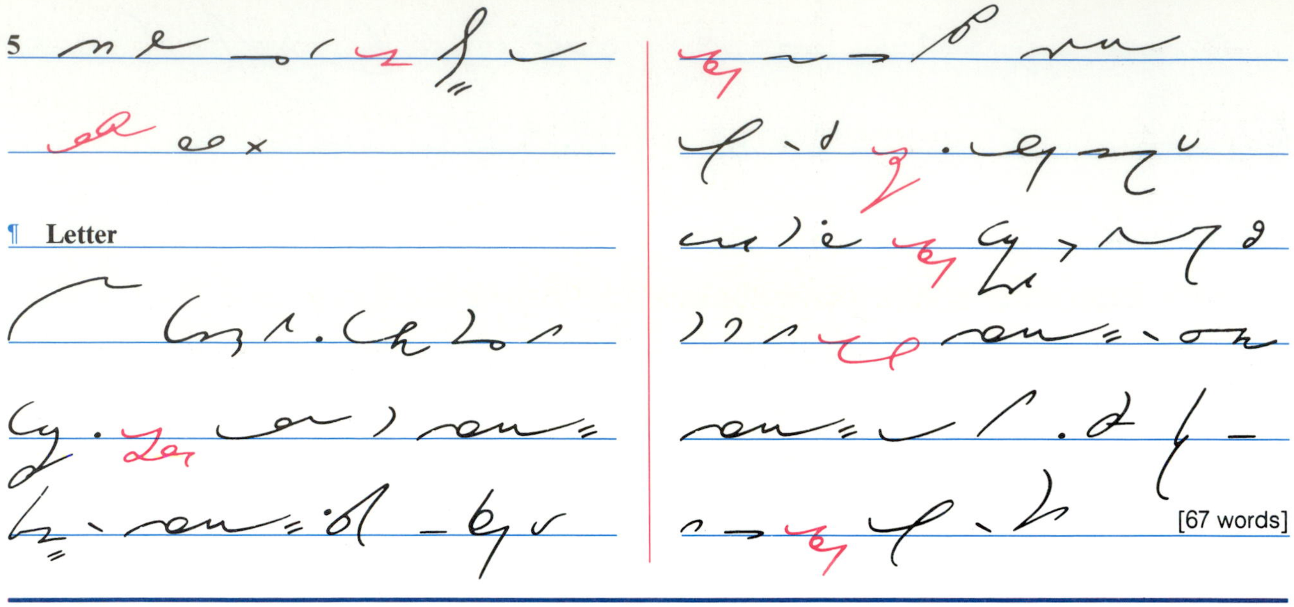

Using Shorthand to Compose Rough Drafts

Anyone who has ever completed a writing assignment knows that writing can be a difficult job. Much thought is required to formulate clear sentences and paragraphs. All too often those thoughts are fleeting. You might spend several minutes trying to mentally compose a smooth sentence, only to have the thoughts disappear during the slow, laborious process of writing them down in longhand. You could compose a rough draft by dictating to a tape recorder, but tape recorded thoughts are very difficult to review when you are trying to compose one sentence after another with grammatical precision, a certain progression of ideas, and a smooth style.

Shorthand, then, is the perfect medium for capturing those fleeting thoughts—those bursts of genius that you may never be able to create verbatim again. The rough draft in shorthand also provides the hard copy that you need for continual review in those instances when elements of grammar, logic, and style are critical.

Executives who know how to write shorthand find it a useful skill when outlining responses to communications received via electronic mail.

Reading and Writing Practice

13.4 Dictation Speed Letter

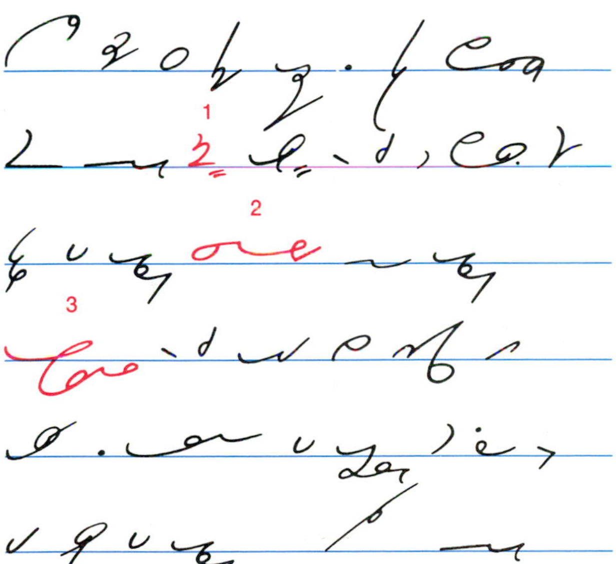

1 Susan 2 analyst 3 laboratory

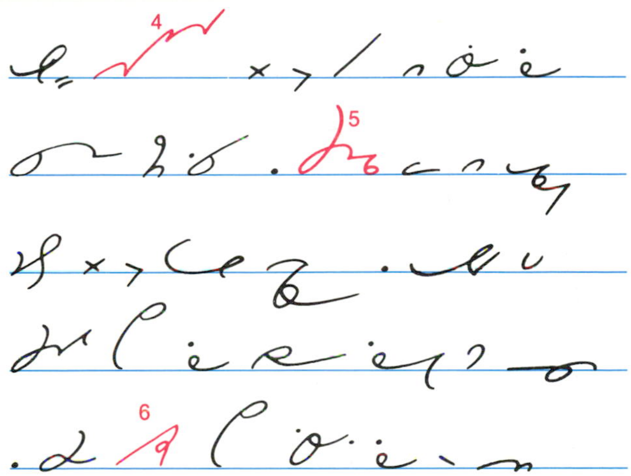

[88 words]

4 conduct 5 vacancy 6 decision

13.5 Business Letter

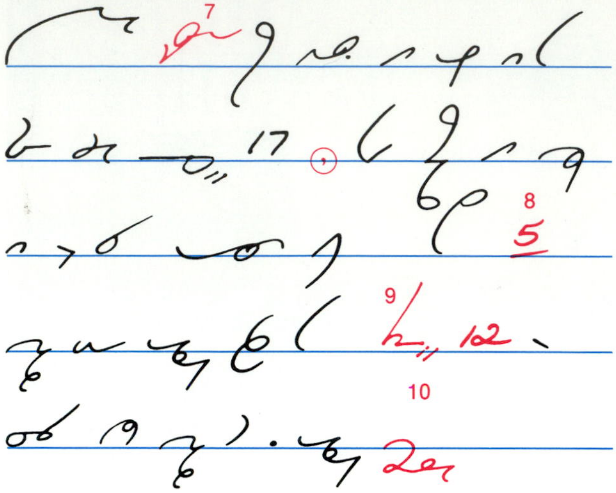

7 Steiner 8 500 9 June 12 10 conference

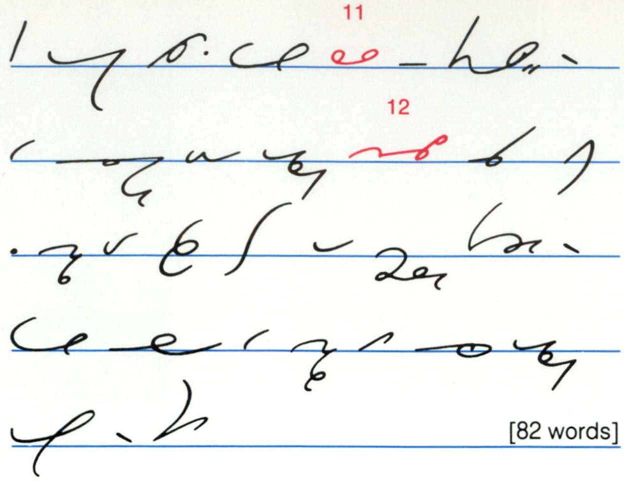

[82 words]

11 early 12 committee

LESSON 14

NEW IN LESSON 14

- **Eight brief forms**
- **Eliminated-word phrases**
- **Blend symbol for the sounds of *ted*, *ded*, and *dit***
- **Differentiating between *there* and *their***

BRIEF FORMS

doctor, Dr., during	they	yesterday
there, their	was	one, won ■
office	where	

■ In shorthand, only the numbers *one* and *two* are written with shorthand symbols. All other numbers are written with arabic numerals.

Brief-Form Derivatives

doctors	offices	once

Brief-Form Phrases

there is	here is	they are not
there was	here are	they will
I was	is there	they will be
it was	they are	they will not

Brief-Form Practice

14.1

1 2 3 4 5

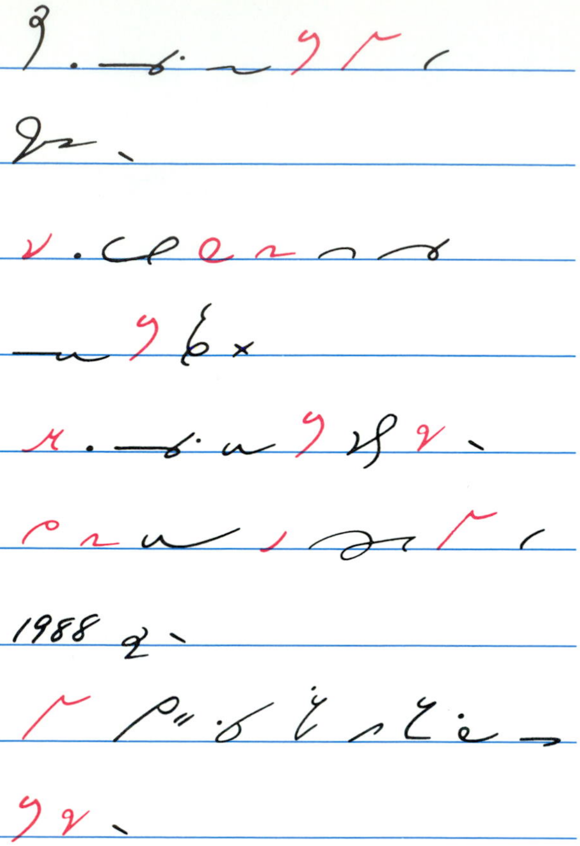

¶ Letter

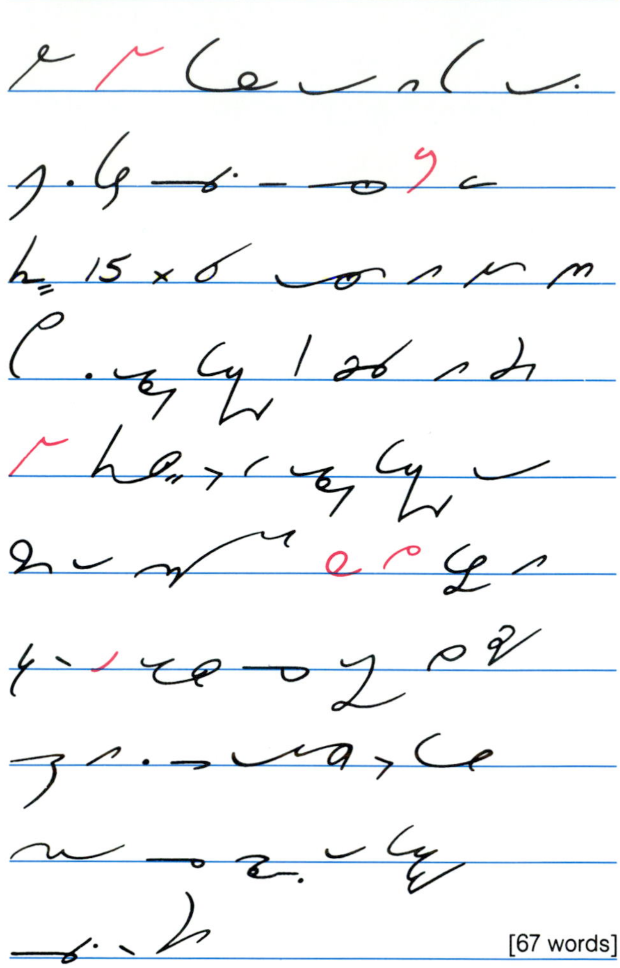

[67 words]

ELIMINATED-WORD PHRASES

In several common phrases the middle word is eliminated.

one of the 

one of them 

one of our 

up to date 

Phrase Practice

14.2

1 2 3 4 5

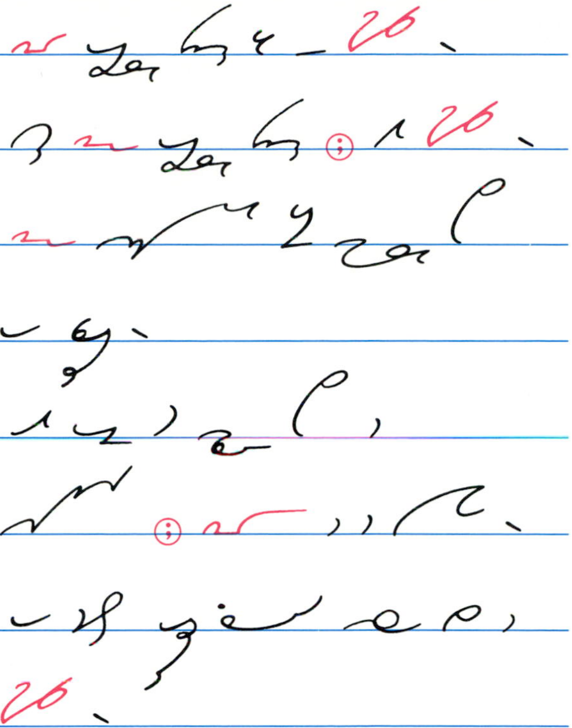

¶ **Memo**

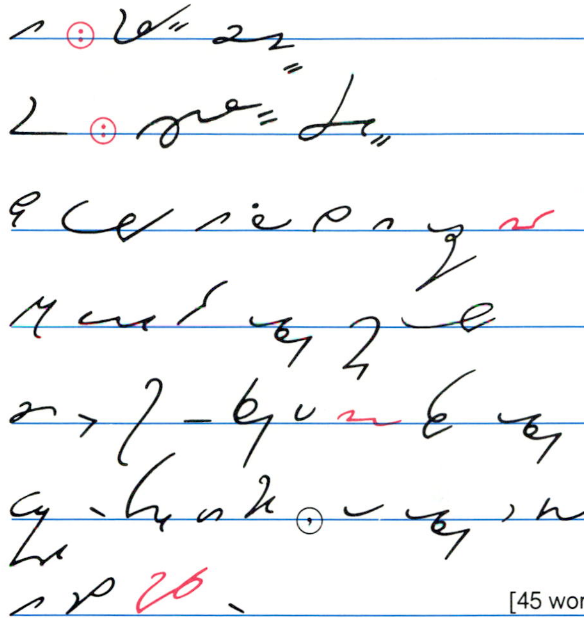

[45 words]

SOUNDS OF TED, DED, DIT

The sounds of *ted* as in *started*, *ded* as in *guided*, and *dit* as in *credit* are represented by a blend of the *t* and *d* symbols.

t d ted

Examples: started guided credit

Ted Words

started rested acted

listed tested accepted

drafted | today | studied

omitted ■ | steady, study

■ Transcription Alert.

Ded Words

guided | graded | deduct

needed | dead | deduction

added | deadline | provided

Dit Words

credit | audited ■ | editor

credited ■ | auditor | detail

audit | edit | debt

■ Note that the past tense *d* joins the *dit* with a jog.

Ted, Ded, Dit Practice

14.3

1

2

3

4

5

¶ **Letter**

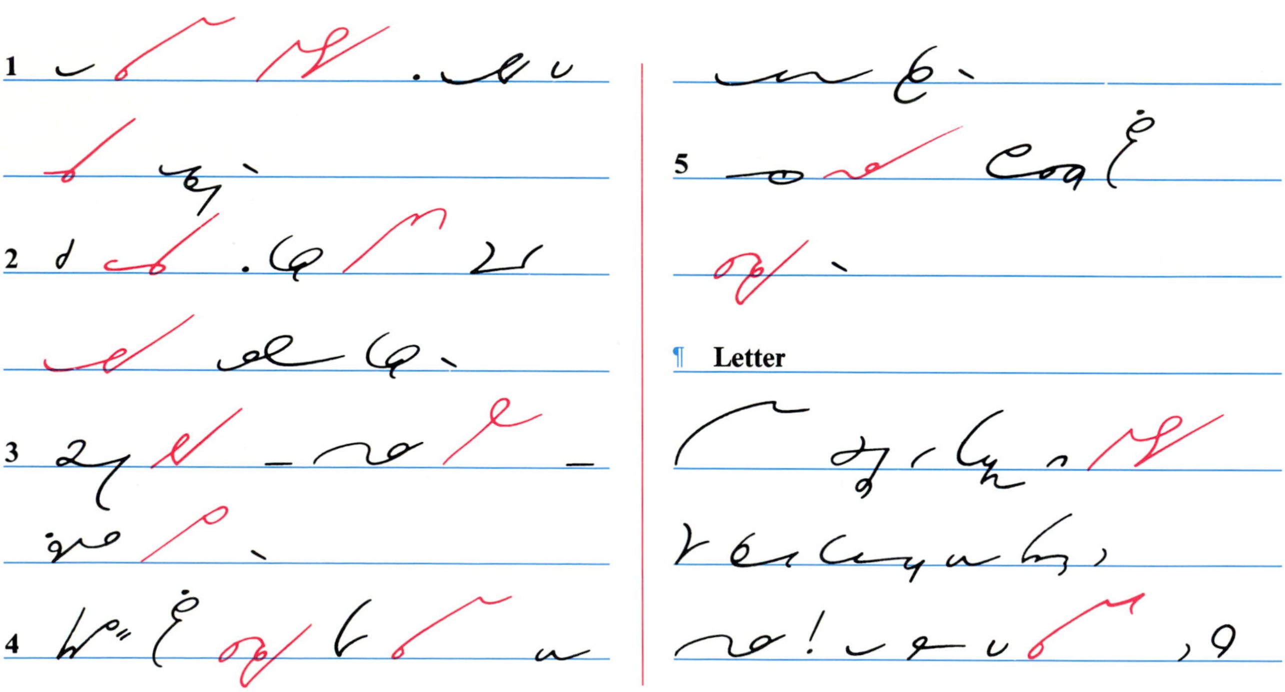

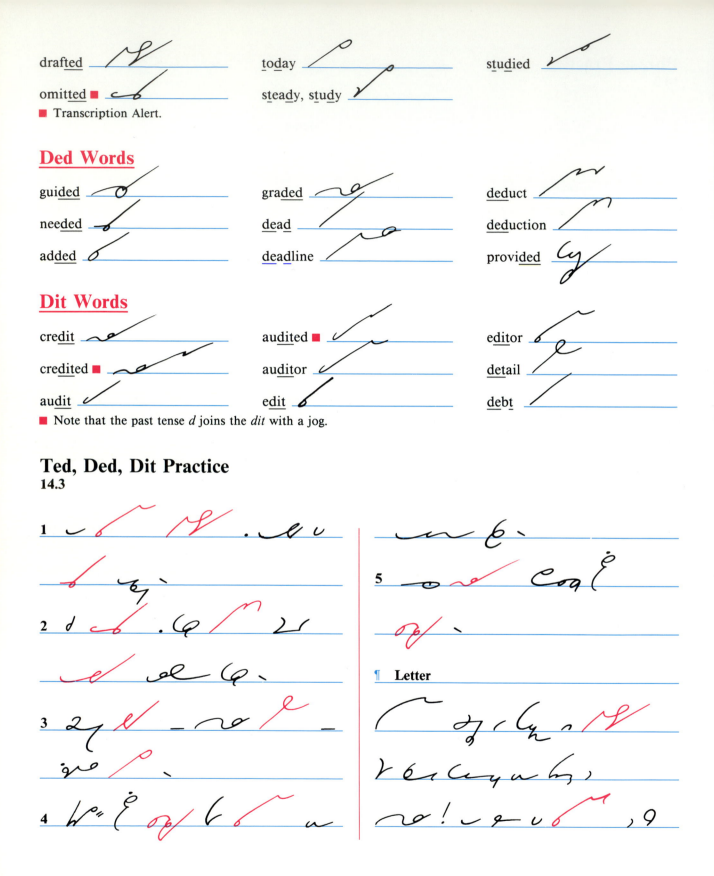

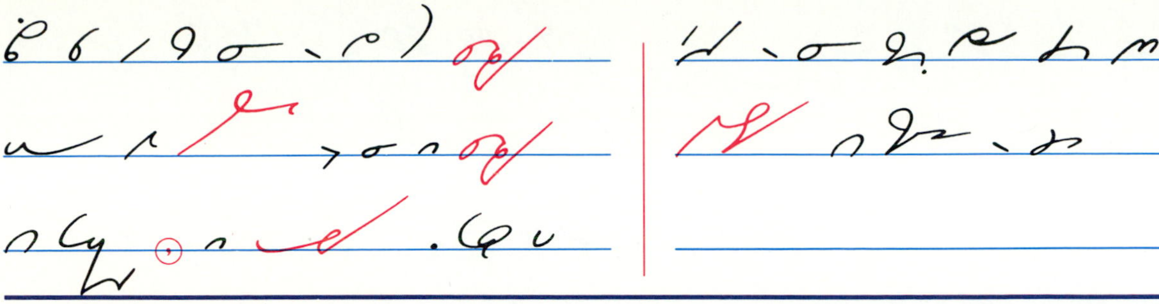

[60 words]

Communication Skill Builder

Similar Words: there, their

there: function word used to introduce a thought; (adv.) at that place

their: possessive pronoun meaning belonging to them

There should be a place listed for the meeting.

Place the book *there*.

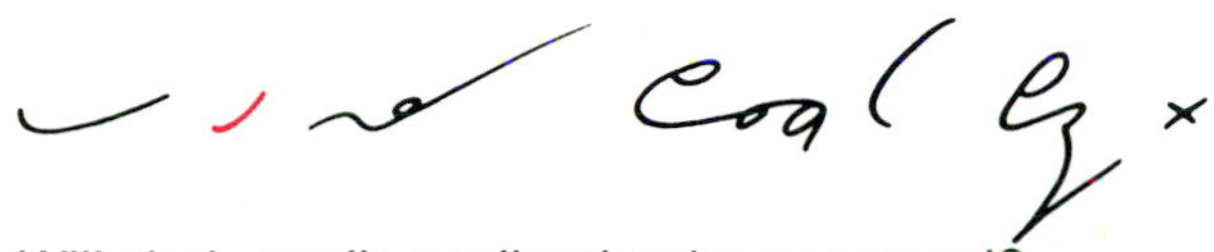

Will *their* credit application be approved?

Reading and Writing Practice

14.4 Dictation Speed Letter

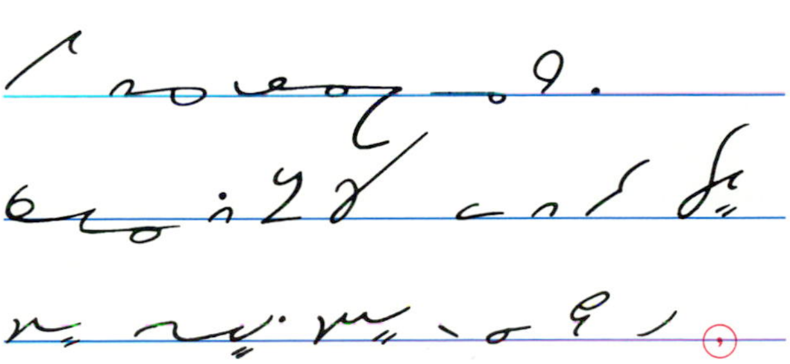

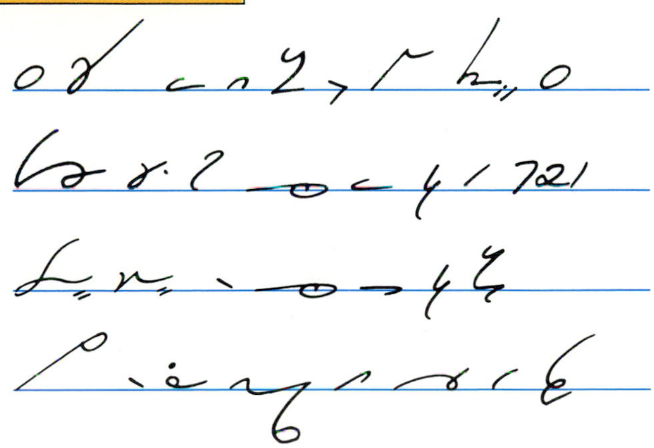

[72 words]

14.5 A Page From a Real Estate Agent's Notebook

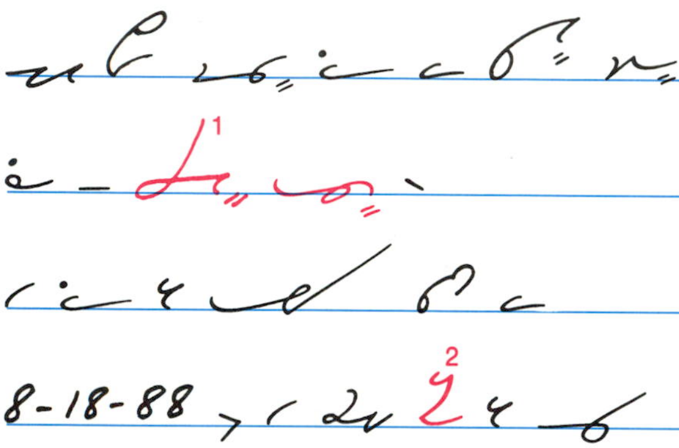

1 James Lake 2 offer

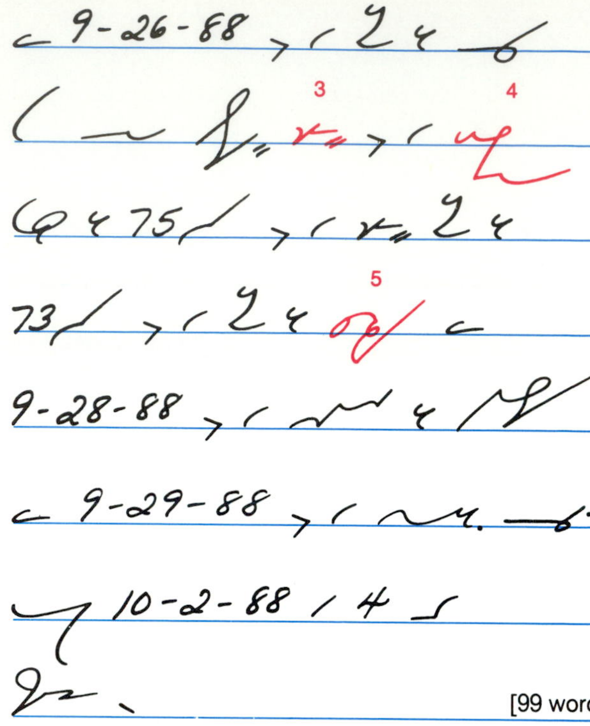

[99 words]

3 Stone 4 original 5 accepted

Shorthand is a portable skill, and busy executives often dictate on the run.

LESSON 15

NEW IN LESSON 15

- Word ending *-ther*
- Word beginning *fur-*
- Symbol for the sound of *ow*
- Differentiating between *weather* and *whether*

WORD ENDING -THER

The word ending *-ther* as in *rather* and *father* is represented by both the *under ith* and the *over ith* symbols.

-ther or

Examples: rather father

-ther Words

rather	weather, whether	either
father	brother	author
other	another	authors
gather	together	bother
neither	mother	bothers

-ther Practice

15.1

1 2 3 4 5

¶ **Letter**

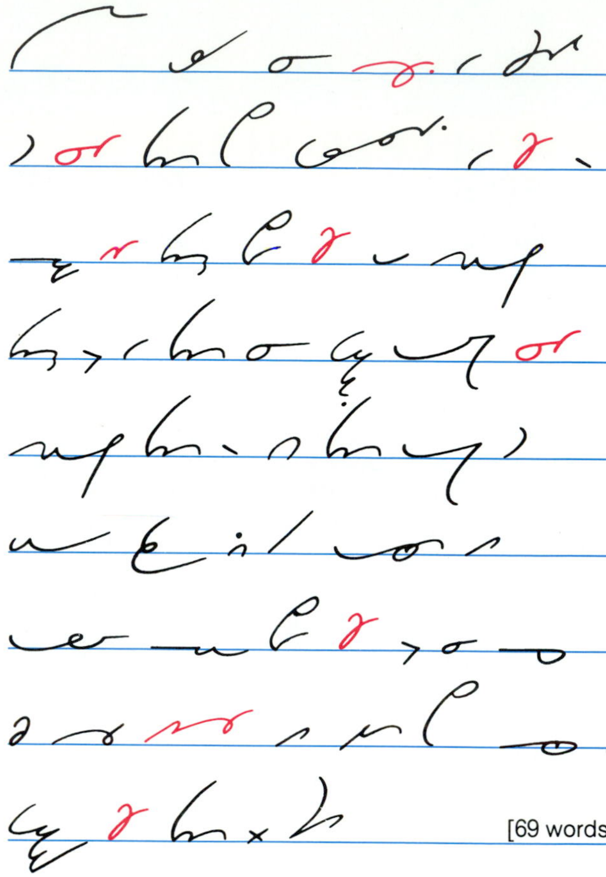

[69 words]

WORD BEGINNING FUR-

The word beginning *fur-* as in *further* is written with the *f* symbol, which you have already been using as an abbreviation for the similar sound *for*.

fur- 

Example: further 

Fur- Words

further 

furthermore 

furnace 

furnish 

furnishes 

refurnish 

Fur- Practice

15.2

1 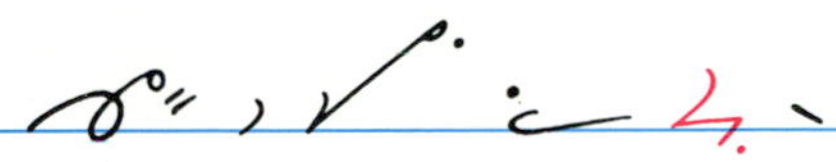

2 

3 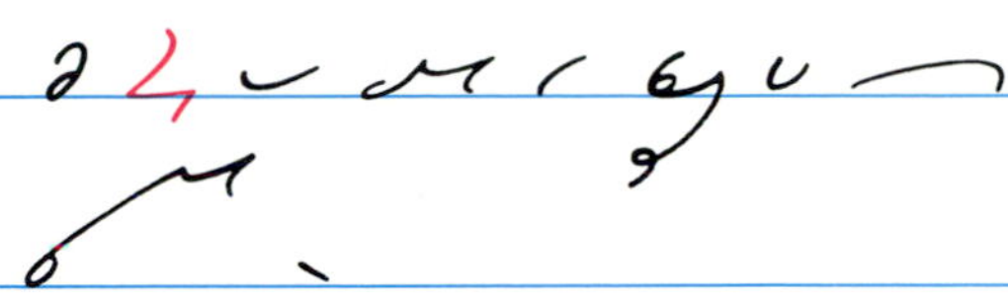

4 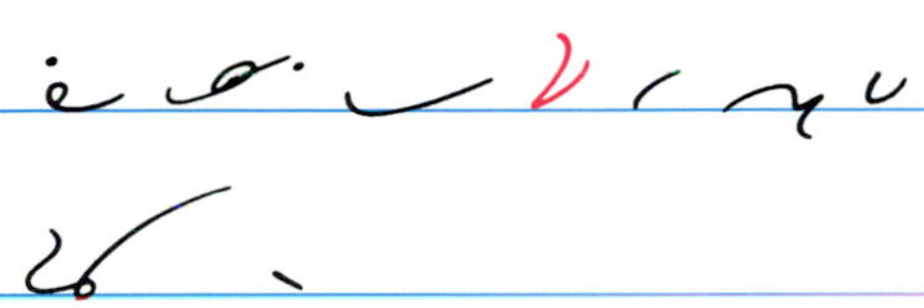

5 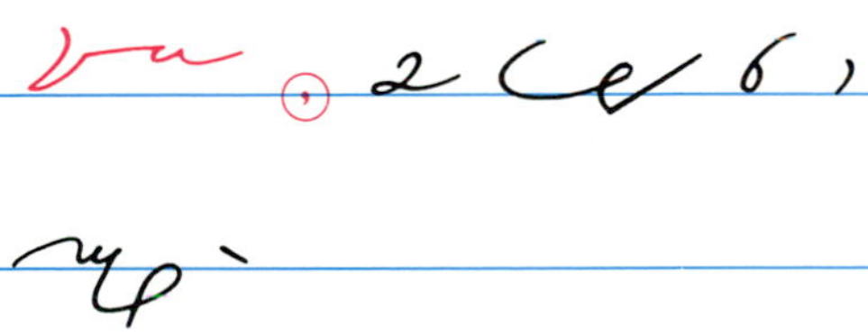

¶ **Letter**

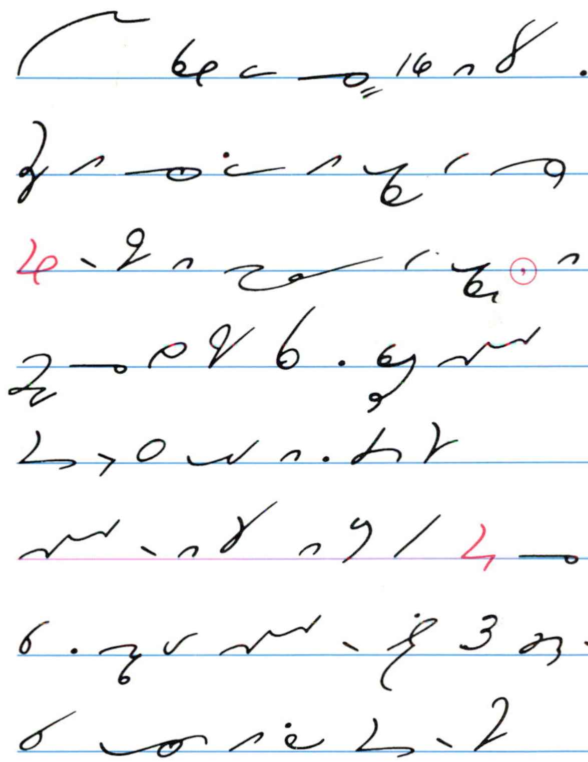

[65 words]

SOUND OF OW

The sound of *ow* as in *south* is written with the *a* and *oo* symbols.

a + oo = ow

Example: how

Ow Words

how	announce	doubt
now	announced	doubts
south	town	crowd
house	down	brown

Ow Practice

15.3

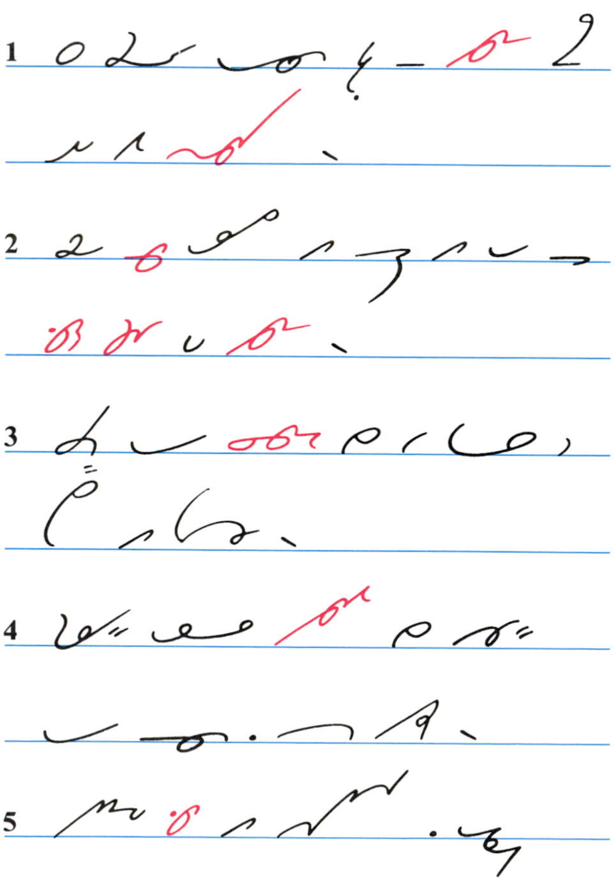

¶ **Rough Draft for a School News Release**

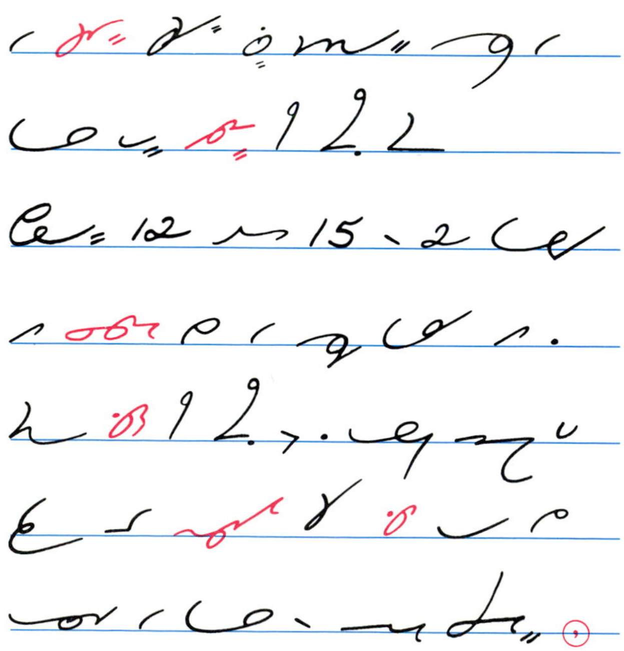

[62 words]

Communication Skill Builder

Similar Words: weather, whether

weather: state of the atmosphere

whether: if

The *weather* is cloudy.

Lee cannot decide *whether* he should buy a new camera.

Executives realize that a secretary who possesses shorthand skill is valuable in the electronic office.

Reading and Writing Practice

15.4 Dictation Speed Letter

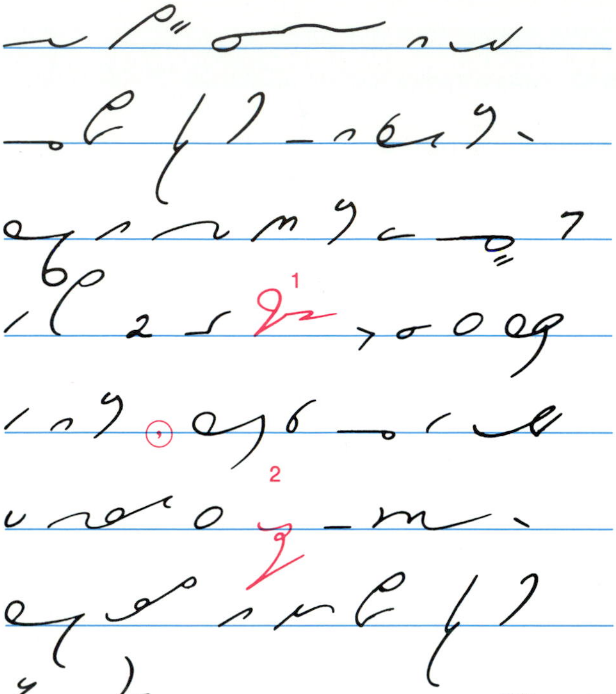

[60 words]

15.5 Business Letter

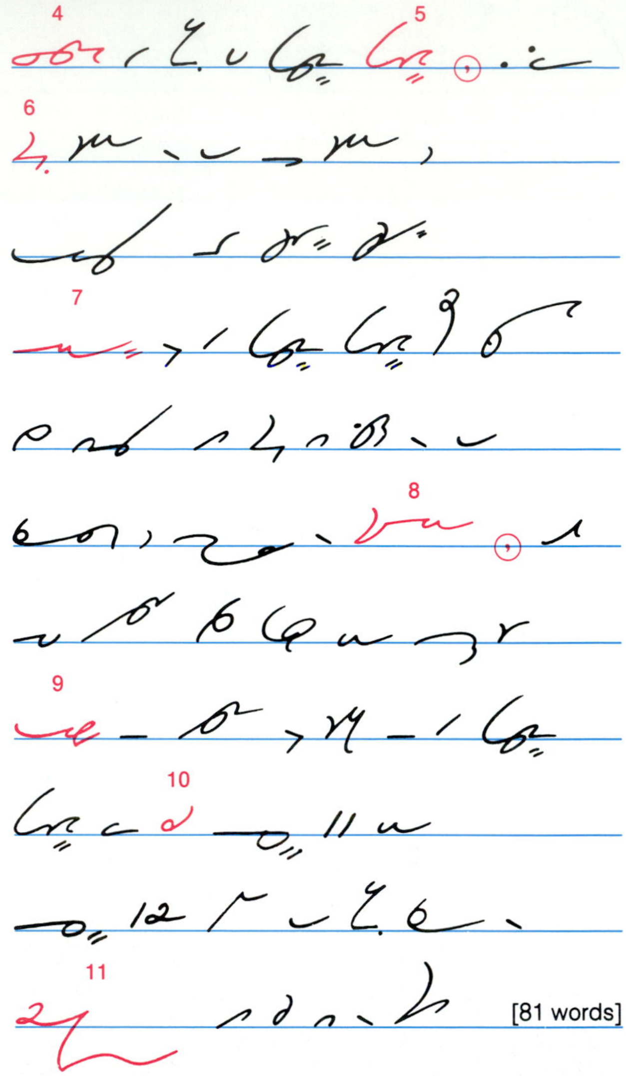

[81 words]

1 afternoon 2 received 3 Customer

4 announce 5 Brothers 6 furnishing 7 Mall 8 Furthermore 9 lowest 10 either 11 We will be glad

LESSON 16

NEW IN LESSON 16

- Eight brief forms
- Special phrases
- Word endings *-ure* and *-ual*
- Transcription tips

BRIEF FORMS

company

work

ever, every

state

communicate

soon

recommend

direct

Brief-Form Derivatives

companies

accompany

worker

everywhere

whenever

stated ■

communication

communications

communicated

sooner

recommends

recommended

recommendation

recommendations

directed

director

directly

direction

■ Note the jog which distinguishes the *t* and *d*.

Brief-Form Practice
16.1

¶ **Notes for a News Story**

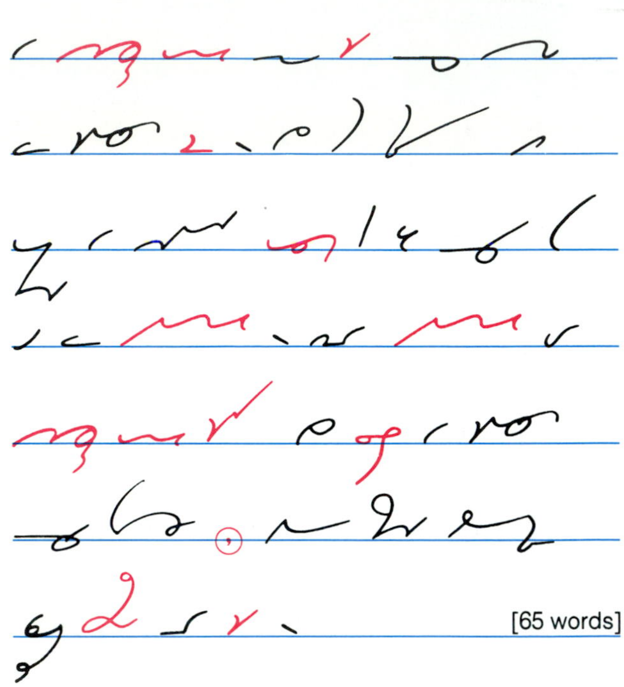

[65 words]

SPECIAL PHRASES

The following phrases contain shorthand symbols representing one or two sounds from each word.

to us 

as soon as 

let us 

of course 

as soon as possible 

let me 

A phrase beginning with *to* followed by the sound of *m* is written with the *tem* blend. A phrase beginning with *to* followed by the sound of *d* as in *do* is written with the *ted* blend.

to me 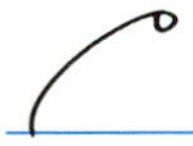

to make 

to do 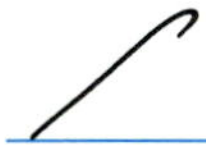

Phrase Practice
16.2

1 

2 

3 

4 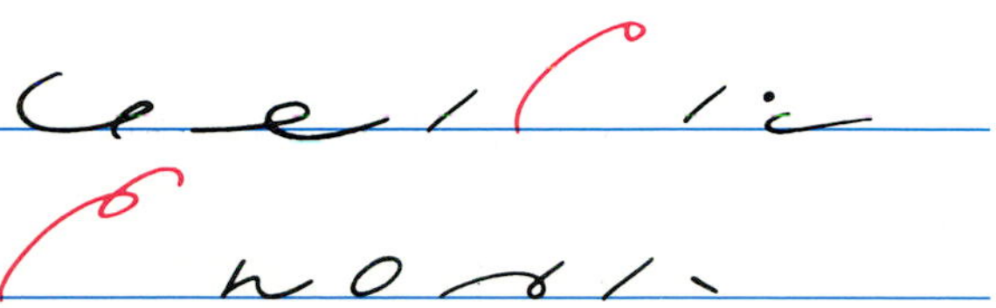

5 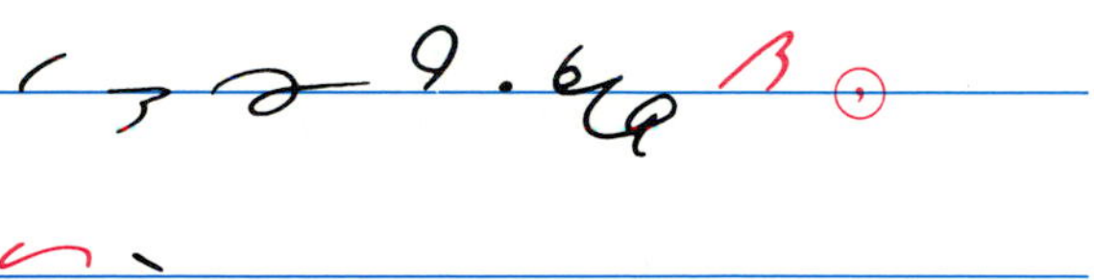

¶ **Note to Secretary**

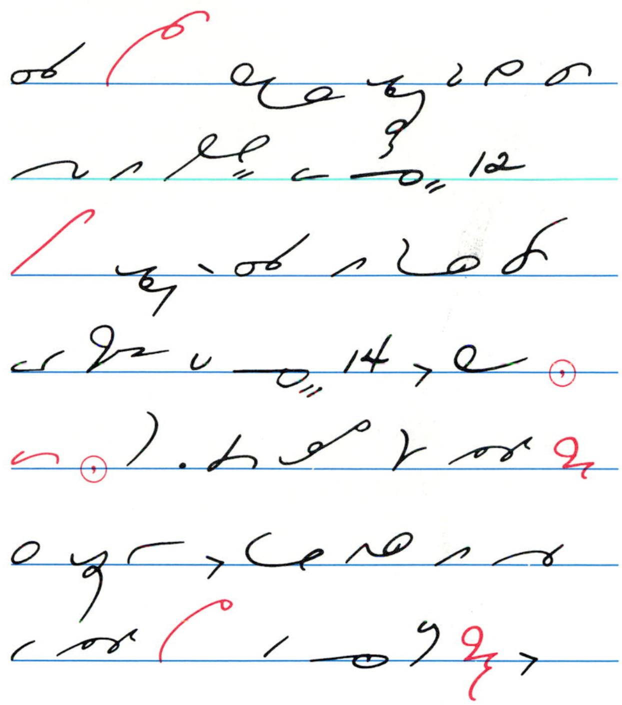

[58 words]

WORD ENDINGS -URE, -UAL

The word ending *-ure* as in *procedure* is written with an *r;* the word ending *-ual* as in *annual* is written with an *l.*

-ure  -ual 

Examples: procedure  annual 

-ure Words

procedure | picture | natural
failure | nature | feature

-ual Words

annual | actually | gradual
annually | factual | gradually
actual | equal | contractual

But: After a downstroke, the *oo* is written.

pleasure | pressure | visual

-ure, -ual Practice

16.3

¶ **Class Notes From a Marketing Course**

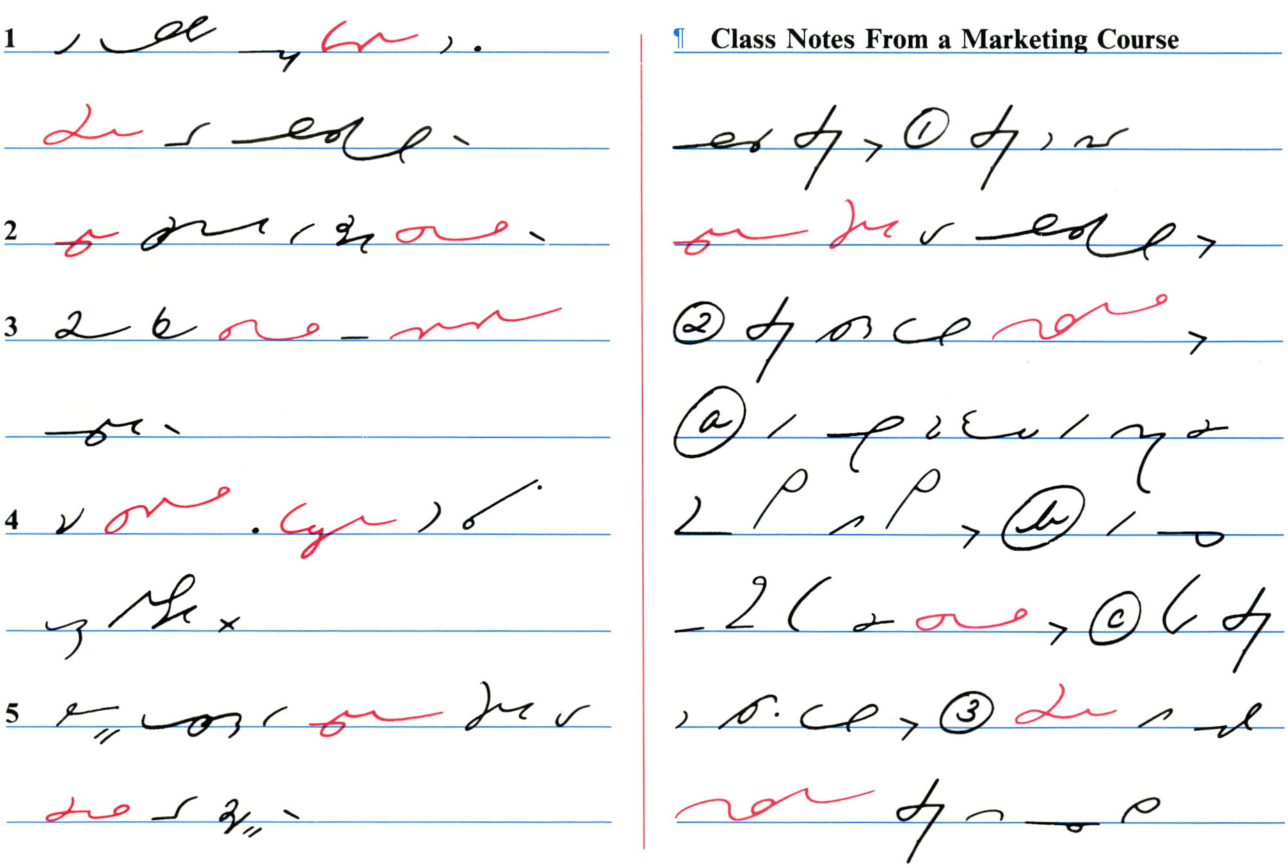

[73 words]

Transcription Tips

Transcription is the process of "translating" shorthand notes into standard English. The ultimate measure of transcription skill is called *mailable-letter production*. This term is broadly defined since not everything that is transcribed at a keyboard is a letter and not every transcript is mailed.

Many of the personal and administrative uses of shorthand do not require that shorthand be transcribed at a keyboard. But all shorthand notes are written with the intention that they will at least be read at some later time. Reading shorthand is the most basic component of transcription skill. In order to make your shorthand skill as useful as possible, you should practice reading your own shorthand notes until you can read them fluently.

If any outlines are difficult to read, or if they are missing from the notes entirely, the context of the sentence should serve as a clue in helping you to fill in the missing words.

If an outline in your notes does not make sense, you may have made an error in writing proportion. Failure to curve the *ith* will make it appear as a *t*, turning *father* into *fat*, for example.

One of the best ways to learn the meanings of the shorthand symbols is through reading. Practice reading. It will make you a faster shorthand writer in the next few weeks and a better transcriber later on.

Shorthand becomes an important productivity tool for an executive to record all pertinent information.

16.4 Phone Message

To: 

From: 

Date: 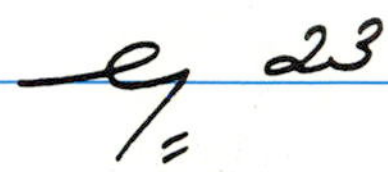

Time: 12:15

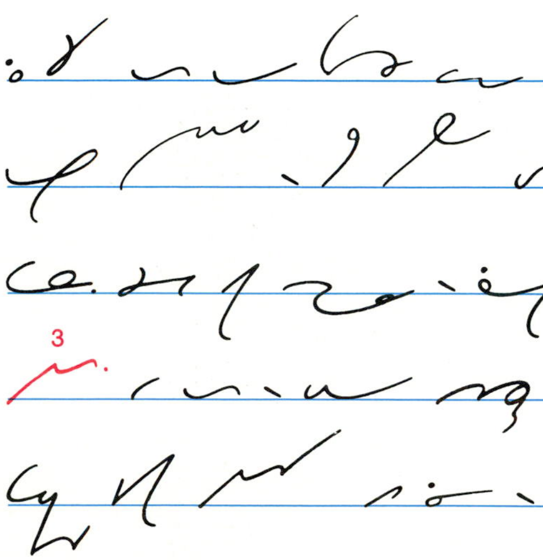

[53 words]

16.5 Business Letter

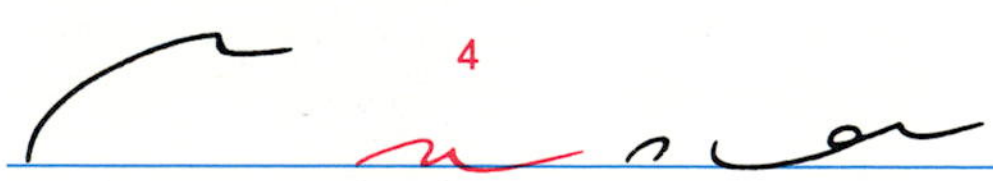

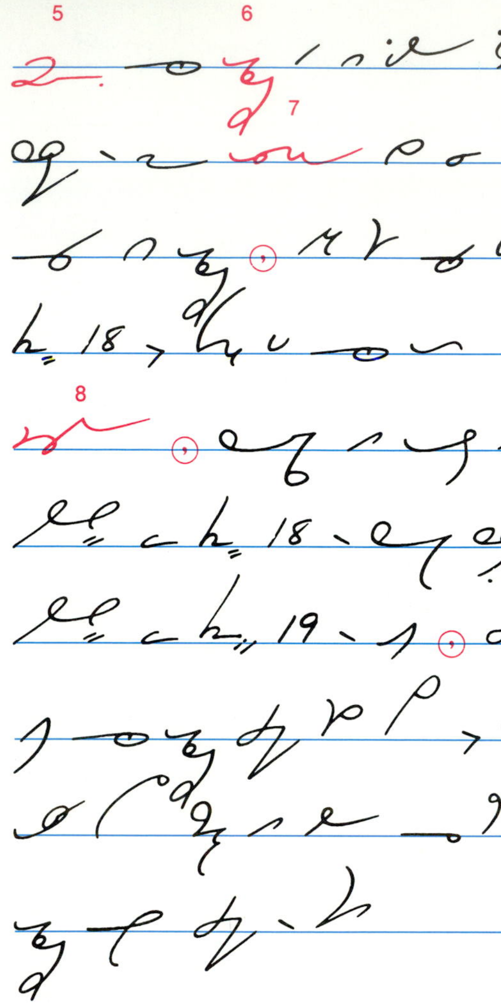

[85 words]

1 Carson 2 communications 3 directing
4 Cole

5 confirming 6 reservation 7 recall
8 schedule

UNIT V

LESSON 17

NEW IN LESSON 17

- Symbol for the sounds of *nd* and *nt*
- Sound of short *u* omitted
- More minor vowels omitted
- Differentiating between *personal* and *personnel*

SOUNDS OF ND, NT

The sound of *nd* (end) as in *sound* and the sound of *nt* (ent) as in *sent* are both written with a blend of *n* and *t*.

n + t = nt

Examples: sound sent

Nd Words

sound	end	grand
found	planned	friend
signed	trained	friendly
assigned	kind	mind
find	kindly	remind
agenda	kindness	spend

Nt Words

sent	currently	agent
print	apparent	spent
printer	account	into
rental	accountant	entire
current	amount	entirely

Nd, Nt Practice

17.1

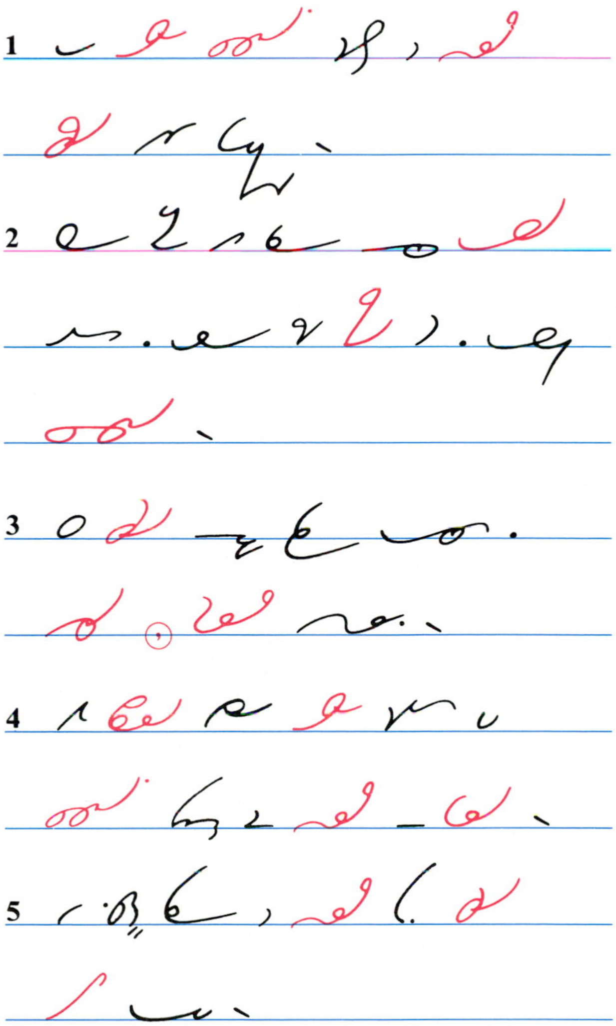

¶ **Memo**

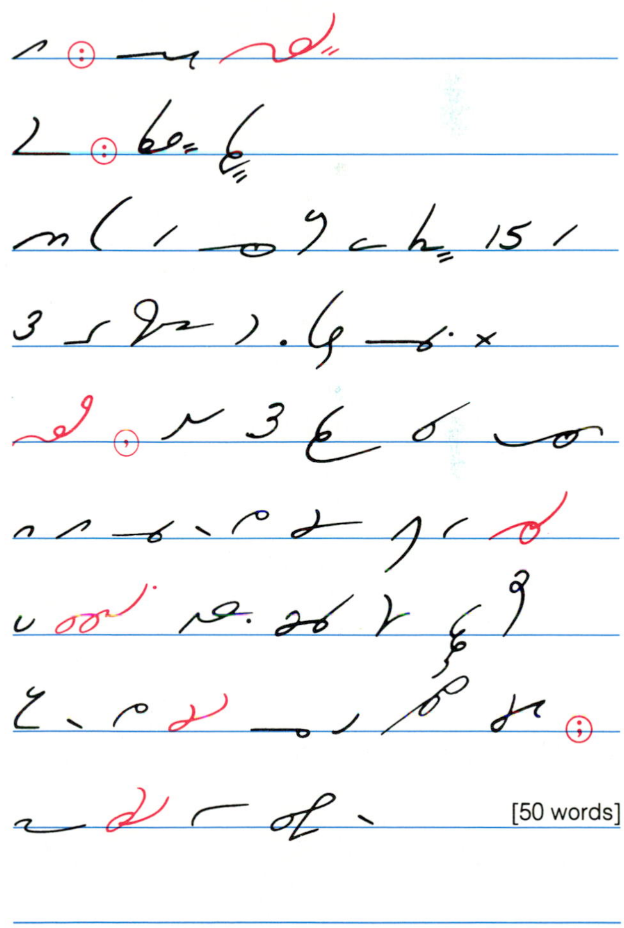

OMISSION OF SHORT U

The short sound of *u* as in *some* is omitted before *n*, *m*, and straight downstrokes (*ish*, *chay*, *j*).

Examples: some much

Short U Omitted Before N and M

some
summer
fun
done
lunch
run
begun
refund
come
income
become
welcome

But: *Number* retains the *oo* to facilitate the joining of *n* and *m*.

number
numbers
numbering

Short U Omitted Before a Straight Downward Symbol

much
such
touch
rush
judge
budget

Short-U-Omitted Practice

17.2

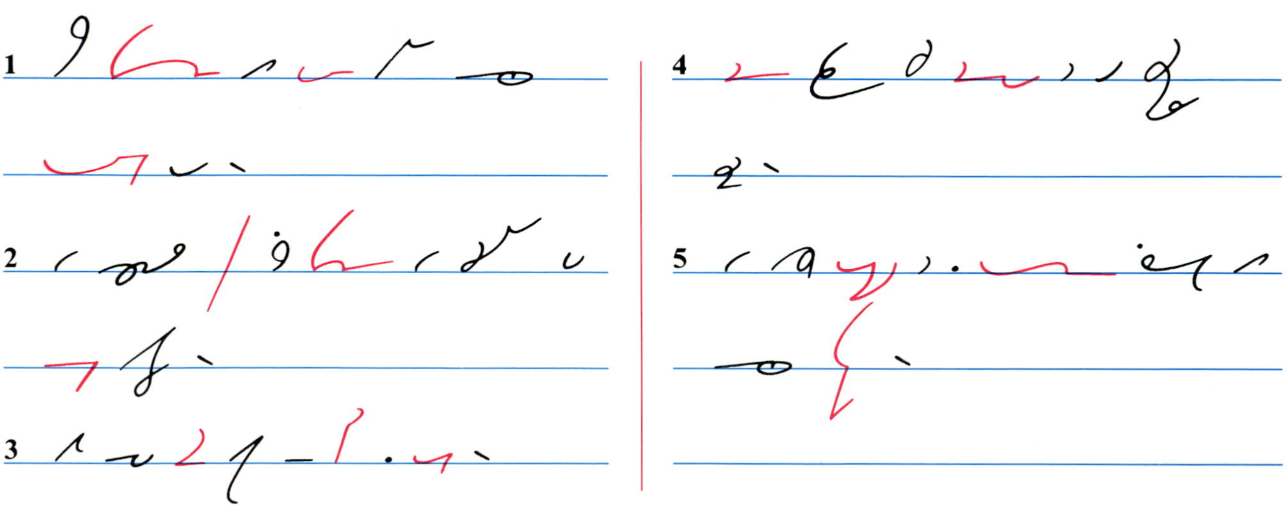

¶ Student Meeting

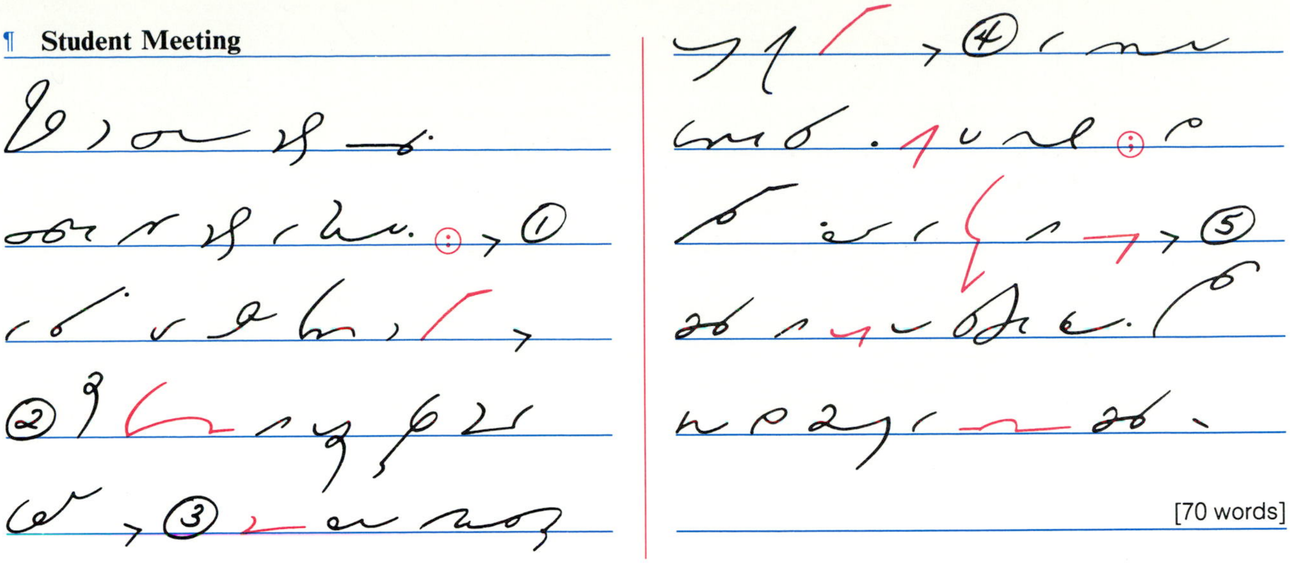

[70 words]

MINOR VOWELS OMITTED

In Lesson 3 you were taught to omit minor vowels. Here is a brief review of minor-vowel-omitted words you have been reading and writing:

reader — final — delay

writer — total — reason

Here are some more minor-vowel-omitted words:

person — purchase — disturb

personal — courtesy — describe

personnel — secretary — description

pursue — display — agency

Minor-Vowel-Omitted Practice

17.3

1 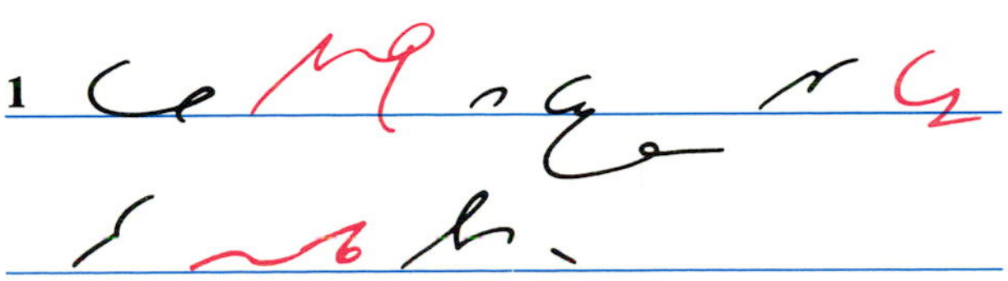

2 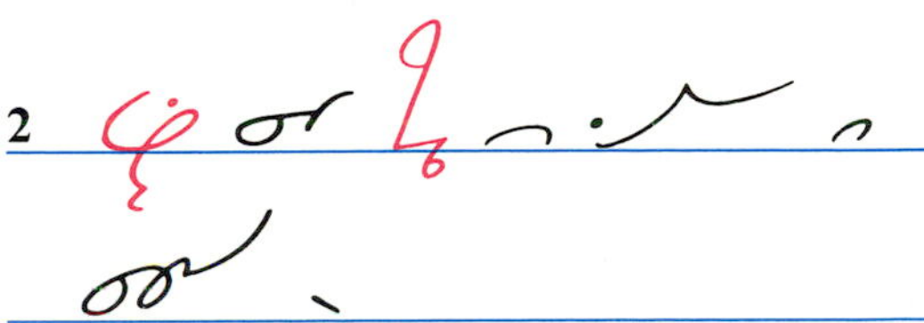

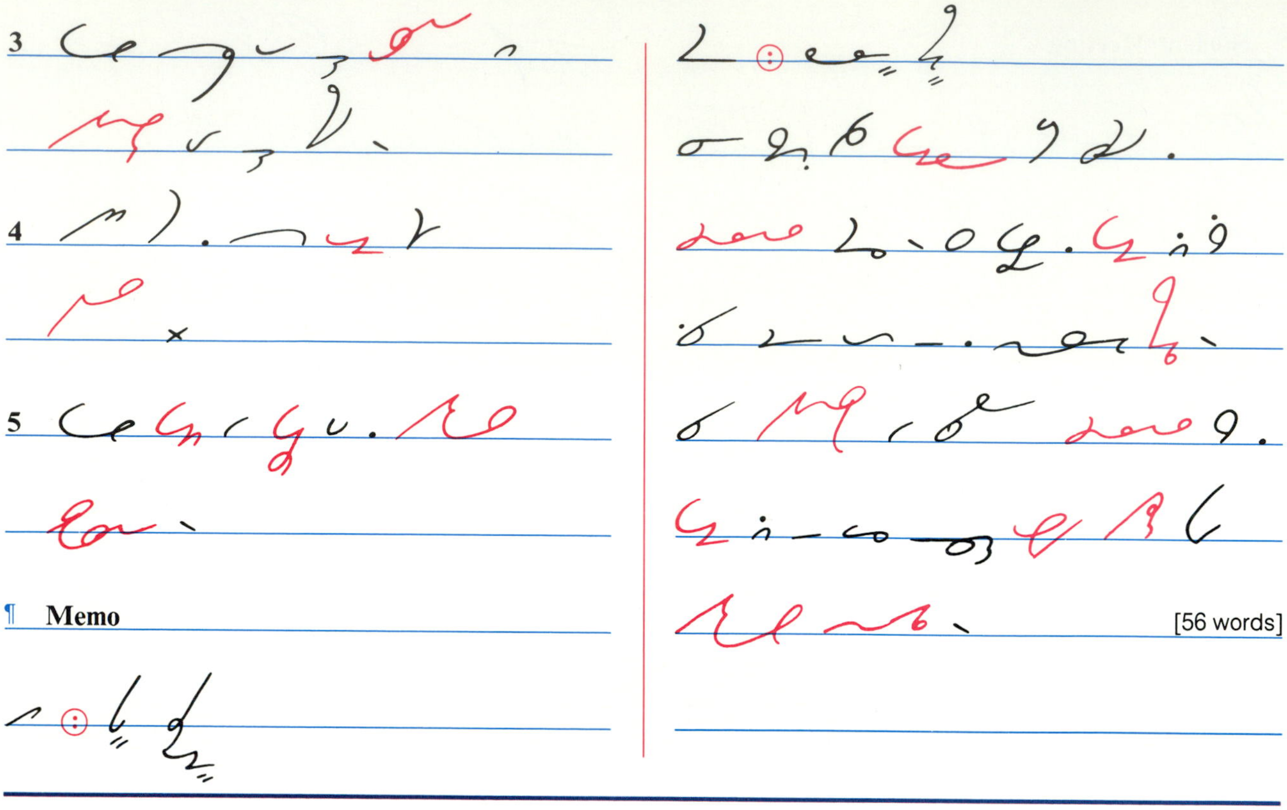

Communication Skill Builder

Similar Words: personal, personnel

personal: belonging to a person; private

personnel: people who make up an organization, such as military personnel; the staff

Do not leave *personal* items in your office.

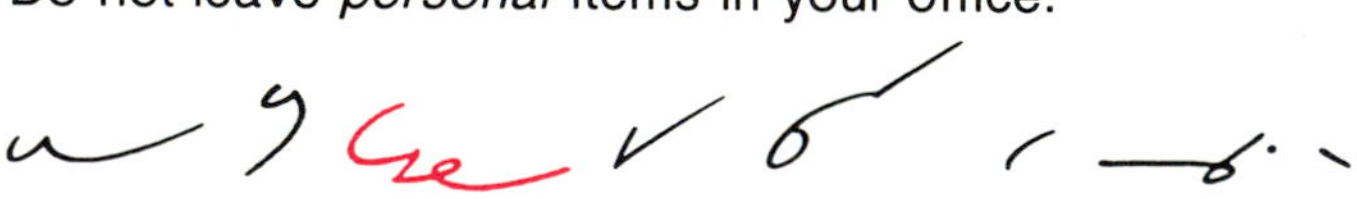

All office *personnel* should attend the meeting.

An attorney with shorthand skills can save valuable time by writing research notes in shorthand.

Reading and Writing Practice

17.4 Dictation Speed Memo

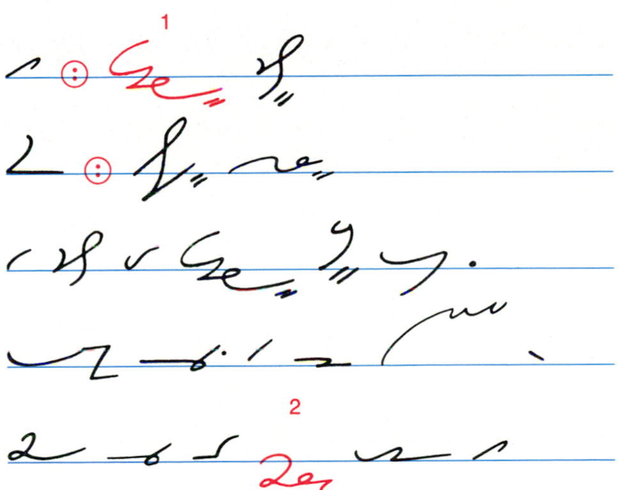

1 Personnel 2 conference

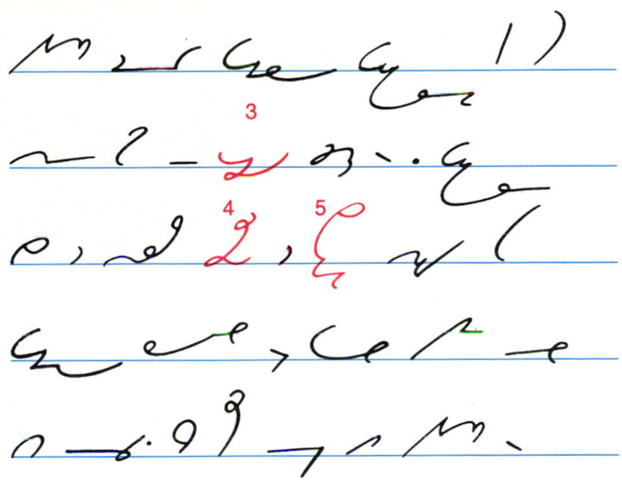

[66 words]

3 recent 4 severe 5 absence

17.5 Letter of Complaint

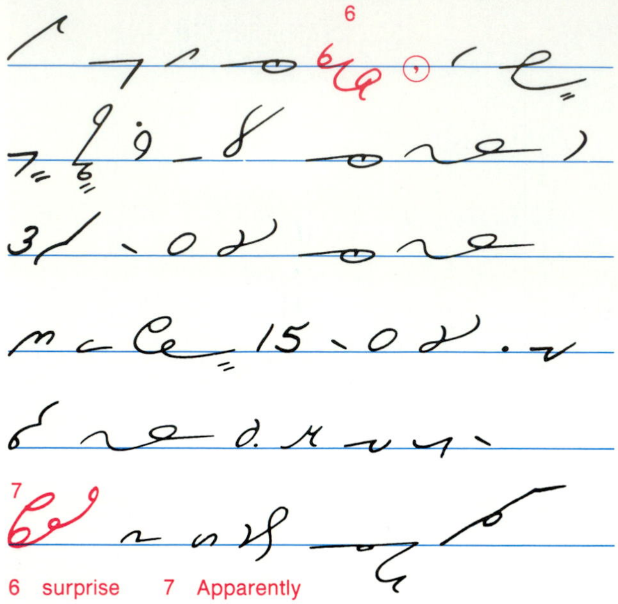

6 surprise 7 Apparently

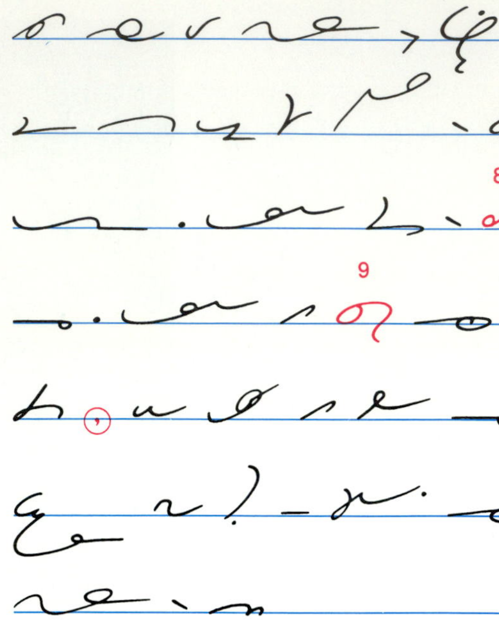

[90 words]

8 Either 9 accompany

LESSON 18

NEW IN LESSON 18

- Eight brief forms
- Word ending *-ble*
- Word ending *-ment*
- Using number as first word of sentence

BRIEF FORMS

and 

part 

advantage 

several 

immediate 

were 

advertise 

value 

Brief-Form Derivatives

partly, party 

partner 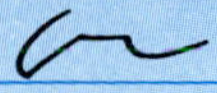

depart 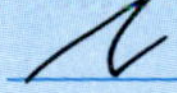

advantages 

disadvantage 

immediately ■ 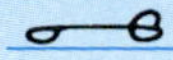

values 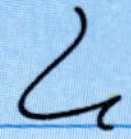

advertising 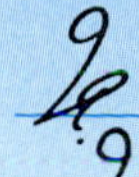

advertises 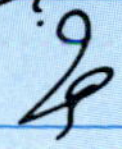

■ Transcription Alert.

Brief-Form Practice

18.1

1 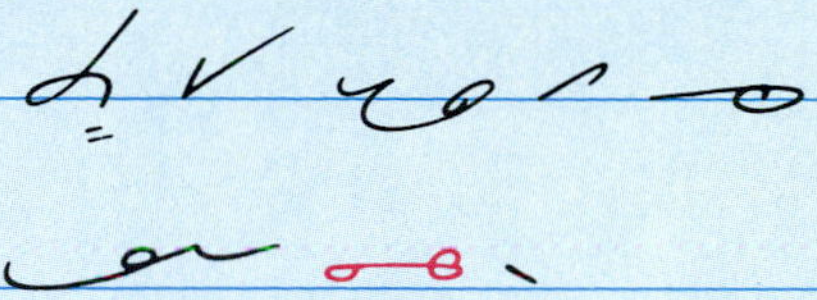

2 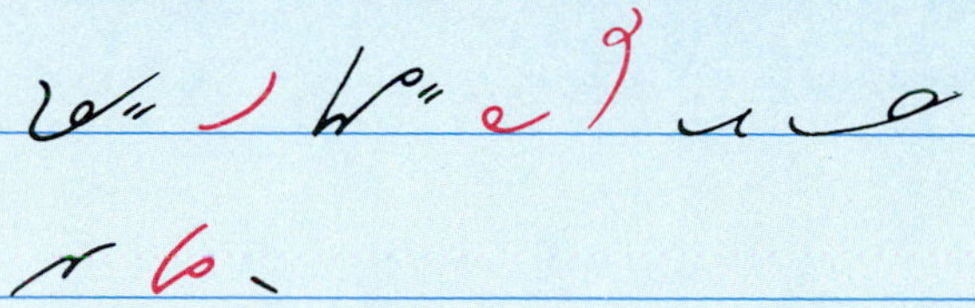

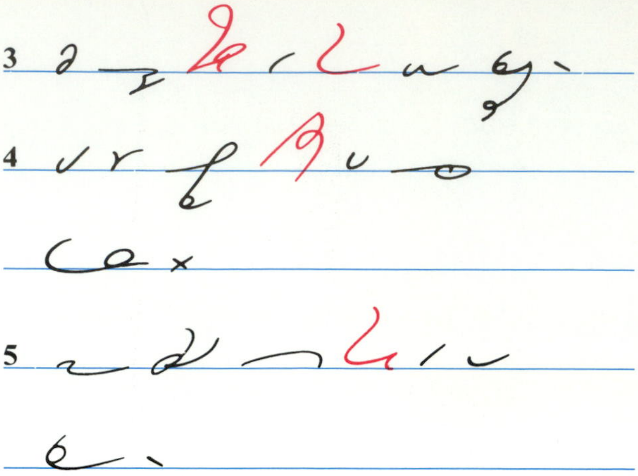

¶ **Rough Draft of an Idea for a Term Paper**

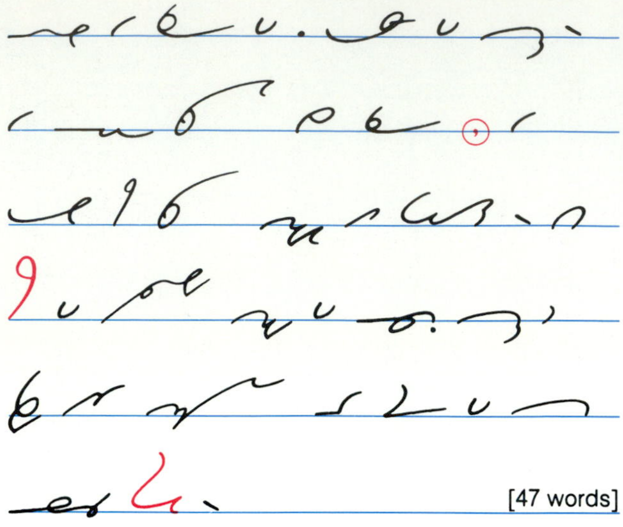

[47 words]

WORD ENDING -BLE

The word ending *-ble* as in *available* is written with the *b* symbol.

-ble 

Example: available 

-ble Words

availa<u>ble</u>	sensi<u>ble</u>	considera<u>ble</u>
possi<u>ble</u>	ta<u>ble</u>	considera<u>bly</u>
capa<u>ble</u>	trou<u>ble</u>	suita<u>ble</u>
relia<u>ble</u>	trou<u>bled</u>	valua<u>ble</u>
favora<u>ble</u>	reasona<u>ble</u>	desira<u>ble</u>

-ble Practice
18.2

1 

2 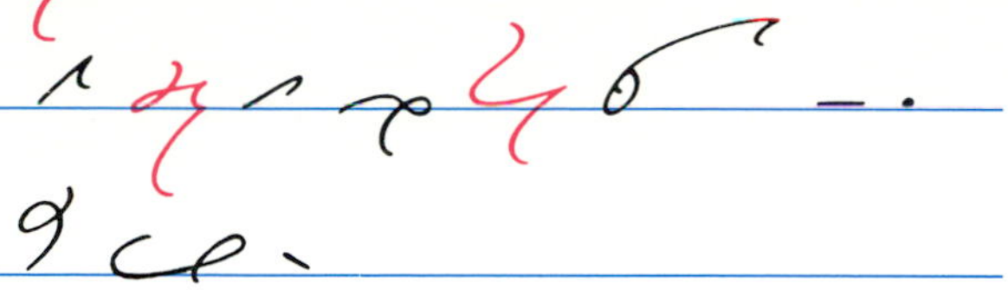

3 

4 

5 

¶ **Personal Note**

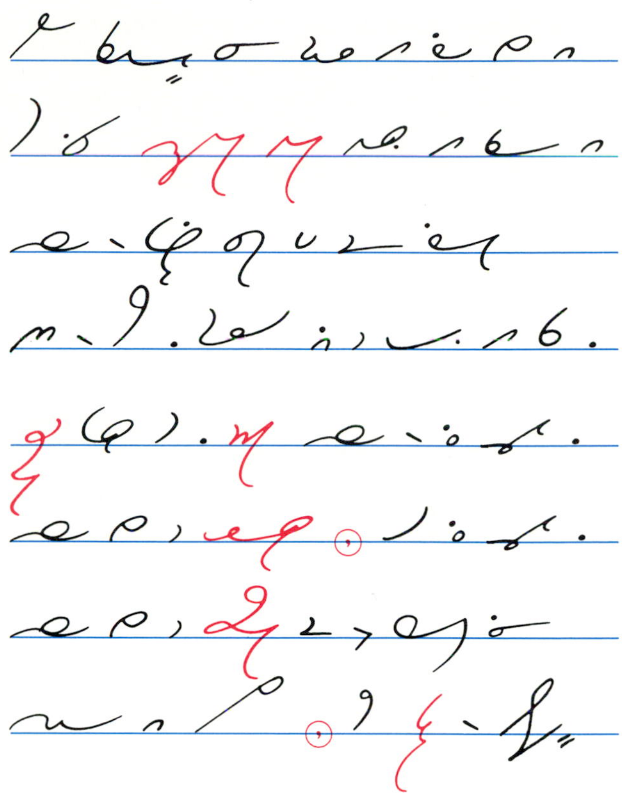

[68 words]

WORD ENDING -MENT

The word ending *-ment* as in *shipment* is represented by the *m* symbol.

-ment

Example: shipment 

-ment Words

shipment	**	commitment ■	**	basement	**
statement	**	retirement	**	payment	**
advertisement	**	replacement	**	payments	**
department	**	investment	**	arrangement	**
judgment ■	**	assignment	**	installment	**
agreement	**	settlement	**	attachment	**

■ Transcription Alert.

-ment Practice
18.3

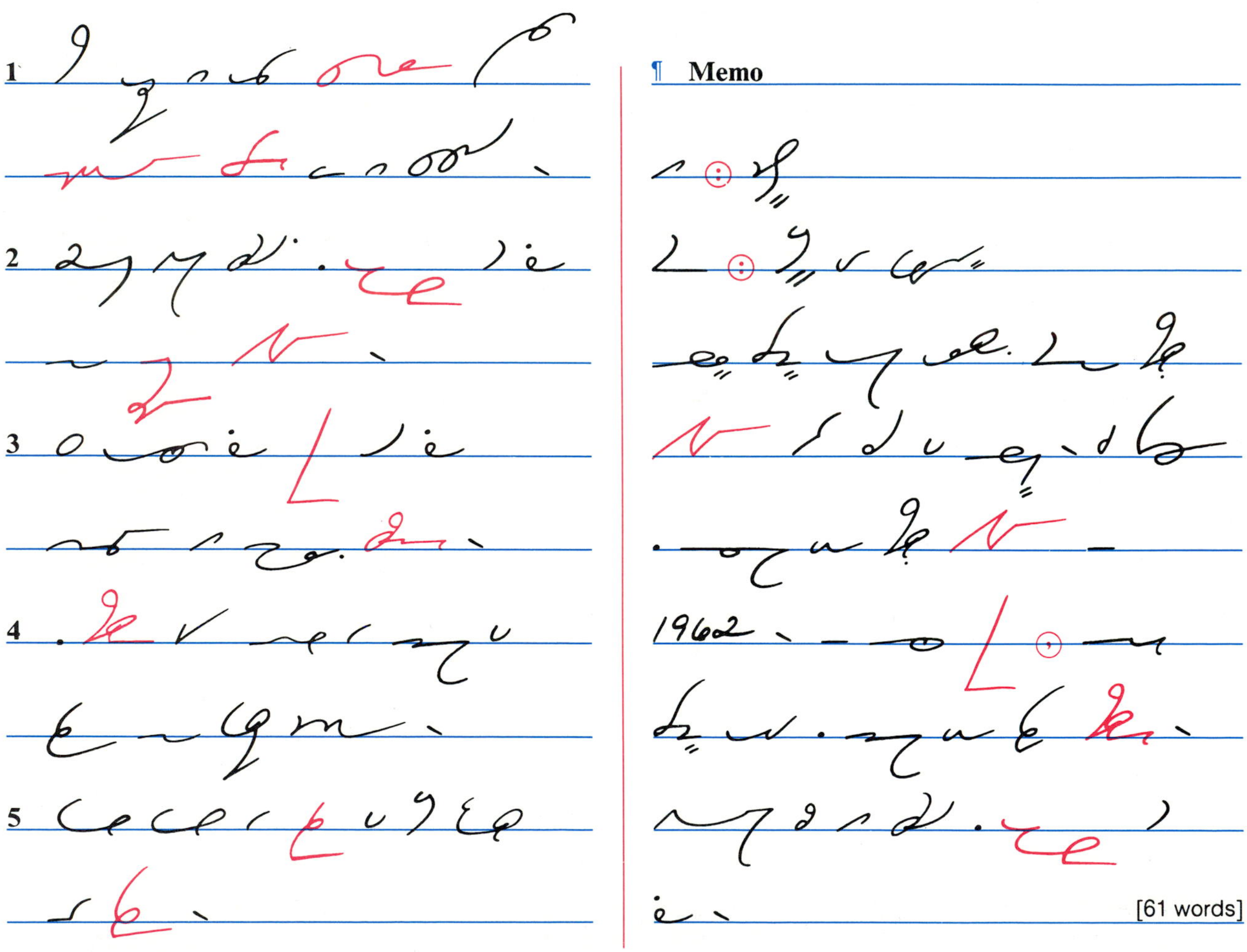

1 **

2 **

3 **

4 **

5 **

¶ **Memo**

1962

[61 words]

Number as First Word of Sentence

One exception to the basic number rule is a number at the beginning of a sentence. When a number is the first word of a sentence, it is spelled out.

5 

Five years have gone by since her retirement.

17 

Seventeen members signed up for the meeting.

24 

Twenty-four books need to be put back on the shelves.

Legal secretaries assist with the signing of legal documents.

18.4 Dictation Speed Letter

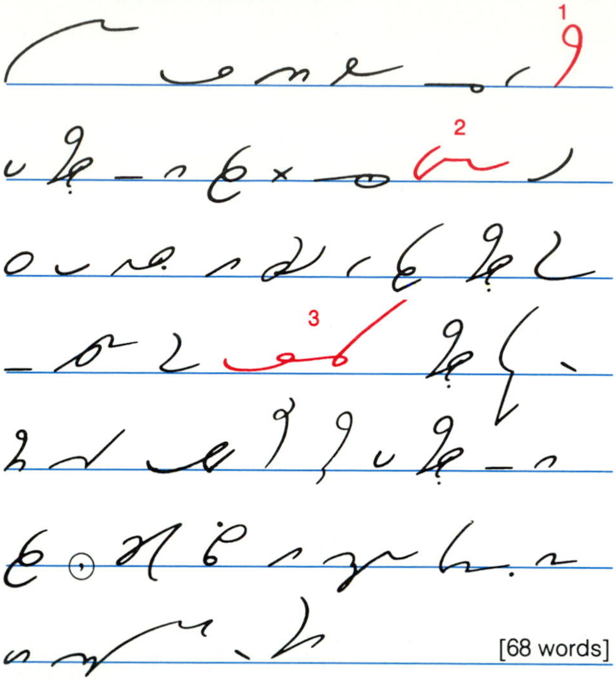

[68 words]

18.5 Business Letter

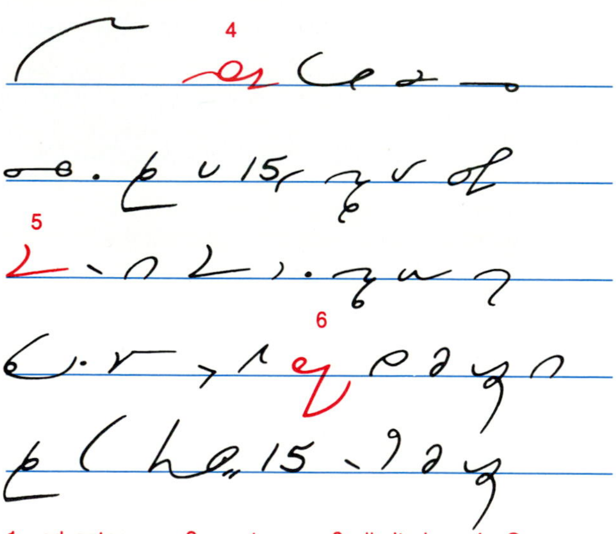

1 advantage 2 partner 3 limited 4 Carson
5 form 6 urgent

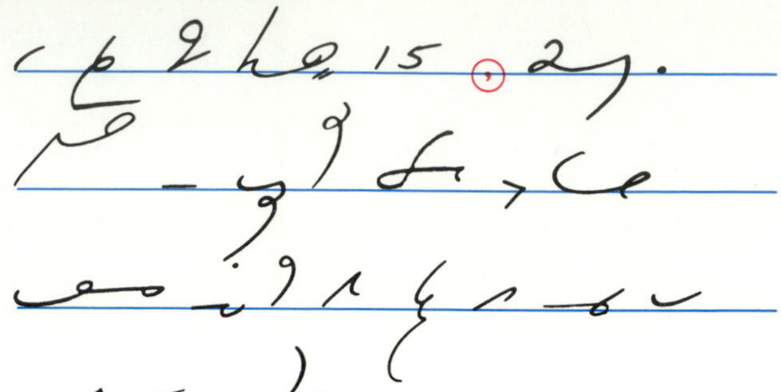

[75 words]

18.6 Business Letter

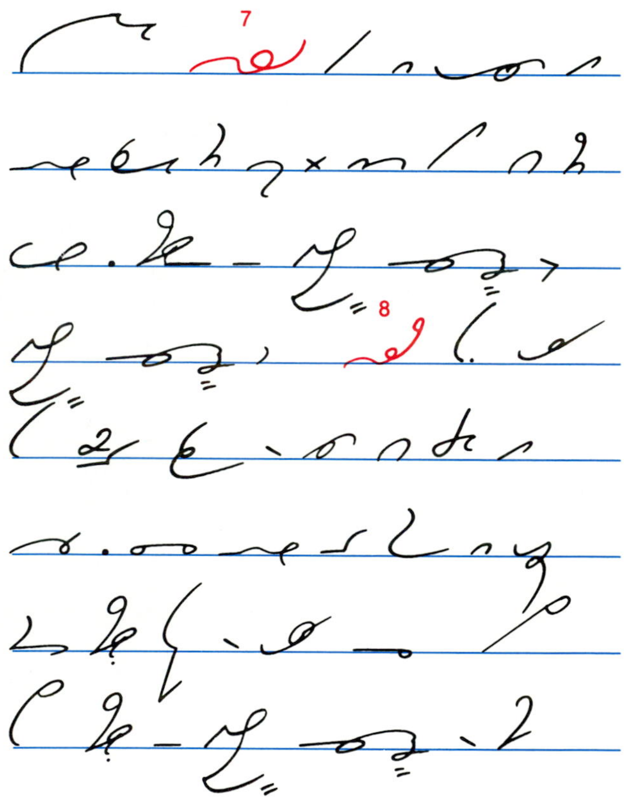

[72 words]

7 Grant 8 currently

LESSON 19

NEW IN LESSON 19

- **Nine new phrases**
- **Blends for the sounds of *rd* and *ld***
- **Blend for the sound of *sez***

PHRASES

Writing speed is gained by representing the word *hope* with the *p* symbol in the following phrases.

I hope

I hope the

I hope that

I hope that the

we hope

we hope the

we hope that

we hope that the

we hope you will

The middle word is eliminated in the following phrases to gain writing speed.

some of the

some of our

some of them

Phrase Practice

19.1

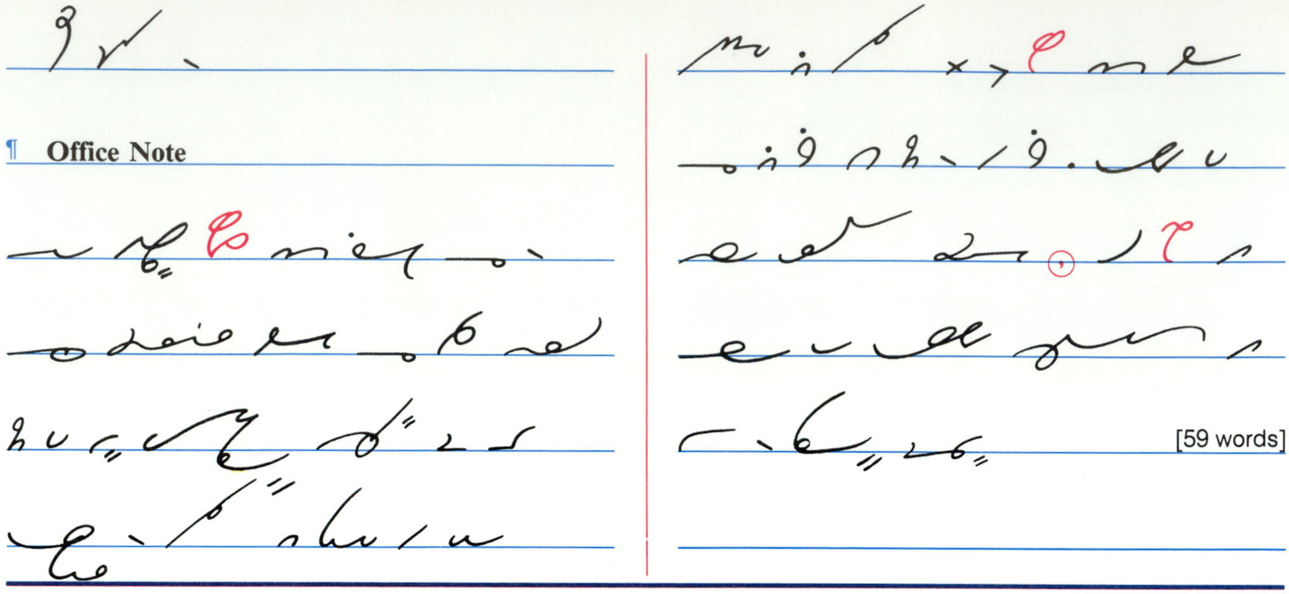

¶ Office Note

[59 words]

SOUNDS FOR RD, LD

The sound of *rd* as in *heard* and the sound of *ld* as in *old* are written with blends in which the end of the *r* and *l* curl upward to represent the *d*.

rd   ld

Examples: heard   old

Rd Words

heard
hard
harder
answered
ignored
assured
toward
prepared
tired
word
record
recorded

Ld Words

old
told
sold
build, billed
folder
folded
failed
stored
held
child
children
called, cold

Rd, Ld Practice

19.2

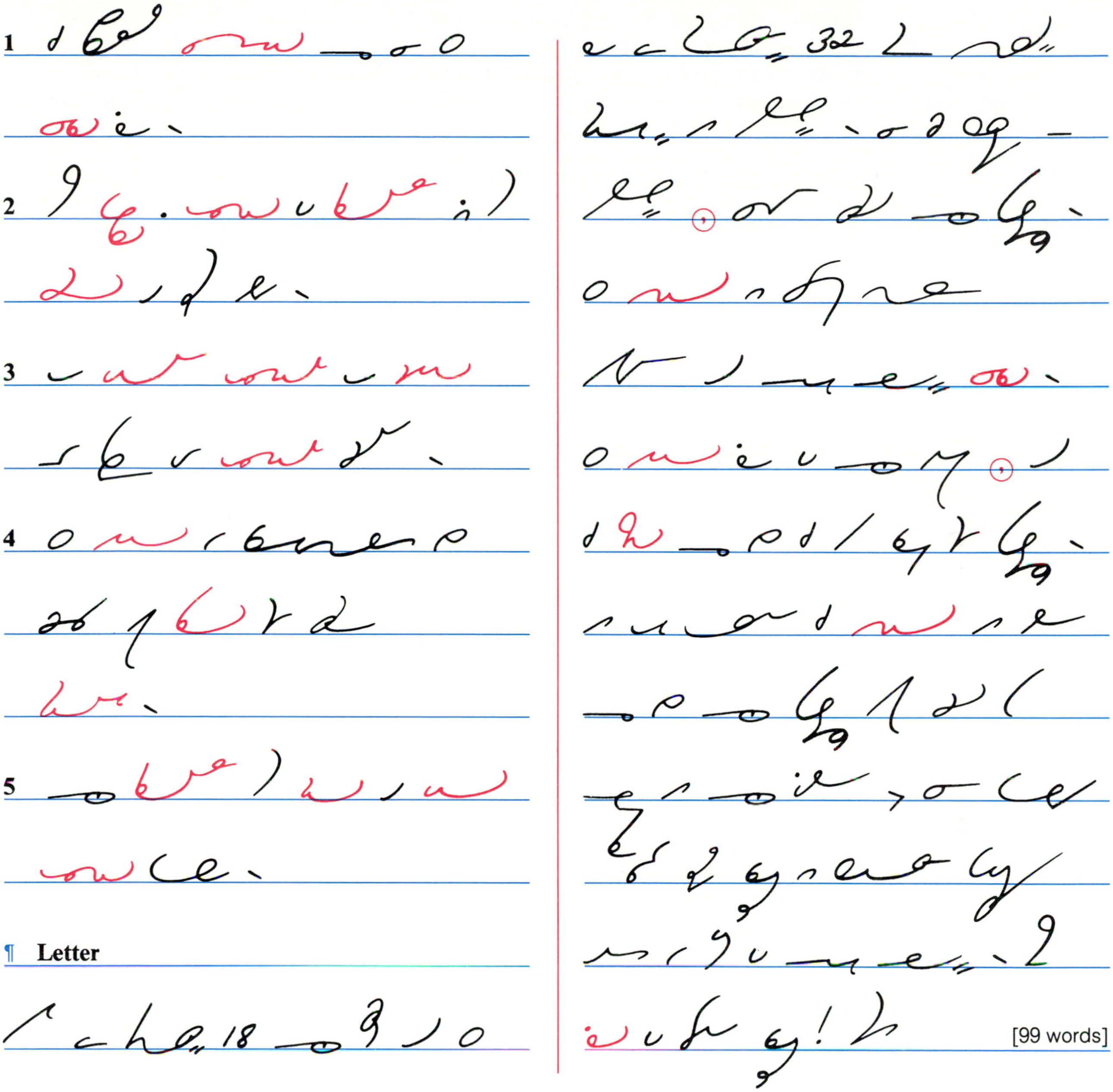

1

2

3

4

5

¶ **Letter**

[99 words]

SOUND OF SEZ

The two forms of *s* are joined—and called the *sez* blend—in order to represent the sounds of *ses*, *sis*, and *sus* as in *senses*, *basis*, and *versus*. Notice the *right sez* begins with the *right s* and ends with the *left s*. The *left sez* begins with the *left s* and ends with the *right s*.

right sez or left sez

Examples: services spaces

Right Sez Words

services

faces

suspend

advises

suspect

cases

Left Sez Words

spaces

insist

basis, bases

says

system

assist

senses

versus

assisted

process

promises

losses

processes

necessary

Moses

sister

analysis

crisis

Sez Practice

19.3

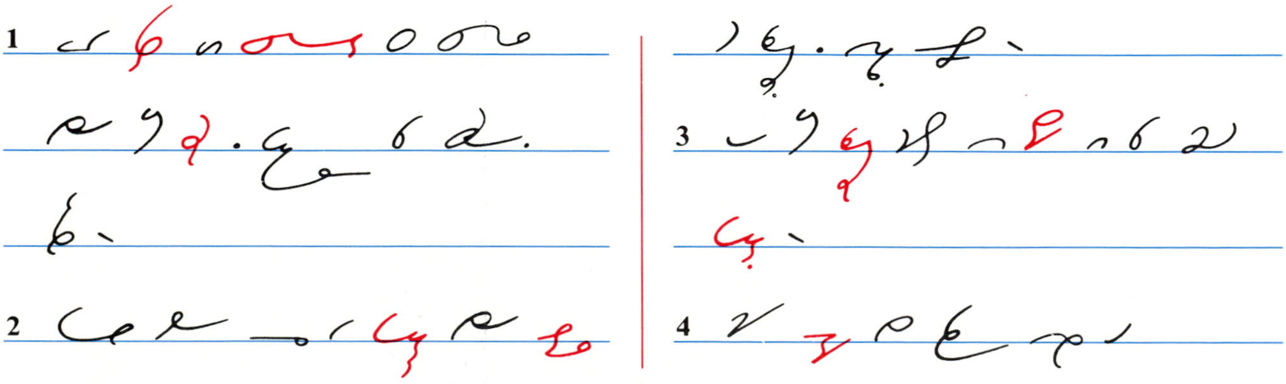

5

¶ Note

[78 words]

Legal secretaries are often called upon to witness legal documents.

Reading and Writing Practice

19.4 Dictation Speed Letter

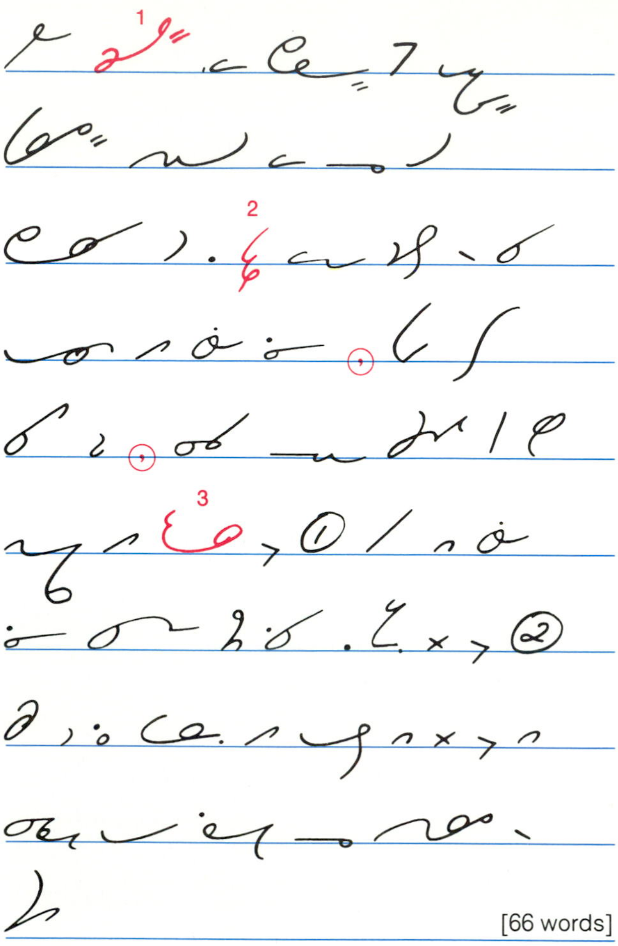

1 Wendy 2 position 3 supply

19.5 Business Letter

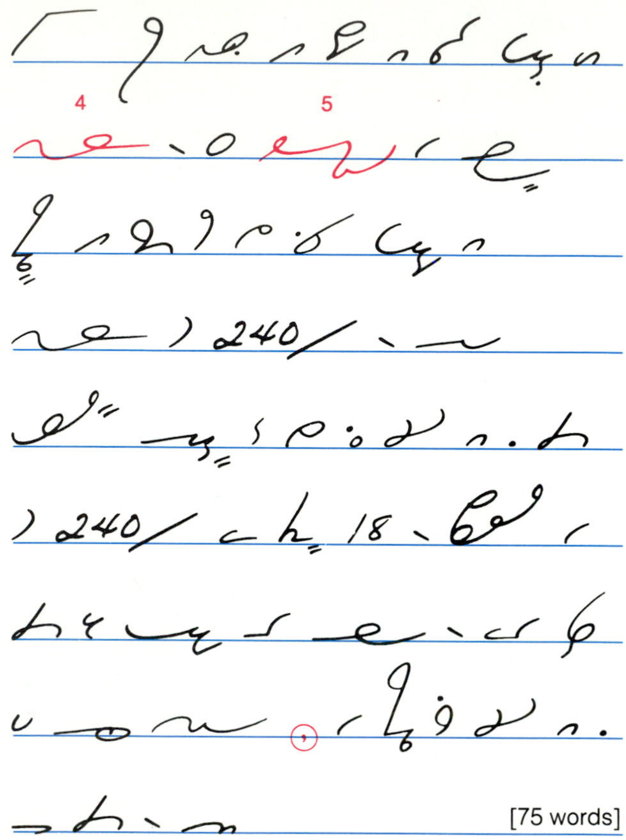

4 claim 5 telephoned

LESSON 20

NEW IN LESSON 20

- Seven brief forms
- Symbol for the sounds of *dev*, *div*, *def*, and *dif*
- Symbol for the sound of *u* (pronounced *you*) as in *few*
- Using shorthand to record instructions

BRIEF FORMS

organize 

present 

general 

govern 

opportunity ■ 

however 

acknowledge ■ 

■ Transcription Alert.

Brief-Form Derivatives

organization 

presented 

acknowledged 

organized 

represented 

acknowledges 

government 

representative 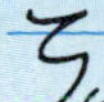

acknowledgment 

presently 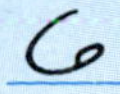

opportunities 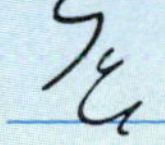

generally 

Brief-Form Practice

20.1

1 

2 

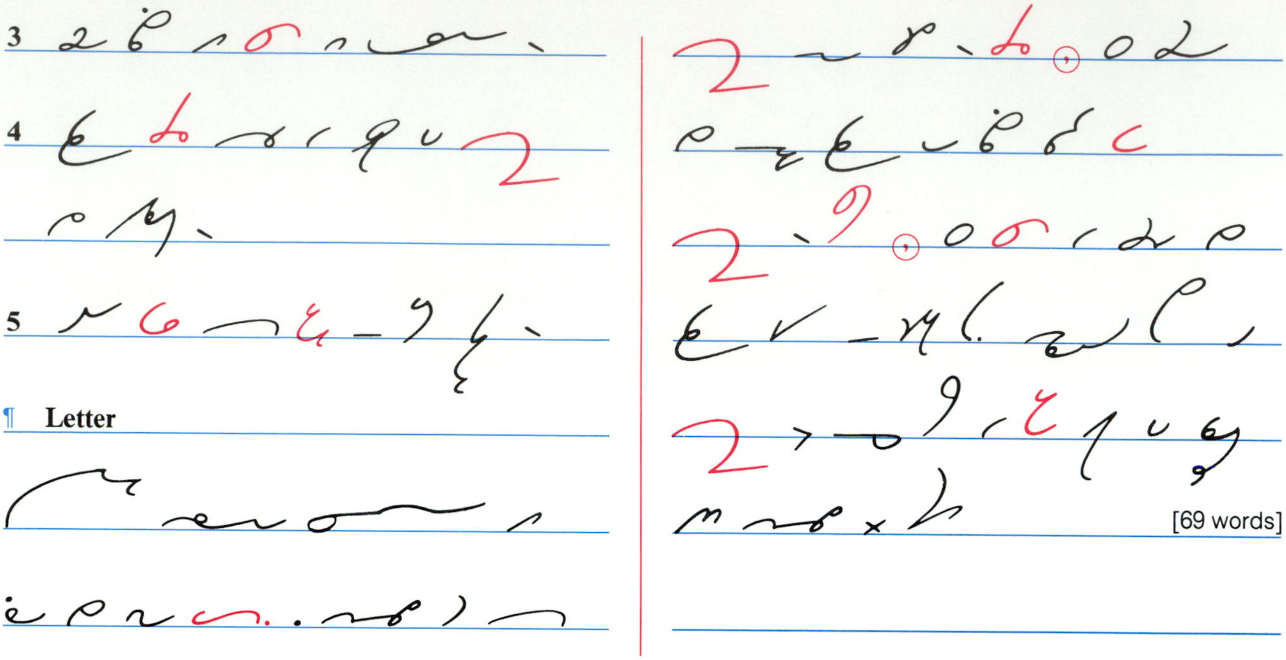

3

4

5

¶ Letter

[69 words]

SOUNDS OF DEV, DIV, DEF, DIF

The sounds of *dev*, *div*, *def*, and *dif* as in *devote*, *divide*, *definite*, and *differ* are all expressed with a blend which represents a rounded *d v* joining. It is called the *dev* blend.

d + v = dev

Examples: devote divide definite differ

Dev, Div Words

devote

devoted

devise, device

devised

devising

devises

develop

development

developing

divide

divided

dividing

division

divisions

divorce

Def, Dif Words

definite ■	defeated	different
definitely	defend	difference
defeat	differ	differences

■ Transcription Alert.

Dev, Div, Def, Dif Practice

20.2

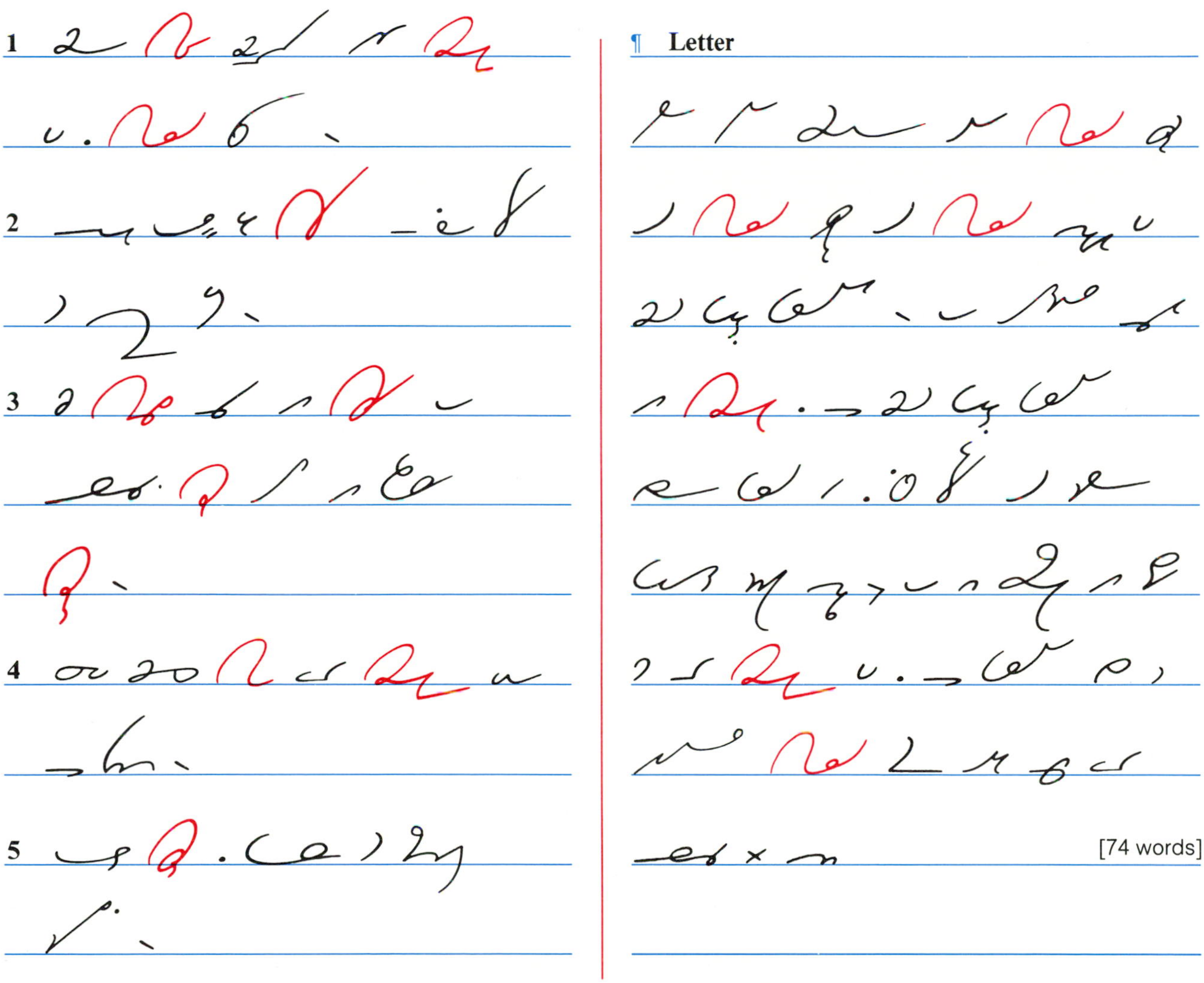

¶ Letter

[74 words]

SOUND OF U

The sound of *u* as in *few* is written with a combination of the *e* and *oo* symbols. This *e oo* combination is called *u* (pronounced *you*).

Example: few

U Words

few	unit	refuse
use	unite	review
used	unique	Hughes

U Practice
20.3

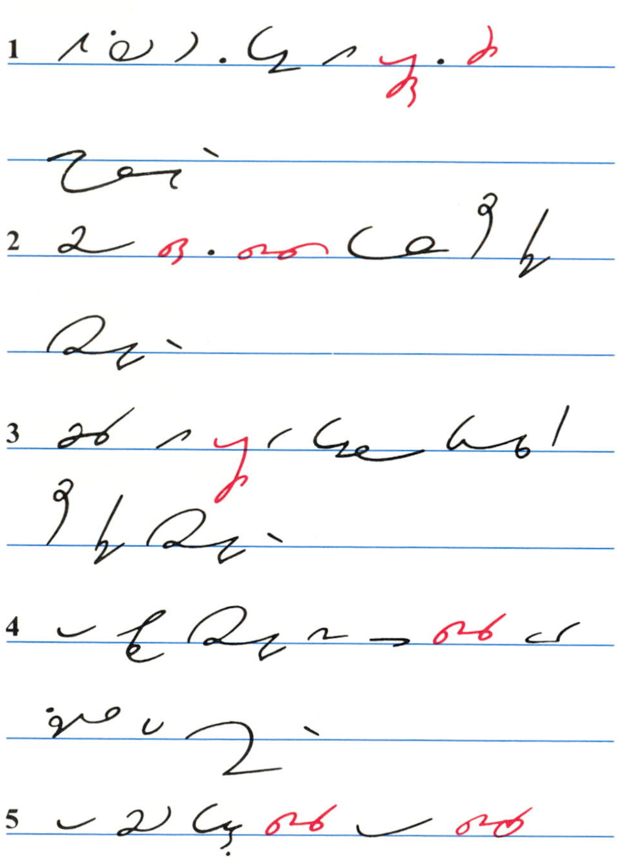

¶ **Business Letter**

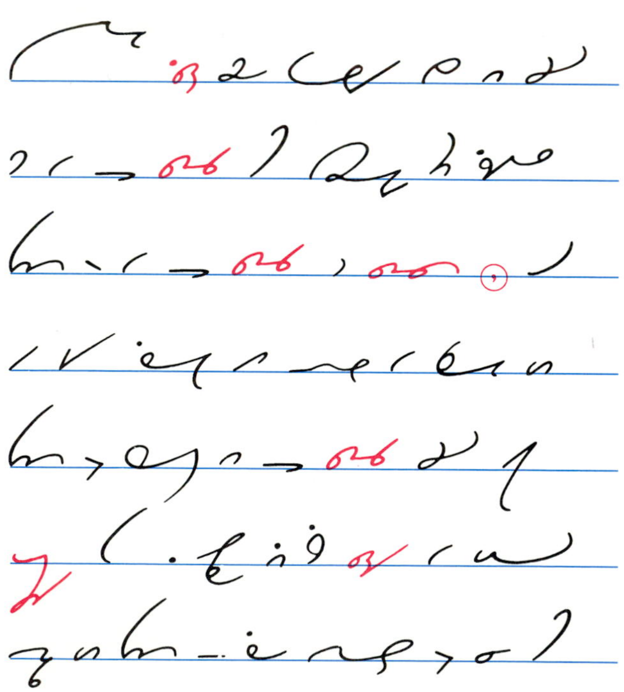

[83 words]

Using Shorthand to Record Instructions

One of the most valuable uses for shorthand is the recording of instructions on the job. This skill is equally useful for people at all levels of the organization.

Shorthand enables you to record your supervisor's instructions without having to ask the speaker to slow down or repeat major points. You will also know that the instructions are accurate and much more likely to be complete. You will thus avoid the embarrassment of having to go back to the supervisor to ask for the instructions a second time.

Finally, recording instructions in shorthand is a mark of professionalism. The supervisor who sees you recording instructions in shorthand knows that you are well prepared for the job, conscientious, and competent.

Shorthand skill is a valuable asset to paralegal assistants and secretaries in the legal office.

Reading and Writing Practice

20.4 Dictation Speed Letter

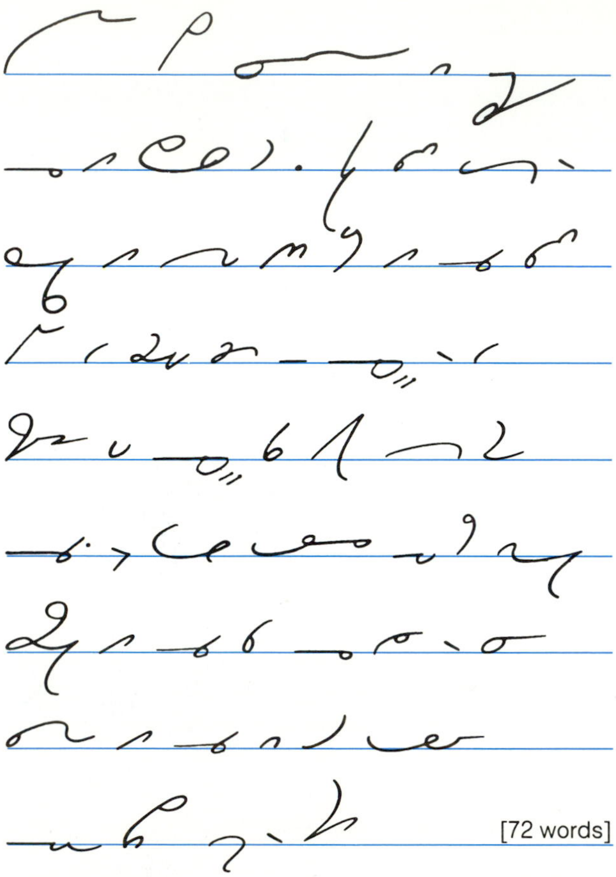

[72 words]

20.5 Business Memo

1 Butler

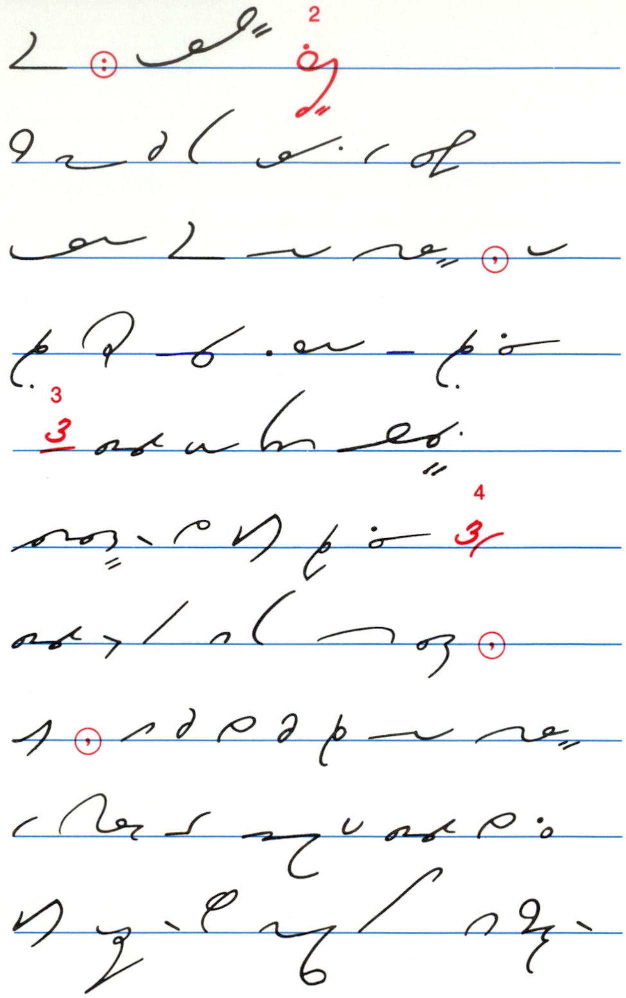

[80 words]

2 Harvey 3 300 4 3,000

UNIT VI

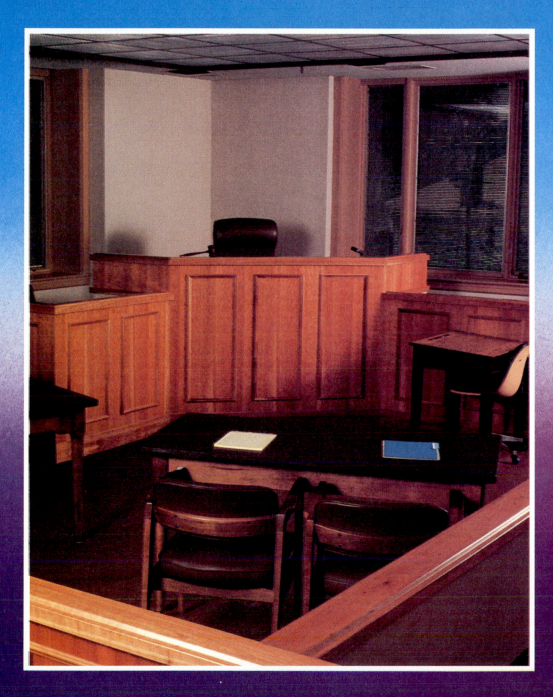

LESSON 21

NEW IN LESSON 21

- Blends for the sounds of *ten*, *den*, and *tain*
- Word ending *-ical*
- Special phrase *to know*
- Using shorthand to record information

SOUNDS OF TEN, DEN, TAIN

The sounds of *ten* as in *tent* and *bulletin* and *den* as in *sudden* are represented by the same blend—a blend of the *t* and *n* symbols. The *ten* blend is also used for the word ending *-tain* as in *obtain*. The curved *ten* blend symbol represents a rounding of the angle of the *t* and *n* joining.

t n ten

Examples: tent sudden obtain

Ten Words

tent
tonight
attend
attention
intend

intention
stand ■
standard
written
bulletin

maintenance
assistance
assistant
Fenton
Trenton

■ Although an *a* is heard in the word *stand* and its derivatives, for ease of writing it is written with the *ten* blend.

Den Words

sudden

suddenly

deny

denies

dentist

dinner

danger ■

evident

evidently

evidence

student

students

confident

president

presidency

■ Although an *a* is heard in the word *danger*, for ease of writing it is written with the *den* blend.

Tain Words

obtain

obtains

obtainable

attain

attained

contain

contains

container

certain

certainly

maintain

retain

Ten, Den, Tain Practice

21.1

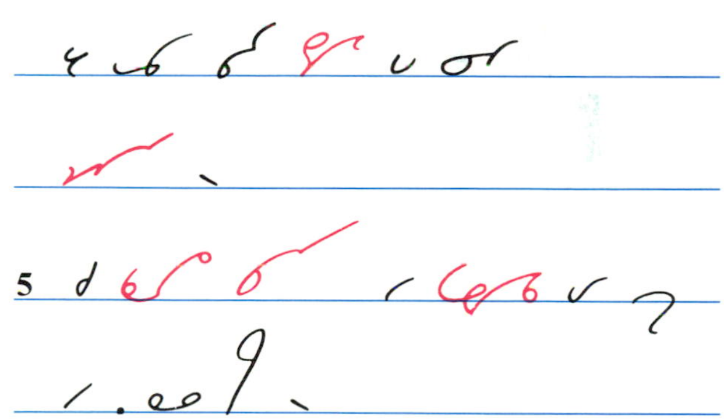

¶ **Notes From a Visitor to the Office**

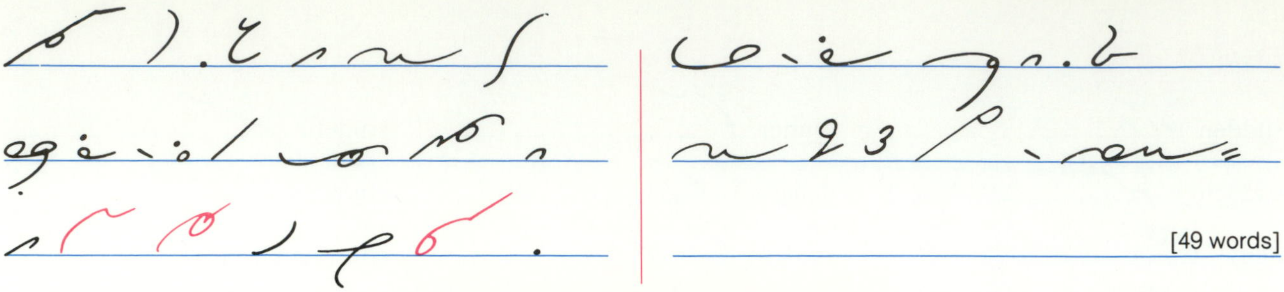

[49 words]

WORD ENDING -ICAL

The word ending *-ical* as in *medical* and *article* is written with a *disjoined k.* A disjoined word ending such as *-ing* or *-ical* should be written close to its root word so that it is not mistaken for a separate outline.

-ical

Example: medical

-ical Words

medical
logical
logically
typical
typically
article
articles
physical
political
radical
technical
chemical

-ical Practice
21.2

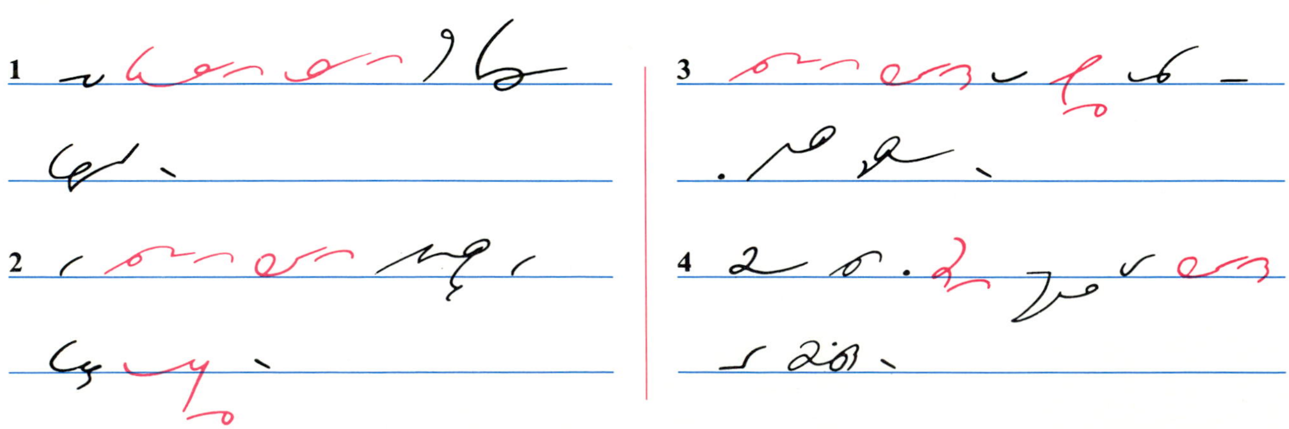

5 

¶ **Notes of Library Orientation**

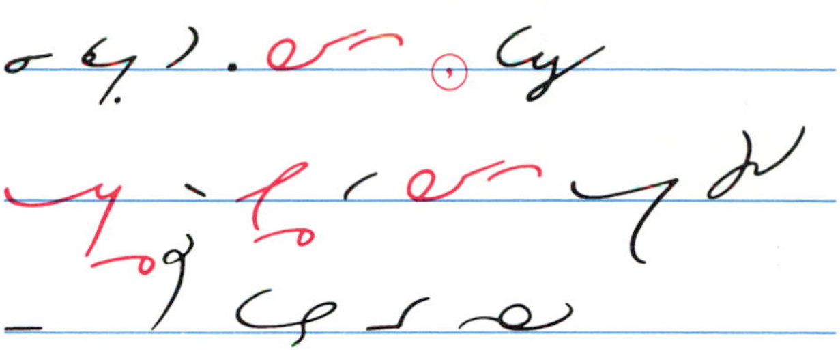

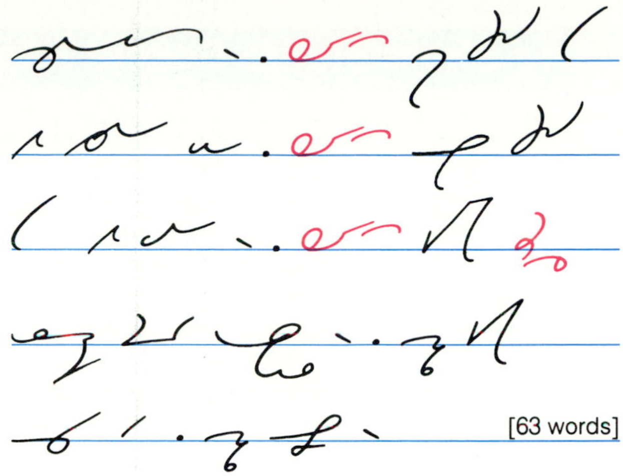

[63 words]

SPECIAL PHRASE

The *ten* blend is used in the frequent phrase *to know.*

to know 

Phrase Practice

21.3

1 

2 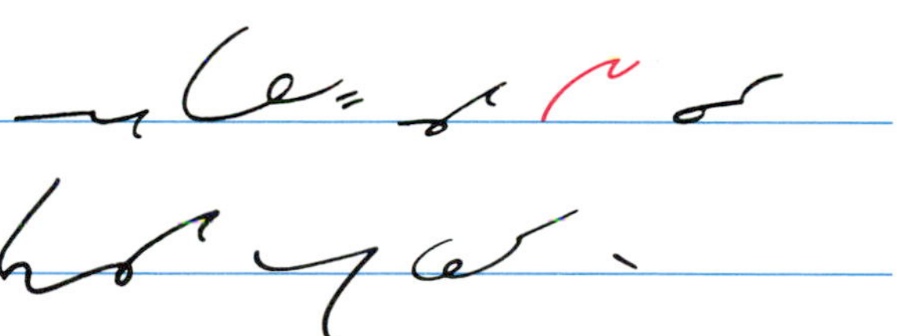

3 

4 

5 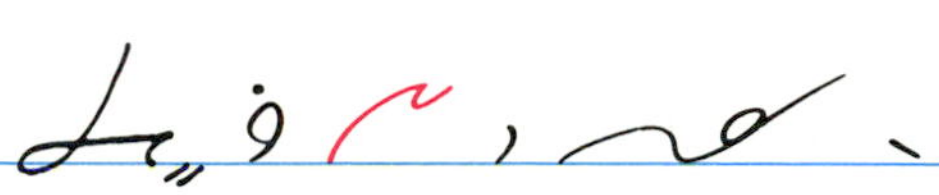

¶ **Personal Note**

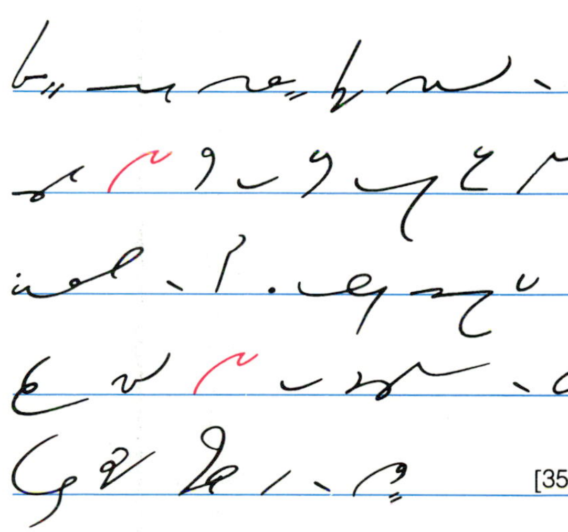

[35 words]

Using Shorthand to Record Information

One of the very valuable uses for shorthand skill is the recording of information from visitors to the office or from people who call on the telephone. People talk several times faster than you are able to write in longhand. Without shorthand skill, you would be forced to ask visitors and callers to repeat information where you failed to make complete notes.

By combining shorthand skill with good listening habits, you can write down all of the important facts that visitors and telephone callers give you. In this way information is complete, facts are accurate, and commitments may be kept. Moreover, using shorthand is evidence of being a competent professional and creates the best possible image for the company.

Reading and Writing Practice

21.4 Dictation Speed Letter

[61 words]

1 President's 2 Sutton 3 Trenton

21.5 Business Letter

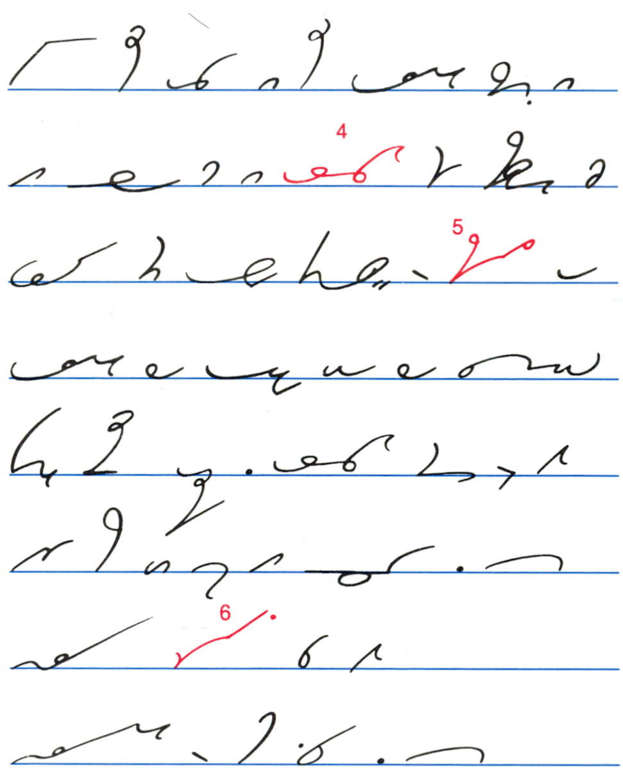

4 remittance 5 Evidently 6 standing

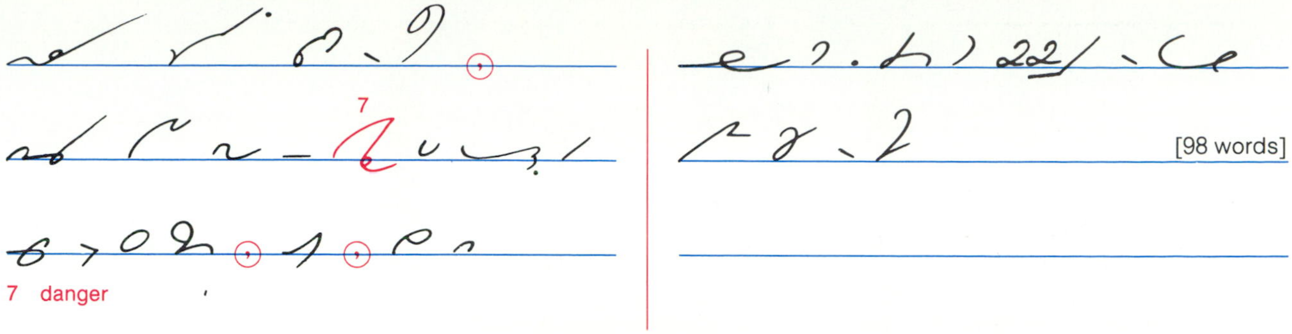

[98 words]

7 danger

Before dictating a letter to a legal secretary, an attorney uses shorthand to outline the points to be covered.

LESSON 22

NEW IN LESSON 22

- Seven brief forms
- Word ending *-tial*
- Symbol for the sound of *oi*

BRIEF FORMS

Ms.

business

out

than

over

what

difficult

Brief-Form Derivatives

businesses

businesslike

outside

outcome

outstanding

without

overhead

overlook

overlooked

whatever

difficulty

difficulties

Brief-Form Practice

22.1

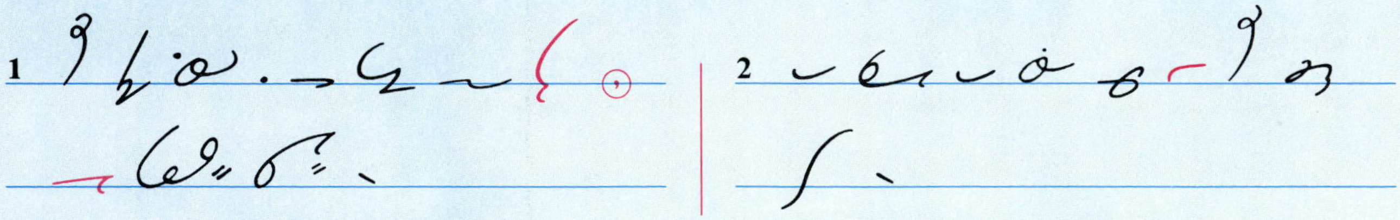

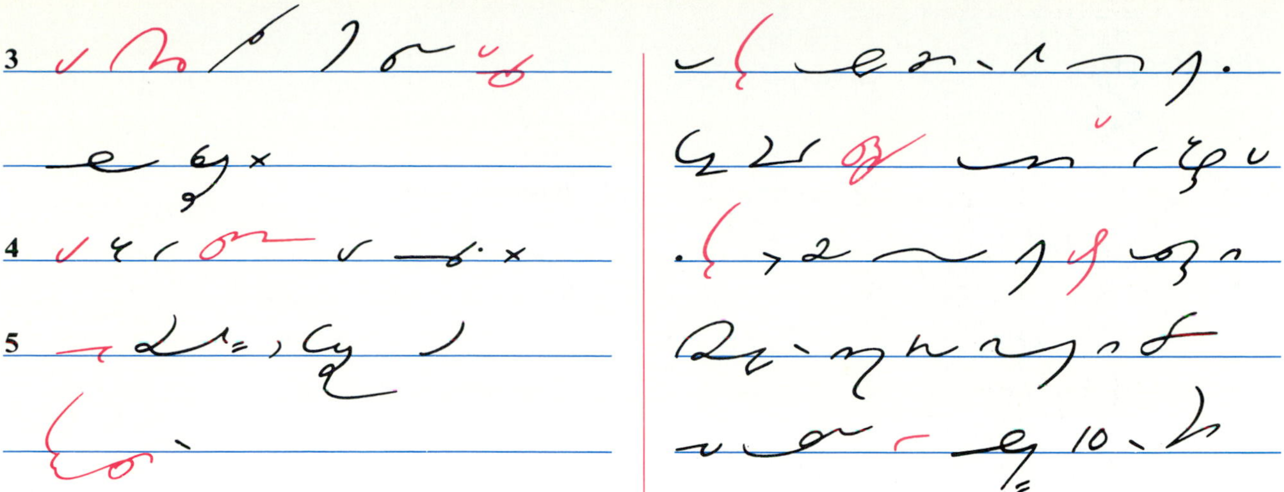

¶ **Business Letter** [57 words]

WORD ENDING -TIAL

The word ending *-tial* (pronounced *shul*) as in *special* is represented by the *ish* symbol. The context of the sentence tells the reader whether the *ish* represents *-tial* or whether it represents *-tion*, which was presented in Lesson 11.

-tial

Example: special

-tial Words

special

especially

initial

initialed

partial

partially

financial

financially

official

officially

social

essential

-tial Practice
22.2

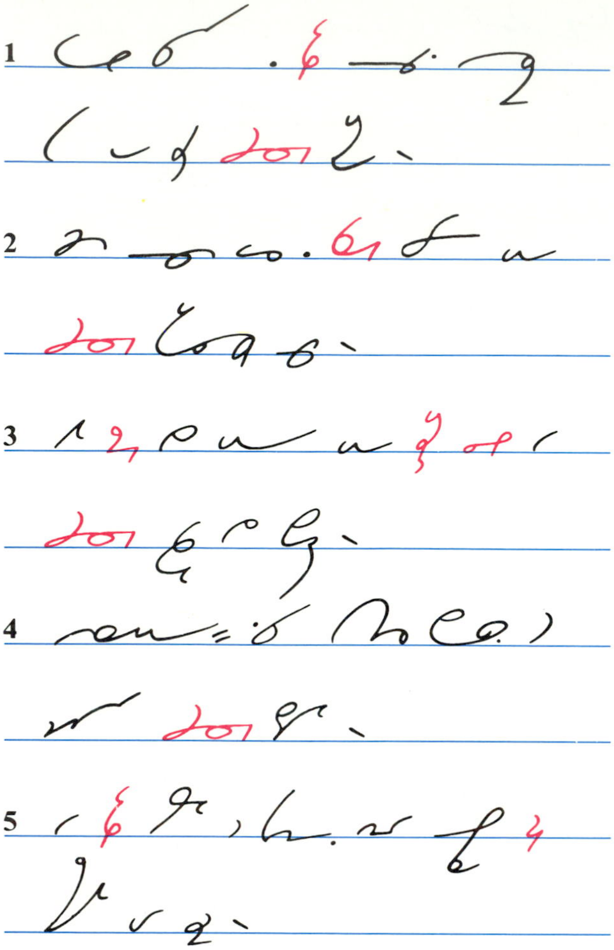

¶ **Business Letter**

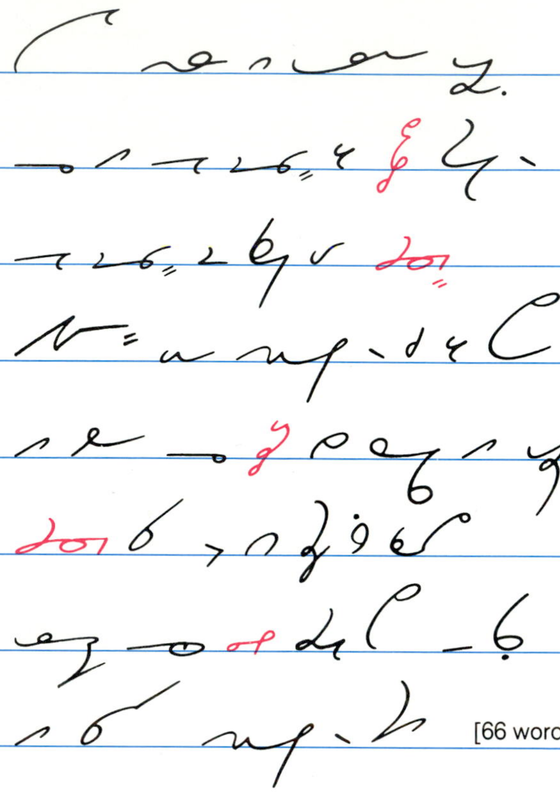

[66 words]

SOUND OF OI

The sound of *oi* as in *toy* is written with a joining of the *o* and *e* symbols. 

Example: toy 

Oi Words

toy	royal	appointment
joy	noise	invoice
join	annoy	invoices
boy	point	Roy
oil	appoint	void
soil	appointed	avoid

Oi Practice

22.3

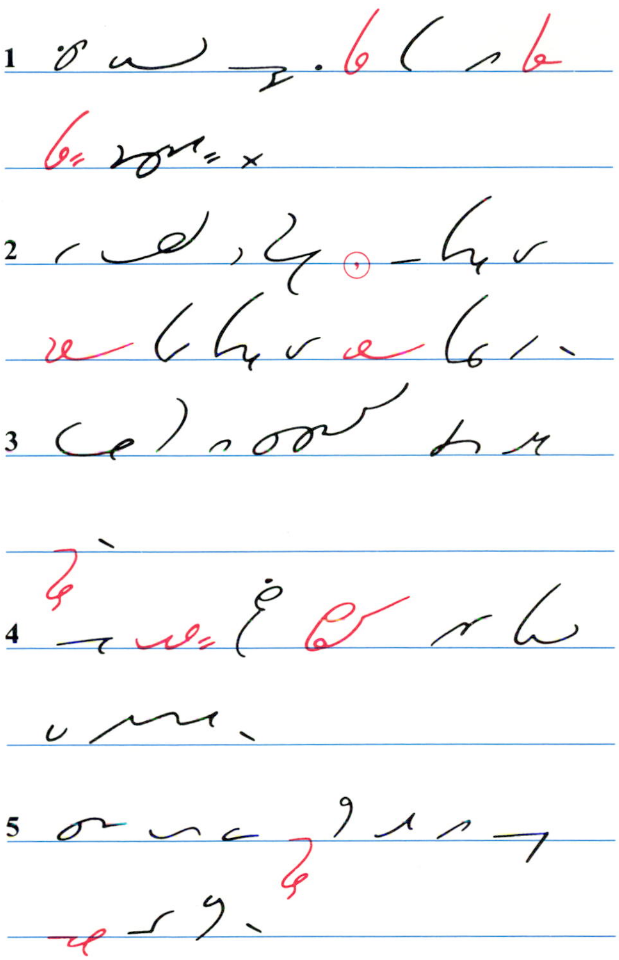

¶ **Business Letter**

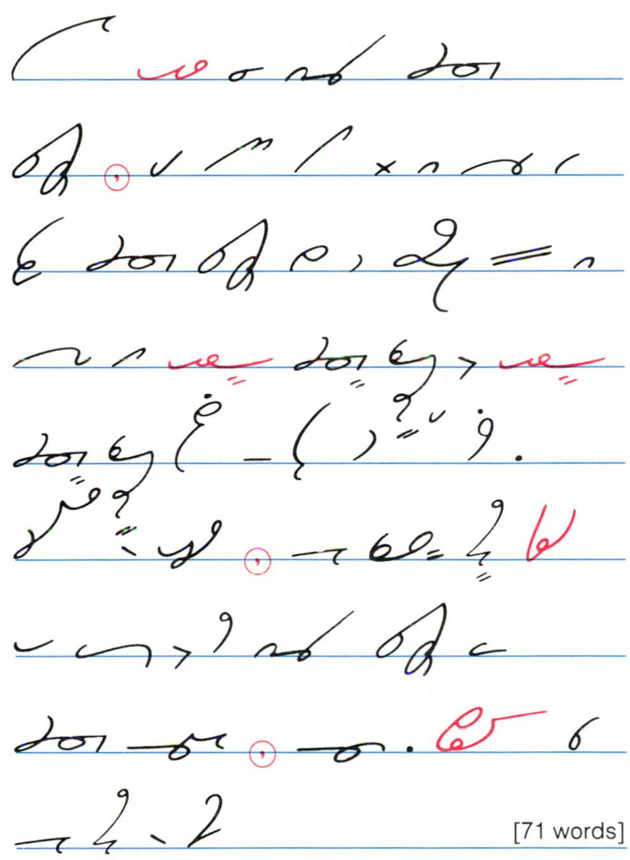

[71 words]

An attorney can quickly record information and draft questions in shorthand.

Reading and Writing Practice

22.4 Dictation Speed Letter

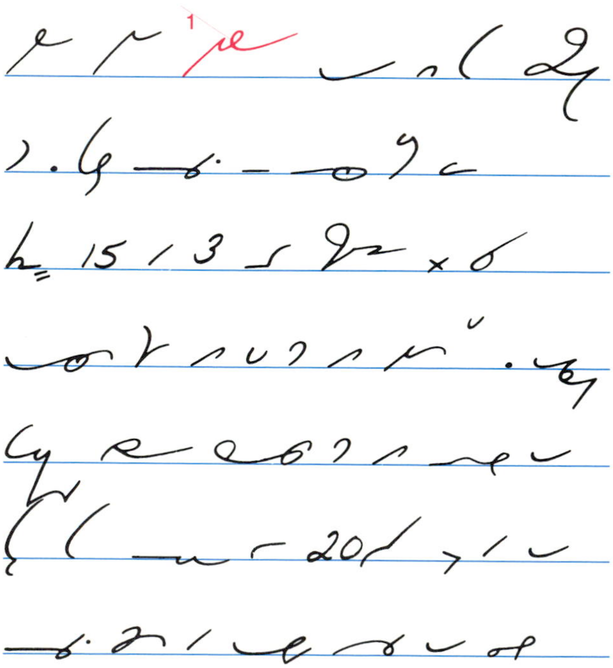

1 Doyle

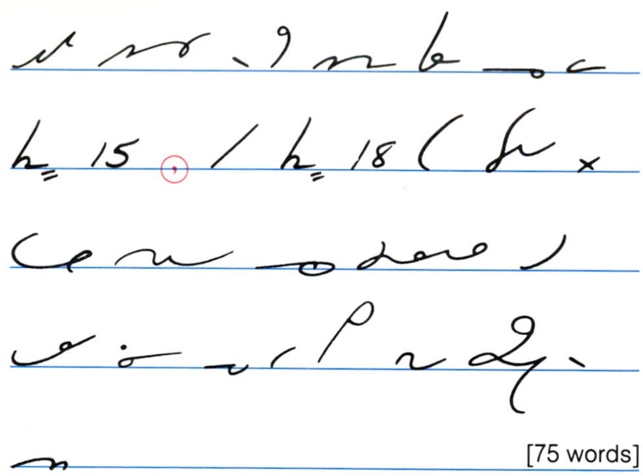

[75 words]

22.5 Minutes Taken During a Meeting

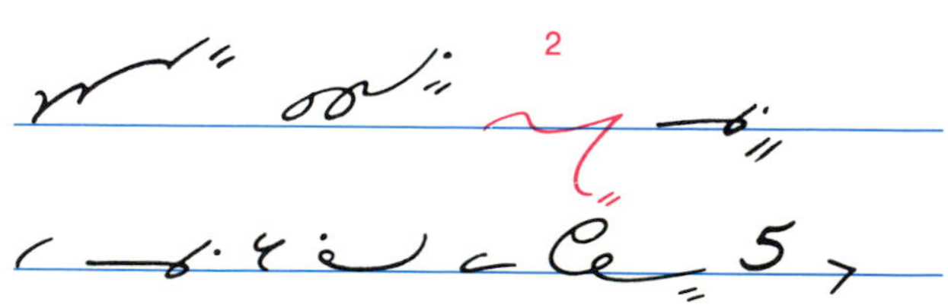

2 Club

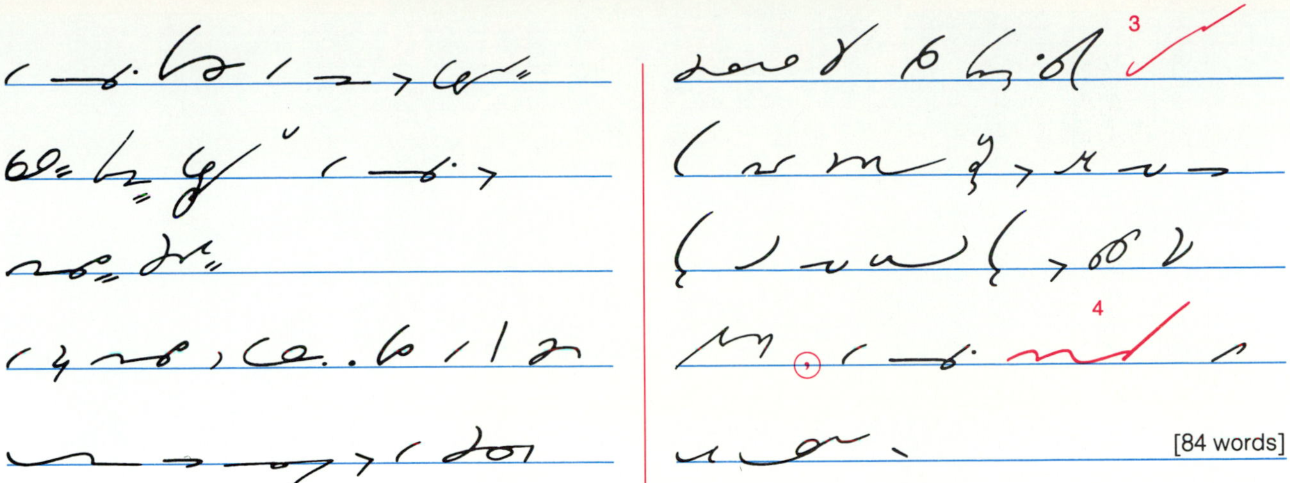

3 audited 4 concluded

LESSON

23

NEW IN LESSON 23

- **Expressing measures of time, percent, feet, and pounds**
- **Symbol for the sound of *men***
- **Word ending *-ward***
- **Transcribing expressions of time and amounts**

MEASURES

Special shorthand abbreviations are used for expressing time, percent, feet, and pounds.

Time

Hours and minutes are expressed in normal-size figures. Shorthand symbols are used for *a.m.*, *p.m.*, and *o'clock*.

The shorthand outline for *a.m.* is *a* with an intersected *m.*

The shorthand outline for *p.m.* is *p* with an intersected *m.*

The *o* is used for *o'clock* and is placed above the number.

11:30 a.m. ______ 5 p.m. ______ 5 o'clock ______

Feet

The word *feet* is represented by the *f* symbol and is placed at the base of the number.

5 feet ______ 200 feet ______

Percent

The word *percent* is represented by the *comma s*. It is placed at the base of the number and should intersect the line. The *comma s* is not used when writing the entire outline for percent.

75 percent    100 percent ■ 

■ In *100 percent* the *n* for *hundred* is placed below the number and followed by the *commas s*.

Pounds

The word *pounds* is represented by the *p* symbol and is placed at the base of the number.

3 pounds    500 pounds 

Measures Practice

23.1

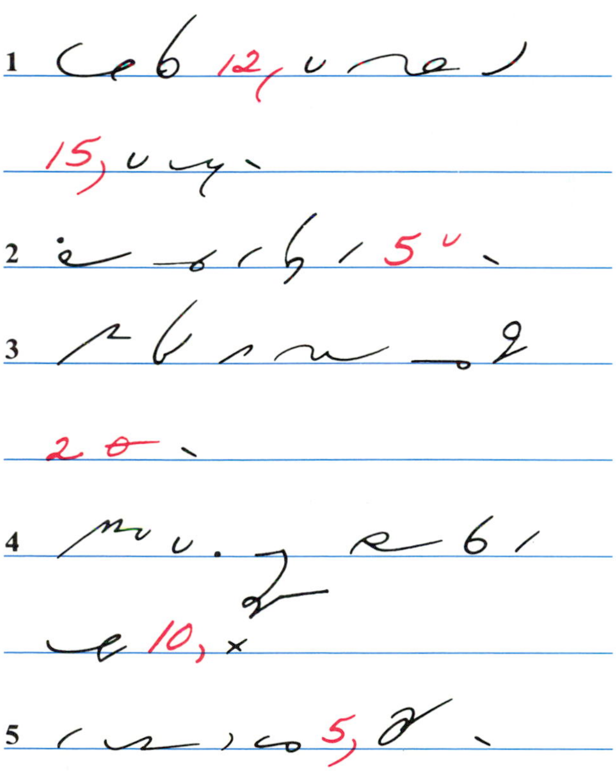

¶ **Notes for Placing a Phone Call**

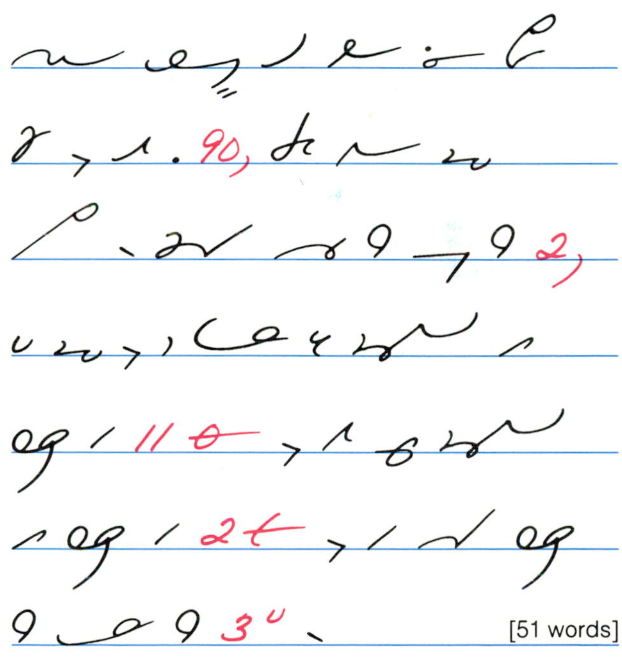

[51 words]

Shorthand can be used to record testimony during legal proceedings.

MEN BLEND

The sounds of *men*, *min*, *man*, and *mon* as in *mention*, *minute*, *manner*, and *month* are represented by a blend of the *m* and *n* symbols called the *men* blend.

m n = men

Examples: mention minute manner month

Men Words

men	mentions	mental
mention	many	mentally
mentioned	meant	women

Min, Man, Mon Words

minute

manner

manage

manager

woman

month

monthly

money

Men, Min, Man, Mon Practice

23.2

WORD ENDING -WARD

The word ending *-ward* as in *backward* is written with a disjoined *d.*

-ward

Example: backward

-ward Words

backward

onward

afterward

afterwards

upward

inward

reward

rewarding

forward

forwarded

forwarding

downward

Edward

Woodward

awkward

-ward Practice

23.3

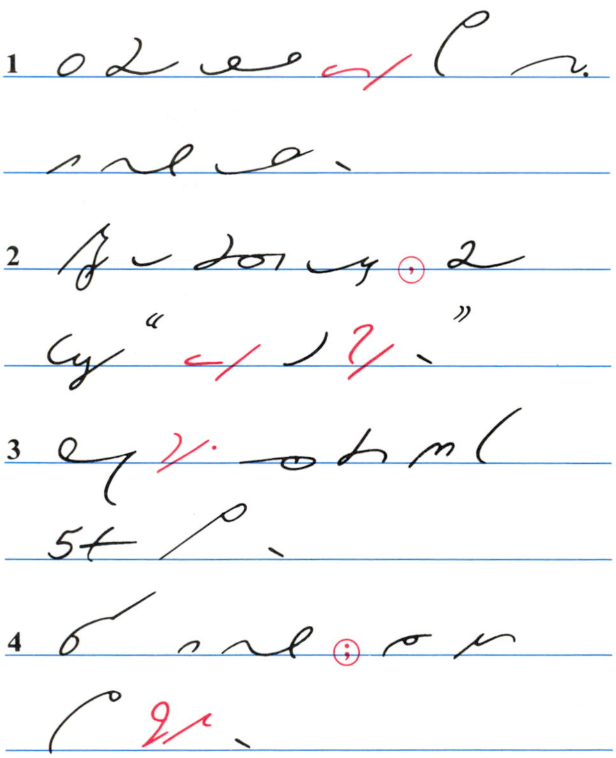

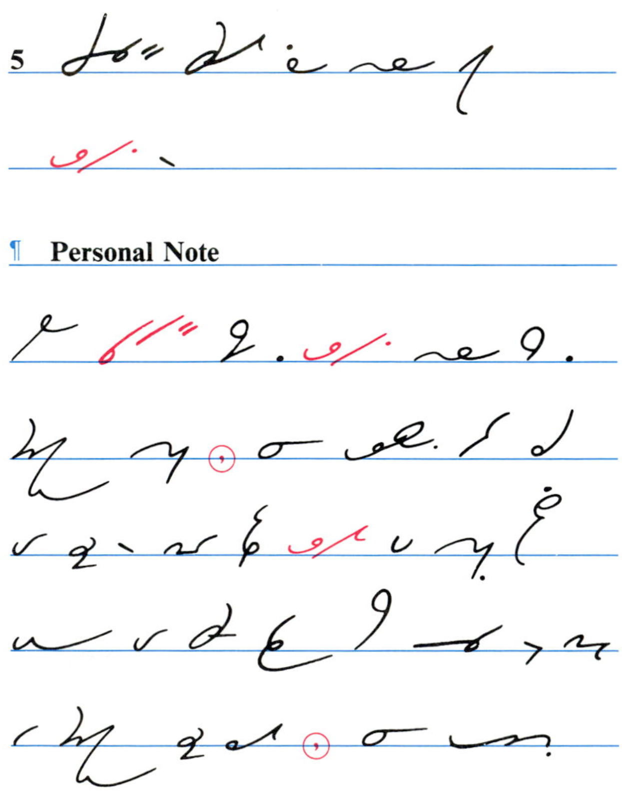

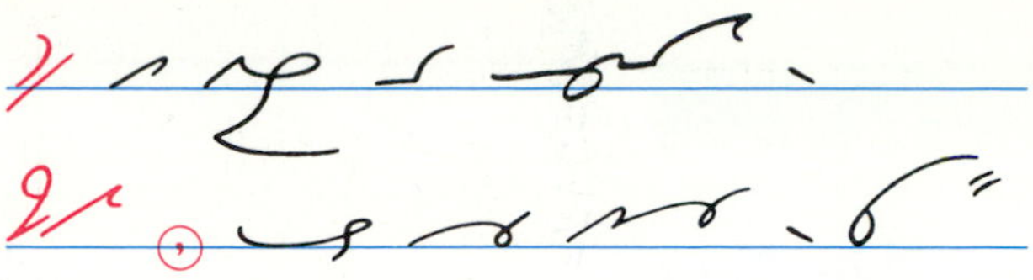

[37 words]

Numbers: Time and Amounts

The basic number rule presented in Lesson 11 specifies that the numbers from one through ten are to be spelled out, while numbers higher than ten are to be written in figures. In Lesson 18 you learned that one exception to this basic number rule is that a number must be spelled out if it is the first word of a sentence.

Another exception to the basic rule is that expressions of time with *a.m.*, *p.m.*, or *o'clock* and percents and distances all may be written in figures for quick comprehension. The words *percent* and *feet* are spelled in full. Note that *a.m.* and *p.m.* appear in lowercase.

7:30 a.m.	7 o'clock	6 feet
6:17 p.m.	8 percent	23 feet
5 p.m.	17 percent	100 feet

Meet me at *11:30 a.m.* or *2 p.m.*

The price has been reduced by *20 percent.*

The cost of *5 feet* of nylon rope is $5.25.

Reading and Writing Practice

23.4 Dictation Speed Letter

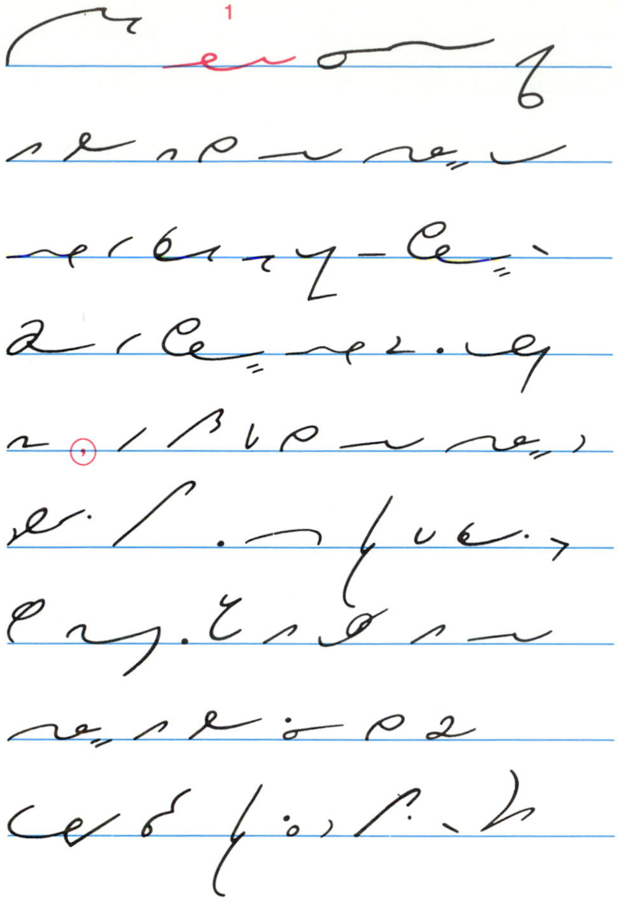

[66 words]

1 Miller

23.5 Sales Letter

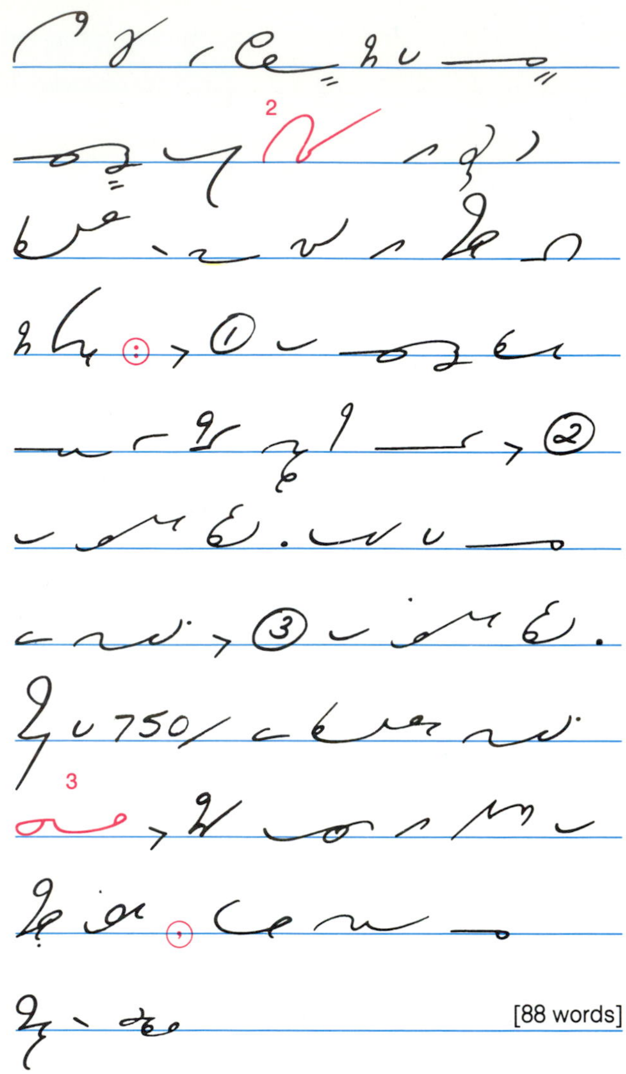

[88 words]

2 devoted 3 annually

LESSON 24

NEW IN LESSON 24

- **Seven brief forms**
- **Word ending *-ings***
- **Word endings *-rity*, *-lity*, and *-lty***

BRIEF FORMS

thing, think

success

between

responsible

request

send

regard

Brief-Form Derivatives

thinking

things, thinks

nothing

successes

requests

requested

requesting

sending

sends

regarding

regarded

regardless

Brief-Form Phrases

I think

we think

send the

send us

send you

sending you

Brief-Form Practice
24.1

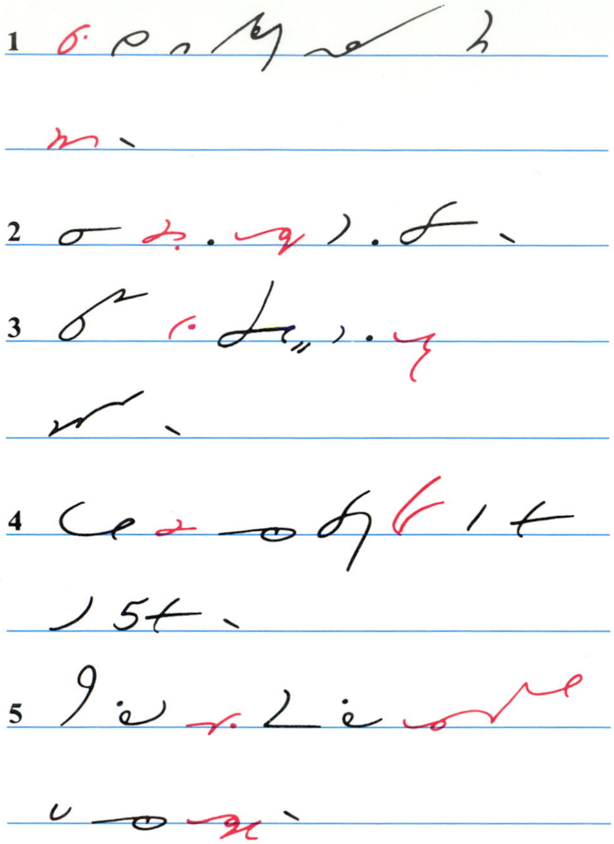

¶ Business Letter

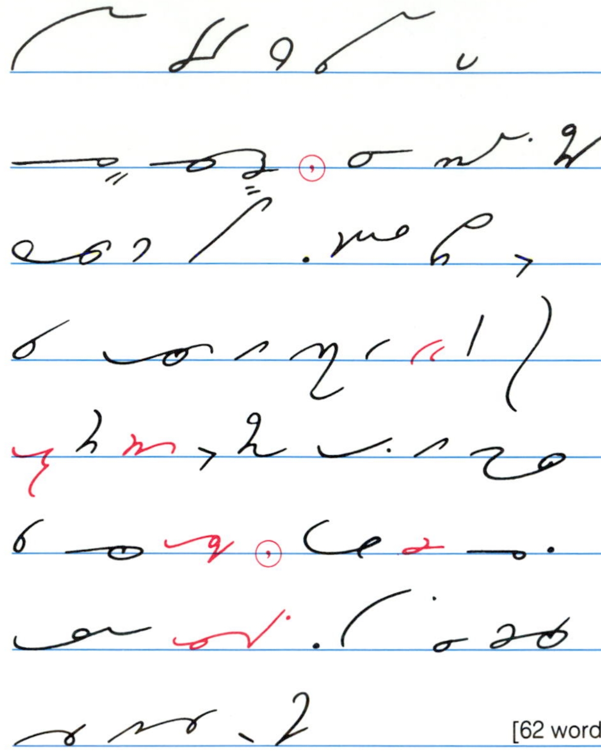

[62 words]

WORD ENDING -INGS

The word ending *-ings* as in *sayings* is represented by a disjoined *left s* and is written close to the last symbol in the root word.

Example: sayings

-ings Words

sayings

listings

earnings

meetings

proceedings ■

openings

■ Transcription Alert.

feelings  savings  drawings 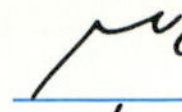

buildings  findings  Jennings 

-ings Practice

24.2

1
2
3
4
5

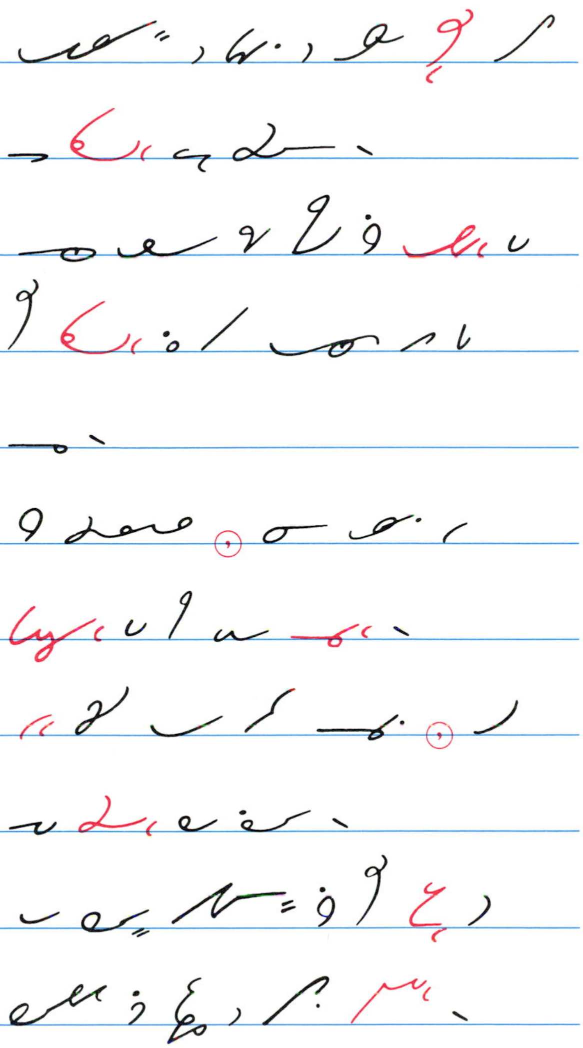

¶ **Memo**

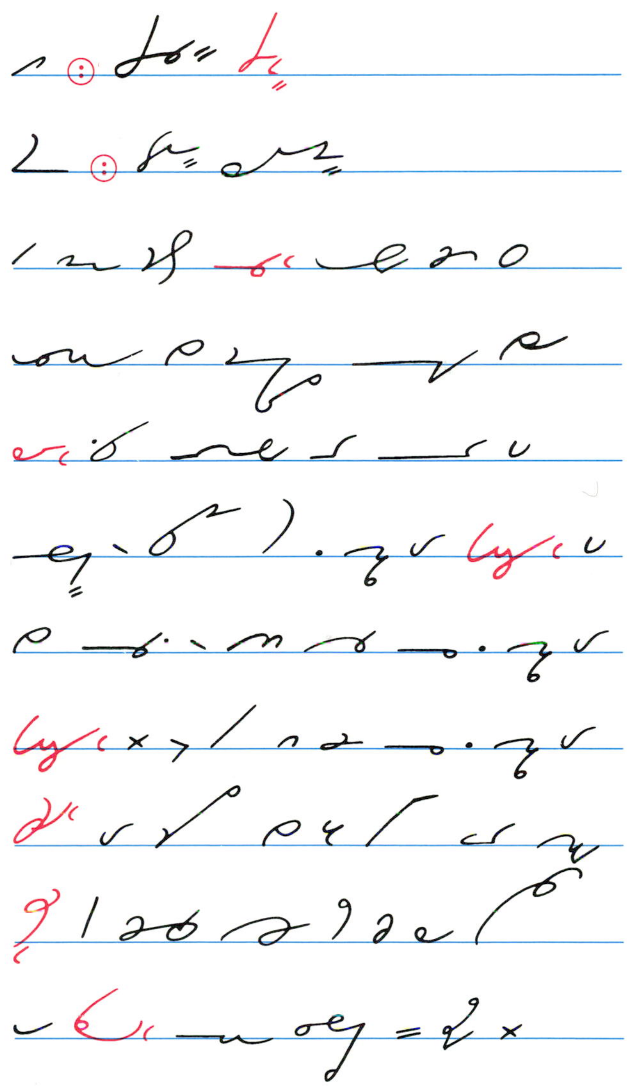

[81 words]

WORD ENDINGS -RITY, -LITY, -LTY

The word ending *-rity* as in *majority* is written with a disjoined *r*. The word endings *-lity* as in *ability* and *-lty* as in *penalty* are written with a disjoined *l*. The disjoined *r* and *l* are written close to the last symbol.

-rity -lity, -lty

Examples: majority ability penalty

-rity Words

majority
sincerity
authority
security
charity
prosperity

-lity Words

ability
dependability
utility
facility
locality
quality
possibility
personality
responsibility ■

■ Brief-form derivative.

-lty Words

penalty
faculty
royalty

-rity, -lity, -lty Practice

24.3

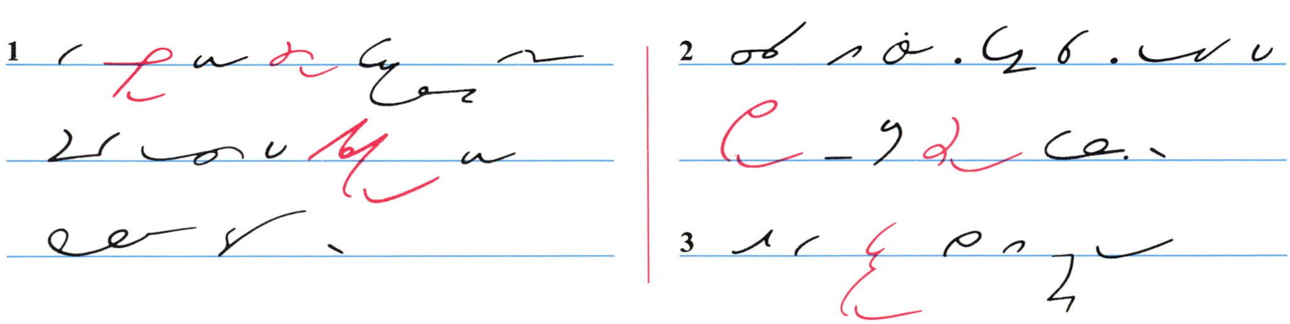

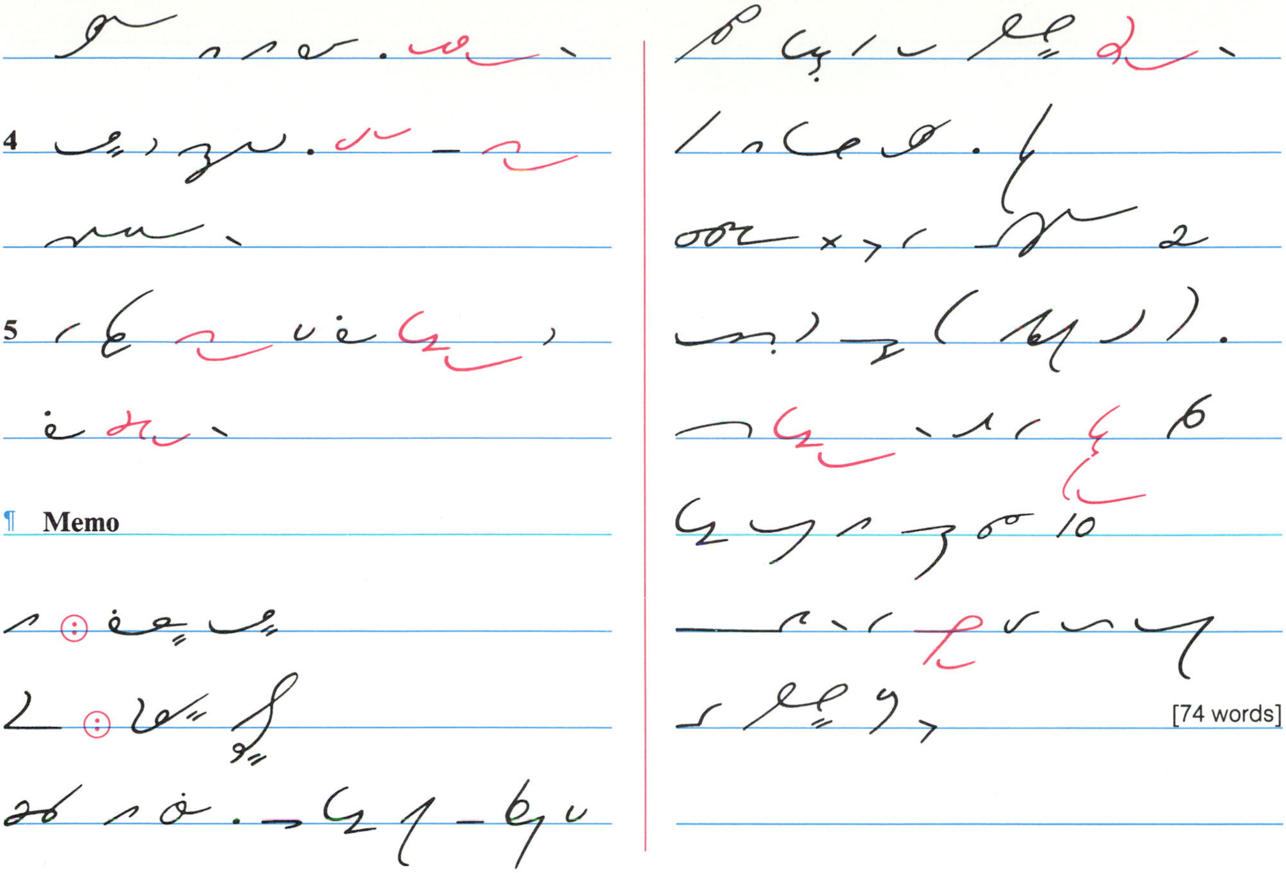

4

5

¶ Memo

[74 words]

Shorthand-writing secretaries are valuable to attorneys who wish to capture legal details quickly and accurately.

Reading and Writing Practice

24.4 Dictation Speed Letter

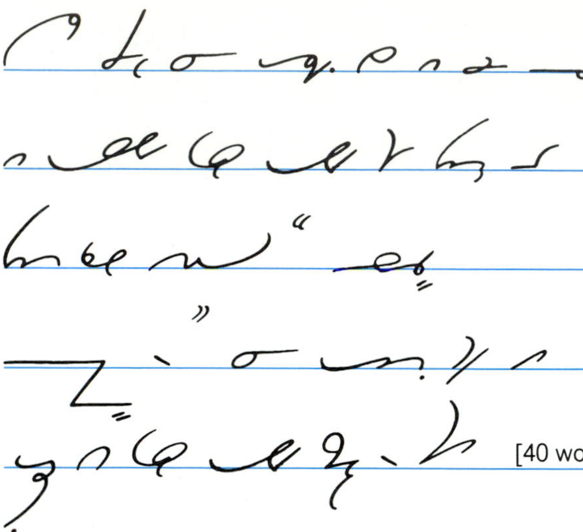

[40 words]

24.5 Personal Note

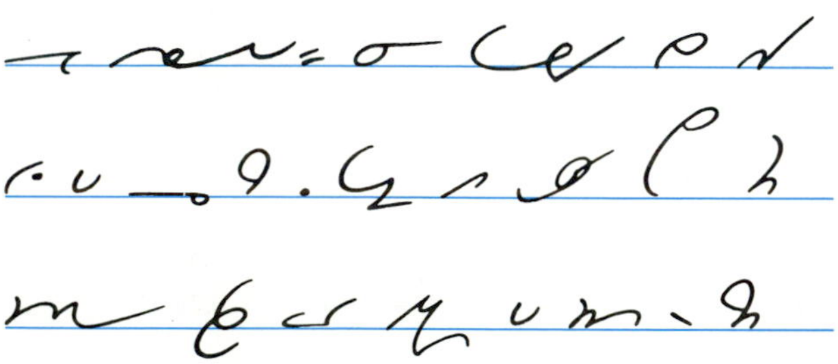

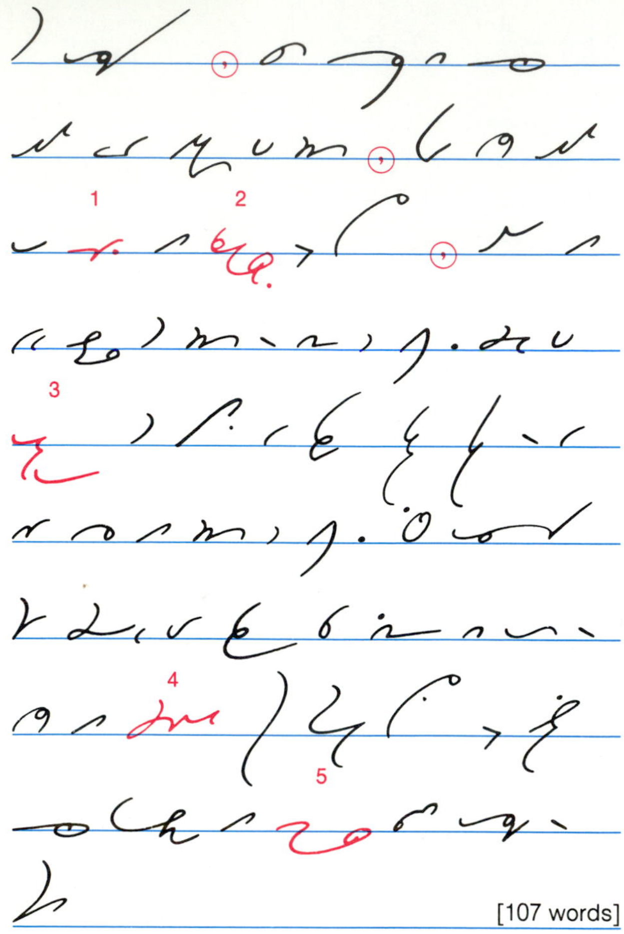

[107 words]

1 nothing 2 surprising 3 responsibility
4 factors 5 comply

UNIT VII

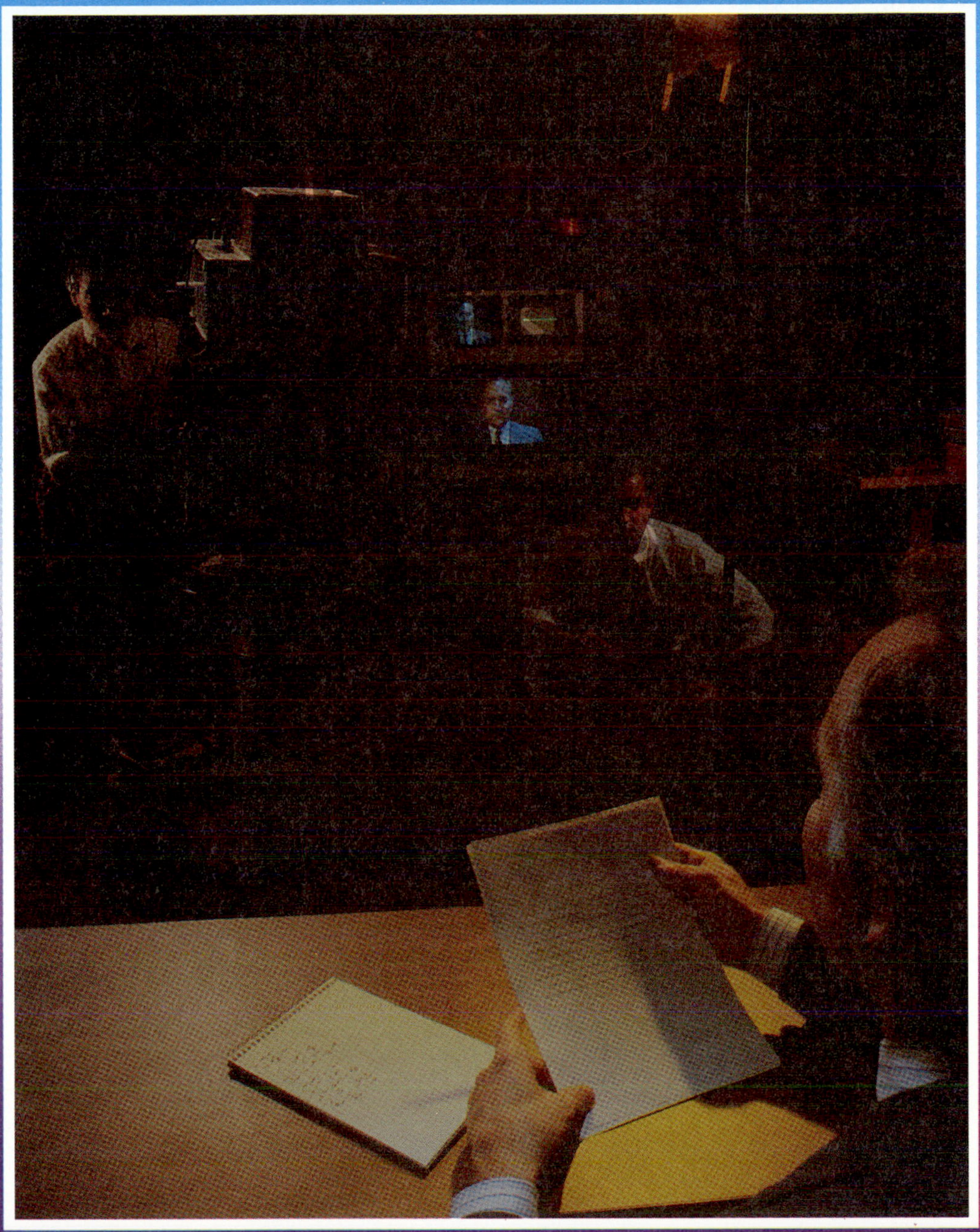

LESSON 25

NEW IN LESSON 25

- Sound of *ort*
- Symbol for the sound of *ea*
- Outlines for days and months

SOUND OF ORT

The sound of *ort* as in *port* is written with the *o* and *t* symbols. For ease of writing, the *r* is not written.

Example: port

Ort Words

port	reporter	sort
portable	support, sport	resort
deport	sports	assort
report	airport	assorted
reported	airports	assortment

Ort Practice

25.1

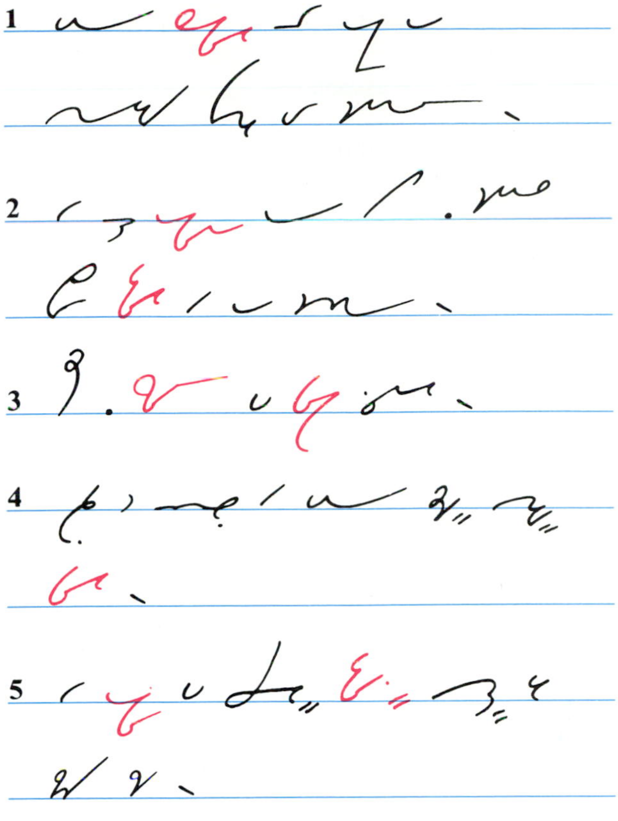

¶ **Office Note**

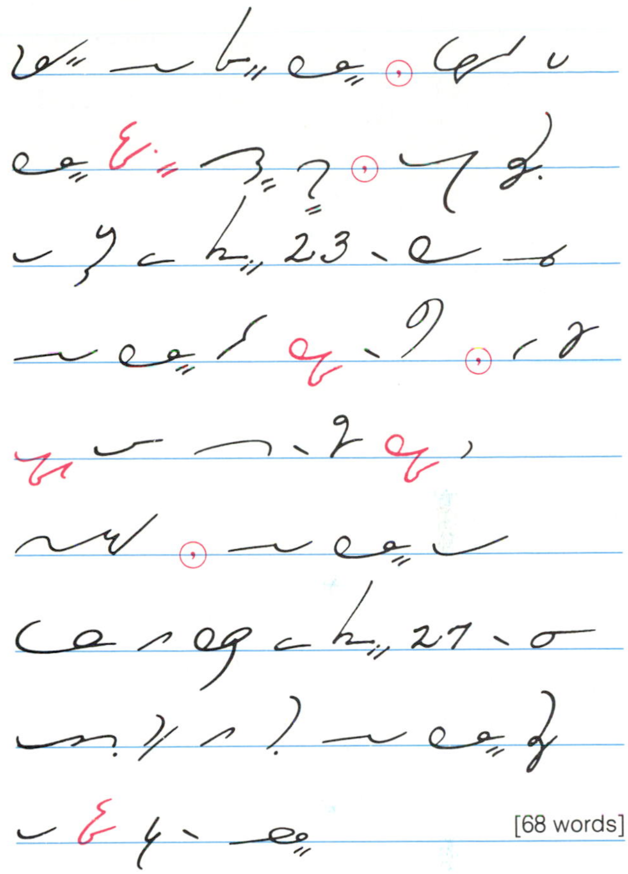

[68 words]

SOUND OF EA

The sound of *e* followed by an *a* as in *area* is represented by an *a* circle with a dot in it. The dot is added after the body of the outline has been written. We call this symbol *e ah.* 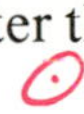

Example: area 

Ea Words

area
areas
create
created
creation
piano
appreciate
appreciates
appreciated
Gloria
associate
Garcia

Ea Practice

25.2

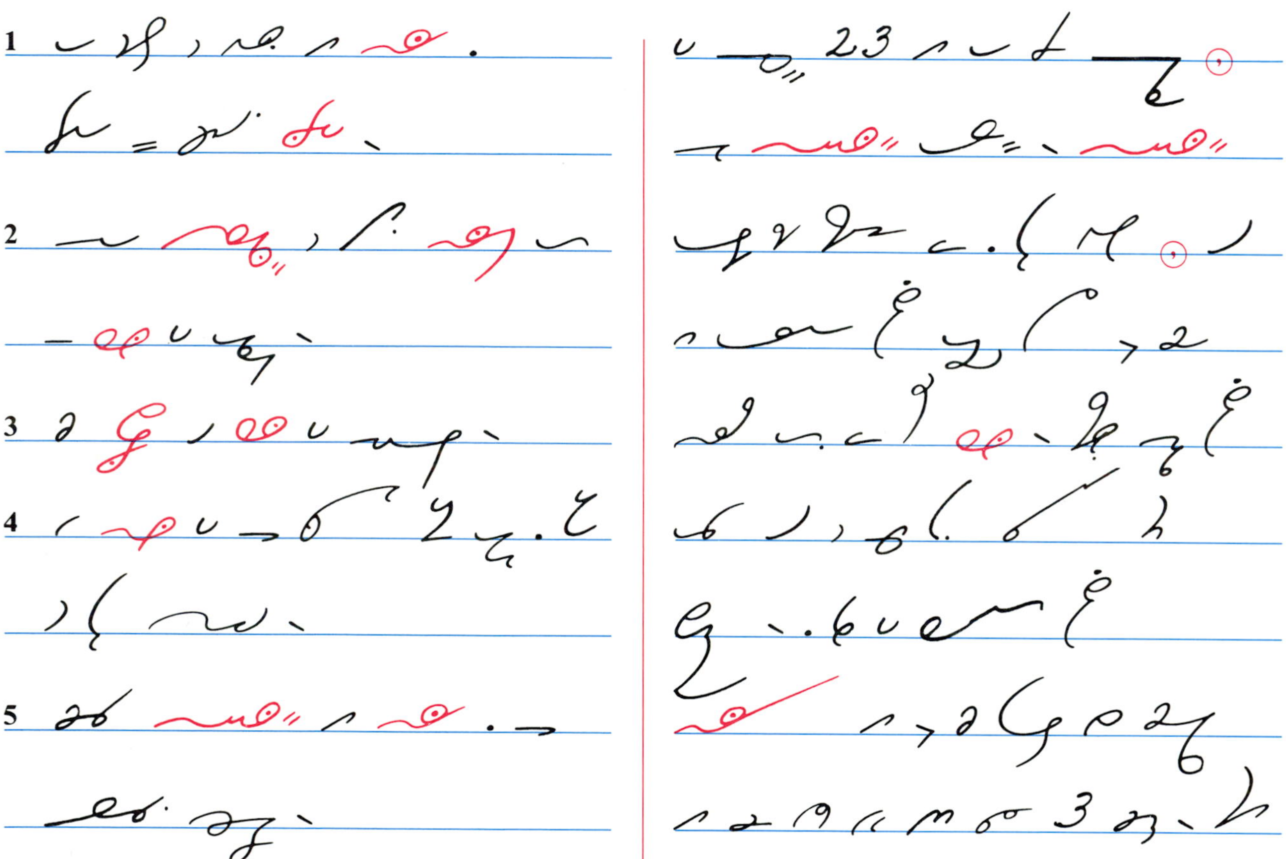

¶ Business Letter

[91 words]

DAYS AND MONTHS

The sound of the first syllable is written for each day of the week; *fri* for *Friday*, for example. The sound of the first syllable is written for each month of the year except for the five months *March* through *July*, which are easy to write in full.

Days

Sunday ___

Monday ___

Tuesday ___

Wednesday ___

Thursday ___

Friday ___

Saturday ___

Months

January ___

February ___

March ___

April ___

May ___

June ___

July ___

August ___

September ___

October ___

November ___

December ___

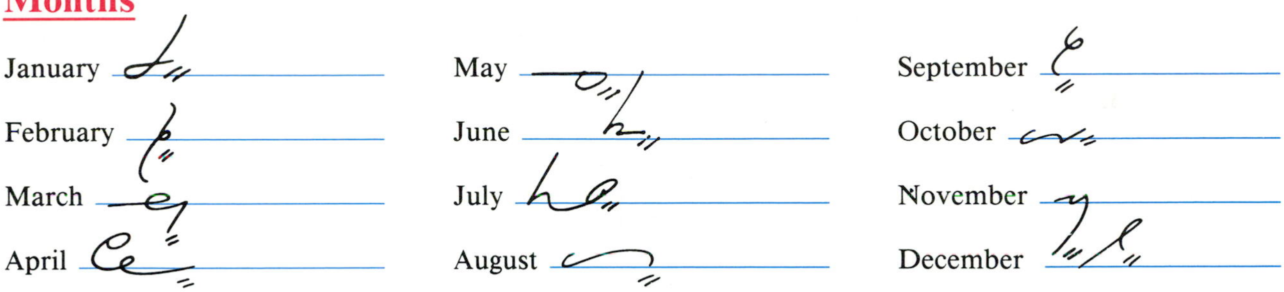

Days and Months Practice

25.3

1

17 .

2

19 .

3

4

5

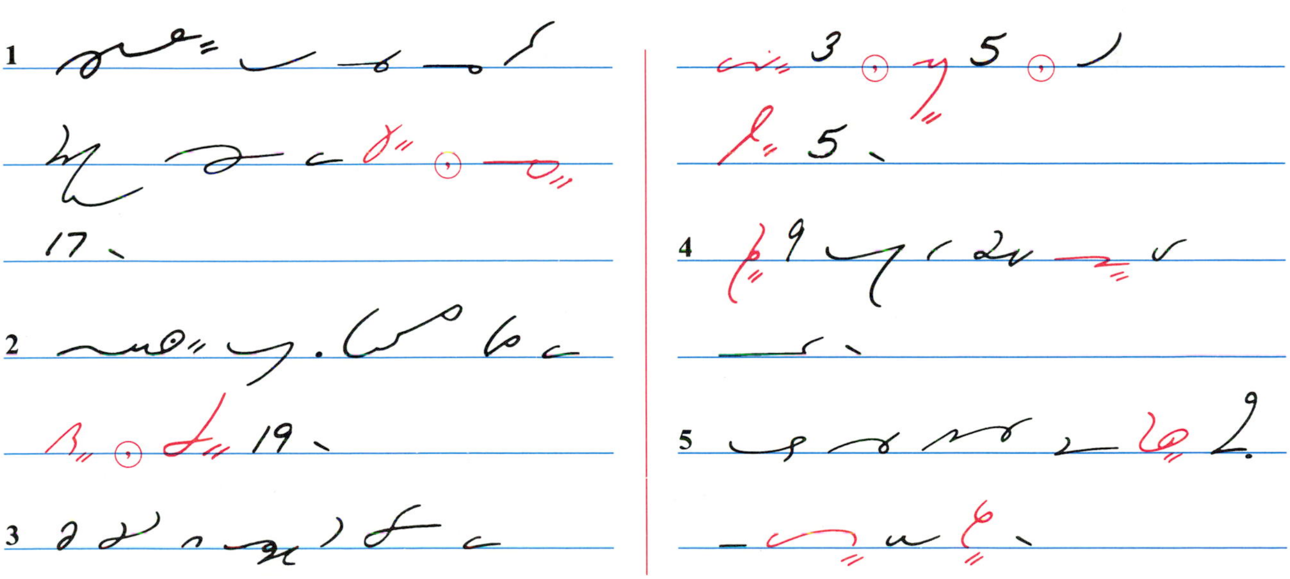

¶ **Letter**

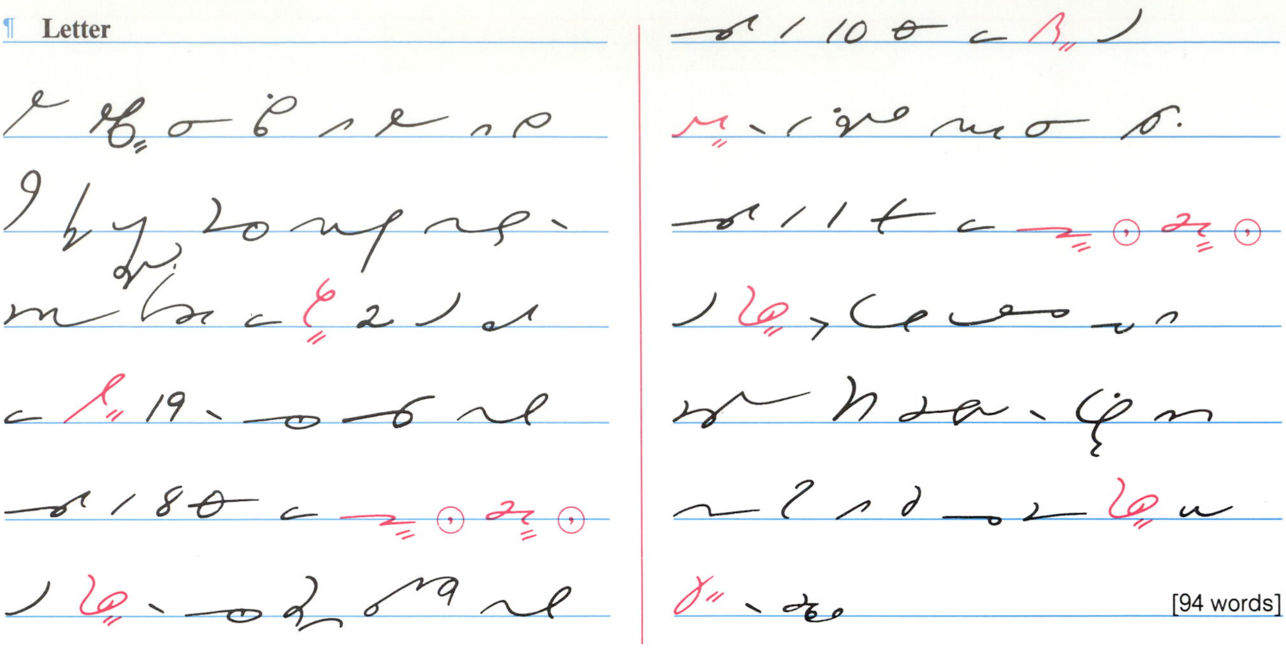

[94 words]

A newsroom can be exciting and hectic. If a reporter uses shorthand, strokes can be recorded quickly.

Reading and Writing Practice

25.4 Dictation Speed Letter

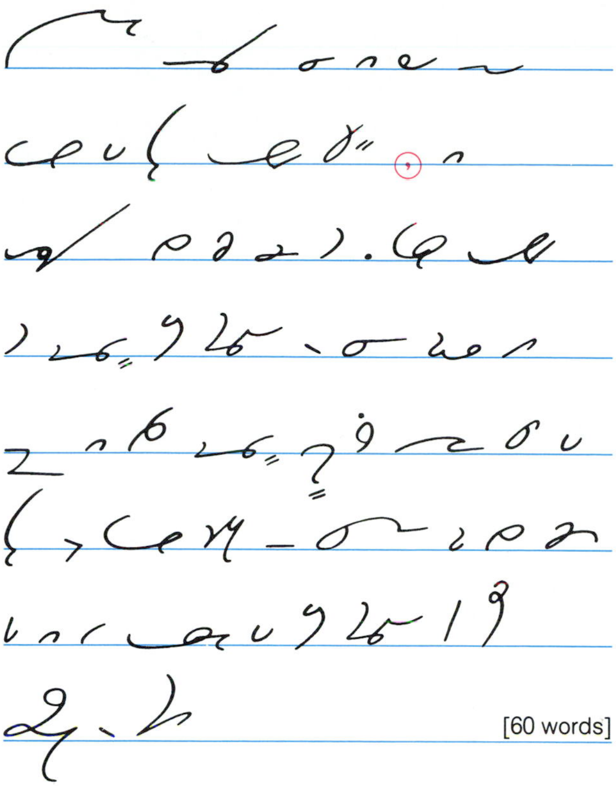

[60 words]

25.5 Business Letter

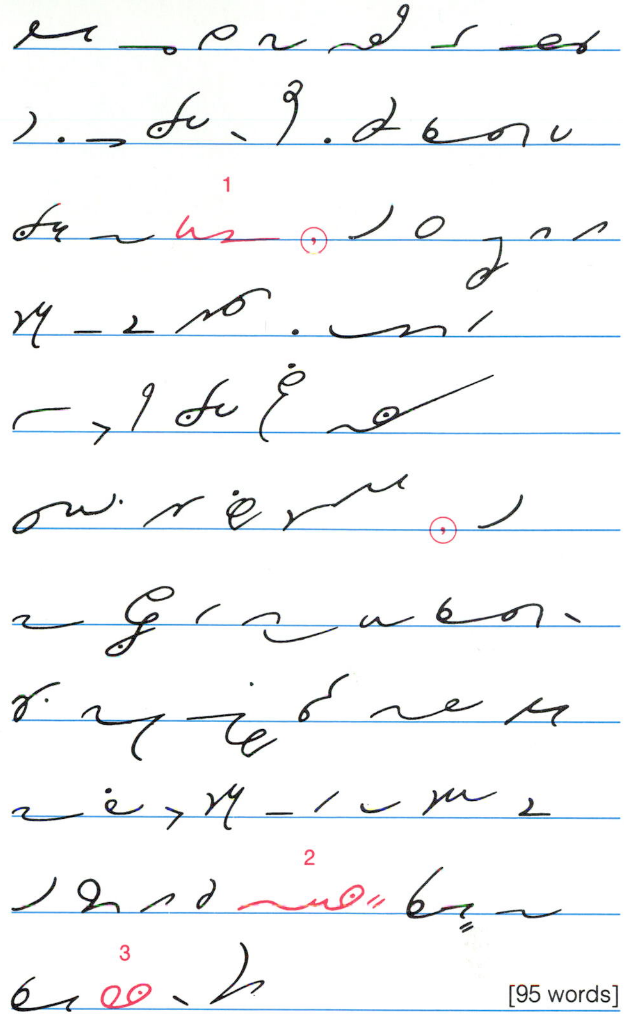

[95 words]

1 showroom 2 Gloria 3 area

LESSON 26

NEW IN LESSON 26

- Seven brief forms
- Word beginnings *en-* and *un-*
- Symbols for the sounds of *ya* and *ye*
- Shorthand for personal use

BRIEF FORMS

gentlemen

time

very

any

manufacture

morning

insure, insurance

Brief-Form Derivatives

anybody

anytime

manufacturer

anyone

timed

insuring

anything

timely

insured

anyway

sometime

gentleman

anywhere ■

manufactured

mornings

■ In the compound word *anywhere*, the *e* is dropped from *any* for ease of writing.

Brief-Form Phrases

at this time

by this time

very much

Brief-Form Practice

26.1

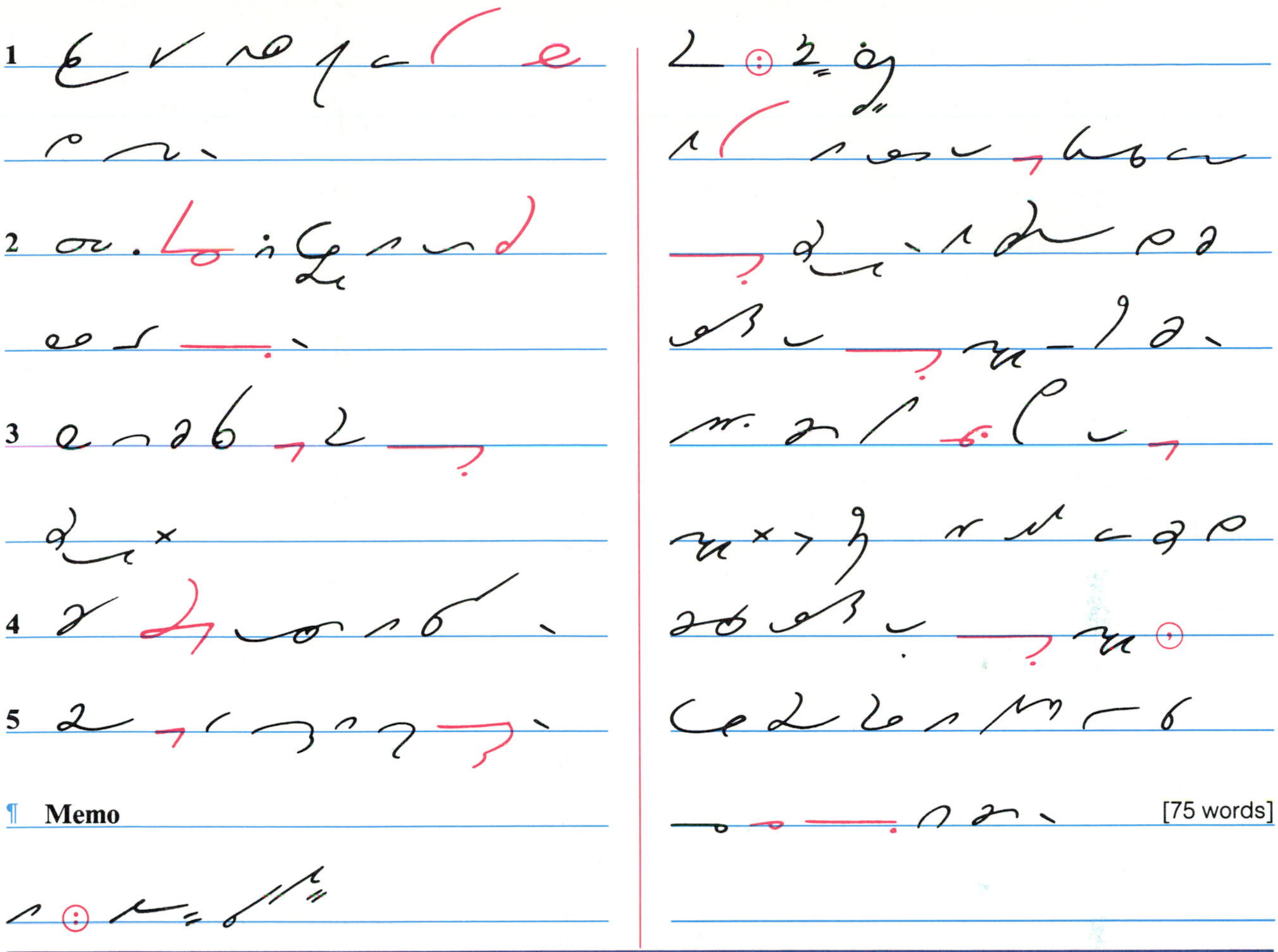

WORD BEGINNINGS EN-, UN-

The word beginning *en-* as in *enjoy* and the word beginning *un-* as in *until* are represented by the *n* symbol. You have been using the letter *n* for the similar word beginning *in-* ever since you learned the brief form *in* in Lesson 4.

Examples: enjoy 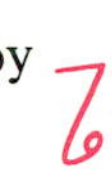 until 

En- Words

enjoy
enroll
enrolled
enrollment
engine
engineers
encourages
encouragement
endeavor
engagement
enforce
environment

Un- Words

until
unless
unlikely
unload
unloaded
unrelated
unfair
unwilling
unpaid

But: When a vowel follows *in-*, *en-*, or *un-*, the initial vowel is also written.

innovative
enable
unable

En-, Un- Practice

26.2

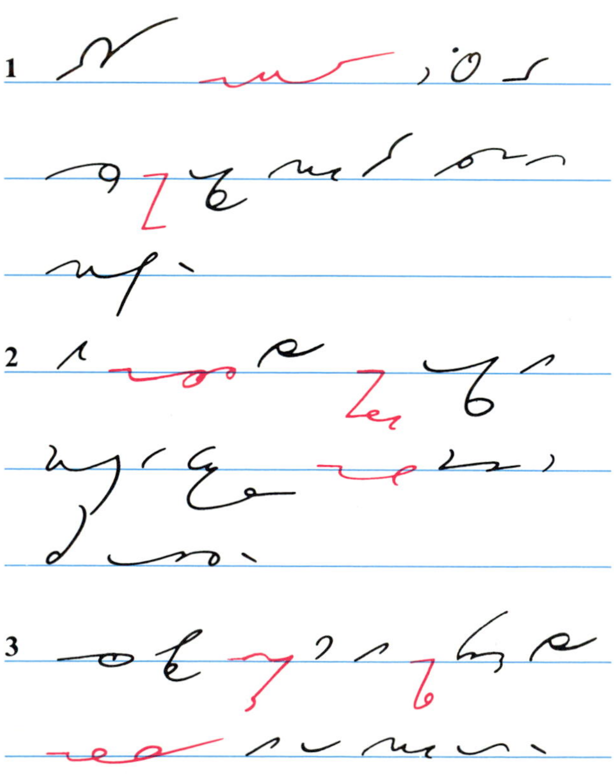

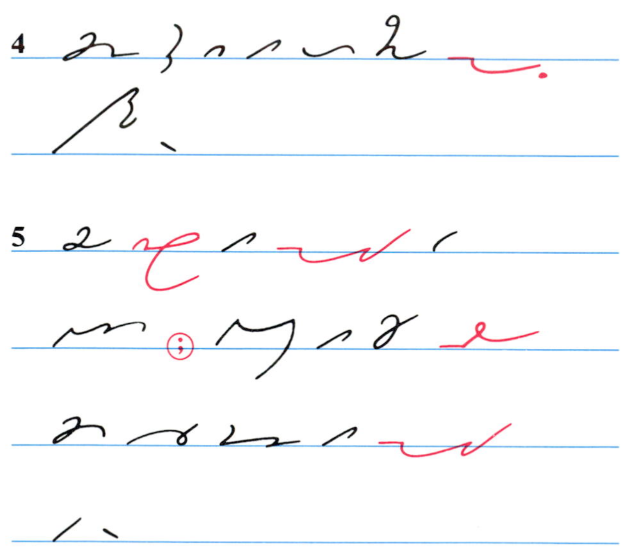

¶ **Business Letter**

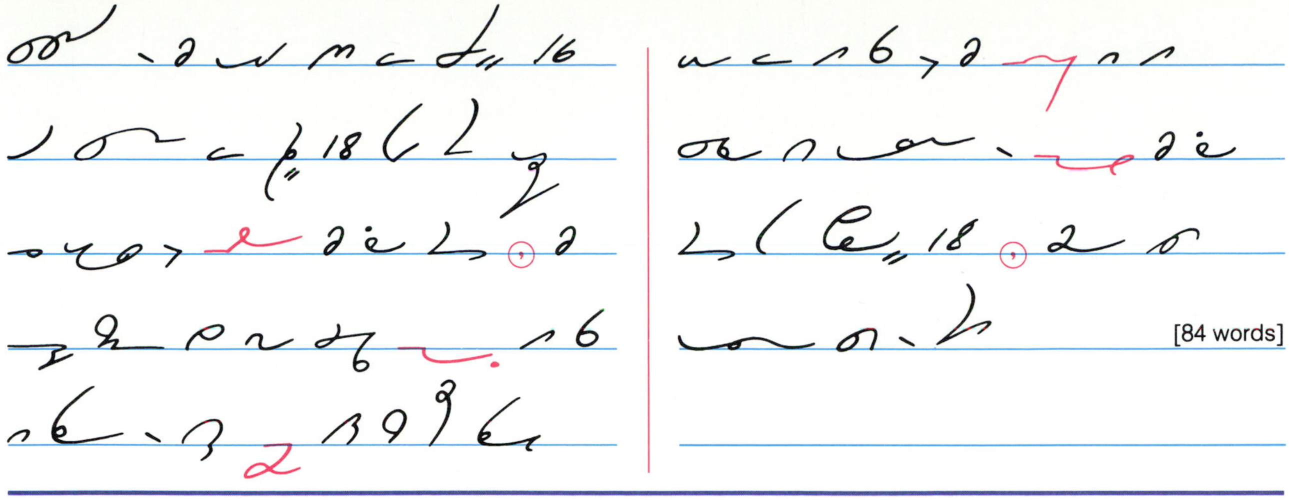

[84 words]

SOUNDS OF YA, YE

The sounds of *ya* as in *yard* and *ye* as in *year* are expressed by dropping the *y* and simply writing the *a* or the *e* that follows.

ya ye

Examples: yard year

Ya Words

yard

yarn

Yale

Ye Words

year

yield

yielded

years

yielding

yes

yellow

yields

yet

Ya, Ye Practice
26.3

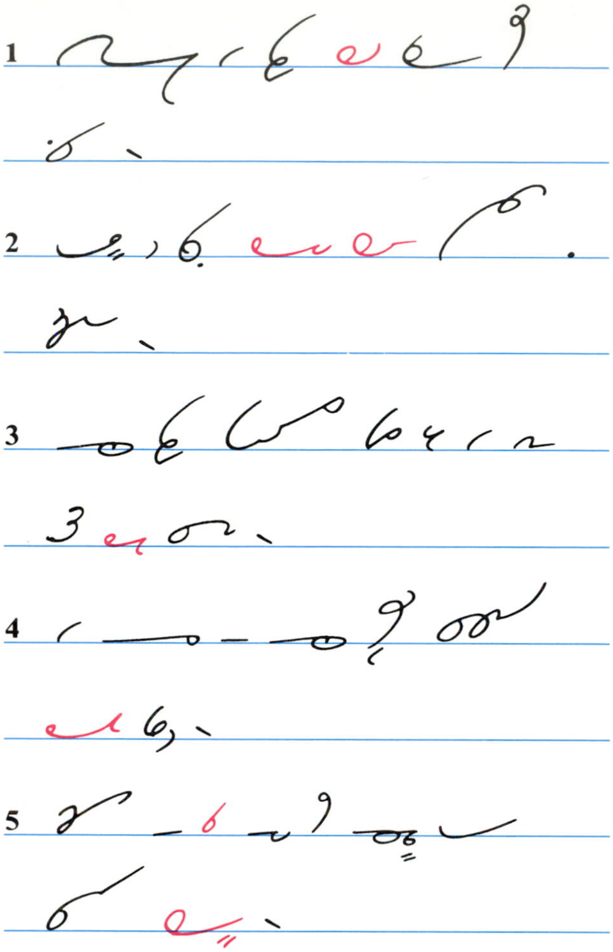

¶ Business Letter

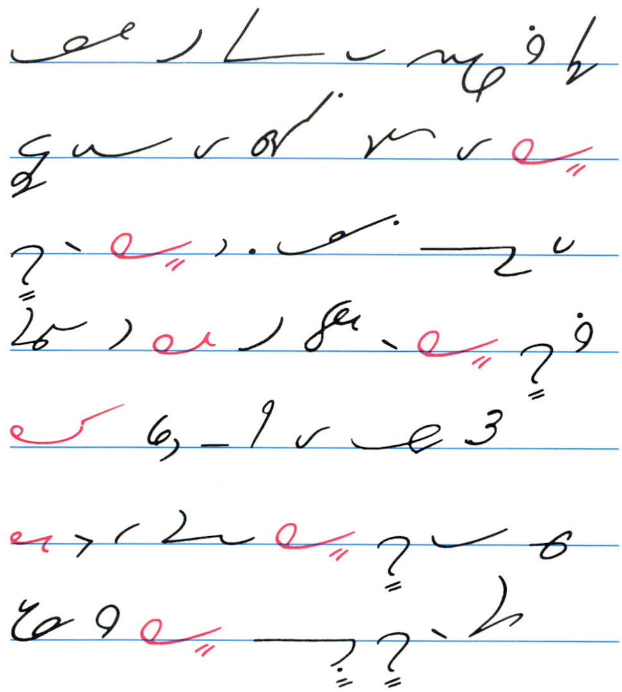

[66 words]

Using Shorthand for "To Do" Lists

Shorthand has many valuable uses both on the job and in one's personal life. Instructions about projects that need to be done, shopping lists, lists of appointments, and other personal reminders can all be easily written in shorthand.

In order to really learn and to retain shorthand, you must write it all the time. Once you have acquired the habit of using shorthand for all your personal notes, you will become so proficient in its use that you will wish you never had to write longhand again!

Here is an example of a personal "to do" list:

Done	Priority	To Do December 16
	A	
	B	
	B	

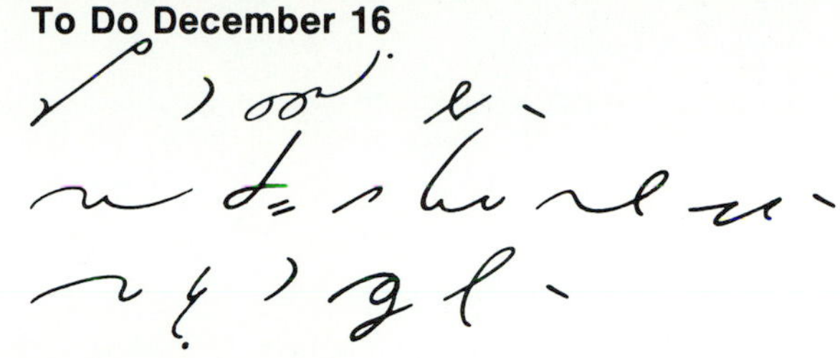

Reading and Writing Practice

26.4 Dictation Speed Letter

[55 words]

1 Leo 2 Boyd 3 anywhere 4 early 5 year

26.5 Personal Note

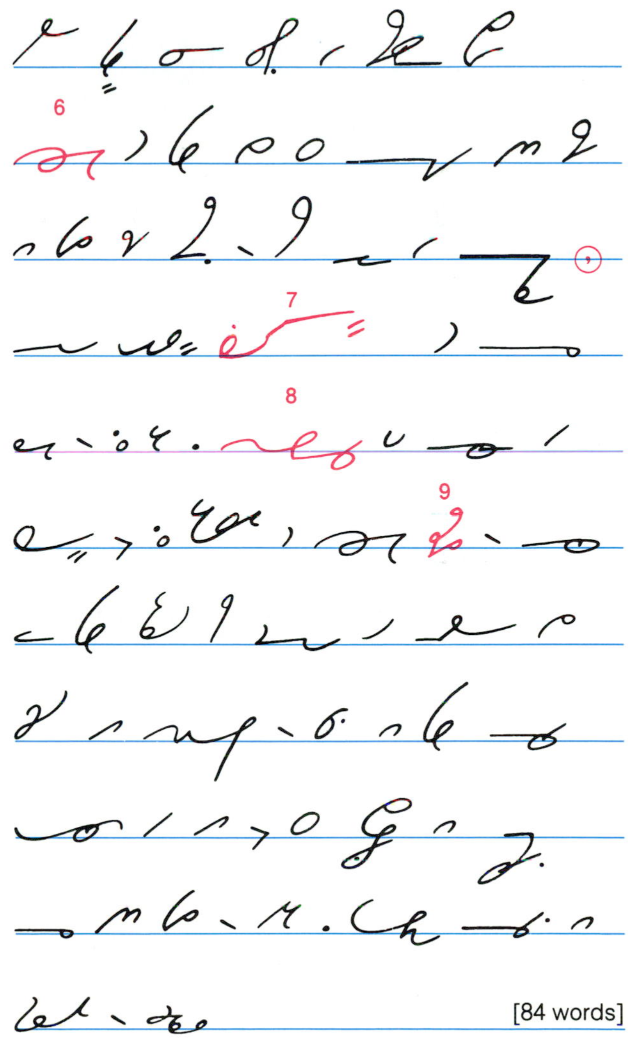

[84 words]

6 camp 7 Hartman 8 classmate 9 efficiently

LESSON 27

NEW IN LESSON 27

- Word ending *-ification*
- Word beginning *mis-*
- New symbol for *w*
- Handling interruptions during dictation

WORD ENDING -IFICATION

The word ending *-ification* as in *ratification* is represented by a disjoined *f* and is written close to the last symbol.

Example: ratification 

-ification Words

ratification 	classification 	clarification 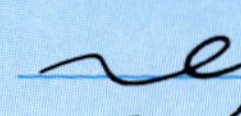
identification 	classifications 	specification 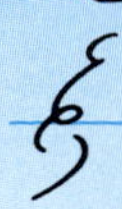
modification 	notification 	specifications 
modifications 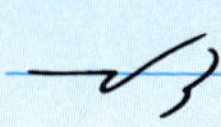	certification 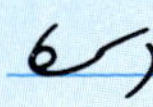	justification 

However, note that the word ending *-ify* is written according to the "minor-vowel-omitted" rule.

Example: ratify 

Minor-Vowel-Omitted Words

ratify
ratified
notify
specify
specifies
classify
justify
modify
clarify

-ification Practice

27.1

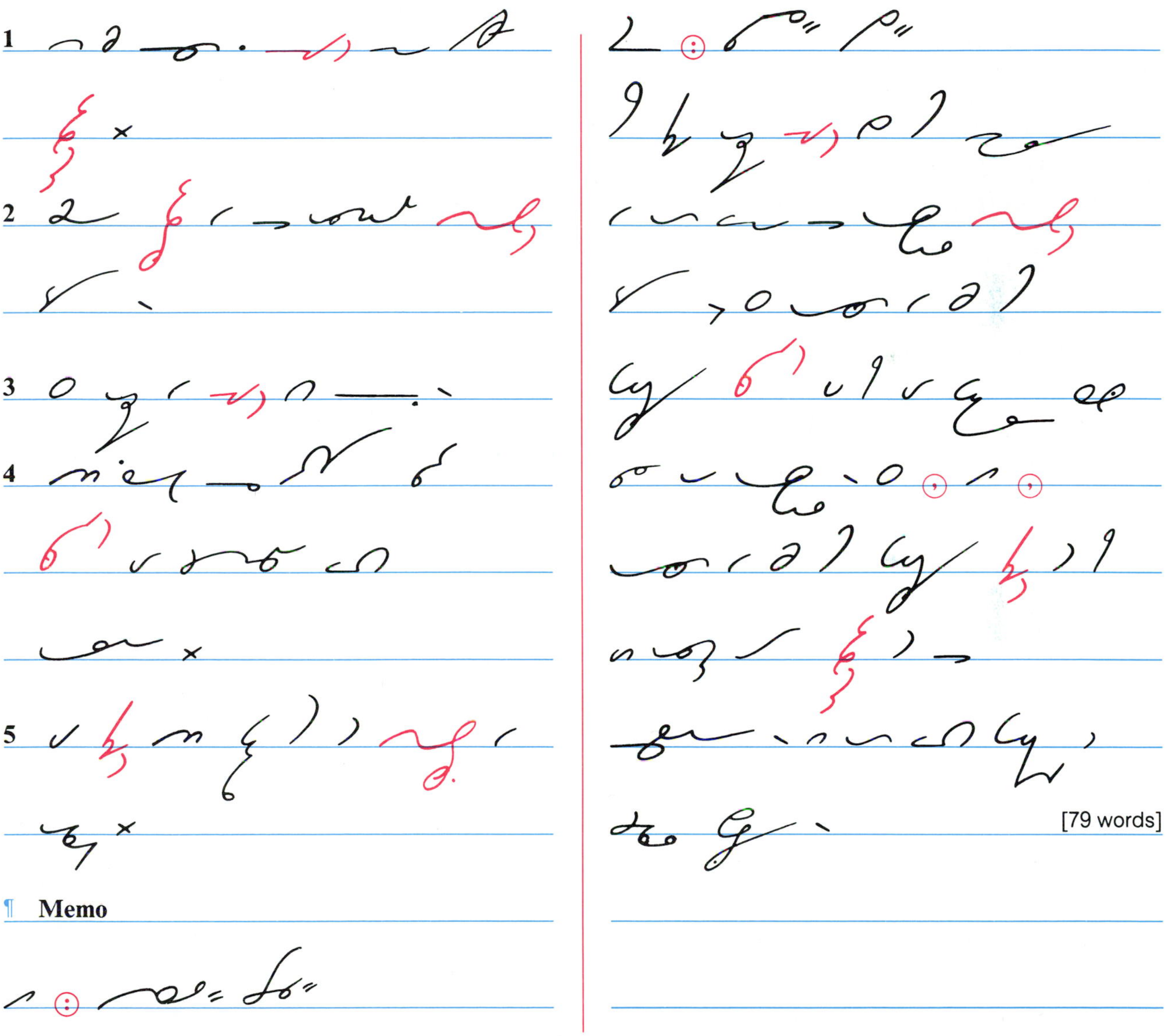

[79 words]

¶ **Memo**

The word beginning *mis-* as in *mistake* is abbreviated with the *m* and *s* symbols.

Example: mistake

Mis- Words

mistake	misplace	misprint
mistakes	mislead	mystery
mistaken	misleading	misrepresent

Mis- Practice

27.2

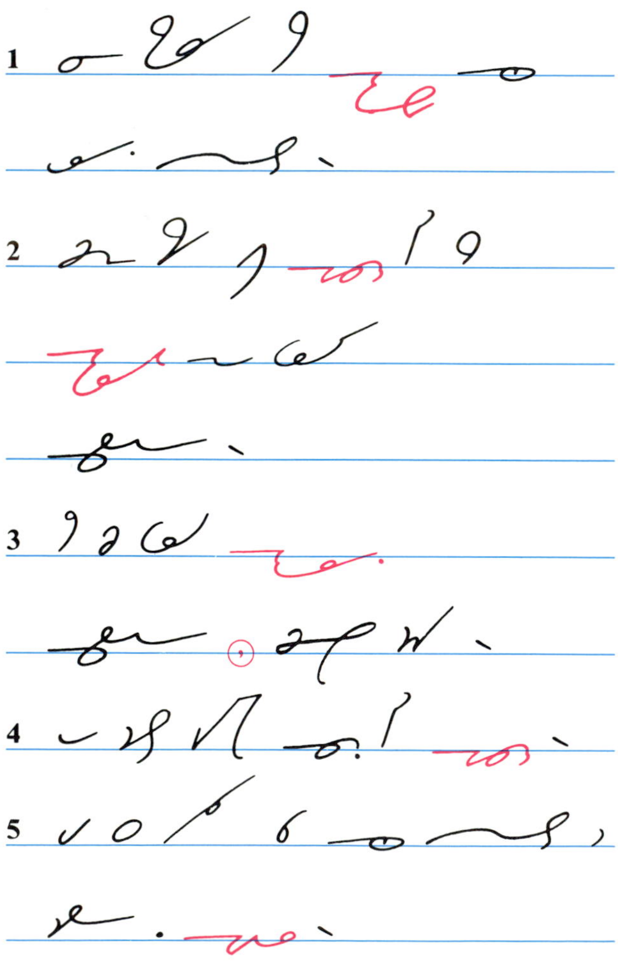

¶ **Business Letter**

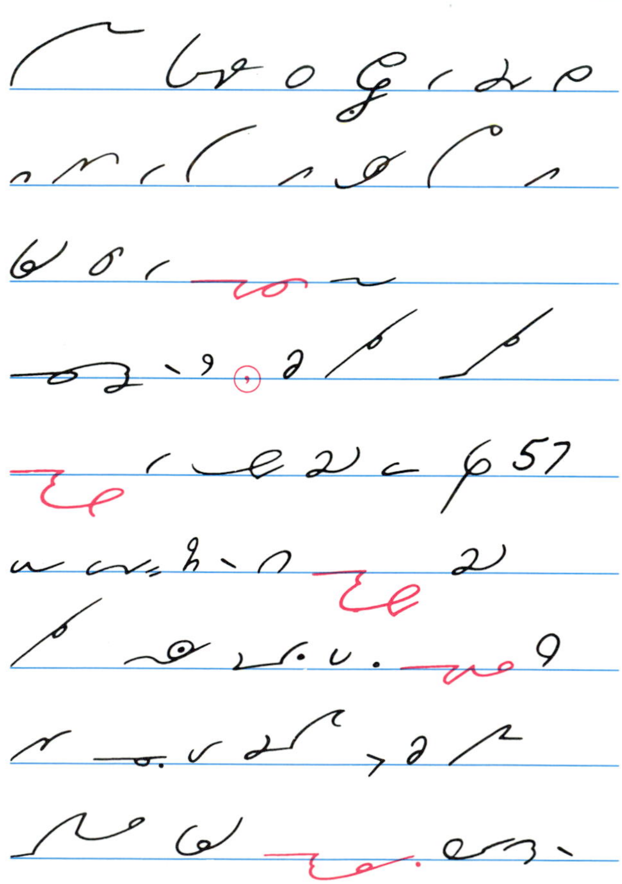

[88 words]

W DASH

In Lesson 6 you learned that the *oo* symbol represents the sound of *w* or *wh* at the beginning of words. A *w* within the body of a word is represented by a short dash *underneath the following vowel*. The dash is written after the body of the outline.

Example: quick

W Dash Words

quick

quickly

quit

quote, quart

quoted

quarterly

qualify

quite

always

Broadway

square

hardware

W Dash Practice

27.3

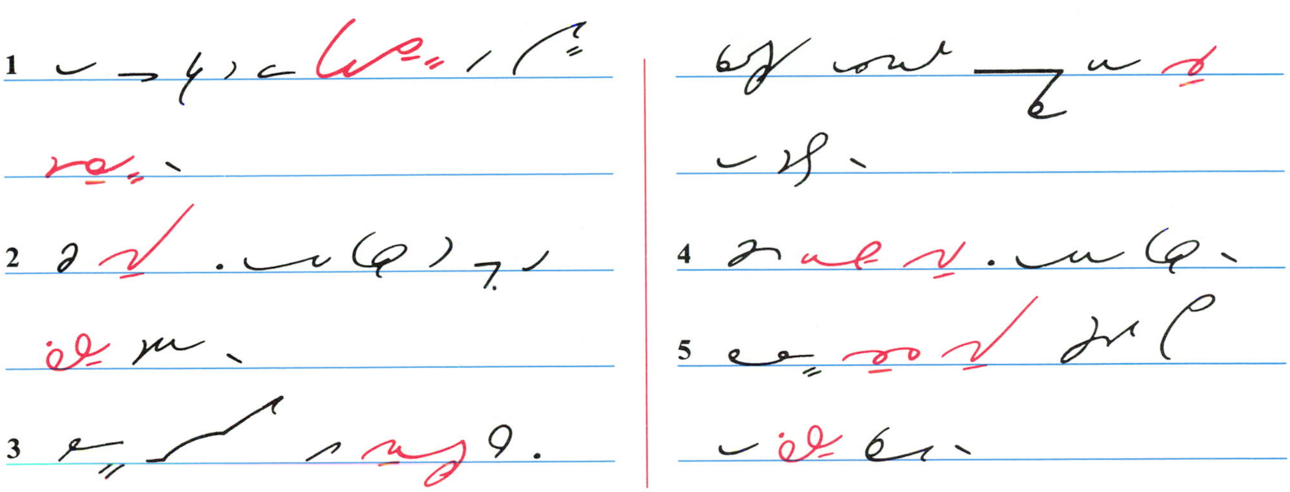

¶ **Business Letter**

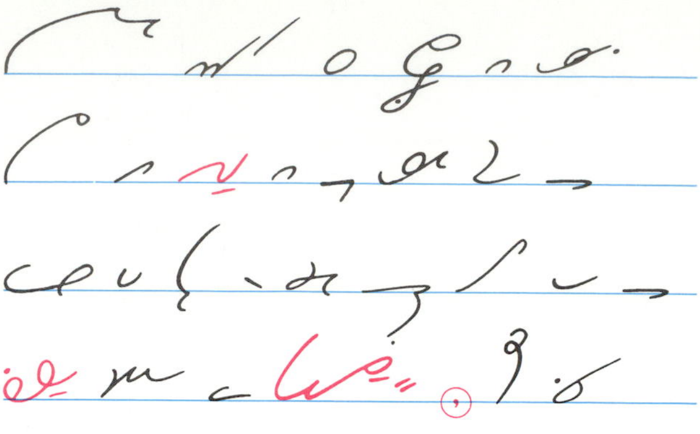

[78 words]

A reporter uses shorthand to obtain a complete and accurate record of the interview.

Handling Interruptions During Dictation

One of the realities of taking dictation in an office is that executives are frequently interrupted. They may be interrupted by the telephone, they may search for a file, or they may simply take a long pause in order to collect their thoughts. These interruptions can be of benefit to the secretary who is writing shorthand.

During a pause, the secretary should quickly scan the notes that have just been written to see if they are readable. Missing outlines can usually be supplied from memory while the dictation is "fresh." Poorly written outlines may be rewritten so that they will be readable during transcription later on. If it is found that outlines are missing or unreadable, the interruption is a good time for the secretary to ask for clarification before the dictation resumes.

Reading and Writing Practice

27.4 Dictation Speed Letter

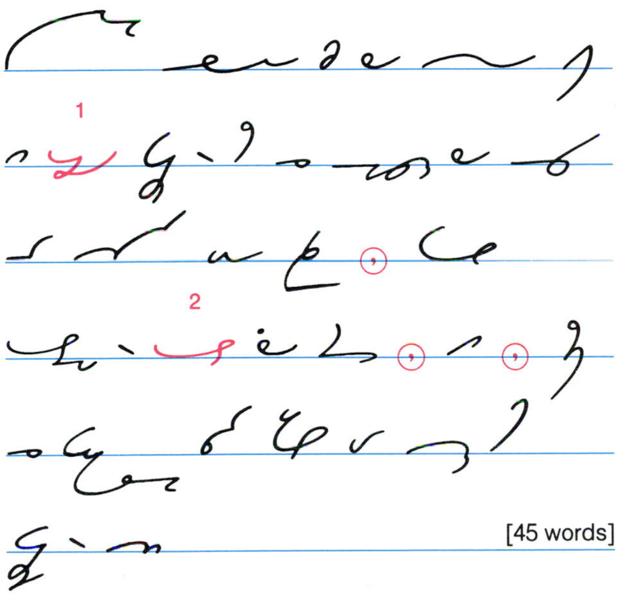

[45 words]

27.5 Business Letter

1 recent 2 Let us 3 Garcia

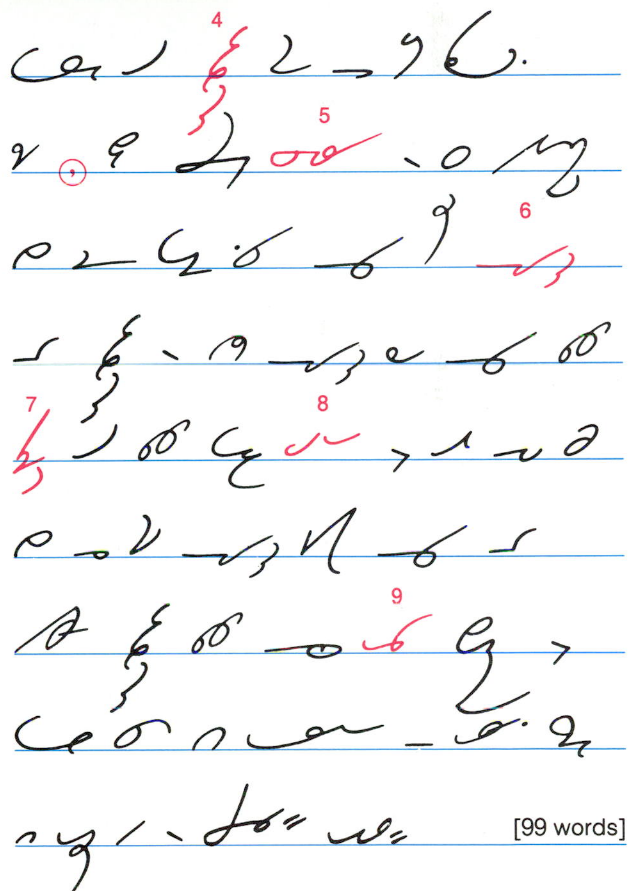

[99 words]

4 specifications 5 annoyed 6 modifications
7 justification 8 authority 9 written

LESSON 28

NEW IN LESSON 28

- Eight brief forms
- *Thank* phrases
- Word beginning *ex-*
- Salutations and complimentary closings
- Differentiating between *correspondence*, *correspondents* and *accept*, *except*

BRIEF FORMS

order

product

equip

never

regular

opinion

thank

correspond, correspondence

Brief-Form Derivatives

orders

ordered ■

ordering

products

production

equipment

equipped

regularly

opinions

thanks ■ ■

thanking

corresponds

corresponded

correspondent

correspondents

■ The jog is used to distinguish the *d* in *order* from the *d* representing past tense.

■ ■ The *dot* is dropped and replaced by the *s*.

Brief-Form Phrase

in order 

Brief-Form Practice

28.1

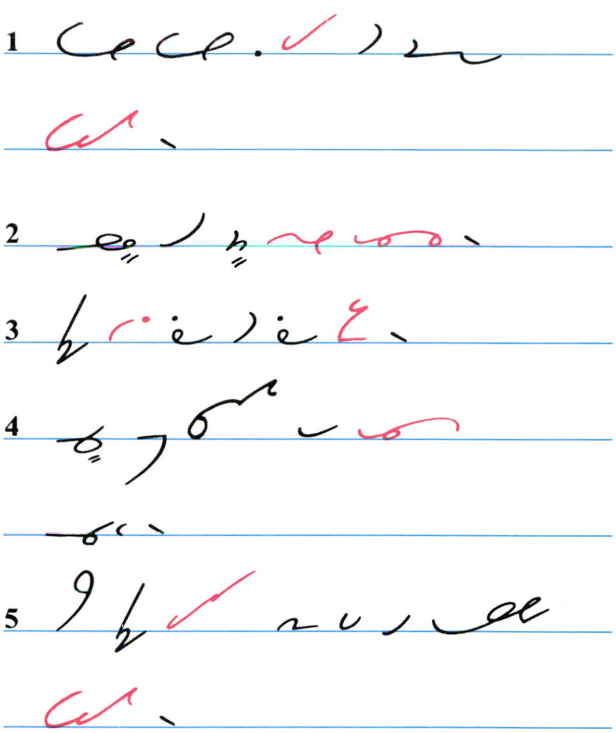

¶ **Business Letter**

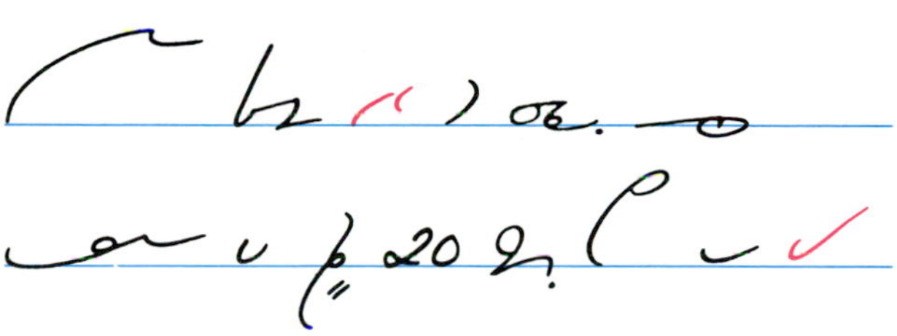

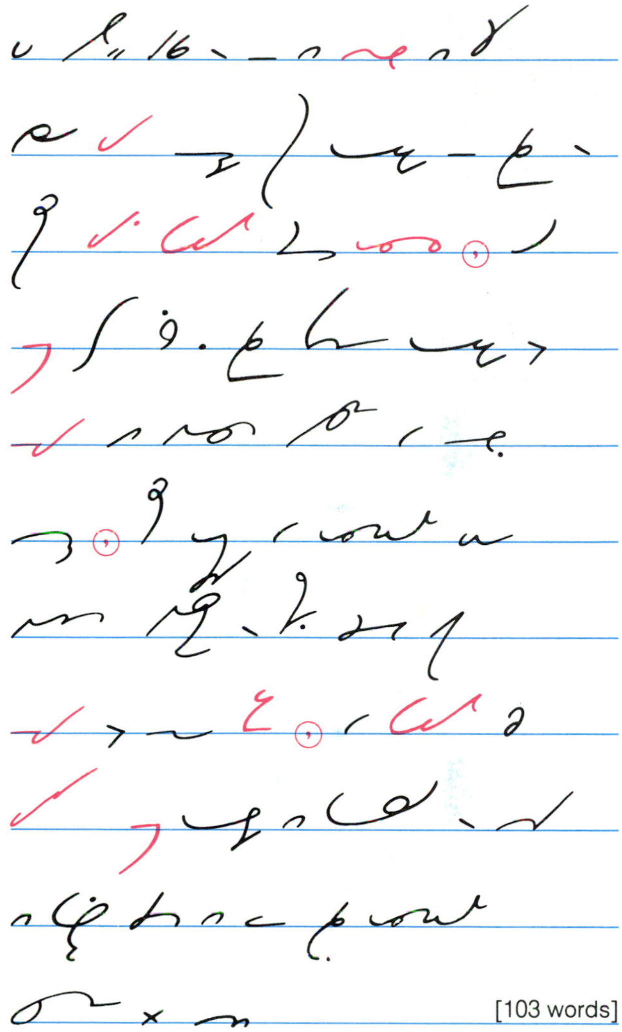

[103 words]

THANK PHRASES

In order to increase writing speed, the dot is omitted from the brief form *thank* in the following phrases.

thank you

thank you for

thank you for the

thank you for your

thank you for your order

thank you for your letter

Phrase Practice

28.2

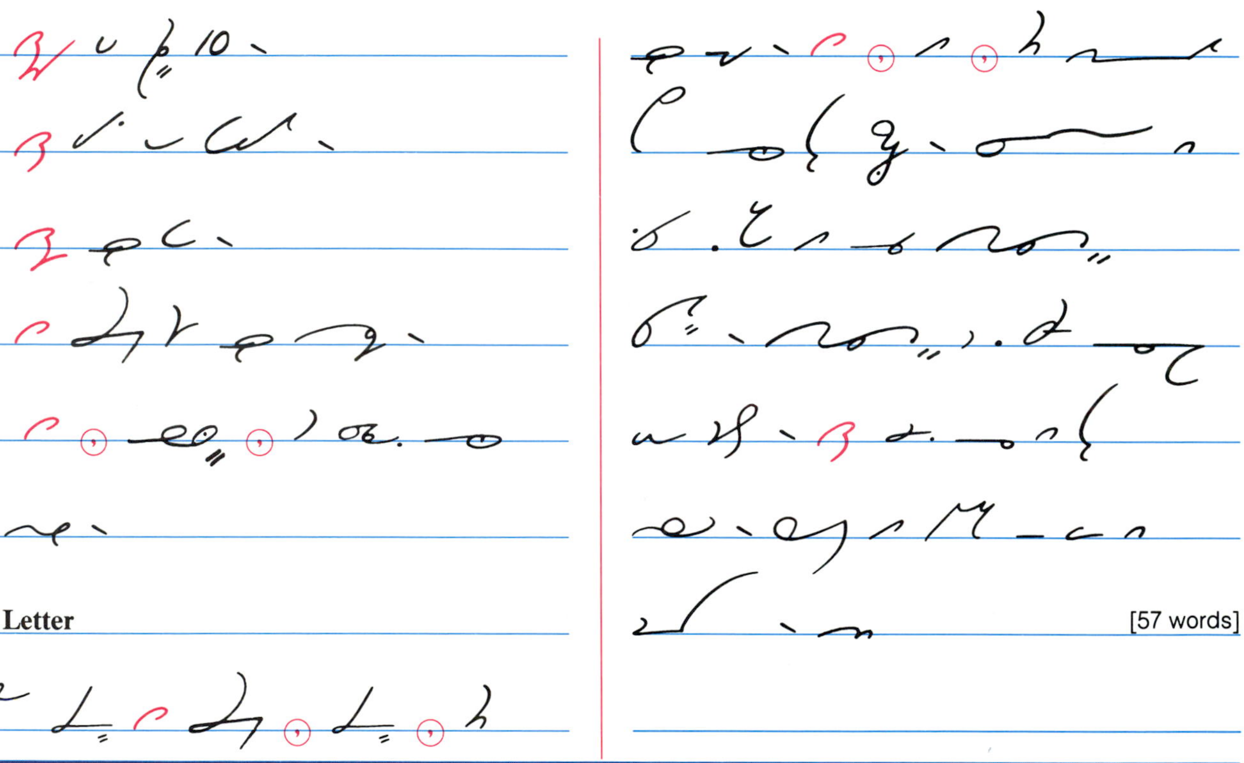

1
2
3
4
5

¶ **Letter**

[57 words]

WORD BEGINNING EX-

The word beginning *ex-* as in *extra* is written with the *e* and *left* or *right* *s* symbols, depending on the symbol that follows *ex.*

ex- or

Examples: extra expire

Ex- Words

extra
exam
examine
extreme
extremely
exact
exactly
exciting
expand
expire
expired
expert
export
expect
expected
expense
expenses
expensive

Ex- Practice

28.3

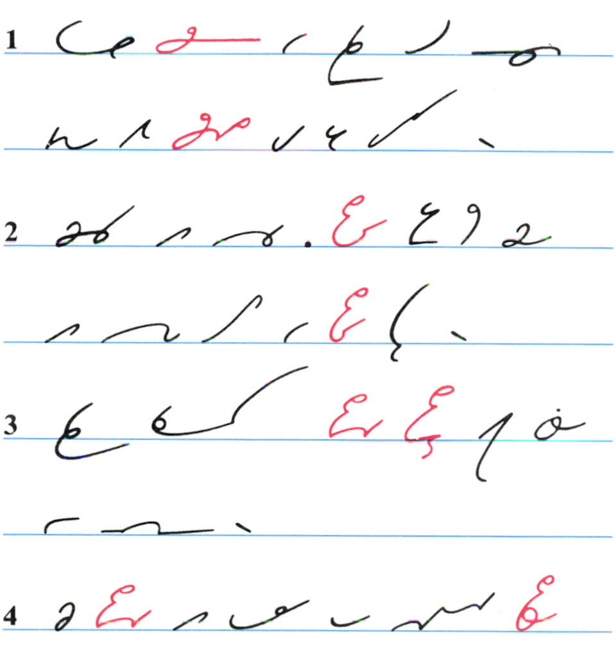

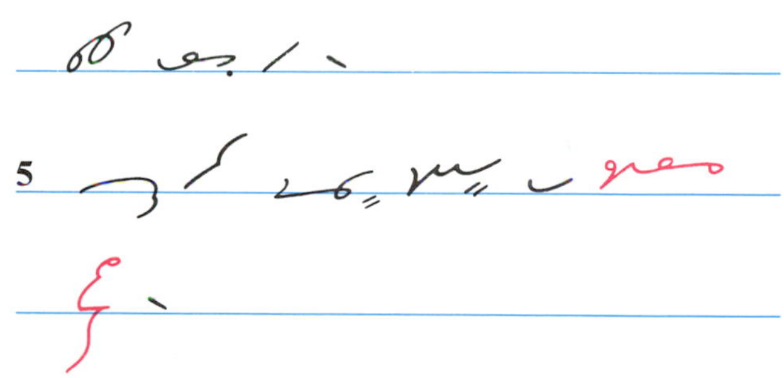

¶ **Study Notes**

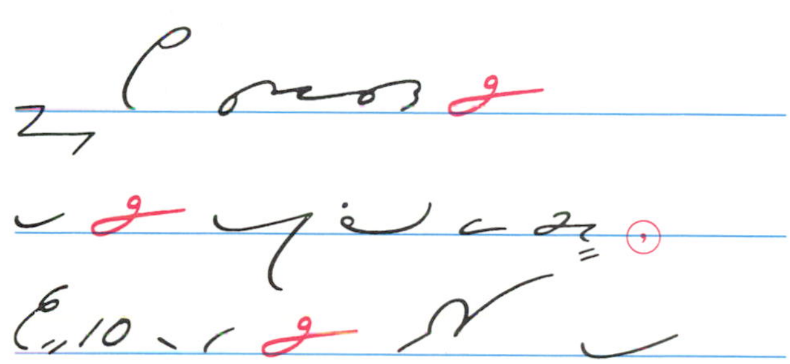

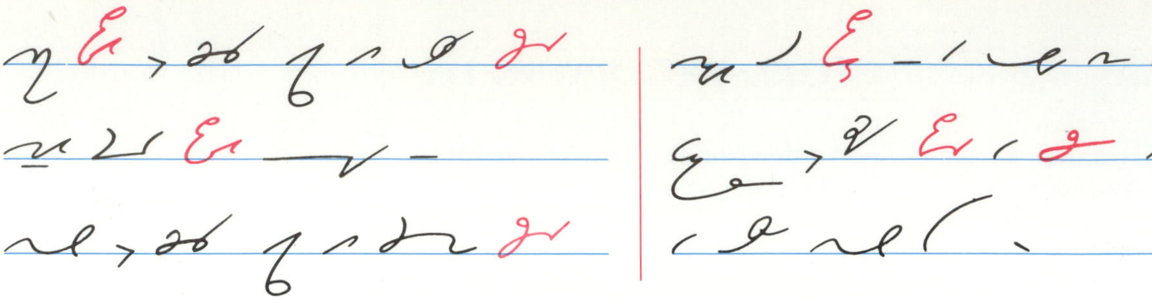

[65 words]

SALUTATIONS AND COMPLIMENTARY CLOSINGS

Eight salutations and complimentary closings were presented in Lesson 12. Here are the remaining six for which we have special outlines.

Dear Ms. 

Sincerely yours 

Yours sincerely 

Very cordially yours 

Very sincerely yours 

Yours very sincerely 

Salutation and Complimentary Closing Practice

28.4

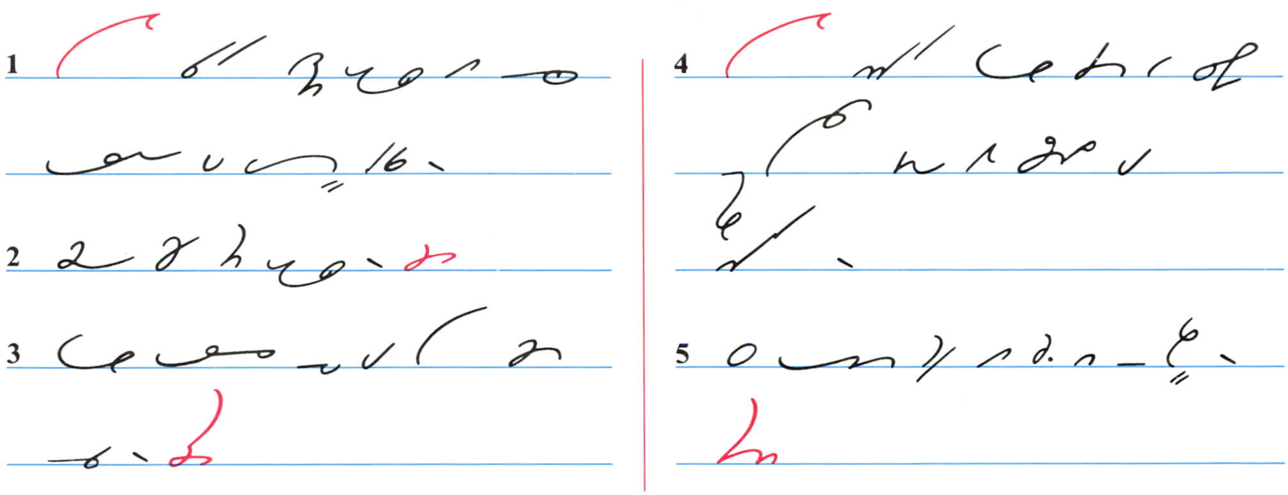

Communication Skill Builder

Similar Words: correspondence, correspondents

correspondence: letters and other communications

correspondents: people who communicate by letter or who contribute news and articles to the news media; plural of *correspondent*

I have much *correspondence* to read by Friday.

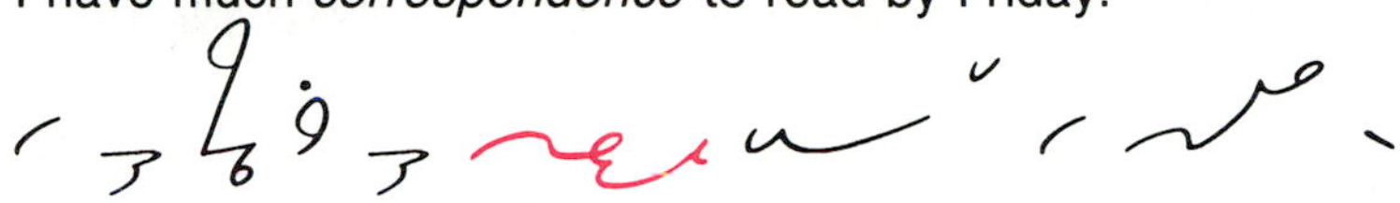

The news agency has news *correspondents* all over the country.

Similar Words: accept, except

accept: to agree to; to receive

except: (prep.) other than; excluding

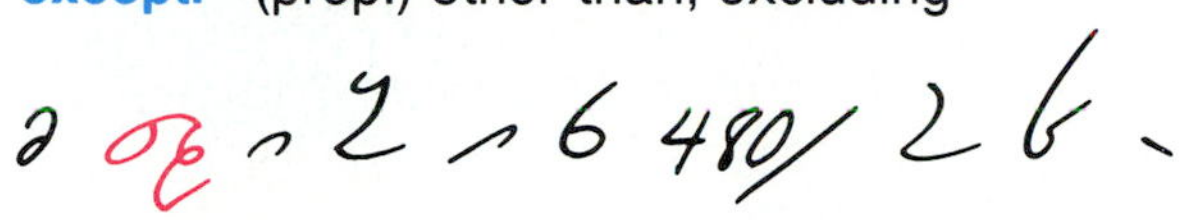

We *accept* your offer to pay $480 for our boat.

Everyone *except* Bill enjoyed the book.

Reading and Writing Practice

28.5 Dictation Speed Letter

1 appreciation 2 quality 3 opinions

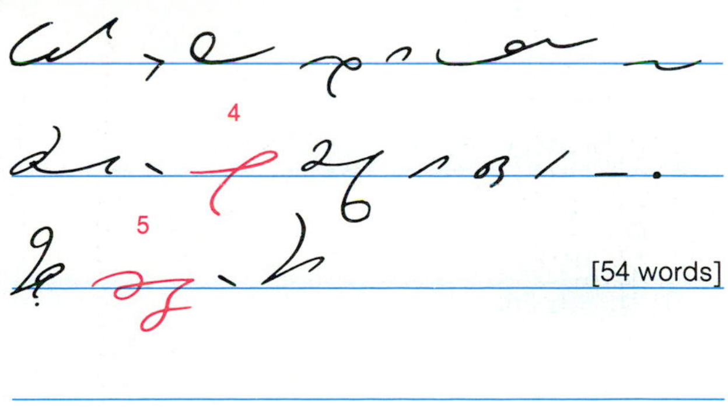

[54 words]

4 Maybe 5 campaign

28.6 Business Letter

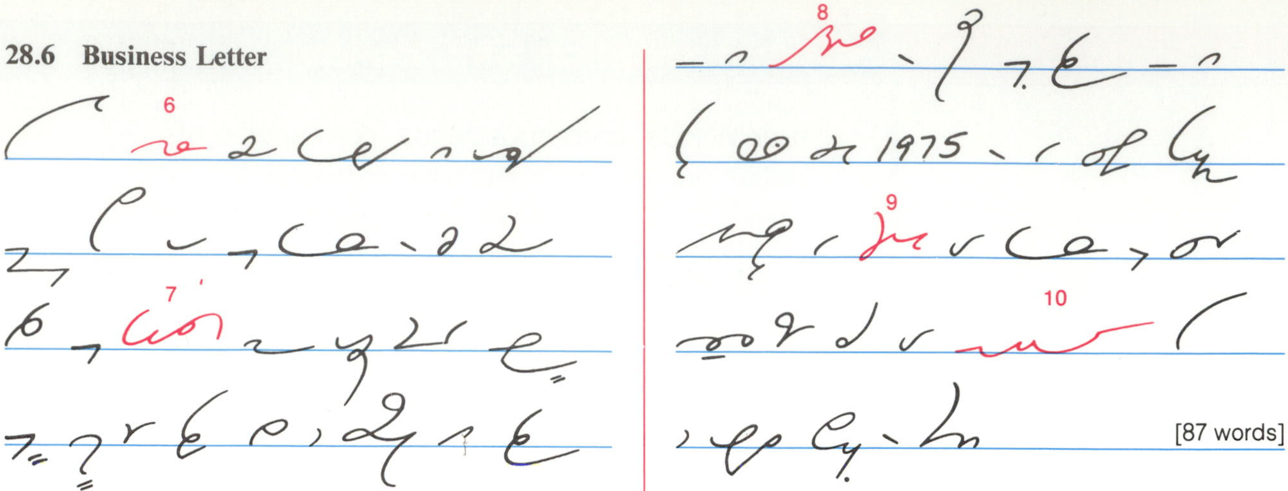

6 Cohen 7 protection 8 industry 9 features 10 enrollment

Newscasters can use shorthand to annotate typed copy.

UNIT VIII

LESSON 29

NEW IN LESSON 29

- Symbol for the sound of *ia*
- Word beginnings *inter-* and *enter-*
- Outlines for cities and states
- Differentiating between similar words *quit*, *quite*, and *quiet*

SOUND OF IA

The sound of *long i* followed by soft *a* as in *riot* is represented by the *long i* symbol in which the tail of the *i* is closed as a second circle.

ia 

Example: riot 

Ia Words

riot 	trial 	quiet 
prior 	appliances 	client 
dryer 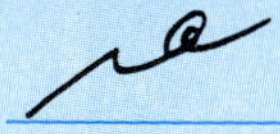	reliance 	O'Bryan 
dryers 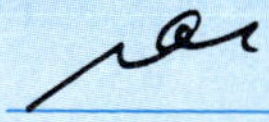	science 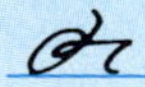	Ryan 

Ia Practice

29.1

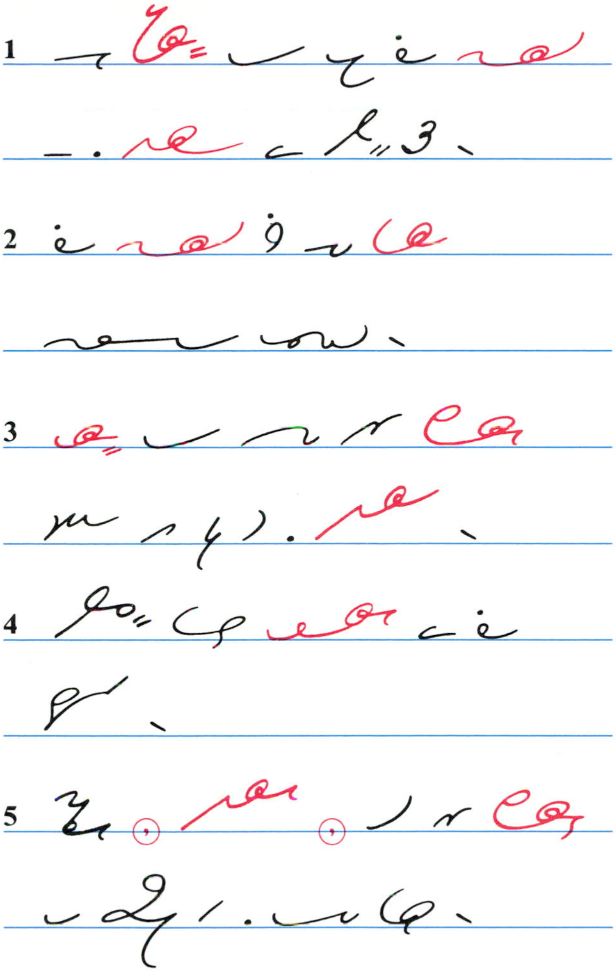

¶ **Business Letter**

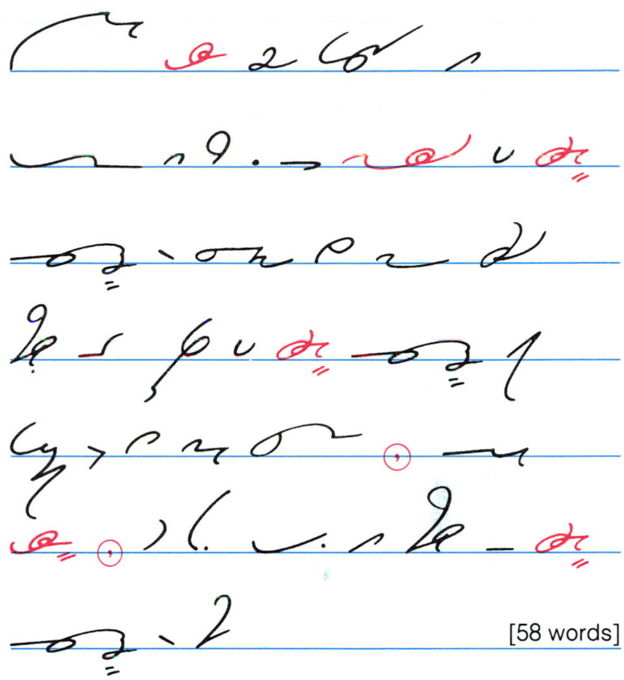

WORD BEGINNINGS INTER-, ENTER-

The word beginnings *inter-* as in *interest* and *intr-* as in *introduce* are written with a disjoined *n*. The word beginnings *enter-* as in *entertain* and *entr-* as in *entrance* are also written with a disjoined *n*. Line placement of the *inter-* word beginning is generally halfway between the lines of writing.

Examples: interest  introduce  entertain  entrance 

Inter- Words

interest	interviewing	international
interested	interfere	interrupted
interests	interferes	introduce
interview	interval	introduction

Enter- Words

enter	entertain	enterprises
entering	entertainment	entrance
entered	enterprise	entrances

Inter-, Enter- Practice

29.2

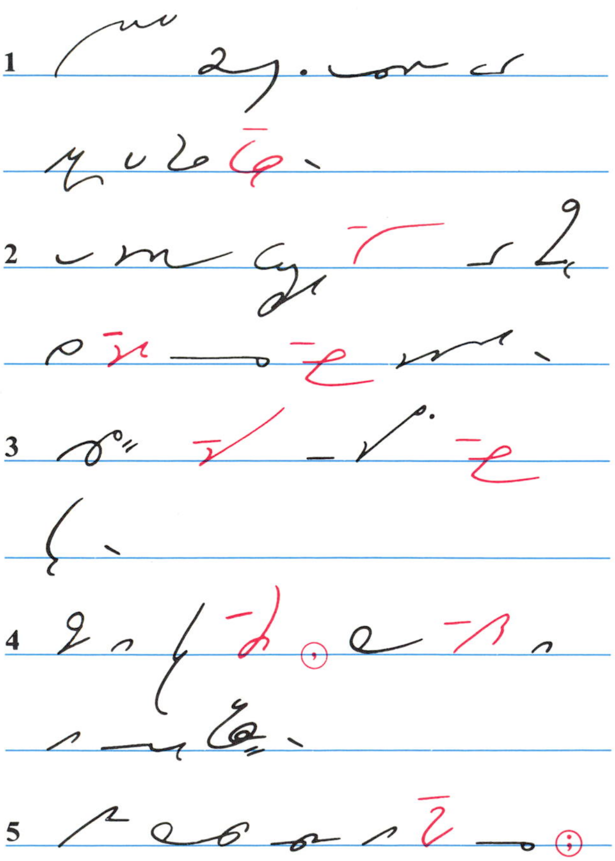

¶ **Business Letter**

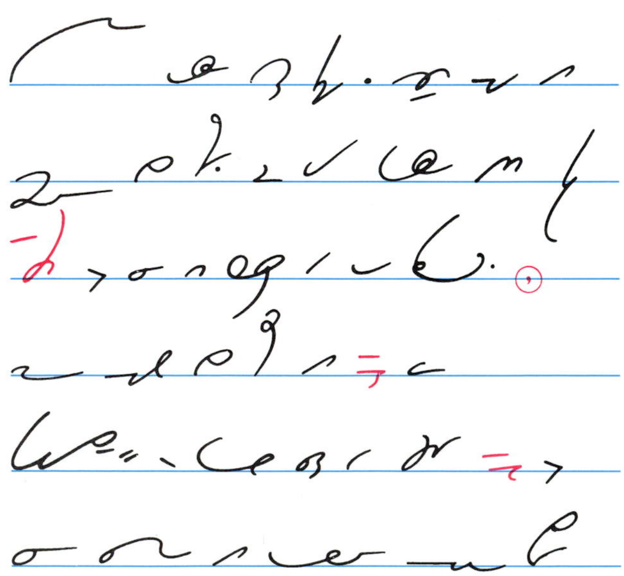

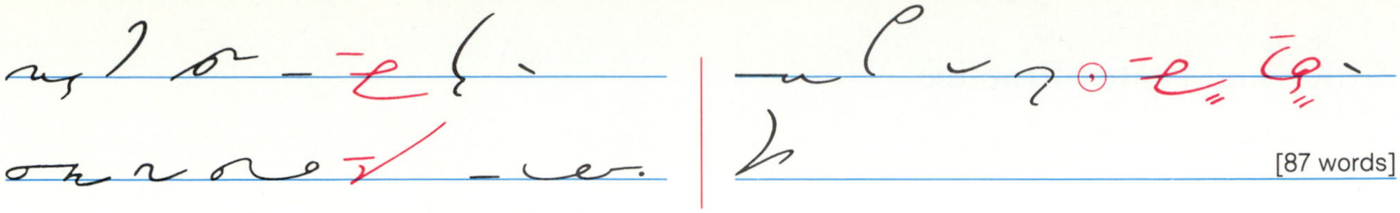

[87 words]

CITIES AND STATES

The state abbreviations are simply shorthand versions of the standard two-letter state abbreviations used with ZIP Codes. The complete lists of state abbreviations and abbreviations for many cities are appendices to the *Gregg Shorthand Dictionary*. Here are several examples.

Cities

Chicago

San Francisco

Denver

Boston

Los Angeles

New Orleans

Philadelphia

St. Louis

Seattle

States

The shorthand outline for each state abbreviation is based upon the two-letter ZIP Code abbreviation. The following guidelines were used to determine the shorthand symbol:

1 The *c* is represented by *k* in CA, CO, CT, NC, and SC.
2 The *y* is represented by *i* in KY, NY, and WY.
3 The *short i* is represented by *e* in IL, IN, and WI.
4 The *w* is represented by *oo* in WA, WV, WI, and WY.

Massachusetts

California

Georgia

Illinois

Missouri

Florida

Pennsylvania

Wyoming

New York

Similar abbreviations are used for the following:

America

American

United States

Cities and States Practice

29.3

1

2

3

4

5

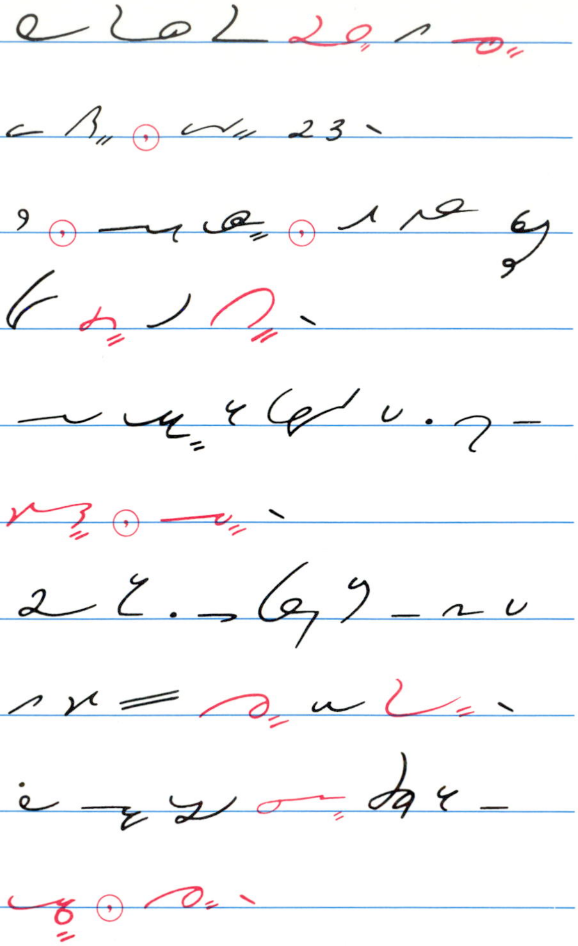

¶ **Geography Class Notes**

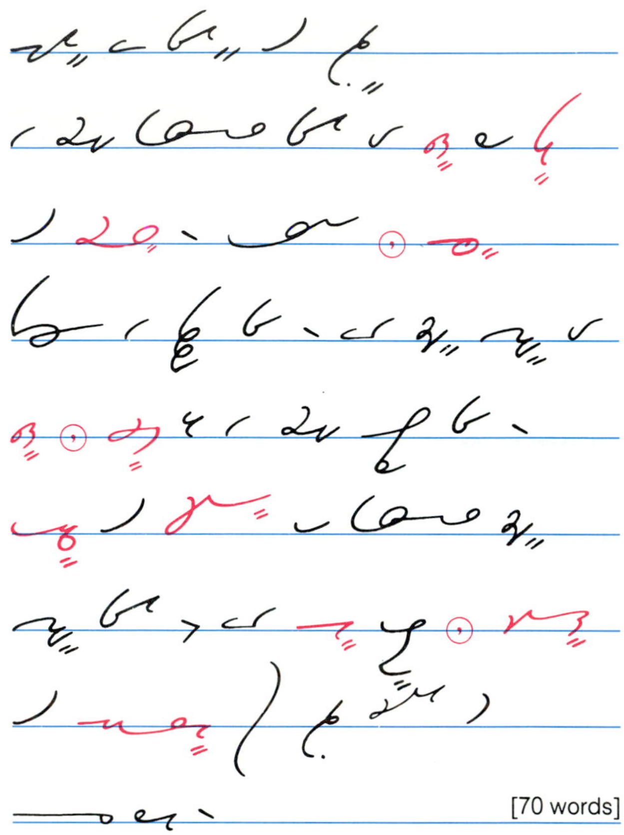

[70 words]

Communication Skill Builder

Similar Words: quit, quite, quiet

quit: to stop

quite: entirely; somewhat or rather

quiet: without noise

Mark says he will *quit* smoking.

I am *quite* pleased with my grades.

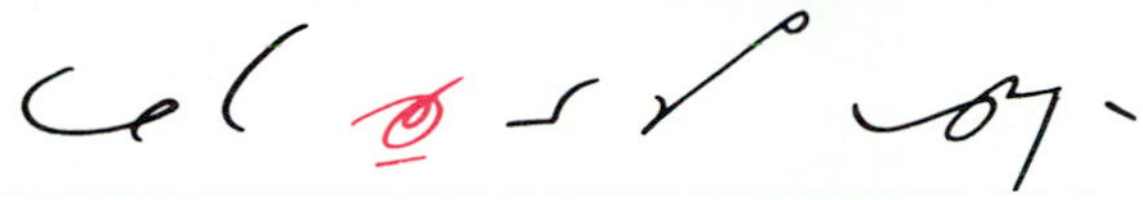

Please be *quiet* in the study lounge.

Reading and Writing Practice

29.4 Dictation Speed Letter

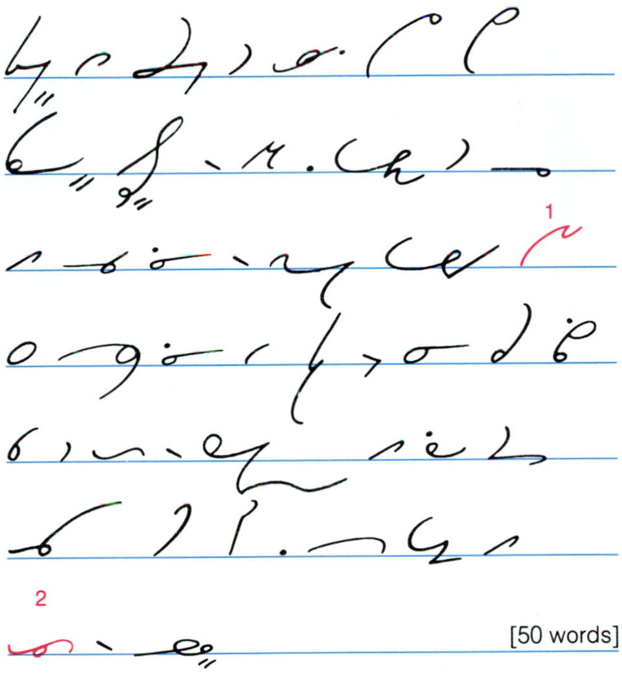

[50 words]

29.5 Professional Letter

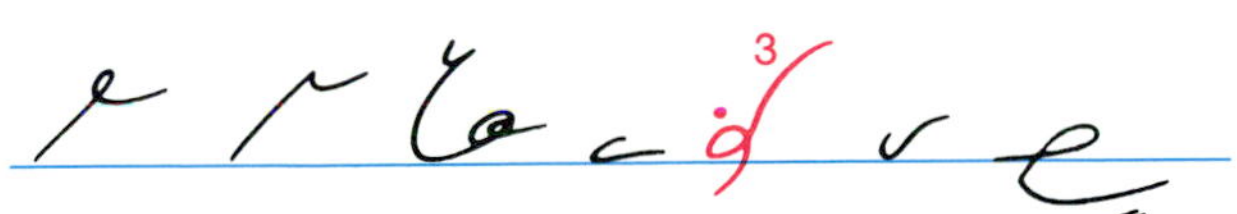

1 to know 2 recommend 3 behalf

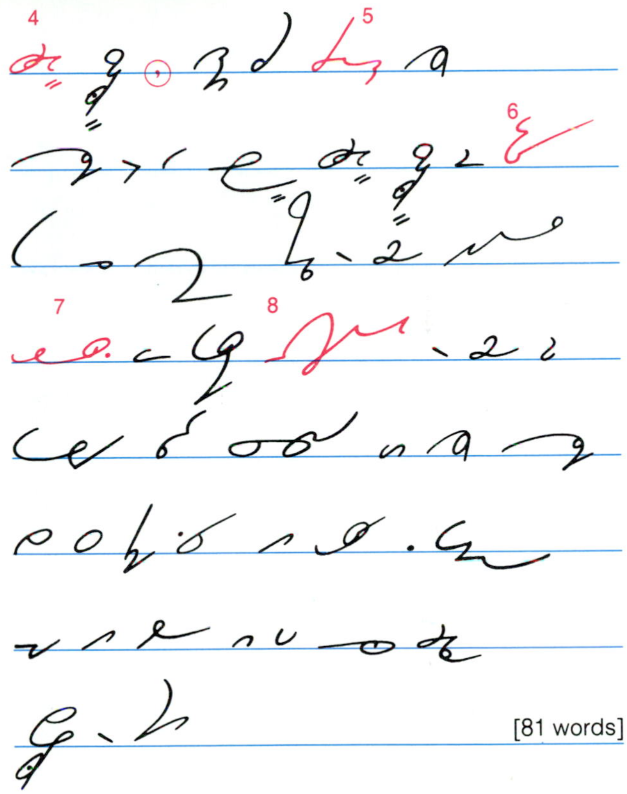

[81 words]

4 Science 5 generous 6 supported 7 relying
8 individuals

LESSON 30

NEW IN LESSON 30

- Eight brief forms
- Word ending *-tribute*
- Word ending *-ful*
- Using shorthand for confidentiality

BRIEF FORMS

enclose	usual	property
envelope	newspaper	probable
throughout	recognize	

Brief-Form Derivatives

enclosed	usually	recognition
enclosure	unusual	recognizes
envelopes	recognized	probably

Brief-Form Practice

30.1

1 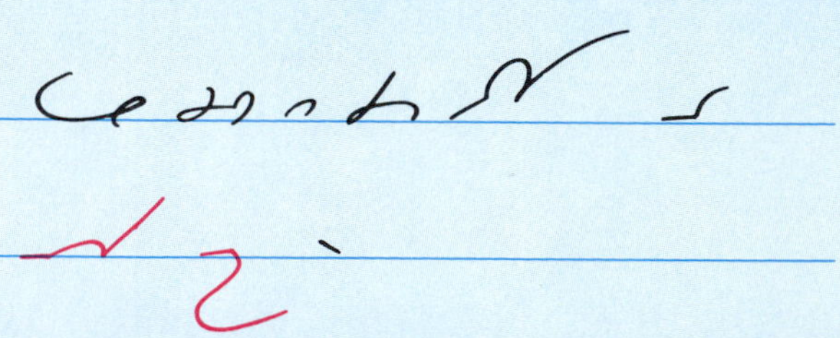

2 

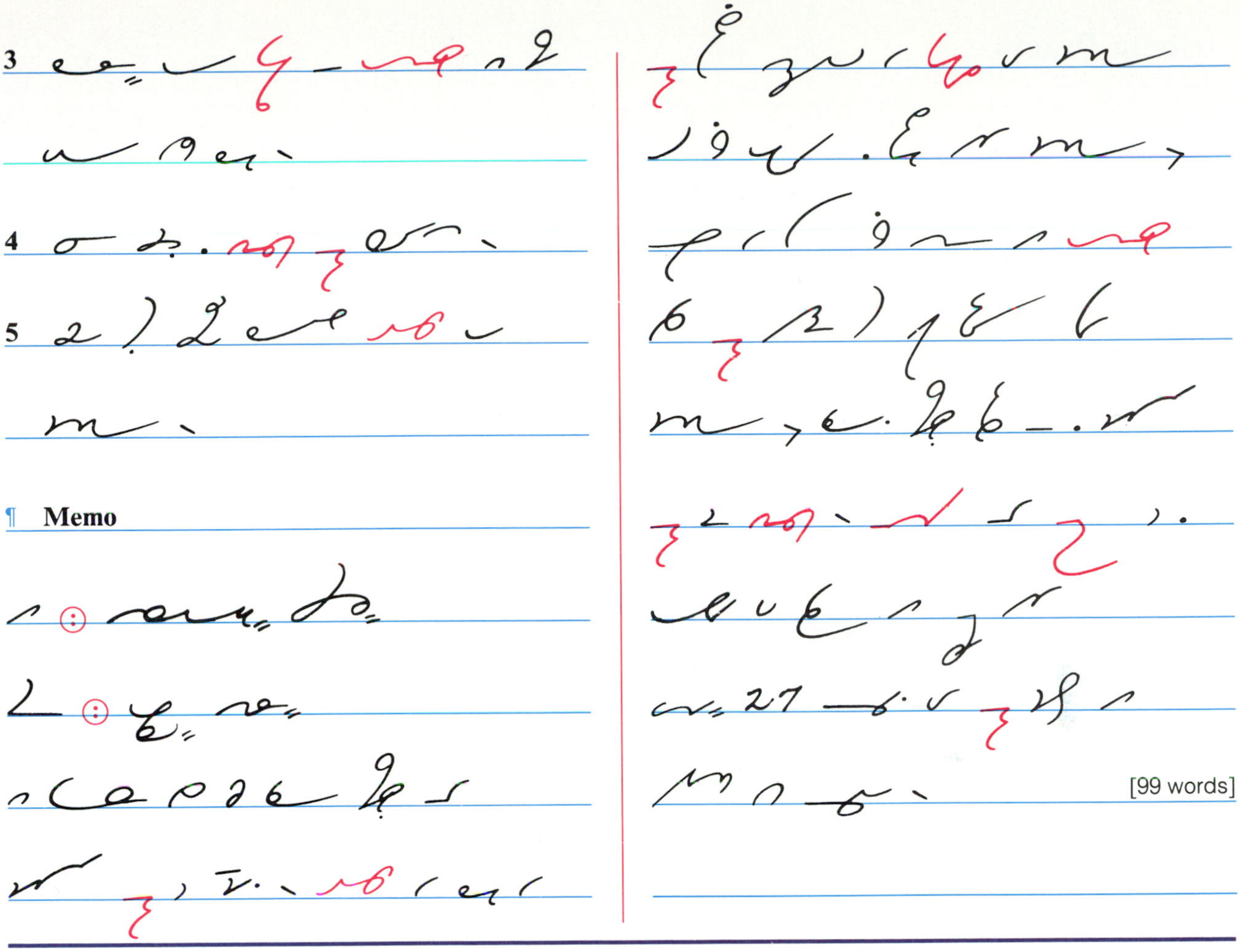

WORD ENDING -TRIBUTE

The word ending *-tribute* as in *contribute* is written with the *t r e b* symbols.

-tribute

Example: contribute

-tribute Words

contribute	distribute	distributes
contribution	distributed	attributes
contributor	distribution	attributed

-tribute Practice
30.2

1 2 3 4 5

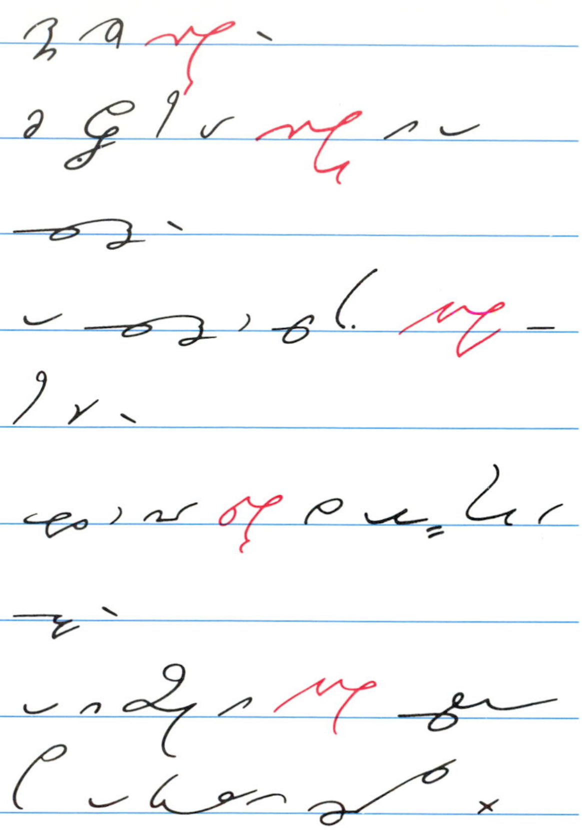

¶ **Letter**

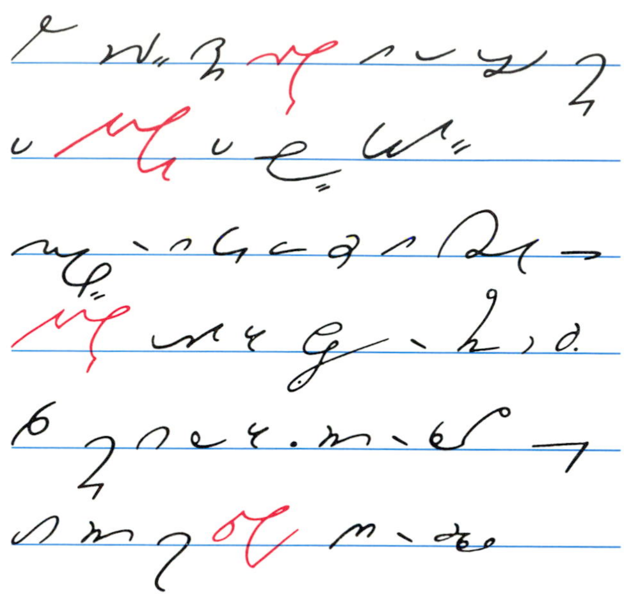

[64 words]

Regardless of their chosen careers, many people study shorthand because they recognize its usefulness in any job.

WORD ENDING -FUL

The word ending *-ful* as in *grateful* is expressed with the *f* symbol.

Example: grateful 

-ful Words

grateful 
successful ■ 
successfully ■ 
helpful 
useful 
careful 
carefully 
meaningful 
beautiful 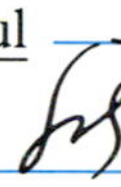
wonderful 
hopefully 
delightful 
thoughtful 
doubtful 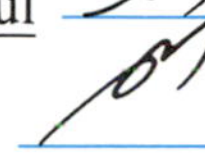
thankful ■ 

■ Brief-form derivative.

-ful Practice

30.3

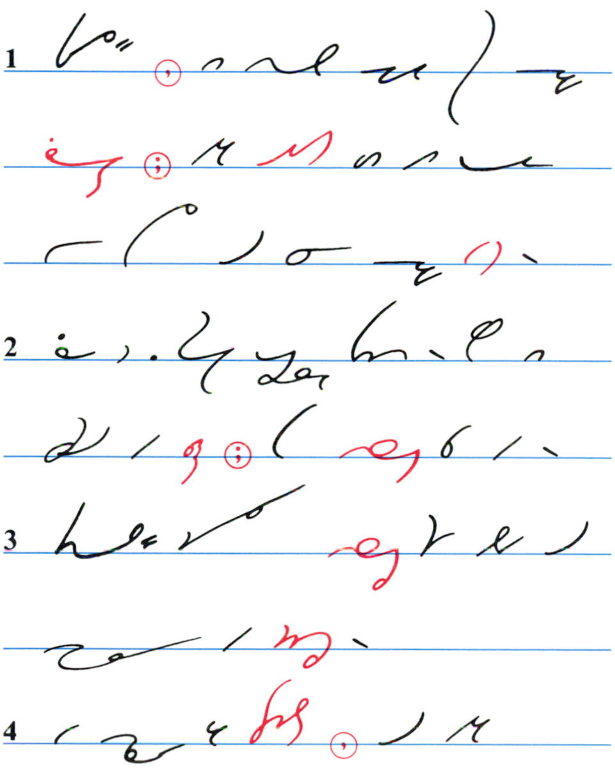

¶ **Personal Note**

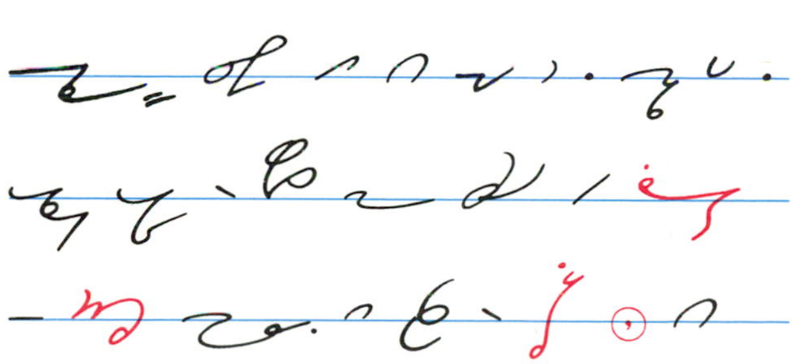

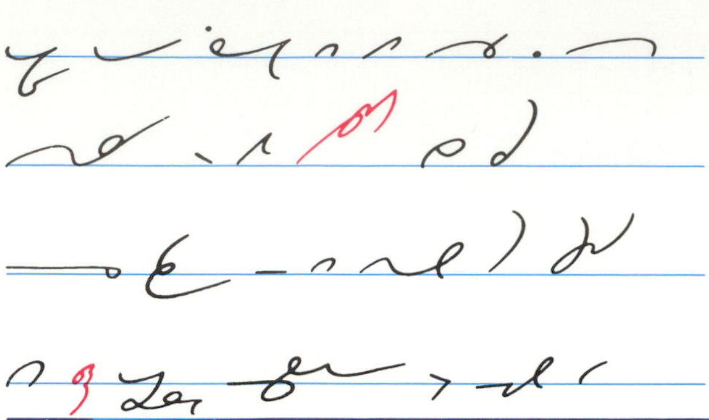

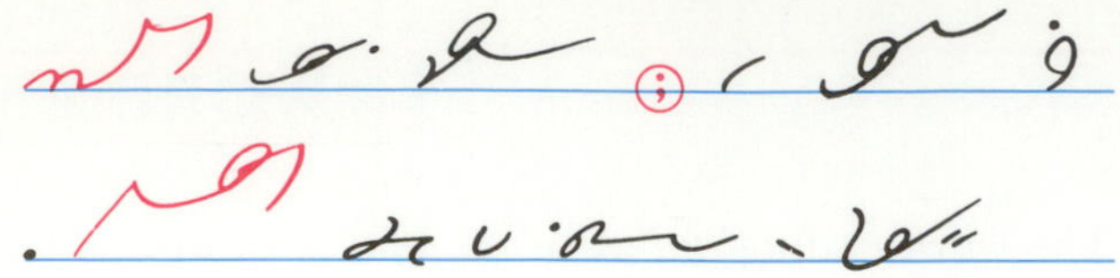

[69 words]

Using Shorthand for Confidentiality

A practical definition of a secretary or an administrative assistant is "the executive's closest and most trusted employee." By working so closely with an executive, a secretary naturally learns information that must be kept confidential. This is one more aspect of office work in which shorthand proves to be valuable.

When an executive wants to dictate a document, the strictest confidentiality may be important. The executive can then dictate to the private secretary who takes shorthand rather than have an anonymous person in a steno pool or word processing center transcribe a voice recording.

Reading and Writing Practice

30.4 Dictation Speed Letter

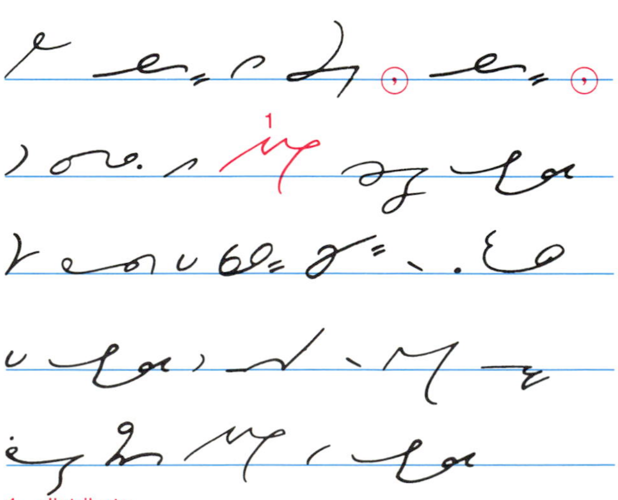

1 distribute

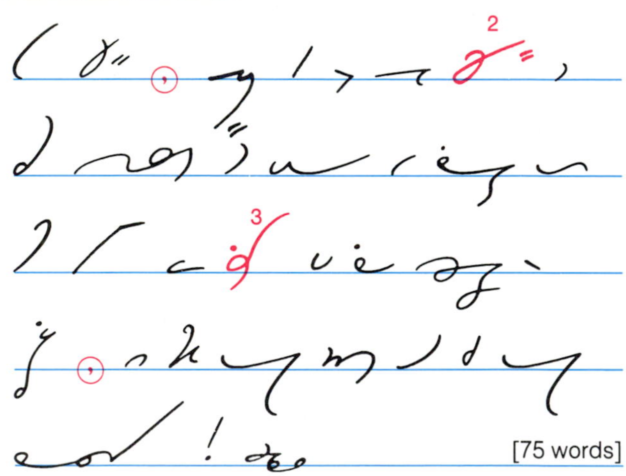

[75 words]

2 Wade 3 behalf

30.5 Personal Note

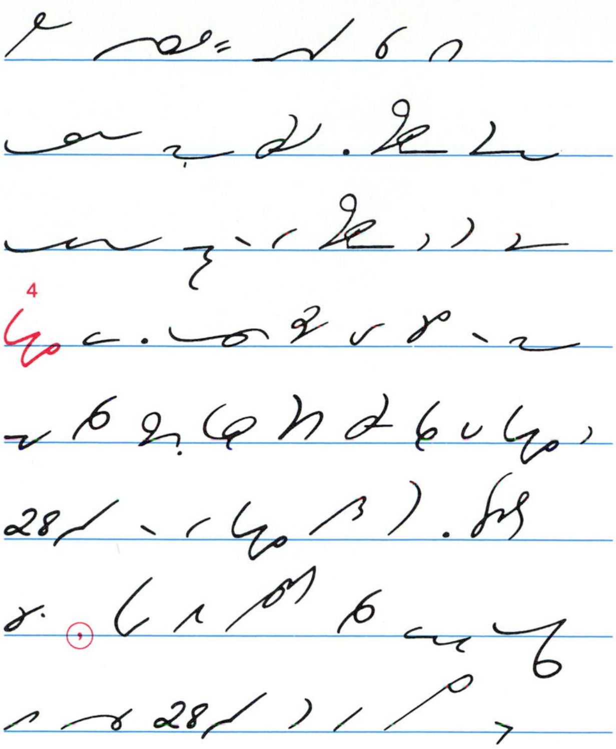

4 property

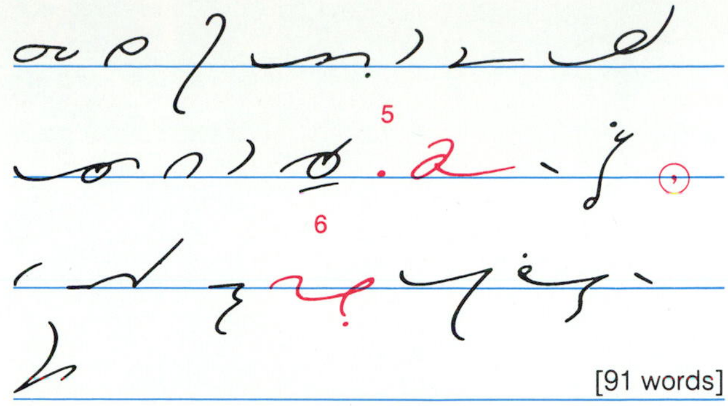

[91 words]

30.6 Message

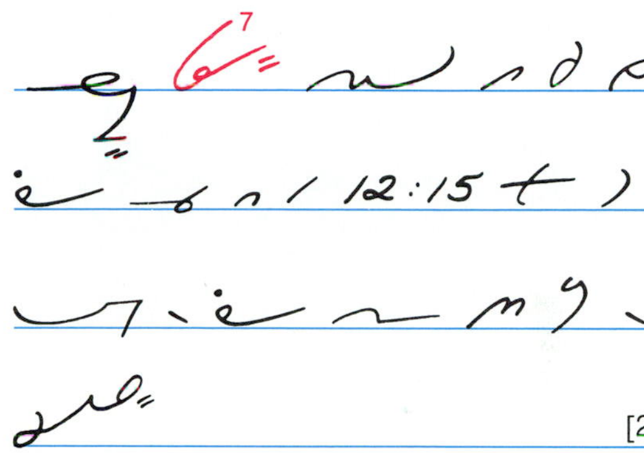

[22 words]

5 a while 6 clipping 7 Boyd

LESSON 31

NEW IN LESSON 31

- **Symbol for the sounds of *md* and *mt***
- **Symbol for the sound of *x***
- **Word beginning *al-***
- **Coding notes**

SOUNDS OF MD, MT

The sounds of *md* as in *seemed* and *mt* as in *empty* are written with a blend that represents a combination of the *m* and *d* symbols. The same symbol represents both sounds and is a long under curve written on the slope of the *d* symbol.

m — d  = md, mt 

Examples: seemed  empty 

Md, Mt Words

seemed 
named 
blamed 
framed 
claimed 
informed 
confirmed 
unconfirmed 
welcomed 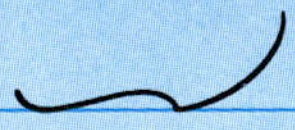
empty 
prompt 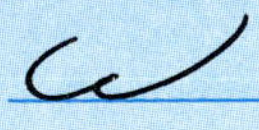
promptly 

Md, Mt Practice

31.1

1 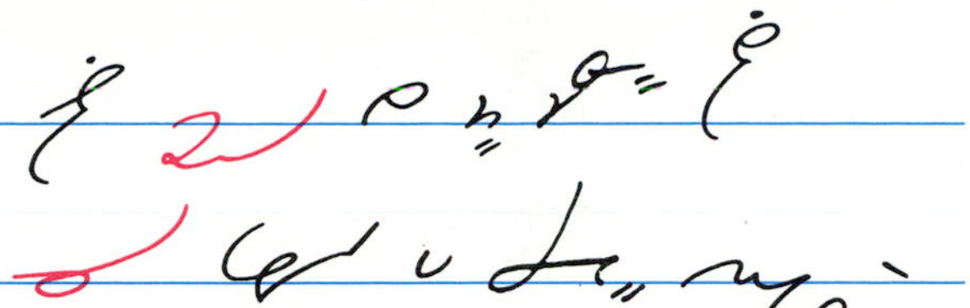

2 

3 

4 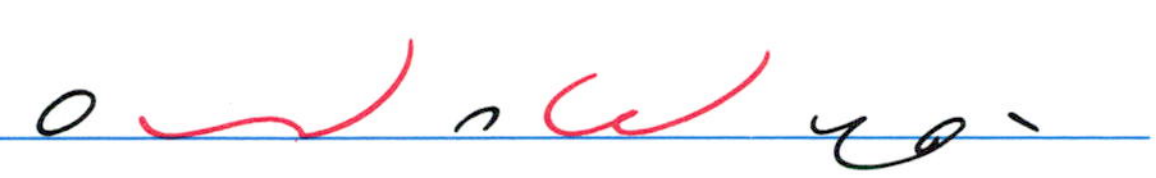

5 

¶ **Letter of Recommendation**

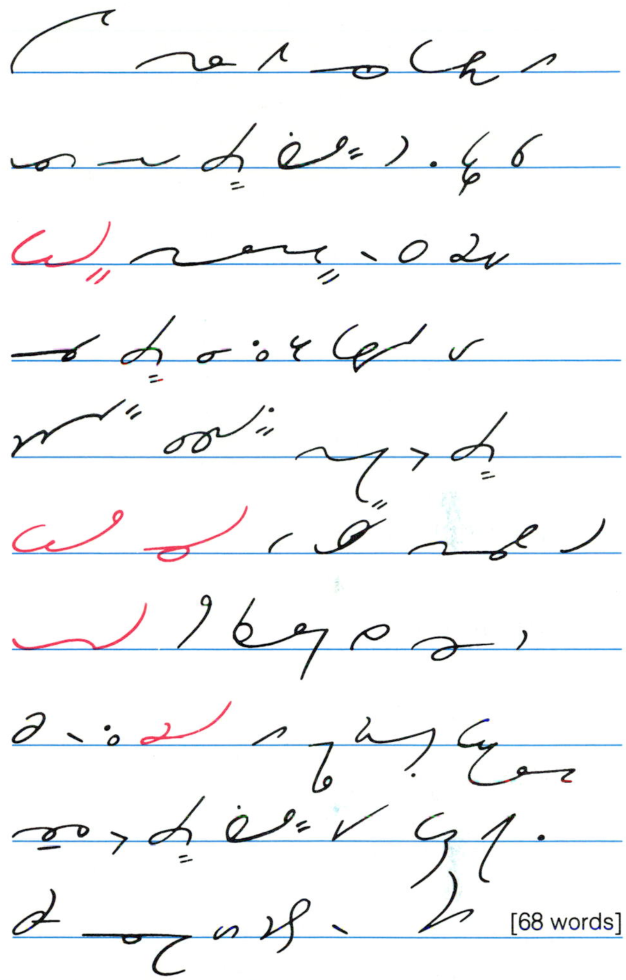

[68 words]

SOUND OF X

The letter *x* in shorthand is represented by a slanted right or left *s* symbol. Compare the examples below.

Examples: mess  mix 

fees  fix 

X Words

mix

tax

taxes

index

indexing

box

boxes

fix

fixed

X Practice

31.2

1 2 3 4 5

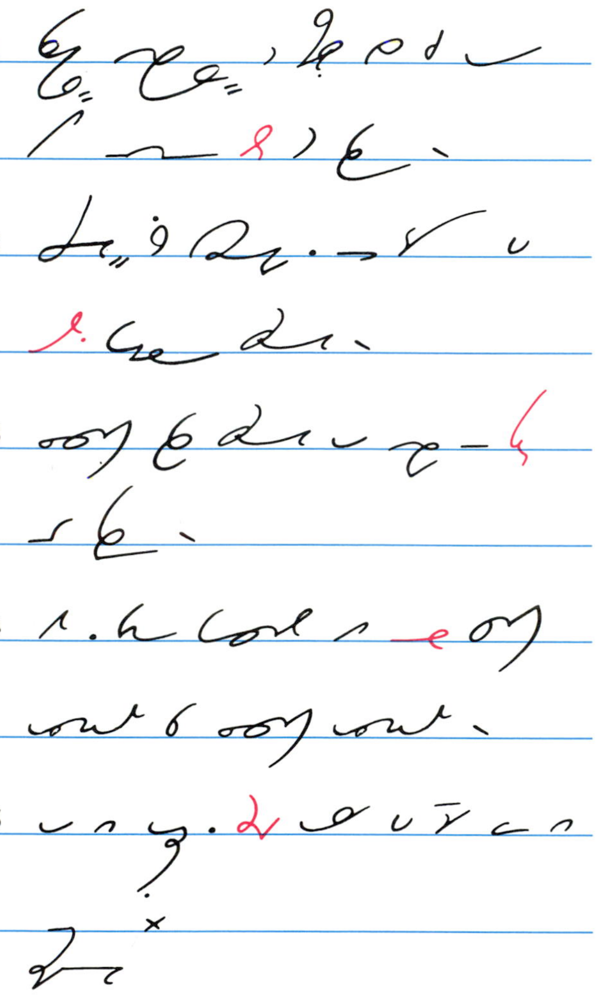

¶ **Memo**

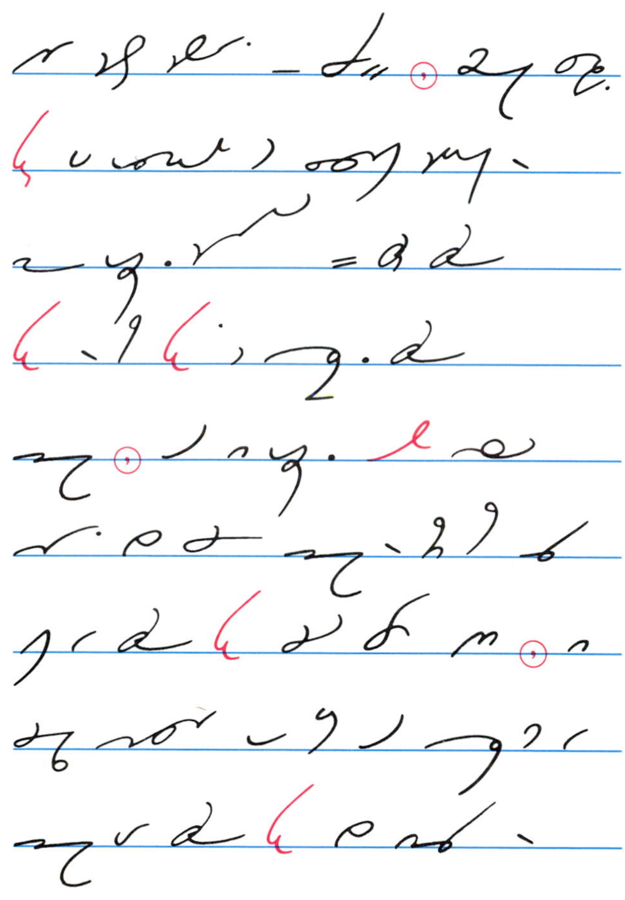

[71 words]

WORD BEGINNING AL-

The word beginning *al-* as in *also* is represented by the *o* symbol for ease of writing.

Example: also

Al- Words

also	altogether	although
already	almost	altered

But: *Always* retains the *l* to make a more readable outline.

always

Al- Practice

31.3

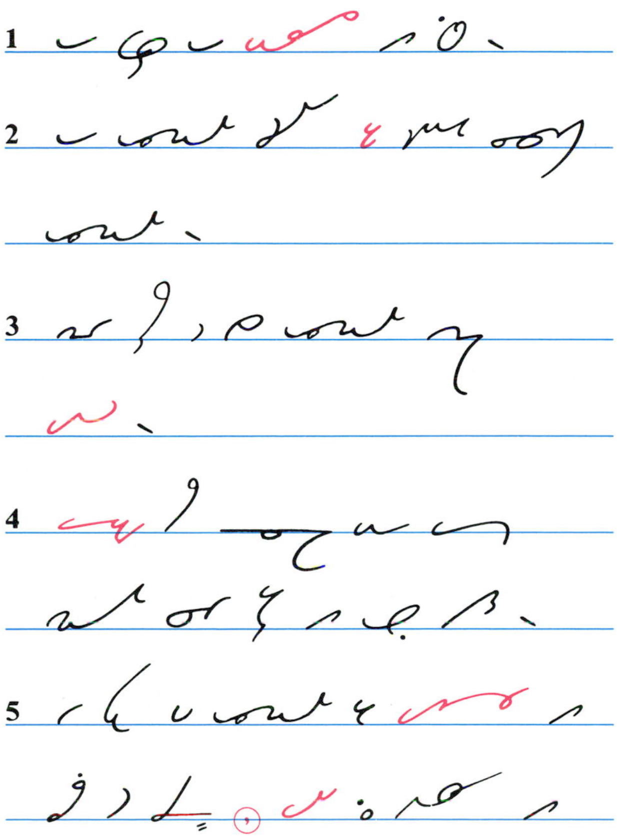

¶ **Personal Note**

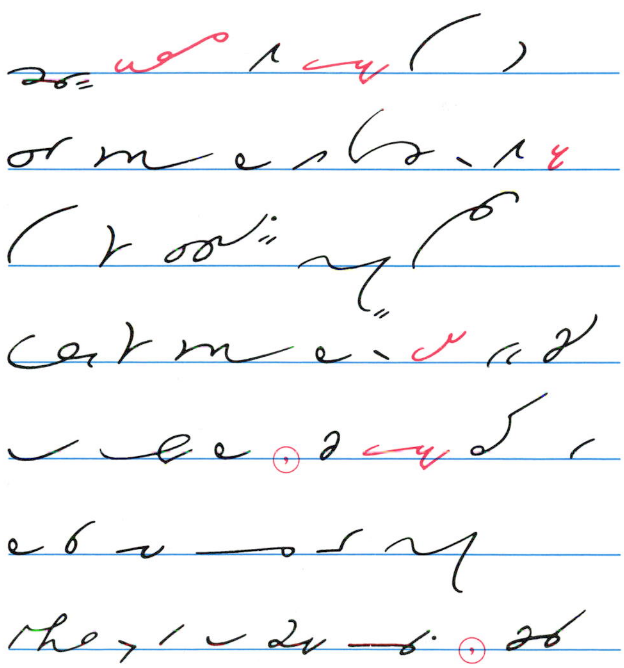

[78 words]

Coding Notes

A person who knows shorthand and has good listening habits has a tremendous advantage over other people in terms of personal efficiency. To the student, knowing shorthand means that all the key points of a lecture can be recorded in class notes for later study. In order to make notes even more useful, they should be coded.

Whenever an assignment is made by the instructor, the student should print an *A* and draw a circle around it. Such an assignment code stands out clearly when the student quickly scans the notebook pages later.

While the student may assume that anything presented in a class is likely to be tested, sometimes an instructor will specifically state that information will be on a test. Information that will be tested should be preceded in the notes by a printed letter *T* with a circle drawn around it. During later study, the items preceded by the test code can be given the most careful review.

Often during meetings people receive instructions from their supervisors or make commitments to complete projects on behalf of the group. Notes explaining such commitments should be preceded by a printed letter *C* with a circle drawn around it.

Students, secretaries, and executives all benefit from coding notes. Coded notes ensure that once a class or meeting has been concluded, details of agreements will be remembered and commitments met.

People in the medical field find shorthand a useful tool to record information from patients.

Reading and Writing Practice

31.4 Dictation Speed Letter

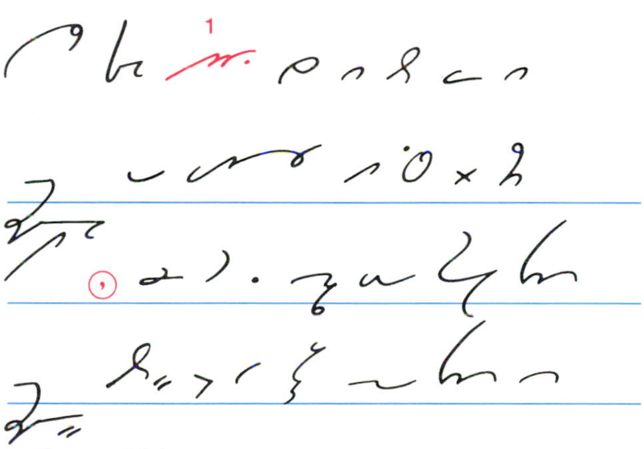

1 Do you think

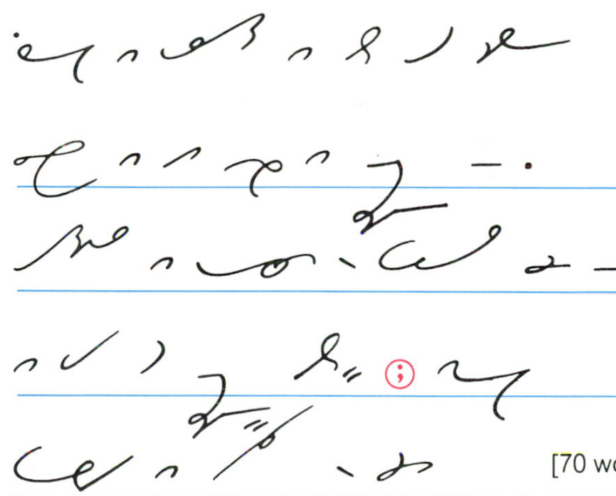

[70 words]

31.5 Business Letter

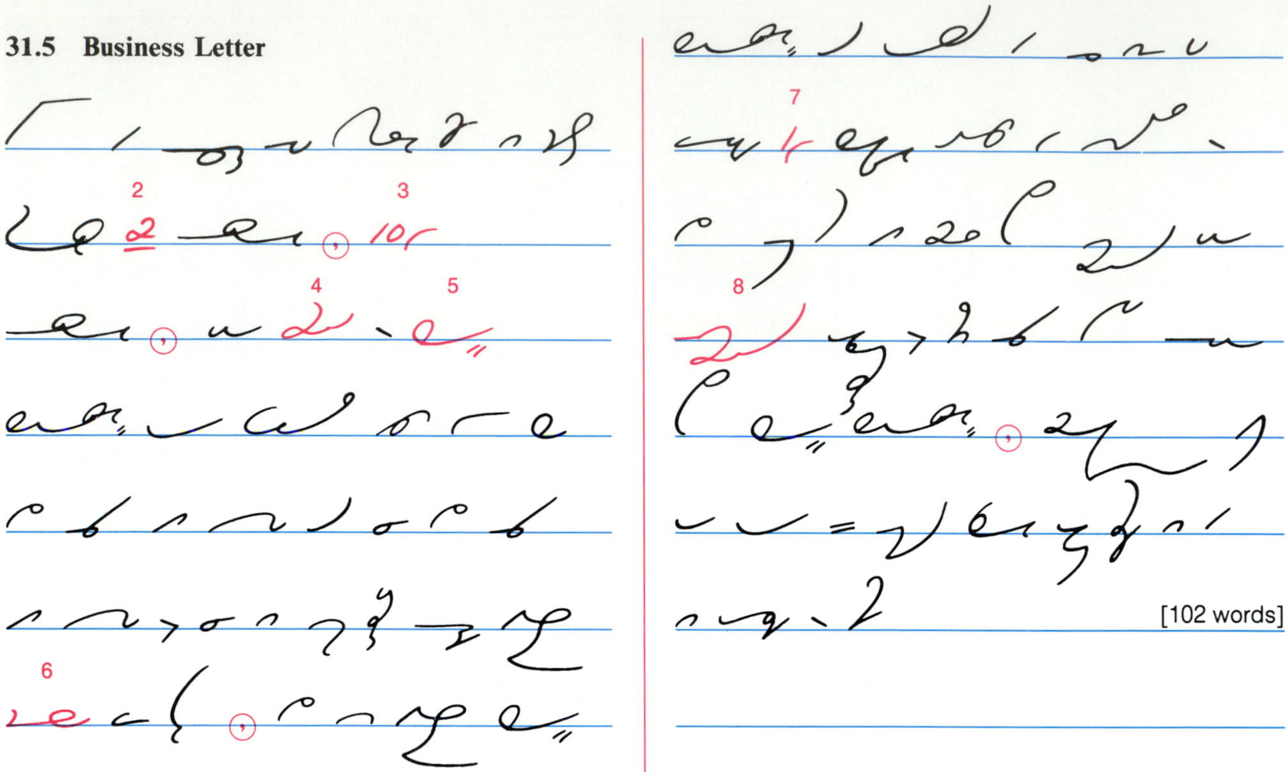

2 200 3 10,000 4 farther 5 Yale
6 somewhere

7 1,000 8 unconfirmed

LESSON 32

NEW IN LESSON 32

- **Eight brief forms**
- **Word ending *-quire***
- **Symbols for the sounds of *ng* and *nk***
- **Differentiating between *some* and *sum***

BRIEF FORMS

suggest	short	experience
satisfy, satisfactory	worth	under
include	progress	

Brief-Form Derivatives

suggested	inclusion	worthwhile ■
suggestion	shortage	progressed
satisfied	shortly	progressive
includes	shorthand	underneath
included	worthless	understand

■ In the compound word *worthwhile*, *while* has been simplified for ease of writing.

Brief-Form Practice

32.1

¶ **Personal Note**

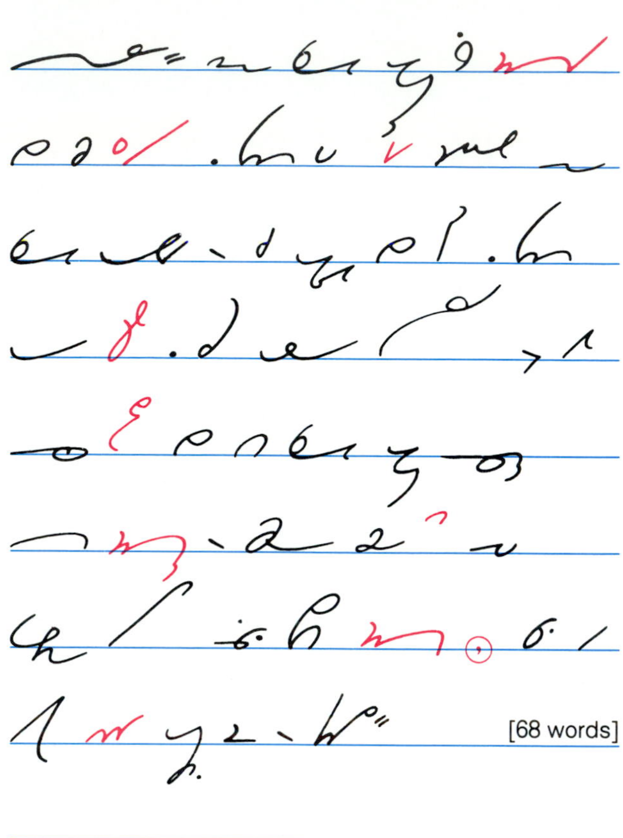

[68 words]

WORD ENDING -QUIRE

The word ending *-quire* as in *acquire* is represented by the *k* and *i* symbols. 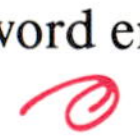

Example: acquire 

-quire Words

acquire	inquiry	requires
inquire	inquired	required
inquires	require	requirements

-quire Practice

32.2

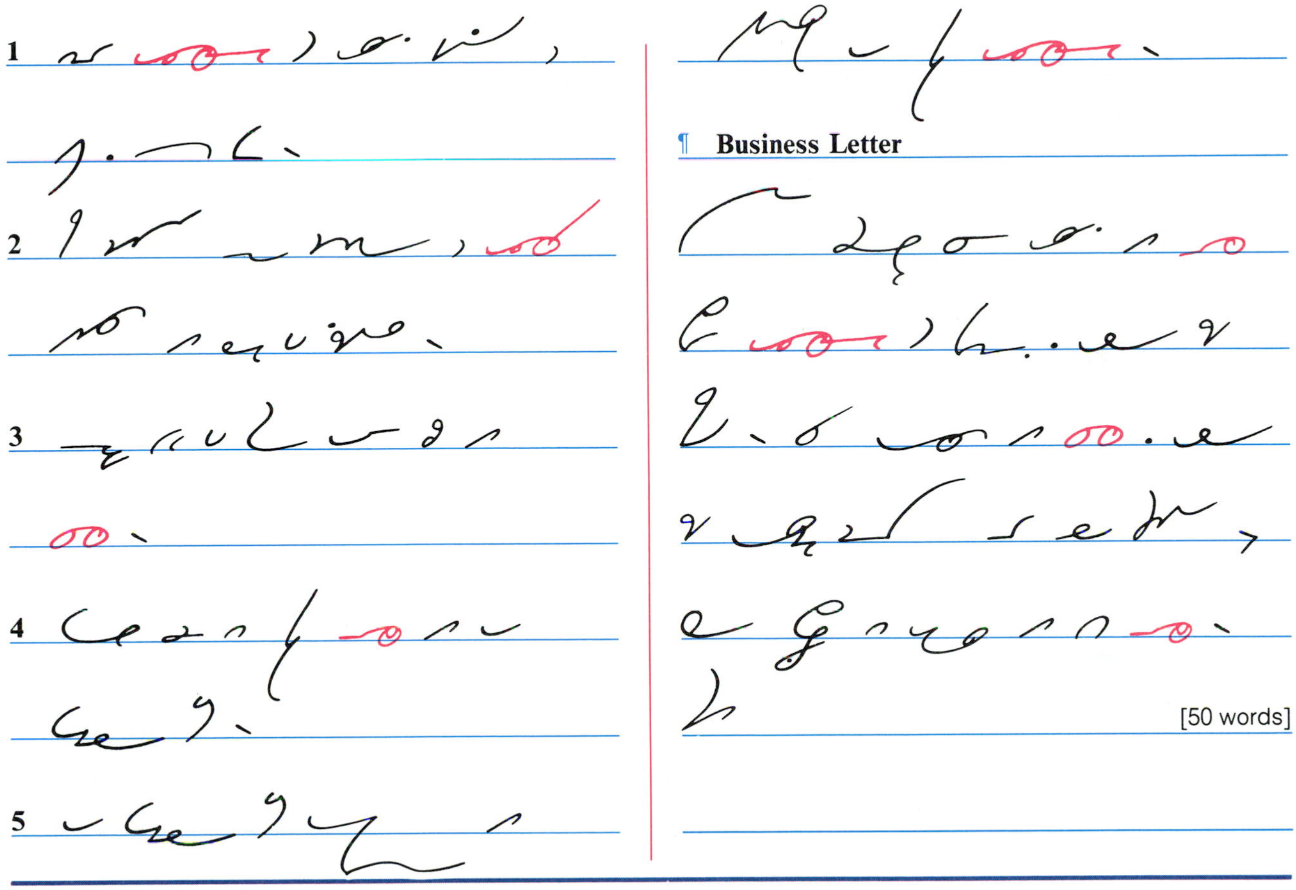

¶ Business Letter

[50 words]

SOUNDS OF NG, NK

The sounds of *ng* as in *single* and *nk* as in *sink* are represented by *downward* slanting straight strokes the size of *n* and *m*.

ng nk

Examples: single sink

Ng Words

single	belong	strong
long	spring	stronger
longer	bring	younger

Nk Words

sink	Franklin	anxious
rank	bank	ink
frank	banker	uncle
frankly	blank	Lincoln

Ng, Nk Practice

32.3

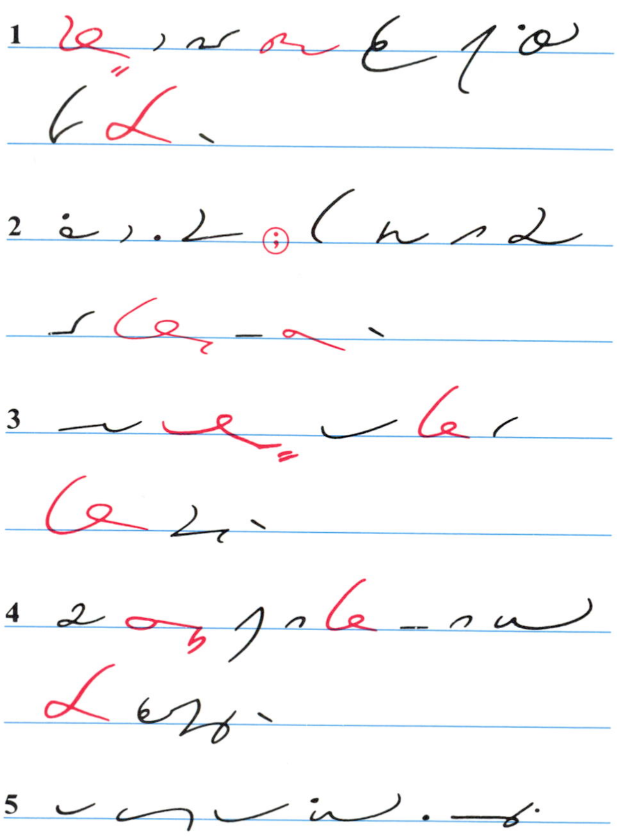

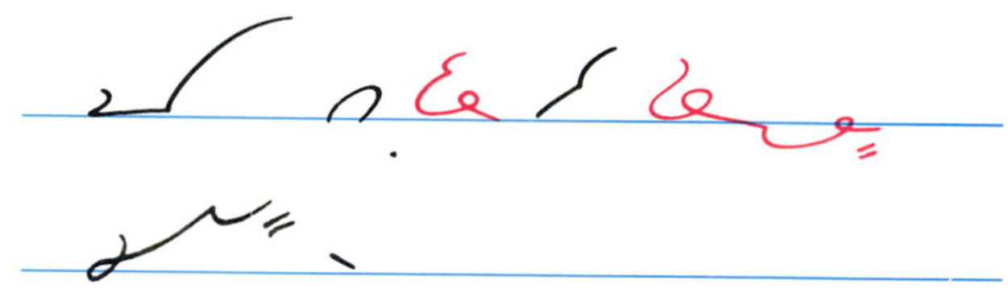

¶ **Letter**

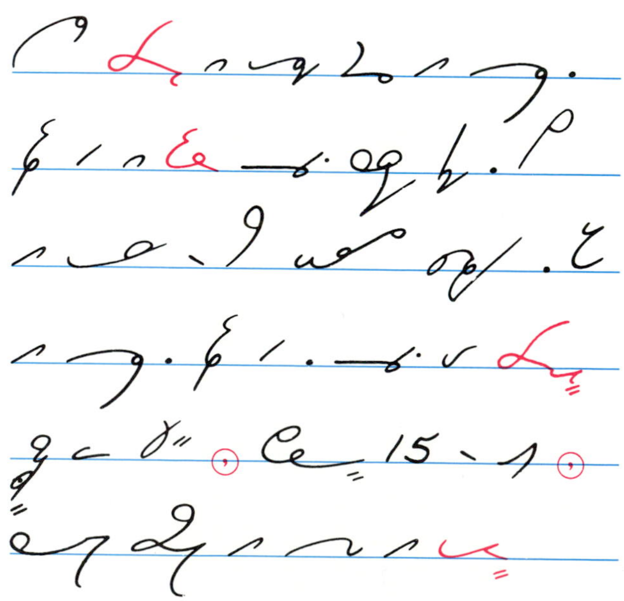

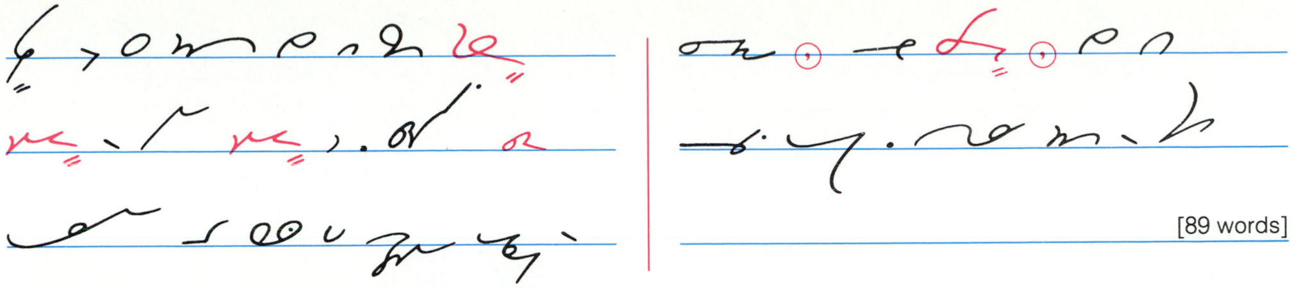

[89 words]

Communication Skill Builder

Similar Words: some, sum

some: a few; a part of

sum: a total; an amount of money

The students raised *some* concerns about the test.

Please send me *some* forms.

Mark received a large *sum* of money.

Reading and Writing Practice

32.4 Dictation Speed Letter

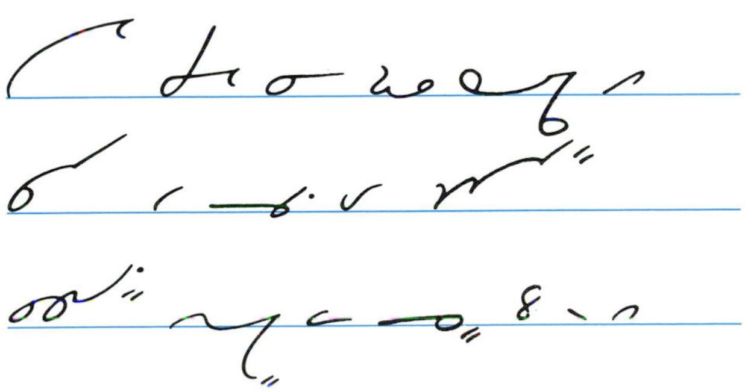

1 organization 2 however

[64 words]

32.5 Student Note

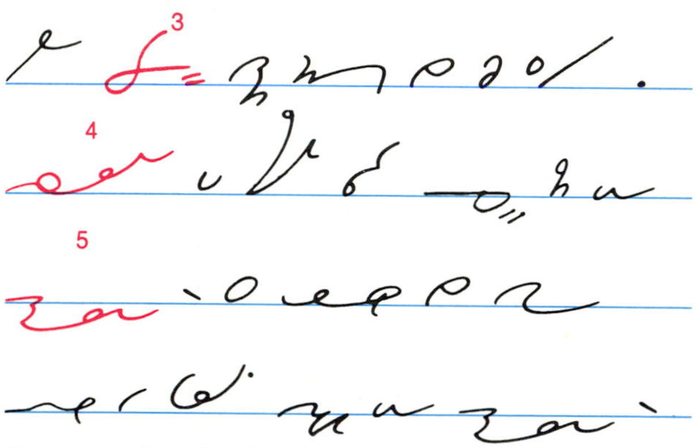

3 Pam 4 calendar 5 newsletter

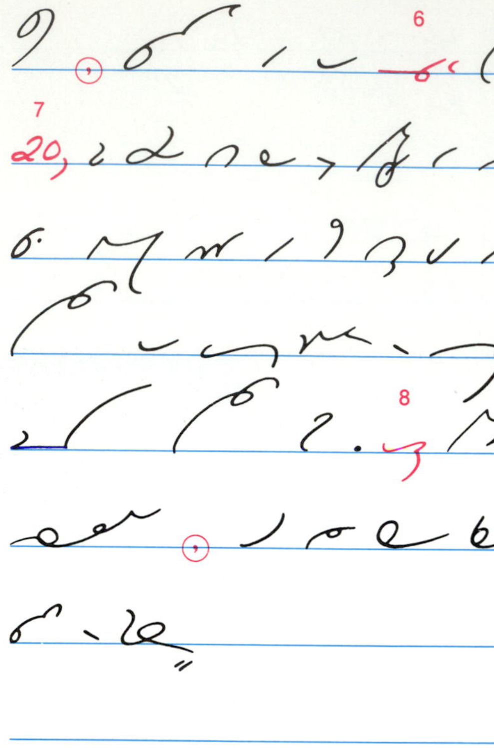

[84 words]

6 meetings 7 20 percent 8 rough

UNIT IX

LESSON 33

NEW IN LESSON 33

- **Word endings *-ition* and *-ation***
- **Word ending *-hood***
- **Symbol for the sound of *ul***
- **Shorthand as an aid to research**

WORD ENDINGS -ITION, -ATION

The circle vowel sounds *a* and *e* are omitted between *t*, *d*, *n*, *m* and the word ending *-tion*. The following eight word endings are thus abbreviated: *-tition*, *-tation*, *-dition*, *-dation*, *-nition*, *-nation*, *-mition*, and *-mation*.

Example: condition

-ition, -ation Words

condition	invitation	permission ■ ■
conditions	station	donation
conditional	stationed	automation
addition	presentation ■	information
additional	reputation	accommodation
edition	admission ■ ■	repetition

■ Brief-form derivative.

■ ■ Although *admission* and *permission* end in *-mission, -mission* has the same sound as *-mition* words and the same rule applies.

-ition, -ation Practice

33.1

¶ **Personal Note**

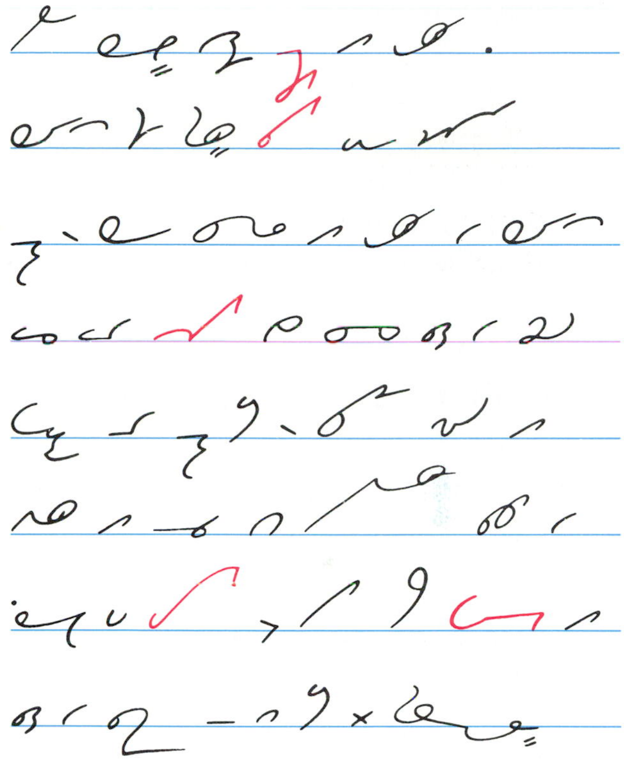

[73 words]

Secretaries are often required to attend important meetings in order to record the minutes.

WORD ENDING -HOOD

The word ending *-hood* as in *neighborhood* is represented by a disjoined *d*.

Example: neighborhood 

-hood Words

neighbor<u>hood</u>

neighbor<u>hoods</u>

boy<u>hood</u>

likeli<u>hood</u> ■

child<u>hood</u>

girl<u>hood</u>

parent<u>hood</u>

mother<u>hood</u>

father<u>hood</u>

■ Transcription Alert.

-hood Practice

33.2

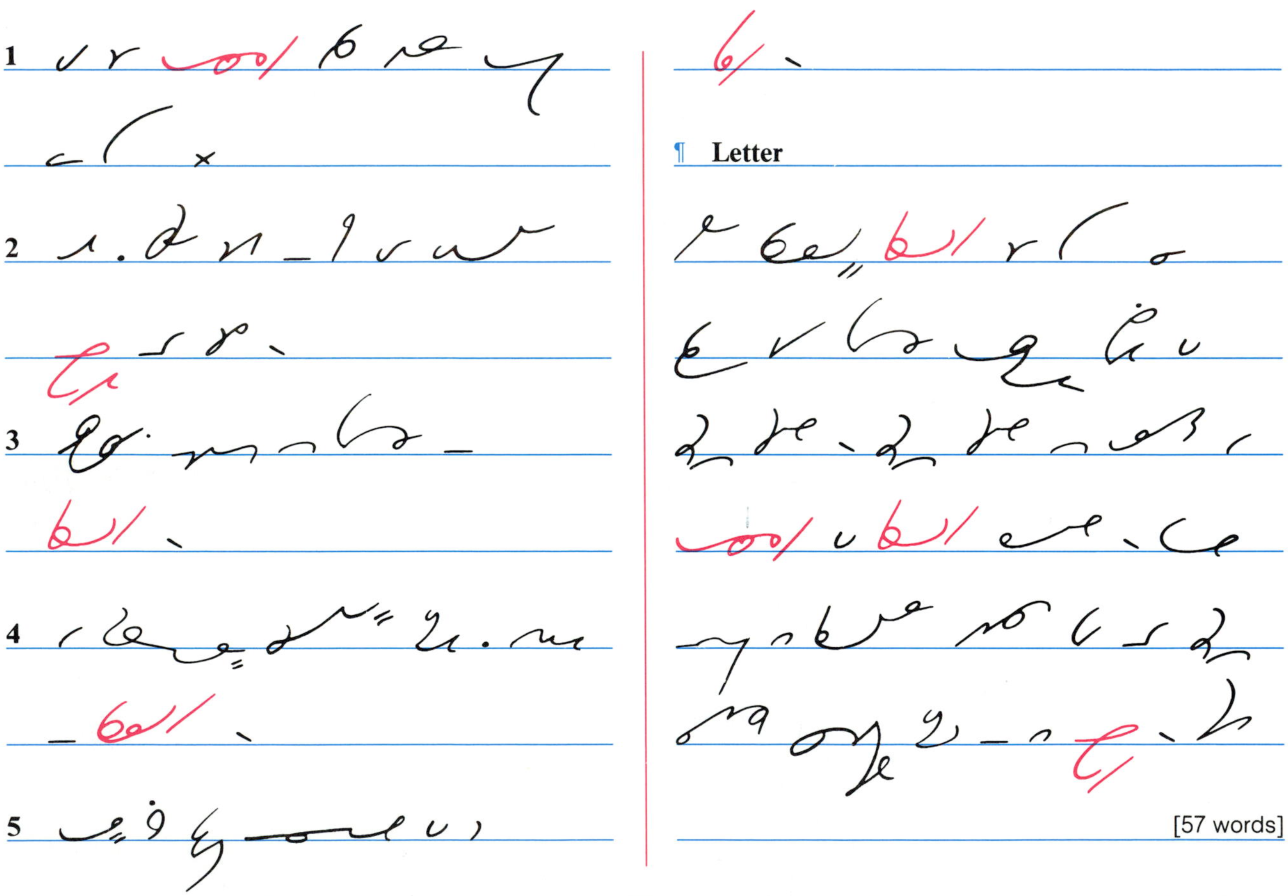

SOUND OF UL

The sound of *ul* as in *result* is represented by the *oo* symbol.

Example: result

Ul Words

result
results
resulted
ultimate
ultimately
consult
consulting
consultant
insult
adult
adulthood
multiply

Ul Practice

33.3

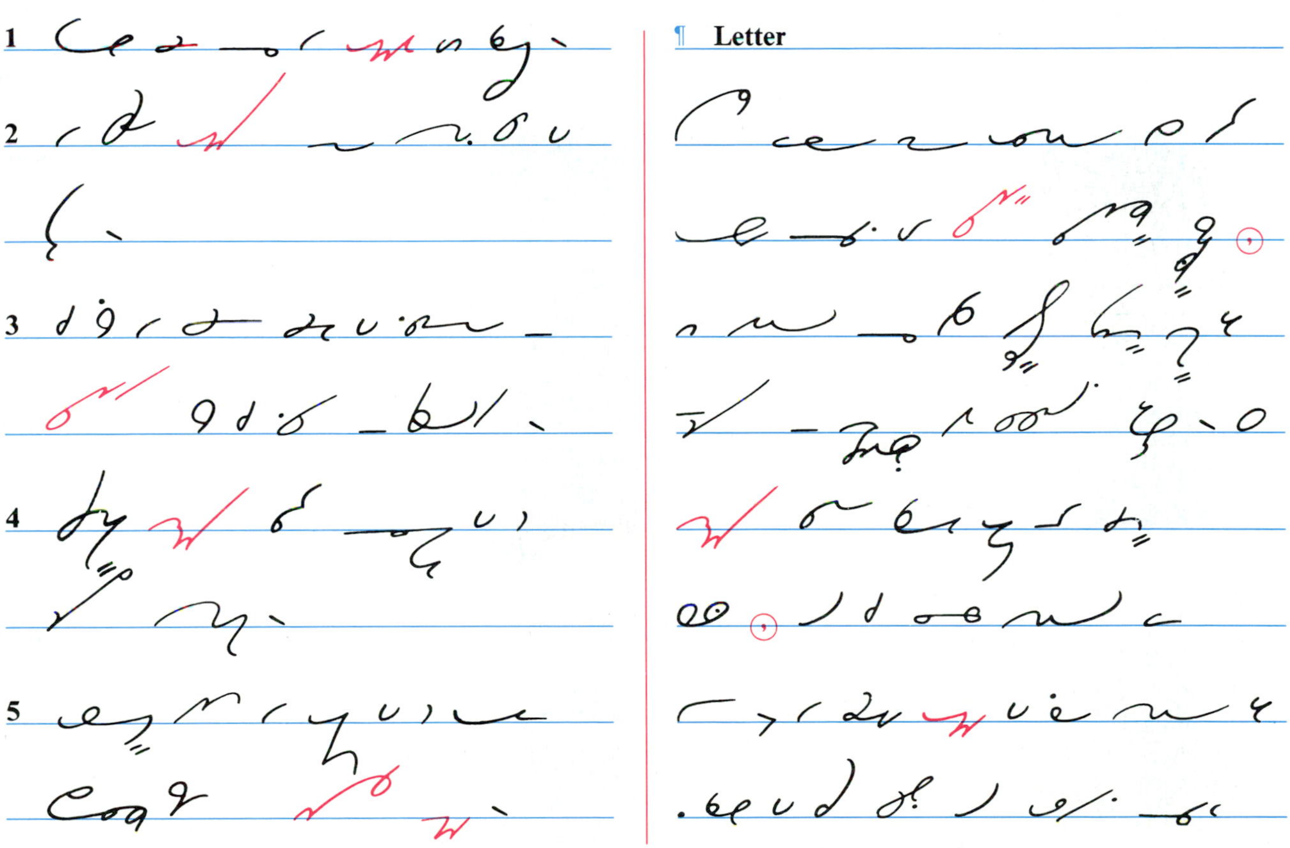

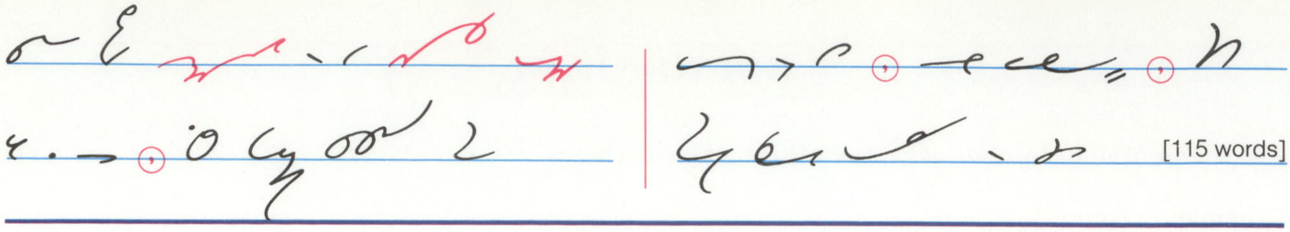

[115 words]

Using Shorthand for Research Notes

An assignment that most students face is to write a research paper based upon resources available in the library. Business people—executives and secretaries—are also called upon to prepare reports that involve extensive research. Anyone who has written such a paper knows the long hours of painstaking work that can be involved in taking longhand notes from research data. While photocopies can be made, this becomes a costly process if a great number of pages must be copied, for photocopy machines cannot edit. They copy an entire page, even though the researcher may desire to quote only a sentence or two.

The person who knows shorthand has an advantage when it comes to taking research notes. Data can be quickly scanned, with major points noted in shorthand. Crucial data and quotations that support those major points are also easily noted in shorthand. Since shorthand can be written at a speed several times that of longhand, it can easily cut research time in half. Virtually everyone can appreciate that kind of contribution to more effective time management.

Reading and Writing Practice

33.4 Dictation Speed Letter

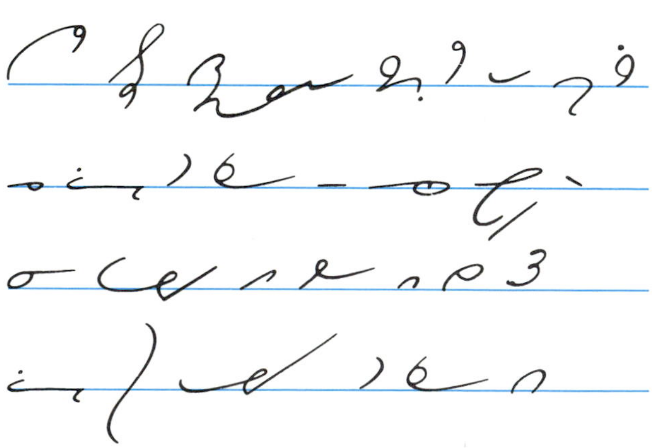

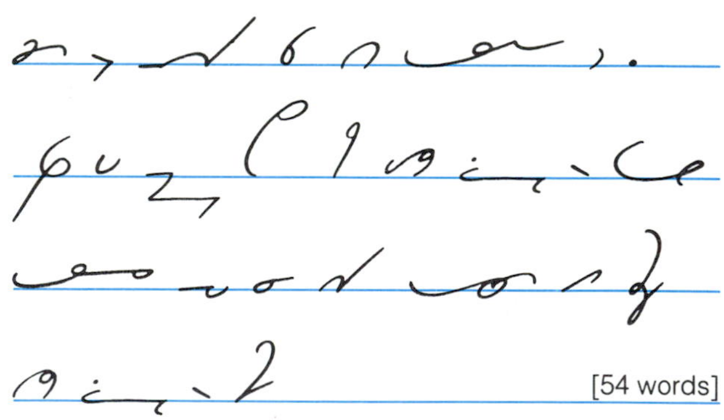

[54 words]

33.5 Business Letter

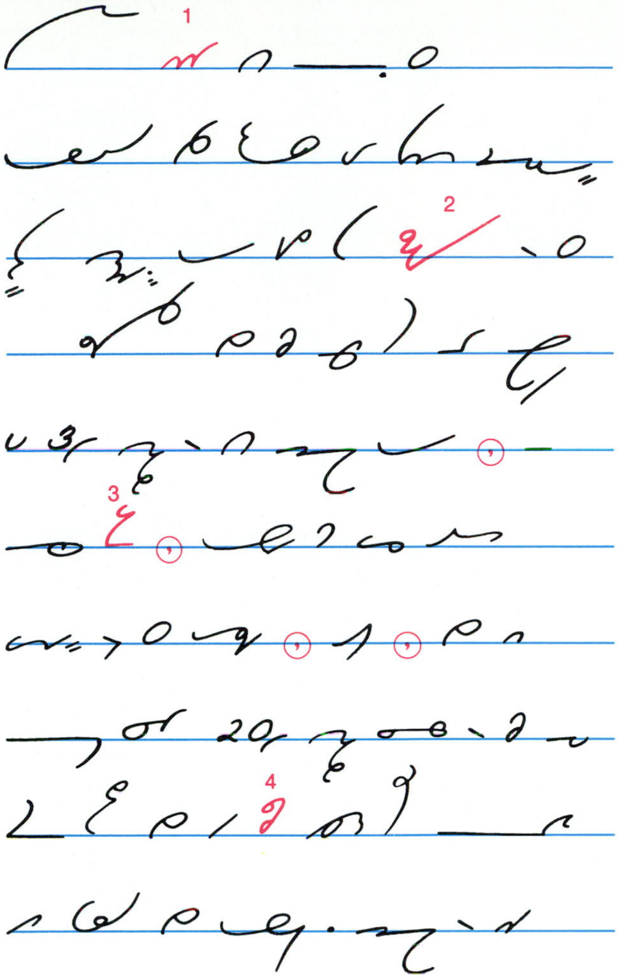

[87 words]

1 Worth   2 exhausted   3 opinion   4 usually

33.6 Agenda for Meeting

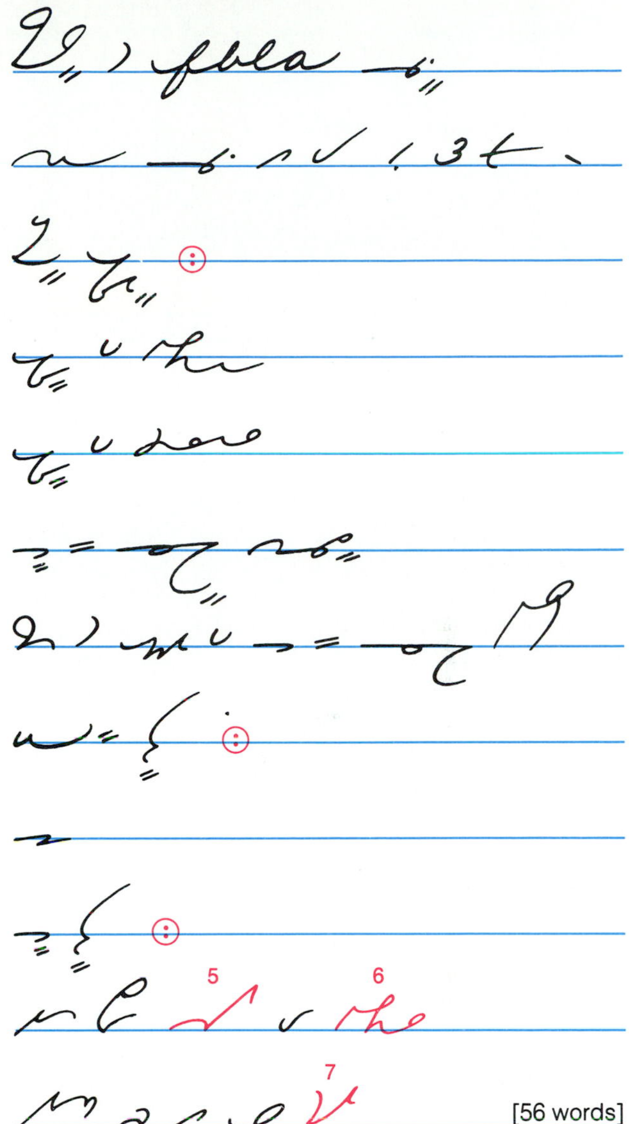

[56 words]

5 condition   6 treasury   7 funds

LESSON 34

NEW IN LESSON 34

- Eight brief forms
- Symbols for the sounds of *ern, erm*
- Word endings *-titute* and *-titude*
- Differentiating between *know* and *no*

BRIEF FORMS

quantity

appropriate ■

executive

wish

object

subject

particular ■

program

■ Transcription Alert.

Brief-Form Derivatives

quantities

appropriately

appropriation

executives

wishes

wished

wishful

objects

objected

objection

objective

subjects

subjected

particularly

programs

programmed

programmer

programming

Brief-Form Practice
34.1

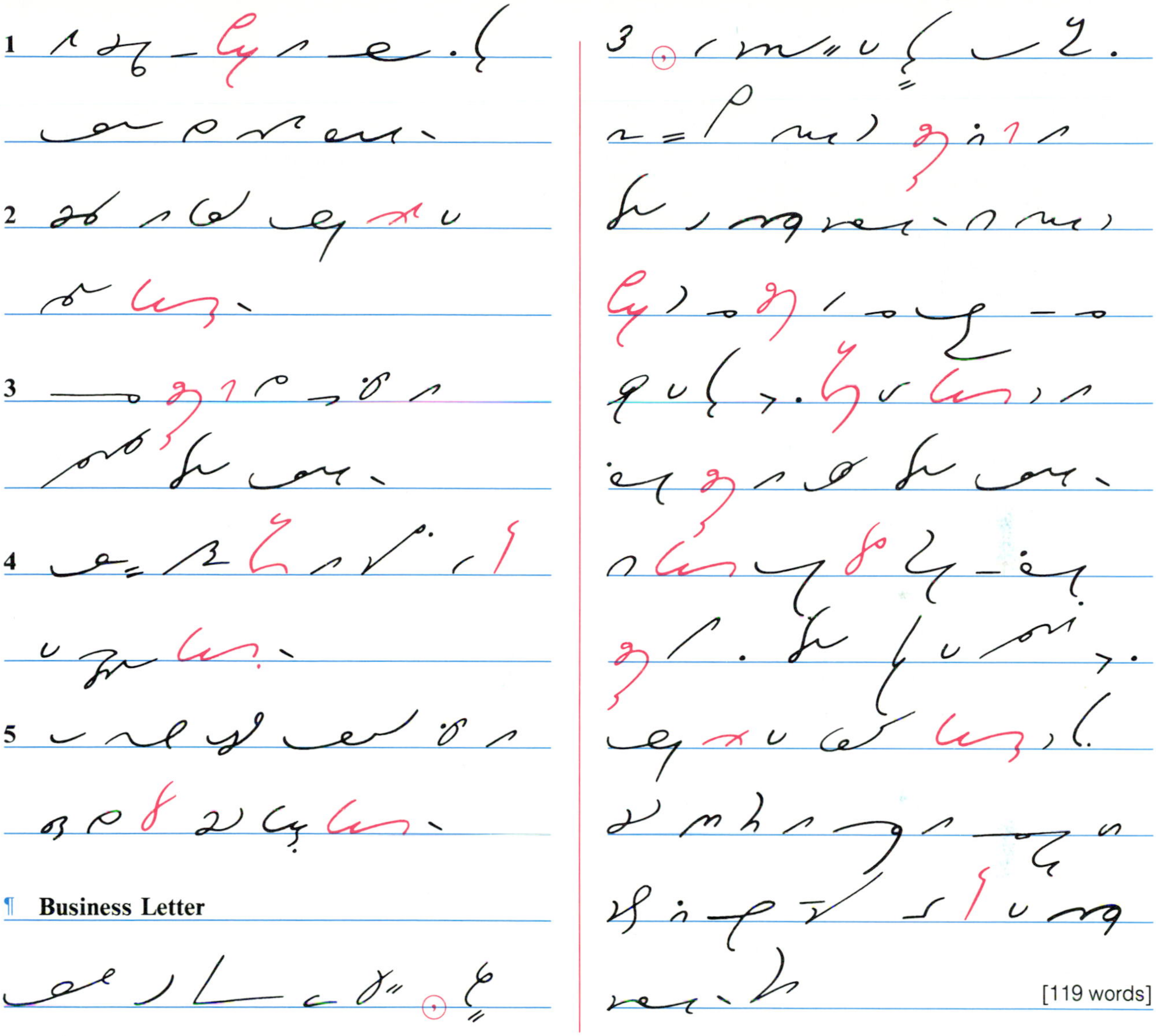

SOUNDS OF ERN, ERM

The sounds of *ern* and *erm* as in *eastern* and *determine* are abbreviated by the deletion of the *r* symbol.

Examples: turn  term 

Ern, Erm Words

turn	modern	terminal
turns	southern	termination
return	alternate	determine
returning	alternated	determined
eastern	alternative	determination
western	term	thermometer

Ern, Erm Practice

34.2

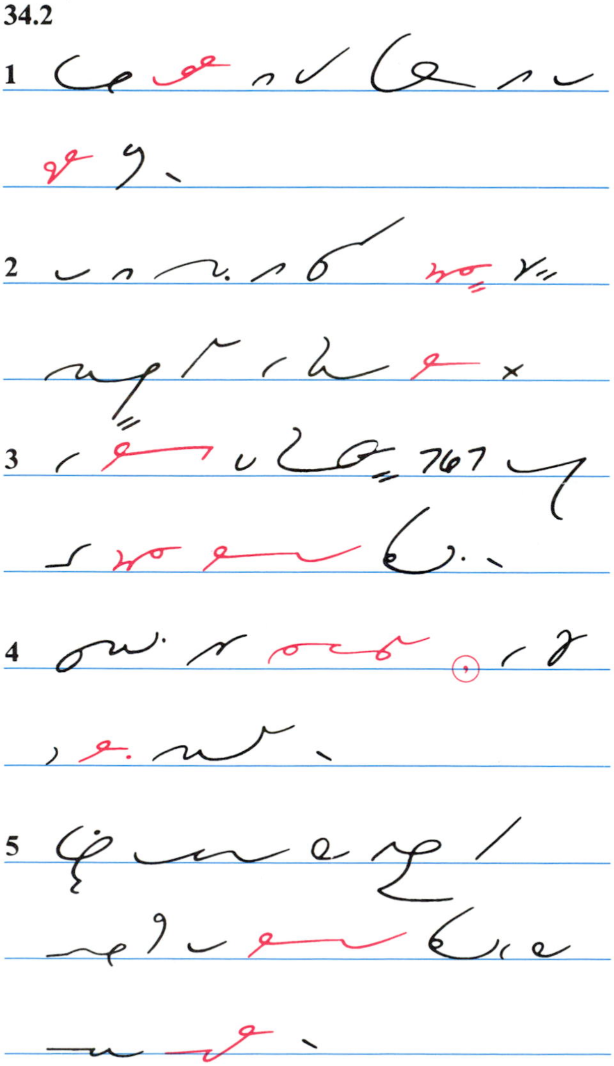

¶ **Business Note**

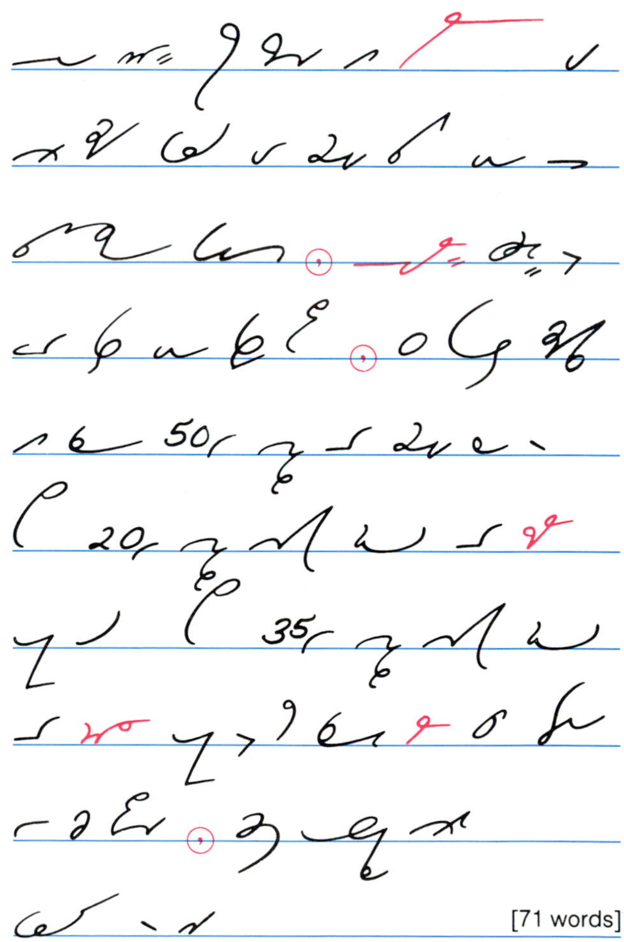

[71 words]

WORD ENDINGS -TITUTE, -TITUDE

The word endings *-titute* and *-titude* as in *institute* and *gratitude* are abbreviated *t e t*.

-titute, -titude

Examples: institute gratitude

-titute, -titude Words

institute	constitute	aptitude
instituted	constitution	attitude
institution	gratitude	attitudes

-titute, -titude Practice

34.3

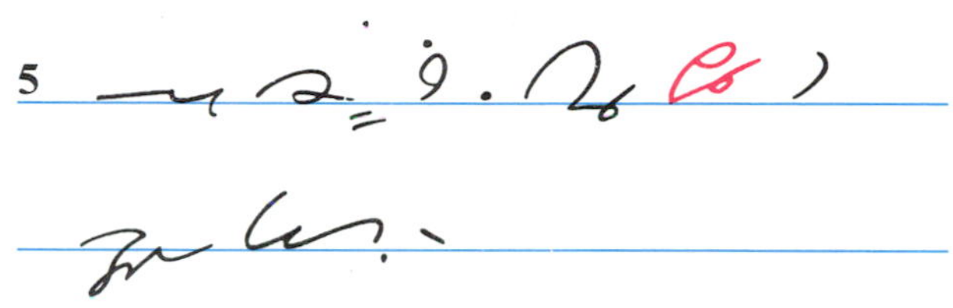

¶ **Personal Note**

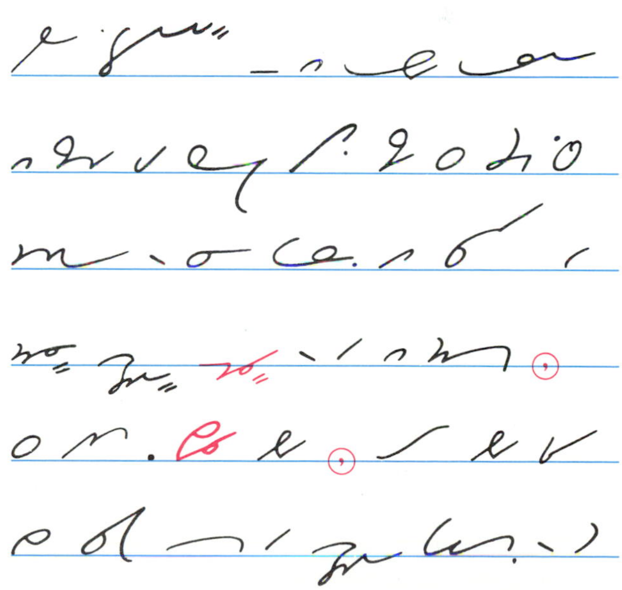

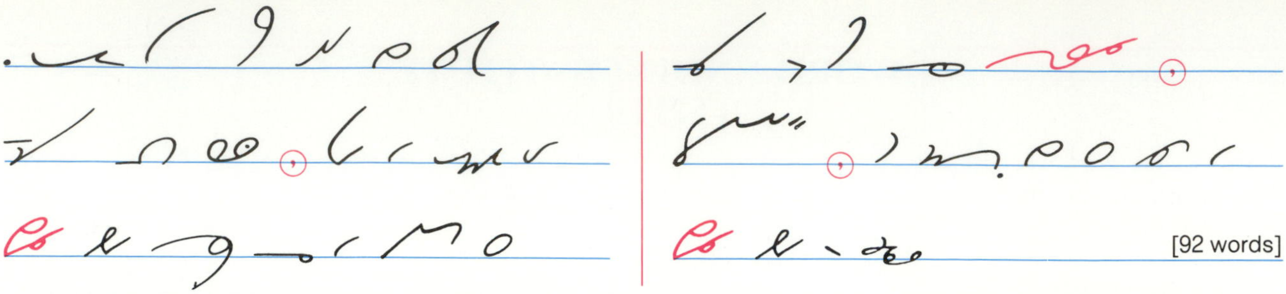

[92 words]

Communication Skill Builder

Similar Words: know, no

know: to have knowledge

no: not any

Floyd does not *know* that typing class has been canceled.

There will be *no* typing class on Wednesday.

Reading and Writing Practice

34.4 Dictation Speed Message

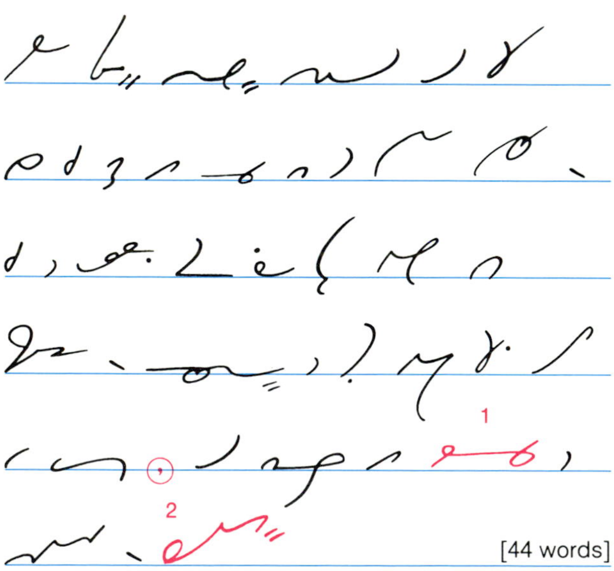

[44 words]

1 terminate 2 Andrew

34.5 Business Letter

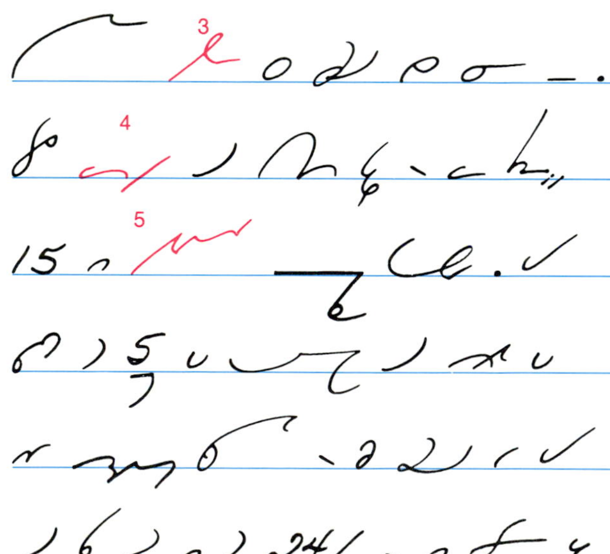

3 Dixon 4 awkward 5 district

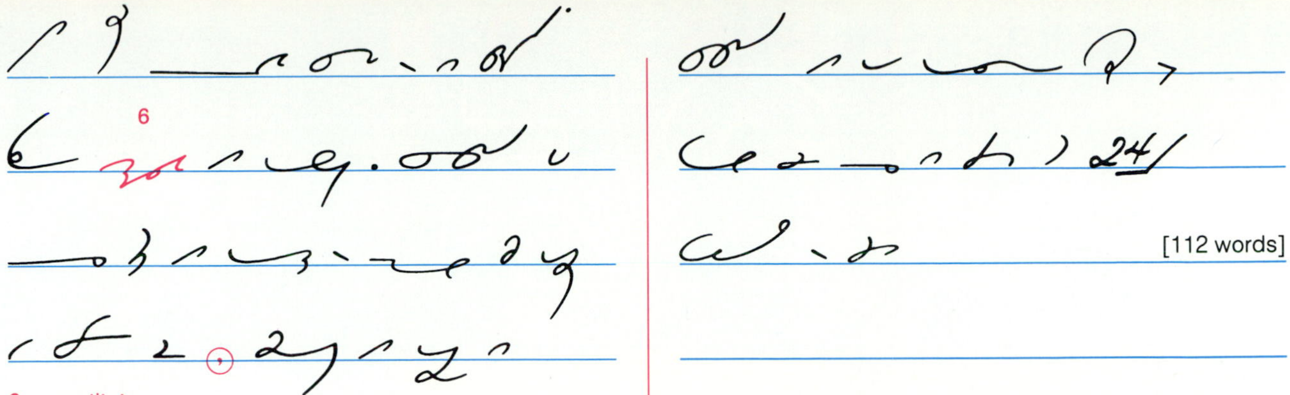

6 constitutes

[112 words]

LESSON 35

NEW IN LESSON 35

- Minor vowels omitted
- Word beginnings *ah-* and *aw-*
- Word ending *-ingly*
- Differentiating between *principle* and *principal*

MINOR VOWELS OMITTED

When two vowels occur together, such as the *e us* sounds in *previous*, the minor vowel may be omitted.

Example: previous

Minor-Vowel-Omitted Words

previous	seriously	situated
previously	period	situation
various	genuine	continue
serious	theory	continues

Minor-Vowel-Omitted Practice

35.1

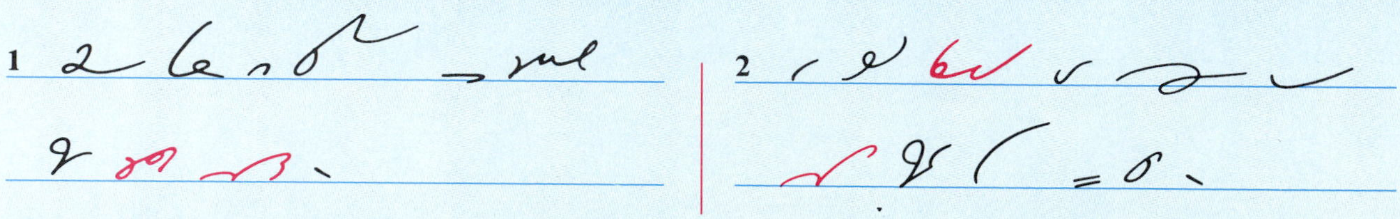

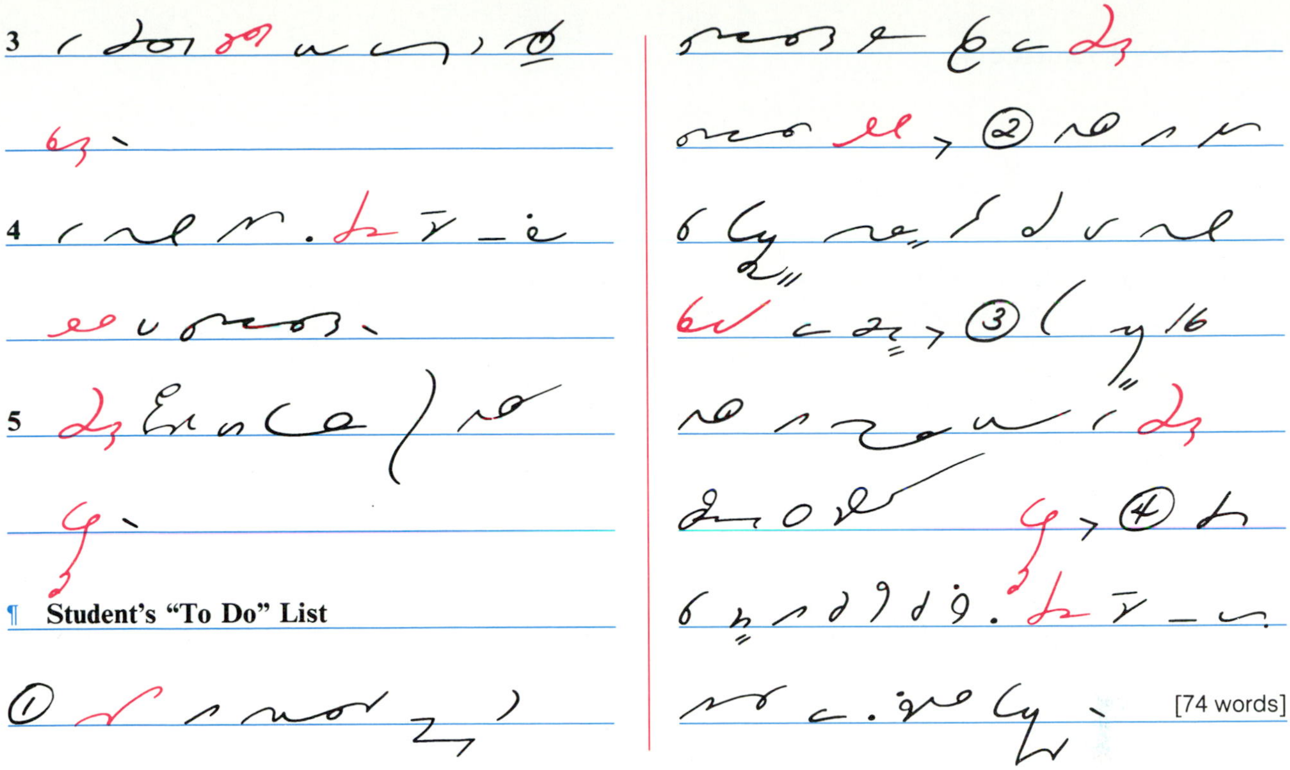

WORD BEGINNINGS AH-, AW-

In the word beginnings *ah-* and *aw-*, the sound of *a* is represented by a dot (the same as the brief form *a*).

Examples: ahead away

Ah-, Aw- Words

ahead	awaken	aware
away	await	award
awake	awaits	awards

Ah-, Aw- Practice
35.2

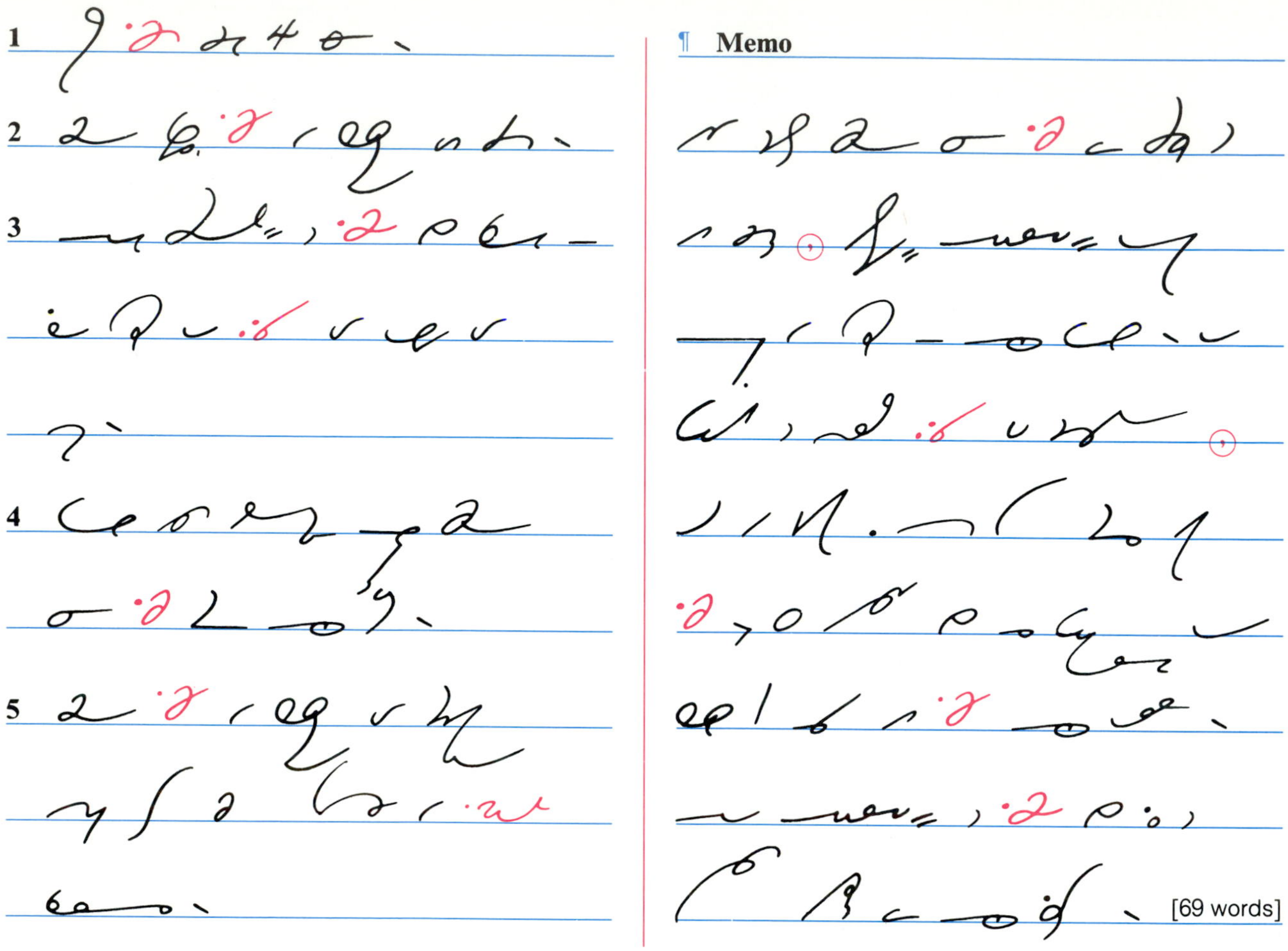

WORD ENDING -INGLY

The word ending *-ingly* as in *knowingly* is represented by a disjoined *-ly* circle.

Example: knowingly

-ingly Words

knowingly 
increasingly 
interestingly 
willingly 
exceedingly 
convincingly 

-ingly Practice

35.3

1 2 3 4 5

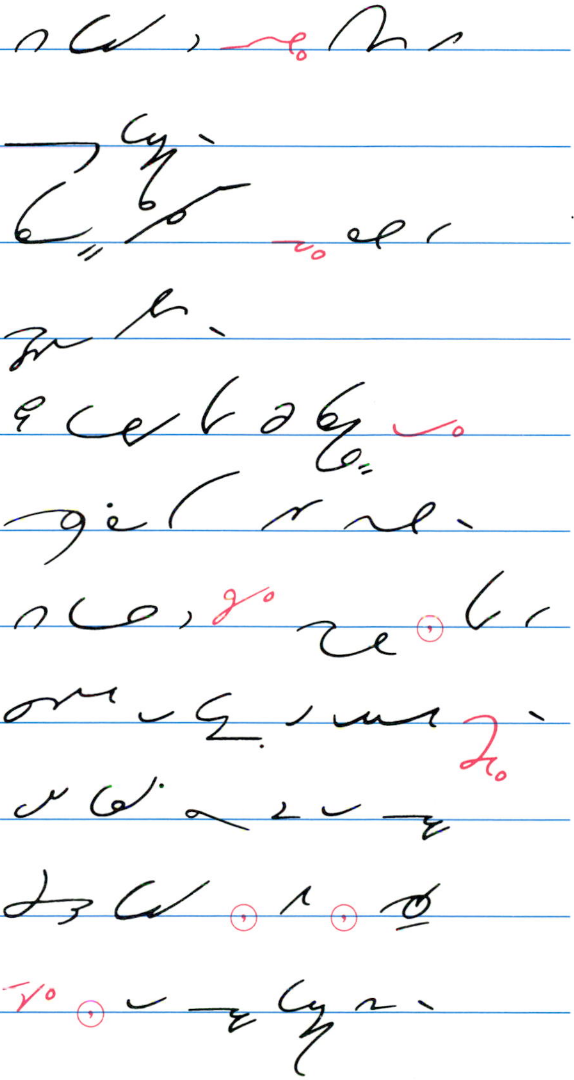

¶ **Letter**

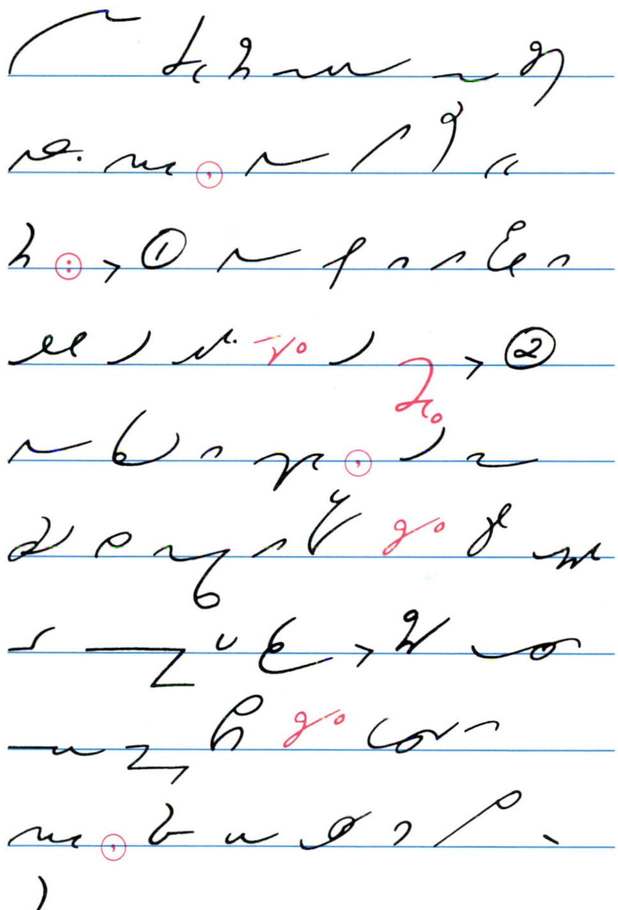

[87 words]

Communication Skill Builder

Similar Words: principle, principal

principle: a rule or fundamental belief

principal: (n.) sum of money that earns interest; chief official of a school; (adj.) chief

She believes in the *principle* of free speech.

Your loan payment equals *principal* plus interest.

Her father was the *principal* of the high school.

Leo will be the *principal* actor in the play.

Reading and Writing Practice

35.4 Dictation Speed Letter

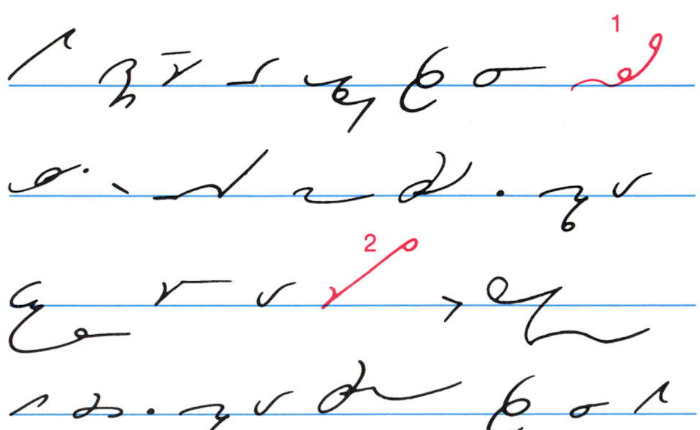

1 currently 2 study

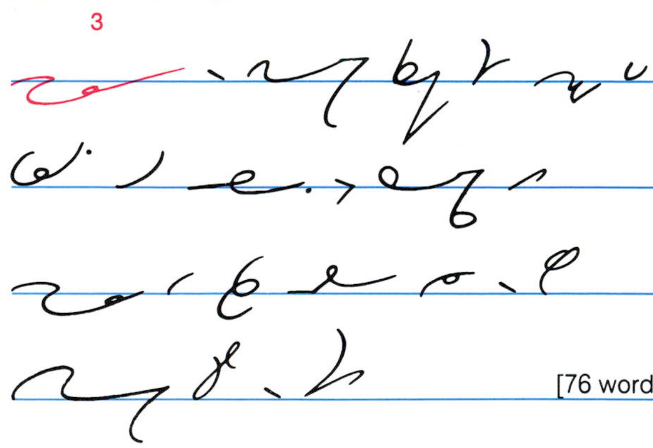

[76 words]

3 completed

35.5 Business Letter

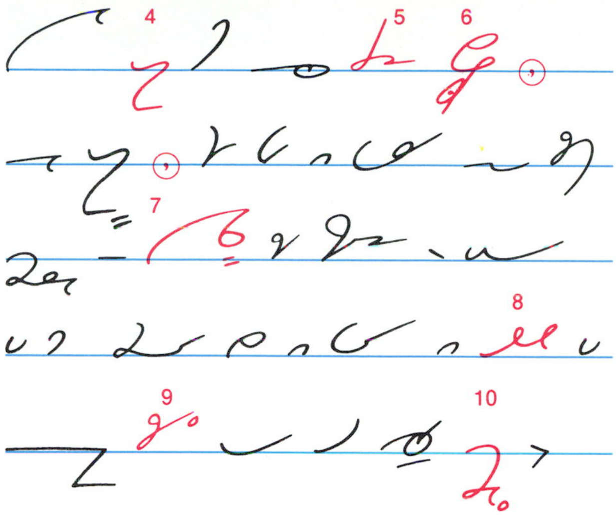

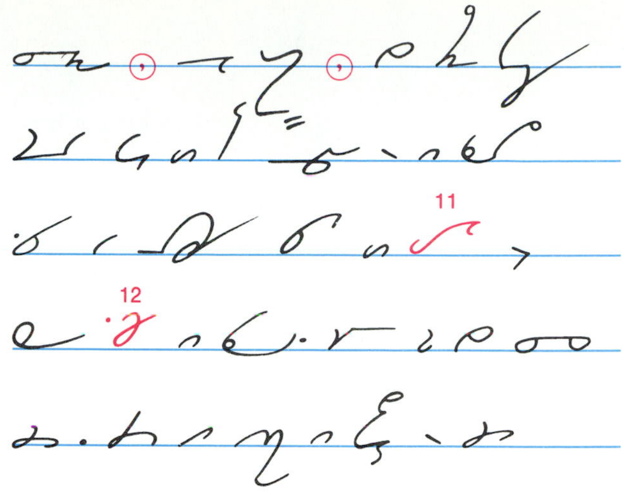

[100 words]

4 Rubin 5 genuine 6 appreciation 7 Tampa
8 theories 9 exceedingly 10 convincingly

11 audience 12 await

An executive may leave a meeting in order to dictate information that must be transcribed and brought back into the meeting.

LESSON 36

NEW IN LESSON 36

- Six brief forms
- Word beginning *super-*
- Word ending *-ulate*
- Word ending *-quent*
- Differentiating between *advise* and *advice*

BRIEF FORMS

reluctant, reluctance

anniversary

public

next

incorporate

convenient, convenience ■

■ Transcription Alert.

Brief-Form Derivatives

reluctantly

incorporated

inconvenient

publicly

conveniently

inconvenience

Brief-Form Phrases

next time

next year

next month

Brief-Form Practice

36.1

1 2 3 4 5

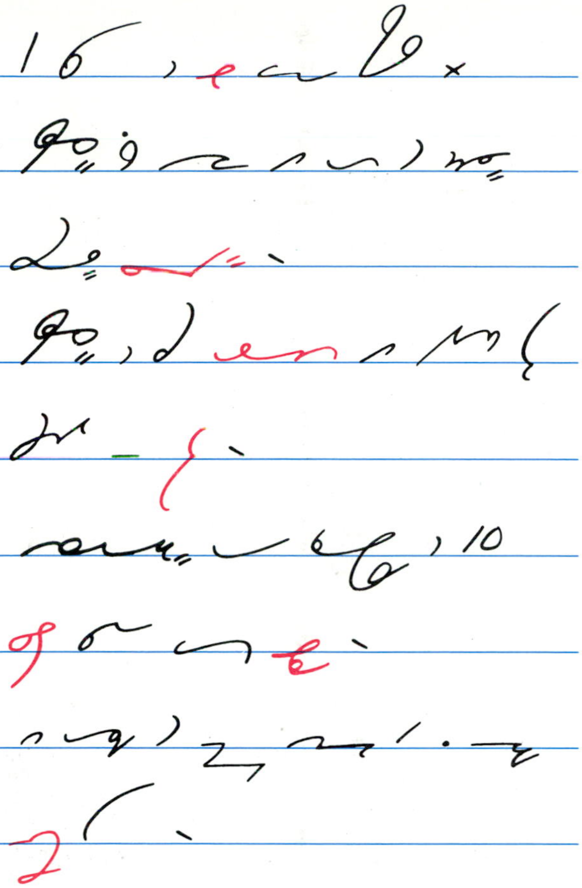

¶ **Personal Letter**

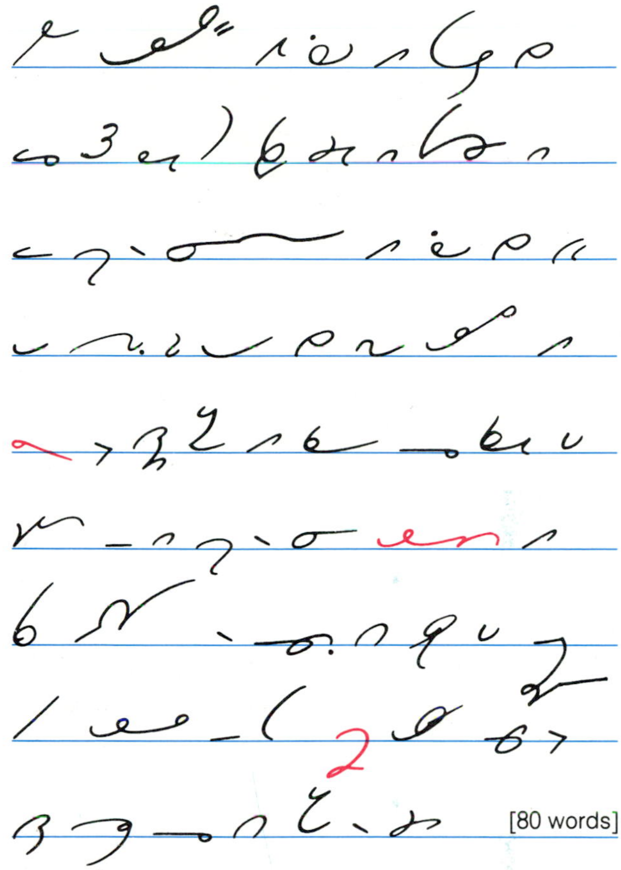

[80 words]

WORD BEGINNING SUPER-

The word beginning *super-* as in *supervise* is written with a disjoined comma *s*.

Example: supervise 

Super- Words

supervise 

supervision 

superintendent 

supervised 

supervises 

superior 

supervisor 

supersede ■ 

superb 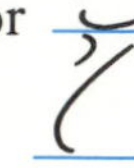

■ Transcription Alert.

Super- Practice

36.2

1 2 3 4 5

¶ **Personal Note**

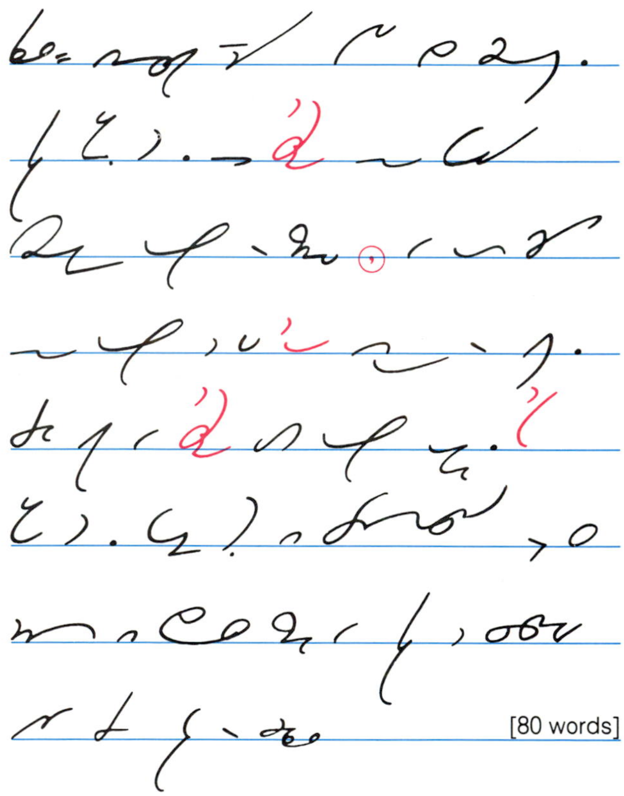

[80 words]

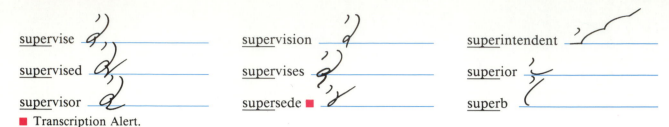

WORD ENDING -ULATE

The word ending *-ulate* as in *congratulate* is represented by a disjoined *oo* and is written close to the last symbol. The word ending *-ulation* is represented by the disjoined *oo* and *ish.*

Examples: congratulate congratulations

-ulate Words

congratulate

congratulations

regulate

regulates

regulation

circulate

circulation

calculate

calculations

calculator

formulate

formulated

-ulate Practice

36.3

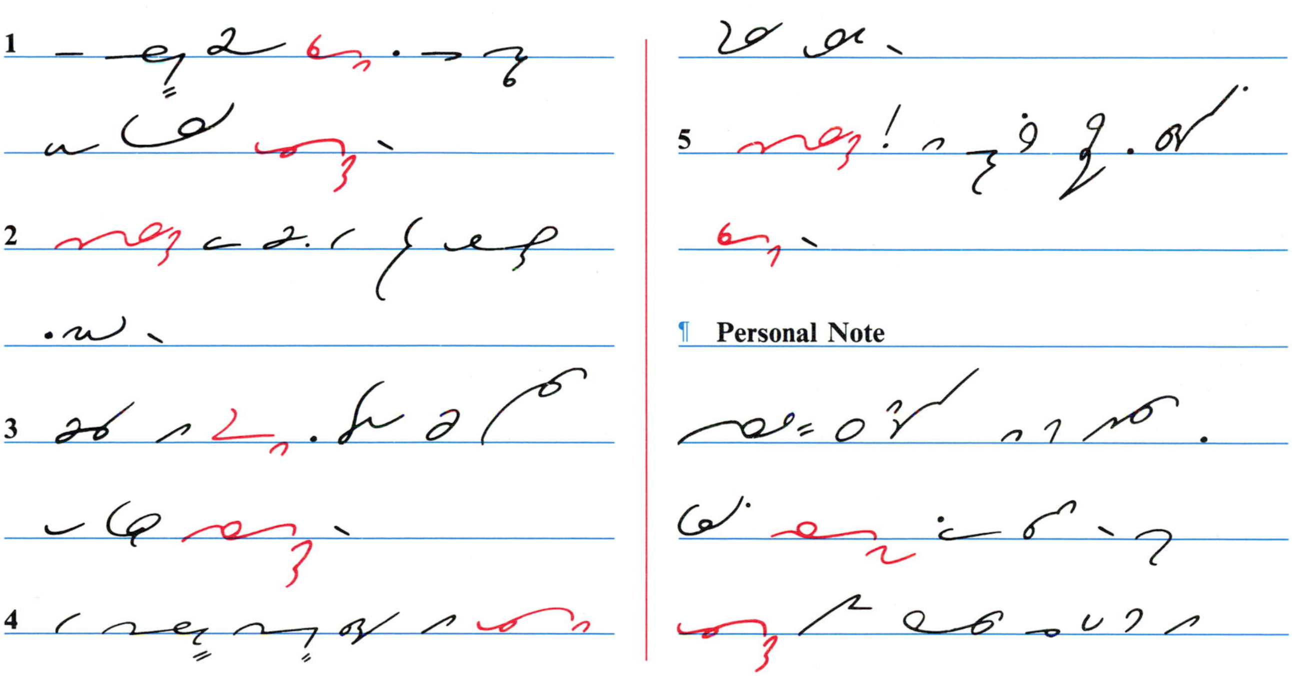

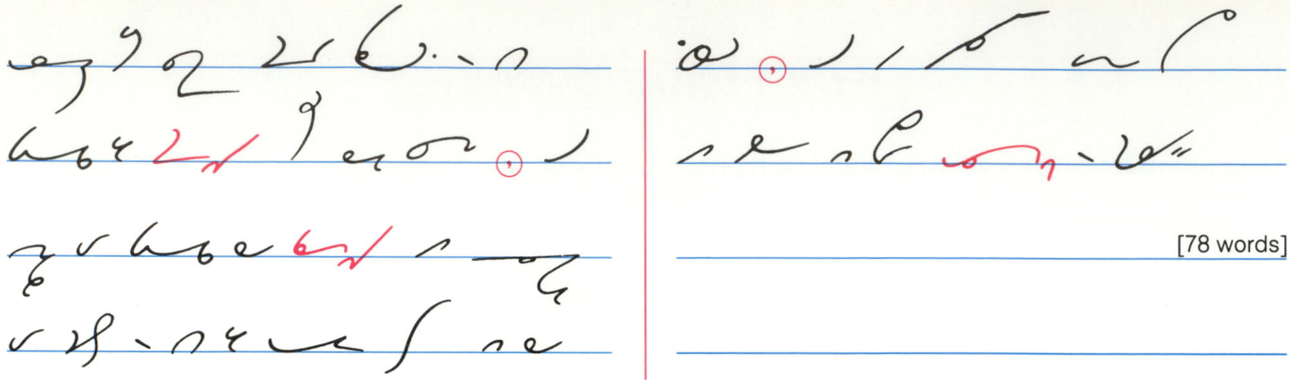

[78 words]

WORD ENDING -QUENT

The word ending *-quent* as in *frequent* is represented by a joined *k*.

-quent 

Example: frequent 

-quent Words

frequent 

frequently 

frequency 

consequent, consequence 

consequently 

eloquent 

-quent Practice

36.4

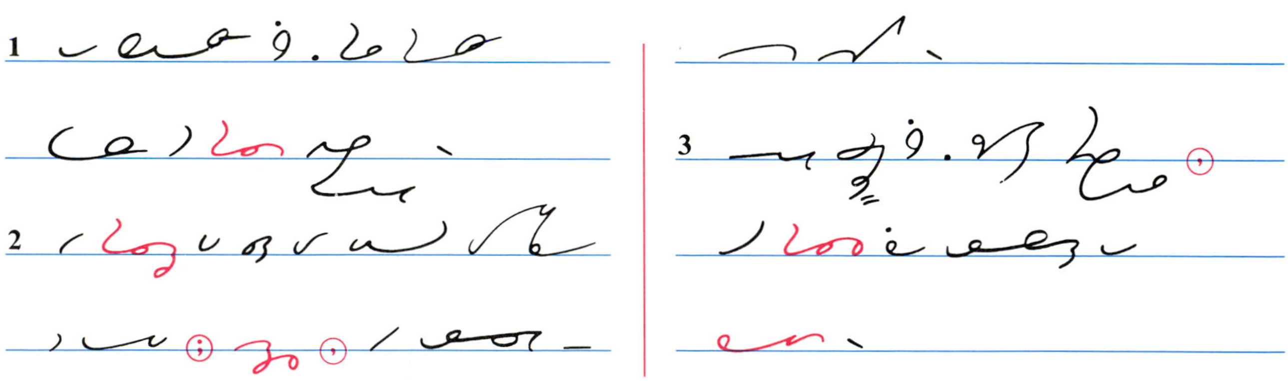

4

5

¶ Letter

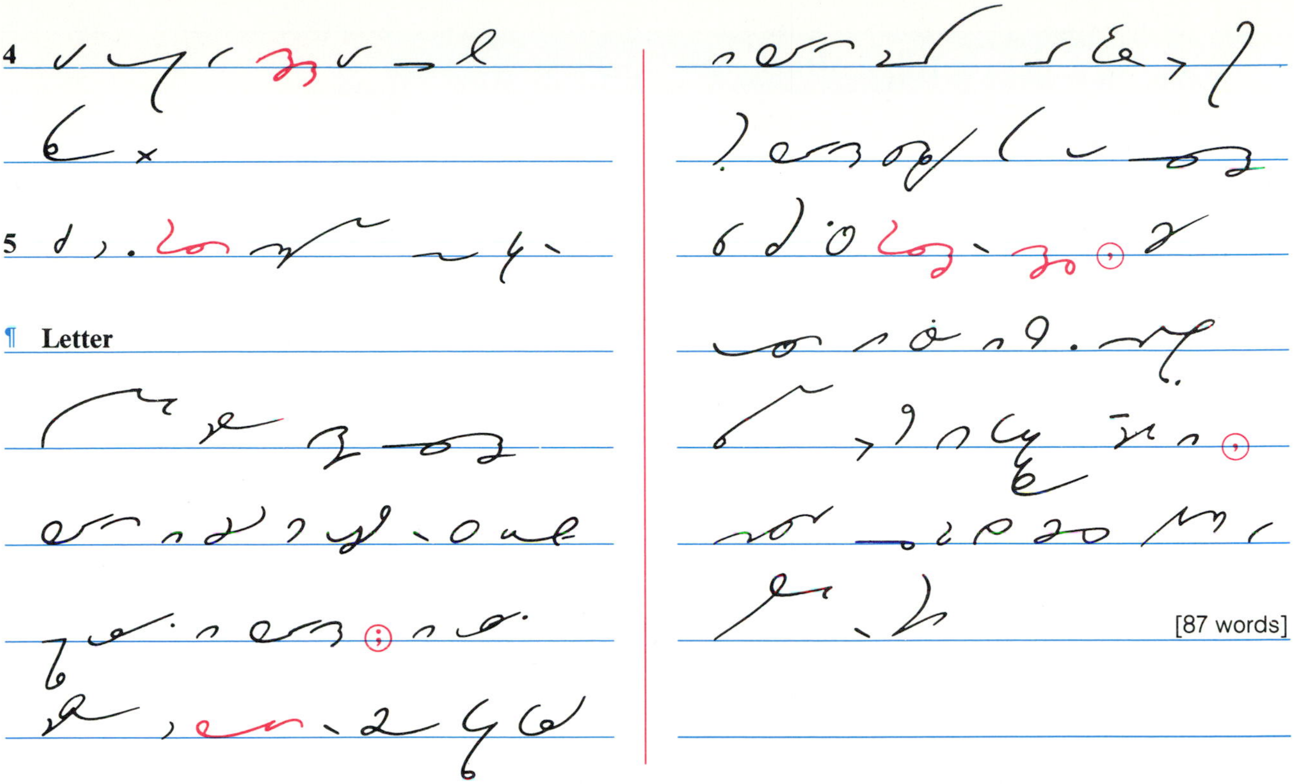

[87 words]

Shorthand enables a busy executive to single out important points during a business meeting.

Communication Skill Builder

Similar Words: advise, advice

advise: (v.) to inform; to give counsel

advice: (n.) information; recommendation

Please *advise* me about your discount policy.

Thank you for giving me *advice* about my career.

Reading and Writing Practice

36.5 Dictation Speed Note

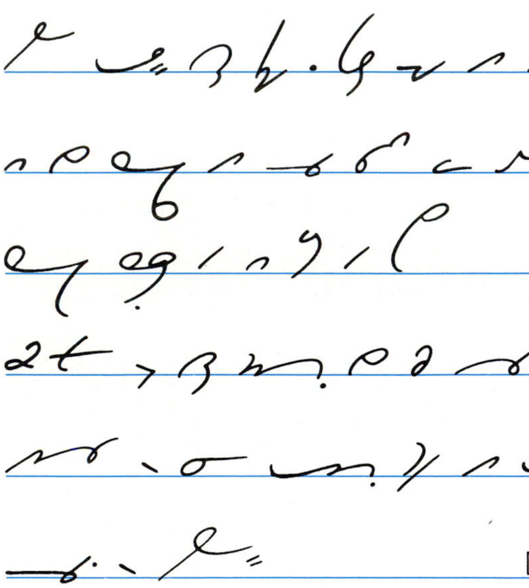

[45 words]

36.6 Business Letter

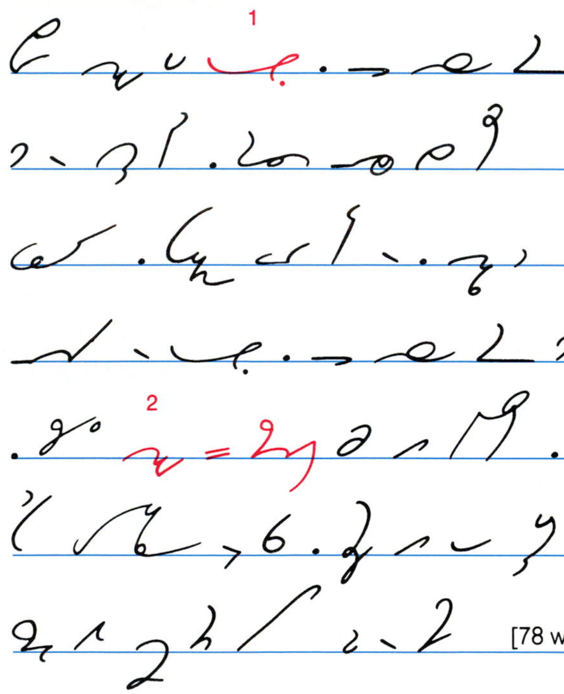

[78 words]

1 leasing 2 cost-effective

UNIT X

LESSON 37

NEW IN LESSON 37

- Word ending *-ship*
- Word beginnings *im-* and *em-*
- Word beginning *trans-*
- Shorthand and the immediate deadline

WORD ENDING -SHIP

The word ending *-ship* as in *leadership* is represented by a disjoined *ish* and is written close to the last symbol in the root word.

Example: leadership 

-ship Words

leader<u>ship</u>	author<u>ship</u>	relation<u>ships</u>
owner<u>ship</u>	member<u>ship</u>	fellow<u>ship</u>
friend<u>ship</u>	relation<u>ship</u>	steam<u>ship</u>

-ship Practice

37.1

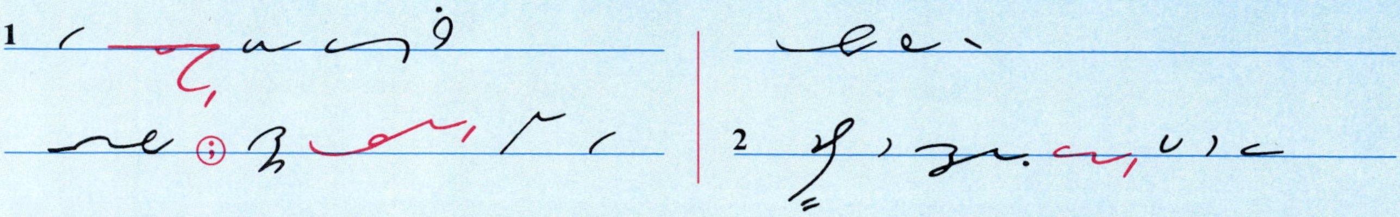

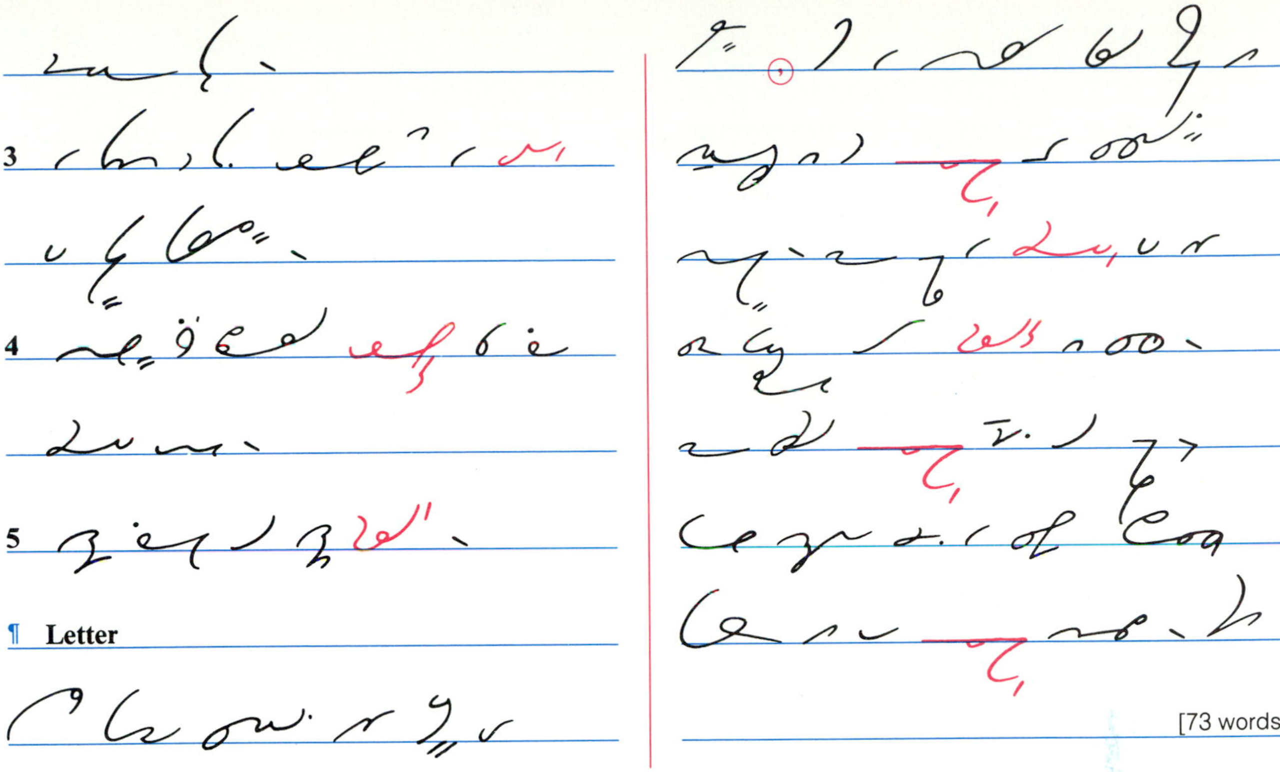

[73 words]

WORD BEGINNINGS IM-, EM-

The word beginnings *im-* and *em-* as in *import* and *empire* are represented by the *m* symbol.

Examples: import  empire 

Im- Words

import 
imports 
impress 
impressed 
impressive 
improve 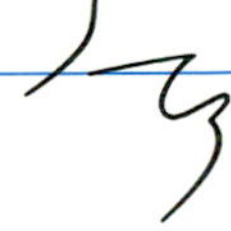
improvement 
impact 
impartial 

Em- Words

empire	**em**ployment	**em**ployees
employ	**em**ploys	**em**barrass
employed	**em**ployee	**em**phatically

But: *Im-* and *em-* are written in full when followed by a vowel.

immodest	**em**otional

Im-, Em- Practice

37.2

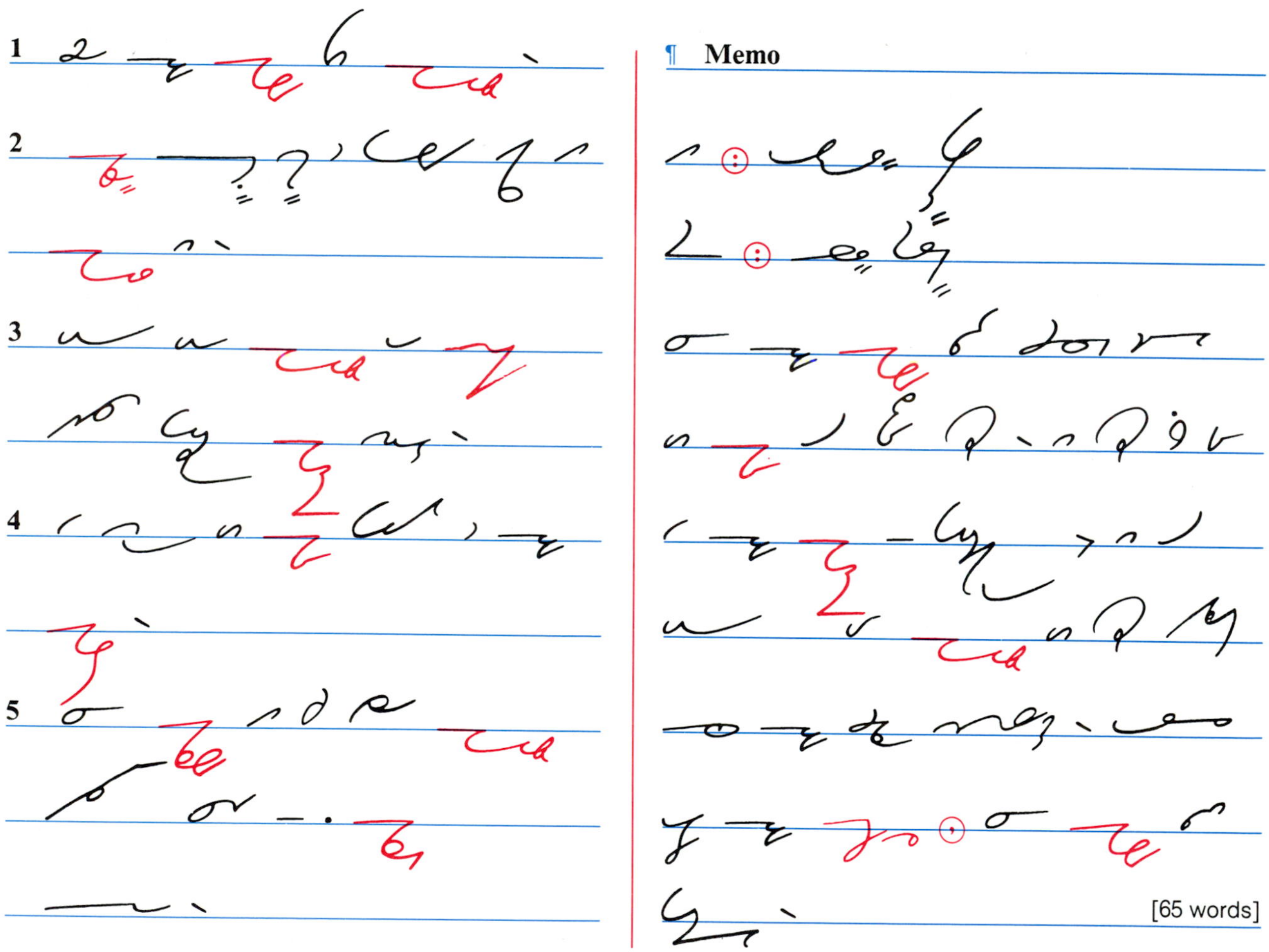

WORD BEGINNING TRANS-

The word beginning *trans-* as in *transfer* is represented by a disjoined *t*. The disjoined *t* is written in the middle of the writing line and close to the first symbol in the second outline.

Example: transfer 

Trans- Words

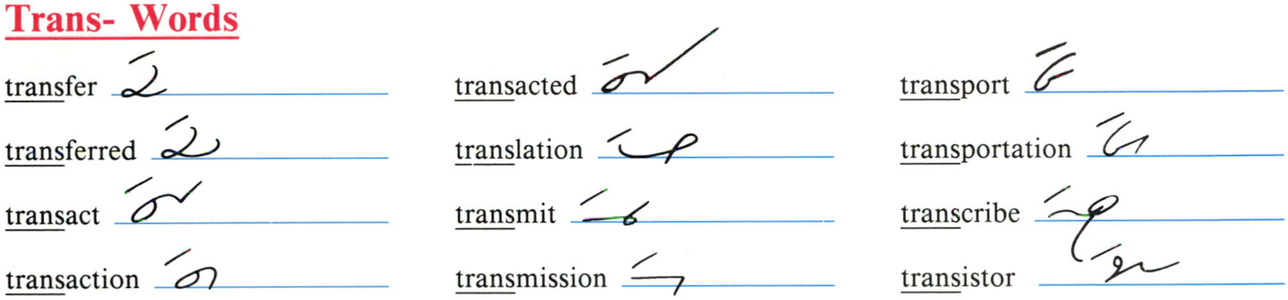

Trans- Practice

37.3

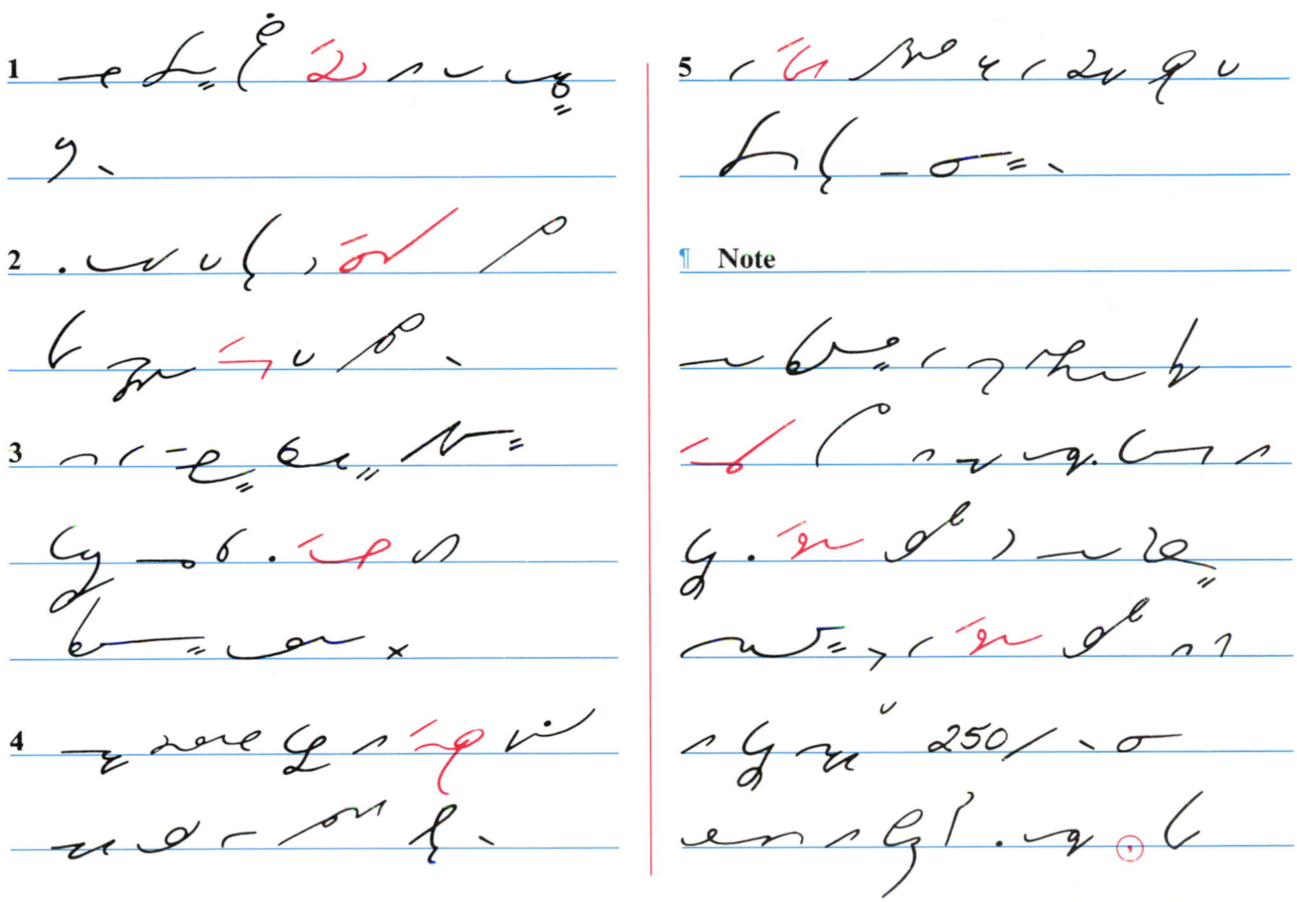

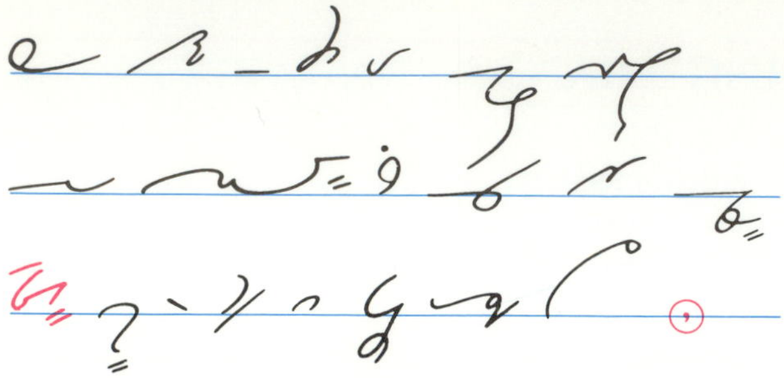

[99 words]

Shorthand and the Immediate Deadline

The concept of "turnaround time" is becoming more and more important as people are increasingly concerned with office productivity. Simply put, turnaround time is the number of minutes or hours that elapse from the time an executive finishes dictating a letter until that letter is ready for the executive's signature.

The executive who knows how to dictate and the secretary who is a good transcriber form an unbeatable team in the quest for rapid turnaround time. An executive with a private secretary knows exactly what the secretary's work priorities are. The executive with a private secretary also knows from experience what level of productivity to expect when the secretary is under pressure. No steno pool or word processing center is likely to beat the turnaround time of a private secretary who has just been told, "Take this letter in shorthand and give me a typewritten transcript now!"

Reading and Writing Practice

37.4 Dictation Speed Letter

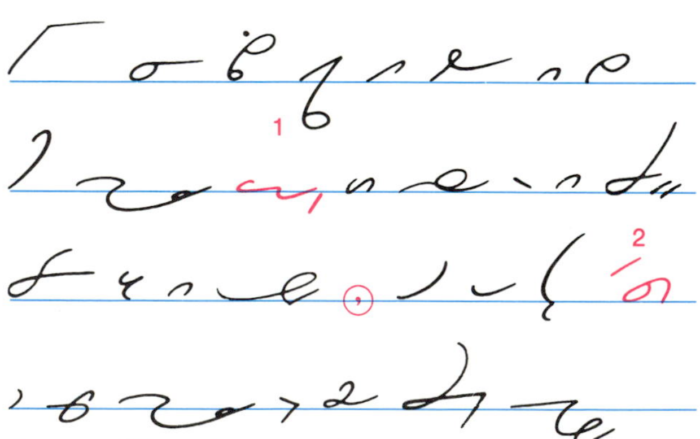

1 ownership 2 transaction

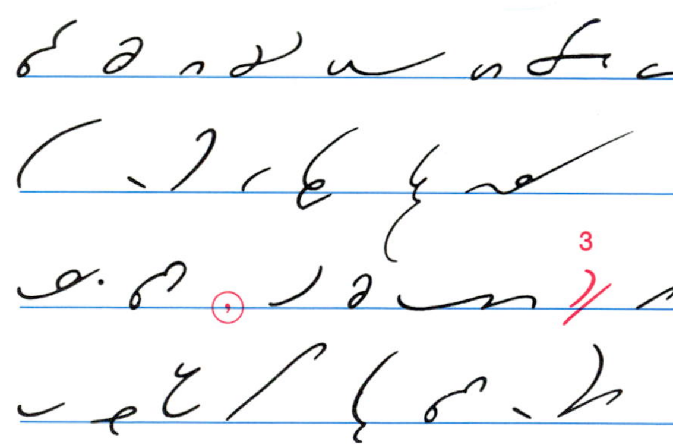

[75 words]

3 forward

37.5 Personal Letter

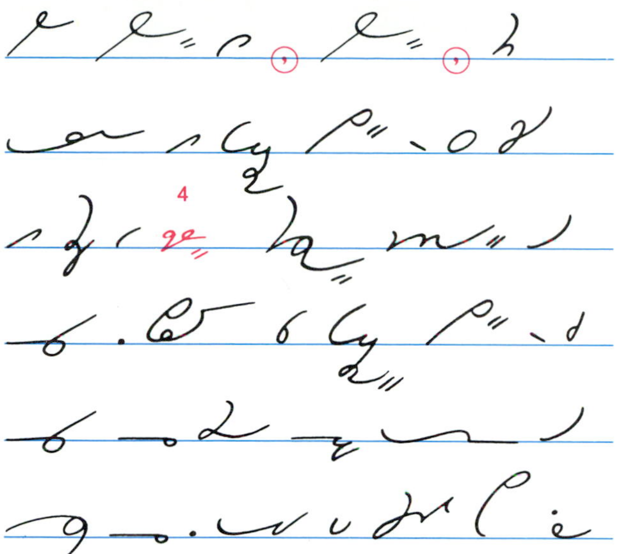

4 Eastern

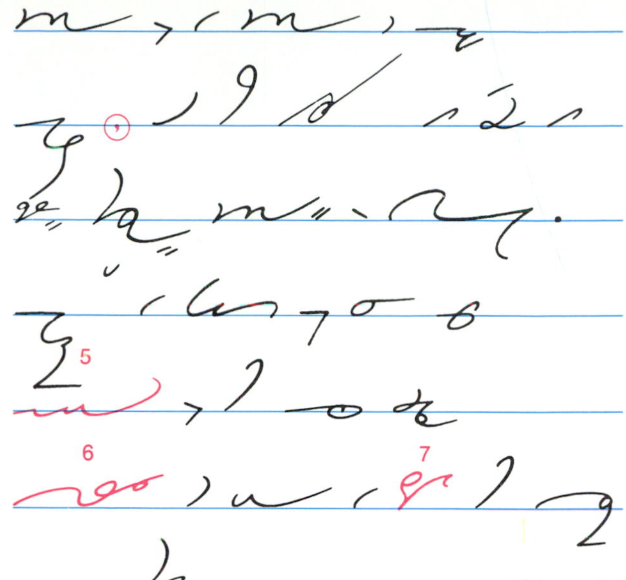

[91 words]

5 enrolled 6 gratitude 7 assistance

Shorthand skill and word processing expertise are combined to increase office productivity.

LESSON 38

NEW IN LESSON 38

- Eight brief forms
- Word ending *-ily*
- Word beginning *sub-*
- Differentiating between *piece* and *peace*

BRIEF FORMS

important, importance		memorandum	
significant, significance		equivalent	
speak		world	
idea		electric	

Brief-Form Derivatives

significantly		ideas ■	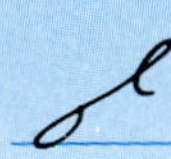	electronic	
speaks		worldwide	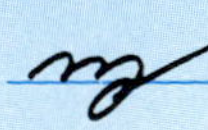	electronically	
speakers		electrical		electricity	

■ The *e* in *ideas* is written counterclockwise for ease of writing the *s*.

Brief-Form Practice

38.1

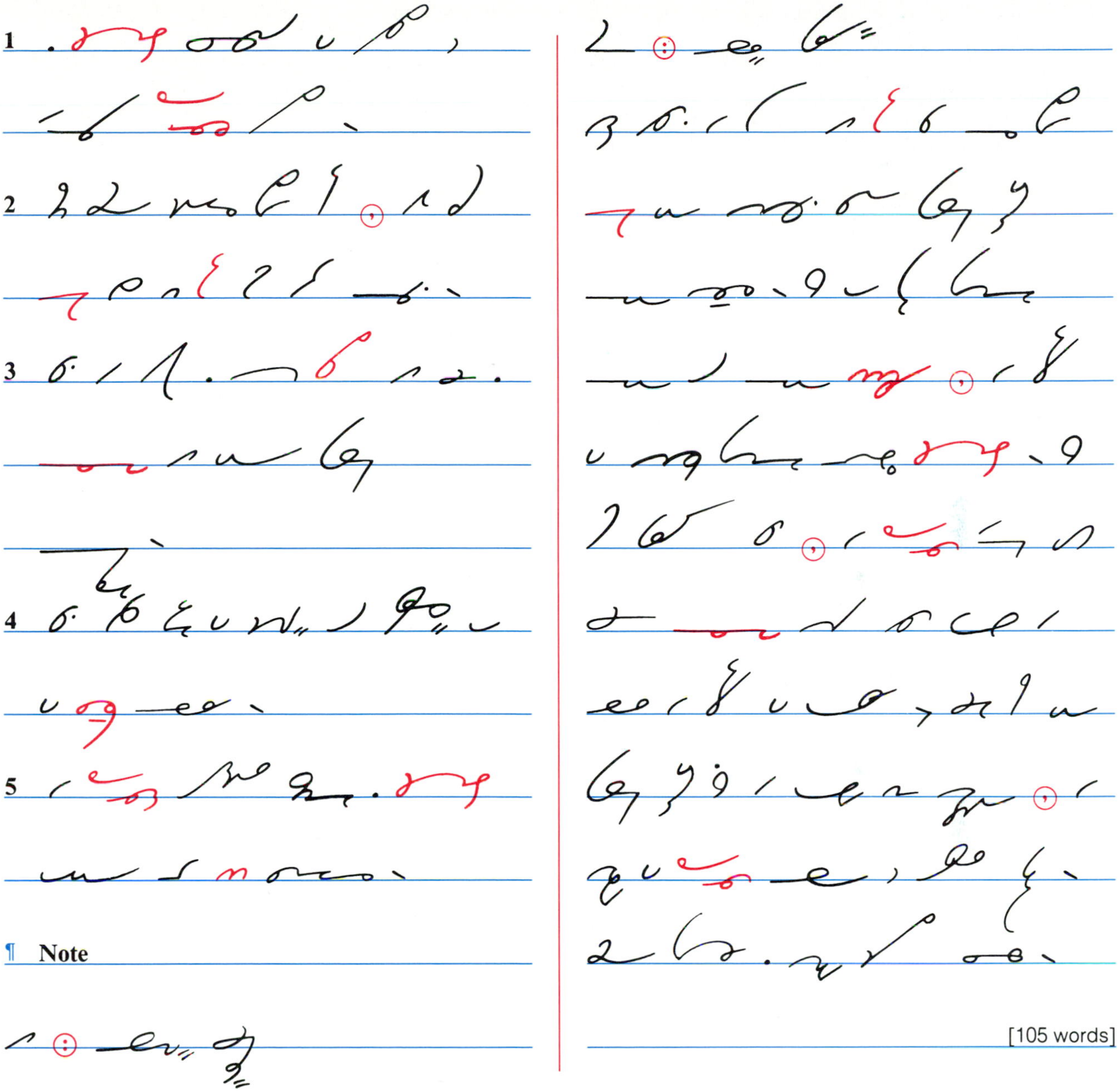

WORD ENDING -ILY

The word ending *-ily* as in *readily* is represented by a *-ly* circle which is flattened into a loop.

Example: readily

Compare with *ready*

-ily Words

readily — family — easily

steadily — families — temporarily

-ily Practice
38.2

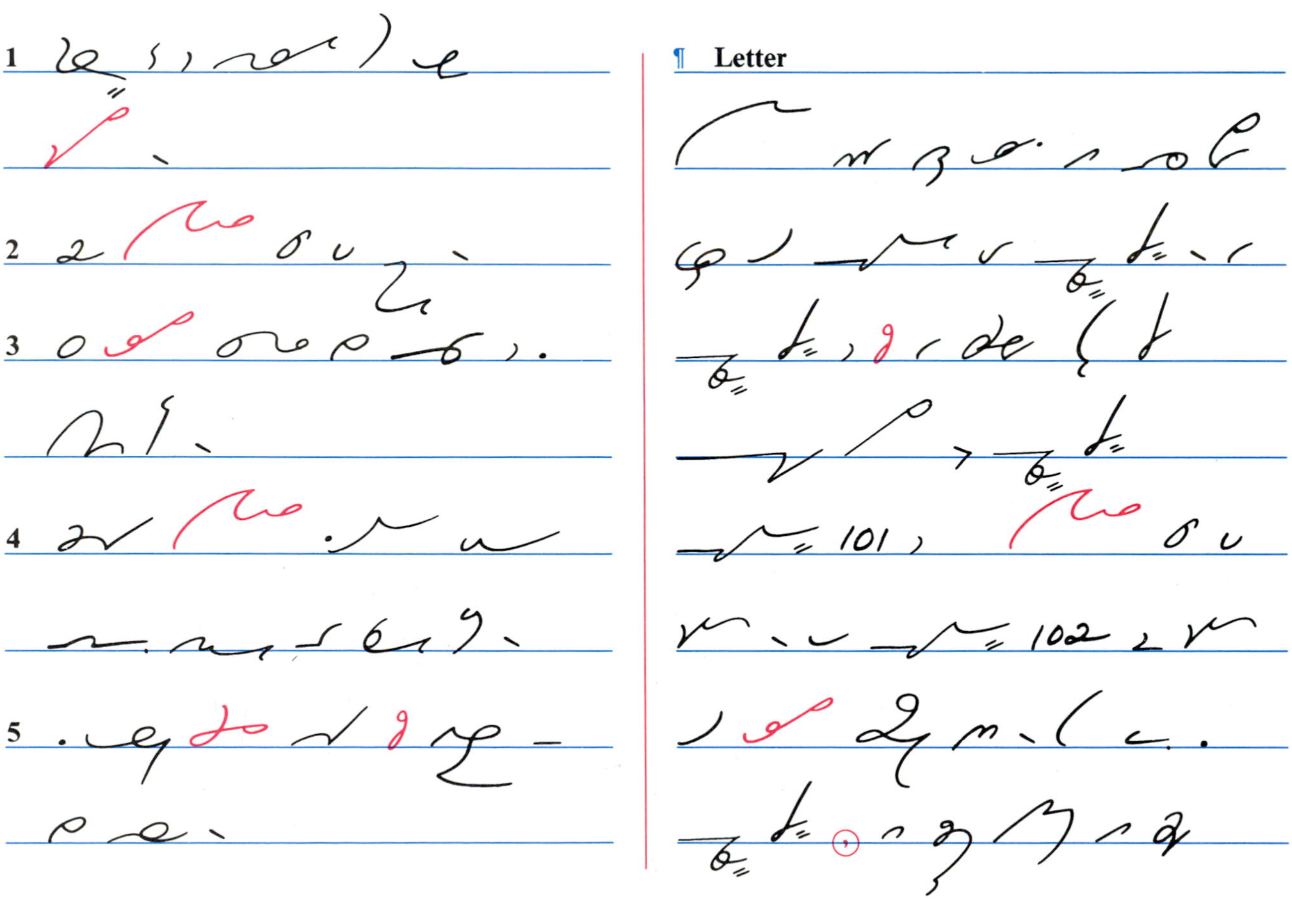

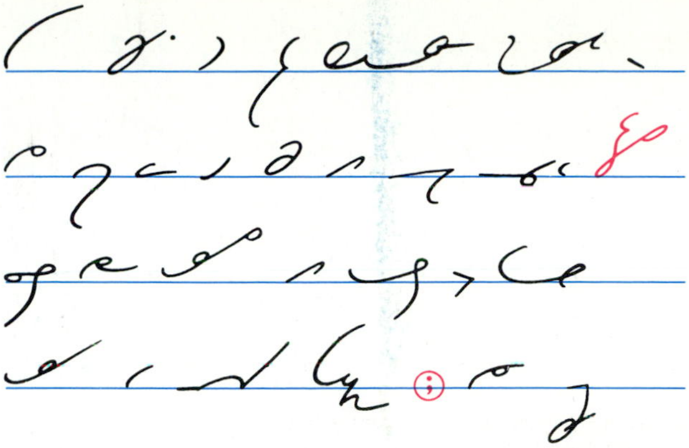

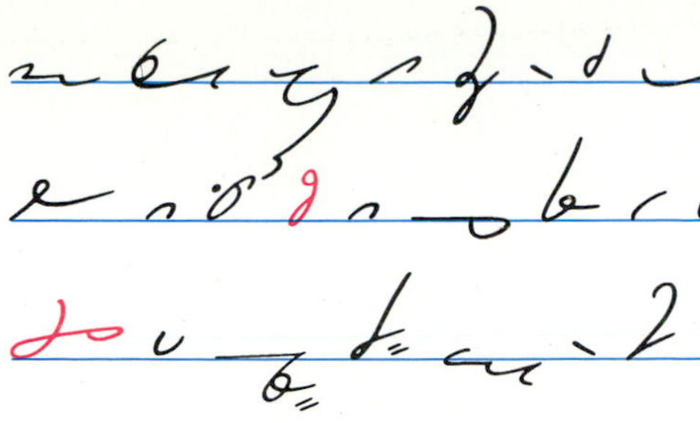

[129 words]

WORD BEGINNING SUB-

The word beginning *sub-* as in *subway* is written with a *left* or *right* *s* symbol, depending on the symbol that follows.

Examples: subway  suburb 

Sub- Words

subway 
submit 
subsequent 
subscribe 
subscribes 
subscription 
subdivide 
subdivision 
substance 
substantial 
suburb 
suburban 

Sub- Practice

38.3

1 

2 

3 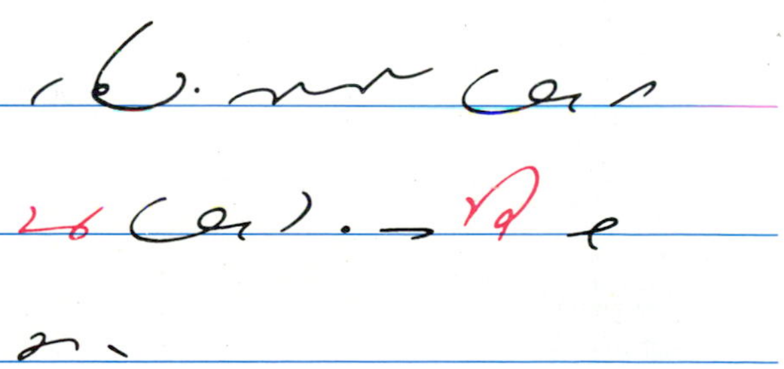

4 

5

¶ Letter

[91 words]

Secretaries and their managers often work as a team in the development of documents, such as reports.

Communication Skill Builder

Similar Words: piece, peace

piece: a single part; a portion

peace: the absence of conflict

Please attach your photograph to this form with a *piece* of tape.

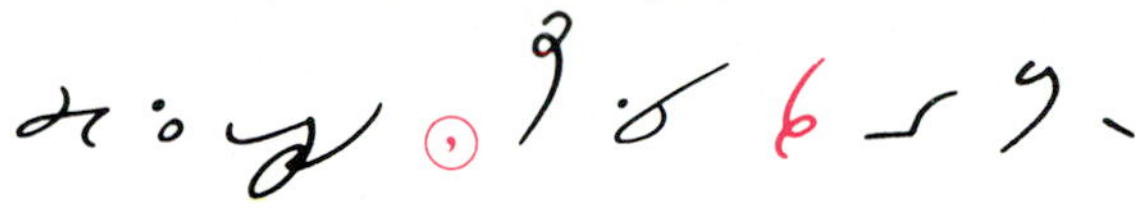

Since he resigned, we have had *peace* in the office.

Reading and Writing Practice

38.4 Dictation Speed Letter

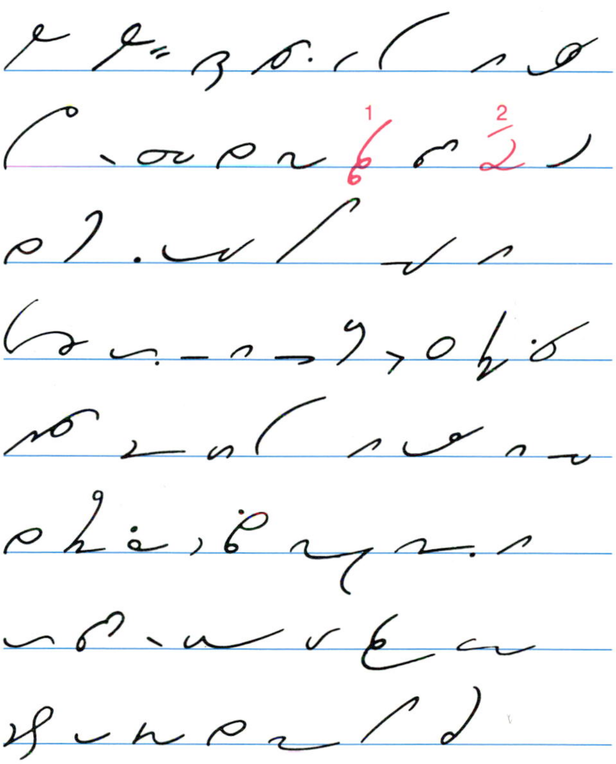

1 busy 2 transfer

[67 words]

38.5 "To Do" List

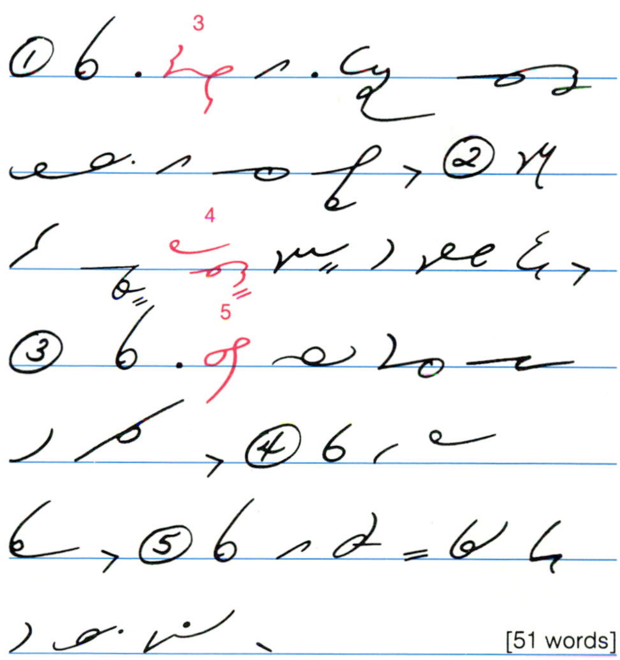

[51 words]

3 subscription 4 Electronics 5 anniversary

LESSON

39

NEW IN LESSON 39

- Word ending *-ology*
- Word beginning and ending *self*
- Word ending *-iety*
- Linking shorthand and English competence

WORD ENDING -OLOGY

The word ending *-ology* as in *psychology* is abbreviated with the *o* and *l* symbols.

Example: psychology

-ology Words

psychology

psychological ■

psychologically ■

apology

apologies

apologize

sociology

biology

technology

technological ■

■ Notice that the disjoined *k* is added for the *-ical* ending.

-ology Practice
39.1

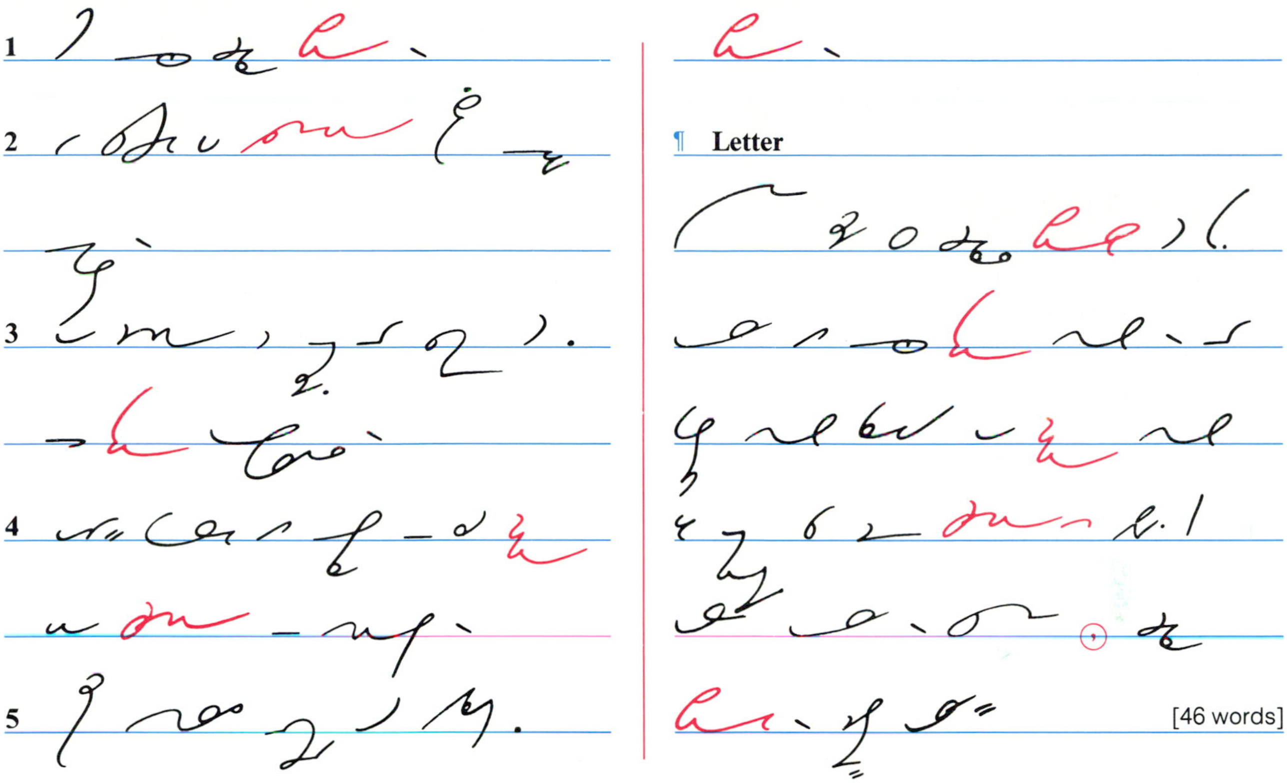

WORD BEGINNING AND ENDING SELF

The word beginning *self-* as in *selfish* is represented by a disjoined left *s* and is written in the middle of the line.

Example: selfish

Self- Words

selfish

selfishness

self-addressed

self-control

self-confidence

self-improvement

The word ending *-self* as in *himself* and *yourself* is represented by a joined *s*.

Examples: himself yourself

-Self Words

himself myself ourselves

herself yourself themselves

itself yourselves

Self-, -self Practice
39.2

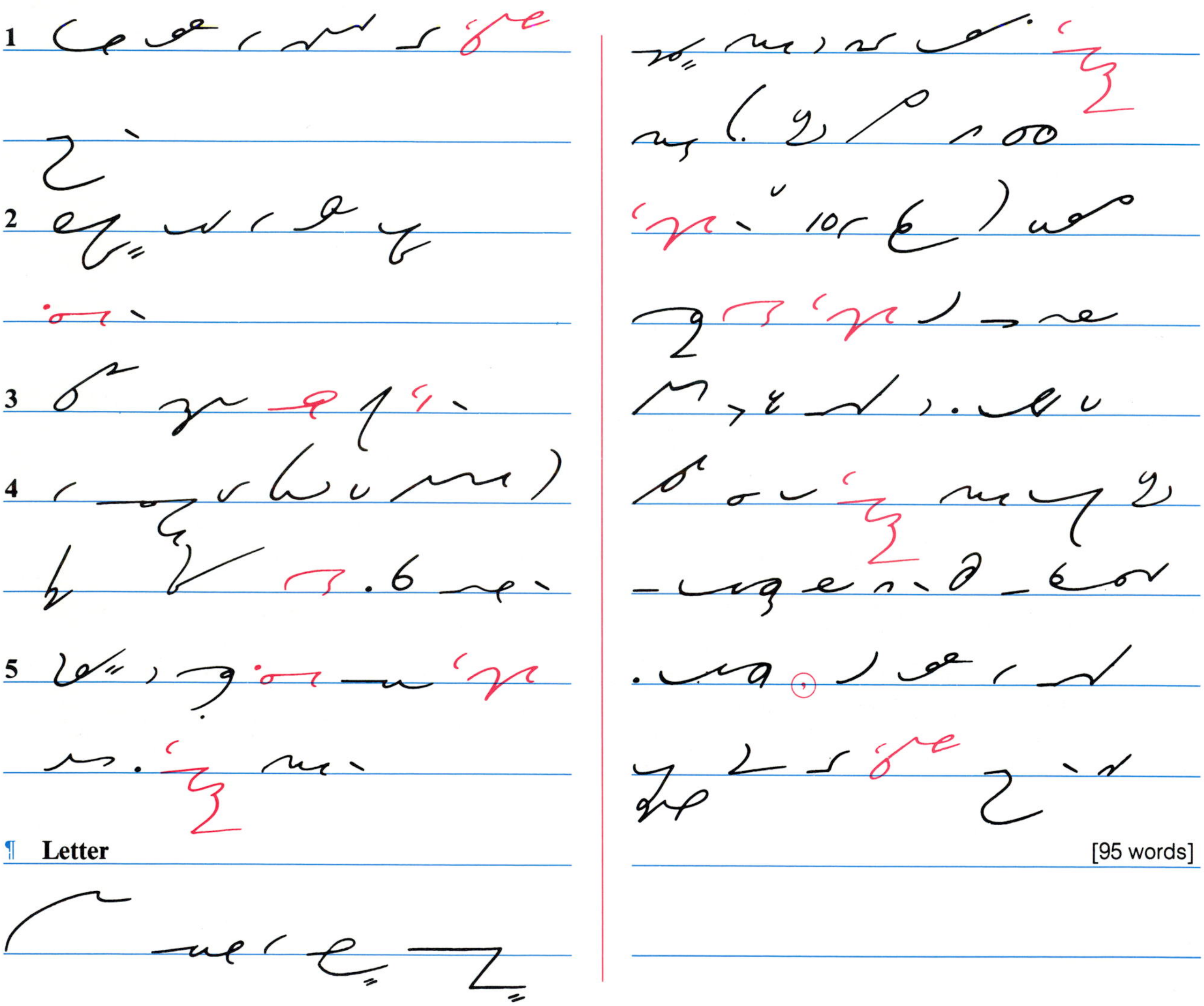

1

2

3

4

5

¶ **Letter**

[95 words]

WORD ENDING -IETY

The word ending *-iety* as in *society* is abbreviated with the *i* symbol.

Example: society

-iety Words

society
anxiety
notoriety
variety

-iety Practice

39.3

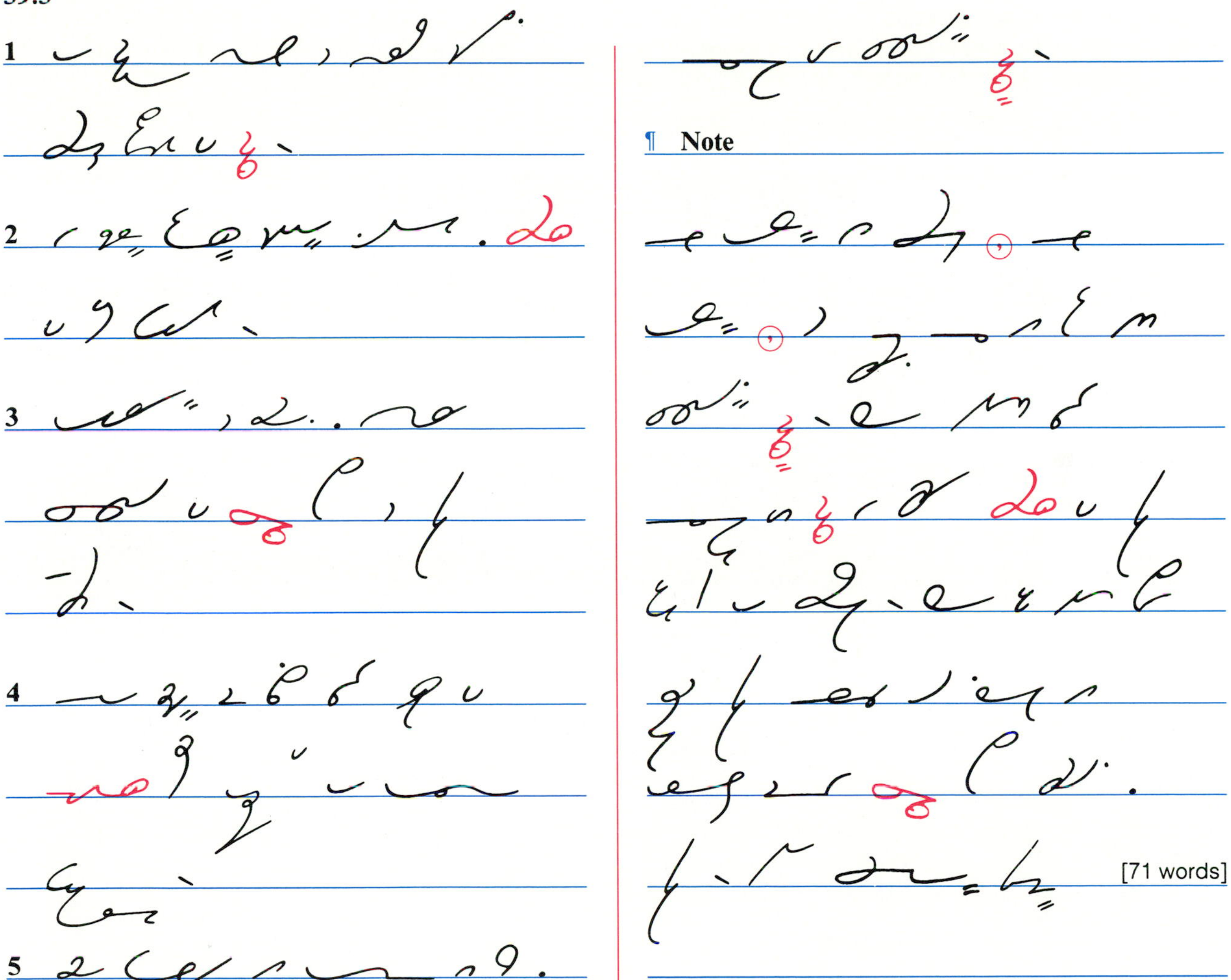

Shorthand and English Competence

For many people, the study of shorthand is the event that makes them feel that they are really beginning to master the English language. Students cannot help but improve their knowledge of the English language by studying Gregg Shorthand, and they apply that knowledge when transcribing their shorthand notes.

Employers recognize the value of the study of shorthand in a secretary's background. In a recent survey, an overwhelming majority of business executives stated that they believe the study of shorthand makes a better secretary.

Because of the English competence gained through the study of Gregg Shorthand, people who have studied Gregg Shorthand make better typists, better word processing operators, better editors of their bosses' correspondence, and better writers of communications that are delegated to them for composition. Best of all, employers appreciate these advantages.

A secretary who has studied Gregg Shorthand has the best chance of being hired, being promoted, and being self-assured on the job.

Reading and Writing Practice

39.4 Dictation Speed Letter

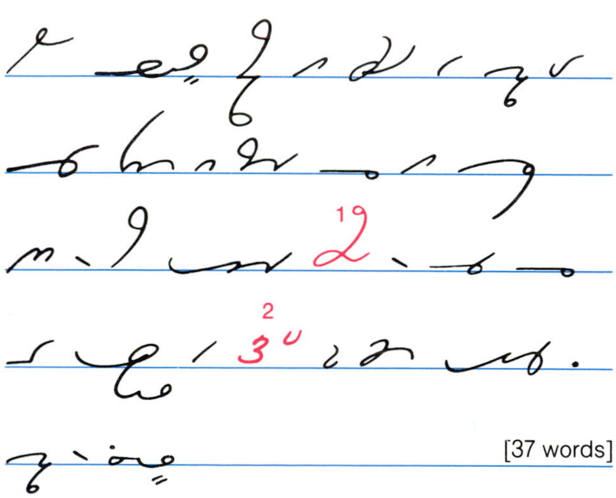

[37 words]

39.5 Sales Letter

1 everywhere 2 3 o'clock

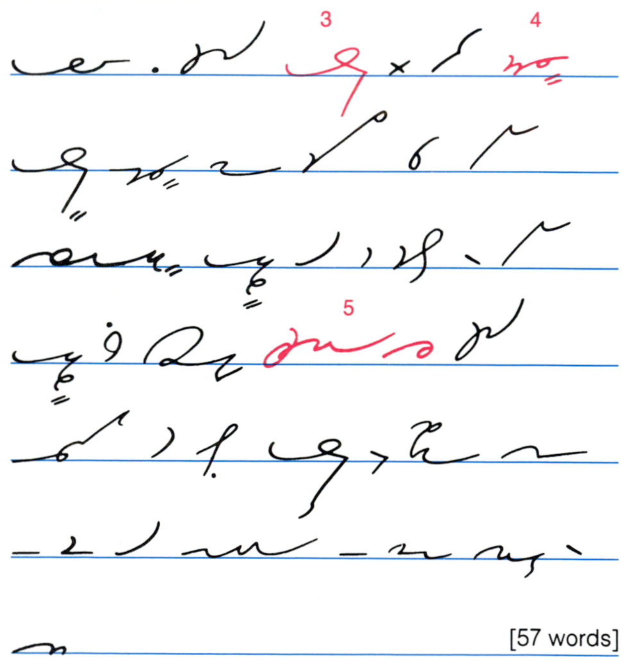

[57 words]

3 language 4 Southern 5 psychologically

LESSON 40

NEW IN LESSON 40

- Eight brief forms
- Common name endings *-ington*, *-ingham*, *-ville*, and *-burgh*
- Differentiating between *sense* and *cents*

BRIEF FORMS

circular	privilege ■	question
circumstance	ordinary	publish, publication
statistic	character	

■ Transcription Alert.

Brief-Form Derivatives

circulars	ordinarily	questionable
circumstances	extraordinary ■	questionnaire ■
statistical	characters	published
privileges	questions	publications, publishes

■ Transcription Alert.

Brief-Form Practice

40.1

1 

2 

3 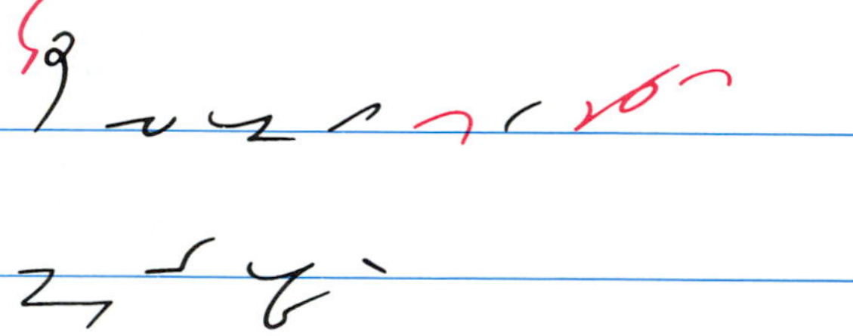

4 

5 

¶ **Letter**

[108 words]

NAMES

-ington

The name ending *-ington* is represented by a disjoined *ten* blend. 

Washington  Lexington  Wilmington 

-ingham

The name ending *-ingham* is represented by a disjoined *m*.

Buckingham 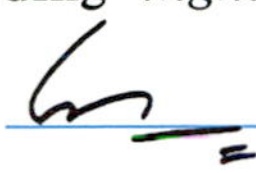 Cunningham  Framingham 

-ville

The name ending *-ville* is represented by the *v* symbol. 

Nashville  Jacksonville  Evansville 

-burgh

The name ending *-burg(h)* is represented by the *b* symbol. 

Pittsburgh, Pittsburg  Harrisburg  Greensburg 

Names Practice

40.2

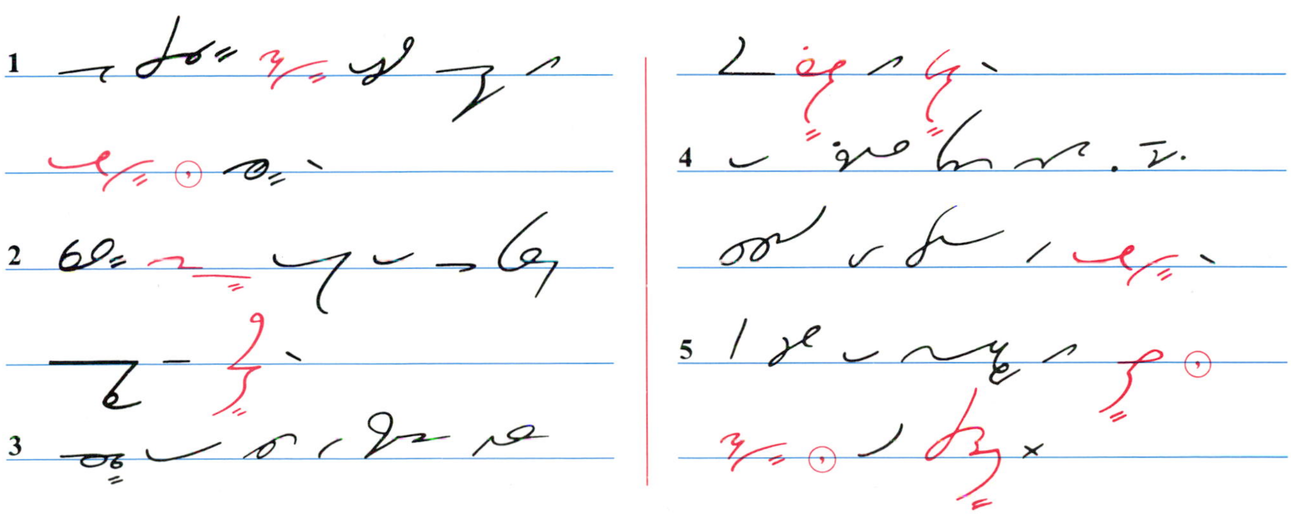

¶ **Business Letter**

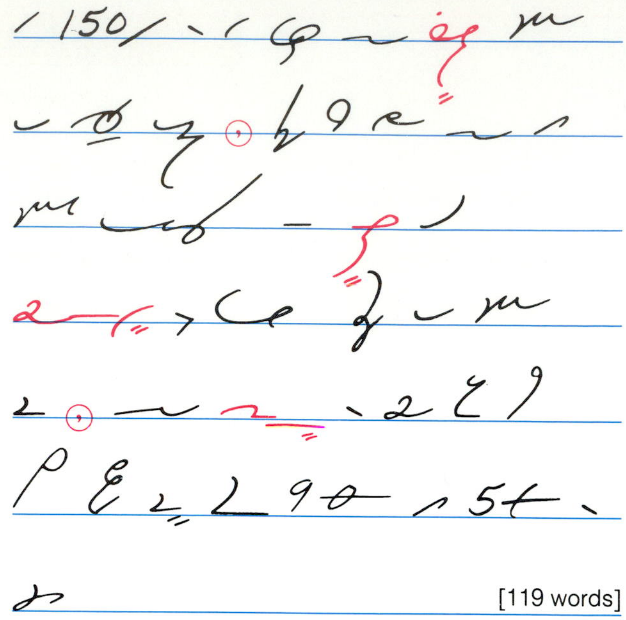

[119 words]

Communication Skill Builder

Similar Words: sense, cents

sense: good judgment

cents: pennies

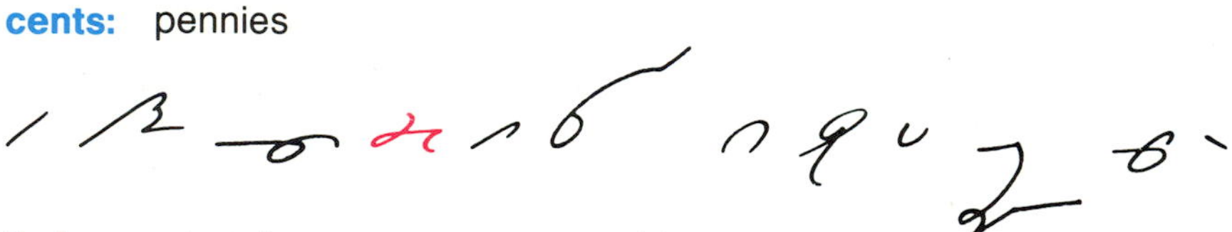

It does not make *sense* to attempt this type of investment now.

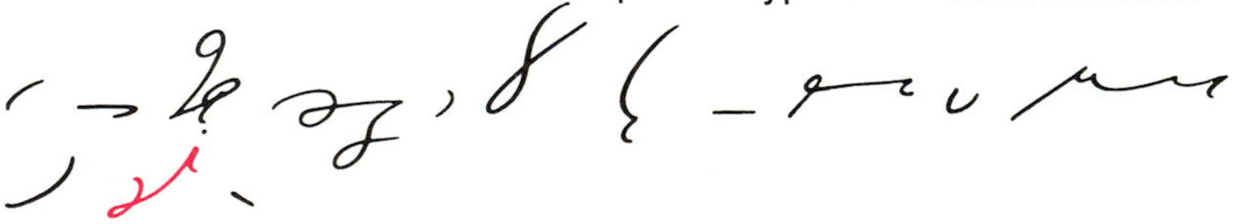

The new advertising campaign is bad business in terms of dollars and *cents*.

Congratulatory Message

Congratulations! Your study of Gregg Shorthand theory is complete. Though millions of people have learned Gregg Shorthand before you, you still have the satisfaction of acquiring knowledge that places you in an elite class of professionals who handle communications most efficiently.

At this point you probably feel that you know the basic Gregg alphabet, as well as most of the early brief forms, quite well. You may not yet have complete confidence in your knowledge of many of the abbreviated word beginnings and endings and some of the recent brief forms. As you continue your shorthand study, your knowledge of the system will become more and more certain and your writing speed will increase.

Documents stored on magnetic media, such as floppy disks, should be labeled both on the disk and in the shorthand notes.

Reading and Writing Practice

40.3 Speed Dictation Memo

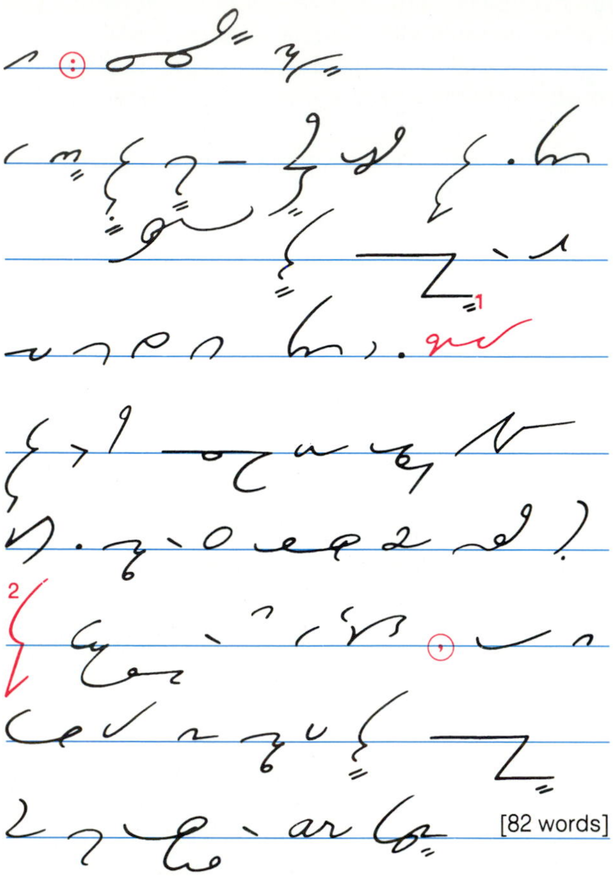

[82 words]

40.4 Professional Letter

1 extraordinary 2 budget 3 privilege

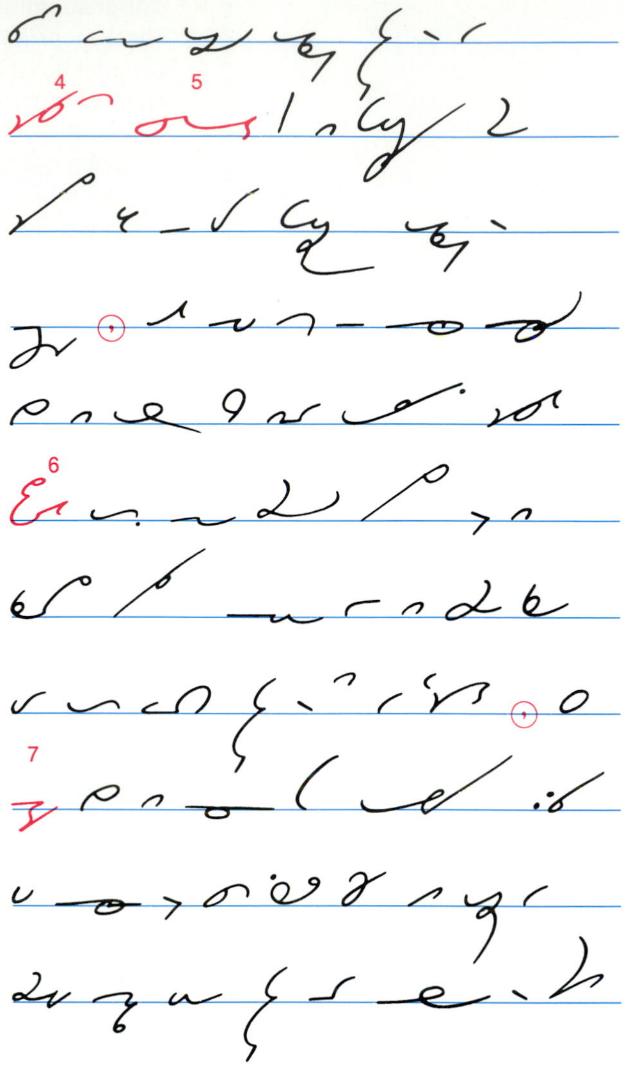

[107 words]

4 statistical 5 analysis 6 experts 7 insist

UNIT XI

LESSON 41

NEW IN LESSON 41

- **Related numbers in a sentence**

DICTATION SPEED BUILDING

The shorthand outlines below appear in the speed dictation practice which follows. Practice writing these words using the shorthand outlines. Then, using the key below, dictate the words to yourself.

Theory Words

Brief Forms

Phrases

Key *Theory*: Mike, locker, second, 11 a.m., useful, return
Brief Forms: hours, this, where, there, after, when, with, them
Phrases: I will be glad, you have, I am sure, you will be able, on the

Speed Dictation Practice

41.1 Personal Note

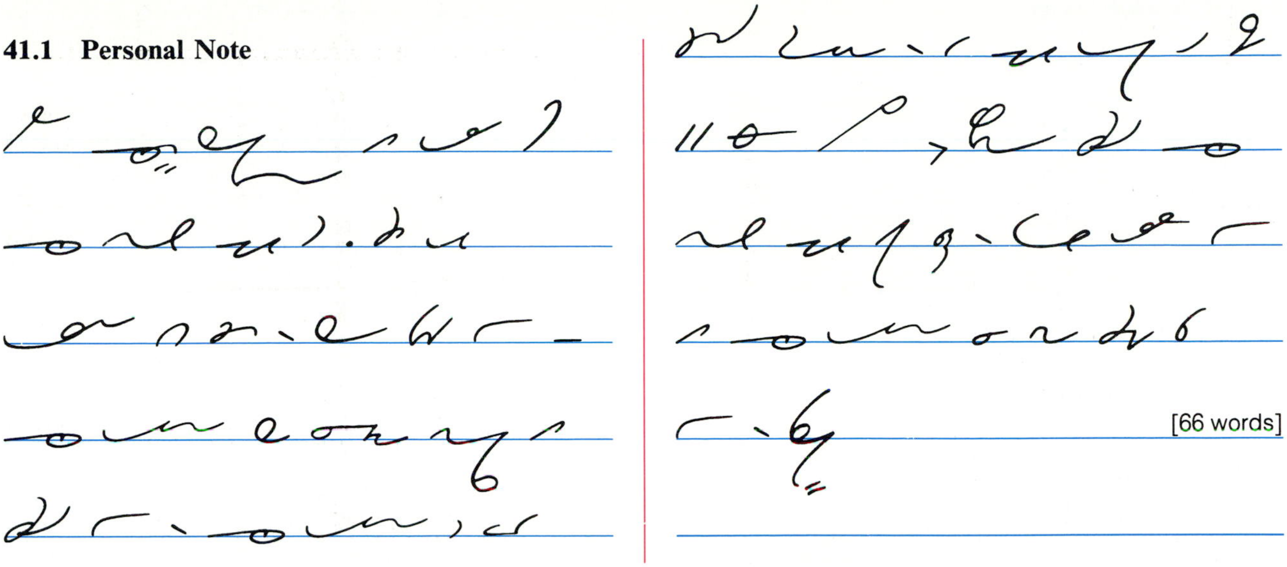

[66 words]

TRANSCRIPTION SKILL DEVELOPMENT

Transcribe the following words and phrases, noting spelling and capitalization. Then transcribe the transcription letter which follows.

Transcription Warmup

41.2

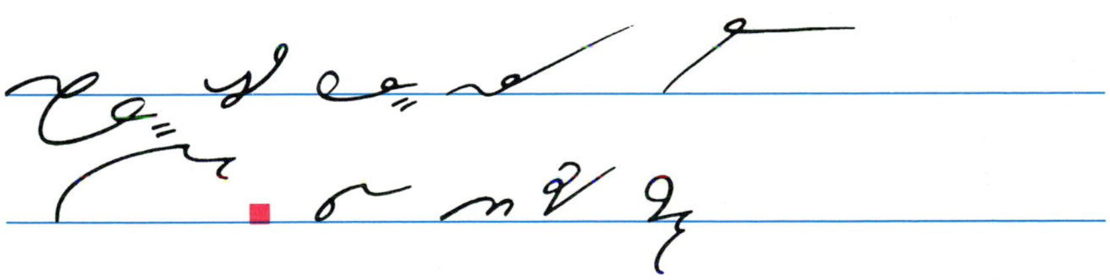

■ Transcription Hint: *Mrs.* will be capitalized and followed by a period.

Transcription Practice

41.3 Reference Letter

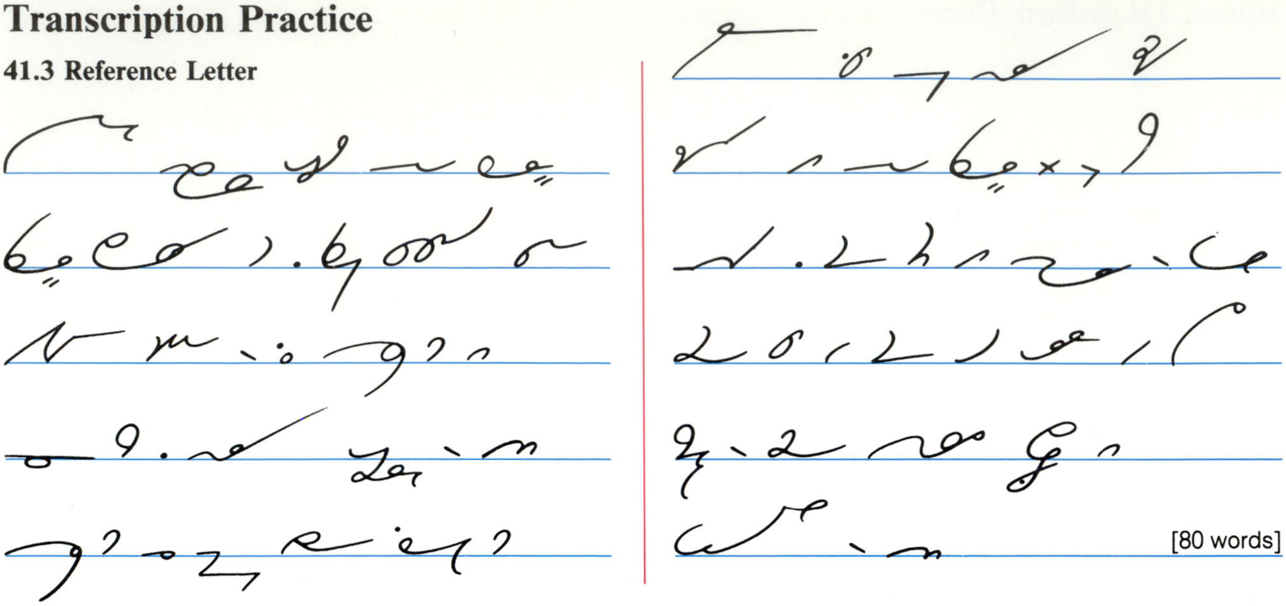

[80 words]

Related Numbers in a Sentence

In previous lessons the following number rules were presented:

Spell out the numbers *one through ten* within a sentence.
Use figures for the numbers *11 and above* within a sentence.
If a number is used at the *beginning of a sentence*, spell it out.

An additional number rule is listed below with examples:

If there is a series of related numbers *one through ten* in a sentence, express all of them in words. If one or more of the related numbers is *above ten*, write all of them in *figures*.

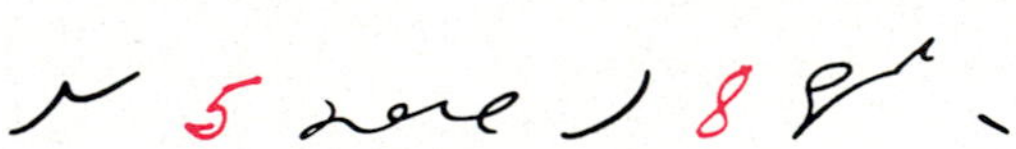

There are *five* secretaries and *eight* assistants.

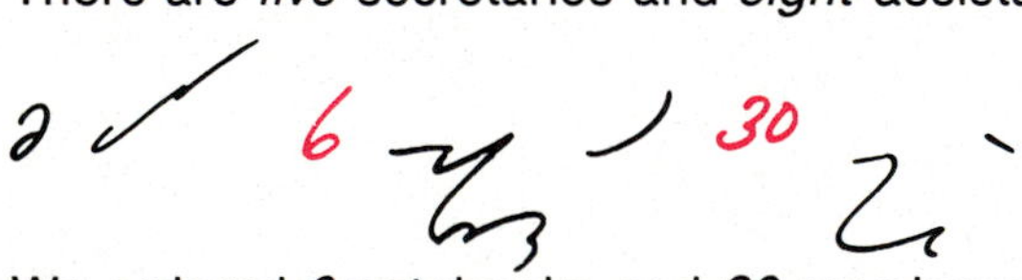

We ordered *6* notebooks and *30* envelopes.

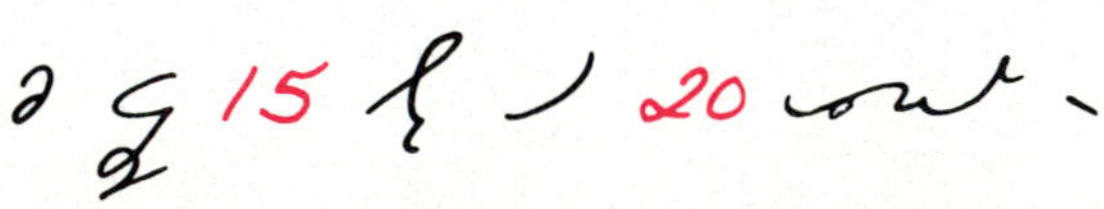

We purchased *15* tapes and *20* records.

Reading and Writing Practice

41.4 Personal Letter

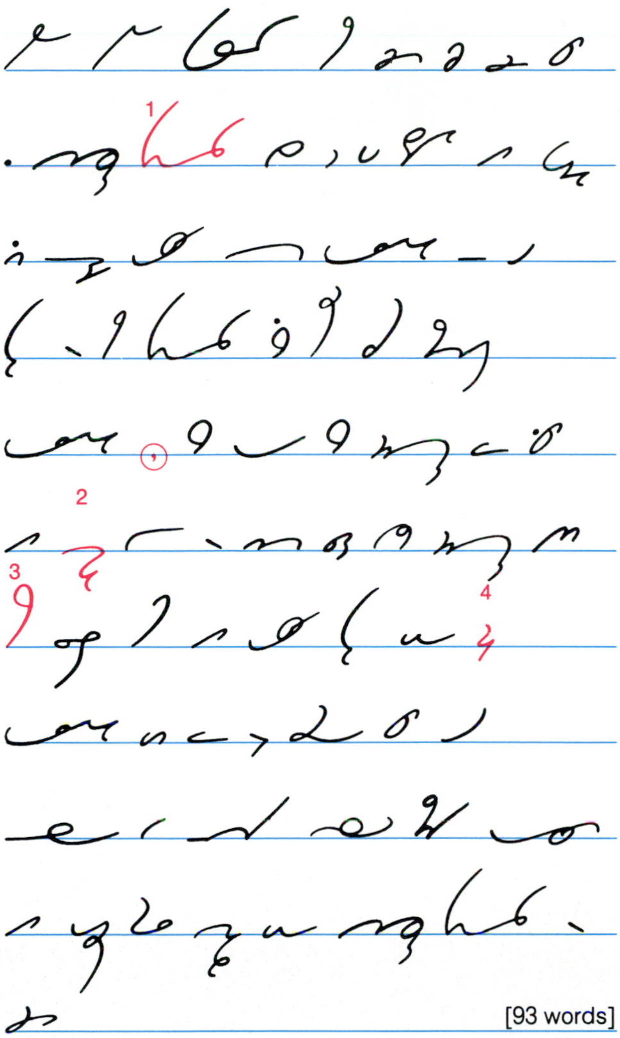

[93 words]

1 bulletin 2 compose 3 advantage 4 social

41.5 Business Letter

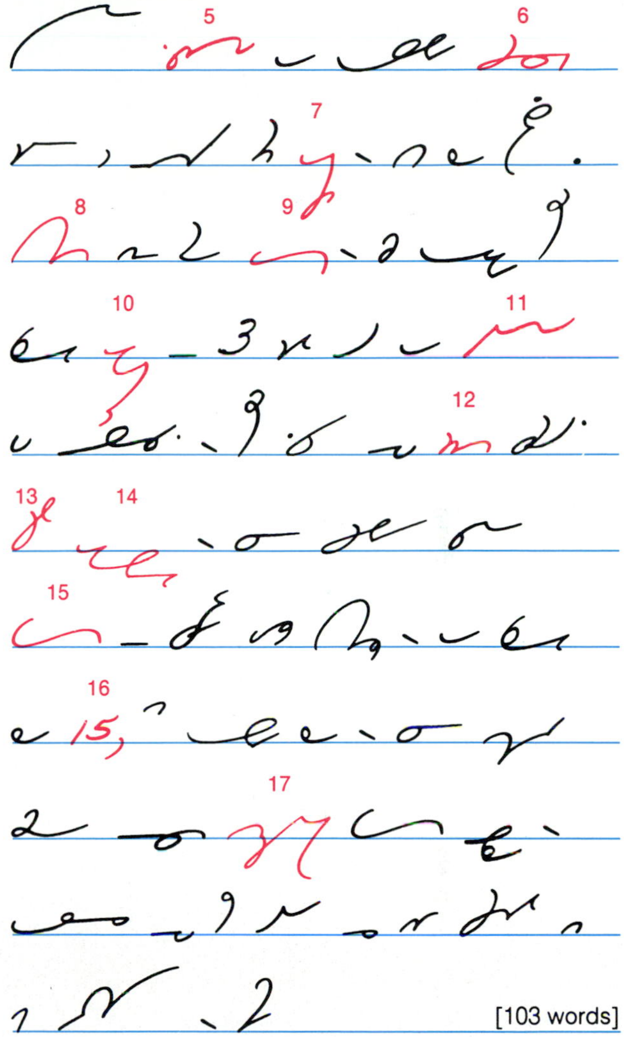

[103 words]

5 Hugo 6 financial 7 review 8 difficult
9 organization 10 representatives 11 director
12 success 13 satisfactory 14 replacements
15 progress 16 15 percent 17 considerable

LESSON 42

NEW IN LESSON 42

- **Punctuation: commas in a series (series comma)**

DICTATION SPEED BUILDING

The shorthand outlines below appear in the speed dictation practice which follows. Practice writing these words using the shorthand outlines. Then, using the key below, dictate the words to yourself.

Theory Words

Brief Forms

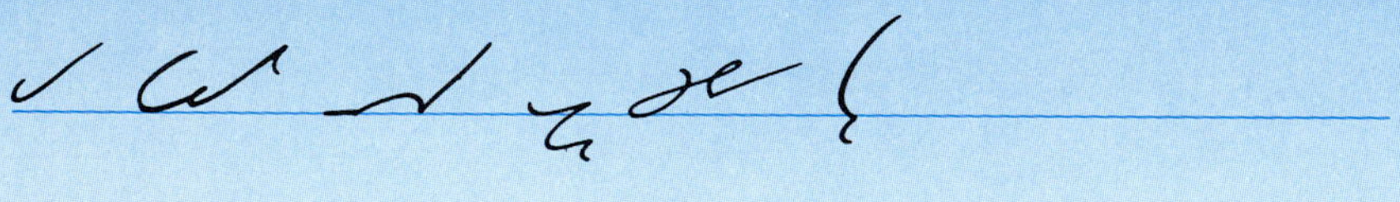

Phrases

Key *Theory*: Garcia, pleasure, receive, various, items, return, handle, forward

Brief Forms: order, products, enclosed, represents, satisfied, business

Phrases: Dear Ms., to us, this will, we hope that, with our, Cordially yours

Speed Dictation Practice

42.1 Business Letter

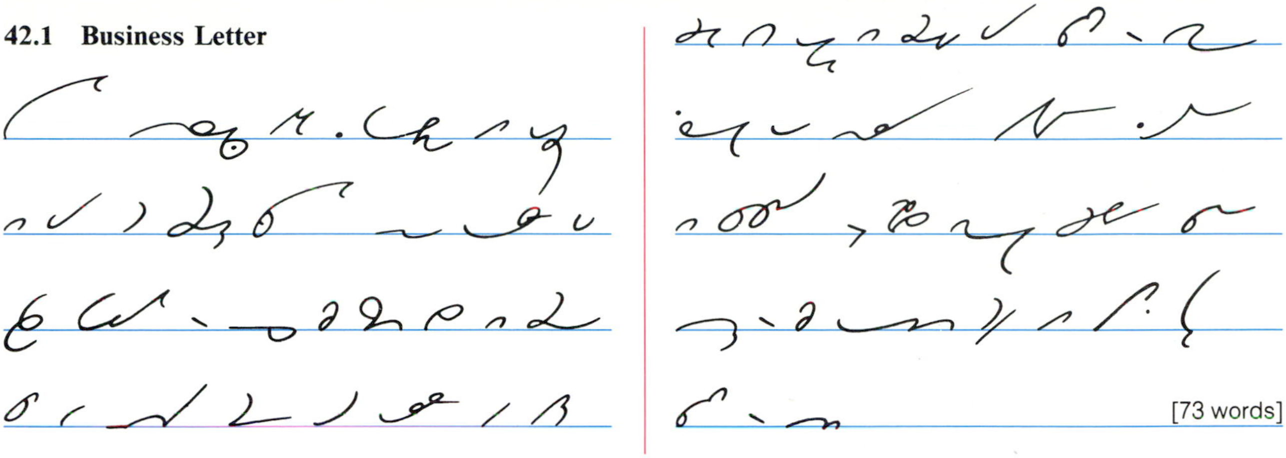

[73 words]

Students learning shorthand can be bilingual secretaries and assistants.

TRANSCRIPTION SKILL DEVELOPMENT

Transcribe the following words and phrases, noting spelling and capitalization. Then transcribe the transcription letter which follows.

Transcription Warmup

42.2

■ Capitalize when used as a closing.

Transcription Practice

42.3 Business Letter

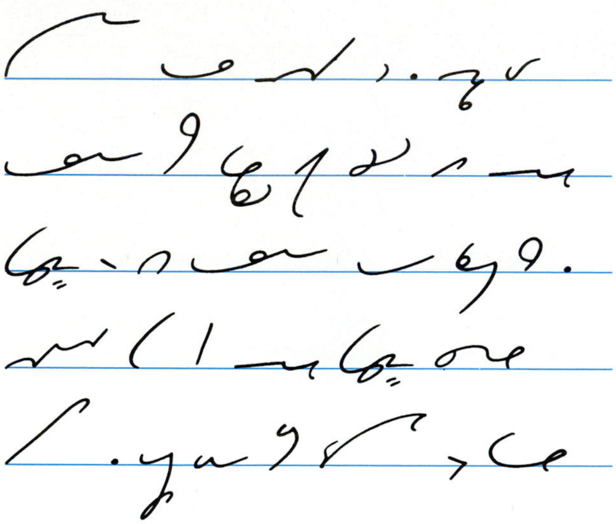

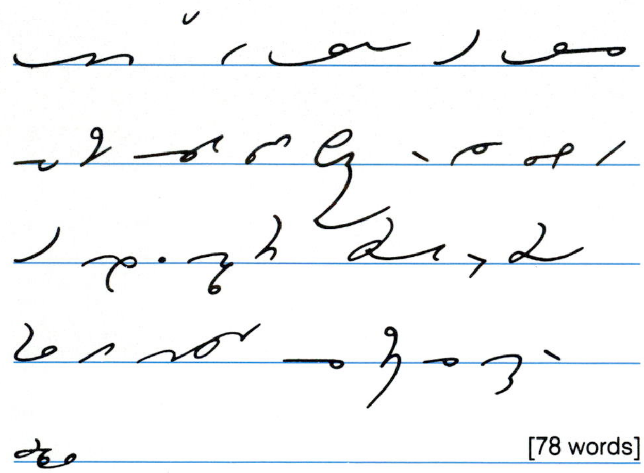

[78 words]

Punctuation: Commas in a Series

When three or more items are listed in a series and the last item is preceded by the word *and*, *or*, or *nor*, place a comma before the conjunction and between the other items.

The *series comma* is indicated by ser ,

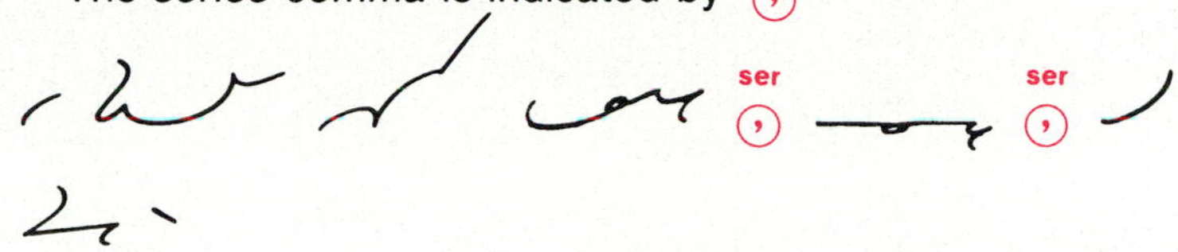

The folder contained *letters*, *memos*, and *forms*.

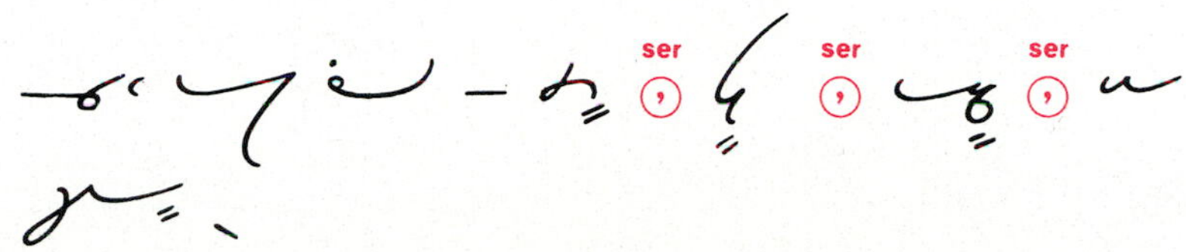

Meetings will be held in *Chicago*, *Boston*, *Los Angeles,* or *Seattle.*

Reading and Writing Practice

42.4 Business Letter

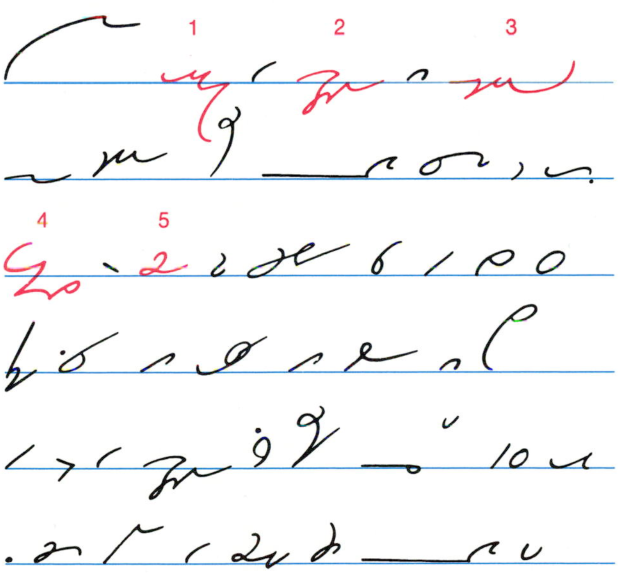

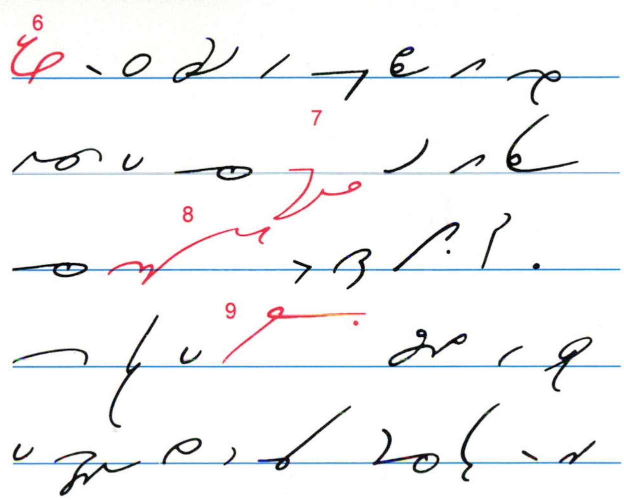

[92 words]

1 Rosenberg 2 computer 3 installed
4 perfectly 5 We are

6 operation 7 inventory 8 customers
9 determining

42.5 Business Memo

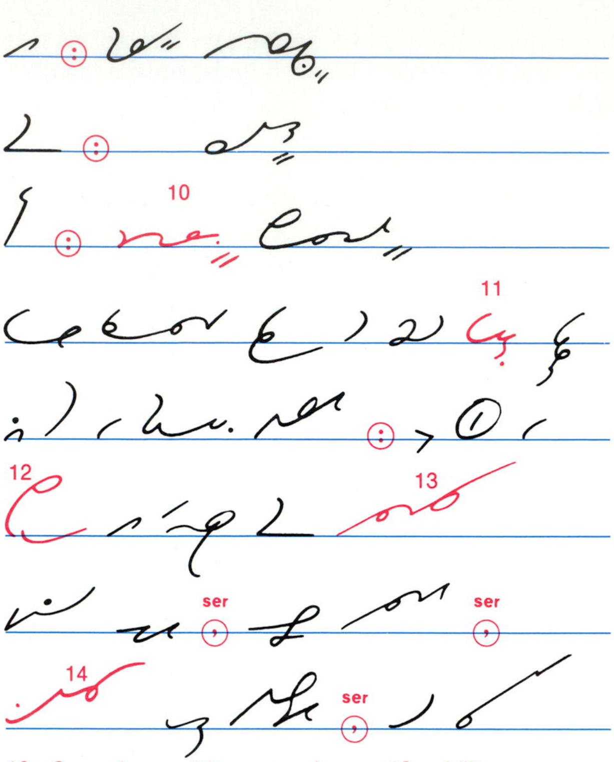

10 Screening 11 processing 12 ability
13 dictated 14 handwritten

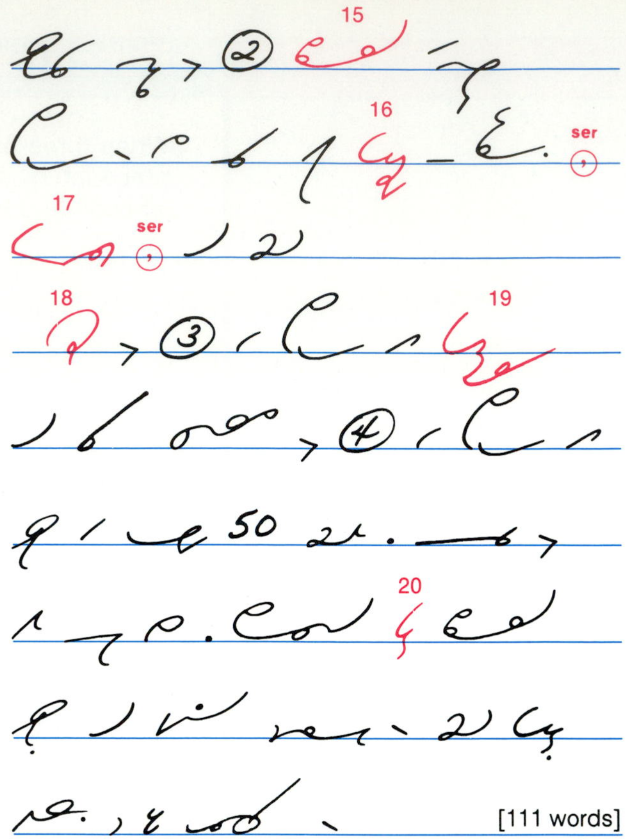

[111 words]

15 Excellent 16 proficient 17 punctuation
18 division 19 proofread 20 possess

LESSON 43

NEW IN LESSON 43

- **Differentiating between *stationary* and *stationery***

DICTATION SPEED BUILDING

The shorthand outlines below appear in the speed dictation practice which follows. Practice writing these words using the shorthand outlines. Then, using the key below, dictate the words to yourself.

Theory Words

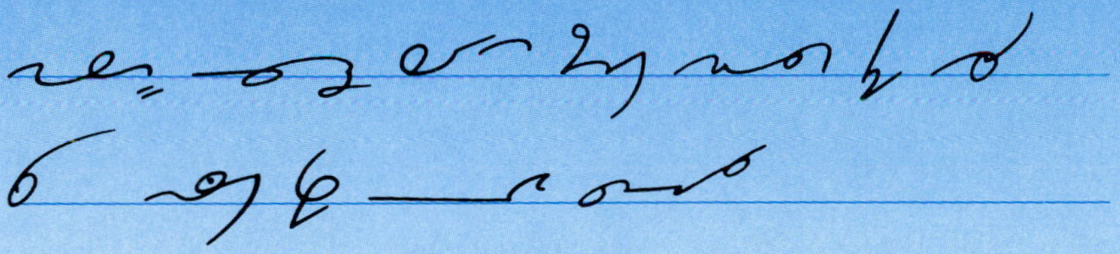

Phrases

Key *Theory*: Clark, magazine, article, effective, collection, just, kind, item, creative, patient, months, accommodate

Phrases: thank you, very much, from our, at this time, that will

Speed Dictation Practice

43.1 Business Letter

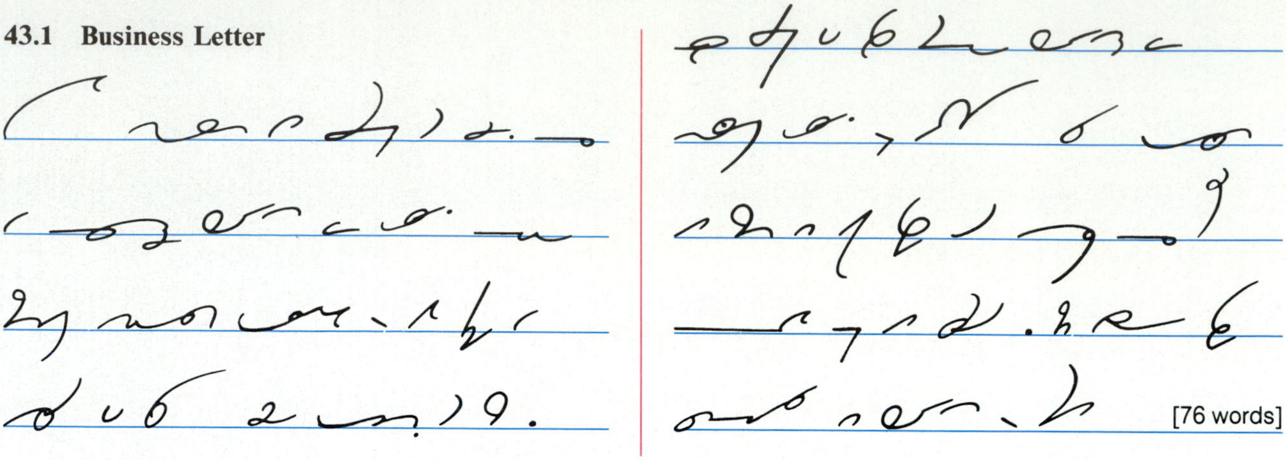

[76 words]

TRANSCRIPTION SKILL DEVELOPMENT

Transcribe the following words and phrases, noting spelling and capitalization. Then transcribe the transcription letter which follows.

Transcription Warmup

43.2

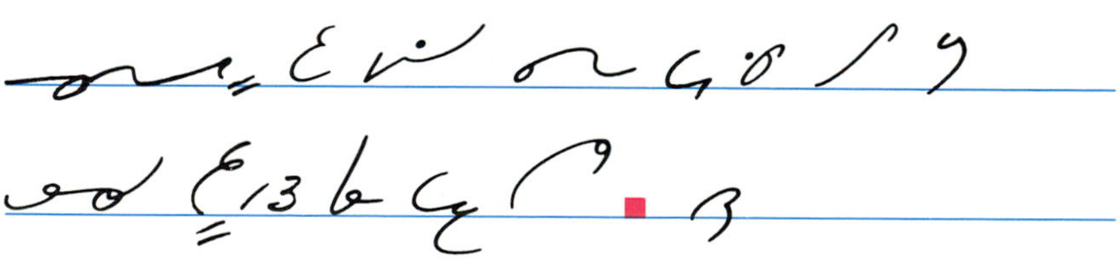

■ *Miss* is not an abbreviation and does not have a period.

Transcription Practice

43.3 Business Letter

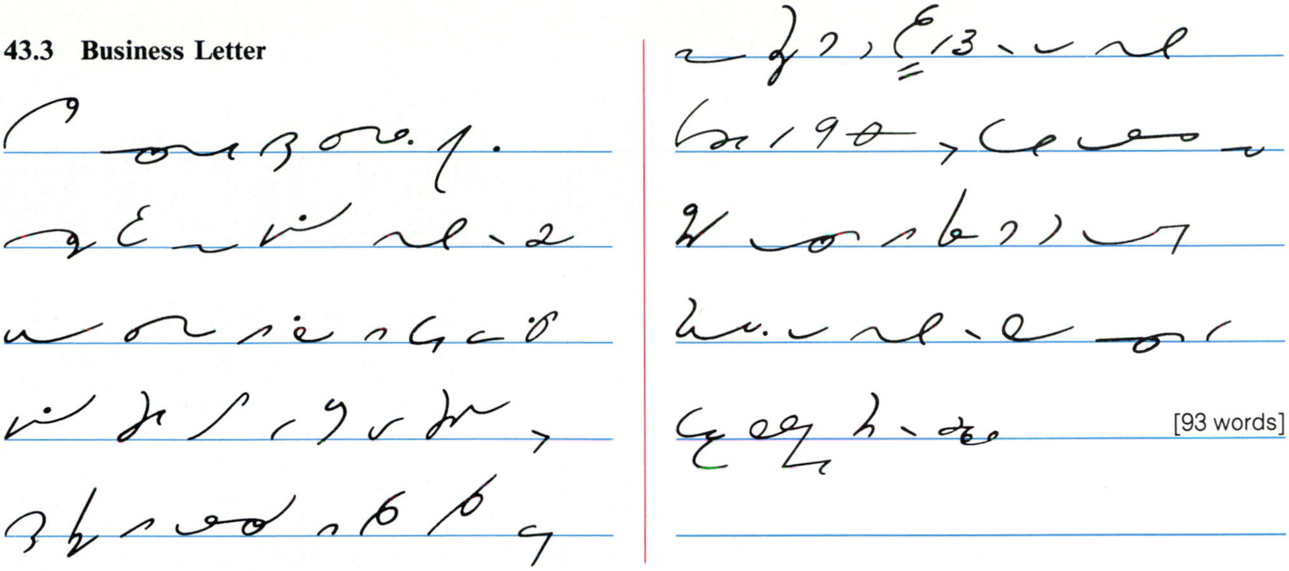

[93 words]

Communication Skill Builder

Similar Words: stationary, stationery

stationary: fixed; not movable
stationery: writing materials

The price index is *stationary*.

I have ordered *stationery* with our new address.

Reading and Writing Practice

43.4 Business Letter

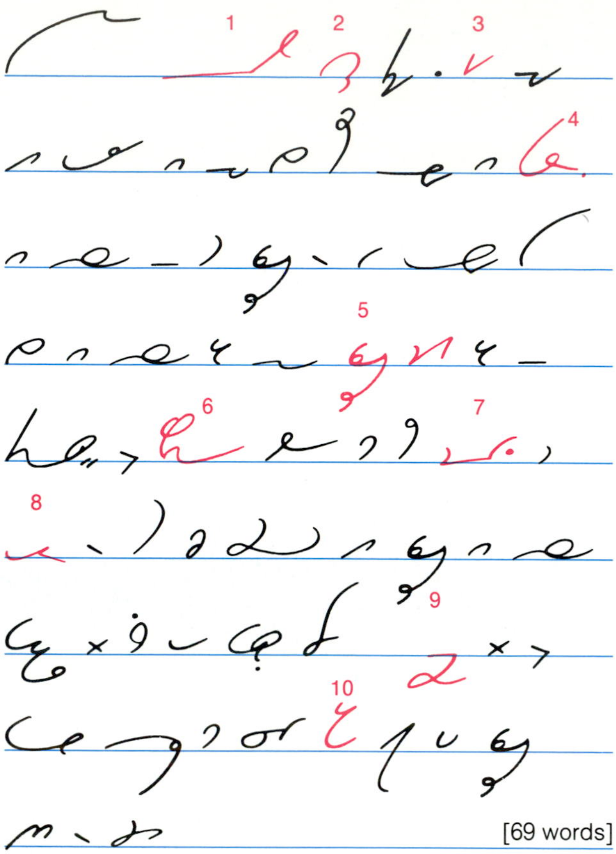

[69 words]

43.5 Business Letter

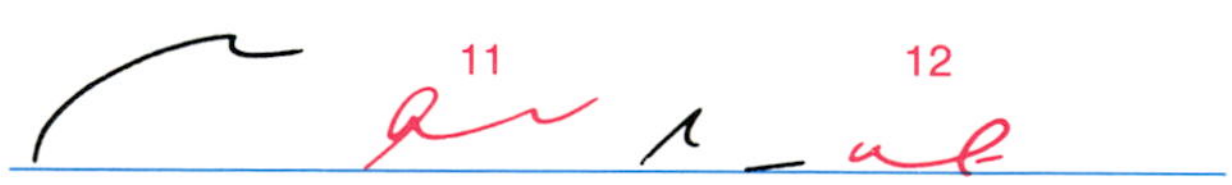

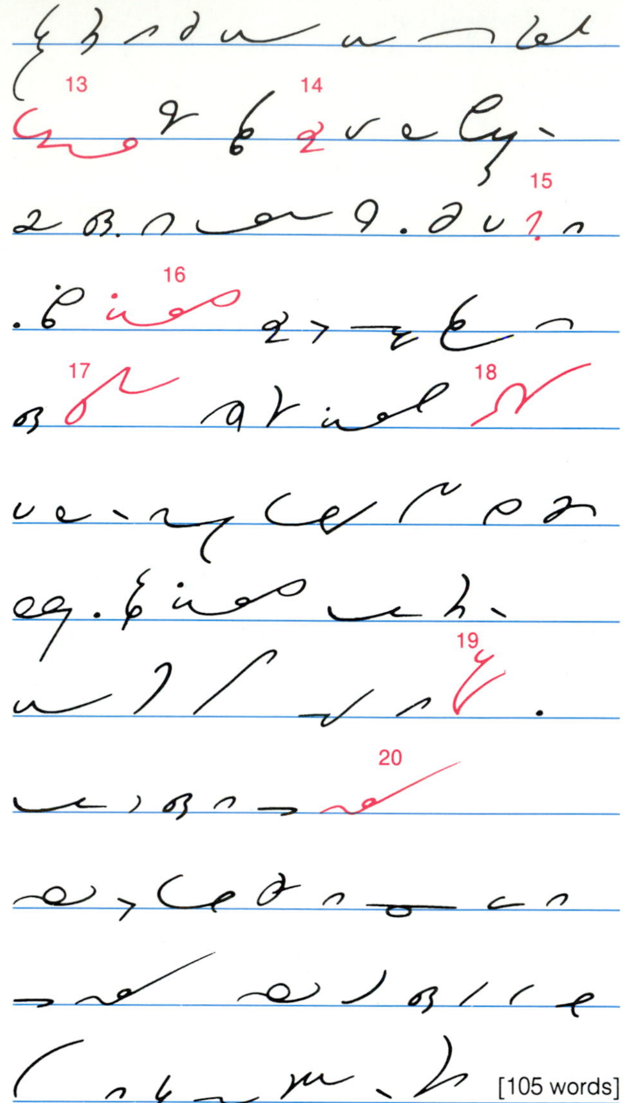

[105 words]

1 Mendez 2 This is 3 short 4 bringing
5 service station 6 I hope you will 7 something
8 wrong 9 unfair 10 opportunity 11 Tyler
12 always

13 personally 14 season 15 wishing
16 holiday 17 additional 18 at this time
19 obtain 20 credit

LESSON 44

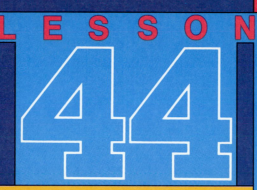

NEW IN LESSON 44

- **Punctuation:** ***as*****,** ***if*****, and** ***when*** **clauses**

DICTATION SPEED BUILDING

The shorthand outlines below appear in the speed dictation practice which follows. Practice writing these words using the shorthand outlines. Then, using the key which follows, dictate the words to yourself.

Theory Words

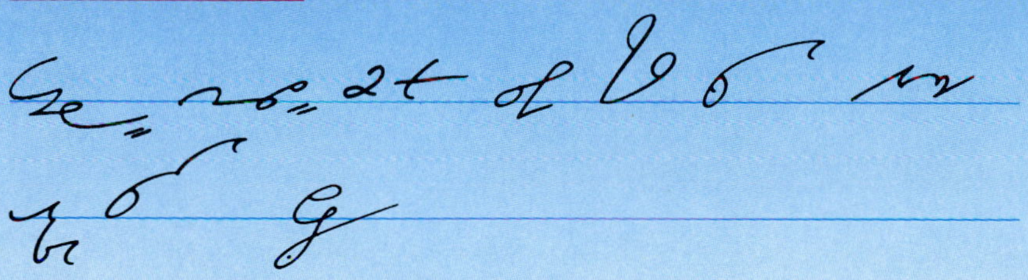

Brief Forms

Phrases

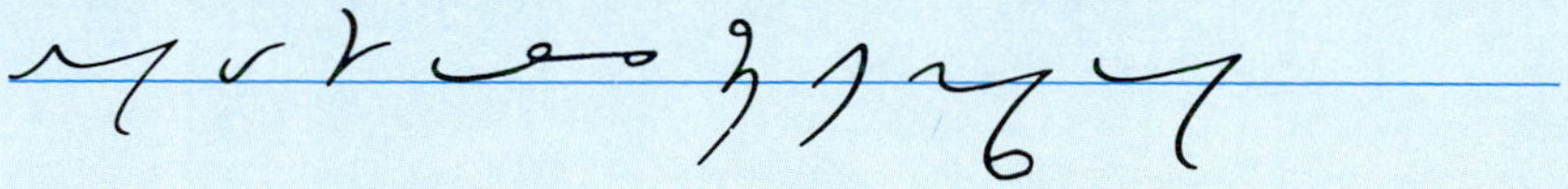

Key *Theory*: Personnel Committee, 2 p.m., attached, agenda, items, discussed, response, attendance, appreciated
Brief Forms: memorandum, immediate, regarding
Phrases: there will be, of the, for the, let me, if you have, to have, you will be able, will be

Speed Dictation Practice

44.1 Memo

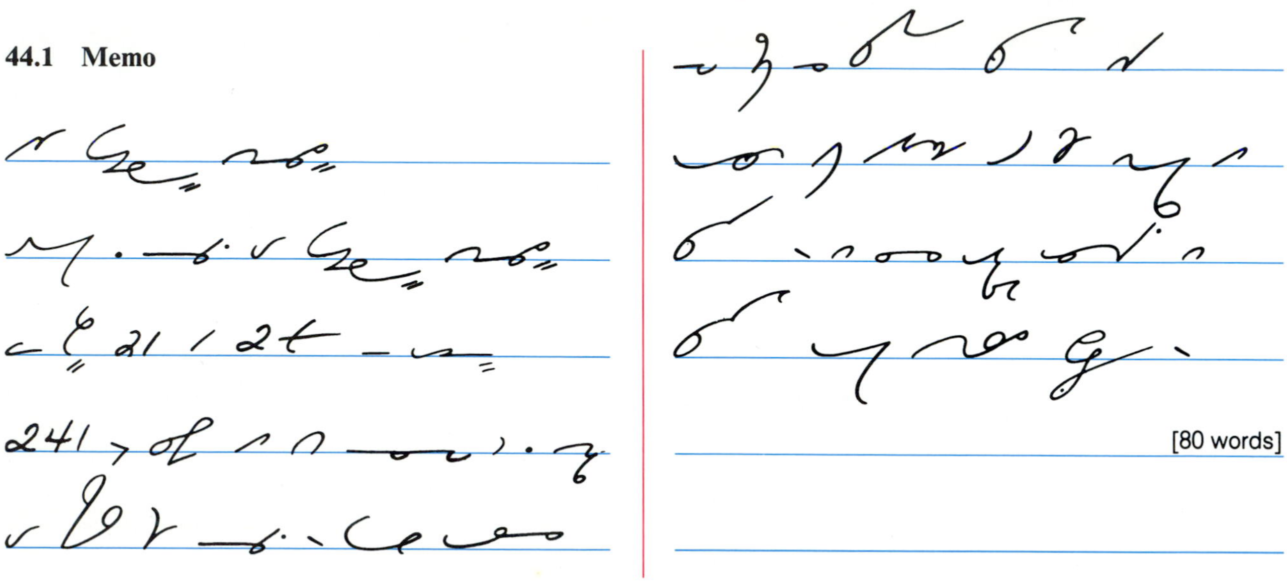

[80 words]

TRANSCRIPTION SKILL DEVELOPMENT

Transcribe the following words and phrases, noting spelling and capitalization. Then transcribe the letter which follows.

Transcription Warmup

44.2

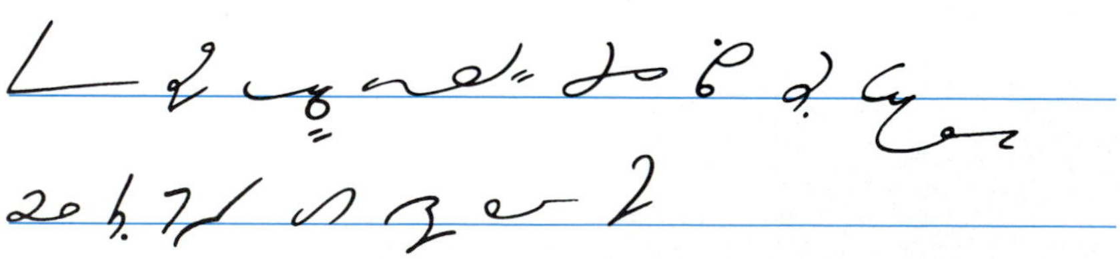

Transcription Practice

44.3 Personal Letter

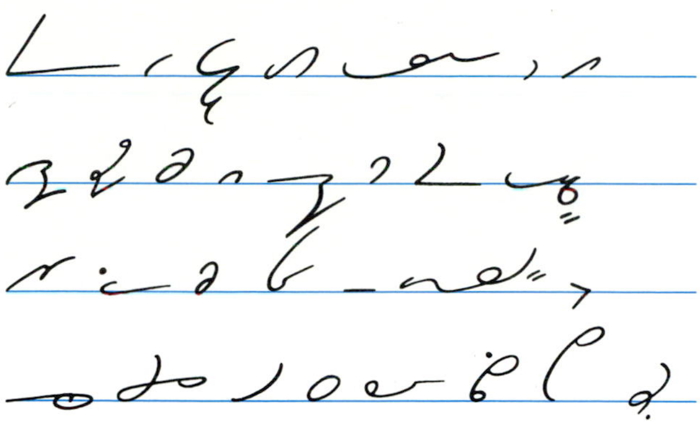

[78 words]

Punctuation: *As, If, When* Clauses

A group of words that begin a sentence with *as*, *if*, or *when* followed by a subject and a predicate is an introductory clause. An introductory clause is dependent on the remaining part of the sentence and should have a comma to set it aside from the rest of the sentence. Be sure the comma is placed at the end of the clause that is introduced by *as*, *if*, or *when*.

The *as clause comma* is indicated by 

The *if clause comma* is indicated by 

The *when clause comma* is indicated by 

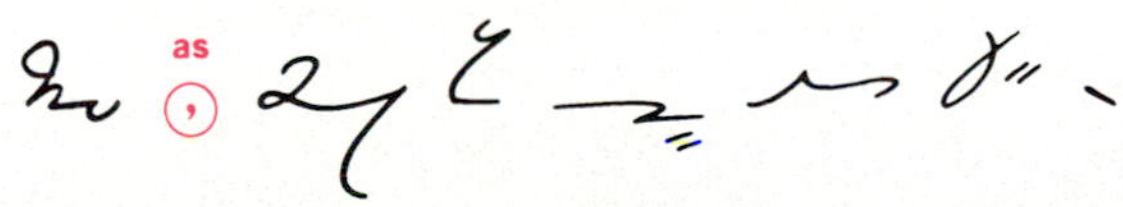

As you know, we will be open Monday through Saturday.

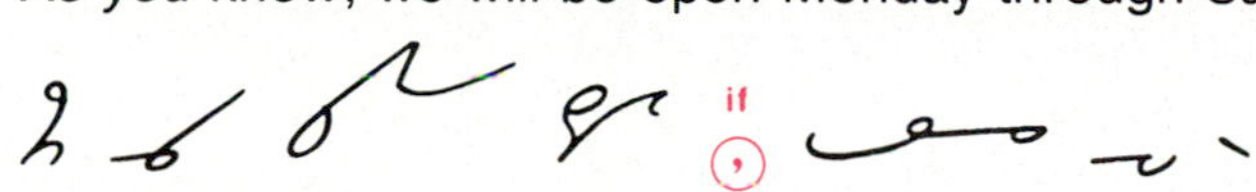

If you need additional assistance, let me know.

When the shipment is received, I will notify you.

Reading and Writing Practice

44.4 Business Letter

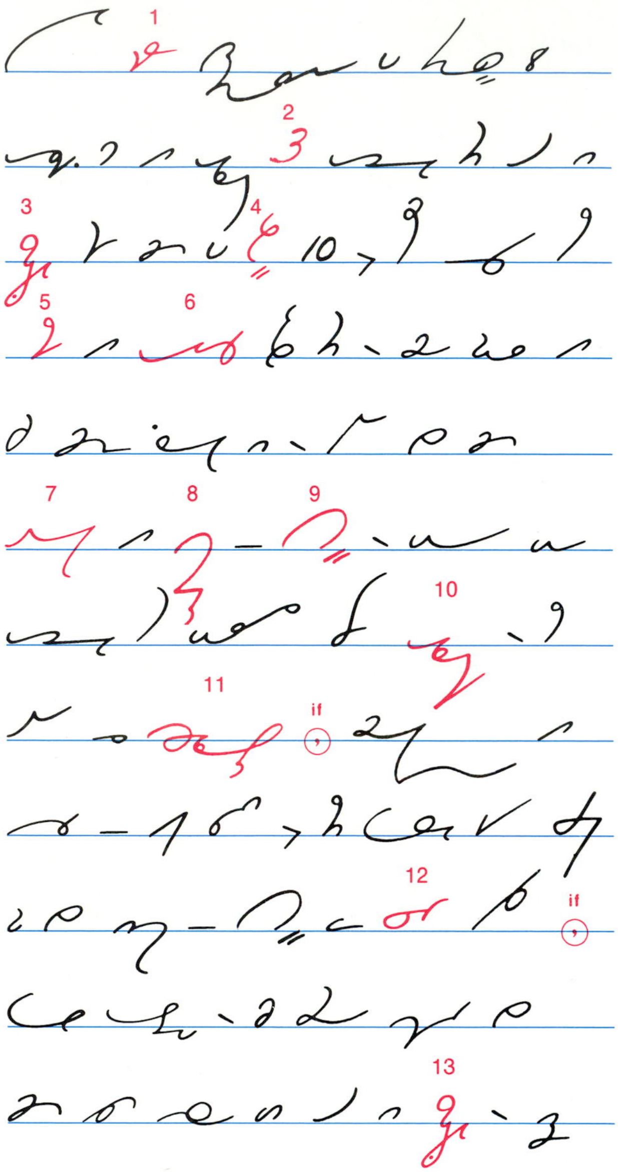

[107 words]

1 Stern 2 three 3 associates 4 September
5 effort 6 locate 7 there will be
8 conventions 9 Denver 10 reserved
11 cancellations 12 another 13 associates

44.5 Business Letter

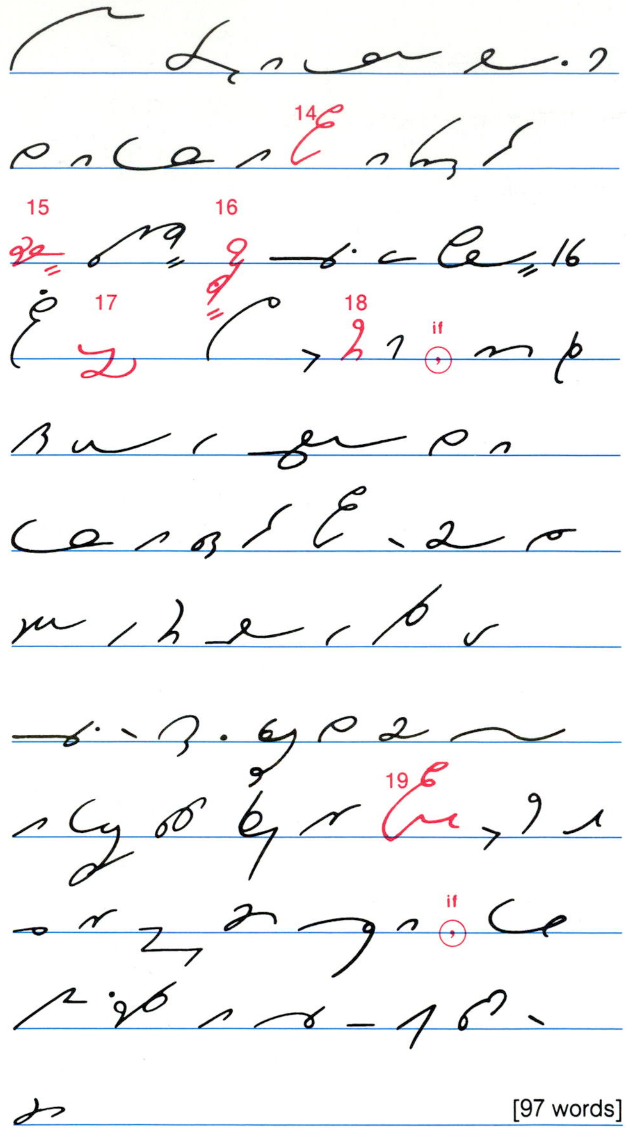

[97 words]

14 exhibit 15 Western 16 Association
17 referred 18 If you 19 exhibitors

UNIT XII

LESSON 45

NEW IN LESSON 45

- **Differentiating between *past* and *passed***

DICTATION SPEED BUILDING

The shorthand outlines below appear in the speed dictation practice which follows. Practice writing these words using the shorthand outlines. Then, using the key which follows, dictate the words to yourself.

Theory Words

Brief Forms

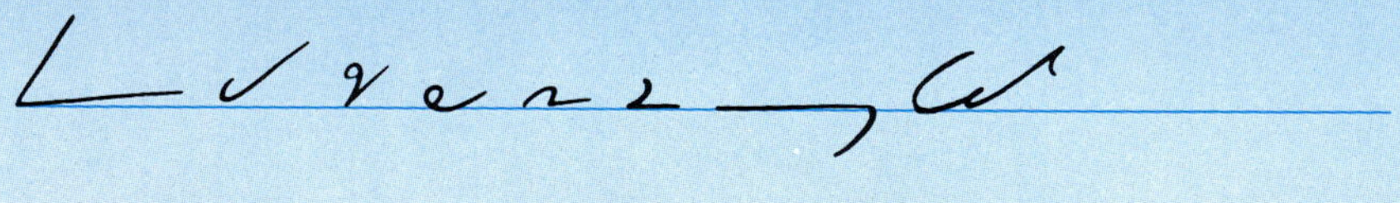

Phrases

Key *Theory*: 100 reams, bond, delighted, first, received, firm, processed, sincere, also, catalog, lowest, industry
Brief Forms: Gentlemen, order, yesterday, were, one, soon, manufacture, products
Phrases: from you/from your, it was, has been, you should have, this will be, Yours very truly

Speed Dictation Practice

45.1 Business Letter

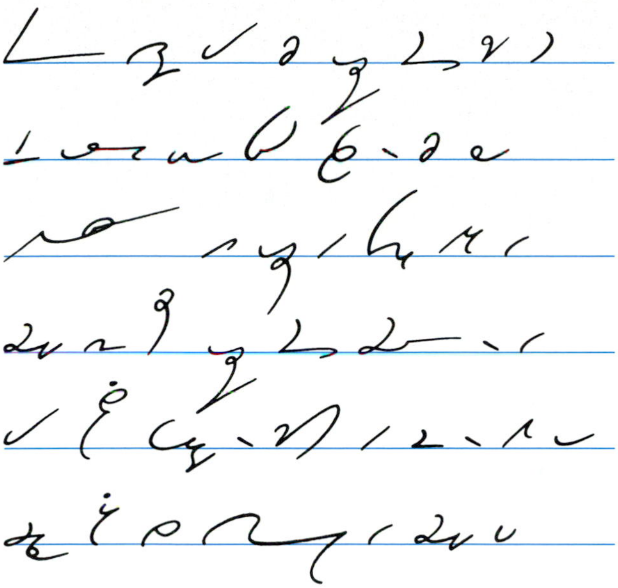

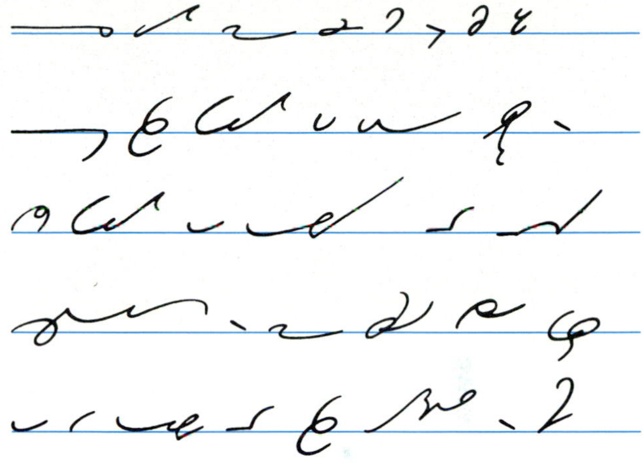

[96 words]

TRANSCRIPTION SKILL DEVELOPMENT

Transcribe the following words and phrases, noting spelling and capitalization. Then transcribe the transcription letter which follows.

Transcription Warmup

45.2

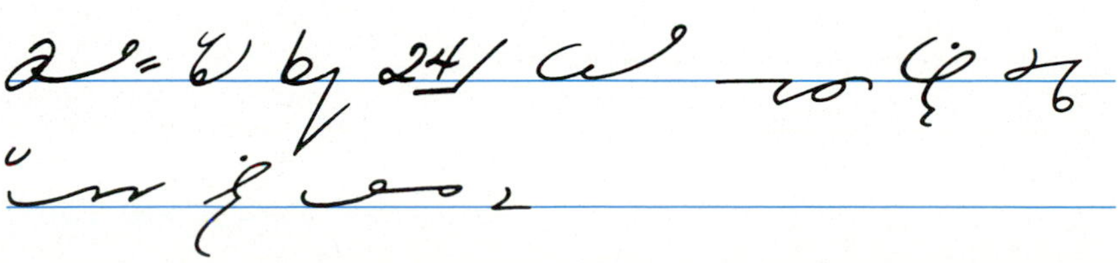

Transcription Practice

45.3 Letter

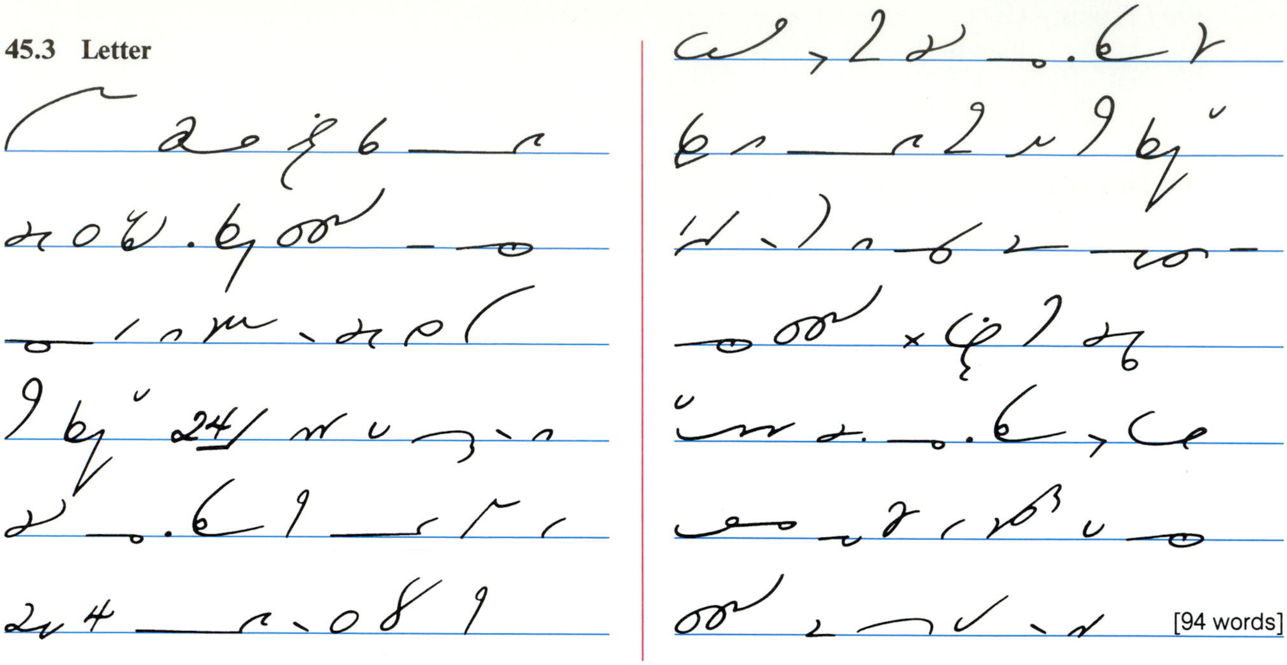

[94 words]

Communication Skill Builder

Similar Words: past, passed

past: (n.) time gone by

passed: (v.) moved from one point to another (past tense of *pass*)

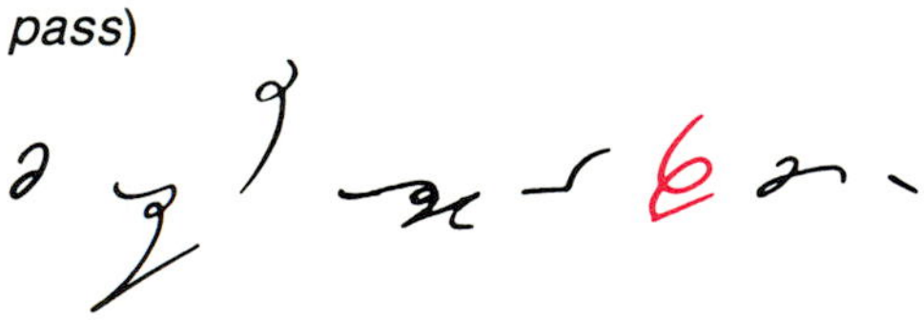

We received several requests in the *past* week.

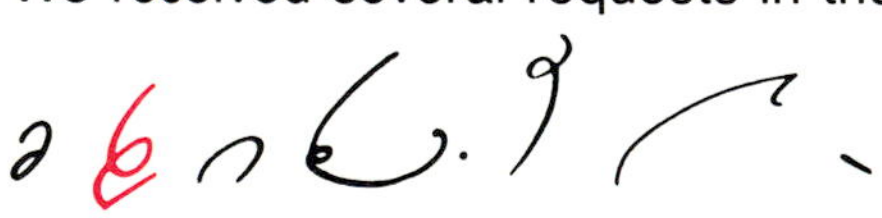

We *passed* this building several times.

Reading and Writing Practice

45.4 Business Letter

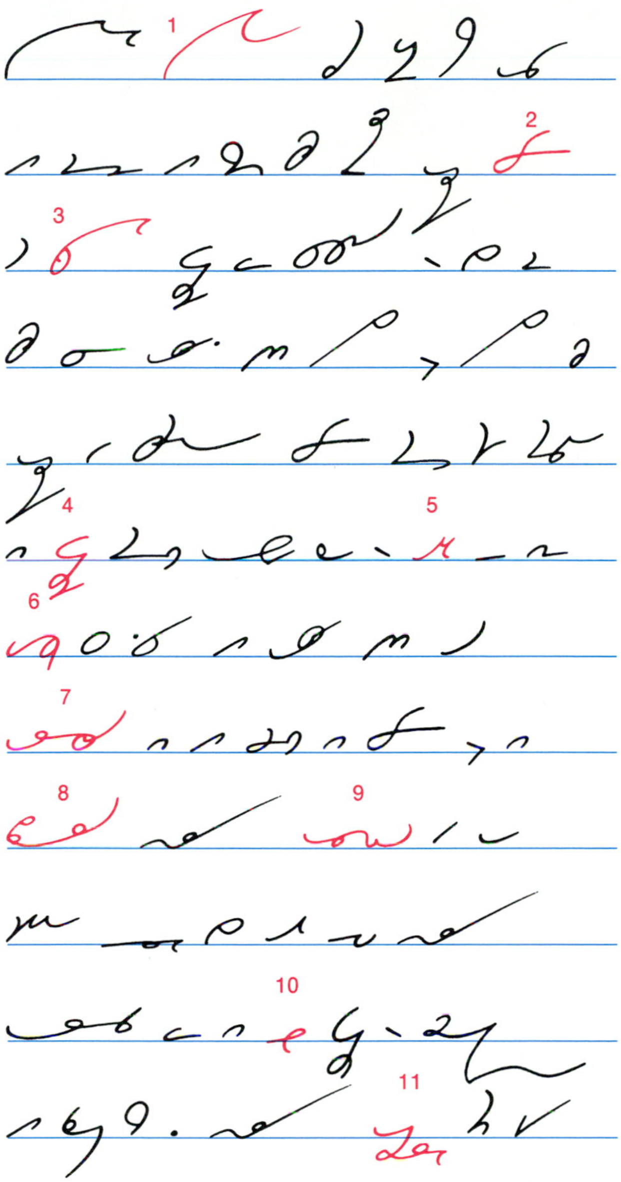

[102 words]

45.5 Business Letter

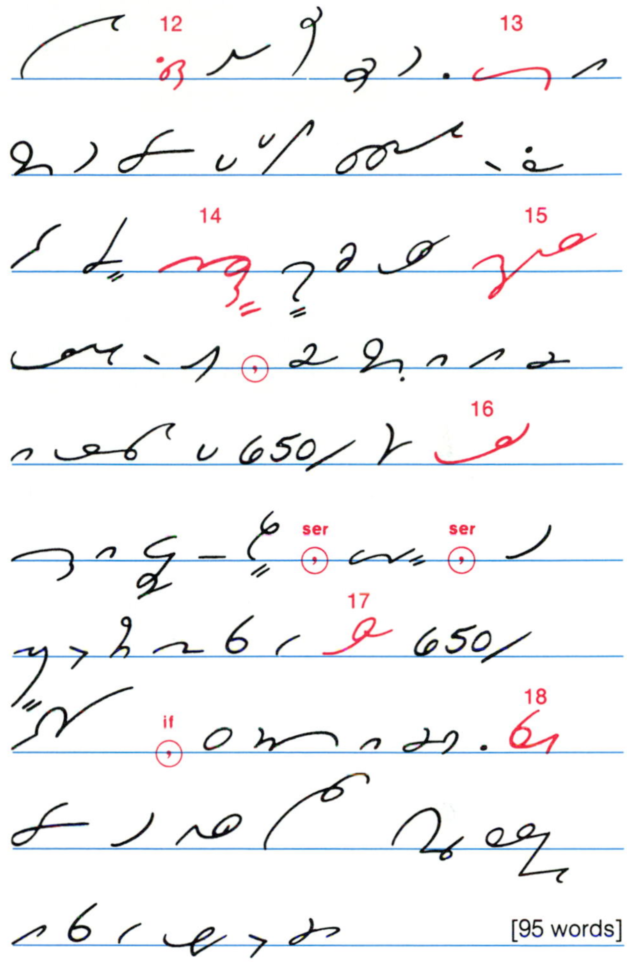

[95 words]

1 Temple 2 payment 3 items 4 purchased
5 There was 6 occasion 7 remind
8 excellent 9 record 10 next 11 reference

12 Hughes 13 organization 14 Communications
15 considerate 16 leather 17 entire
18 partial

LESSON 46

NEW IN LESSON 46

- **Differentiating between *council* and *counsel***

DICTATION SPEED BUILDING

The shorthand outlines below appear in the speed dictation practice which follows. Practice writing these words using the shorthand outlines. Then, using the key which follows, dictate the words to yourself.

Theory Words

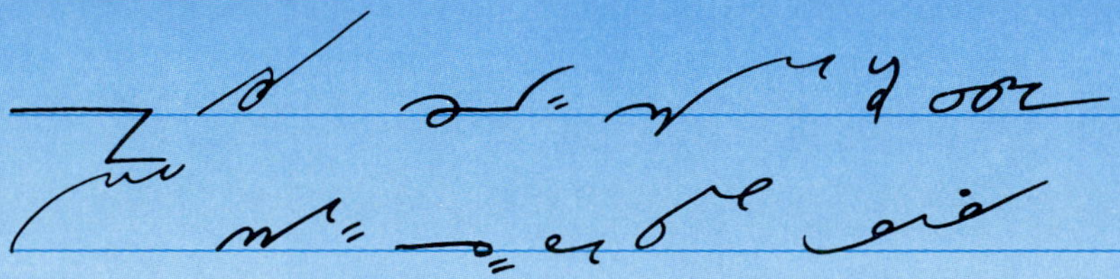

Brief Forms

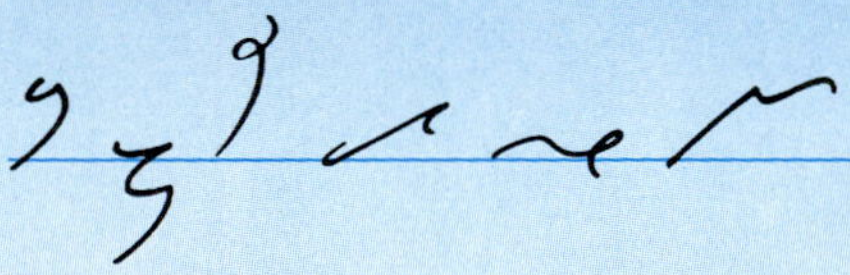

Phrases

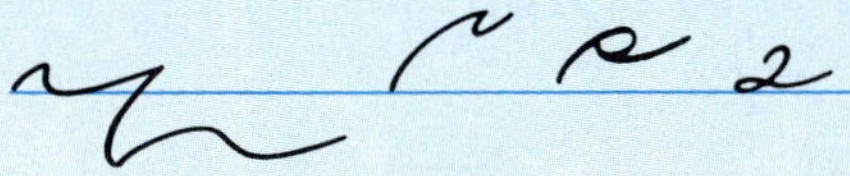

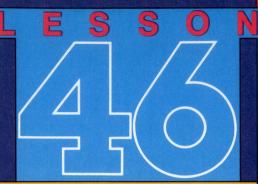

Key *Theory*: management, decided, Camden, customers, official, announcement, tomorrow, Woods, Maine, years, address, letterhead

Brief Forms: office, representative, several, orders, correspondence, direct

Phrases: you will be glad, to know, that our, we are

Speed Dictation Practice

46.1 Business Letter

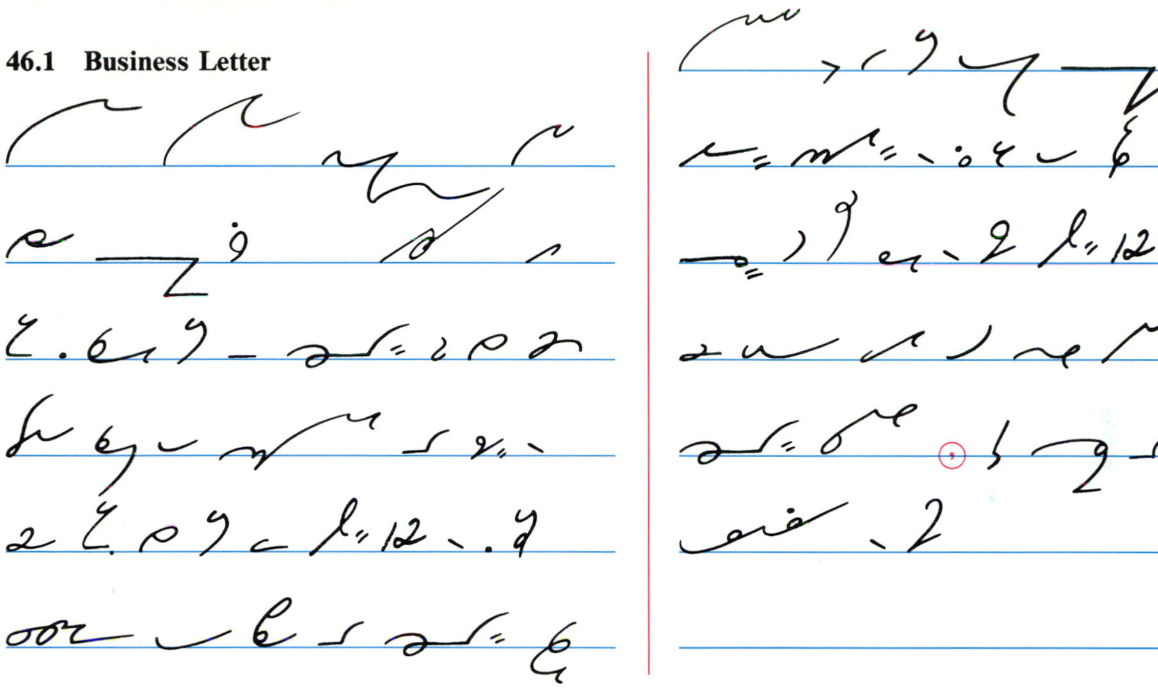

[93 words]

TRANSCRIPTION SKILL DEVELOPMENT

Transcribe the following words and phrases, noting spelling and capitalization. Then transcribe the letter which follows.

Transcription Warmup

46.2

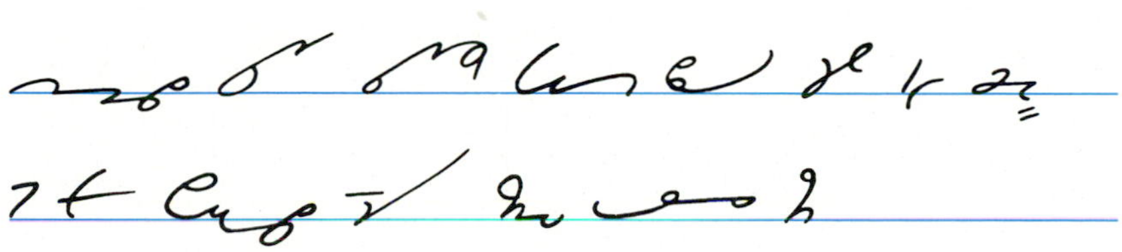

Transcription Practice

46.3 Business Letter

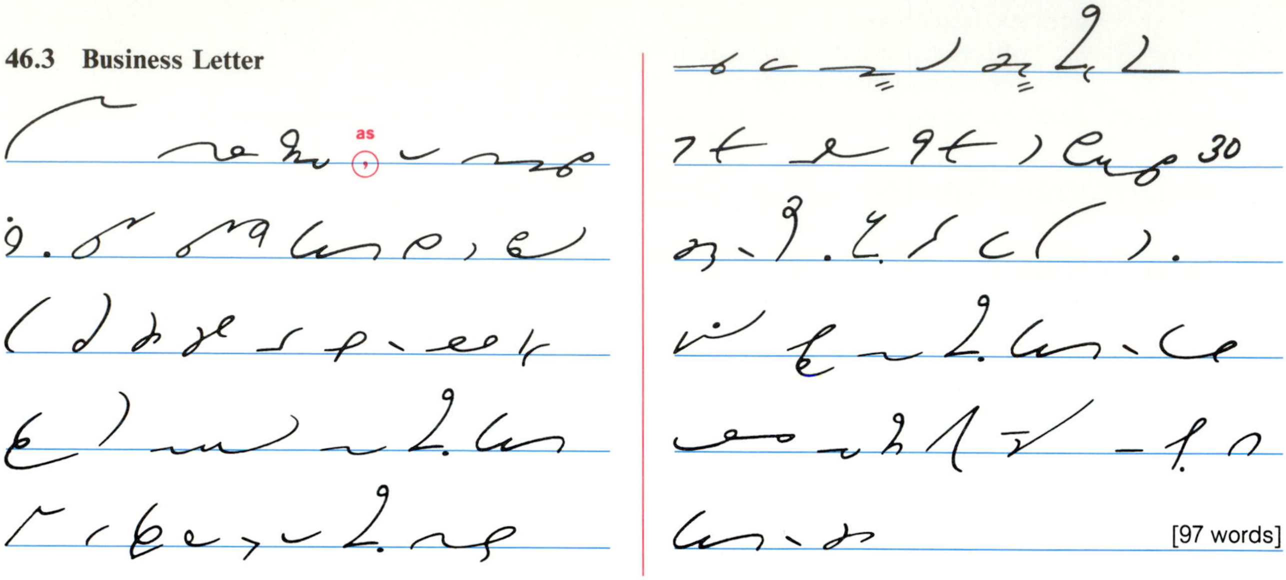

[97 words]

Communication Skill Builder

Similar Words: council, counsel

council: (n.) an assembly

counsel: (v.) to give advice

The meeting of the city *council* will be held in February.

Dr. Jennings will *counsel* my daughter.

Reading and Writing Practice

46.4 Business Letter

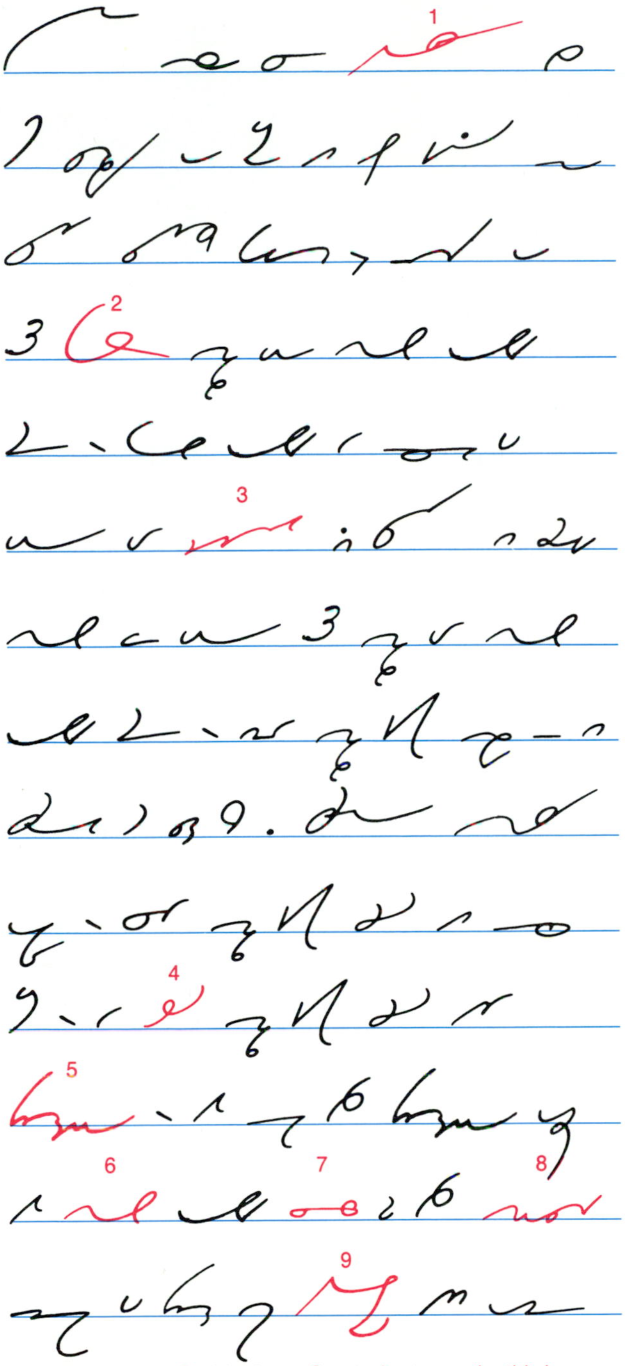

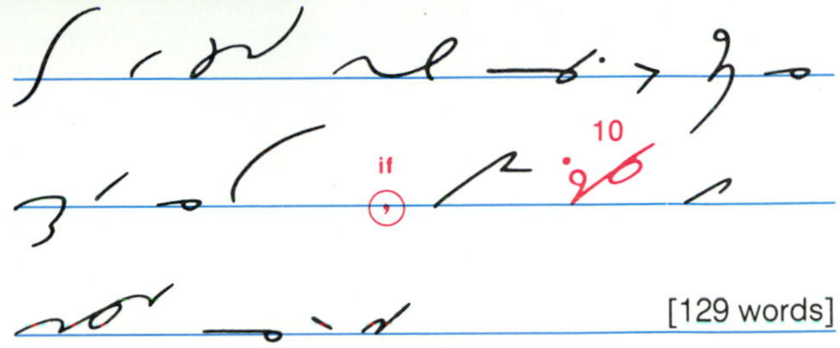

[129 words]

1 delighted 2 blank 3 students 4 third
5 bookstore 6 class 7 immediately 8 correct
9 delivered

46.5 Business Letter

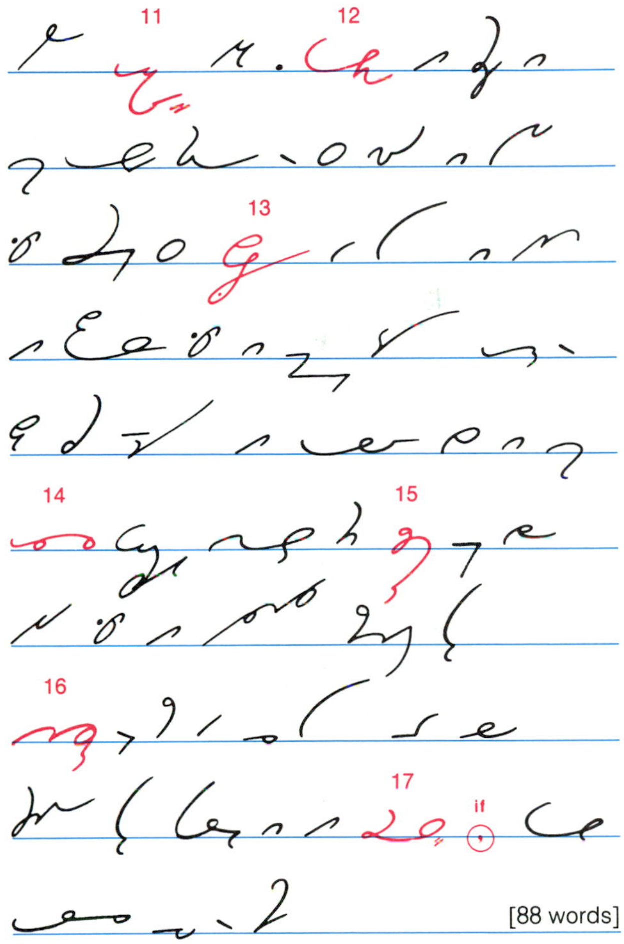

[88 words]

10 hesitate 11 Robert 12 pleasure
13 appreciated 14 regularly 15 executives
16 communications 17 Philadelphia

LESSON 47

NEW IN LESSON 47

- Punctuation: words or phrases in apposition (apposition comma)

DICTATION SPEED BUILDING

The shorthand outlines below appear in the speed dictation practice which follows. Practice writing these words using the shorthand outlines. Then, using the key which follows, dictate the words to yourself.

Theory Words

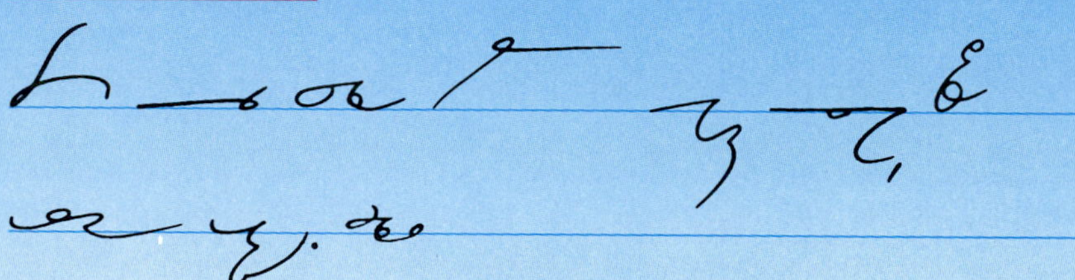

Brief Forms

Phrases

Key *Theory*: big, minute, answer, determine, improve, membership, expire, renewal, responding, Sincerely
Brief Forms: organization, questionnaire, short, questions, where, nevertheless, idea, requests
Phrases: for your, will you please, to the, if you, you will be

Speed Dictation Practice

47.1 Form Letter

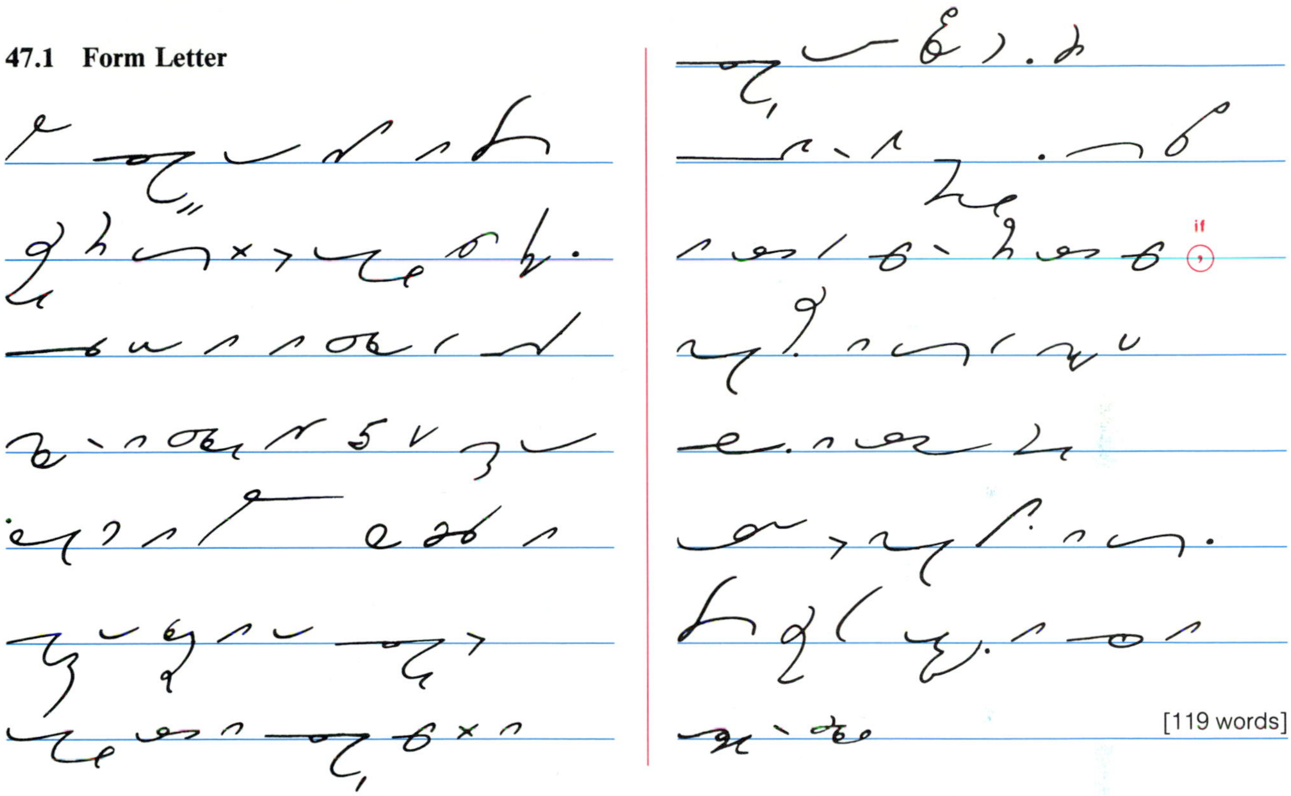

[119 words]

TRANSCRIPTION SKILL DEVELOPMENT

Transcribe the following words and phrases, noting spelling and capitalization. Then transcribe the transcription letter which follows.

Transcription Warmup

47.2

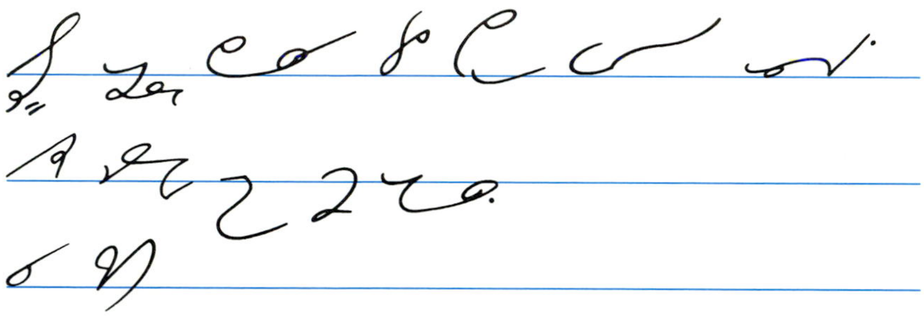

Transcription Practice

47.3 Reference Letter

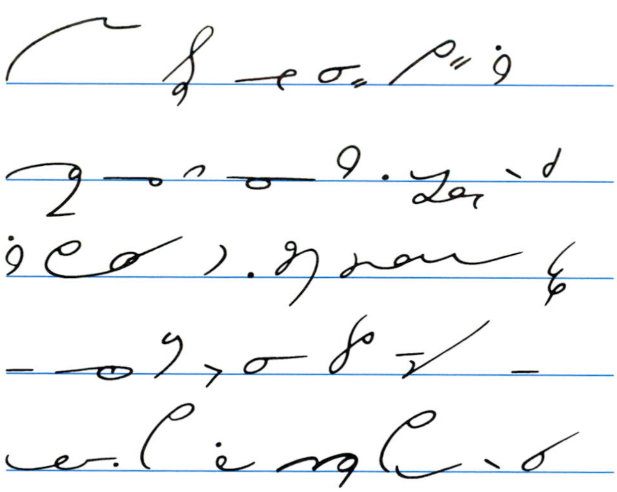

[88 words]

Punctuation: Words or Phrases in Apposition

A word or phrase used in apposition is one that explains or identifies other terms. When it occurs within a sentence, it is set off by two commas. When it occurs at the end of a sentence, only one comma is used.

The *apposition comma* is indicated by 

Our auditor, *Mr. Santiago*, is ill today.

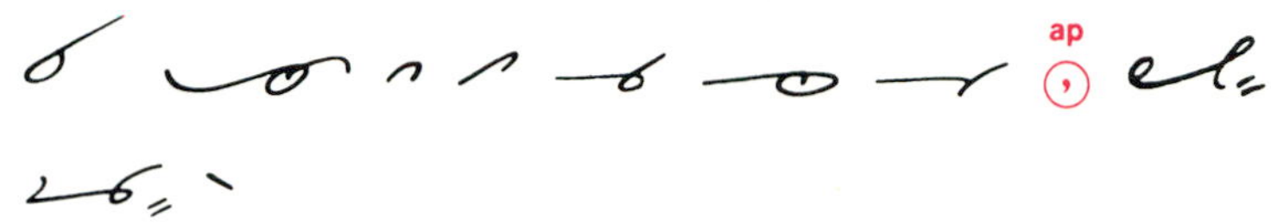

I would like you to meet my mother, *Elise Smith*.

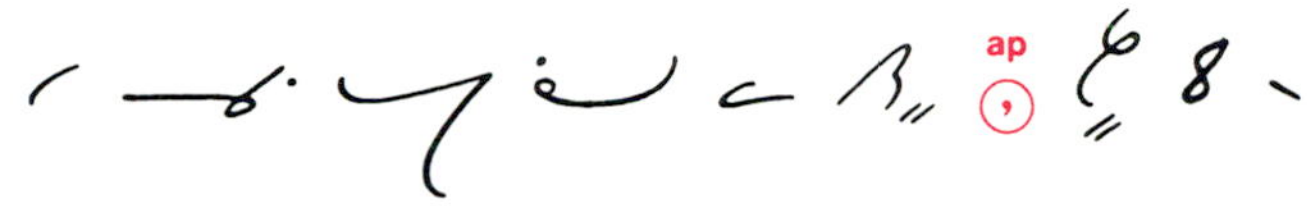

The meeting will be held on Tuesday, *September 8*.

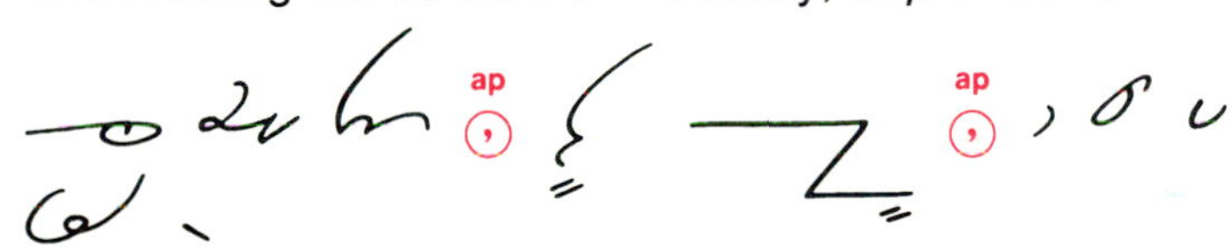

My first book, *Business Management*, is out of print.

Reading and Writing Practice

47.4 Business Letter

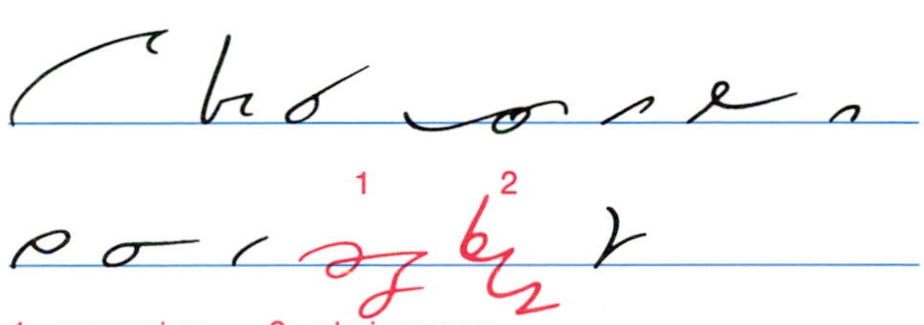

1 campaign 2 chairperson

3 United 4 pledge

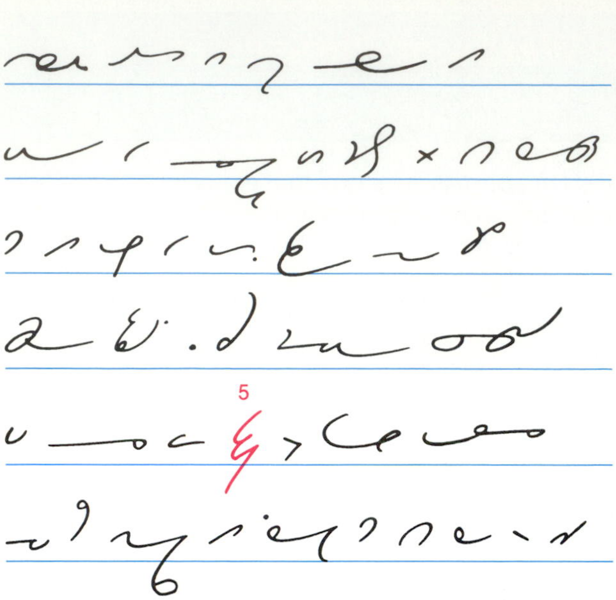

[81 words]

47.5 Business Memo

5 postage 6 Steve

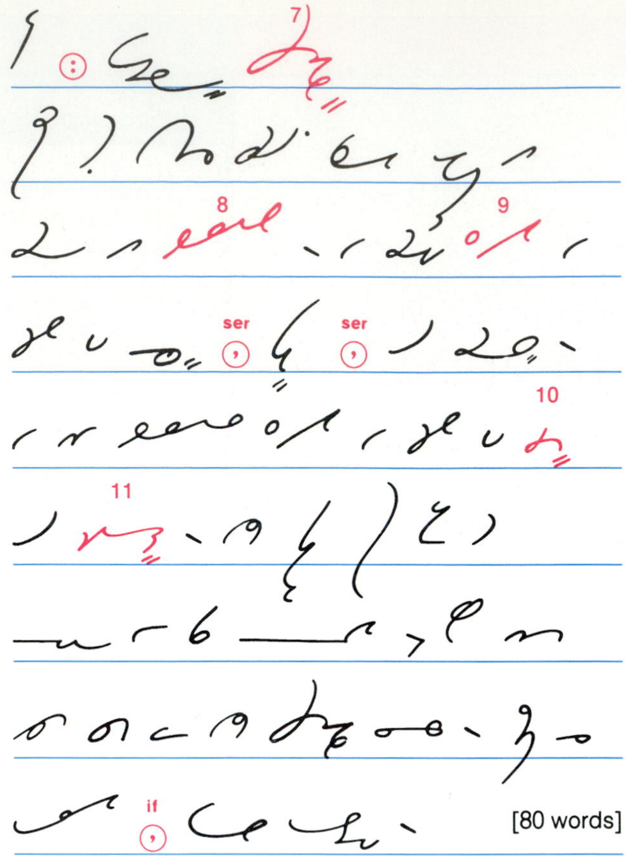

[80 words]

7 Vacancies 8 territories 9 includes
10 Chicago 11 St. Louis

The need for shorthand-writing secretaries is prominent in the fashion industry.

LESSON 48

NEW IN LESSON 48

- **Differentiating between *lose*, *loose*, and *loss***

DICTATION SPEED BUILDING

The shorthand outlines below appear in the speed dictation practice which follows. Practice writing these words using the shorthand outlines. Then, using the key which follows, dictate the words to yourself.

Theory Words

Brief Forms

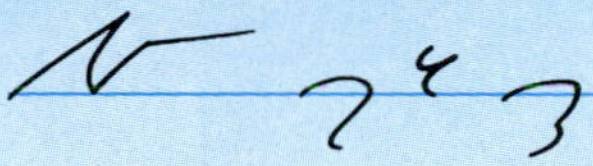

Phrases

Key *Theory*: Monroe, determined, legally, obligated, expenses, injured, Chicago, medical, $5,300, issue, additional
Brief Forms: department, company, was, questions
Phrases: Dear Mrs., that our, as soon as possible, if you have, Very truly yours

Speed Dictation Practice

48.1 Business Letter

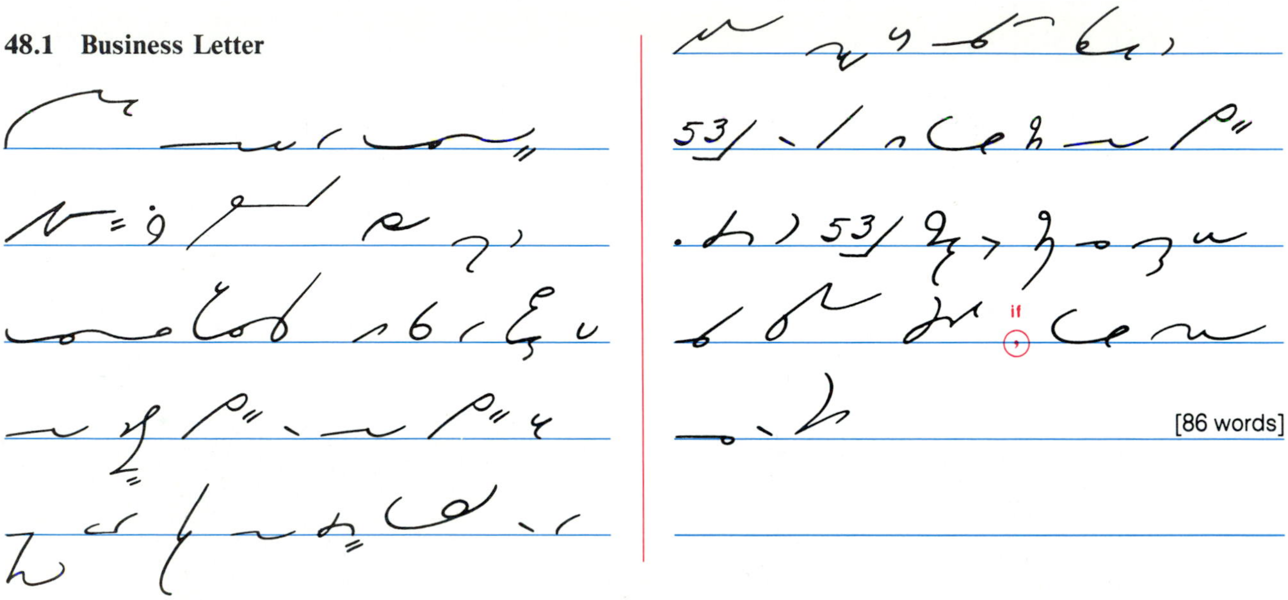

[86 words]

TRANSCRIPTION SKILL DEVELOPMENT

Transcribe the following words and phrases, noting spelling and capitalization. Then transcribe the transcription letter which follows.

Transcription Warmup

48.2

Transcription Practice

48.3 Business Letter

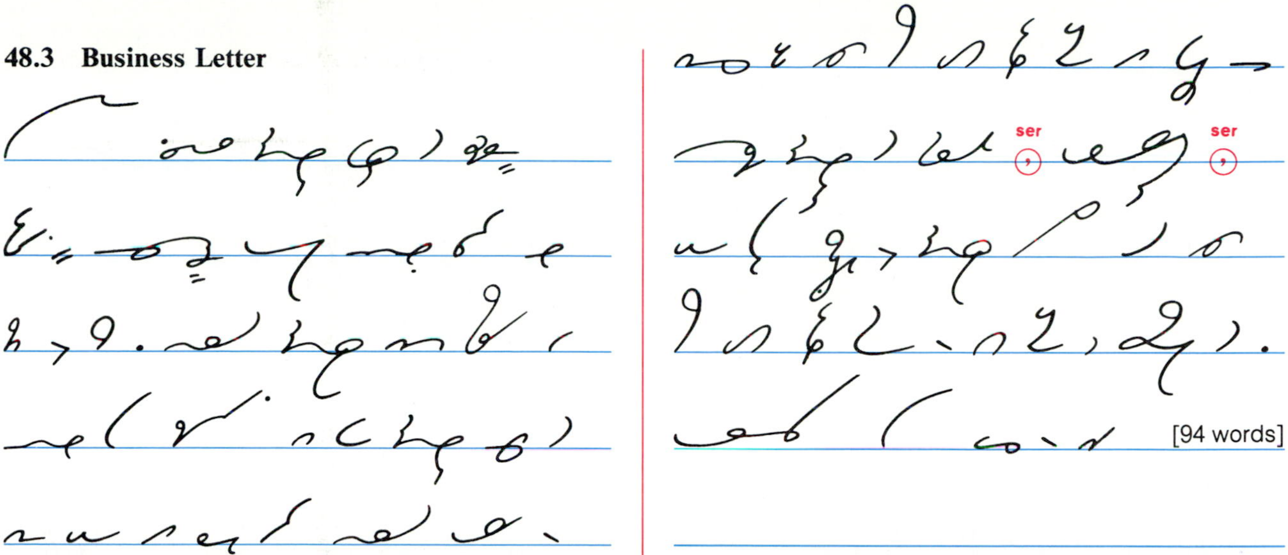

[94 words]

Communication Skill Builder

Similar Words: lose, loose, loss

lose: (v.) to part with unintentionally

loose: (adj.) not tight

loss: (n.) something lost

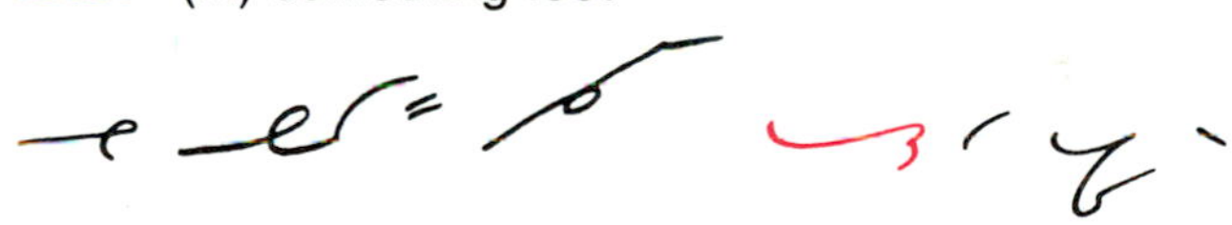

Miss Martin did not *lose* the report.

The coat is too *loose* for me to wear.

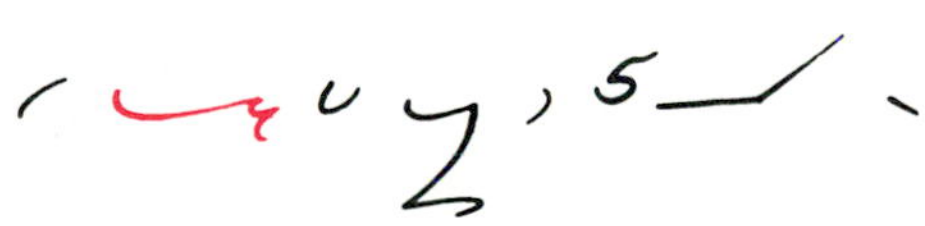

The *loss* of revenue is $5 million.

48.4 Business Letter

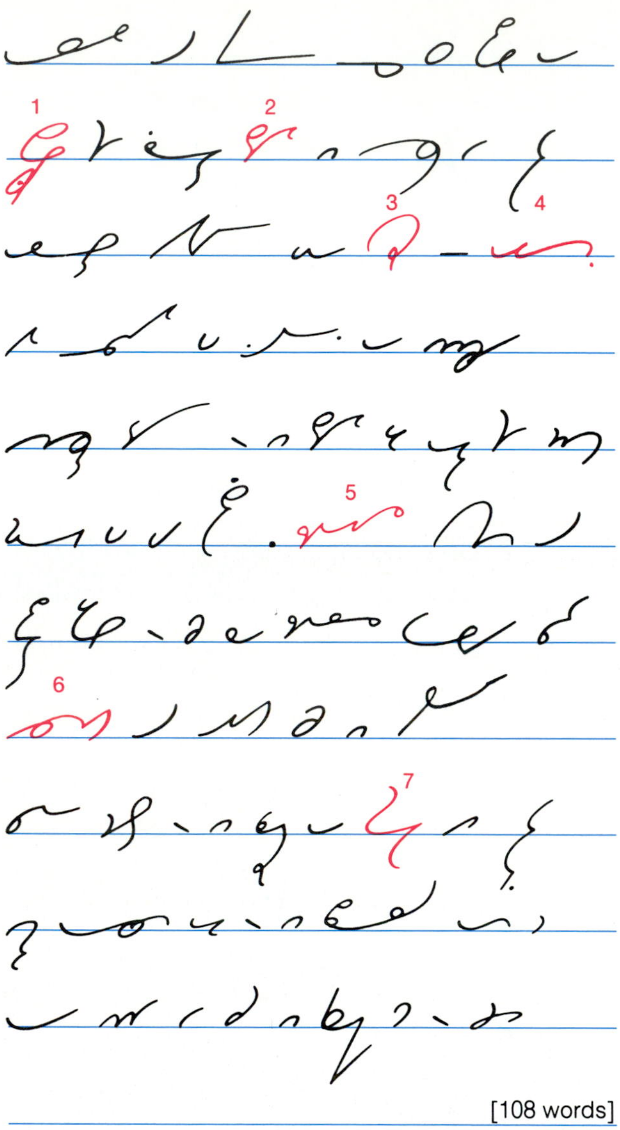

1 appreciation 2 assistance 3 division
4 reorganizing 5 extraordinarily 6 tactful
7 valuable

48.5 Business Letter

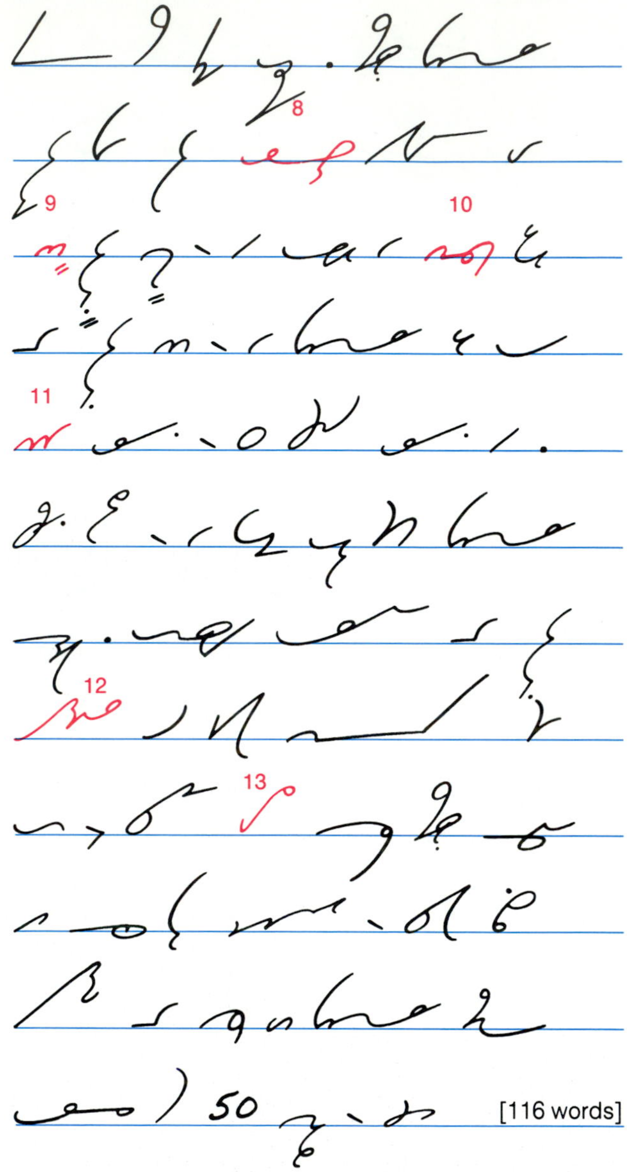

8 relations 9 World 10 unusual 11 worth
12 industry 13 ordinarily

UNIT XIII

LESSON 49

NEW IN LESSON 49

- **Punctuation: commas with conjunctions (conjunction comma)**

DICTATION SPEED BUILDING

The shorthand outlines below appear in the speed dictation practice which follows. Practice writing these words using the shorthand outlines. Then, using the key below, dictate the words to yourself.

Theory Words

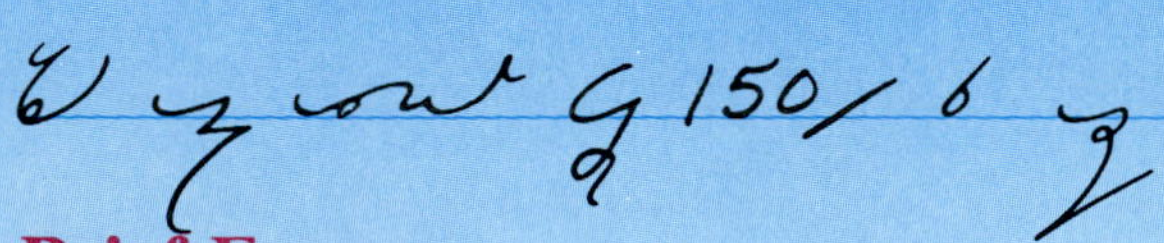

Brief Forms

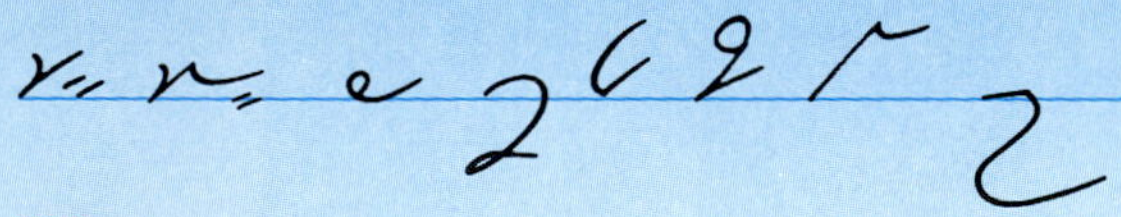

Phrases

Key *Theory*: opened, reasonable, records, purchases, $150, yet, received

Brief Forms: State Street, were, convenience, part, after, during, envelope

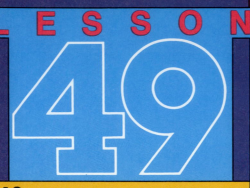

Phrases: to do so, we have not, send us

Speed Dictation Practice

49.1 Letter

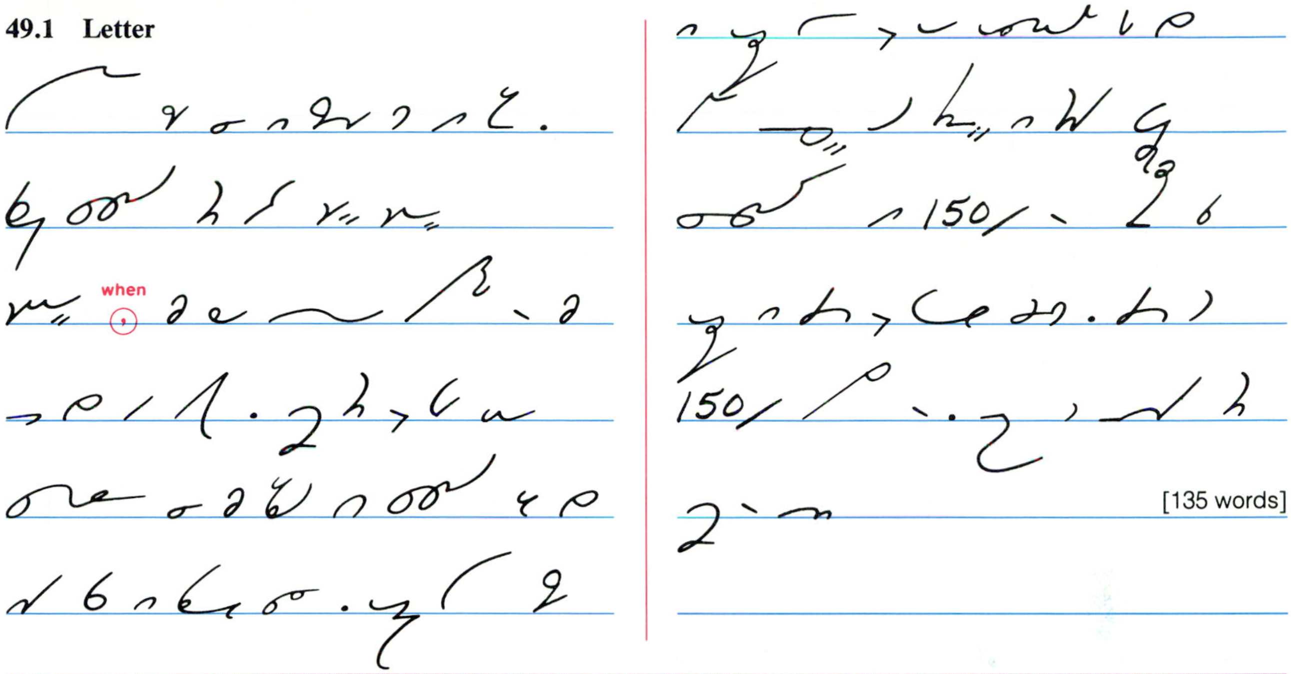

[135 words]

TRANSCRIPTION SKILL DEVELOPMENT

Transcribe the following words and phrases, noting spelling and capitalization. Then transcribe the transcription letter which follows.

Transcription Warmup

49.2

Transcription Practice

49.3 Letter

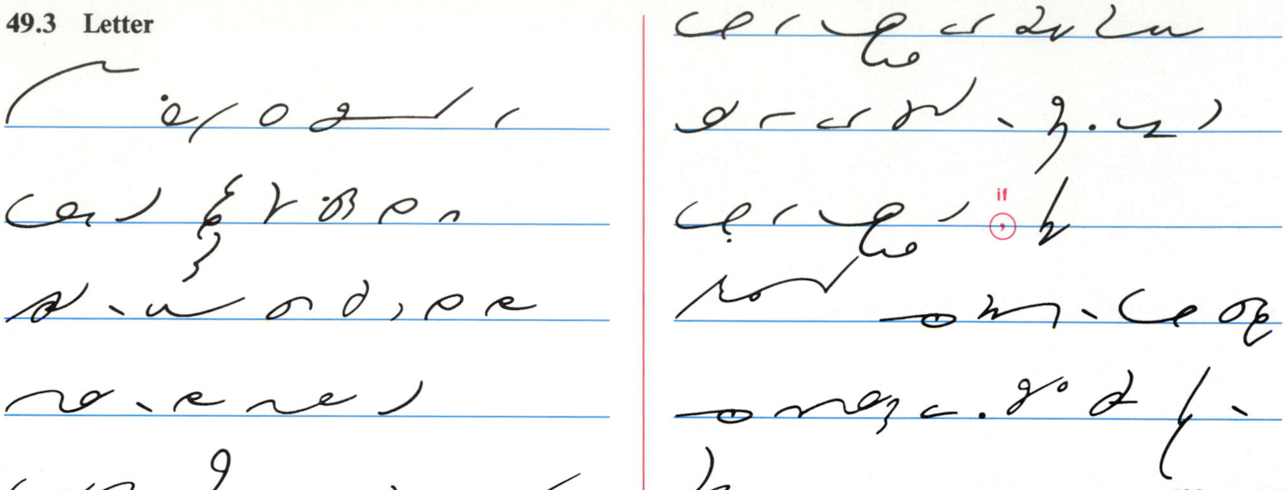

[80 words]

Punctuation: Commas With Conjunctions

Sometimes two simple sentences are joined together. Usually the sentences are joined by a conjunction such as *and*, *or*, or *but*. This type of sentence is called a compound sentence, and the conjunction is preceded by a comma.

The *conjunction comma* is indicated by 

Today the weather is stormy, *and* I want to stay home.

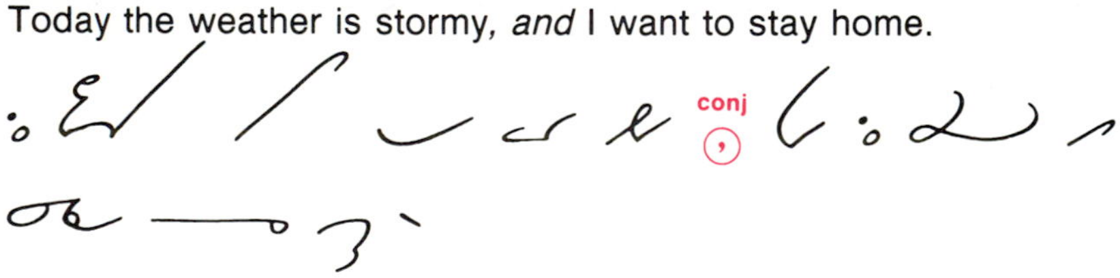

He expected to do well on the test, *but* he failed to answer many questions.

Reading and Writing Practice

49.4 Business Letter

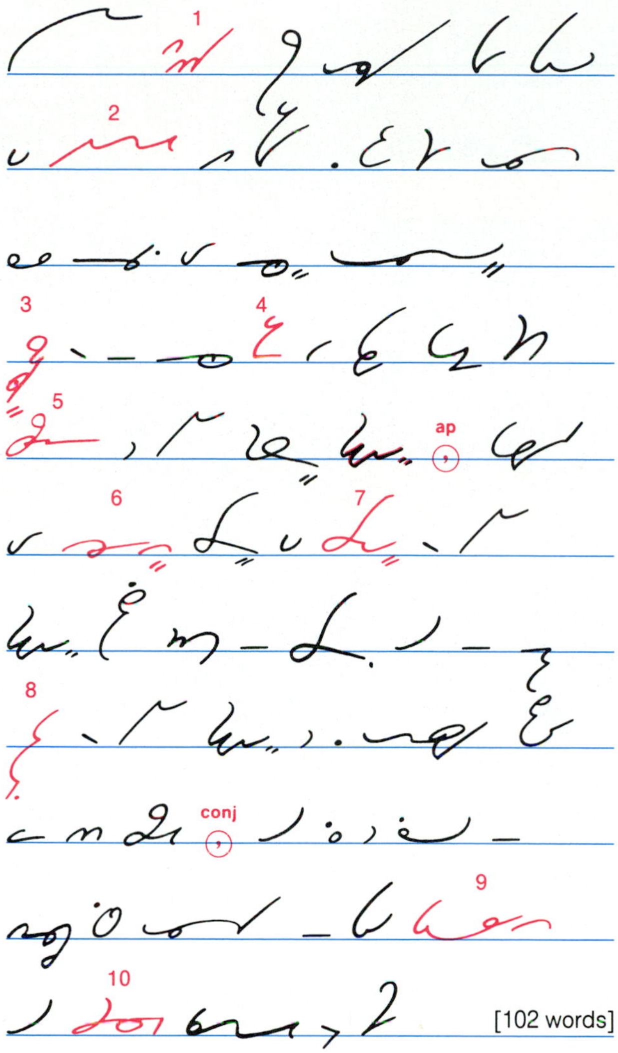

[102 words]

49.5 Business Letter

1 Underwood 2 directors 3 Association
4 opinion 5 assignment 6 Chemical
7 Bangor 8 publishing 9 political 10 financial

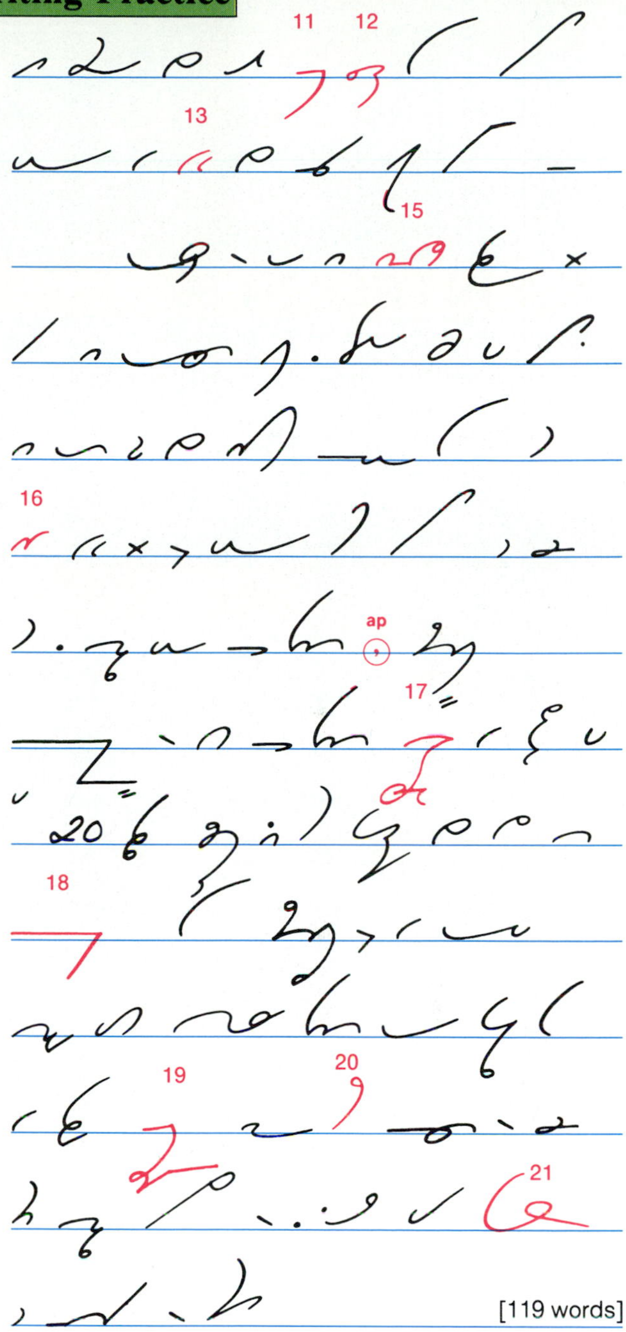

[119 words]

11 never 12 enough 13 things
14 professional 15 one of these 16 other
17 combines 18 manage 19 investment
20 ever 21 blank

LESSON 50

NEW IN LESSON 50

- **Punctuation: introductory expressions**

DICTATION SPEED BUILDING

The shorthand outlines below appear in the speed dictation practice which follows. Practice writing these words using the shorthand outlines. Then, using the key which follows, dictate the words to yourself.

Theory Words

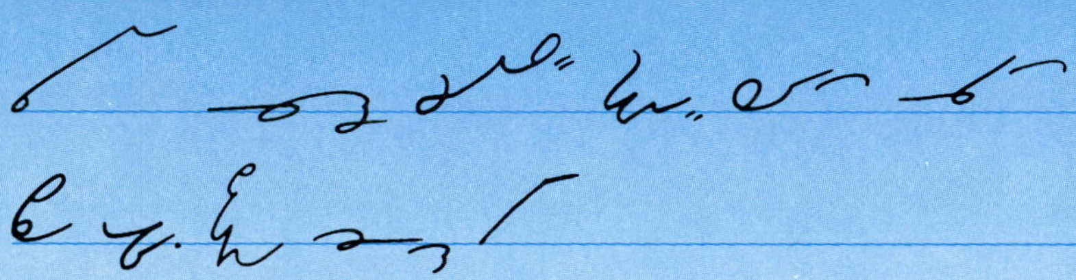

Brief Forms

Phrases

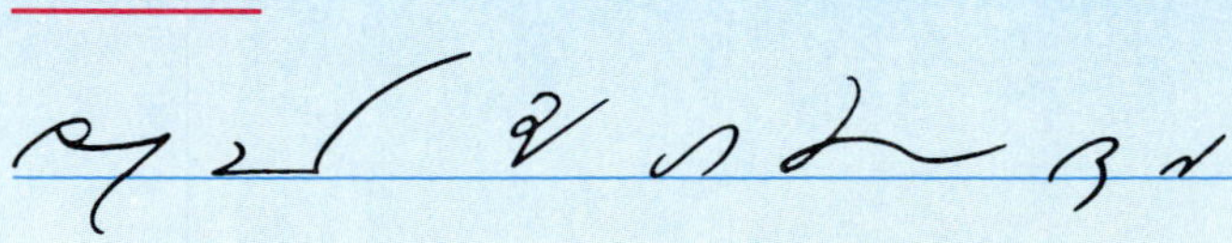

Key *Theory*: editor, magazine, Sandra Foster, article, medical, appear, reporting, exposure, chemicals, done
Brief Forms: Dr., published, publish/publication, about, thinking
Phrases: that will be, some time, we should, of this, very glad, thank you for, Yours truly

Speed Dictation Practice

50.1 Business Letter

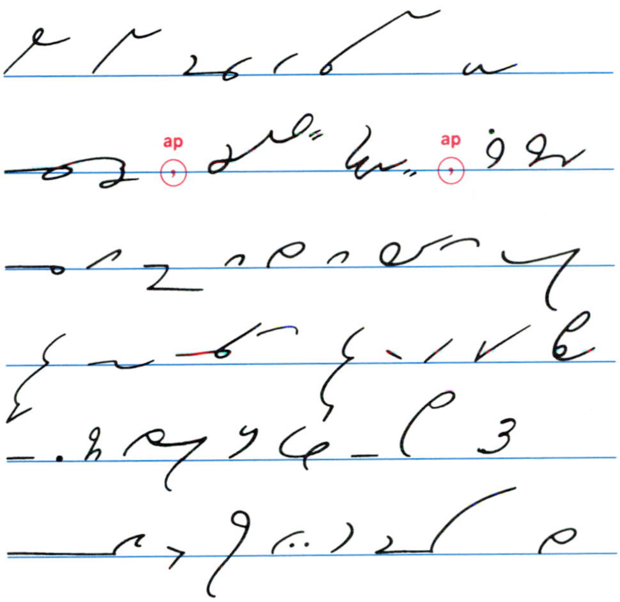

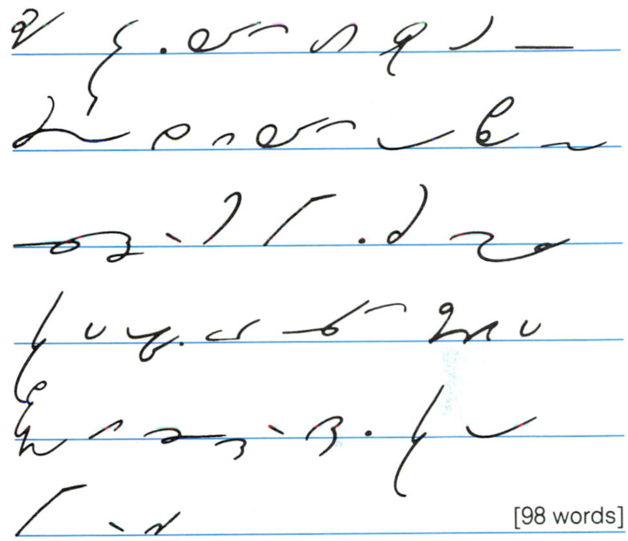

[98 words]

The need for shorthand is industrywide in the travel business.

TRANSCRIPTION SKILL DEVELOPMENT

Transcribe the following words and phrases, noting spelling and capitalization. Then transcribe the transcription letter which follows.

Transcription Warmup

50.2

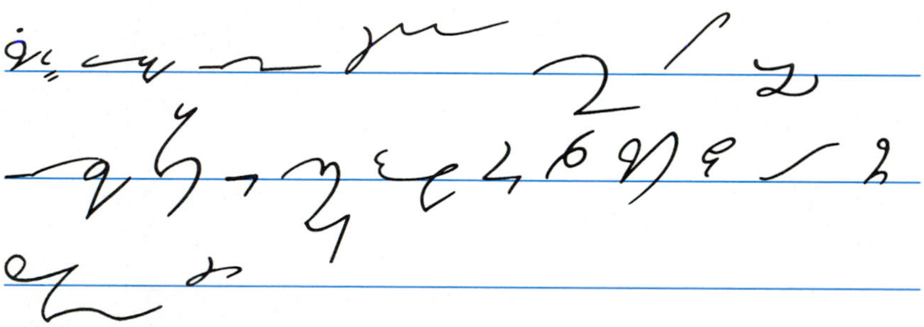

Transcription Practice

50.3 Business Letter

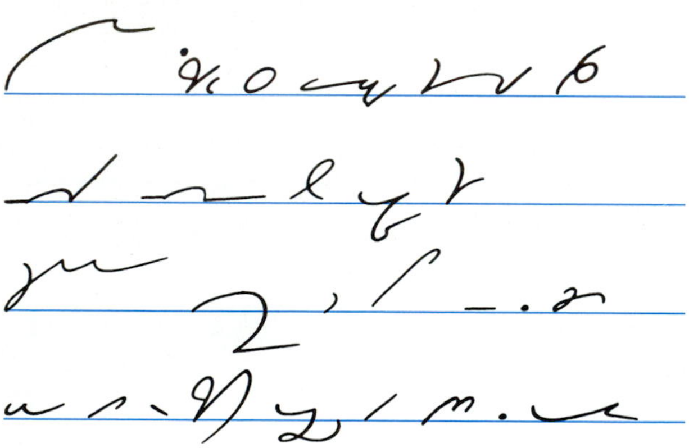

[80 words]

Punctuation: Introductory Expressions

Introductory expressions are elements such as single words, phrases, or clauses that begin a sentence and come before the subject and verb of the main clause. The comma is placed after the introductory expression.

An *introductory comma* is indicated by intro ,

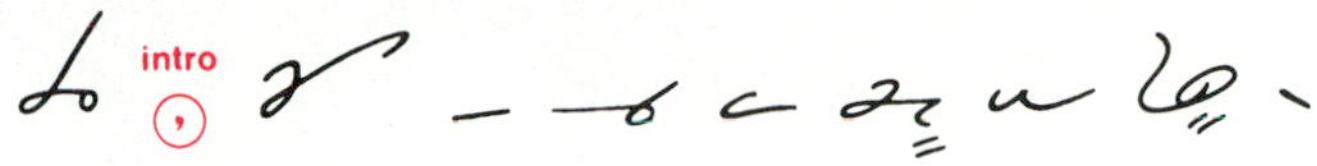

Generally, we do not meet on Wednesday or Friday.

To determine the publication dates, we need to meet with the entire team.

Before we make the final collection, check with the advertising department.

Reading and Writing Practice

50.4 Business Letter

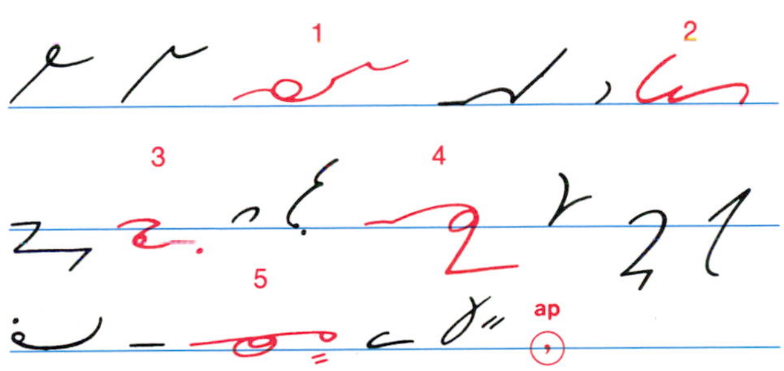

1 Carter 2 program 3 concerning
4 engagement 5 Miami

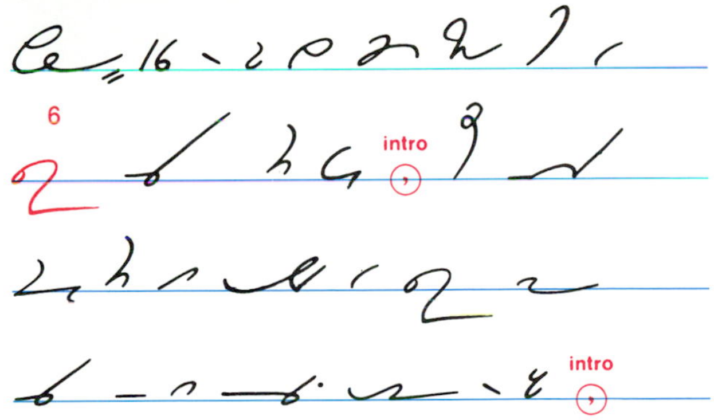

6 equipment

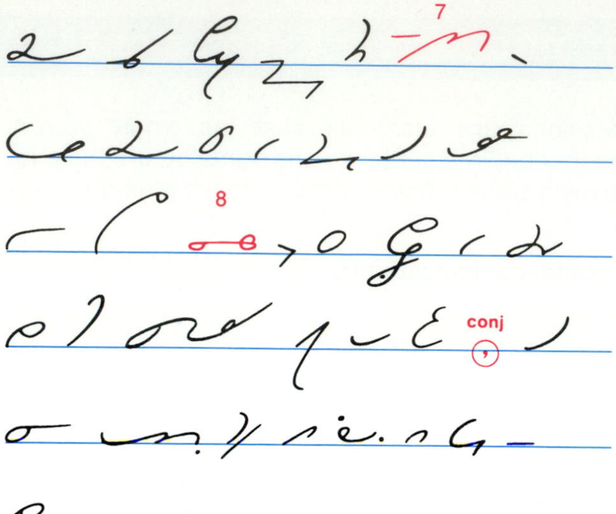

[115 words]

50.5 Business Letter

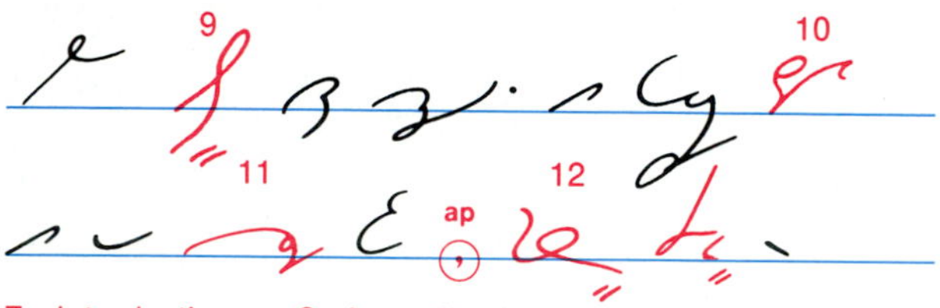

7 introduction 8 immediately 9 Dave
10 assistance 11 guest 12 Frank Jennings

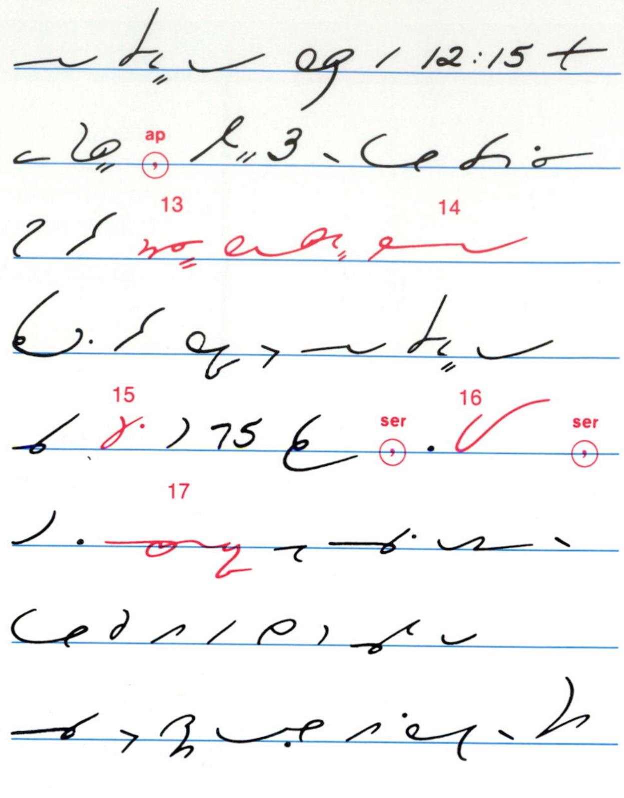

[82 words]

13 Southern Airlines 14 terminal 15 seating
16 podium 17 microphone

LESSON 51

NEW IN LESSON 51

- **Punctuation: commas with parenthetical expressions**

DICTATION SPEED BUILDING

The shorthand outlines below appear in the speed dictation letter which follows. Practice writing these words using the shorthand outlines. Then, using the key which follows, dictate the words to yourself.

Theory Words

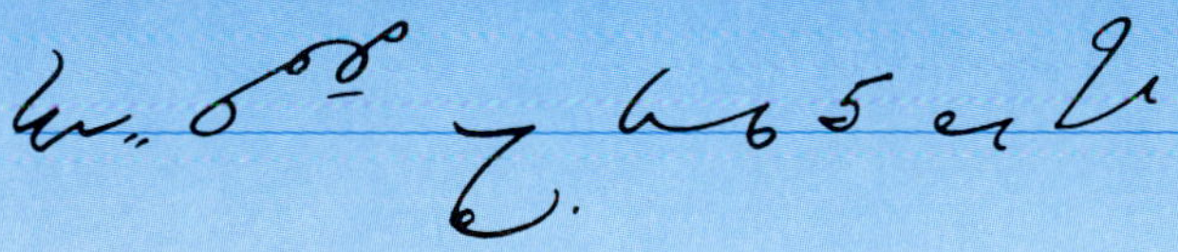

Brief Forms

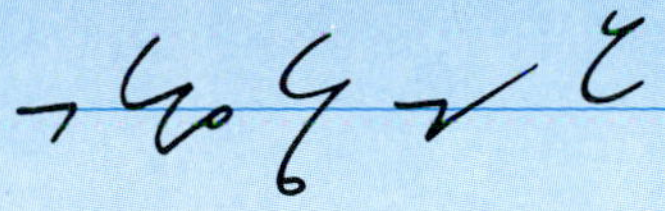

Phrases

Key *Theory*: Foster, adequately, rebuilding, policy, five years, agents

Brief Forms: insurance, property, probably, insured, opportunity

Phrases: you have not, you will have, has not been, one of our

Speed Dictation Practice

51.1 Insurance Letter

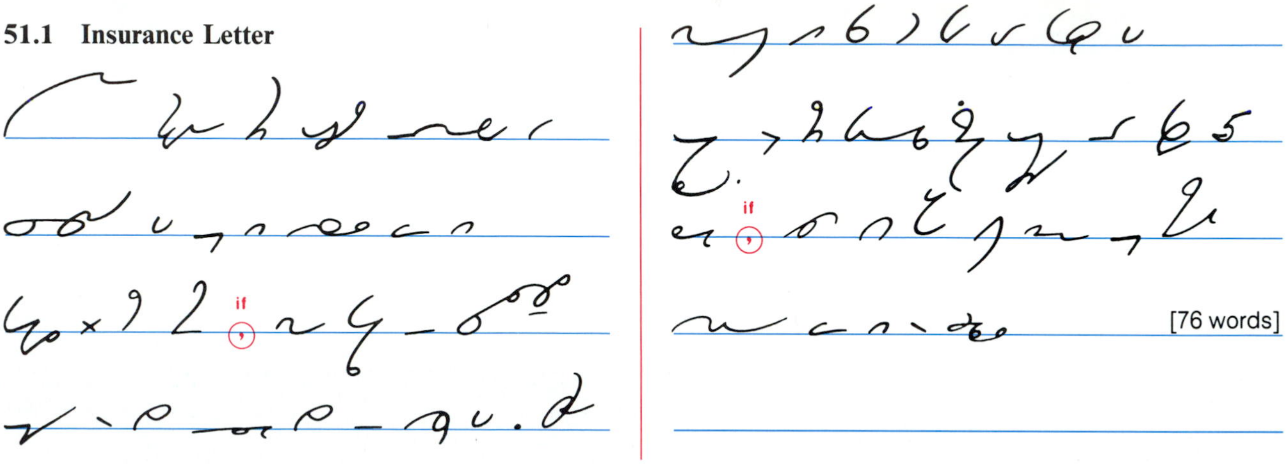

TRANSCRIPTION SKILL DEVELOPMENT

Transcription Warmup

51.2

Transcribe the following words and phrases, noting spelling and capitalization. Then transcribe the transcription letter which follows.

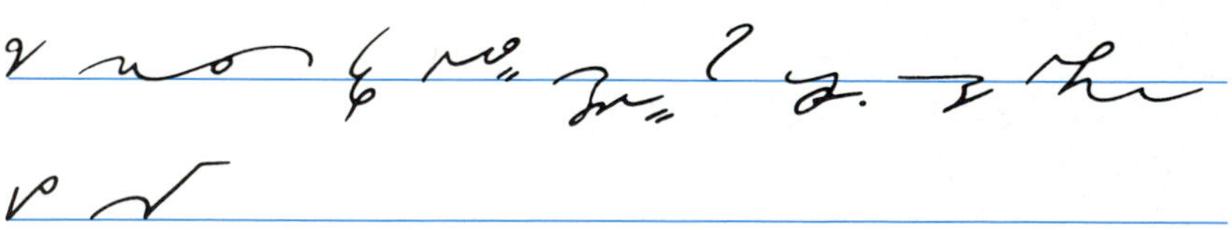

Transcription Practice

51.3 Business Letter

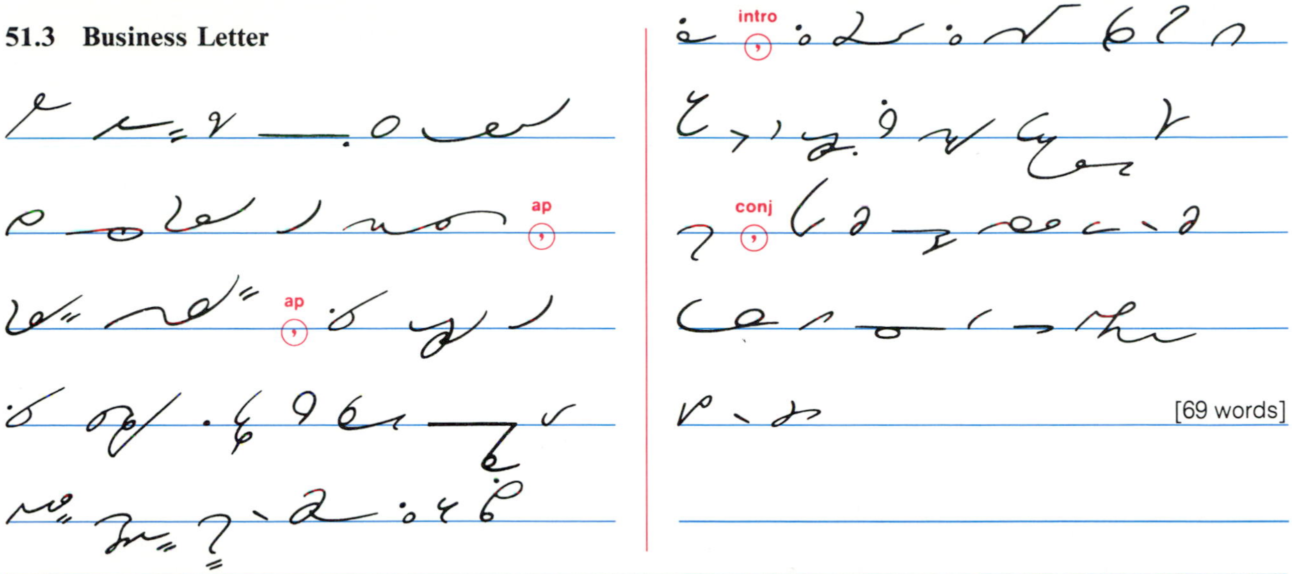

Punctuation: Commas With Parenthetical Expressions

Parenthetical expressions are words or phrases that are not needed for the meaning or the grammatical completeness of the sentence. They are set off by commas. A parenthetical expression occurring at the end of a sentence needs only one comma.

A *parenthetical comma* is indicated by par (,)

Today is, *of course*, a holiday.

Tell me, *Tom*, what time you will arrive.

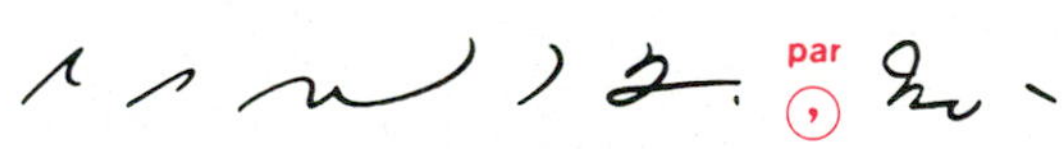

It is too cold for swimming, *as you know*.

Reading and Writing Practice

51.4 Personal Letter

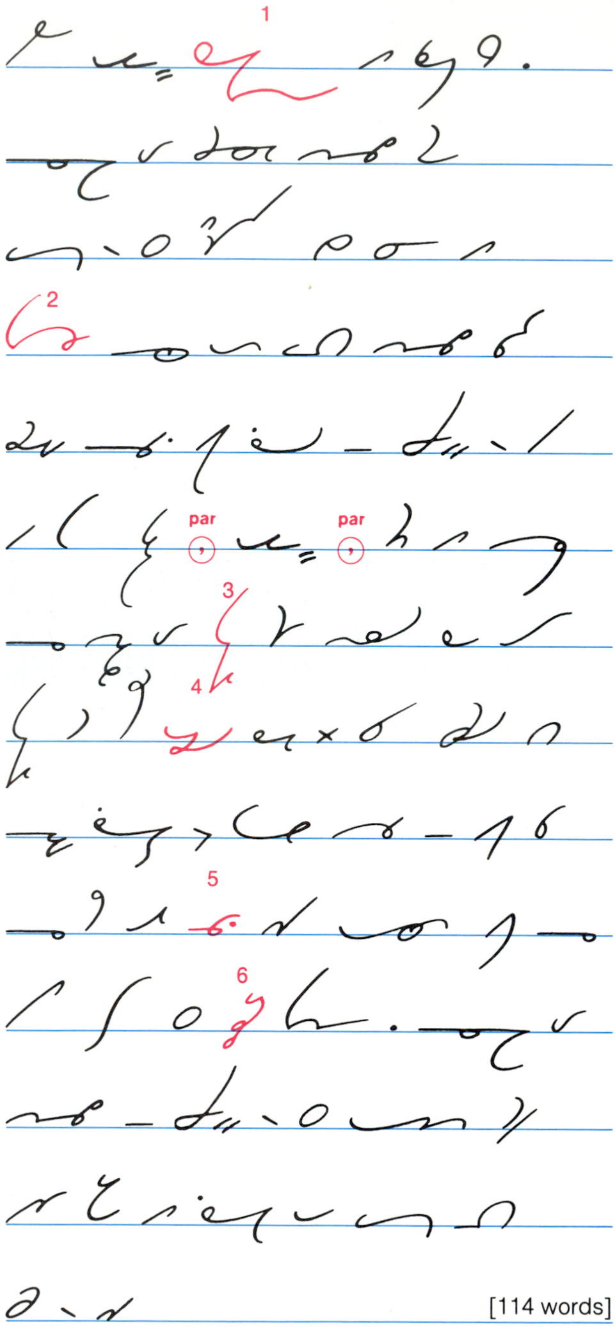

[114 words]

1 I will be glad 2 begin 3 budgets 4 recent 5 anything 6 officially

51.5 Business Letter

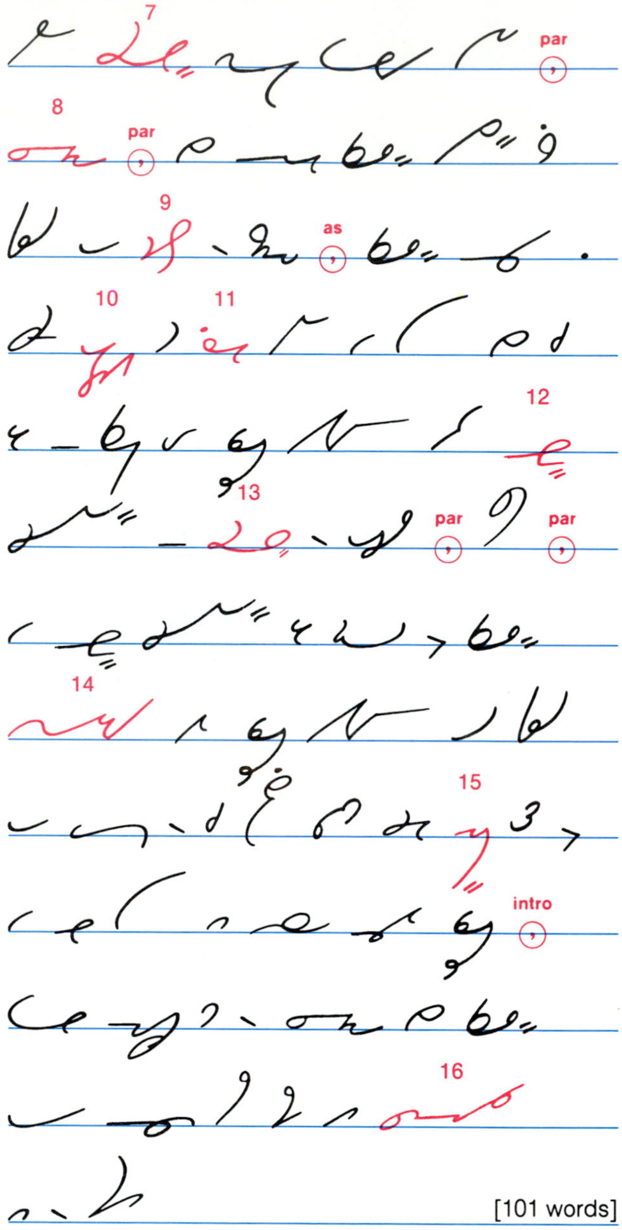

[101 words]

7 Phyllis 8 I am sure 9 staff 10 reputation 11 herself 12 Mason 13 Philadelphia 14 closed 15 November 16 accommodate

LESSON 52

NEW IN LESSON 52

- Geographic references

DICTATION SPEED BUILDING

The shorthand outlines below appear in the speed dictation practice which follows. Practice writing these words using the shorthand outlines. Then, using the key below, dictate the words to yourself.

Theory Words

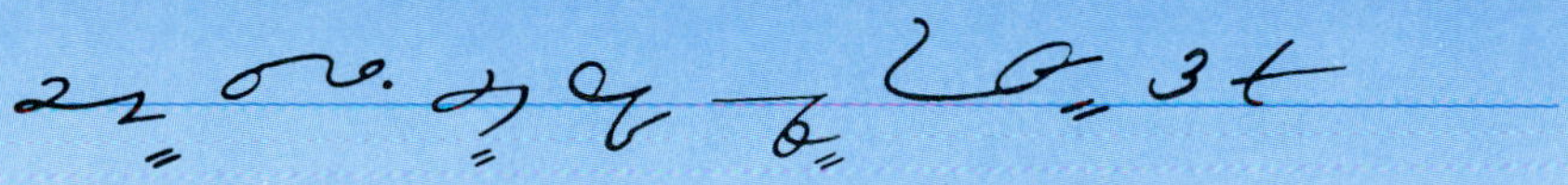

Brief Forms

Phrases

Key *Theory*: Wilson, agreeing, San Francisco, airport, Empire, Flight, 3 p.m.
Brief Forms: office, presenting, which, company, with, what, after
Phrases: thank you for, I will be, I know, I hope, to be

Speed Dictation Practice

52.1 Business Letter

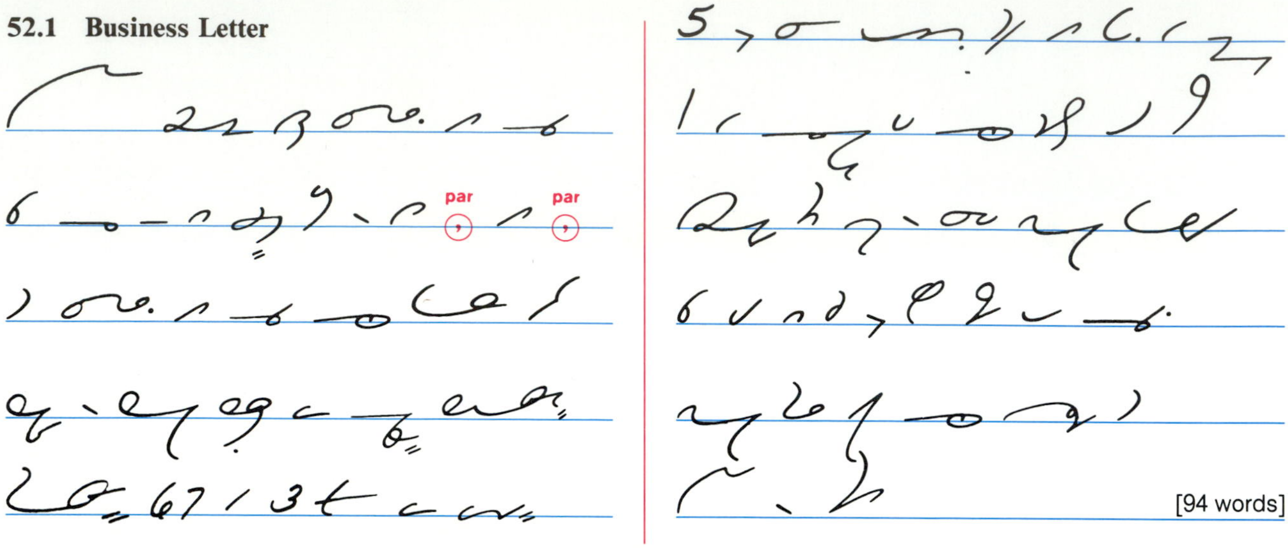

[94 words]

TRANSCRIPTION SKILL DEVELOPMENT

Transcribe the following words and phrases, noting spelling and capitalization. Then transcribe the transcription letter which follows.

Transcription Warmup

52.2

Transcription Practice

52.3 Letter

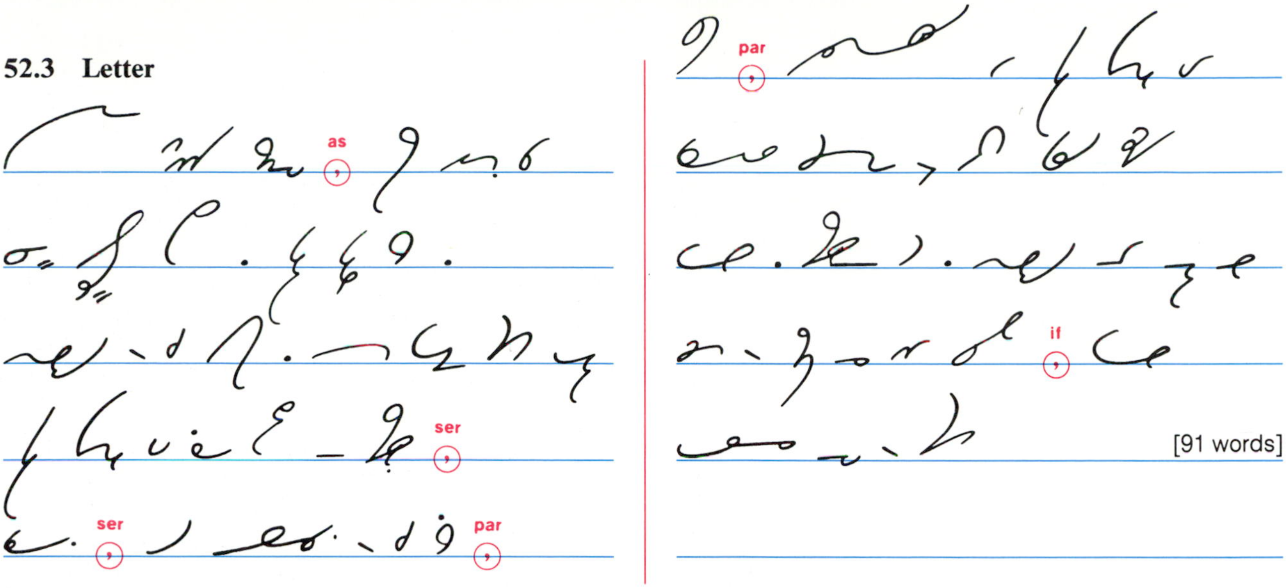

[91 words]

Geographic References

A comma is used to separate a city and a state. If the name of the state does not end the sentence, place a comma after the state also.

A *geographic comma* is indicated by 

We will meet in *Dallas, Texas.*

We will meet in *Dallas, Texas,* on Wednesday.

52.4 Business Memo

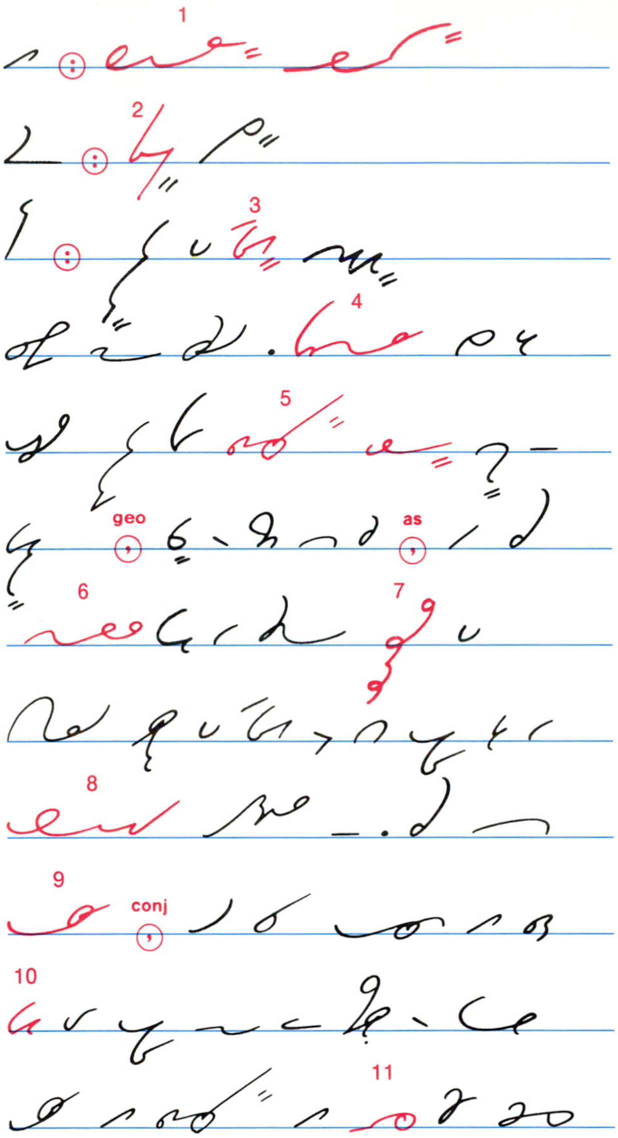

1 Arlene Milton 2 George 3 Transportation
4 booklet 5 United Oil 6 clearly 7 efficiencies
8 railroad 9 light 10 parts 11 inquire

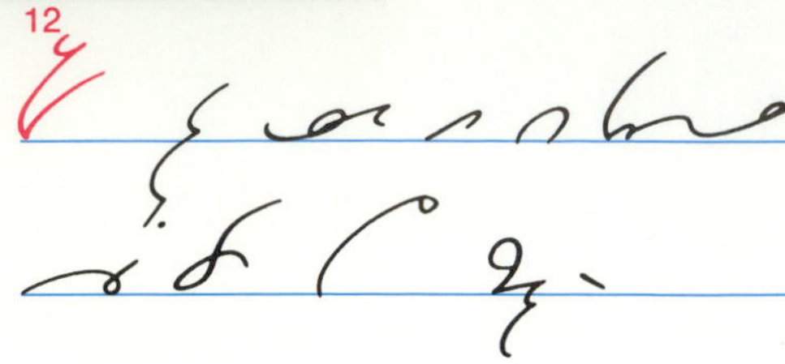

[105 words]

52.5 Business Letter

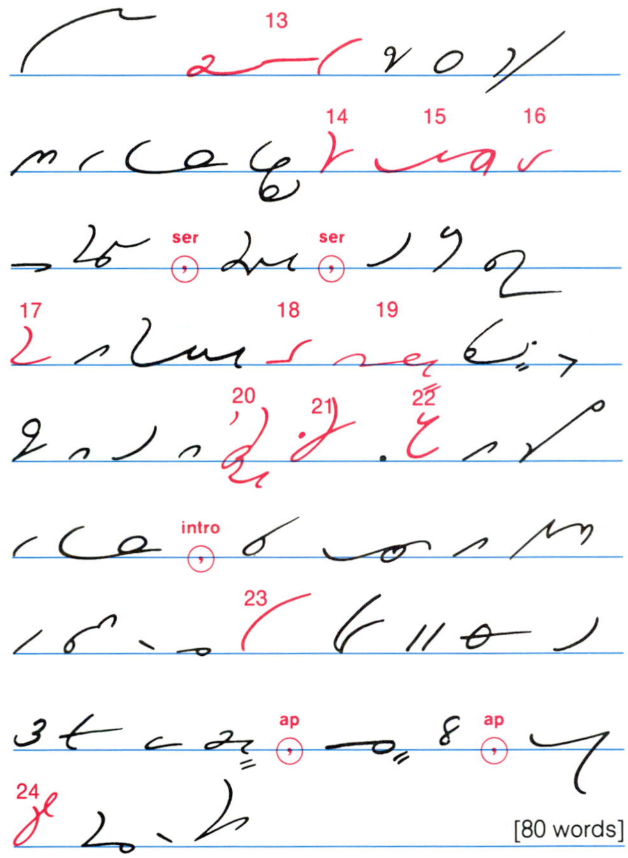

[80 words]

12 obtain 13 Wilmington 14 for the
15 location 16 of the 17 for our 18 in the
19 Commerce 20 supervisors 21 have had
22 opportunity 23 time 24 satisfactory

TRANSCRIPT

The material is counted in groups of 20 standard words or 28 syllables for convenience in timing the reading or dictation.

LESSON 1

1.1

1 I aim to please.
2 She may go to the game.
3 My knee hurts.
4 He did not meet me.
5 What is her name?
6 Meet me at 3 o'clock.
7 The main gate is open.
8 His name is Jim.
9 He is not mean.
10 I may name the dog.

1.2

1 The tiger is tame.
2 The deed has been signed.
3 The chef made tea.
4 Leon will meet the train.
5 The day is warm.
6 Check the date on the calendar.
7 Our team won!
8 When will you eat lunch?
9 Steve is a nurse's aide.
10 We ate lunch late.

1.3

1 Amy won the track meet for her team.
2 Put your name on the deed next to the date.
3 Nate ate meat.
4 Dean made a date with Amy.
5 Our friend, Amy Dean, made the team.
6 Dean made the team.
7 Meet me for a day in May.
8 Can Dean meet me too?
9 Amy is mean.
10 What made Amy mean?

1.4

1 My knee may stop me from going.
2 Dean will meet me any day.
3 Meet me at 4 o'clock for tea.
4 Nate may meet me.
5 Amy may be on the team.
6 Dean may sign the deed in May.
7 He will need the date of the track meet.
8 Nate made tea for the team.
9 Meet me on East Main to sign the deed.
10 Mark the date on the deed.

LESSON 2

2.1

1 He may be meeting me at lunch on that day.
2 Amy is dating Dean.
3 Nate enjoys taming wild animals all day.
4 He may hate the meeting.

5 May is not heeding our warning about Dean.
6 The date for the meeting is in May.
7 Who is naming the team?
8 He may repair the heating.
9 A team meeting was held in May.
10 I hate missing the meeting with Amy.

2.2

1 He might write Amy at night in May.
2 My deed is in the safe at night.
3 Dean tied a fancy knot in my tie.
4 The price of my deed is too high.
5 My team ended the game in a tie.
6 The date is in May.
7 Amy might go out at night to dye her tie.
8 He did not dye my tie before the meeting.
9 The rate on my deed might be high.
10 He might learn to tie his tie.

2.3

1 Amy might be at the team meeting.
2 My team may meet me at 10 at night.
3 The meeting will be held with Dean.
4 We need heat in the room at night.
5 The tie is not mine.
6 Dean will name the team.
7 May tied her tie.
8 Nate will heed the warning of Amy.
9 The rate Amy gave me is high.
10 The price of the tie is too high.

LESSON 3

3.1

1 Nate wrote a note home.
2 He may mail the note.
3 Dale may read without a light.
4 Do not try reading without a light.
5 Dale made a deal with Ray.
6 He will trade the team in May.
7 Lee may write a note about the low rate.
8 At night Dale rode the train to his home.
9 Nate was late in writing the note.
10 Leo was late for the meeting.

3.2

1 Ray will write Mary later.
2 Will Dale make a trade with a car dealer?
3 Lane is known as a leader.
4 A delay will make Amy even later.
5 Lee made a fast rate as a speed writer.
6 The leader of the team is not known.
7 The total of the account is not known.
8 Dale may delight in reading the title.
9 He will trade the car for a trailer.
10 Lee spoke to the dealer about the low rate.

3.3

1 Mary did knit a sweater for Lee.
2 The team is hitting a little better than they did.
3 The baseball hit him on the ankle last night.
4 Lee did better than Tim on writing the deed.
5 Did Tim pick up litter on the train?
6 Did the team choose him last night?
7 He did not trade the trailer.
8 Is Ray eating at home with his little sister?
9 Tim did not write the note to Dean.
10 Lee will need a little light to write.

3.4

1 Lee is mailing his writing to me late.
2 He will delay the leader at the train.
3 We are deciding the title of the book in May.
4 The total price is not known.
5 We will need the date of the meeting.
6 Ray may write a new title.
7 I know who will own the home.
8 The leader will delay the meeting.
9 Mary rode the train at night.
10 Leo may try to write.

LESSON 4

4.1

1 Nate will meet me in an hour.
2 Will Amy Dean lead our team?
3 You and I are doing well at reading.
4 I am the leader of a meeting.
5 I would not miss it.
6 He is willing to lead the meeting in an hour.
7 Would Leo meet me in an hour?
8 Will Lee read our note?

9 Our train will leave in an hour.
10 We are trading in our car.

4.2

1 Nate ran home to get a hammer.
2 My dad bought a new ladder.
3 Is something the matter with his arm?
4 Matt ran to strengthen his heart.
5 She had an old hat from the Army.
6 A man will write the story in May.
7 Matt had a low reading rate.
8 Will my dad go to the meeting at night?
9 The matter will be settled in May.
10 My dad had a leading role in a play.

4.3

1 Her dad was in the Army.
2 Let Amy have the red ladder.
3 Matt hurt his head on the ladder.
4 He read her letter.
5 He met her dad, Matt Dean.
6 Let Tim meet the leader.
7 He will mail a letter to Leo.
8 A letter was sent to my home.
9 My red tie is missing.
10 What will be the net rate on the loan?

4.4

1 Lee will meet Dean in an hour.
2 Will Leo read our note?
3 Would Lee Dean meet me at the train?
4 The leader is willing to hold a meeting in May.
5 Ray and I are writing a story.
6 We will trade our car in at the sale in May.
7 A letter did arrive in the mail.
8 A man in a red hat will mail our letter.
9 Matt would be willing to read the letter.
10 Mary will hold a meeting in May at her home.

LESSON 5

5.1

1 I am not well.
2 Meet me in our home.
3 I will not try writing in our trailer.
4 It will delay my meeting. It will not matter.
5 I would not try reading in low light.

¶ Paragraph

I made a deal. I will trade Matt my trailer. Matt will not need a deed in our trade. He wrote it will not matter.[1] I will not try writing a deed. [25 words]

5.2

1 Fay has seen Lee write a letter at night.
2 Steven ran as fast as Dave.
3 Did Steven say Amy will see Lee?
4 Our team has faced a Navy team.
5 Dave will not even say if Dale will sign a deed.

¶ Note

Dale wrote to Steven. Her letter made him laugh as he read it. Her fame will not make her vain. Steven will save her[1] letter. Steven will even save her letter in a safe. [29 words]

5.3

1 Dave will fry ham.
2 Fred will fly home.
3 Has Fred flown free?
4 I am afraid of flying.
5 He may own a frame home.

¶ Phone Message

To: Fred Tate
From: Mary Lowe
Date: May 6
Time: 12:15
I am afraid I will not see Dave in Reno. I had[1] a flat tire. Dave's flight leaves in an hour or so. I may see him at a later date. [34 words]

5.4

1 I saw Tom at home.
2 He met Tom on a rainy day.
3 He saw a small tame deer.
4 I hear a lot of laughter in our home.
5 Tom taught in a small city.

¶ Letter

Dear Dave I hear Tom owns a small farm near our city. I will need a home site. Will Tom save me a small lot? Write me[1] in a day or so. Dale
[24 words]

5.5 Agenda for Yearbook Staff Meeting

1. Start meeting at three.
2. Vote on title of scene.

3. Will late photo mailing hurt final date?
4. See if Steven[1] will lead May meeting.
5. Decide on date of staff meeting in May.

[31 words]

5.6 "To Do" List

Write Dale in Army.
Decide on meeting site.
Tell Amy I will see her in Reno.
Tell her I am not[1] afraid of flying. [22 words]

LESSON 6

6.1

1 I will invest in a motor home.
2 If Fred arrives, invite him in.
3 Rain has made our river high indeed.
4 Light a fire inside our stove.
5 Invite him to our home.

¶ Phone Message

To: David Lane
From: Ann Cline
Date: May 13
Time: 11:30
Dale will invest in a hotel in Reno.[1] He said he will tell me more in May. [26 words]

6.2

1 Sue will move to Reno.
2 Sue will clean her car.
3 I may move to a new room.
4 Mike may make a cake.
5 Mike will take care of our legal file.

¶ Note

Dear Dale I regret to say a heavy rainstorm hit our farm. It moved a great deal of dirt in our lane. A road grader[1] will need to clear our lane.

I am eager to get our lane clear again.

Call me. Mike [35 words]

6.3

1 We may not waste food.
2 Why are we waiting so late?
3 Our hot fire has a white flame.
4 Her hurt arm may swell.
5 Will Matt read while waiting?

¶ Note

Dear Sue Dave White has asked why it has taken two weeks to get a railroad car to him ready to load. Tell him[1] we had to wait while our railroad got legal title to our new railroad car fleet. Mike

[35 words]

6.4 List of Points for Phone Call

1. Why did Dave leave school at noon?
2. I got a new white suit. I hate my green suit.
3. Give history notes to Sue.[1]
4. I got a lot of law notes. [25 words]

6.5 Personal Letter

Dear Tom I am eager to go to an Army-Navy game in May. I will get a free ticket if I see Fred[1] Lee. Will Sue go if I get her a free ticket? I will not decide to go till I hear if Sue will go too. Mike

[40 words]

6.6 Memo

To Our Staff Green Airline will not start flying to Reno in a week. We regret making a delay.

I am[1] eager to take care of our legal matter so we may start flying to Reno in May. [36 words]

LESSON 7

7.1

1 My neighbor may buy my boat.
2 Please place a piece of paper on my desk.
3 Most people hope to please.
4 It pays most of our readers to lease space.
5 Our sale price beats our best list price.

¶ Memo to a Sales Manager

In May we raised our base price of our leading suit label. Despite our price increase, our suits are still sales leaders. Our[1] high sales are based on sales people.

Please write nice brief letters to all sales staff people who made our May sales great. [39 words]

7.2

1 Janet took her new plan up to our boss.
2 May we increase sales of our cookbook?
3 Not enough people seem to like our high rates.

4 Please put us on a new list.
5 We put a number of new books in our store.

¶ Memo

To Our Staff Our book sales are off again in May. New books will increase our sales. We must locate a number of new[1] writers who will put us back in a leading role in selling books.

If all of us would try to locate two new writers,[2] it would make enough of an increase in book sales to keep us a market leader. [55 words]

7.3 Letter

Dear David Last night I read my copy of our new sales letter. We plan to mail it to our book[1] dealers in May.

I am pleased to read of our new low base price on our line of books. It will help us to sell our books[2] better.

May we mail our sales letter in a day or so? Our sales staff will like it. Fay [56 words]

7.4 Notes From a Meeting

Sales Staff Meeting on 9-30

1. Need names of a number of people we might hire in Dallas.
2. Most people[1] seem to hate our new labels.
3. Most people still like our paper labels.
4. Fred has sales leads[2] in Reno.
5. People still like our books best; price will not matter. [51 words]

7.5 Note to a Roommate

Matt needs a place to write school papers. May we let him write in our spare room? He has a desk. Matt will put it in our[1] spare room.

He may pay us a small price so he may write here. [30 words]

LESSON 8

8.1

1 Mr. Lee can sell his boat for a good price.
2 Mr. Lee cannot forget his trip.
3 Are you able to go to Dallas?
4 Dave became a good player.
5 Please call me by ten if Dave is late.
6 Mr. Baker believes in having a good sales force.
7 Please call me before calling Tom White.
8 Please inform me of your telephone number.
9 Nate is being given a pay increase.
10 Our game is being delayed because of rain.

¶ Personal Note

Dear Fay Please forgive my delay in writing you. School has kept me busy. Because of my class load, I will not go[1] to Dallas before May.

I will inform you of my travel plans later. I will not forget our plans for a good[2] visit. Paul [43 words]

8.2

1 I will be reading a book while I wait for you.
2 You can have my spare tire if you would like it.
3 I will be happy if I can meet our new neighbor.
4 You will not have a meeting at your home.
5 I have an airline ticket for you.

¶ Note

Dear Sue I have good news for you. I will be moving to Erie in May. I will be looking for a place to live[1] in Erie in April. May I stay at your home for two days while I am looking for a place of my own?

I will not be[2] in Erie before April 16. Please tell me if I can stay at your home. Ellen [56 words]

8.3 Personal Note

Mr. Stein It will be three weeks since you wrote us to say you would buy our sailboat. Do you still hope to buy our boat? It is[1] a great boat. Its price is low.

Please tell us if you plan to buy our boat. Janet Bailey [35 words]

8.4 Business Letter

Dear Matt May I ask a big favor of you, Matt?

A member of our staff, Alice White, will be moving to Dallas[1] in April. If you will help her locate a new home, we will be happy for your help.

If you can be of help, please[2] call me at my home. David Bailey [47 words]

LESSON 9

9.1

1 We will be flying to Reno in May.
2 We cannot see people in our rooms.
3 Do you have a legal problem for our staff?
4 We will not be in our home, so we will have our heat off.
5 We are afraid we cannot be of help to you.

¶ List of Points to Discuss With the Boss

1. We have a legal problem on our copyright for our new magazine title.
2. We might have to delay[1] our sales meeting till May.
3. We might have a price increase on our mailing labels. [34 words]

9.2

1 I took these nȯtes in my math class.
2 I have faith in our sales staff.
3 Beth has Mr. Smith for math.
4 Keith will read his lesson, then go to class.
5 Try to write in thin, smooth lines.

¶ Personal Note

Dear Ruth I know you are taking a math course in school. Do you have Mr. Smith for math? Here are five math problems[1] Mr. Smith gave us.

Can you help me do these problems? Keith [29 words]

9.3

1 She showed me her new suit.
2 Jane changed jobs in search of higher pay.
3 She teaches in a large college.
4 Check each page of our math papers.
5 We will be charged for each page.

¶ Personal Letter

Dear Jane A Smith College evening class in French will start in March. Are you willing to teach our French class again? [1]

Please call if you will teach our class. Keith [27 words]

9.4 Business Letter

Mr. French On March 5 you bought goods at our store. On April 3 we gave you our bill. Your check arrived on April [1] 7. You put a date of March 5 on your check.

Please mail us a check having a proper date on it. Carol Smith [39 words]

9.5 Personal Note

Dear Beth My math teacher, Ruth Jones, plans to leave her teaching job here at Keith High School. She will open a store in[1] Great Falls in March or April.

Since you are so good in math, you might really like a job in her store. Jane [38 words]

LESSON 10

10.1

1 The school is small, but the class is good.
2 Did you know that Jean could fly a plane?
3 Our team should beat them in football.
4 I had a delay in writing this paper.
5 Fay did forget which book is mine.

¶ Agenda for a Meeting

Begin the meeting at three.
Take the roll call of members.
Read the letter which Sue James wrote us.
Ask the members:
Should[1] we increase our fees?
Could a member write a newsletter?
Could a member make copies of our newsletter?
Could a[2] member mail them?
Tell them that this meeting is our last meeting before fall. [53 words]

10.2

1 This is the first day of our new French course.
2 You have the same chance as the best member of the class.
3 Will the airline increase the number of flights to the East?
4 Is this the paper that you will give to the teacher?
5 By the way, this will be the first test of our new factory.

¶ Business Letter

Mr. Black This is a hard letter for me to write. Your March bill arrived in the mail last week. I wrote a check to[1] you on the same day.

I noticed I forgot to mail the check. I will mail the check in this letter. Please accept my[2] regrets. James Goodman [45 words]

10.3

1 In only three weeks we will begin meeting daily.
2 If you are really early, go to the meeting room.
3 Sales have finally increased; we are greatly relieved.
4 Beth is likely to finish the job properly.
5 I am highly pleased by the totally new look of our store.

¶ Interoffice Note

Ann In only two days our weekly meeting will take place. All members of our staff who will be involved in our project[1] will be at the meeting.

If we are totally ready for this meeting, we can greatly increase the chance that our[2] plan will succeed.

Please arrive at the meeting room early on the day of the meeting. Beth [55 words]

10.4 Interoffice Note

To Fred Lee Attached are the travel plans of the members of the sales staff. As you can see, all of them plan to[1] travel to the meeting by airline. This will make it easy for you to get all of our people to the hotel.[2] The attached plans are the best we could make. Keith [48 words]

10.5 Insurance Adjuster's Notes About Accident

Car Crash of Keith Smith

Keith Smith owns the car.

The car crash took place at noon on June 7.

Mr. Smith is clearly at[1] fault.

He got a ticket for driving too fast.

He drove at 65 miles an hour. The speed limit on this road is[2] 45 miles an hour.

The Smith car is totally wrecked.

Mr. Smith did not have injuries. [58 words]

LESSON 11

11.1

1 Your application for a position in our collection agency has arrived.
2 The promotion of our new fashion book is being delayed.
3 The National Education Corporation will move to a new location.
4 Who made the decision to operate on the patient?
5 Her typing proficiency helps make her an efficient member of the staff.

¶ Letter

Mr. James Attached is a collection of photos that I took on my vacation. A portion of the photos shows[1] the normal vacation spots. Most of the photos show locations that most people on vacation do not[2] normally see.

If these photos appear in your national paper, it will help promote travel. You have often said[3] that you are in favor of a national promotion of vacations.

Please tell me if I have given you a[4] sufficient number of photos. I will be waiting to hear your decision. Sincerely [95 words]

11.2

1 Only 600 people bought a ticket for the play.
2 Fred paid a dollar for my book.
3 The check is for $7,000.
4 The small nation has only 900,000 people.
5 Beth will sell a stamp for $4.50.

¶ Letter

Mr. Jones We are pleased that you asked us for facts on the cost of selling your art collection. Our rates are[1] $8 for each $1,000 of the cost of your collection. If your collection would cost $3,000,[2] then our fee would be $24.

Please call if we can sell your art collection. Sincerely [57 words]

11.3

1 We have to be sure we are right.
2 Mark has to have $8 for the book.

3 If you have been in class lately, you know we will have a test in a week or so.
4 You have been late for each class, so you have not been able to take good notes.
5 People have not been able to be in class.

¶ **Personal Note**

Dear Mike I am afraid you have not been easy to reach. I am eager to tell you the grade I got in my French[1] class. I have not been able to talk to the French professor. I will not be able to talk to her for a day[2] or so.

I suppose you have not been able to get your grade in math this early. In a day or so we will have[3] all of our grades. Bill [64 words]

11.4 News Reporter's Notes

A robbery took place at the Smith Food Store at eight in the evening on July 18. Only three members of the[1] staff of the store saw the robber. The names of these three people are not being made known.

The robber took nearly[2] $3,000 in cash. The robber left the scene on foot. The police will have a news release in an hour or[3] so. [61 words]

11.5 Business Memo

To: Jean Day
From: Nancy Barnes
Attached are the vacation plans of the staff members on my floor.

I would like to[1] begin my own two-week vacation on July 21. Before I can do this, I will have to ask if you[2] are willing to fill in for me at a meeting. I am to be in charge of a sectional meeting of the[3] National Retail Store Owners in Reno on July 23.

Please call me if you are able to help me.

[80 words]

LESSON 12

12.1

1 I am glad to have a letter from Mrs. Jones.
2 After all these weeks, it is good to hear from Mrs. Lake.
3 I will not be able to talk with you about the answers to the test.
4 Please get the facts about the game from the team.
5 I have not had a call from you.

¶ **Letter**

Dear Jody I am writing about the meeting of the sales staff starting on April 14. We will be meeting[1] with our sales staff about the plans for selling our latest fashions.

I am glad to hear you will be able to talk[2] with our staff. I will be glad to be with you in Dallas on the day we meet with the sales staff. Betty

[58 words]

12.2

1 Jack lost his temper because of the damage to his car.
2 Our customers seldom arrive at our store by automobile.
3 Sarah will attempt to have a cost estimate for us tomorrow.
4 The large cat had temporary freedom after escaping from the zoo.
5 Each item for sale in our store is in the medium price range.

¶ **Letter**

Mrs. Adams We are glad to have the estimate of $350 to take care of the damage to[1] your car. I am happy with the low cost of the estimate. Seldom does a customer demonstrate good faith with[2] a low-cost estimate.

Your cost estimate is low enough that we do not have to have an itemized [3] estimate. I will have a check in the mail to you by tomorrow at the latest.

In spite of the damage to your car,[4] I am hoping you will remain our good customer. Keith Temple

[92 words]

12.3

1 Dear Mr. Jones I will mail you the estimate for the damage to your car. Very truly yours
2 Dear Mrs. Black We were glad to learn about the new items for sale. Cordially yours
3 Dear Madam The demonstration will be on April 15. Yours very truly
4 Dear Sir We have two new staff members. Very truly yours
5 Dear Miss Dempsey We are pleased to have you as a customer. Cordially yours

12.4 Business Letter

Dear Mr. Temple I am sorry for the problems you have been caused by a temporary staff member. I can[1] assure you, Mr. Temple, that we make a sincere effort to hire the best temporary staff people.

We will[2] not charge you when you again have occasion to fill a temporary staff position. We are sincerely glad[3] to have you as our customer. Very truly yours [70 words]

12.5 A Student's "To Do" List

Do June 10

1. Prepare for history test tomorrow.
2. Get gas for the automobile.
3. Go to physics[1] class demonstration.
4. Try to get news items for the school paper.
5. Agree to be a temporary[2] helper in the library.

[45 words]

12.6 Business Letter

Dear Mrs. Dempsey We are happy to tell you that we are opening a new store on March 17. Our new[1] store will be on Main Street here in Mason City.

We are inviting you to a demonstration of our new line even before our[2] new store is open. Show this letter to the member of our staff who will greet you at the door.

I will be glad to[3] see you at the opening of our new store. Cordially yours [71 words]

LESSON 13

13.1

1 Following our conversation, I will sign the contract.
2 Please compile complete data for the committee.
3 The committee considers our data to be complete.
4 Fred controls the committee completely.
5 Do not complain about his conduct; it compares nicely with the rest of the class.

¶ Memo

To: Nancy Robbins
From: Elaine Rice
This note is to tell you about my concern for Judy Page. She does not seem[1] to have consideration for people. She has completely lost her temper in dealing with good customers.

She[2] often complains about the rest of the people on our staff.

On two occasions I had a conference with her.[3] These conversations have not helped matters.

I believe we should release her from her contract. If you agree completely, [4] I will proceed with letting her go. [86 words]

13.2

1 The cost of health coverage seems high.
2 Our clothing factory will be closed through May.
3 We will mail a brochure to all those on our mailing list.
4 It is a great book, though it takes a while to read.
5 Roberta thought the clothes had a high price.

¶ Memo

To: Esther Goodman
From: James Casey
I have thought through the problem of increasing health care costs. I would like to share[1] my thoughts with the members of our planning committee early in June.

Attached is a list of those people who should be[2] at the meeting to hear my thoughts on health care. [49 words]

13.3

1 Please replace me on the research committee.
2 I need to reply to the letters I received.
3 Can you refer me to a place which will repair my car?
4 Robin will receive a good letter of reference from Mrs. Smith.
5 Can you tell me the reason Dave will retire early?

¶ Letter

Dear Mr. Brooks It is a pleasure for me to provide a reference letter for Carol Johnson. Carol had been[1] in charge of the research in our new data control lab. She received a large number of honors for her[2] research projects.

It will not be easy for us to replace Carol. I am sure Carol will do a fine job in[3] your new research lab. Very truly yours [67 words]

13.4 Dictation Speed Letter

Dear Miss West I just received a job application from Mrs. Susan Rice. She is applying for the position[1] of research analyst in our research laboratory. She wrote that you would be able to write a letter [2] of reference for her.

What type of research did Mrs. Rice conduct?

Would you hire her again if you had a[3] vacancy on your research staff?

Please compile a list of facts about her that will help us make a fair decision[4] about hiring her. Cordially yours [88 words]

13.5 Business Letter

Dear Mrs. Steiner I have been trying to reach you by phone since May 17, but I have not been able to[1] catch you.

I would like to have about 500 copies of our research paper by June 12. I need these copies[2] for a research conference which will be taking place early in July. The members of our research committee need[3] to have a copy of the paper before our conference begins. Please mail the copies to my research lab.[4] Very truly yours [82 words]

LESSON 14

14.1

1 We have a meeting in our office during the afternoon.
2 Is there a place where one can get more office space?
3 There was a meeting of our office staff yesterday.
4 They won all their games during the 1988 season.
5 Dr. Day had hoped to open her new office yesterday.

¶ Letter

Dear Dr. Blair Will you be willing to have a brief meeting in my office on June 15? I would like to talk to you[1] about a research project which we need to finish during July.

The research project will ask our customers[2] where they prefer to shop. Their replies may reveal that we should move to a new location.

Please call me[3] concerning our proposed meeting. Very truly yours [67 words]

14.2

1 One of the reference books was not up to date.
2 This is one of our reference books; it is up to date.
3 One of our customers often complains about our service.
4 There is reason for concern about his conduct; one of them is his temper.
5 Our staff receives health care that is up to date.

¶ Memo

To: Fred Wilson
From: Katherine James
I was pleased to hear that you received one of the top honors at the research[1] convention last week.

You have been in charge of one of our best research projects. Because of your efforts, our research[2] is sure to stay up to date. [45 words]

14.3

1 Our editor drafted a list of needed research.
2 She omitted a price deduction from the listed retail price.
3 We will be tested in great detail in history today.
4 Judy has been accepted by the editor of our local paper.
5 My credit application has been accepted.

¶ Letter

Dear Mr. Sanchez The brochure you drafted for the sales promotion of our books is great! Our team of editors[1] is as happy with it as I am. They have accepted all its details.

When you accepted this project, you[2] listed a price of $1,000. I am asking that our check to you be drafted this afternoon. Sincerely yours[3] [60 words]

14.4 Dictation Speed Letter

Dear Sir You may remember me as a salesman who often waited on you at the Bates Street Clothing Store. When[1] I was there, I waited on you often.

During June I began setting up my own shop at 721[2] Baker Street. My new shop opens today. Here you will be able to get the best clothing buys in our city.[3]

I will be glad to have you as one of our customers at our new store. Very truly yours [77 words]

14.5 A Page From a Real Estate Agent's Notebook

Notes about the Smith home on Adams Street here in James Lake.

The home was listed with us on[1] 8-18-88.

The first offer was made on 9-26-88.

The offer was made by Mr.[2] David Stone.

The original price was $75,000.

The Stone offer was[3] $73,000.

The offer was accepted on 9-28-88.

The contract was drafted on[4] 9-29-88.

The closing meeting will be 10-2-88 at four in the afternoon. [99 words]

LESSON 15

15.1

1 Give my bill to either my mother or my father.
2 We will get together on another day when the weather is better.
3 I would rather not bother my brother with my problems.
4 Paul likes to get together with other authors.
5 I gather from your reply that you would rather get together on another day.

¶ Letter

Dear Mr. Reed I am gathering the facts for another book about predicting the weather. Most other books[1] about the weather are college books.

The book I am proposing will not be another college book.[2] This book will be for all people who would like to learn more about the weather.

When may we get together to[3] talk about my proposed weather book? Very truly yours [69 words]

15.2

1 Kathy is studying home furnishing.
2 Our home is heated with a gas furnace.
3 We furnish our authors the service of good editors.
4 Her writing will further the cause of freedom.
5 Furthermore, we are pleased with his cooperation.

¶ Letter

Dear Mr. Perez On May 16 you paid a visit to my home to repair the gas furnace. After you[1] completed the repairs, you convinced me that I should buy a service contract from you.

I wrote you a check for the[2] contract. You said your office would furnish me with a copy of the contract. It has been three weeks. I would like to[3] hear from you. Yours very truly [65 words]

15.3

1 I felt like shopping in town even though it is crowded.
2 We are now ready to move to our new house south of town.
3 Jack will announce that the play is about to begin.
4 Fred really doubts that Keith will make a good decision.
5 Do you know how to conduct a research study?

¶ Rough Draft for a School News Release

The South Side High School gave the play Our Town each evening from April 12 through 15. We are pleased to announce that[1] the cast played to a full house each evening.

A large number of people in the crowds said how well they liked the play.[2] Mrs. James, principal of South Side High School, said, "There is no doubt that this is one of the best plays in the history[3] of our school!" [62 words]

15.4 Dictation Speed Letter

Mr. Day I am glad you wrote me about the job you have in your sales office. I will be able to go to your[1] office on May 7 at about two in the afternoon.

When I arrive at your office, I will have with me[2] the list of grades I received in school. I will be ready to talk about the job you have open. Very truly yours[3] [60 words]

15.5 Business Letter

Dear Customer We are pleased to announce the opening of Brown Brothers, a home furnishing store. Our new store is[1] located in the South Side Mall.

At Brown Brothers we have items that you need to furnish your house. Our selection[2] is complete. Furthermore, there is no doubt that the price of our goods is the lowest in town.

Stop in at Brown Brothers[3] on either May 11 or May 12 during our opening sale. We will be glad to see you. Very truly yours [80 words]

LESSON 16

16.1

1 Laura works for a company in town.
2 Our communications teacher will direct our class play.
3 Every communications worker in the state may go on strike.
4 I recommend that we meet soon.
5 My little brother stated that he would accompany me everywhere today.

¶ Notes for a News Story

The communications workers in our state may go on strike soon. They have voted to reject the contract[1] recommendation which was made by their own directors. One of the[2] directors of the communications workers stated that whenever the strike might begin, it will affect telephone[3] service everywhere in the state. [65 words]

16.2

1 Please communicate with us as soon as possible.
2 We will reply as soon as we hear from you.
3 I will give it to my secretary to do tomorrow.
4 Please mail it to me at home to make sure I get it.
5 The news came as a surprise to us, of course.

¶ Note to Secretary

I need to make airplane reservations so that I can go to Dallas on May 12 to do research. I need to[1] fly back on the afternoon of May 14.

I will, of course, have a check ready for the tickets as soon as I[2] receive them.

Please try to get the tickets to me at my office as soon as possible. [56 words]

16.3

1 Their latest motion picture is a failure in the marketplace.
2 Nature cycles the seasons annually.
3 We will share equally in contractual matters.
4 Is there actually a procedure for editing rough drafts?
5 Tim likes the natural features of the scenery in the West.

¶ Class Notes From a Marketing Course

Market Change

1. Change is one of the natural features of the marketplace.
2. Change takes place gradually.
    a. It[1] may be so slow it cannot be seen from day to day.
    b. It may not even be seen annually.
    c. But change is[2] taking place.
3. Failure to notice gradual change can mean that items gradually lose their appeal.
4. There are[3] procedures for getting an accurate picture of the market change. [73 words]

16.4 Phone Message

To: Mrs. Carson
From: David Santos
Date: March 23
Time: 12:15
He said work will begin on our communications lab[1] tomorrow. Every detail of the planning seems to be complete. He will be directing the work. All[2] communications about the project should be directed to him. [53 words]

16.5 Business Letter

Dear Mr. Cole Your letter confirming my reservation at your hotel has arrived. You will recall that when[1] I made this reservation, it was for the night of June 18.

Because of my work schedule, I will not be able[2] to leave for Dallas on June 18. I will be arriving in Dallas on June 19. Therefore, I need to have my[3] reservation changed for that day.

Please write to me as soon as possible to tell me if my reservation may be[4] changed. Very truly yours [85 words]

LESSON 17

17.1

1 Our entire accounting staff is currently assigned to the project.
2 I will offer to sell my land through a real estate agent for a large amount.

3 I find most people like a kind, friendly greeting.
4 It is apparent that our entire stock of accounting books is not currently in print.
5 The House bill is currently being signed into law.

¶ Memo

To: Mrs. Grand
From: Jerry Best
Can you be at my office on June 15 at three in the afternoon for a brief meeting? Currently, there are three people[1] I would like you to meet. They seem to have the kind of accounting training we need for the positions we have open.[2] They sent me their data sheets; you will find them attached.
[50 words]

17.2

1 I have begun to run during my lunch hour.
2 The county judge has become the center of much debate.
3 It is no fun to be in such a rush.
4 Some people say summer is their favorite season.
5 The cash refund is a welcome help to my budget.

¶ Student Meeting

Agenda for Annual Staff Meeting
Announce to the staff the following:
1. The editing of the entire book[1] is done.
2. We have begun to receive pages from the printer.
3. Some error corrections will have to be done.[2]
4. The color pictures add a touch of class; they did not hurt the budget too much.
5. We need to rush our advance[3] selling to make sure that we will have the income we need.
[70 words]

17.3

1 Please describe your problem to the person at the courtesy desk.
2 Perhaps another agency can handle your account.
3 Please give our news writer your description of the news event.
4 Do you have a good reason for the delay?
5 Please pursue the purchase of a display typewriter.

¶ Memo

To: Joe Jefferson
From: Ellen Evans
I am asking that the personnel office find a secretary[1] for me. I prefer a person who has had some work in a claims agency. I would describe the ideal[2] secretary as a person who not only makes rapid decisions but displays courtesy. [56 words]

17.4 Dictation Speed Memo

To: Personnel Staff
From: David Green
The staff of the Personnel Office will have a luncheon meeting at noon[1] tomorrow. We will meet in the conference room to discuss some of the personnel problems which have come up in[2] recent weeks. A problem that is currently severe is absence caused by personal illness.

Please do not miss this[3] meeting as we have much to discuss. [66 words]

17.5 Letter of Complaint

Dear Sir Much to my surprise, the National Insurance Agency has not paid my claim for $3,000.[1] I sent my claim to you on April 15. I sent a note with the claim saying there was no rush. Apparently one[2] of your staff members did not take care of the claim.

Perhaps there is some good reason for the delay. I would welcome[3] a letter from you. Either write me a letter to accompany my check, or write to tell me about the problem[4] you are having in settling my claim. Cordially yours [90 words]

LESSON 18

18.1

1 Jack should reply to my letter immediately.
2 Fred and Judy were several hours late to the party.
3 We must advertise the value of our service.
4 What is the major disadvantage of my plan?
5 You will find good values at our sale.

¶ Rough Draft of an Idea for a Term Paper

Part of the value of advertising is that it may increase the sale of a line of goods. The more items that[1] sell, the less each item costs to produce. This advantage of decreased cost of making goods is passed to the customer [2] in the form of good market values. [47 words]

18.2

1 Is it possible to find a suitable home at a reasonable price?
2 It is sensible to keep valuable items in a safe place.
3 My doctor is highly capable and reliable.
4 Our office furniture is available at a considerably reasonable price.
5 I am not able to get a favorable offer to buy my table.

¶ Personal Note

Dear Charles I am sorry to hear that you have had considerable trouble trying to sell your car. Perhaps I can be[1] of some help to you. I have a friend who is willing to pay a favorable price for a suitable[2] car. He needs a car that is reliable, and he needs a car that is available soon.

I will have him call[3] you today, if possible. David [68 words]

18.3

1 I have received your written agreement to make installment payments on your account.
2 We will have trouble finding a replacement for her in our investment department.
3 I like her judgment and her commitment to completing assignments.
4 An advertisement should increase the number of people in our private school.
5 Please place the shipment of office supplies in the basement.

¶ Memo

To: Staff
From: Office of the President
Mary Benson will be retiring from our advertising[1] department at the end of March. She became a member of our advertising department in 1962.[2] In my judgment, Mrs. Benson wrote a number of our best advertisements. It will not be easy to find a[3] replacement for her. [63 words]

18.4 Dictation Speed Letter

Dear Mr. Lee Can you tell me the advantage of advertising in your paper? My partner and I are trying[1] to find the best advertising value in town for our limited advertising budget. If you could list[2] several advantages of advertising in your paper, we would be happy to consider becoming[3] one of your customers. Very truly yours [68 words]

18.5 Business Letter

Dear Mr. Carson Please send me immediately a shipment of 15,000 copies of the attached form.[1] This form is a copy of our company billing statement.

It is urgent that we receive this shipment by July[2] 15. If we receive the shipment after July 15, we will have a delay in receiving several payments.[3]

Please let me know if it is possible to meet our schedule. Very truly yours [75 words]

18.6 Business Letter

Dear Mrs. Grant Would you like to increase sales for your company? You can do this if you place an advertisement[1] in Travel Magazine.

Travel Magazine is currently being read by 200,000 people. Take this[2] chance to get an immediate increase in the value you receive from your advertising budget. Write me today[3] about advertising in Travel Magazine. Yours very truly [72 words]

LESSON 19

19.1

1 I hope to meet some of the staff for lunch.
2 I hope that you will take advantage of some of our recommendations.
3 I hope that the office assigned to you is acceptable.
4 I hope the weather cooperates for the gathering this weekend.
5 I hope that you have decided to accept the price we have stated.

¶ Office Note

Mr. Tracy I hope that you can help me. My secretary tells me that the current issue of The Automobile[1] Guide is not in the library. Did you borrow it or do you know who did?

I hope you can tell me who has[2] this issue. It has a list of car rental firms, and we hope to mail our latest catalog to them. Bill Smith [59 words]

19.2

1 She apparently ignored me when I answered her.
2 I have prepared a record of children who have failed their vision test.
3 Our older records are stored in the basement of the records center.
4 I told the salesclerk that we need to be billed for the file folders.
5 My children have sold their old record player.

¶ Letter

Dear Sir On July 18 my wife and I were on Flight 32 from Grand Falls to Dallas. When we arrived[1] in Dallas, I could not find my briefcase. I called your baggage claim department and Mrs. Neal answered. I told her[2] of my trouble, and she assured me that she would search for the briefcase. Two hours later she called to tell me that my[3] briefcase would be sent by messenger to my hotel.

I am pleased with the efficient service your airline provided[4] through the office of Mrs. Neal. I have not heard of better service! Very truly yours [99 words]

19.3

1 On the basis of your analysis I agree that our office faces a problem with filing space.
2 Please tell me the processes that are necessary for servicing a copying machine.
3 Our office services staff can assist you with word processing.
4 You should insist that people keep their promises.
5 I suspect we will have to suspend telephone services to your offices for a week.

¶ Note

Barbara According to Fred the biggest problem our offices face is in word processing services. He[1] suspects it will be necessary for us to train some of our own staff people. His analysis reveals that there[2] are not enough people available with the necessary office skills.

We will have to do an analysis[3] of the steps that will be necessary for us to begin an office training department. Janice [78 words]

19.4 Dictation Speed Letter

Dear Wendy On April 7 Robert Brady called on me and applied for a position on our staff. I would[1] like to hire him, but before I do so, I need more facts which I hope you will be able to supply.

1. Would you[2] hire him again if you had an opening?
2. Why is he planning to leave you?

Your answers will help me greatly.[3] Very truly yours [64 words]

19.5 Business Letter

Dear Madam I have been trying to assist you with the processing of your claim. I telephoned the National[1] Agency to ask if they had processed your claim for $240. Mr. Randy Moses says that [2] he sent you a check for $240 on June 18. Apparently the check was lost in the [3] mail. On the basis of my call, the agency has sent you a new check. Cordially yours [75 words]

LESSON 20

20.1

1 Our present opportunity may not come again, however.
2 We should organize a committee of government leaders.
3 We are happy to acknowledge your letter.
4 People generally get the type of government they deserve.
5 There are presently good opportunities in office jobs.

¶ Letter

Dear Mrs. Keller I am glad to hear that you are organizing a committee for good government in our[1] city. Generally, I feel that most people are happy with the present government. However, I acknowledge the fact[2] that people should not stop being concerned about their government.

May I have the opportunity to be[3] of service to your committee? Very truly yours [69 words]

20.2

1 We will devote $200,000 to the development of a different item.

2 Mrs. Lee was defeated in her bid for government office.
3 We definitely need to divide our marketing division into two separate divisions.
4 I know we may differ on the development of our new book.
5 Let us devise a plan for effective studying.

¶ Letter

Dear Dr. Farrell There are different sizes and different types and different costs of word processing printers. Our[1] industry needs to develop a new word processing printer that will print at a high speed and still produce[2] suitable copy.

Are you available to assist us in the development of a new printer that is [3] totally different from those now on the market? Cordially yours [70 words]

20.3

1 It is hard for a person to refuse a few compliments.
2 We will use a unique plan we have just developed.
3 We need to review the personnel policy which we have just developed.
4 Our teacher developed one new unit on the history of government.
5 Our word processing unit will unite with our data processing unit.

¶ Business Letter

Dear Mrs. Hughes We are pleased that you sent us the new unit you have developed for your history book. The new unit[1] is unique, and it should help to increase the sales of your book.

I will have your new unit sent to be reviewed[2] by a teacher who has used the old copy of your book in her classes.

When you have the opportunity to do[3] so, please provide us with a few samples of the type of pictures you will want to use with the new[4] unit. Very truly yours [83 words]

20.4 Dictation Speed Letter

Dear Mr. Day I am glad you invited me to apply for a job with your organization. I will be able[1] to go to your office to meet with you during the first week in May. The afternoon of May 6[2] would be good for our meeting.

Please let me know if you will be available to meet with me then. I am eager[3] to meet you and learn more about your company. Very truly yours [72 words]

20.5 Business Memo

To: Brenda Butler
From: Linda Harvey
As you will see by reading the attached letter from Mr. Green, our shipping[1] division made an error in shipping him 300 units of our book Marketing Techniques. They should have shipped[2] him 3,000 units.

Would you be good enough, therefore, to see that we ship Mr. Green the difference in the[3] number of units that he should have received. I hope you will be able to do this as soon as possible.[4] [80 words]

LESSON 21

21.1

1 We intend to maintain the market position we attained.
2 I am sure that the bulletin will get their attention.
3 This letter contains a maintenance contract.
4 My paper on the history of the presidents was written with the assistance of another student.
5 She certainly attained the presidency of the company at an early age.

¶ Notes From a Visitor to the Office

Mr. Fulton stopped at the office to see you. He came to town suddenly and did not have an opportunity[1] to call before arriving here. He would like to take you to dinner tonight and maybe attend a play. He will[2] give you a phone call after three today. Carol [49 words]

21.2

1 No political radical ever became president.
2 The technical article describes the process logically.
3 Technical articles are typically written in a dry style.
4 We will take a physical inventory of the articles in the warehouse.

5 The medical bills at that hospital are typically high.

¶ Notes of Library Orientation

When searching for an article, proceed logically. Typically the article will be found in several[1] places in the card catalog. An article can be found by its title or an article may be found by[2] its author. An article should not be physically removed from the library. A copy should be made at[3] a copy machine. [63 words]

21.3

1 I need to know the price of the article.
2 Mrs. Blair needs to know when the bulletins will be printed.
3 I would like to know the address.
4 I want to know when you will call.
5 James has to know his grade.

¶ Personal Note

John Mrs. Green just called. She needs to know if our office will be open during the holidays.[1] Such a large number of people want to know our schedule. I believe we should advertise it. Dennis [35 words]

21.4 Dictation Speed Letter

Dear Miss Fry You are invited to the President's Dinner to be held on June 15. I would like to attend[1] but I cannot.

Yesterday I was invited by Dr. Sutton to talk to the student body at Fenton[2] High School in Trenton on June 15. I will attend a dinner that will follow the meeting. Yours very truly[3] [60 words]

21.5 Business Letter

Dear Madam We have written you several letters asking you to mail us your remittance for the advertisements[1] we printed for you last July. Evidently our letters were lost or were ignored because we have not[2] received a remittance from you.

It is to the advantage of your company to maintain a good credit standing with its creditors.[3] You have had a good credit standing with us. However, you need to know you are in danger of losing it now.[4]

I ask, therefore, that you mail us a check for $2,200. Please do not wait. Yours very truly [98 words]

LESSON 22

22.1

1 We have just hired a new person in our business, Ms. Brenda Adams.
2 Our sales are higher now than several weeks before.
3 What difficulty did you have with our overnight mail service?
4 What was the outcome of the meeting?
5 Ms. Fields is professional and businesslike.

¶ Business Letter

Dear Miss Fields It was a pleasure to have you visit our business last week. It is good to have a person from the outside[1] look over the operations of a business.

We are glad to have whatever recommendations you[2] developed. You can be sure you will have your payment no later than March 10. Very truly yours [57 words]

22.2

1 Please attend a special meeting given by our chief financial officer.
2 We can make only a partial payment of our financial obligation now.
3 It is essential that all of our officials initial the financial papers they approve.
4 Carol had difficulty applying for student financial assistance.
5 The special dance is becoming one of the major social events of the season.

¶ Business Letter

Dear Ms. Crane Your letter referring me to Ms. Smith was especially valuable. Ms. Smith is in charge of the[1] Financial Department of our college. She was able to tell me officially that I will be able to[2] receive financial aid.

This visit has certainly removed my initial fears about not being able to[3] attend college. Very truly yours [66 words]

22.3

1 How old must a boy be to join Boy Scouts?
2 The land is valuable, not because of the soil but because of the oil beneath it.

3 Please have your accountant check those invoices.
4 Ms. Roy has been appointed to the board of directors.
5 I cannot work on invoices if there is too much noise in the office.

¶ Business Letter

Dear Ms. Roy When you need financial advice, what do you do? You get the best financial advice that is[1] available—you go to Royal Financial Services.

Royal Financial Services has been in business for[2] over half a century. Recently, Ms. Sara Evans joined our organization.

If you need advice on[3] financial matters, make an appointment with Ms. Evans. Yours very truly [71 words]

22.4 Dictation Speed Letter

Dear Dr. Doyle Will you be available for a brief meeting in my office on June 15 at three in the[1] afternoon? I would like for the two of us to talk over a research project that will allow us[2] to increase our business by more than $20,000. At our meeting we can at least get our initial[3] thoughts together. If you cannot join me on June 15, would June 18 be better? Please call my secretary[4] and let him know the day you are available. Cordially yours [92 words]

22.5 Minutes Taken During a Meeting

Student Accounting Club Meeting

The meeting was held on April 5.

The meeting began at noon.

President[1] Sarah Johnson presided over the meeting.

Committee Facts

The social committee is planning a party[2] at which we can welcome new members.

The financial secretary said that the books had been audited by one of the[3] school officials.

There was no new business and no old business.

Without further discussion, the meeting[4] concluded two hours later. [84 words]

LESSON 23

23.1

1 Please buy 12 pounds of grain and 15 feet of rope.
2 He will meet the bus at 5 o'clock.
3 Do not bother to call me after 2 a.m.
4 Do you know of an investment that will pay at least 10 percent?
5 The room is only 5 feet wide.

¶ Notes for Placing a Phone Call

Call Ralph and tell him about the weather.

There is a 90 percent chance it will snow today. We could get as much as 2 feet[1] of snow.

His plane was scheduled to arrive at 11 a.m.

It is now scheduled to arrive[2] at 2 p.m.

It could arrive as late as 3 o'clock. [51 words]

23.2

1 The men and women of our club meet monthly.
2 Many people have mentioned that they like our bus schedule.
3 Did I ever mention that you are a good money manager?
4 Can you mentally solve that math problem within a minute?
5 Our new sales representative deals with people in a pleasing manner.

¶ Personal Note

Dear Roy Our college food service organization has hired a new manager, Ruth Lloyd.

Within a month Mrs.[1] Lloyd will be hiring college men and women to work in food service. She mentioned that she is looking for people who[2] have an easy personal manner in dealing with other people, who can be trusted to handle money,[3] and who are available to work about 40 hours a month.

It sounds like a great opportunity for you;[4] let me know if you decide to apply. Floyd [88 words]

23.3

1 I feel really awkward about going to class late.
2 Despite our financial losses, we will proceed "onward and upward."
3 I will be forwarding my check to you by 5 p.m. today.

4 Attend your class; then talk to me afterwards.
5 Janet finds her career to be rewarding.

¶ Personal Note

Dear Edward After a rewarding career as a football coach, I am retiring at the end of the season.[1] One of the special rewards of coaching has been all of the fine people I have met.

Once the football season ends,[2] I am looking forward to travel in the mountains. Afterwards, let us get together. Adam [57 words]

23.4 Dictation Speed Letter

Dear Mrs. Miller I am glad to be able to tell you that Mr. Green will increase the sales in his region in April.[1] While the April increase is not a large one, it does show that Mr. Green is starting to do a good job of selling.[2]

I hope you will have an opportunity to write to Mr. Green to tell him that we are pleased with the job[3] he is doing. Very truly yours [66 words]

23.5 Sales Letter

Dear Miss Wade The April issue of Money Magazine will be devoted to fashions for children. You will[1] want to advertise in this issue because:

1. Our magazine sells more than 900,000 copies each month.[2]
2. Our readers spend a lot of money on clothing.
3. Our readers spend an average of $750[3] on children's clothing annually.

If you would like to discuss our advertising rates, please call me[4] as soon as possible. Sincerely [84 words]

LESSON 24

24.1

1 I think that you deserve credit for your success.
2 I am sending you a request for a payment.
3 I do not think James is a responsible student.
4 Please send my package between 1 p.m. and 5 p.m.
5 I have heard nothing from her regardless of my requests.

¶ Business Letter

Dear Mr. Benton As editor of Money Magazine, I am wondering if you would allow us to do[1] a story about you.

I would like to cover the things which have been responsible for your success.

If you are[2] willing to comply with my request, please send me a letter regarding a time when we might get together.[3] Yours very truly [62 words]

24.2

1 Lloyd is putting his entire savings into new buildings on his farm.
2 My real estate agent has listings of several buildings he would like to show me.
3 As secretary, I am writing the proceedings of each of our meetings.
4 Things went well at the meeting, and no feelings were hurt.
5 Our Art Department has several openings for artists whose specialty is doing drawings.

¶ Memo

To: Janet Jennings
From: Peter Anderson
At one of our staff meetings last week I recall that somebody[1] mentioned that our earnings had increased in the month of March. I do not have a copy of the proceedings of[2] that meeting. Can you get me a copy of the proceedings?

Would you send me a copy of the findings of the study[3] that was done on the cost savings which we might gain if we were to make our buildings more energy-efficient? [80 words]

24.3

1 The majority of our security problems come from the lack of dependability of our alarm system.
2 I need to hire a person with a lot of ability in office facility planning.
3 There is the possibility that your invention will entitle you to earn a royalty.
4 Lee is considered an authority in quality control.
5 The best quality of her personality is her sincerity.

¶ Memo

To: Helen Lee
From: Fred Davis
We need to hire a new person to be in charge of data processing at our[1] Dallas facility. Would you please write a job announcement?

The individual we are looking for must[2] be dependable and have a good personality. There is the possibility that the person will have to[3] move within ten months. The majority of the work will be in the Dallas office. [74 words]

24.4 Dictation Speed Letter

Dear Miss Jennings I am requesting that you send me your latest price list for the books in the book series called "Market[1] Management." I am looking forward to receiving this price list as soon as possible. Very truly yours[2] [40 words]

24.5 Personal Note

Ms. Keller I am pleased that you would think of me as a person to write about for your school paper on the topic[1] of success. As you have requested, I can give you my thoughts on the topic of success, but these thoughts are nothing[2] too surprising.

To me, there are two things necessary for success. One is to have a sense of responsibility[3] for doing the best possible job. The other key to success is to have a high regard for the feelings[4] of the people with whom you work. These two factors have been valuable to me.

It has been my pleasure to[5] comply with your request. Very truly yours [107 words]

LESSON 25

25.1

1 All airports in the region are closed because of the storm.
2 The news reporter will do a story about the sports at our school.
3 We have an assortment of portable heaters.
4 Shipping is increasing at all West Coast ports.
5 The report of James Sporting Goods was issued yesterday.

¶ Office Note

Fred Mr. John Allen, president of Allen Sporting Goods Company, will be visiting our offices on[1] June 23. I will meet Mr. Allen at the airport. However, the weather reports are not good.[2] If the airport is closed, Mr. Allen will plan to arrive on June 27. I am looking forward to[3] having Mr. Allen visit our sport shop. Mary [68 words]

25.2

1 Our staff is trying to create a better-sounding piano.
2 Mr. Garcia is doing creative work in areas of research.
3 We appreciate their area of knowledge.
4 The creation of new items often represents an opportunity for business growth.
5 We need Gloria to create a new marketing campaign.

¶ Business Letter

Dear Madam This letter acknowledges your letter of May 23 to our general manager, Ms. Gloria[1] Lane. Gloria left yesterday afternoon on a business trip, and your letter has been referred to me.

We are[2] currently working on several areas. Advertising copy has been written and is now being[3] edited for your approval. A piece of artwork has been created too.

We believe that we will be able[4] to send these things to you within three weeks. Very truly yours [91 words]

25.3

1 Kathleen will meet me at the football game on Saturday, May 17.
2 Gloria will have a birthday party on Tuesday, January 19.
3 We sent you requests for payment on October 3, November 5, and December 5.
4 February 9 will be the first Monday of the month.
5 Let us get together some Friday evening in August or September.

¶ Letter

Dear Theresa I am happy to tell you that I have just registered for my college classes. School begins[1] on September 2 and ends on December 19. My math class meets at 8 a.m. on Monday, Wednesday, and[2] Friday. My physical education class meets at 10 a.m. on Tuesday and Thursday. The history course I am[3] taking meets at 1 p.m. on Monday, Wednesday, and Friday.

Please let me know your schedule for this semester.[4] Perhaps you can come up to see me some Friday or Saturday. Sincerely [94 words]

25.4 Dictation Speed Letter

Dear Mrs. Mead When you were in our place of business last Saturday, you requested that we send for a price list[1] for Smith office furniture. I am sorry to inform you that the Smith Company has gone out of business.[2]

Please stop in again so that we can show you the lines of office furniture which we have available. Very truly yours[3] [60 words]

25.5 Business Letter

Dear Mrs. Garcia A friend of ours tells me that you are currently in the market for a new piano.[1] We have a fine selection of pianos in our showroom, and I invite you to stop in soon to take a[2] look at them.

Each piano has been created according to the highest standards, and you will appreciate[3] the quality of our selection. We think you will be impressed with the clear tones you will hear.

Stop in at[4] our store soon and ask to see Gloria Barnes in our sales area. Very truly yours [95 words]

LESSON 26

26.1

1 People should try to be on time anywhere they go.
2 I know a gentleman who prefers to work very early in the morning.
3 Where can we buy insurance for our manufacturing facilities?
4 We would very much like to attend.
5 We will insure the goods your company manufactures.

¶ Memo

To: Tom Edwards
From: Susan Harvey
It is time to renew our insurance policy on our manufacturing[1] facilities. It is vital that we reduce our manufacturing costs in every way. Do you think[2] we can do anything about our insurance costs?

If you have any other thoughts on ways that we might reduce our[3] manufacturing costs, please feel free to discuss them with me any morning this week. [75 words]

26.2

1 At this time enrollment is high in the gas engine repair course at the technical college.
2 It is unlikely that our engineers will be able to solve the problem unless someone is very lucky.
3 My teacher encourages us to enjoy books that are unrelated to our course work.
4 We cannot force you to work if you are unwilling to do so.
5 We are unable to unload the truck; it will have to wait until we can get someone to unload it.

¶ Business Letter

Gentlemen Our company is concerned about your unpaid account. We wrote to you on January 16 and[1] again on February 18 but have not received any reply.

Until we hear from you, we[2] must assume that you are simply unwilling to pay your bill. This is unfair to us as we have bills of our own[3] to pay.

We encourage you to answer this letter. Unless we hear from you by April 18, we will take legal[4] action. Very truly yours [84 words]

26.3

1 This will be the best yard sale we have had.
2 Lee is buying yellow yarn to make a sweater.
3 My best birthday party was the one three years ago.
4 The money in my savings account yields 6 percent.
5 We do not yet know if Nancy will attend Yale.

¶ Business Letter

Ladies and Gentlemen Our corporation has just purchased all of the outstanding stock of the Yale Company.[1] Yale is a leading manufacturer of furniture for yards and patios. Yale Company has[2] yielded 6 percent in each of the last three years.

The former Yale Company will now operate as Yale[3] Manufacturing Company. Very truly yours [66 words]

26.4 Dictation Speed Letter

Dear Leo Could you mail me the name of the woman who was appointed credit manager of the Boyd Toy Manufacturing[1] Company last week? I made a note of her name, but I cannot find it anywhere.

I would appreciate your[2] help at this time as I would like to write to her sometime early in the new year. Fred [55 words]

26.5 Personal Note

Dear Joyce I am attaching the advertisement about the camp for boys that I mentioned to you after your party[1] yesterday evening. I have known the manager, Mr. Roy Hartman, for many years. He was a classmate of mine[2] at Yale.

He operates his camp efficiently. My own boys spent each summer there until they went to college. I think[3] your boys might like it too.

I appreciate your inviting me to your party. It was a pleasure meeting[4] your friends. Sincerely [84 words]

LESSON 27

27.1

1 Can we make a modification in our design specifications?
2 We will specify the new records classification system.
3 I received the notification this morning.
4 Can you help me at this time with the identification of the signature on this letter?
5 What justification can you possibly have for classifying the research?

¶ Memo

To: Gary Bennett
From: Edna Day
I have just received notification that you have completed the work on[1] our new library classification system.

I like the way you have provided identification of each[2] of the problem areas within our library. I, too, like the way you have provided justification[3] for each of your recommendations and the specifications for new material. Your work on this project[4] is sincerely appreciated. [87 words]

27.2

1 I am afraid I have misplaced my reading glasses.
2 We cannot afford to have mistakes such as misprints in our printed material.
3 If we print misleading material, we may be sued.
4 Our staff should not be making such mistakes.
5 What I did with my glasses is still a mystery.

¶ Business Letter

Dear Mr. Bernstein I appreciate the fact that you took the time to write to me to point out the mistake in our[1] magazine. Yes, we did indeed misplace the last word on page 57 of our October issue. This misplaced [2] word did create something of a mystery as to the meaning of the sentence.

We do not intentionally[3] print misleading articles. We have a fine staff of editors, but despite their best efforts mistakes can[4] occasionally occur. Very truly yours [88 words]

27.3

1 Our new shop is on Broadway at Times Square.
2 We quoted a low price for insuring their hardware store.
3 Tim intends to qualify as a certified records manager or quit our staff.
4 We can always quote a lower price.
5 Ellen quickly quoted facts about our hardware sales.

¶ Business Letter

Dear Mrs. Woodward I appreciate your writing to me to quote your insurance rates for our new place of[1] business. Since moving into our new hardware store on Broadway, we have had quite a few quotes to review. We had to[2] quit reviewing quotes and make a decision.

Despite the fact that we cannot accept your quoted rates, it is[3] reassuring to know that we qualify for insurance with your company. Very truly yours [78 words]

27.4 Dictation Speed Letter

Dear Mrs. Miller We were glad to have your recent purchase. If any mistakes were made in the content of our shipment,[1] please let us know. Let us hear from you, too, if you have any problems with the operation of the goods you have[2] purchased. Cordially yours [45 words]

27.5 Business Letter

Dear Miss Garcia When I looked at the plans and specifications for our new office building yesterday, I was[1] very much annoyed. I discovered that some person had made several modifications in the specifications.[2] These modifications were made without justification and without proper authority.[3]

There is no way that any further modifications should be made in the design specifications without[4] my written approval.

Please acknowledge this letter in writing as soon as you receive it. Janet Roy [99 words]

LESSON 28

28.1

1 Please place an order for some of our products.
2 Mary and Sue correspond regularly.
3 Just thank her for her opinion.
4 Nate never attends our regular meetings.
5 I have just ordered one of their latest products.

¶ Business Letter

Dear Mr. Johnson Thanks for answering my letter of February 20 asking about our order of[1] December 16. In your correspondence you said that our order must have been lost in shipment. We have been[2] ordering products from you regularly, and never before has a shipment become lost.

In order to track[3] down the missing goods, we have reviewed the records of our truck driver. Everything seems to be in order.

In our[4] opinion, the products we ordered never left your plant. Could you perhaps check your own shipping records again?[5] Cordially yours [103 words]

28.2

1 Thank you for your order of February 10.
2 Thank you for ordering our products.
3 Thank you for the nice present.
4 Thank you very much for the nice gift.
5 Thank you, Maria, for answering my correspondence.

¶ Letter

Dear Jim Thank you very much, Jim, for your nice note. Thank you, too, for your comments about my business associate.[1] I am glad you had an opportunity to meet Greg Adams. Greg is a fine member of our staff. Thank you for[2] sending me your business card. I will have to drop in on you sometime. Cordially yours [57 words]

28.3

1 Please examine the shipment and make sure it is exactly what was ordered.
2 We need to get an expert opinion if we are to go into the export business.
3 People seldom expect expenses to be higher than income.
4 We expect to let our contract expire without renewing it.
5 Goods at the Smith Store are extremely expensive.

¶ Study Notes

Information About Economics Exam

Our exam will be held on Wednesday, September 10. The exam[1] at this time will cover exports.

We need to be able to write exact quotes from the experts mentioned in class.

We need[2] to be able to figure exact costs and expenses in at least one case problem.

We should expect the exam[3] to take the entire class time. [65 words]

28.4

1 Dear Ms. Edward Thank you for your reply to my letter of August 16.
2 We will wait for your reply. Sincerely yours
3 Please let me know what time we can meet. Very sincerely yours
4 Dear Ms. Woodward Please check the attached invoice to make sure it is exactly what you ordered.
5 I look forward to seeing you in September. Very cordially yours

28.5 Dictation Speed Letter

Dear Ms. Golden Thank you for your letter expressing appreciation for the quality of our products.[1] We value the opinions of people who regularly order our products.

I will keep your letter in our files.[2] Maybe we will be able to use it in an advertising campaign. Very truly yours [54 words]

28.6 Business Letter

Dear Ms. Cohen We are pleased you requested information about our insurance plan. We feel that the insurance[1] protection you will receive from the

National Insurance Company is the best that is available to[2] people in your industry. We have been insuring people in your business area since 1975.[3] The attached brochure describes the features of the plan.

Act quickly as the end of the enrollment time is rapidly[4] approaching. Very cordially yours

[87 words]

LESSON 29

29.1

1 Ms. O'Brien will represent her client in a trial on December 3.
2 Her client has no prior criminal record.
3 Ryan will go to the appliance store to shop for a dryer.
4 Dana places reliance on her assistant.
5 Washers, dryers, and other appliances are available at a low price.

¶ Business Letter

Dear Mrs. Ryan We are proud to welcome you as a new client of Science Magazine. I am sure that you will[1] find advertising in the pages of Science Magazine to be profitable.

Thank you once again,[2] Mrs. Ryan, for being willing to advertise in Science Magazine. Yours very truly [58 words]

29.2

1 Tomorrow we will have a lecture on the topic of free enterprise.
2 Our school provides entertainment in the evenings that interests many international students.
3 Kathy is interested in studying international business.
4 After your job interview, I will introduce you to Mrs. O'Bryan.
5 Do not allow anyone to interrupt me; I do not like anything that interferes with my work.

¶ Business Letter

Dear Mr. Ryan This is just a quick note to confirm that everything is in order prior to your job[1] interview.

When you arrive at our building, you will notice that we have two entrances on Broadway. Please use the[2] south entrance.

I am eager to learn more about the courses you have taken in international business.[3] I am sure you are equally interested in learning more about our company, International[4] Enterprises. Very truly yours [87 words]

29.3

1 I will fly from Philadelphia to New York on Tuesday, October 23.
2 Yes, Mrs. Ryan, there is train service between Chicago and Denver.
3 Mr. Rosen was president of a company in St. Louis, Missouri.
4 We will open a new branch office in one of two states—Georgia or Florida.
5 Her most recent American vacation was in Los Angeles, California.

¶ Geography Class Notes

Notes on Ports and Shipping

The first primary ports of the United States were Boston and Philadelphia.[1] Later, New York became the busiest port. On the West Coast of the United States, San Francisco was the[2] first major port. Los Angeles and Seattle are primary West Coast ports.

On the Mississippi River,[3] St. Louis and New Orleans have been shipping centers for many years.

[70 words]

29.4 Dictation Speed Letter

George Thank you very much for writing to me about Bill Davis. It was a pleasure for me to meet him. You will be[1] pleased to know I gave him the job.

I am very happy with his work. I will be glad to hear from you anytime[2] you have such a good person to recommend. Mary [50 words]

29.5 Professional Letter

Dear Dr. O'Brien On behalf of the National Science Association, thank you for your very[1] generous cash gift.

The National Science Association is not supported by any government[2] agency. We are totally relying on private individuals. We are so pleased with the amount of your cash[3] gift that I just had to write a personal note to tell you of my sincere appreciation. Very truly yours[4] [80 words]

LESSON 30

30.1

1 Please send us your check at this time in the enclosed envelope.
2 What brochure do we usually use as an enclosure?
3 Ellen will probably not recognize you after all these years.
4 I am sending you an unusual newspaper article.
5 We are having severe illness throughout our school.

¶ Memo

To: Carlos Vega
From: Richard Cohen
Your plan that we sell advertising in the student newspaper is[1] interesting. Throughout the years the newspaper has been considered the property of the school and has represented[2] an expense to the school.

Maybe the time has come to recognize that the newspaper does not have to be supported[3] by the school.

Selling advertising space in a student newspaper is not unusual. Enclosed in the[4] envelope is a list of people to invite to the October 27 meeting of the newspaper[5] staff to discuss this matter.
[105 words]

30.2

1 Thank you for your cash contribution.
2 We appreciate each of the contributors to our magazine.
3 Our magazine is now being distributed in every state.
4 Honesty is one of the attributes that Ron values the most.
5 Are you available to distribute material about our political candidate?

¶ Letter

Dear Scott Thank you for your contribution to our recent convention of distributors of National Products[1] Corporation. Your presentation on ways to develop new distribution routes was appreciated.[2] Everyone is saying that the convention this year was a success. Certainly much of this success can be attributed[3] to you. Sincerely
[64 words]

30.3

1 Jody, your class notes have been most helpful; it was thoughtful of you to loan them to me and I am most thankful.
2 Here is a valuable reference book. I hope you find it useful; be careful with it.
3 Julie studied carefully for the test and completed it successfully.
4 The concert was beautiful, and it was wonderful of you to invite me to it.
5 The first performance of the play was delightful, but it is doubtful that it will last.

¶ Personal Note

Michelle Attached to this note is a copy of a research report. I hope that you will find it helpful in successfully[1] completing your paper. Hopefully, this report will help you to get a good grade. It is doubtful that very[2] many people in your class have found this useful reference material.

Notice the wonderful writing style;[3] the writer has a delightful sense of humor. Fred [69 words]

30.4 Dictation Speed Letter

Dear Mark Thank you very much, Mark, for agreeing to distribute campaign leaflets for the election of Sarah Wade.[1] A supply of leaflets is enclosed. It will be most helpful if you can distribute the leaflets by Saturday,[2] November 1.

Ms. Wade is very grateful for all the helpful work you have done on behalf of her campaign.[3] Hopefully, your efforts will be successful and she will be elected! Sincerely [75 words]

30.5 Personal Note

Dear Gary Enclosed with this letter you will find an advertisement from our local newspaper. The advertisement[1] is for some property on a lake west of the city. You will note that the asking price for this fine piece of[2] property is $28,000. The property does have a beautiful setting, but it is doubtful[3] that the owners will be able to get $28,000 for it today.

I know that you have been looking[4] for some land like this for quite a while. Hopefully, the enclosed newspaper clipping will be helpful. Very truly yours[5]
[101 words]

30.6 Message

Marvin Boyd called to say that he will meet you at 12:15 p.m. for lunch. He will come to your[1] office. Sandra [22 words]

LESSON 31

31.1

1 It has been confirmed that Sue Stein has been named president of James Corporation.
2 We have an unconfirmed report that bad weather may be blamed for the late arrival of the airplane.
3 Carol was excited about the new painting and promptly framed it.
4 I welcomed your prompt reply.
5 I have been informed that the treasury is empty.

¶ Letter of Recommendation

Dear Ms. Green It is my pleasure to recommend Mr. Jack Haley for a position with Prompt Cleaners. I first[1] met Jack when he was president of the Student Accounting Club.

Jack promptly named the right committees and welcomed[2] every challenge that came his way. He seemed to enjoy solving problems quickly.

Jack Haley should prove to be a[3] fine member of your staff. Very truly yours [68 words]

31.2

1 Barbara Kaplan is advertising that she will do income taxes for people.
2 James has developed a new system of indexing personnel files.
3 Inactive paper files are kept in boxes in the basement.
4 It is a poor practice to mix active records with inactive records.
5 Are you receiving a fixed rate of interest on your investments?

¶ Memo

To the Staff Starting in January, we will be accepting boxes of records for inactive storage.[1] You will receive a standard-size file box. Each box is given a file number, and you receive an index card[2] containing that same number. If you ever need to have the file box sent back to you, you simply contact our[3] office and give us the number of the file box that you need. [68 words]

31.3

1 Our prices are already too high.
2 Our records center also stores inactive records.
3 One of the advantages is that records cannot be altered.
4 Almost every member of our organization wants another option to raising dues.
5 The box of records was altogether too heavy for Jim, although he tried to lift it.

¶ Personal Note

Kenneth Already it is almost time for another school year to begin. It is also time for the[1] Accounting Club to make plans for the school year. Although things went well last year, we almost ended the year with no[2] money in the club treasury.

At our first meeting, we need to discuss other ways for raising money.[3] Let us get together to discuss what we can present to the members at the first meeting. Dave [78 words]

31.4 Dictation Speed Letter

Dear Miss Jones Do you think that your taxes on your investments are altogether too high? If you do, send for a[1] copy of our valuable book Investment Taxes.

The options in our book can help you reduce your[2] taxes and still enable you to keep your investment in an industry you like. Promptly send in your order[3] for Investment Taxes; You will be pleased you did. Sincerely yours [70 words]

31.5 Business Letter

Dear Madam It makes no difference whether your staff flies 200 miles, 10,000 miles, or farther. Yale Airlines will[1] promptly take them where they need to go and when they need to go.

When your company officials must travel somewhere[2] on business, they can travel Yale Airlines and land at any one of almost 1,000 airports throughout the[3] country. They never have to worry about confirmed or unconfirmed reservations.

If you need to know more about[4] Yale Airlines, we will be glad to have our well-informed sales representative visit you at your request.[5] Yours very truly [102 words]

LESSON 32

32.1

1 Mike suggests that nearly everyone could benefit from the study of shorthand.
2 Many people have found the study of shorthand to be a worthwhile experience.
3 I do not understand your book report; it should include a short summary of the story.
4 I understand that you are making satisfactory progress at this time.
5 The short report I received on the progress of the project is worthless.

¶ Personal Note

Glenn One of our sales representatives has suggested that we include a book of short stories in our sales list.[1] She reports that such a book will satisfy a very real demand.

It is my experience that this sales[2] representative makes good suggestions. While we are under no pressure to do anything about this suggestion,[3] I think it would be worth reviewing soon. Judy

[68 words]

32.2

1 One of the requirements for writing shorthand is to have a good pen.
2 Each student in our school is required to take two years of history.
3 Most things of value are not easy to acquire.
4 Please send your job inquiry to our personnel office.
5 Our personnel office will be glad to describe our job requirements.

¶ Business Letter

Dear Mr. Phillips I am writing to inquire about the requirements for becoming a real estate agent.[1] I would like to acquire a real estate license sometime in the near future.

I will appreciate your reply[2] to this inquiry. Very truly yours [48 words]

32.3

1 Frank is one of the younger people to be hired by the bank.
2 Here is a form; be sure to fill in the blanks in ink.
3 Mr. Lincoln will bring the blank forms.
4 We are anxious to have you bring in your old bank certificate.
5 Our organization will hold a meeting sometime this spring at the Franklin Center.

¶ Letter

Dear Miss Banks Your request for me to give a speech at your spring meeting arrived just a day too late. I have[1] already accepted an opportunity to give a speech at a meeting of the Bankers Association on[2] Saturday, April 15. Therefore, I will not be available to go to Long Beach.

I suggest that you ask[3] Frank Strong. Dr. Strong is an outstanding young leader in the area of computer research. I am sure,[4] Miss Banks, that this meeting will be a great success. Very truly yours

[89 words]

32.4 Dictation Speed Letter

Dear Ms. James I am sorry I will not be able to attend the meeting of the Student Accounting Club on May 8. Your[1] organization is one of the most active clubs in our school. I would like to take part in one of your meetings[2] sometime.

On May 8, however, I will be out of town. Please invite me to attend one of your meetings again[3] soon. Sincerely yours [64 words]

32.5 Student Note

Dear Pam Thank you for your suggestion that we include a calendar of events with the May issue of our[1] newsletter. I realize that this will increase the printing costs of our newsletter. However, attendance at[2] our meetings has been under 20 percent so far this year.

Despite the cost, I think it will be worth it if this[3] is what it takes to make our organization strong. Give me some time to make up a rough draft of the calendar,[4] and then I will share it with you. Frank

[84 words]

LESSON 33

33.1

1 I am sure you will make a fine addition to our news station!
2 Did you read the Saturday edition?

3 If you accept our invitation, we will meet you at the station.
4 May I have permission to alter some of the conditions of the contract?
5 Ron made a sizable donation to the fund.

¶ Personal Note

Dear Alice Thank you for the invitation to write an article for the Friday edition of our student[1] newspaper. I will agree to write the article only on the condition that I may use the word processor[2] in the newspaper office. I do not want to try to meet this deadline without the help of automation.

Do[3] I have permission to use the equipment in your office? Franklin [73 words]

33.2

1 What is the likelihood that the train will be on time?
2 There is a fire station in each of the older neighborhoods in the city.
3 Typewriting instruction can begin in childhood.
4 The Franklin Center offers a course in parenthood.
5 Lee has positive memories of his boyhood.

¶ Letter

Dear Parent Childhood is the time when people should begin lifelong habits of physical fitness. Physical[1] fitness can reduce the likelihood of childhood illness. Please encourage your children to take part in the physical [2] education activities offered in your neighborhood. Very truly yours [57 words]

33.3

1 Please send me the results of your survey.
2 The fire resulted in our going out of business.
3 She has the same sense of humor in adulthood as she had in childhood.
4 Jacob consulted with the members of his study group.
5 Ralph took the rejection of his loan application as the ultimate insult.

¶ Letter

Dear Miss O'Neal You will recall that at the last meeting of the Adult Education Association, you[1] told me that the Davis Book Company was interested in computerizing its accounting operations.[2] I consulted with our sales representative in the Chicago area, and she immediately called[3] on them.

The first result of her call was a series of very satisfying and rewarding meetings with our[4] experienced consultants. The ultimate result was a new, highly profitable account for our[5] organization.

Thank you, Miss O'Neal, for this valuable sales lead. Sincerely yours [115 words]

33.4 Dictation Speed Letter

Dear Miss Davis Thank you for your letter asking if our company has any homes for sale in my neighborhood.[1] I am pleased to tell you that three homes have been listed for sale this week.

Enclosed with this letter is a page of[2] information about each of these homes. Please let me know when you would like to visit these homes. Yours very truly [59 words]

33.5 Business Letter

Dear Mr. Worth This morning I learned that the supply of the book Small Business Consulting will shortly be[1] exhausted. I estimate that we now have in the neighborhood of 3,000 copies. This number will, in my[2] opinion, last us only through October.

I request, therefore, that you manufacture another 20,000[3] copies immediately. We know from experience that it usually takes several months to print that large[4] a number. Yours truly

[82 words]

33.6 Agenda for Meeting

Agenda for FBLA Meeting
Call meeting to order at 3 p.m.
Officer Reports:
Report[1] of treasurer
Report of secretary
New-Member Committee
Ask for results of new-member drive
Old Business: [2]
None
New Business:
Talk about the condition of the treasury
Discuss ways to raise funds [56 words]

LESSON 34

34.1

1 It is simply not appropriate to mail a business letter that contains errors.
2 We need to print large quantities of theater programs.
3 Many executives wish they knew how to dictate better letters.
4 Lynn does not object to studying the subject of computer programming.
5 Our class recently learned how to use that particular word processing program.

¶ Business Letter

Ladies and Gentlemen On Saturday, September 3, the School of Business will offer a one-day course for[1] executives who wish to better their communication skills. This course is appropriate for any executive[2] at any level in any type of business.

An objective of the program is to help executives to write[3] better letters. This program will be particularly valuable in helping executives do a better[4] job of dictation.

A large quantity of printed programs is being sent to you for you to give to members[5] of your staff who may be interested in the subject of communication skills. Very truly yours [119 words]

34.2

1 Please return your order blank to our eastern office.
2 Are you going to attend Southern State College during the fall term?
3 The termination of Flight 767 will be in the southern terminal building.
4 According to the thermometer, the weather is turning colder.
5 Perhaps local air travel would increase if our terminal buildings were more modern.

¶ Business Note

Mr. Worth I have been asked to determine what quantity we should print of the first edition of our new[1] educational program, Modern Science.

On the basis of our past experience, I believe we should be able[2] to sell 50,000 copies in the first year. About 20,000 copies could be sold in the eastern[3] region and about 35,000 copies could be sold in the southern region.

If sales turn out better than[4] we expect, we can have larger quantities printed. Yours truly

[91 words]

34.3

1 Southern Airlines is going to institute a free-flight plan.
2 Thanks for giving me a copy of the constitution of our organization; you have my gratitude.
3 Most people look for a positive attitude when hiring someone.
4 Failure to make installment payments on time constitutes a breach of contract.
5 Mrs. King has a definite aptitude for computer programming.

¶ Personal Note

Dear Pedro In your last letter you asked what I will be doing after I finish high school. I am planning to[1] attend the Southern Computer Institute. At your suggestion, I took an aptitude test, and the test showed that[2] I would be good at computer programming. For a long time I have thought that I would be interested in this[3] area, but the results of the aptitude test gave me the direction I needed.

You have my gratitude,[4] Pedro, for suggesting that I take the aptitude test. Sincerely [92 words]

34.4 Dictation Speed Message

Dear John Chris called and said that she wishes to meet you for dinner tonight. She is returning from her business trip[1] this afternoon. Michael is having trouble fitting into the organization, and you may have to[2] terminate his contract. Andrew

[44 words]

34.5 Business Letter

Dear Mr. Dixon I find that I am in a particularly awkward and difficult position. On June[1] 15 your district manager placed an order with us for 500 feet of lumber and quantities of[2] other construction items. We filled the order and billed you for $2,400.

Your payment was due[3] several months ago. Your outstanding bill constitutes too large an amount of money for us to lose. Unless[4] we receive the payment soon, we will have to refer your account to our legal division.

Please send me your check[5] for $2,400 promptly. Sincerely yours [112 words]

LESSON 35

35.1

1 We will bring you additional new stories as the situation continues.
2 The third period of the game will continue after the time-out.
3 The financial situation of our organization is quite serious.
4 The class took a genuine interest in her theory of economics.
5 Various aspects of your plan have been tried previously.

¶ Student's "To Do" List

1. Continue to collect information for economics term paper on various[1] economic theories.
2. Try to talk with Professor Green at the end of the class period on Wednesday.
3. By November 16 try[2] to complete all the various assignments I started previously.
4. Check with Sue to see if she has a[3] genuine interest in working together on a history project.

[74 words]

35.2

1 I have been awake since 4 a.m.
2 We will patiently await the arrival of your check.
3 Mrs. Valdez is aware that sales in her division are ahead of the rest of the company.
4 Please take telephone messages while I am away from my office.
5 We will await the arrival of the football coach before we begin the awards ceremony.

¶ Memo

To the Staff While I am away on vacation for two weeks, David Moreno will be managing the[1] division in my place. Our production is currently ahead of schedule, and it should be a good time for me[2] to be away.

I doubt that any problems will arise which need to await my return. Mr. Moreno[3] is aware that he is to make decisions on my behalf. [69 words]

35.3

1 This product is increasingly difficult to manufacture profitably.
2 Bill did not knowingly erase the computer disk.
3 I was pleased by the way Barbara willingly gave her time to the class.
4 This play is exceedingly complex, but the actors are performing their roles convincingly.
5 Although printing ink is not our most famous product, it is, quite interestingly, our most profitable one.

¶ Letter

Dear Mr. Jennings If you enroll in our executive training course, it will do several things for you:

1. [1] It will teach you to express your theories and thoughts interestingly and convincingly.
2. It will build your[2] confidence, and you will find that you will be able to obtain exceedingly satisfactory results in the[3] management of people.

If you would like more information about this exceedingly practical course, phone[4] or write us today. Very truly yours [87 words]

35.4 Dictation Speed Letter

Dear Sir Thank you for your interest in the research paper I am currently writing. Enclosed you will find a[1] copy of the problem statement of the study.

I will be glad to send you a copy of the final paper[2] when it is completed. You will not be charged for the cost of printing and mailing.

I will not be able to[3] complete the paper until then. I hope this will be satisfactory. Very truly yours [76 words]

35.5 Business Letter

Dear Ms. Rubin You have my genuine appreciation, Ms. Rubin, for the part you played in our executive[1] conference in Tampa yesterday afternoon. All of us felt that you presented your theories of management[2] exceedingly well and quite convincingly.

I am sure, Ms. Rubin, that everyone benefited from the[3] presentation of your subject matter. You certainly had the undivided attention of your audience.[4]

I will await your billing statement so that I may send you a check to cover your expenses. Sincerely yours [99 words]

LESSON 36

36.1

1 Which item is next on our agenda?
2 Diana has gone to work for Southern Valley Incorporated.
3 Diana is very reluctant to discuss business facts in public.
4 Carlos will celebrate his tenth anniversary with our organization next year.
5 Your request for information comes at a most inconvenient time.

¶ Personal Letter

Dear Linda It is hard to believe that only three years have passed since you began your own company. I am glad to[1] hear that things are going so well that you are ready to incorporate.

Thank you for your offer to sell me shares[2] of stock in your company. I am reluctant to buy at this time. Making this type of investment would[3] really not be convenient right now.

Thank you for giving me this[4] opportunity. Sincerely yours [86 words]

36.2

1 You are doing a superb job, John, as supervisor of your department.
2 The authority of the plant superintendent does not supersede that of the vice president.
3 Our old product line will be superseded by a superior new product design.
4 Fred does an excellent job of supervision.
5 He should be able to supervise the sales division.

¶ Personal Note

Jerry You might be interested to know that we will have a job opening for a new supervisor[1] in our product development lab. As you know, the work we do in our lab is of superior quality.[2] To have a chance to be the supervisor of this lab represents a superb opportunity for a[3] person having your background.

I suggest you apply as soon as the job is announced to the general public. Sincerely[4] [80 words]

36.3

1 In March we will circulate a new copy of our plant regulations.
2 Congratulations on winning the public relations award.
3 We need to formulate a better way to make our price calculations.
4 The Commerce Commission used to regulate freight rates.
5 Congratulations! Your newspaper has achieved an outstanding circulation.

¶ Personal Note

Gary I understand you wish to take a printing calculator home with you. Company regulations do not[1] allow any of us to remove office equipment from the building. This policy was formulated[2] several years ago, and copies of the policy were circulated to members of the staff. This was long[3] before you were hired, and it did not occur to me to tell you about the regulation. Fred [78 words]

36.4

1 Our airline has a free flight plan for frequent travelers.
2 The frequency of use of the old automobile is low; consequently, it remains in good condition.
3 Mrs. Sanchez has an extensive vocabulary, and frequently her remarks are eloquent.
4 What will be the consequences of the new tax bill?
5 She is a frequent customer in our shop.

¶ Letter

Dear Mrs. Steele Thank you for the magazine article you sent us recently. I always enjoy reading your[1] articles; your writing style is eloquent. We will probably print your article sometime in the spring.

You have been[2] having articles accepted by our magazine with very high frequency. Consequently, we would like[3] to hire you as a contributing editor.

If this proposal interests you, contact me so that we may[4] discuss the details. Very truly yours [87 words]

36.5 Dictation Speed Note

Dear Lee This is just a brief note to tell you that I will be able to meet with you on Thursday. I will be[1] arriving at your office at about 2 p.m.

Thank you for suggesting that we get together. I am[2] looking forward to our meeting. Dale

[45 words]

36.6 Business Letter

Dear Mr. Samuels Thank you for your letter inquiring about the cost of leasing a new car from us.[1] This is such a frequent inquiry that we have printed a brochure on the subject. A copy is enclosed. [2] Leasing a new car from us is an exceedingly cost-effective way to drive a superb automobile.

Pay[3] a visit to our offices as soon as it is convenient for you to do so. Yours very truly

[78 words]

LESSON 37

37.1

1 The membership of our organization has increased; thank you for your leadership during the last year.
2 Steve is considering ownership of his own small business.
3 The book is being released under the authorship of Bob Brady.
4 Chris has excellent relationships with her fellow workers.
5 Thank you for the help and thank you for your friendship.

¶ Letter

Dear Miss Brewer According to the Office of the Dean, you have the grade point average to qualify you for[1] membership in the Accounting Club. You will enjoy the fellowship of other young professionals and the[2] friendships you acquire. You will find membership interesting and enjoyable.

Please consider sending the[3] attached application blank to our membership committee. Very truly yours [73 words]

37.2

1 We are most impressed by your employees.
2 Empire Manufacturing Company is pleased to be able to employ you.
3 All of our employees are encouraged to take professional improvement courses.
4 The quality of your import products is most impressive.
5 I am embarrassed to say that our employees did not act in an impartial manner.

¶ Memo

To: Leslie Bridges
From: Mary French
I am most impressed with the financial statements of your Import and Export[1] Division. Your division has shown the most improvement in profitability.

You and all of the[2] employees of your division deserve my most sincere congratulations. Let me repeat most[3] emphatically, I am impressed with your performance. [69 words]

37.3

1 Miss Baker has been transferred to our Los Angeles office.
2 A lot of business is transacted today by the computer transmission of data.
3 Can the International Sales Department provide me with a translation of this German letter?
4 Most secretaries prefer to transcribe shorthand notes rather than dictation tapes.
5 The transportation industry was the first type of big business in America.

¶ Note

Mr. Bentley The company treasurer just transmitted to me your note requesting permission to purchase[1] a transistor radio for Mr. Frank Golden.

The transistor radio you wish to purchase costs over[2] $250. I am reluctant to approve such a request, but I will do so in view of the[3] impressive contribution Mr. Golden has made to the Empire Transportation Company. Forward your[4] purchase request to me, and I will have our purchasing department complete the transaction. James French [99 words]

37.4 Dictation Speed Letter

Dear Madam I am happy to be able to tell you that you have complete ownership of your car. Your January[1] payment was your last, and our business transaction is now complete.

We are very much impressed with the way[2] you sent all of your payments on time. You have the best possible credit rating with us, and we look forward[3] to our next opportunity to do business with you. Very truly yours [75 words]

37.5 Personal Letter

Dear Dale Thank you, Dale, for your letter to Professor Day. I went to visit the Eastern Vocational School and[1] made an appointment with Professor Day. She made me feel most welcome and gave me a lot of facts about her school.[2]

The school is most impressive, and I have decided to transfer to Eastern Vocational School. This will be an[3] improvement over the program in which I am now enrolled.

You have my sincere gratitude for all the assistance[4] you have given me. Very truly yours [88 words]

LESSON 38

38.1

1 A significant amount of data is transmitted electronically today.
2 If you feel strongly about the subject, it is very important that you speak up at the meeting.
3 I think it would be a good idea to send a memorandum to all branch managers.
4 I think that the opinions of Scott and Diana are of equivalent merit.
5 The electronics industry assumes a significant role in the world economy.

¶ Note

To: Marco Sanchez
From: Mary Boyd
Thank you for taking the time to speak with me about the importance of our[1] communicating with our branch offices more quickly. As our business becomes more and more worldwide, the speed of[2] communication becomes increasingly significant. As you have pointed out, the electronic transmission[3] of this same memorandum could take place at nearly the speed of light.

Since each of our branch offices has[4] at least one computer, the concept of electronic mail is entirely possible. We will begin a cost[5] study immediately. [105 words]

38.2

1 Frank says his grades have risen steadily.
2 We are temporarily out of envelopes.
3 I readily agree that math is a difficult subject.
4 We could temporarily handle all incoming calls in the sales office.
5 A large family could easily travel in that car.

¶ Letter

Dear Mr. Worth Thank you for writing to inquire about the prices and models of the Empire Jet. The Empire[1] Jet is easily the finest business jet manufactured today.

Empire Jet Model 101 is[2] temporarily out of stock. Our Model 102 is in stock and readily available to you. By owning[3] an Empire Jet, your executives do not have to waste time waiting for public airline flights. They can be on their[4] way to important meetings speedily whenever they are ready to leave.

Please read the enclosed brochure; then invite[5] one of our sales representatives to visit. She will tell you how easily you may join the happy[6] family of Empire Jet owners. Yours very truly [129 words]

38.3

1 The cost of the subscription to Empire Magazine is substantial.
2 The city transit line will extend service to several suburban area subdivisions.
3 The building contractor plans to submit plans for a new subdivision next week.
4 Ellen does not subscribe to the attendance policy of our school.
5 Less than 1 percent of our subscribers have ever submitted an article to our magazine.

¶ Letter

Dear Mr. and Mrs. Sanford Your name has been submitted to us as the parents of a child who is the proper[1] age to be a newspaper carrier. The Suburban Daily is a new newspaper that is just now selling[2] its first subscriptions. We already have many subscribers in your subdivision.

If your son or daughter[3] would like to deliver newspapers on a daily basis to about thirty subscribers in your neighborhood,[4] please submit the attached application form. Cordially yours

[91 words]

38.4 Dictation Speed Letter

Dear Dan Thank you for taking the time to write to me. I know that you are busy with your transfer and that you have[1] a lot to do in order to begin working in your new office.

I just had to take some of your[2] time to let you know that everyone here is happy you will be coming to work with us. All of the people[3] on our staff are sure that you will do very well. Mike

[67 words]

38.5 "To Do" List

1. Buy a subscription to a professional magazine relating to my major.
2. Stop at the Empire[1] Electronics Store for stereo speakers.
3. Buy an anniversary card for my Mom and Dad.
4. Pay the[2] electric bill.
5. Buy two fine-point pens for writing shorthand.

[51 words]

LESSON 39

39.1

1 You have my sincere apology.
2 The advance of technology has been most impressive.
3 Our school is investing in the equipment for a new biology laboratory.
4 Ruth plans to major in either sociology or psychology in college.
5 We have been greatly inconvenienced and deserve an apology.

¶ Letter

Dear Mr. West I sincerely apologize for being late to my biology class. In the previous[1] class period our sociology class was involved with some psychological testing which ran late. Again,[2] sincere apologies. Steven Wright [46 words]

39.2

1 Please return the contract in the self-addressed envelope.
2 Albert wrote the entire report himself.
3 I do not consider myself to be selfish.
4 The members of the board of directors have just voted themselves a pay increase.
5 Fred is giving himself more self-confidence through a self-improvement course.

¶ Letter

Dear Mr. Morris The National Management Institute course is one of the leading self-improvement courses[1] being offered today to acquire self-confidence. Over 10,000 people have already given themselves[2] self-confidence and new career direction.

Also enclosed is a list of dates when our self-improvement course will be[3] offered in locations near you. Why not select a location, and return the[4] enclosed registration form in the self-addressed envelope. Yours truly [95 words]

39.3

1 Our sociology class is currently studying various aspects of society.
2 The Eastern Supply Store handles a variety of office products.
3 Lloyd is feeling a great amount of anxiety about his job interview.
4 Mr. West is not happy with the type of notoriety we have received over our legal problems.
5 We are pleased to welcome you as a member of the Accounting Society.

¶ Note

Miss Lane Thank you very much, Miss Lane, for inviting me to speak to your Accounting Society. I will[1] discuss with the members of your society the wide variety of job opportunities which are[2] available. I will also talk about the favorable job market and help to relieve some of the [3] anxiety about finding a job. Dr. Samuel Johnson [70 words]

39.4 Dictation Speed Letter

Dear Martha I have not been able to find the copy of the math book you asked me to give to you. I have looked[1] everywhere. Meet me in the library at 3 o'clock so we can locate a copy. Henry

[37 words]

39.5 Sales Letter

Dear Ms. Bell Would you like to learn a second language? At the Southern Language Institute you will study with[1] Dr. Carlos Lopez and his staff. Dr. Lopez has developed psychologically sound methods for teaching[2] languages.

We hope you will come in soon and enroll in one of our courses. Cordially yours [56 words]

LESSON 40

40.1

1 We will begin publishing our new magazine in the spring.
2 Our new magazine will be no ordinary publication.
3 We have no reason to question the statistical information in the report.
4 It is a privilege to work with a person of such extraordinary character.
5 Under the circumstances we will have to take a look at our pricing.

¶ Letter

Dear Sir This letter is to announce the publication of an extraordinary new magazine. This magazine[1] has been designed specifically for the modern advertising executive. Careful statistical [2] analysis of our intended readership has shown us exactly the type of magazine to publish.

There is[3] no question that Advertising Today will have wide circulation among leading advertising[4] executives.

Under these circumstances, you will not want to miss a single issue. Plan on becoming a[5] subscriber today. Very cordially yours [108 words]

40.2

1 Ms. Janet Washington recently moved to Lexington, Kentucky.
2 Sarah Cunningham will be our new branch manager in Evansville.
3 Nancy will take the afternoon train from Harrisburg to Pittsburgh.
4 Our history book contains an interesting account of the Battle at Lexington.
5 Which cities are closest to Nashville, Washington, and Jacksonville?

¶ Business Letter

Dear Mr. Cunningham Many think that the Lexington Store in Harrisburg is very expensive. This is[1] definitely not the case. We invite you to make price comparisons between our store and any other[2] quality stores in Harrisburg.

As you will see by the enclosed circular, our prices for sport coats start at[3] $90 and our executive suits start at $150. The prices in our Harrisburg[4] store are quite reasonable, just as they are in our two stores located in Nashville and Wilmington.

Please visit[5] our store soon, Mr. Cunningham. We are open every day except Sunday from 9 a.m. to 5 p.m. Sincerely yours[6] [120 words]

40.3 Speed Dictation Memo

To: Amanda Washington
The World Publishing Company in Evansville recently published a book[1] entitled Business Management. There is no question that this book is an extraordinary publication.

Each[2] member of our research department should have a copy. I realize we are currently having budget problems.[3] Under the circumstances, will you please order one copy of Business Management for our company library.[4] A. R. Brown

[82 words]

40.4 Professional Letter

Dear Mrs. Lexington It was a privilege to work with you on our recent research publication. The[1] statistical analysis which you provided for our study was not ordinary professional[2] research. In fact, there is no question in my mind that you rank as one of the leading statistics experts working[3] in our field today.

You certainly did more than your fair share of the work on this publication. Under the[4] circumstances, I insist that your name be listed ahead of mine.

I can hardly wait to receive the first[5] copy of our publication in the mail. Very truly yours

[107 words]

LESSON 41

41.1 Personal Note

Dear Mike I will be glad to let you have my class notes for a few hours later this week. I will put them in my locker[1] where I am sure you will be able to find them. My locker is on the second floor. The notes will be there after[2] 11 a.m. today.

I hope you will find my class notes to be useful. Please return them to my locker[3] when you are finished with them. Barb [66 words]

41.2

Kaplan recently Allen credit determine
Dear Mrs. with our can you we should
as soon as possible

41.3 Reference Letter

Dear Mrs. Kaplan Recently Mr. Allen Bailey applied for a charge account with our department store. He[1] gave us your name as a credit reference. Can you give us any information that will help us determine how[2] much credit we should extend to Mr. Bailey?

I have enclosed a form for you to complete. Please fill out the form[3] and return it to me as soon as possible. We will greatly appreciate your promptness. Cordially yours[4] [80 words]

41.4 Personal Letter

Dear Dr. Brandon Every week we send out a communications bulletin that is of assistance to[1] persons who must write good letters in their business. Each bulletin has several very effective[2] letters, as well as suggestions on how to compose them. You can use these suggestions to your advantage whenever[3] you have to write business or social letters of your own.

Fill out and mail the enclosed card if you would like to[4] receive free copies of our communications bulletin. Sincerely yours [93 words]

41.5 Business Letter

Dear Mr. Hugo Our latest financial statement is enclosed for your review. This year has been a difficult[1] one for our organization. We lost several sales representatives in three states and our director[2] of marketing. We have had no success finding satisfactory replacements. I am satisfied with our[3] progress in spite of these difficulties. Our sales were 15 percent under last year. I am confident we will[4] make considerable progress next year. Let me know if there are any other facts you wish about our finances at this time. Yours very truly [5]
[100 words]

LESSON 42

42.1 Business Letter

Dear Ms. Garcia It was a pleasure to receive your order for various items in our line of paper[1] products. May we ask that you fill out the enclosed form and return[2] it to us since this represents your first order with us. This will help our credit department handle your account. We hope that you will be satisfied with our[3] goods. We look forward to doing business with you. Cordially yours [73 words]

42.2

copy Mrs. Brown serve contract agrees
systems approval initial questions
Sincerely Dear Mr. of the I have to do
let me if you have

42.3 Business Letter

Dear Mr. Lee Enclosed is a copy of the letter I have prepared to be sent to Mrs. Brown. This letter[1] will serve as a contract by which Mrs. Brown agrees to do a review of our office systems.

Please look over[2] the letter and let me know if it meets with your approval. Then initial it and keep a copy for your files.[3]

Feel free to contact me if you have any questions. Sincerely [71 words]

42.4 Business Letter

Dear Mr. Rosenberg The computer you installed in our store several months ago is working perfectly.[1] We are so satisfied with it that I just had to write to tell you about it.

The computer has saved me over[2] ten hours a week during the first few months of operation. I find it much easier to keep track of[3] my inventory and to bill my customers.

Thank you for doing such a good job of determining[4] exactly the type of computer that is needed for my business. Yours truly [92 words]

42.5 Business Memo

To: Fred Garcia
From: Bob Andrews
Subject: Screening Applicants
Please select people for word processing positions[1] who have the following traits:

1. The ability to transcribe from dictated shorthand notes, machine dictation,[2] handwritten rough drafts, and edited typewritten copy.
2. Excellent transcription ability. They need to be[3] proficient in spelling, punctuation, and word division.
3. The ability to proofread and edit[4] accurately.
4. The ability to type at least 50 words a minute.

It is important that an[5] applicant possess excellent typing and shorthand skills. Word processing training is also required. [119 words]

LESSON 43

43.1 Business Letter

Dear Ms. Clark Thank you very much for sending me the magazine article on writing more effective[1] collection letters. It is just the kind of item we are looking for as a nice change of pace from our[2] articles on creative writing.

At this time I would like to ask you to be patient and give me several[3] months in which to find an issue that will best accommodate your article. Very truly yours [76 words]

43.2

Michaels	speaker	shorthand	eager
presentation	how	into	office
remind			
September 13	join	proper	Dear Miss
thank you for			

43.3 Business Letter

Dear Miss Michaels Thank you for agreeing to be a guest speaker in our shorthand class. We are all eager to hear[1] your presentation on how shorthand fits into the office of the future.

This is just to remind you that the[2] date on which you will visit us is September 13. Our class begins at 9 a.m.

Please let me know if you would[3] like to join us for lunch following our class. I will make the proper arrangements for you. Sincerely [79 words]

43.4 Business Letter

Dear Mr. Mendez This is just a short note to let you know that we have missed your bringing your car in for service.[1] The last time that your car was in our service station was in July.

I hope you will tell us if something is wrong.[2] Have we failed to service your car properly? Has our pricing been unfair?

Please give us another opportunity[3] to be of service to you. Sincerely yours [69 words]

43.5 Business Letter

Dear Mr. Tyler It is not always possible for us to see all of our good friends personally as the[1] busy season of the year approaches. We are using this letter as a way of wishing you a happy[2] holiday season.

Most people can use additional cash for the holidays at this time of year. You will be[3] pleased to know that we can arrange a special holiday loan for you. All you have to do in order to obtain[4] a loan is use your new credit card.

Please sign your name on your new credit card and use it the next time you shop[5] in our store. Very truly yours [105 words]

LESSON 44

44.1 Memo

To the Personnel Committee There will be a meeting of the Personnel Committee on September 21[1] at 2 p.m. in Room 241.

Attached to this memorandum is a copy of the agenda for the[2] meeting. Please let me know if you have any additional items you would like to have discussed and whether[3] you will be able to attend. Your immediate response regarding your attendance will be greatly appreciated.[4] [80 words]

44.2

Gentlemen efficient Los Angeles Oakland family happy facing problems worry choosing $7,000 of this thank you for the were not Yours very truly

44.3 Personal Letter

Gentlemen The purpose of this letter is to thank you for the efficient way you moved us from Los Angeles[1] to the home we bought in Oakland.

My family and I were not happy about facing the problems of moving. We[2] learned quickly that we had nothing to worry about.

We knew after we moved in that we had made a wise decision[3] in choosing your company. Your check for $7,000 is enclosed. Yours very truly [78 words]

44.4 Business Letter

Dear Ms. Stern Thank you for your letter of July 8 requesting us to reserve three rooms for you and your associates[1] for the week of September 10.

We have made every effort to locate space for you. We are sorry[2] to say we cannot help you. During that week there will be two conventions in Denver. All of our rooms have already[3] been reserved. If there are any cancellations, we will be glad to get in touch with you.

If your plans should change so that[4] you can be in Denver on another date, please let us know. We feel confident that we can take care of you[5] and your associates. Yours sincerely [107 words]

44.5 Business Letter

Dear Mr. Banks Your letter telling us that you plan to exhibit your books at the Western Education[1] Association meeting on April 16 has been referred to me.

If you wish, you can ship to us all the[2] material that you plan to use at the exhibit. We will then store it for you until the date of the[3] meeting. This is a service that we are glad to provide without charge to the exhibitors.

If there is any[4] other information we can give you, please do not hesitate to get in touch with us. Sincerely yours [97 words]

LESSON 45

45.1 Business Letter

Gentlemen Thank you for the order we received from you yesterday for 100 reams of our bond paper. We[1] were delighted to receive it because it was the first one we have received from your firm. The order has been[2] processed. You should have it soon. It is our sincere hope that this will be the first of many orders you will send us.[3]

We also manufacture paper products of all types. These products are listed in the enclosed catalog.[4] You will find that our prices are the lowest in the paper industry. Yours very truly [96 words]

45.2

Wiley opened charged $2,400 promptly mistake perhaps simply overlooked it has been let me is in

45.3 Letter

Dear Mr. Wiley It has been six months since I opened a charge account in my name at your store. Since that time[1] I have charged over $2,400 worth of goods. You sent me a bill each month during the first four months. I paid[2] each promptly.

You have not sent me a bill for the past two months even though I have charged over $1,000.[3] Have you made some mistake in my account? Perhaps you have simply overlooked sending me a bill.

Please let me know[4] whether the status of my account is in good order. Yours truly [94 words]

45.4 Business Letter

Dear Mrs. Temple Very often I have written to someone to ask why we have not received payment for[1] items purchased on account. That is not why I am writing to you today.

Today we received the final[2] payment from you for the furniture you purchased from us last year. There was not one occasion I had to write to you[3] and remind you to send us your payment.

Your excellent credit record at our store means that there is no credit [4] limit on your next purchase. We will be glad to serve as a credit reference for you should the need arise.[5] Cordially yours [102 words]

45.5 Business Letter

Dear Ms. Hughes There are several ways for an organization to ask for payment of overdue accounts. Here at the[1] General Communications Company we write considerate letters. Therefore, we are asking you to send your [2] remittance of $650 for the leather goods you purchased in September, October, and[3] November.

If you cannot pay the entire $650 at this time, I suggest you send us a[4] partial payment and try to make definite arrangements to pay the rest. Sincerely yours [95 words]

LESSON 46

46.1 Business Letter

Dear Mr. Temple You will be glad to know that our management has decided to open a sales office in[1] Camden so that we can better serve our customers in the East. We are opening that office on December 12.[2] An official announcement will appear in the Camden papers tomorrow.

The office will be managed by Tom[3] Woods. He was our special representative in Maine for several years. After December 12 please send all orders[4] and correspondence direct to the Camden address, which is given in this letterhead. Yours very truly[5] [100 words]

46.2

community adult education program
excelled cities 1,000 Wednesday 7 p.m.
approximately interested as you know
let me if you

46.3 Business Letter

Dear Mr. Green As you know, our community has an adult education program that is excelled by[1] very few cities in the nation. Nearly 1,000 people have enrolled in our evening program during the past[2] year.

Our evening classes meet on Monday and Wednesday evenings from 7 p.m. until 9 p.m. for[3] approximately 30 weeks. We have an opening at the present time for a shorthand teacher in our evening[4] program. Please let me know if you would be interested in teaching this program. Sincerely yours [97 words]

46.4 Business Letter

Dear Mr. Carr I am delighted that you have accepted our offer to teach shorthand in our adult[1] education program.

Enclosed are three blank copies of our class list form. Please list the names of all of the students[2] who attend your first class on all three copies of the class list form. One of the copies should be kept in your files for use[3] as a final grade report. Another copy should be sent to my office. The third copy should be sent to the[4] bookstore.

It is important that the bookstore receive its class list immediately so that the correct number[5] of books can be delivered to your room before the second class meeting.

If you have any questions at any time,[6] do not hesitate to contact me. Yours truly [129 words]

46.5 Business Letter

Dear Robert It was a pleasure to visit your company last fall. I want you to know how very much I[1] appreciated the time you took to explain how your information system works. I was very interested[2] to learn that your company regularly provides classes for your executives in which they are taught how to dictate[3] effective business communications.

If at any time in the near future business brings you to Philadelphia,[4] please let me know. Yours very truly [88 words]

LESSON 47

47.1 Form Letter

Dear Member Will you do two big favors for your organization?

Will you please take just a minute or two[1] to answer the enclosed questionnaire. Your answers to the five short questions will help us to determine where we need[2] to improve our services to our members.

Will you please renew your membership now? Your membership will not expire[3] for a few months. It is nevertheless a good idea to renew it now. If you renew now, you will be[4] saving your organization the cost of mailing you renewal forms later.

You will be doing your[5] organization a big favor by responding to my two requests. Sincerely [113 words]

47.2

Davis	reference	applied	particularly
ability	pertinent	regarding	decision
stamped	envelope	convenience	replying
I would	I should have		

47.3 Reference Letter

Dear Mr. Davis Miss Ann Day has given me your name as a reference. She has applied for an executive[1] secretarial position in my office.

I am particularly interested in learning about her[2] communication ability. I would also like to have any other pertinent information you[3] think I should have regarding my decision to hire Miss Day.

I have enclosed a stamped self-addressed envelope for your[4] convenience in replying. Sincerely [88 words]

47.4 Business Letter

Dear Ms. Jones I would like to tell you that I am the campaign chairperson for the United Way Drive. There is[1] something that you can do to help the United Way.

Would you please send United Way pledge cards through your company[2] mail to all the members of your staff? This allows us to reach the working people in our city while spending[3] a very small amount of money on postage.

Please let me know if you will be able to help us this year. Yours truly[4] [81 words]

47.5 Business Memo

To: Bob Richards
From: Steve Ryan
Subject: Personnel Vacancies
We have been having difficulty finding sales[1] representatives to fill two territories. The first includes the cities of New York, Boston, and Philadelphia.[2] The other territory includes the cities of Chicago and St. Louis. These jobs have been open[3] for more than six months. I hope you can take action on these vacancies immediately. If you have any leads,[4] please let us know. [83 words]

LESSON 48

48.1 Business Letter

Dear Mrs. Monroe The Legal Department has determined that our company is legally obligated[1] to pay the expenses of Mr. Steven Day. Mr. Day was injured on the job in our Chicago plant. The[2] total cost of his medical bills is $5,300. Would you please issue Mr. Day a check for[3] $5,300 as soon as possible.

If you have any questions or need additional facts, please[4] call me. Very truly yours [86 words]

48.2

Henry	subscription	Sporting	next	current
subscriber	avoid	advantage	special	
relatives	associates	value	limited	
you can	of this	Yours truly		

48.3 Business Letter

Dear Mr. Henry Subscription prices for Western Sporting Magazine will be increasing with the next issue.[1]

As a current subscriber you can avoid the increase by extending your present subscription now for one or two[2] years at the current rate. You may also take advantage of this special offer to purchase new gift[3] subscriptions for friends, relatives, or business associates.

Subscribe today and take advantage of this special[4] value. This offer is available for a limited time only. Yours truly [94 words]

48.4 Business Letter

Ladies and Gentlemen May I express our appreciation for the helpful assistance you gave the public[1] relations department of our division in reorganizing its methods of handling our worldwide[2] communications system. Your assistance was responsible for the successful solution of what has been an[3] extraordinarily difficult and expensive operation. We were extremely pleased with the tactful and[4] thoughtful way you dealt with our staff. Your services are valuable to publishing companies like ours. Your excellent[5] work is well worth the fee you charged us. Sincerely yours [110 words]

48.5 Business Letter

Gentlemen I have just received an advertising booklet published by the public relations department[1] of the World Publishing Company. It lists the unusual opportunities in the publishing world. The booklet[2] was well worth reading. I found reading it an exciting experience. The person responsible for this[3] booklet must be a recognized leader in the publishing industry and should be commended for the work.[4]

I do not ordinarily give advertising matter to my business students. I would be happy to do so[5] in the case of your booklet if you will let me have 50 copies. Sincerely yours [116 words]

LESSON 49

49.1 Letter

Dear Mr. East When you asked us to open a charge account for you at the State Street Store, we were glad to do so.[1] We knew that it would be a convenience for you.

Part of our agreement when we opened this account was that you would[2] pay your bills within a reasonable time after you received them.

Our records show that during May and June[3] your food purchases amounted to $150. We have not yet received your check.

Please send us a[4] check for $150 today. An envelope is enclosed for your convenience. Cordially yours [99 words]

49.2

Harrington examined specifications designed practical library first second disregard suggestion accept congratulations exceedingly if you have

49.3 Letter

Dear Mr. Harrington I examined the plans and specifications for the house that you designed. All I can[1] say is that they are great. They are clear and practical. I have only one suggestion. I would place the library[2] on the first floor rather than on the second. If you have a reason for placing the library there, just disregard[3] my suggestion. Please accept my congratulations on an exceedingly fine job. Very truly yours [78 words]

49.4 Business Letter

Dear Mr. Underwood I have been requested by the board of directors to obtain a speaker for the[1] regular yearly meeting of the New York Legal Association. In my opinion the best person for this[2] assignment is Dr. Frank Foster, president of the Chemical Bank of Bangor. Dr. Foster has been[3] successful in banking and in newspaper publishing. Dr. Foster is a recognized expert on world affairs,[4] and he is held in unusually high regard in both political and financial circles. Yours very truly[5] [100 words]

49.5 Business Letter

Dear Mrs. Gray Most people seem to feel that there is never enough time to do all the things that need to be done[1] in professional life. Are you one of these people? Would you like to have a better way of doing your work[2] so that you would have more time for other things?

All you have to do is send for a copy of our new book, Effective[3] Management. This new book combines the experiences of over 20 busy executives who have proved[4] that they can manage time effectively.

The low cost of this great book will probably be the best investment[5] you will ever make. Send for your copy today. A handy order blank is enclosed. Very truly yours [119 words]

LESSON 50

50.1 Business Letter

Dear Dr. Smith The editor of our magazine, Sandra Foster, has asked me to inform you that your[1] article will be published in our medical publication. It should appear in an issue that will be off[2] press in about three months.

I have been thinking for some time that we should publish an article of this type and am[3] very glad that your article will appear in our magazine. You have done a very complete job of reporting[4] on the medical effects of exposure to chemicals. Thank you for a job well done. Yours truly [98 words]

50.2

Hastings	almost	income	federal
government	due	referred	engaged
objective	insurance	coverage	slipped
furnish	that the	I should have	I was
and the	if you need	I will be glad	
Sincerely yours			

50.3 Business Letter

Dear Mr. Hastings I almost forgot that the enclosed income tax report for the federal government is[1] due in a week or two. I should have referred it to you a long time ago. I was engaged in making an[2] objective study of our insurance coverage, and the report slipped my mind. If you need any other information[3] from me, I will be glad to furnish it. Sincerely yours [70 words]

50.4 Business Letter

Dear Dr. Carter Enclosed is program information concerning your speaking engagement for the convention[1] to be held in Miami on Saturday, April 16. So that we can assure you have the equipment needed[2] for your presentation, we have enclosed forms for you to list the equipment you will need in your meeting room.[3] Also, we will need appropriate information for your introduction. Please fill out the forms and return them[4] to me immediately.

I appreciate the fact that you have agreed to be our speaker, and I am[5] looking forward to hearing your presentation in April. Sincerely yours [115 words]

50.5 Business Letter

Dear Dave Thank you for consenting to provide assistance to our guest speaker, Frank Jennings. Mr. Jennings will[1] arrive at 12:15 p.m. on Friday, December 3. Please pick him up at the Southern Airlines terminal [2] building at the airport.

Mr. Jennings will need seating for 75 people, a podium, and a[3] microphone in his meeting room. Please see to it that his needs are met.

Thank you for your willingness to help. Very truly yours[4] [80 words]

LESSON 51

51.1 Insurance Letter

Dear Mr. Foster Have you recently increased the amount of insurance you carry on your property? If[1] you have not, you are probably not adequately insured. That means that in case of a fire you will have to[2] pay for part of the price of rebuilding.

If your policy has not been reviewed in the past five years, take this[3] opportunity to have one of our insurance agents call on you. Sincerely [76 words]

51.2

yesterday	colleague	position	Troy
Computer	up	resigning	must	treasurer
shortly	could not		

51.3 Business Letter

Dear Tom Yesterday morning I learned that my friend and colleague, Fred Grant, had resigned and had accepted a position[1] as sales manager of the Troy Computer Company. While he was happy here, he felt he could not pass up[2] this opportunity.

His resigning has caused problems for the company, but we must carry on. We plan to[3] name the new treasurer shortly. Sincerely yours [69 words]

51.4 Personal Letter

Dear Ron I will be glad to serve as a member of the finance committee for our organization. I[1] understand that I am to begin my work on this committee with the first meeting to be held in[2] January. Would it be possible, Ron, for you to give me copies of the budgets for the current year and the budgets for[3] several recent years? I would find this most helpful.

Please get in touch with me if there is anything you would like[4] to have me do before I officially become a member of the committee in January. I look[5] forward to the opportunity to help our organization in this way. Yours truly [114 words]

51.5 Business Letter

Dear Phyllis You will be pleased to know, I am sure, that Mrs. Sherry Day has joined our staff. As you know, Sherry made[1] a fine reputation for herself during the time that she was in charge of the service department at the[2] Mason Center in Philadelphia. Recently, however, the Mason Center was sold.

Sherry closed its[3] service department and joined our organization. She has been with us since November 3.

The next time your car[4] needs service, please notify us. I am sure that Sherry will make every effort to accommodate you. Very truly yours[5]

[100 words]

LESSON 52

52.1 Business Letter

Dear Mr. Wilson Thank you for agreeing to meet with me in your San Francisco office. Thank you, too, for[1] agreeing to meet my plane at the airport. I will be arriving on Empire Airlines Flight 67 at[2] 3 p.m. on October 5.

I am looking forward to presenting the information which the members[3] of my staff and I have developed for your company. I know you will be pleased with what you see.

I hope after our meeting[4] you will be free to be my guest for dinner. Very truly yours [94 words]

52.2

Underwood talking Davis possible correspondent responsible experience advertising marketing declined salary figure newspaper ideas as you know would have been at this if you let me

52.3 Letter

Dear Mr. Underwood As you know, I have been talking with Ann Davis about a possible position as[1] a correspondent. She would have been a good person for this responsible job because of her experience[2] in advertising, selling, and marketing. She has, however, declined the job because of the salary[3] figure.

At this point we should place an advertisement for a correspondent in the newspaper next week. If you have[4] any other ideas, please let me know. Very truly yours [91 words]

52.4 Business Memo

To: Arlene Milton
From: George Day
Subject: Publication of Transportation Costs
Attached you will find a booklet [1] that was recently published by the United Oil Company in Pittsburgh, Pennsylvania. As you can see, it[2] very clearly presents the fuel efficiencies of different types of transportation.

This report shows the[3] railroad industry in a very good light, and I would like to use parts of the report in our own advertising.[4] Please write to United to inquire whether we may obtain publishing rights to this booklet and get back to me[5] as soon as possible. [105 words]

52.5 Business Letter

Dear Mr. Wilmington Yesterday I forwarded to you the plan prepared for the location of the new[1] furniture, fixtures, and office equipment for our two floors in the Commerce Building.

After you and your supervisors[2] have had an opportunity to study the plan, I would like to discuss it with you. Any time between[3] 11 a.m. and 3 p.m. on Wednesday, May 8, will be satisfactory for me. Very truly yours[4] [80 words]

APPENDIX

BRIEF FORMS

The number indicates the lesson in which the brief form was introduced.

a 4
about 12
acknowledge 20
advantage 18
advertise 18
after 12
am 4
an 4
and 18
anniversary 35
any 26
appropriate 34
are 4
at 4
be 8
between 24
business 22
but 10
by 8
can 8
character 40
circular 40
circumstance 40
communicate 16
company 16
convenience 35
convenient 35
correspond 28
correspondence 28
could 10
difficult 22
direct 16
doctor 14
Dr. 14
during 14
electric 38
enclose 30
envelope 30
equip 28
equivalent 38
ever 16
every 16
executive 34
experience 32
for 8
from 12
general 20
gentlemen 26
glad 12
good 8
govern 20
have 8
his 8
hour 4
however 20
I 4
idea 38
immediate 18
importance 38
important 38
in 4
include 32
incorporate 35
insurance 26
insure 26
is 8
it 4
manufacture 26
memorandum 38
morning 26
Mr. 8
Mrs. 12

PHRASES

The number indicates the lesson in which the phrase was introduced.

INDEX TO WORDS

The number indicates the lesson in which the theory word was introduced.

B

C

D